Lecture Notes in Computer Science

Lecture Notes in Computer Science

Vol. 167: International Symposium on Programming. Proceedings, 1984. Edited by C. Girault and M. Paul. VI, 262 pages. 1984.

Vol. 168: Methods and Tools for Computer Integrated Manufacturing. Edited by R. Dillmann and U. Rembold. XVI, 528 pages. 1984.

Vol. 169: Ch. Ronse, Feedback Shift Registers. II, 1–2, 145 pages. 1984.

Vol. 170: Seventh International Conference on Automated Deduction. Edited by R.E. Shostak. IV, 508 pages. 1984.

Vol. 171: Logic and Machines: Decision Problems and Complexity. Proceedings, 1983. Edited by E. Börger, G. Hasenjaeger and D. Rödding. VI, 456 pages. 1984.

Vol. 172: Automata, Languages and Programming. Proceedings, 1984. Edited by J. Paredaens. VIII, 527 pages. 1984.

Vol. 173: Semantics of Data Types. Proceedings, 1984. Edited by G. Kahn, D.B. MacQueen and G. Plotkin. VI, 391 pages. 1984.

Vol. 174: EUROSAM 84. Proceedings, 1984. Edited by J. Fitch. XI, 396 pages. 1984.

Vol. 175: A. Thayse, P-Functions and Boolean Matrix Factorization. VII, 248 pages. 1984.

Vol. 176: Mathematical Foundations of Computer Science 1984. Proceedings, 1984. Edited by M.P. Chytil and V. Koubek. XI, 581 pages. 1984.

Vol. 177: Programming Languages and Their Definition. Edited by C.B. Jones. XXXII, 254 pages. 1984.

Vol. 178: Readings on Cognitive Ergonomics – Mind and Computers. Proceedings, 1984. Edited by G.C. van der Veer, M.J. Tauber, T.R.G. Green and P. Gorny. VI, 269 pages. 1984.

Vol. 179: V. Pan, How to Multiply Matrices Faster. XI, 212 pages. 1984.

Vol. 180: Ada Software Tools Interfaces. Proceedings, 1983. Edited by P.J.L. Wallis. III, 164 pages. 1984.

Vol. 181: Foundations of Software Technology and Theoretical Computer Science. Proceedings, 1984. Edited by M. Joseph and R. Shyamasundar. VIII, 468 pages. 1984.

Vol. 182: STACS 85. 2nd Annual Symposium on Theoretical Aspects of Computer Science. Proceedings, 1985. Edited by K. Mehlhorn. VII, 374 pages. 1985.

Vol. 183: The Munich Project CIP. Volume I: The Wide Spectrum Language CIP-L. By the CIP Language Group. XI, 275 pages. 1985.

Vol. 184: Local Area Networks: An Advanced Course. Proceedings, 1983. Edited by D. Hutchison, J. Mariani and D. Shepherd. VIII, 497 pages. 1985.

Vol. 185: Mathematical Foundations of Software Development. Proceedings, 1985. Volume 1: Colloquium on Trees in Algebra and Programming (CAAP'85). Edited by H. Ehrig, C. Floyd, M. Nivat and J. Thatcher. XIV, 418 pages. 1985.

Vol. 186: Formal Methods and Software Development. Proceedings, 1985. Volume 2: Colloquium on Software Engineering (CSE). Edited by H. Ehrig, C. Floyd, M. Nivat and J. Thatcher. XIV, 455 pages. 1985.

Vol. 187: F.S. Chaghaghi, Time Series Package (TSPACK). III, 305 pages. 1985.

Vol. 188: Advances in Petri Nets 1984. Edited by G. Rozenberg with the cooperation of H. Genrich and G. Roucairol. VII, 467 pages. 1985.

Vol. 189: M.S. Sherman, Paragon. XI, 376 pages. 1985.

Vol. 190: M.W. Alford, J.P. Ansart, G. Hommel, L. Lamport, B. Liskov, G.P. Mullery and F.B. Schneider, Distributed Systems. Edited by M. Paul and H.J. Siegert. VI, 573 pages. 1985.

Vol. 191: H. Barringer, A Survey of Verification Techniques for Parallel Programs. VI, 115 pages. 1985.

Vol. 192: Automata on Infinite Words. Proceedings, 1984. Edited by M. Nivat and D. Perrin. V, 216 pages.1985.

Vol. 193: Logics of Programs. Proceedings, 1985. Edited by R. Parikh. VI, 424 pages. 1985.

Vol. 194: Automata, Languages and Programming. Proceedings, 1985. Edited by W. Brauer. IX, 520 pages. 1985.

Vol. 195: H.J. Stüttgen, A Hierarchical Associative Processing System. XII, 273 pages. 1985.

Vol. 196: Advances in Cryptology. Proceedings of CRYPTO '84. Edited by G.R. Blakley and D. Chaum. IX, 491 pages.1985.

Vol. 197: Seminar on Concurrency. Proceedings, 1984. Edited by S.D. Brookes, A. W. Roscoe and G. Winskel. X, 523 pages. 1985.

Vol. 198: A. Businger, PORTAL Language Description. VIII, 186 pages. 1985.

Vol. 199: Fundamentals of Computation Theory. Proceedings, 1985. Edited by L. Budach. XII, 533 pages. 1985.

Vol. 200: J.L.A. van de Snepscheut, Trace Theory and VLSI Design. VI, 0–140 pages. 1985.

Vol. 201: Functional Programming Languages and Computer Architecture. Proceedings, 1985. Edited by J.-P. Jouannaud. VI, 413 pages. 1985.

Vol. 202: Rewriting Techniques and Applications. Edited by J.-P. Jouannaud. VI, 441 pages. 1985.

Vol. 203: EUROCAL '85. Proceedings Vol. 1, 1985. Edited by B. Buchberger. V, 233 pages. 1985.

Vol. 204: EUROCAL '85. Proceedings Vol. 2, 1985. Edited by B. F. Caviness. XVI, 650 pages. 1985.

Vol. 205: P. Klint, A Study in String Processing Languages. VIII, 165 pages. 1985.

Vol. 206: Foundations of Software Technology and Theoretical Computer Science. Proceedings, 1985. Edited by S.N. Maheshwari. IX, 522 pages. 1985.

Vol. 207: The Analysis of Concurrent Systems. Proceedings, 1983. Edited by B.T. Denvir, W.T. Harwood, M.I. Jackson and M.J. Wray. VII, 398 pages. 1985.

Vol. 208: Computation Theory. Proceedings, 1984. Edited by A. Skowron. VII, 397 pages. 1985.

Vol. 209: Advances in Cryptology. Proceedings of EUROCRYPT '84. Edited by T. Beth, N. Cot and I. Ingemarsson. VII, 491 pages. 1985.

Vol. 210: STACS 86. Proceedings, 1986. Edited by B. Monien and G. Vidal-Naquet. IX, 368 pages. 1986.

Vol. 211: U. Schöning, Complexity and Structure. V, 99 pages. 1986.

Vol. 212: Interval Mathematics 1985. Proceedings, 1985. Edited by K. Nickel. VI, 227 pages. 1986.

Vol. 213: ESOP 86. Proceedings, 1986. Edited by B. Robinet and R. Wilhelm. VI, 374 pages. 1986.

Vol. 214: CAAP '86. 11th Colloquium on Trees in Algebra and Programming. Proceedings, 1986. Edited by P. Franchi-Zannettacci. VI, 306 pages. 1986.

Vol. 215: Mathematical Methods of Specification and Synthesis of Software Systems '85. Proceedings, 1985. Edited by W. Bibel and K.P. Jantke. 245 pages. 1986.

Vol. 216: Ch. Fernstrom, I. Kruzela, B. Svensson, LUCAS Associative Array Processor: Design, Programming and Application Studies. XII, 323 pages. 1986.

Vol. 217: Programs as Data Objects. Proceedings, 1985. Edited by H. Ganzinger and N.D. Jones. X, 324 pages. 1986.

Vol. 218: Advances in Cryptology – CRYPTO '85. Proceedings, 1985. Edited by H.C. Williams. X, 548 pages. 1986.

Lecture Notes in Computer Science

Edited by G. Goos and J. Hartmanis

250

TAPSOFT '87

TAPSOFT '87

Proceedings of the International Joint Conference on Theory and Practice of Software Development
Pisa, Italy, March 23–27, 1987

Volume 2:
Advanced Seminar on Foundations of Innovative Software Development II and Colloquium on Functional and Logic Programming and Specifications (CFLP)

Edited by Hartmut Ehrig, Robert Kowalski, Giorgio Levi and Ugo Montanari

Springer-Verlag
Berlin Heidelberg New York London Paris Tokyo

Editors

Hartmut Ehrig
Technische Universität Berlin
Fachbereich 20, Informatik, SWT FR5-6
Franklinstr. 28/29, D-1000 Berlin 10

Robert Kowalski
Imperial College of Science and Technology
180 Queen's Gate, London SW7 2BZ, England

Giorgio Levi
Ugo Montanari
Dipartimento di Informatica, Università di Pisa
Corso Italia 40, I-56100 Pisa

CR Subject Classification (1987): D.3.1-4, F.3.1-3, F.4.1, I.2.3

ISBN 3-540-17611-X Springer-Verlag Berlin Heidelberg New York
ISBN 0-387-17611-X Springer-Verlag New York Berlin Heidelberg

Printed in Germany

Printing and binding: Druckhaus Beltz, Hemsbach/Bergstr.
2145/3140-543210

PREFACE

TAPSOFT '87 is the Second International Joint Conference on Theory and Practice of Software Development.

TAPSOFT '87 is being held from March 23 to March 27, 1987 in Pisa. TAPSOFT '87 has been organized by Dipartimento di Informatica (Università di Pisa), I.E.I. - C.N.R. and CNUCE - C.N.R., and has been supported by AICA and EATCS.

TAPSOFT '87 consists of three parts:

Advanced Seminar on Foundations of Innovative Software Development

New directions in software development have been proposed, on the basis of recent technological and theoretical advances. Following these trends, the software production process should be made more rigorous, and its result should be expressed in a more abstract and understandable form.

The aim of the Advanced Seminar is to bring together leading experts in the various fields which form the foundations of this renovation still in progress and to provide a forum to discuss the possible integration of available theories and methods in view of their applications.

The Advanced Seminar will consist of a number of invited talks, two panel discussions and several working groups. The invited talks will be either long, i.e. comprehensive and general, or short, i.e. dedicated to hot topics.

Invited Speakers

E. Astesiano (Univ. Genova)
K. Clark (Imp. C., London)
K. Furukawa (ICOT, Tokyo)
J. Goguen (SRI, Menlo Park)
G. Huet (INRIA, Paris)
R. Milner (Univ.Edinburgh)
M. Nivat (LITP, Paris)
J. Thatcher (IBM, Yorktown Heights)
D. Warren (Univ. Manchester)

Panels

- On Industrial Activity and Trends. Chairman: J. Goguen (SRI, Menlo Park)
- The Future of Software Engineering. Chairman: D. Bjørner (Lyngby)

The seminar organizers are H. Ehrig (Tech. Univ. Berlin) G. Levi (Univ. Pisa) R. Kowalski (Imperial College, London) U. Montanari (Univ. Pisa)

Colloquium on Trees in Algebra and Programming

Traditionally, the topics of the Colloquium cover a wider area of theoretical Computer Science than that indicated by the title. Actually, topics include the formal aspects and properties of trees and, more generally, of combinatorial and algebraic structures in all fields of Computer Science.
Besides the customary topics, in keeping with the overall theme of TAPSOFT, the program will include contributions related to specifications, communicating systems and type theory.

The preceding eleven colloquia were held in France and Italy as autonomous conferences, except in Berlin 1985, when for the first time CAAP was integrated into the TAPSOFT Conference.

In keeping with the tradition of CAAP as well as with the overall theme of the TAPSOFT conference, the selected papers are presented in the sections listed below.

- Algorithms
- Proving techniques
- Algebraic specifications
- Concurrency
- Foundations

The program committee for CAAP '87 is the following:

A. Arnold, Bordeaux	G. Ausiello, Roma
J. de Bakker, Amsterdam	A. Bertoni, Milano
B. Buchberger, Linz	M. Dauchet, Lille
J. Diaz, Barcelona	H. Ehrig, Berlin
Ph. Flajolet, Paris	N. Francez, Haifa
H. Ganzinger, Dortmund	U. Montanari, Pisa (Chairman)
P. Mosses, Aarhus	M. Nivat, Paris
J. Thatcher, Yorktown Heights	G. Winskel, Cambridge
M. Wirsing, Passau	

Colloquium on Functional and Logic Programming and Specifications

In keeping with the overall theme of the TAPSOFT conferences, CFPL focuses on those aspects of Functional and Logic Programming which are most important in innovative software development. The integration of formal methods and practical aspects of software production is also stressed.

The selected papers are presented in six sessions covering the following topics.

- Theory and Semantics of Functional Languages
- Types, Polymorphism and Abstract Data Type Specifications
- Unification of Functional and Logic Programming Languages
- Program Proving and Transformation
- Language Features and Compilation in Logic Programming
- Implementation Techniques

The Programme Committee for CFLP is the following

C. Böhm, Roma
K. Clark, London
K. Furukawa, Tokyo
H. Gallaire, München
C. Ghezzi, Milano
J. Goguen, Menlo Park
G. Huet, Paris
G. Kahn, Sophia Antipolis
R. Kowalski, London
G. Levi, Pisa (Chairman)
B. Mahr, Berlin
A. Martelli, Torino
R. Milner, Edinburgh
L. Moniz Pereira, Lisboa
E. Sandewall, Linköping
E. Shapiro, Rehovot
D. Warren, Manchester

The TAPSOFT '87 Conference proceedings are published in advance of the conference in two volumes. The first volume includes the final versions of 17 papers from CAAP '87, selected from a total of 51 submitted papers. The second volume includes the final versions of 17 papers from CFLP, selected from a total of 80 submitted papers. Invited papers from the Advanced Seminar are divided between the two volumes.

We would like to extend our sincere thanks to all the Program Committee members as well as to the referees listed below for their care in reviewing and selecting the submitted papers:
J. Alegria, A. Alfons, S. Anderson, J.L. Balcázar, F. Barbic, R. Barbuti, M. Bellia, R. Bird, E. Börger, P.G. Bosco, A. Bossi, G. Boudol, K. Broda, D. Brough, D. Chan, L. Carlucci Aiello, G. Castelli, T. Chikayama, T. Chusho, E. Ciapessoni, N. Cocco, L. Colussi, M. Coppo, T. Coquand, B. Courcelle, G. Cousineau, W. Coy, P.L. Curien, A. Davison, P. Degano, R. De Nicola, M. Dezani, M. Dincbas, M. Ducassé, P. Dufresne, J. Ebert, B. Eggers, P. van Emde Boas, R. Enders, G. Engels, K. Estenfeld, E. Fachini, A. Fantechi, I. Foster, D. Frutos, J. Gabarro, D. Gabbay, F. Galdbay, G. Gambosi, G. Ghelli, P. Giannini, M. Goldwurm, A. Goto, S. Goto, G. Guida, C. Gunter, T. Iato, H. Habel, M. Hagiya, N. Halbwacks, H. Hansen, S. Haqqlund, J. Heering, P. Henderson, R. Hennincker, D. Henry de Villeneuve, C. Hogger, F. Honsell, M. Huntback, H. Hussmann, P. Inverardi, R.C.L. Koymans, L. Kott, H.J. Kreowski, F. Kriwaczek, S. Kunifuji, Y. Lafont, B. Lang, R. Lasas, A.

Laville, P. Le Cheradec, K. Leeb, B. Lennartsson, J.J. Levy, M. Lindqvist, A. Llamosi, G. Lolli, G. Longo, J.A. Makowski, V. Manca, P. Mancarella, D. Mandrioli, M. Manny, A. Marchetti Spaccamela, I. Margaria, M. Martelli, L. Mascoet, Y. Matsumoto, G. Mauri, B.H. Mayoh, F. McCabe, J. Meseguer, J.J.Ch. Meyer, C. Moiso, B. Möller, C. Montangero, K. Moody, A. Mycroft, F. Nickl, M. Nielsen, F. Nielson, F. Nürnberg, M.E. Occhiuto, F.J. Oles, F. Orejas, M. Ornaghi, R. Orsini, P. Padawitz, C. Palamidessi, D. Pedreschi, P. Pepper, A. Pettorossi, A. Poigné, A. Porto, M. Protasi, G. Ringwood, J. Roman, S. Ronchi Della Rocca, G. Rossi, I. Kott, T. Sakurai,D. Sannella, D. Sartini, T. Sato, R. Schuster, M. Sergot, D. Siefkes, M. Smyth, T. Streicher, A. Suarez, Y. Takayama, J. Tanaka, A. Tarlecki, W. Thomas, M. Tofte, S. Tomura, J. Toran, M. Torelli, J.V. Tucker, F. Turini, T. Yuasa, F.W. Vaandrager, B. Vauquelin, B. Venneri, M. Venturini Zilli, H. Wagener, E.G. Wagner, M. Wallace, P. Weis, M. Zacchi, B. Zimmermann

We gratefully acknowledge the financial support provided by the following Institutions and Companies:

- Comune di Pisa
- C.N.R.
  - Presidenza
  - Comitato Nazionale per l'Ingegneria
  - Comitato Nazionale per le Scienze Matematiche
  - CNUCE
  - I.E.I.
- Dipartimento di Informatica, Università di Pisa
- Elsag, Genova
- Enidata, Milano
- IBM Italia, Roma
- List, Pisa
- Olivetti, Ivrea
- Selenia, Roma
- Sipe, Roma
- Systems & Management, Torino
- Tecsiel, Roma
- Università di Pisa

We wish to express our gratitude to the members of the Local Arrangement Committee: P. Asirelli, R. Barbuti, P. Degano (Chairman), A. Fantechi, P. Mancarella, M. Martelli, F. Tarini and F. Turini. Without their help, the Conference would not have been possible.

Pisa, March 1987

Hartmut Ehrig
Institut für Software und Theoretische Informatik
Technische Universität Berlin

Robert A. Kowalski
Dept of Computing and Control
Imperial College London

Giorgio Levi
Dipartimento di Informatica
Università di Pisa

Ugo Montanari
Dipartimento di Informatica
Università di Pisa

CONTENTS OF VOLUME 2

CONTENTS OF VOLUME 1

Models and Equality for Logical Programming[1]

Joseph A. Goguen and José Meseguer
SRI International, Menlo Park CA 94025
Center for the Study of Language and Information, Stanford University 94305

Abstract: We argue that some standard tools from model theory provide a better semantic foundation than the more syntactic and operational approaches usually used in logic programming. In particular, we show how initial models capture the intended semantics of both functional and logic programming, as well as their combination, with existential queries having logical variables (for both functions and relations) in the presence of arbitrary user-defined abstract data types, and with the full power of constraint languages, having any desired built-in (computable) relations and functions, including disequality (the negation of the equality relation) as well as the usual ordering relations on the usual built-in types, such as numbers and strings. These results are based on a new completeness theorem for order-sorted Horn clause logic with equality, plus the use of standard interpretations for fixed sorts, functions and relations. Finally, we define "logical programming," based on the concept of institution, and show how it yields a general framework for discussions of this kind. For example, this viewpoint suggests that the natural way to combine functional and logic programming is simply to combine their logics, getting Horn clause logic with equality.

1 Introduction

This paper argues that some very significant benefits are available to logic programming from using certain concepts from first order model theory, namely:

- order-sorted logic and models;
- initial models;
- interpretation into fixed models for certain fixed sorts, functions and relations; and
- true semantic equality.

These techniques, which are all standard in the theory of abstract data types [17, 22, 14], provide an attractive alternative to the more syntactical and operational approaches generally favored in logic programming. Moreover, they provide a powerful approach that supports:

- user-defined abstract data types;
- built-in data types;
- combined logic and functional programming; and
- constraint-based programming, in a way that can utilize standard algorithms for standard problems, such as linear programming.

In addition, we suggest that the more recent theory of institutions [10] may provide conceptual insight and clarification, as well as a broadening of the general scope of logic programming, so as to encompass any logical system satisfying certain simple restrictions.

In a sense, this paper is an attempt to explicate our previous paper on Eqlog [11], by giving a fuller account of its mathematical semantics, as well as further details, polemics, and comparisons with the

---

[1]Supported in part by Office of Naval Research Contracts N00014-85-C-0417 and N00014-86-C-0450, and a gift from the System Development Foundation.

existing literature. One reason that [11] may have been obscure to many readers, is the large number of new ideas that it tried to introduce all at once; here, we attempt to highlight certain ideas by ignoring others. Among the features of Eqlog deliberately downplayed here are: modules, both hierarchical and generic; theories and views; and "attributes" of operators (e.g., associativity and commutativity). Although these features greatly increase the expressive power of Eqlog, they would also distract from the basic foundational and semantic issues that we wish to emphasize here. For similar reasons, this paper does not develop most issues concerning the operational semantics of the various systems that are discussed. Thus, unification, term rewriting, narrowing and resolution are only touched upon. They are discussed in somewhat more detail in [11], and will receive full treatment in [23] and [26].

1.1 Order-Sorted Logic

Ordinary unsorted logic offers the dubious advantage that anything can be applied to anything; for example,

```
3 * first-name(age(false)) < 2^birth-place(temperature(329))
```

is a well-formed expression. Although beloved by hackers of Lisp and Prolog, unsorted logic is too permissive. The trouble is that the usual alternative, many-sorted logic, is too restrictive, since it does not support overloading of function symbols such as _+_ for integer, rational, and complex numbers. In addition, an expression like

```
(-4 / -2)!
```

does not, strictly speaking, parse (assuming that factorial only applies to natural numbers). Here, we suggest that **order-sorted logic**, with subsorts and operator loading, plus the additional twist of **retracts** (although they are not discussed here; see [14]), really does provide sufficient expressiveness, while still banishing the truly meaningless.

Although the specialization of many-sorted logic to many-sorted algebra has been very successfully applied to the theory of abstract data types, many-sorted algebra can produce some very awkward specifications in practice, primarily due to difficulties in handling erroneous expressions, such as dividing by zero in the rationals, or taking the top of an empty stack. In fact there *is no* really satisfactory way to define either the rationals or stacks with MSA. However, order-sorted algebra overcomes these obstacles through its richer type system, which supports subsorts, overloaded operators, and total functions that would otherwise have to be partial. Moreover, order-sorted algebra is the basis of both OBJ [9] and Eqlog [11]. Finally, order-sorted algebra solves the **constructor-selector problem**, which, roughly speaking, is to define inverses, called selectors, for constructors; the solution is to restrict selectors to the largest subsorts where they make sense. For example, **pop and top** are only defined for non-empty stacks. [15] shows not only that order-sorted algebra solves this problem, but also that many-sorted algebra *cannot* solve it.

The essence of order-sorted logic is to provide a *subsort* partial ordering among the sorts, and to interpret it semantically as subset inclusion, among the carriers of a model, and to support operator overloading that is interpreted as restricting functions to subsorts. Two happy facts are that order-sorted logic is only slightly more difficult than many-sorted logic, and that essentially all results generalize from the many-sorted to the order-sorted case without complication. See [14] for a comprehensive treatment of order-sorted algebra. This paper broadens the logical framework to allow not only algebras, but also models of arbitrary first-order signatures, with both function and predicate symbols, including equality, and gives rules of deduction for Horn clauses in such a logic, proving their completeness and several other basic results that are directly relevant to our model-theoretic account of logic and functional programming, including initiality and Herbrand theorems.

1.2 Models

Perhaps the origins in proof theory explain the obsession of logic programming theorists with syntactic and proof theoretic constructions. In any case, we believe that more semantic and more abstract tools provide a basis that is both broader and more powerful. In particular, we feel that the usual Herbrand Universe construction is too syntactic and is also unnecessarily restrictive, because:

1. it does not provide for built-in types, such as numbers and infinite trees;
2. it does not provide for user-defined abstract data types;
3. it does not (directly) address the phenomenon of representation independence for terms and for data types, whether built-in or user-defined; and
4. the proofs are more concrete and computational than necessary[2].

Of course, these deficiencies can all be patched without great difficulty -- for example, [19] shows how to include built-in numbers -- but after a few such patches, you have something enough like the initial model approach that you might as well, or better, take advantage of the powerful machinery associated with that tradition.

The reason for being interested in models is just that a standard model can provide the implementer with a clear standard for correctness, and can also provide the programmer and user with a clear model for what to expect when programs are actually run.

The reason for being interested in standard interpretations into particular semantic domains on some sorts, functions and relations (while leaving others free) is that then one can use standard algorithms to solve particular problems over such domains, for example, linear programming algorithms over the real numbers. This gives a great deal of flexibility, since one can still use initiality (i.e., abstraction) over other sorts. We argue below that this provides an elegant foundation for constraint-based programming.

1.3 Equality

Equational logic, which is essentially the logic of substitution of equals for equals, provides a foundation for functional programming languages. For example: [18] gives (what can be seen as) an equational description of Backus' FP [2]; [24] describes an "equational programming" language[3]; and [9] describes OBJ2, a language that combines initial algebra semantics for executable "objects" (defined by very general sets of user-supplied conditional order-sorted equations), with "loose" algebra semantics for non-executable "theories" (defined by arbitrary sets of equations).

---

[2] Not everyone will regard this as a deficiency!

[3] This language has some very strong restrictions, including: no repeated variables on lefthand sides, no overlap among equations, only one sort of data, no conditional equations, and a strong sequentiality condition; on the other hand, it is much easier to compile efficient code from sets of equations that satisfy such restrictions.

In the context of first order logic, equality is generally treated as a special relation, interpreted as real semantic equality in models, rather than merely axiomatized. This is the sense in which one speaks of "first order logic with equality" and of "Horn clause logic with equality." Complete sets of rules of deduction are well-known for these logical systems, and the latter has been used to combine logic and functional programming [11]. This paper later gives corresponding rules for order-sorted Horn clause logic with equality.

Equality is also useful in understanding constraint-based programming, because equations can be used to define the basic data structures, and then various relations of special interest can be defined recursively over these data structures, and/or provided as built-ins.

1.4 Initiality

Initial models free one from commitment to any particular representation; that is, they support *abstraction*. In particular, initiality handles abstract data types for logical programming languages with great fluency and convenience, and similarly it can be used to define functions and relations over built-in types [11]. Initial models also provide an account of the conceptual world of a program, in the sense of being "closed worlds" or "standard models." In particular, they provide a standard of correctness for the implementer, as well as a model for what results to expect for the programmer. Finally, initiality is a so-called "universal property," that there exists a unique mapping satisfying certain conditions, and it is well-known that, in many cases, one gets a much cleaner mathematical theory, with simpler and more conceptual proofs, from using universal characterizations of objects of interest, as compared to using concrete constructions for them [21]. In fact, the familiar characterization of "free" by the existence of a unique mapping with certain properties that extends another, is a special case of initiality.

One can better understand initiality through the so-called "no junk" and "no confusion" conditions (originally from [7]); these can also be seen as "completeness" and "soundness" conditions, respectively. Assume that signatures provide symbols for construcing sentences, including functions and constants (in Σ) and relations (in Π), and that models contain "data elements." Given a signature Σ,Π and a set C of Σ,Π-sentences, call a Σ,Π-model **standard** if and only if:

1. **No junk**: Every data item is denoted by a term using the function (and constant) symbols in Σ. (A data item that cannot be so constructed is "junk.")
2. **No confusion**: a predicate holds of some data elements if and only if it can be proved from the given sentences; in particular, two elements are identified if and only if they can be proved equal from the given sentences. (Two data items that are equal but cannot be proved so are "confused.")

For Horn clause logic, either with or without equality, either order-sorted, many-sorted, or unsorted, these two conditions define the data items *uniquely* up to renaming, i.e., they define a model up to isomorphism. Moreover, "no junk" is equivalent to structural induction over the signature, and the two conditions together are equivalent to the "unique homomorphism" condition called **initiality** (see [22] for details).

1.5 Constraints

In its general sense, a **constraint** is a logical relation that one wishes to impose on a set of potential solutions. In principle, such constraints could be arbitrary first order sentences involving arbitrary (interpreted and uninterpreted) relations; but in practice, constraints are limited to sets of atomic sentences, such as

$$a * X + b * Y < c * Z + d,$$
$$a * X * X + b * X + c = 0,$$
$$a * X * Y \cup b * X + c \subseteq Z,$$

where the variables in the first two constraints range over some kind of number (e.g., integers, or rationals, or complexes), and in the second range over sets of strings from some fixed alphabet (* is multiplication in the first two, and is concatenation, extended to sets, in the third). Although Prolog would, in principle, be ideal for *constraint-based programming*, it does not suffice in practice, because of the limited capabilities of the built-in relations. Moreover, the usual semantic basis of Prolog does not extend to built-ins without some extra fuss and awkwardness (e.g., as in [19]).

We refer to sorts, functions, and relations upon which interpretation into a fixed (standard) model are imposed as **built-ins**. Two obvious examples of such models are numbers and infinite trees, with their usual functions and relations. The pioneering work of Jaffar and Lassez [19] and of Jaffar and Michaylov [20] treat these and a number of other examples, in the context of a constraint logic programming language called CLP. These authors also treat a number of other topics, some of which are not considered here, including negation as failure and compactness conditions [19].

1.6 Logical Programming

Various aspects of programming languages are captured by various aspects of logic. The functional aspect of programming is captured by equational logic [9]. Strong typing is captured by many-sorted logic. Logic programming (which might be less misleadingly called relational or Horn clause programming) is captured by Horn clause logic. Object-oriented programming is captured by reflective logic, in which there is an abstract data type of program texts built into the language [12]. The perspective of logical programming suggests that the right way to combine various programming paradigms is to discover their underlying logics, combine them, and then base a language upon the combined logic. This permits one to mix and match various programming language features. For example, combined functional and logic programming is captured by Horn clause logic with equality [11]. Combined functional and object-oriented programming is captured by reflective equational logic (we call this language FOOPS, see [12]). We currently feel that reflective order-sorted Horn clause logic with equality is a good candidate for unifying the functional, relational and object-oriented paradigms into a single simple programming language which also has powerful database capabilities.

The theory of institutions [10] can provide a formal basis for the notion of logical programming. Informally, an institution is a logical system, with formal notions of sentence, model, and satisfaction. Then, a **logical programming language** $\mathcal{L}$ has an associated logical system (i.e., institution) $\mathcal{I}$ such that:

- the statements of $\mathcal{L}$ are sentences from $\mathcal{I}$;
- the operational semantics of $\mathcal{L}$ is (a reasonably efficient) deduction in $\mathcal{I}$; and
- the denotational semantics of $\mathcal{L}$ is given by a class of models in $\mathcal{I}$ (preferably initial models).

2 Order-Sorted Algebra

The following assumes familiarity with S-sorted sets and functions (for S a family of sorts) and with many-sorted algebra signatures (S,Σ), Σ-algebras and Σ-homomorphisms [22], and generalizes these concepts to order-sorted algebra.

Definition 1: An **order-sorted signature** is a triple (S,≤,Σ) such that (S,Σ) is a many-sorted signature, (S,≤) is a partially ordered set[4], and the operators satisfy the following **monotonicity condition**[5]:

if $\sigma \in \Sigma_{w1,s1} \cap \Sigma_{w2,s2}$ and if w1≤w2, then s1≤s2 .

When the sort set S is clear, we write Σ for (S,Σ). Similarly, when the partial order (S,≤) is clear, we write Σ for (S,≤,Σ). Also, we may write σ: w→s for $\sigma \in \Sigma_{w,s}$ to emphasize that σ denotes a function with **arity** w and co-arity (or **value sort**) s. An important special case is w=λ, the empty string; then $\sigma \in \Sigma_{\lambda,s}$ denotes a **constant** of sort s. □

Regular signatures allow one to define the least sort of a term, and to give an order-sorted generalization of the usual term algebra construction. Intuitively, regularity says that overloaded operators with argument sorts greater than a given sort string are consistent under the restriction of arguments to subsorts.

Definition 2: An order-sorted signature Σ is **regular** iff given w0≤w1 in S* and σ in $\Sigma_{w1,s1}$ there a least ⟨w,s⟩∈S*×S such that $\sigma \in \Sigma_{w,s}$ and w0≤w. If, in addition, each connected component[6] of the sort poset has a top element, then the regular signature is called **coherent**. □

Definition 3: Let (S,≤,Σ) be an order-sorted signature. Then an (S,≤,Σ)-**algebra** is an (S,Σ)-algebra A such that

(1) s≤s′ in S implies $A_s \subseteq A_{s'}$ and

(2) $\sigma \in \Sigma_{w1,s1} \cap \Sigma_{w2,s2}$ with s1≤s2 and w1≤w2 implies $A_\sigma: A_{w1} \to A_{s1}$ equals $A_\sigma: A_{w2} \to A_{s2}$ on A_{w1} .

When (S,≤) is clear, (S,≤,Σ)-algebras may be called **order-sorted Σ-algebras**. We may write $A_\sigma^{w,s}$ instead of $A_\sigma: A_w \to A_s$. □

Definition 4: Let (S,≤,Σ) be an order-sorted signature, and let A and B be order-sorted (S,≤,Σ)-algebras. Then a (S,≤,Σ)-**homomorphism** h: A→B is a (S,Σ)-homomorphism satisfying the following **restriction** condition

s≤s′ and $a \in A_s$ imply $h_s(a) = h_{s'}(a)$.

When the partially ordered set (S,≤) is clear, (S,≤,Σ)-homomorphisms are also called **order-sorted Σ-homomorphisms**. The (S,≤,Σ)-algebras and (S,≤,Σ)-homomorphisms form a category that we denote $\mathbf{OSAlg}_\Sigma$. □

Order-sorted algebra *strictly generalizes* many-sorted algebra, in the sense that any many-sorted (S,Σ)-algebra is an order-sorted (S,≤,Σ)-algebra for ≤ the trivial ordering on S, with s≤s′ iff s=s′;

---

[4]We extend the ordering ≤ on S to strings of equal length in S* by $s_1 \ldots s_n \le s'_1 \ldots s'_n$ iff $s_i \le s'_i$ for 1≤i≤n. Similarly, ≤ extends to pairs ⟨w,s⟩ in S*×S by ⟨w,s⟩≤⟨w′,s′⟩ iff w≤w′ and s≤s′.

[5]Although not needed for validity of our results, this very natural condition rules out some bizarre models.

[6]Given a poset (S,≤), let ≡ denote the transitive and symmetric closure of ≤. Then ≡ is an equivalence relation whose equivalence classes are the **connected componets** of (S,≤).

then $\mathbf{OSAlg}_\Sigma = \mathbf{Alg}_\Sigma$ and the forgetful functor $\mathbf{OSAlg}_\Sigma \to \mathbf{Alg}_\Sigma$ is the identity. Similarly, the rules of order-sorted deduction given later specialize to many-sorted rules for this ordering.

Definition 5: For $(S,\leq,\Sigma)$ an order-sorted signature and A an order-sorted Σ-algebra, an **order-sorted Σ-congruence** $\equiv$ on A is a many-sorted Σ-congruence $\equiv=\{\equiv_s \mid s\in S\}$ such that

for each $s,s'\in S$ and $a,a'\in A_{s'}$, whenever $s\leq s'$ then $a\equiv_s a'$ iff $a\equiv_{s'} a'$.

□

Let f: $A\to B$ be an order-sorted Σ-homomorphism. Then the **kernel** of f is an S-sorted family of equivalence relations $\equiv_f$ defined by $a\equiv_{f,s}a'$ iff $f_s(a)=f_s(a')$ and denoted ker(f). It is easy to check that ker(f) is an order-sorted Σ-congruence. For $(S,\leq,\Sigma)$ a coherent order-sorted signature, A an order-sorted Σ-algebra, and $\equiv$ an order-sorted Σ-congruence on A, the **quotient** of A by $\equiv$ is the order-sorted Σ-algebra $A/\equiv$ defined as follows: for each sort s, the carrier of maximal sort in its connected component is $(A/\equiv)_{max(s)} = A_{max(s)}/\equiv_{max(s)}$ and the carrier of sort s is $(A/\equiv)_s = q_{max(s)}(A_s)$, for $q_{max(s)}: A_{max(s)}\to(A/\equiv)_{max(s)}$ the natural projection of each element a into its $\equiv_{max(s)}$-equivalence class. The operations are defined by: $(A/\equiv)_\sigma([a1],...,[an]) = [A_\sigma(a1,...,an)]$, which is well-defined since $\equiv$ is an order-sorted Σ-congruence. The order-sorted algebra $A/\equiv$ has a natural surjective order-sorted Σ-homomorphism q: $A\to A/\equiv$ defined by restricting the $q_{max(s)}$ to the remaining sorts and such that ker(q) = $\equiv$. This homomorphism is called the **quotient map** associated to the congruence $\equiv$.

Lemma 6: <u>Universal Property of Quotients</u>: Let Σ be a coherent order-sorted signature, A an order-sorted Σ-algebra and $\equiv$ an order-sorted congruence on A. Then the quotient map q: $A\to A/\equiv$ satisfies the following universal property: If f: $A\to B$ is any order-sorted Σ-homomorphism such that $\equiv\subseteq$ker(f), then there is a unique Σ-homomorphism u: $A/\equiv\to B$ such that uoq=f. □

Given an order-sorted signature Σ, we construct the **order-sorted Σ-term algebra** $\mathcal{T}_\Sigma$ as the least family $\{\mathcal{T}_{\Sigma,s} \mid s\in S\}$ of sets satisfying the following conditions (note our somewhat pedantic, but temporary, use of (and) for parentheses as formal syntactic symbols):

- $\Sigma_{\lambda,s}\subseteq\mathcal{T}_{\Sigma,s}$ for $s\in S$;
- $\mathcal{T}_{\Sigma,s'}\subseteq\mathcal{T}_{\Sigma,s}$ if $s'\leq s$;
- if $\sigma\in\Sigma_{w,s}$ and if $ti\in\mathcal{T}_{\Sigma,si}$ where $w=s1...sn\neq\lambda$, then (the string) $\sigma(t1...tn)\in\mathcal{T}_{\Sigma,s}$.
- Also, for $\sigma\in\Sigma_{w,s}$ let $\mathcal{T}_\sigma$: $\mathcal{T}_w\to\mathcal{T}_s$ send t1,...,tn to (the string) $\sigma(t1...tn)$.

These terms are ground terms, i.e., they involve no variables. Terms with variables arise from ground terms by enlarging the signature Σ with additional constants for the variables. We assume that each variable comes with a unique associated sort, so that variables form an S-sorted set X with $X_s\cap X_{s'}=\emptyset$ if $s\neq s'$. This gives an extended signature $\Sigma(X)$ (that is also regular) and an algebra $\mathcal{T}_{\Sigma(X)}$ also denoted $\mathcal{T}_\Sigma(X)$. Although a term in an order-sorted term algebra may have many different sorts, we still have

Fact 7: For Σ a regular signature, each term t in $\mathcal{T}_\Sigma$ has a least sort, denoted LS(t). □

Definition 8: Let Σ be an order-sorted signature. Then an order-sorted Σ-algebra I is **initial** in the class of all order-sorted Σ-algebras iff there is a unique order-sorted Σ-homomorphism from I to any other order-sorted Σ-algebra. □

Theorem 9: Let Σ be a regular order-sorted signature. Then $\mathcal{T}_\Sigma$ is an initial order-sorted Σ-algebra. □

Fact 10: Let A be an order-sorted Σ-algebra, X an S-sorted set of variables, and let f: $X\to A$ be an S-sorted function (with X disjoint from Σ); such a function is called an **assignment** from X to A. Then (by initiality) there is a unique order-sorted Σ-homomorphism f^*: $\mathcal{T}_\Sigma(X)\to A$ that extends f. □

This fact is usually expressed by saying that $\mathcal{T}_\Sigma(X)$ is the **free** order-sorted Σ-algebra on X.

For $(S,\leq,\Sigma)$ a coherent order-sorted signature and X,Y two S-sorted variable sets, a **substitution** is an S-sorted map θ: $X \rightarrow T_{\Sigma}(Y)$; this is a special assignment, where the values of variables lie in a term algebra. The unique order-sorted Σ-homomorphism θ^*: $T_{\Sigma}(X) \rightarrow T_{\Sigma}(Y)$ that extends θ is also be denoted θ.

3 Order-Sorted Model Theory

Order-sorted models generalize order-sorted algebras by allowing predicates instead of just function symbols, and order-sorted Horn clause logic allows arbitrary Horn clauses instead of just conditional equations. Order-sorted Horn clause logic has a number of advantages over unsorted logic; in general, these advantages are extensions of the advantages of order-sorted algebra over unsorted algebra, such as the great expressive power given by overloading and strong but still flexible typing, and the capacity to handle errors. An additional advantage of order-sorted Horn clause logic that has great practical importance is that sometimes the search space and required time for theorem proving can by drastically cut by making use of subsorts, and shown, for example, by work of Walther [27] on the steamroller example.

This section first extends the basic notions from algebras to models, and then gives rules of deduction for order-sorted Horn clause logic with equality, with a proof of their completeness. We then construc the initial model associated to a set of Horn clauses, and prove Herbrand's theorem, both in general, and for the special case where all sorts are non-empty. Finally, we prove the existence of free extensions, and apply this to built-ins.

3.1 Basic Definitions

Definition 11: An **order-sorted signature with predicates** is a quadruple $(S,\leq,\Sigma,\Pi)$ such that $(S,\leq,\Sigma)$ is a coherent order-sorted signature, and $\Pi=\{\Pi_w \mid w\in S^+\}$ is a family of **predicate symbols** satisfying the conditions below. We use capital letters $P,Q,P_1,P_2,\ldots$ to denote predicate symbols. We may write "P: w" for $P\in\Pi_w$ and then call w an **arity** of P. As with function symbols, we allow overloading of predicate symbols, i.e., P can have several arities. We assume the following two conditions:

1. There is an equality predicate symbol $=$ of arity ss in Π iff s is the top of a connected component of the sort poset S.
2. Regularity: For each w0 such that there is a P: w1 with $w0\leq w1$, there is a least w such that P: w and $w0\leq w$.

When the sort set S and partial order $\leq$ are clear, we write Σ,Π for $(S,\leq,\Sigma,\Pi)$. □

Definition 12: Let $(S,\leq,\Sigma,\Pi)$ be an order-sorted signature with predicates. Then an $(S,\leq,\Sigma,\Pi)$**-model** is an order-sorted $(S,\leq,\Sigma)$-algebra M together with an assignment to each P: w in Π of a subset $M^w{}_P\subseteq M_w$ such that:

(i) for P the identity predicate $=$: ss the assignment is the identity relation, i.e., $(M^{ss}{}_=)=\{(a,a) \mid a\in M_s\}$; and

(ii) whenever P: w1 and P: w2 and $w1\leq w2$ then $M^{w1}{}_P=M_{w1}\cap M^{w2}{}_P$.

□

Definition 13: Let Σ,Π be an order-sorted signature with predicates and let M and M' be order-sorted Σ,Π-models. Then a Σ,Π**-homomorphism** h: $M\rightarrow M'$ is an order-sorted Σ,Π-homomorphism such that for each P: w in Π,

$f_w(a_1,...,a_n) \in M'^w_P$ whenever $(a_1,...,a_n) \in M^w_P$.

The Σ,Π-models and Σ,Π-homomorphisms form a category that we denote $\mathbf{Mod}_{\Sigma,\Pi}$. □

Order-sorted model theory *strictly generalizes* many-sorted model theory, in the sense that any many-sorted (S,Σ,Π)-model is an order-sorted $(S,\leq,\Sigma,\Pi)$-model for $\leq$ the trivial ordering on S, with $s \leq s'$ iff $s=s'$. Similarly, the rules of order-sorted deduction given later specialize to rules for many-sorted deduction for the trivial ordering.

Given an order-sorted signature Σ,Π with predicates, we can define the Σ,Π-model $\mathcal{T}_{\Sigma,\Pi}$ consisting of the Σ-term algebra $\mathcal{T}_\Sigma$ and having $(\mathcal{T}_{\Sigma,\Pi}{}^w)_P=\emptyset$ for each P: w in Π different from the identity predicate (= is of course interpreted as actual identity). For X an S-sorted set of variables disjoint form Σ, the model $\mathcal{T}_{\Sigma,\Pi}(X)$ is defined in a similar way by enlarging Σ with the constants in X. It is then immediate to generalize to models the notion of an initial algebra and to check the following:

Theorem 14: Let Σ,Π be an order-sorted signature with predicates. Then $\mathcal{T}_{\Sigma,\Pi}$ is an initial order-sorted Σ,Π-model. □

Fact 15: Let M be an order-sorted Σ,Π-model, X an S-sorted set of variables disjoint from Σ, and let f: X→M be an S-sorted assignment. Then, by initiality, there is a unique order-sorted Σ,Π-homomorphism f^*: $\mathcal{T}_{\Sigma,\Pi}(X)\to M$ that extends f. This fact is usually expressed by saying that $\mathcal{T}_{\Sigma,\Pi}(X)$ is the **free** Σ,Π-model on X. □

We now introduce additional notation for atoms and Horn clauses. For Σ,Π an order-sorted signature with predicates we define Σ,Π-**atoms** as expressions $P(t_1,...,t_n)$ such that the $t_1,...,t_n$ are Σ-terms (possibly with variables) and there is a $w=s_1...s_n$ with P: w in Π such that t_i has sort s_i for $i=1,...,n$. Thus, an equation $t=t'$ is an atom where P is the identity relation. We will use symbols $A,B,A_1,A_2,...$ for atoms. For θ a substitution and $A=P(t_1,...,t_n)$ an atom, θA denotes the atom $A=P(\theta[t_1],...,\theta[t_n])$. We interpret a *set* of atoms $\{A_1,...,A_n\}$ as a conjunction. Although we may drop the curly brackets and write $A_1,...,A_n$ we still assume that this denotes a set, so that the order does not matter and there are no repeated atoms. The empty set of atoms has the empty notation, i.e., it is denoted as a blank. By a Σ,Π-**Horn clause** we mean an expression

$$(\forall X)\ A \Leftarrow B_1,...,B_m$$

where X contains all the variables occurring in all the terms in the atoms $A,B_1,...,B_m$. We call A the **head** and the set $B_1,...,B_m$ the **body**. When the body is empty, the Horn clause is called an **atomic** (universal) **sentence** and the notation "$(\forall X)\ A \Leftarrow$" is abbreviated to "$(\forall X)\ A$." When all atoms have the equality predicate as their predicate symbol, the Horn clause is called a **conditional equation**; if, in addition, the body is empty it is called an **equation**.

Definition 16: For Σ,Π an order-sorted signature with predicates, M a Σ,Π-model and $(\forall X)\ A \Leftarrow B_1,...,B_m$ a Σ,Π-Horn clause, we say that M **satisfies** $(\forall X)\ A \Leftarrow B_1,...,B_m$ if (assuming $A=Q(t_1,...,t_n)$, $B_i=P_i(t_{i1},...,t_{in_i})$) for any assignment f: X→M such that[7]

$$(f^*(t_{i1}),...,f^*(t_{in_i})) \in M^{wi}_{P_i} \text{ for } i=1,...,m,$$

then also

$$(f^*(t_1),...,f^*(t_n)) \in M^w_Q.$$

Similarly, for $\mathcal{C}$ a set of horn clauses we say that M **satisfies** $\mathcal{C}$ iff it satisfies each clause in $\mathcal{C}$; such a model is then called a $\Sigma,\Pi,\mathcal{C}$-**model**, and the category of all such models is denoted $\mathbf{Mod}_{\Sigma,\Pi,\mathcal{C}}$. □

---

[7] Note that, by regularity, the least arity wi of P_i is uniquely defined.

3.2 Order-Sorted Deduction

This section presents a new completeness theorem for order-sorted Horn clause logic with equality. This theorem provides a basis for the correctness of implementations for languages like Eqlog [11], as well as the basis for our development of a semantic theory for constraint languages.

Given an order-sorted signature Σ,Π with predicates and a set C of Σ,Π-Horn clauses, the following are the rules for deriving atomic sentences:

(1) Reflexivity: Each equation $(\forall X)\ t=t$ is derivable.

(2) Symmetry: If $(\forall X)\ t=t'$ is derivable, then so is $(\forall X)\ t'=t$.

(3) Transitivity: If the equations $(\forall X)\ t=t'$, $(\forall X)\ t'=t''$ are derivable, then so is $(\forall X)\ t=t''$.

(4) Congruence: If $t_i, t'_i \in \mathcal{T}_\Sigma(X)_{s_i}$ for $i=1,...,n$, and if $(\forall X)\ t_i=t'_i$ is derivable for $i=1,...,n$, then:

- for any $\sigma: s_1...s_n \to s$ in Σ the equation $(\forall X)\ \sigma(t_1,...,t_n)=\sigma(t'_1,...,t'_n)$ is derivable;
- for any $P: s_1...s_n$ in Π (other than the identity predicate) if the sentence $(\forall X)\ P(t_1,...,t_n)$ is derivable, then so is $(\forall X)\ P(t'_1,...,t'_n)$.

(5) Modus Ponens: If $(\forall X)\ A \Leftarrow B_1,...,B_m$ is in C and if $\theta: X \to \mathcal{T}_\Sigma(Y)$ is a substitution such that for each B_i in the body of the clause the atomic sentence $(\forall Y)\ \theta B_i$ is derivable, then so is $(\forall Y)\ \theta A$.

For X an S-sorted set of variables, we define a Σ,Π-model $\mathcal{T}_{\Sigma,\Pi,C}(X)$ as follows: First, notice that for t and t' terms of the same sort, the property

$(\forall X)\ t=t'$ is derivable from C using rules (1)-(5)

defines an order-sorted Σ-congruence $\sim^C_{(X)}$ on $\mathcal{T}_\Sigma(X)$ since, by rules (1)-(4), $\sim^C_{(X)}$ is a many-sorted Σ-congruence relation and, in addition, $\sim^C_{(X)}$ is an order-sorted Σ-congruence relation, since for any sort s such that $t, t' \in \mathcal{T}_\Sigma(X)_s$ we have $t \sim^C_{(X),s} t'$ iff $(\forall X)\ t=t'$ is derivable from C using rules (1)-(5), a property that does not depend on s. Thus, we can define an order-sorted Σ-algebra $\mathcal{T}_{\Sigma,C}(X)$ as the quotient of $\mathcal{T}_\Sigma(X)$ by the order-sorted congruence $\sim^C_{(X)}$. We can then give a Σ,Π-model structure $\mathcal{T}_{\Sigma,\Pi,C}(X)$ to $\mathcal{T}_{\Sigma,C}(X)$ by defining $([t_1],...,[t_n]) \in \mathcal{T}_{\Sigma,\Pi,C}(X)^w{}_P$ iff $(\forall X)\ P(t_1,...,t_n)$ is provable from C by (1)-(5) (where $w=s_1,...,s_n$ and t_i has sort s_i). This definition is independent of the representatives t_i by (4). We can now prove

Lemma 17: $\mathcal{T}_{\Sigma,\Pi,C}(X)$ satisfies C.

Proof: Let $(\forall Y)\ A \Leftarrow B_1,...,B_m$ be a Horn clause in C (with, say, $A=Q(t_1,...,t_n)$, $B_i=P_i(t_{i1},...,t_{in_i})$) and let $\theta_0: Y \to \mathcal{T}_{\Sigma,\Pi,C}(X)$ be an S-sorted assignment such that $(\theta_0{}^*(t_{i1}),...,\theta_0{}^*(t_{in_i})) \in \mathcal{T}_{\Sigma,\Pi,C}(X)^{w_i}{}_{P_i}$ for $i=1,...,m$. By choosing a representative $t \in \mathcal{T}_\Sigma(X)_s$ for each $[t]=\theta_0(y)$, $y \in Y_s$, we then obtain a substitution $\theta: Y \to \mathcal{T}_\Sigma(X)$ such that, by hypothesis (and by initiality of $\mathcal{T}_{\Sigma,\Pi}(Y)$ making $\theta_0{}^*=q\circ\theta$ for q the quotient homomorphism $q: \mathcal{T}_{\Sigma,\Pi}(X) \to \mathcal{T}_{\Sigma,\Pi,C}(X)$) we have $(\forall X)\ \theta B_1$ derivable from C using rules (1)-(5) for $i=1,...,m$. Thus, by (5) we then have $(\forall X)\ \theta A$ derivable from C using rules (1)-(5), i.e., we have $(\theta_0{}^*(t_1),...,\theta_0{}^*(t_n)) \in \mathcal{T}_{\Sigma,\Pi,C}(X)^{wi}{}_Q$ as desired. □

Theorem 18: Completeness Theorem: For Σ,Π an order-sorted signature, C a set of Σ,Π-Horn clauses and $(\forall X)\ A$ a Σ,Π-atomic sentence, the following are equivalent:

- $(\forall X)\ A$ is derivable from C using rules (1)-(5).
- $(\forall X)\ A$ is satisfied by all order-sorted Σ-algebras that satisfy C.

Proof: We leave the reader to check soundness, i.e., that the first assertion implies the second, and concentrate here on proving completeness, i.e., that any sentence that is satisfied is provable. Let $(\forall X)\ P(t_1,...,t_n)$ be a sentence satisfied by all Σ,Π,C-models. Then, it is satisfied by $\mathcal{T}_{\Sigma,\Pi,C}(X)$. In particular, for the assignment $q: X \to \mathcal{T}_{\Sigma,\Pi,C}(X)$ associated to the quotient homomorphism $q: \mathcal{T}_{\Sigma,\Pi}(X) \to \mathcal{T}_{\Sigma,\Pi,C}(X)$) we have

$([t_1],\ldots,[t_n]) \in \mathcal{T}_{\Sigma,\Pi,C}(X)^w{}_P$
which by definition just means that the sentence $(\forall X)\ P(t_1,\ldots,t_n)$ is derivable from C with rules (1)-(5).
□

Corollary 19: Initiality Theorem: For Σ,Π an order-sorted signature with predicates and C a set of Σ,Π-Horn clauses, $\mathcal{T}_{\Sigma,\Pi,C}(\emptyset)$ (henceforth denoted $\mathcal{T}_{\Sigma,\Pi,C}$) is an initial model in the class of all Σ,Π,C-models, and $\mathcal{T}_{\Sigma,\Pi,C}(X)$ is a free model on X in that same class.

Proof: Let M be an order-sorted model satisfying C, and let $\underline{a}$: X→M be an assignment. We have to show that there is a unique order-sorted Σ,Π-homomorphism $\underline{a}^{\&}$: $\mathcal{T}_{\Sigma,\Pi,C}(X) \to M$ extending $\underline{a}$, i.e., such that $\underline{a}^{\&}(q(x))=\underline{a}(x)$ for each $x \in X$, where q denotes the quotient homomorphism q: $\mathcal{T}_{\Sigma,\Pi}(X) \to \mathcal{T}_{\Sigma,\Pi,C}(X)$. Existence of $\underline{a}^{\&}$ follows from the Completeness Theorem, by (i) and (ii) below:

(i) $\underline{a}^*(t)=\underline{a}(t')$ for each equation $(\forall X)\ t=t'$ provable from C by the rules (1)-(5).

This means that $\sim^C_{(X)} \subseteq \ker(\underline{a}^*)$ and by the universal property of quotients (Lemma 6) there is a unique order-sorted Σ-homomorphism $\underline{a}^{\&}$: $\mathcal{T}_{\Sigma,C}(X) \to M$ with $\underline{a}^* = \underline{a}^{\&} \circ q$.

(ii) $([t_1],\ldots,[t_n]) \in \mathcal{T}_{\Sigma,\Pi,C}(X)^w{}_P$ iff (for representatives t_i of sort s_i, with $w=s_1,\ldots,s_n$) $(\forall X)\ P(t_1,\ldots,t_n)$ is provable from C by the rules (1)-(5) iff (by the Completeness Theorem) $(\forall X)\ P(t_1,\ldots,t_n)$ holds in all models that satisfy C.

Thus, $(\underline{a}^{\&}[t_1],\ldots,\underline{a}^{\&}[t_n])=(\underline{a}^*(t_1),\ldots,\underline{a}^*(t_n)) \in M^w{}_P$ which shows that $\underline{a}^{\&}$ is a Σ,Π-homomorphism. Uniquenes of $\underline{a}^{\&}$ then follows by combining the universal property of $\mathcal{T}_{\Sigma,\Pi}(X)$ as a free order-sorted model on X with the universal property of q as a quotient. Indeed, let $\underline{a}^{\$}$: $\mathcal{T}_{\Sigma,\Pi,C}(X) \to M$ be another order-sorted homomorphism such that $\underline{a}^{\$}(q(x))=\underline{a}(x)$ for each $x \in X$. Then, since $\mathcal{T}_{\Sigma,\Pi}(X)$ is a free order-sorted model on X, we have $\underline{a}^* = \underline{a}^{\$} \circ q$ and by the universal property of q as a quotient we have $\underline{a}^{\$} = \underline{a}^{\&}$ as desired. For $X=\emptyset$ the empty S-sorted family, this proves that $\mathcal{T}_{\Sigma,\Pi,C}(\emptyset)=\mathcal{T}_{\Sigma,\Pi,C}$ is an initial model in the class of models that satisfy C. □

3.3 Herbrand's Theorem

Usual logic programming practice considers queries of the form $B_1,\ldots,B_n$. Such queries are answered positively if a substitution θ is found such that each θB_i is provable from the clauses C that constitute the program. Such a query is simply an existential formula of the form $(\exists X)\ B_1,\ldots,B_n$ and what is being established is that the formula holds for all models that satisfy C. Herbrand's theorem reduces provability of such a formula to satisfaction in the initial model. This subsection extends the rules of order-sorted deduction to handle existential quantification of conjunctions of atoms by giving a very simple proof of a general Herbrand's theorem that hold for any order-sorted Horn clause logic with equality specification (Σ,Π,C). Before the advent of resolution in the theorem-proving literature [25], the methods used to prove that an existential formula was satisfied were brute-force, "saturation" methods that enumerated all possible elements of the initial model until a successful instance was found. Assuming that all the sorts of the initial model are nonempty, we can give simpler rules of deduction that dispense with explicit quantification, and we can prove a second version of Herbrand's Theorem. This second version provides a foundation for proofs by resolution in the extended context of order-sorted logic with equality.

Definition 20: For Σ,Π an order-sorted signature with predicates, we call an existential formula of the form $(\exists X)\ B_1,\ldots,B_n$ where X is an S-sorted variable set that contains all variables that appear in terms of the Σ,Π-atoms $B_1,\ldots,B_n$ a Σ,Π-**existential conjunction (of atoms)**. Given a Σ,Π-model M, we say that M **satisfies** the above existential conjunction iff there is an assignment $\underline{a}$: X→M, called a **witness** such that (assuming, say, $B_i=P_i(t_{i1},\ldots,t_{in_i})$ with P: $s_1\ldots s_n$ and t_i of sort s_i) we have

$(\underline{a}^*(t_1),\ldots,\underline{a}^*(t_n)) \in M^w{}_P$. □

Theorem 21: Herbrand's Theorem: For Σ,Π an order-sorted signature with predicates, C a set of Σ,Π-Horn clauses, and $(\exists X)\ B_1,...,B_n$ a Σ,Π-existential conjunction, the following are equivalent:

- $(\exists X)\ B_1,...,B_n$ is satisfied by all Σ,Π,C-models.
- $(\exists X)\ B_1,...,B_n$ is satisfied by the initial Σ,Π,C-model $\mathcal{T}_{\Sigma,\Pi,C}$.

Proof: Of course, if $(\exists X)\ B_1,...,B_n$ is satisfied by all Σ,Π,C-models, it is satisfied by the initial one. Conversely, if θ: $X\rightarrow\mathcal{T}_{\Sigma,\Pi,C}$ is a witness for $(\exists X)\ B_1,...,B_n$, in $\mathcal{T}_{\Sigma,\Pi,C}$ and if M is a Σ,Π,C-model with h: $\mathcal{T}_{\Sigma,\Pi,C}\rightarrow M$ the unique Σ,Π,C-homomorphism, then it follows from the homomorphic property of h that $h\circ\theta$ is a witness for $(\exists X)\ B_1,...,B_n$ in M. □

Corollary 22: Adding the following rule to the rules (1)-(5) of order-sorted deduction gives a sound and complete set of rules to derive, for C a set of Σ,Π-Horn clauses, all valid universal atomic formulas and all valid existential conjunctions of atoms.

(6) Existential Introduction: If, for $1=1,..,n$, $(\forall\emptyset)\theta B_i$ is derivable, with θ: $X\rightarrow\mathcal{T}_{\Sigma}$, then $(\exists X)\ B_1,...,B_n$ is derivable.

□

So far nothing in this paper has required that all sorts of a model are nonempty. There are good reasons for not imposing such a restriction on the models. Indeed, excluding empty sorts one would in general fail to have initial models, and parameterization would be awkward [13]. Nevertheless, in the context of existential quantification there are definite advantages in the case where models do not have empty sorts. This happens exactly when all the sorts of the initial algebra $\mathcal{T}_{\Sigma}$ are nonempty, for Σ the order-sorted signature of function symbols in question; we will then say that the order-sorted signature with predicates Σ,Π has **nonempty sorts**. We will show that the rules of deduction become simpler in this case. We first prove a lemma that holds for any signature at all. The simplest proof of this lemma would be a model-theoretic soundness proof. However, we prefer to give a proof-theoretic proof that shows explicitly why the substitution rule is not needed.

Lemma 23: Substitution Lemma: For Σ,Π an order-sorted signature with predicates and C a set of Σ,Π-Horn clauses,

Substitution: If $(\forall X)$ A is derivable from C by (1)-(5) and if θ: $X\rightarrow\mathcal{T}_{\Sigma}(Y)$ is a substitution, then $(\forall Y)\ \theta A$ is also derivable.

Proof: The derivable formulas can be obtained in a countable number of stages, with stage n+1 adding the new formulas that can be obtained from the those in stage n by (1)-(5) using C. In the first stage, we just have all equations $(\forall X)\ t=t$ (by reflexivity) and all atomic sentences $(\forall Y)\ \theta A$ for each $(\forall X)$ A in C and arbitrary $\theta X\rightarrow\mathcal{T}_{\Sigma}(Y)$ (by Modus Ponens). Consequently, the first stage is trivially closed under substitution. Let us assume as our induction hypothesis that stage n is closed under substitution; we only need to show that stage n+1 also is:

- If $(\forall X)\ t=t'$ is in stage n, then, by symmetry, $(\forall X)\ t'=t$ is in stage n+1 and so is $(\forall Y)\ \theta(t')=\theta(t)$ since $(\forall Y)\ \theta(t)=\theta(t')$ is in stage n by hypothesis.
- If the equations $(\forall X)\ t=t'$, $(\forall X)\ t'=t''$ belong to stage n, then by transitivity, $(\forall X)\ t=t''$ belongs to stage n+1 and so is $(\forall Y)\ \theta(t)=\theta(t'')$ since $(\forall Y)\ \theta(t)=\theta(t')$, $(\forall Y)\ \theta(t')=\theta(t'')$ are in stage n by hypothesis.
- If $t_i,t'_i\in\mathcal{T}_{\Sigma}(X)_{s_i}$, $i=1,...,k$, and if the equations $(\forall X)\ t_i=t'_i$ belong to stage n for $i=1,...,k$, then by congruence:
  - for any σ: $s_1...s_k\rightarrow s$ in Σ the equation $(\forall X)\ \sigma(t_1,...,t_k)=\sigma(t'_1,...,t'_k)$ belongs to stage n+1 and so does the equation $(\forall Y)\ \sigma(\theta(t_1),...,\theta(t_k))=\sigma(\theta(t'_1),...,\theta(t'_k))$, by applying the induction hypothesis to the original equations;

- o for any $P: s_1...s_k$ in Π (other than the identity predicate) if the sentence $(\forall X)\ P(t_1,...,t_k)$ belongs to stage n, then $(\forall X)\ P(t'_1,...,t'_k)$ belongs to stage n+1 and so does $(\forall Y)\ P(t'_1,...,t'_k)$ by applying the induction hypothesis to the original equations and to $(\forall X)\ P(t_1,...,t_k)$.
- If $(\forall X)\ A \Leftarrow B_1,...,B_m$ is in C, and if $\theta: X \to \mathcal{T}_\Sigma(Y)$ is a substitution such that for each B_i in the body of the clause the atomic sentence $(\forall Y)\ \theta B_i$ belongs to stage n, then, by Modus Ponens, $(\forall Y)\ \theta A$ belongs to stage n+1 and so does $(\forall Z)\ \rho\theta A$ by applying the induction hypothesis to the sentences $(\forall Y)\ \theta B_i$ $i=1,...,m$.

□

Using the Substitution Lemma we can now establish the following version of Herbrand's Theorem for signatures with nonempty sorts:

Corollary 24: Herbrand's Theorem for Nonempty Sorts: For Σ,Π an order-sorted signature with predicates and nonempty sorts, C a set of Σ,Π-Horn clauses, and $(\exists X)\ B_1,...,B_n$ a Σ,Π-existential conjunction the following are equivalent:

- $(\exists X)\ B_1,...,B_n$ is satisfied by all Σ,Π,C-models.
- There is a substitution $\theta: X \to \mathcal{T}_\Sigma(Y)$ such that $(\forall Y)\ \theta B_i$ is provable from C using (1)-(5) for $i=1,...,n$.

Proof: By Herbrand's Theorem we only have to prove that the second condition is satisfied by some substitution $\theta: X \to \mathcal{T}_\Sigma(Y)$ iff it is satisfied by some ground term substitution $\theta': X \to \mathcal{T}_\Sigma$. This is so since, by the nonempty sort assumption, we can always define a substitution $\rho: Y \to \mathcal{T}_\Sigma$ and, by the Substitutivity Lemma, we can satisfy the condition with $\theta' = \rho\circ\theta$. □

Nonempty sorts allow dispensing with quantification over sets of variables. This also follows easily from the Substitutivity Lemma, by the following corollary, which says that the choice of a superset X of the set of variables occurring in an atom A is immaterial for the validity of the universally quantified sentence:

Corollary 25: For Σ,Π an order-sorted signature with predicates and nonempty sorts, for A a Σ,Π-atom, and C a set of Σ,Π-Horn clauses, then

$(\forall X)$ A is provable from C using (1)-(5) iff $(\forall vars(A))$ A is also,

where vars(A) is the S-sorted set of variables occurring in A (and, of course, $vars(A) \subseteq X$).

Proof: The "if" part is clear, using rule of substitution applied to the inclusion $vars(A) \subseteq X \subseteq \mathcal{T}_\Sigma(X)$. For the "only if" part, by the nonempty sort assumption one can always define a substitution $X \to \mathcal{T}_\Sigma(vars(A))$ that is the identity on vars(A) by sending the variables in X-vars(A) to ground terms.

□

We finish this subsection with a simplified and generalized set of sound and complete proof rules for the case of nonempty sorts. We leave the universal quantification implicit for atoms and Horn clauses, and treat not only atomic sentences, but also conjunctions $B_1,...,B_n$. Similarly, we simplify existential quantification by omitting the set of variables, since our last corollary, combined with Herbrand's Theorem for nonempty sorts, shows that choice of a superset of variables is also immaterial for existential quantification; we just write $\exists\ B_1,...,B_n$. Here are the rules of deduction for Σ,Π an order-sorted signature with predicates and nonempty sorts and C a set of Σ,Π-Horn clauses to derive (implicitly universal) conjunctions of atoms and existential conjunctions of atoms:

(1) Reflexivity: Each equation $t=t$ is derivable.

(2) Symmetry: If $t=t'$ is derivable, then so is $t'=t$.

(3) Transitivity: If $t=t', t'=t''$ is derivable, then so is $t=t''$.

(4) Congruence: If $t_i, t'_i \in \mathcal{T}_\Sigma(X)_{s_i}$ for $i=1,...,n$, and if $t_1=t'_1,...,t_n=t'_n$ are derivable then:

- for any σ: $s_1...s_n \to s$ in Σ the equation $\sigma(t_1,...,t_n)=\sigma(t'_1,...,t'_n)$ is derivable;
- for any P: $s_1...s_n$ in Π (other than the identity predicate) if $P(t_1,...,t_n)$ is derivable, then so is $P(t'_1,...,t'_n)$.

(5) Modus Ponens: If $A \Leftarrow B_1,...,B_m$ is in $\mathcal{C}$, and if θ: $X \to \mathcal{T}_\Sigma(Y)$ is a substitution such that $\theta B_1,...,\theta B$ is derivable, then so is θA.

(6) Conjunction Introduction: If B_1 and ... and B_m are derivable, then $B_1,...,B_m$ is derivable.

(7) Existential Introduction: If $\theta B_1,...,\theta B_n$ is derivable for some substitution θ, then $\exists\, B_1,...,B_m$ is derivable.

By assigning extra variables from X to elements of a model M denoted by ground terms it is easy to check that, for signatures with nonempty sorts, satisfaction of a Horn clause or an existential conjunction of atoms does not depend on the superset of variables being quantified, and can thus be defined for implicitly quantified sentences. Satisfaction of a conjunction $B_1,...,B_m$ is defined as simultaneous satisfaction of each one of its conjuncts. We then obtain,

Theorem 26: Completeness Theorem for nonempty sorts: For Σ,Π an order-sorted with predicates and nonempty sorts, for $\mathcal{C}$ a set of Σ,Π-Horn clauses and S a (impicitly universal) conjunction $B_1,...,B$ of Σ,Π-atoms, or an existential conjunction of Σ,Π-atoms $\exists\, B_1,...,B_m$ the following are equivalent:

- $(\forall X)$ S is derivable from $\mathcal{C}$ using rules (1)-(7).
- $(\forall X)$ S is satisfied by all order-sorted Σ-algebras that satisfy $\mathcal{C}$.

□

The rules (1)-(7) are the foundation for the much more efficient operational semantics rules for Eqlog, which is based on term rewriting, narrowing, order-sorted unification, and resolution. Since Eqlog computation is restricted to objects, and not allowed for theories, we can allow nonempty sorts in theories for convenience with parameterization, while still requiring nonempty sorts for the executable parts. For example, the theory **POSET** of partially ordered sets can have an empty **Element** sort, but any instantiation along a view from **POSET** to an object should map **Element** to a nonempty sort.

3.4 Operational semantics

The two sets of rules of deduction that we have given, one fully general, and the other for the case where all sorts are non-empty, are not in themsleves efficient enough to implement a langauge that would really be used for programming, although the second is an improvement on the first. Rather, the purpose of these rule sets is to support theoretical developments, such as completeness and Herbrand theorems, and to serve as a bridge to a really efficient operational semantics. Thus, our view is that an operational semantics for a logical programming language is just an efficient proof theory for its logic. For example, order-sorted rewriting [16] provides an efficient proof theory for order-sorted equational logic, and thus for OBJ [9], just as ordinary term rewriting provides an efficien proof theory for ordinary equational logic. Similarly, Horn clause resolution (with some tricks for the incremental accumulation of substitutions, etc.) provides an efficient operational semantics for ordinary Horn clause logic, and thus for Prolog. Finally, the efficient operational semantics for Eqlog [11] is a combination of order-sorted resolution with order-sorted narrowing (which itself is a combination of rewriting and unification); our joint work with Gert Smolka on the order-sorted operational semantics of Eqlog [26], and more specifically on order-sorted unification [23], spells all this out in detail.

3.5 Free Extensions

So far we have considered initial and free models for order-sorted Horn clause logic with equality. However, initiality and freeness can be considered in a relative way: given a model of a subspecification, can we extend it to a model of a superspecification so that the extension is initial or free? This is a question naturally associated with the semantics of parameterized modules, where a model of a (parameter) requirement theory is freely extended to a model of of the theory of the "body." Free extensions are also associated with models that are partly built-in and partly interpreted as initial models of a set of axioms (i.e., a program) in that these models are just free extensions of their built-in parts. This subsection proves that such free extensions exist and can be obtained by a proof-theoretic construction. With slight variations to accomodate changes in syntax and possibly noninjective maps between sorts, our proof generalizes straightforwardly to give a construction of free extensions along a specification morphism (called a view in Eqlog and OBJ) V: $(\Sigma,\Pi,C)\rightarrow(\Sigma',\Pi',C')$, i.e., to a proof that order-sorted Horn clause logic with equality is a *liberal* institution (in the sense of [10]).

Consider a containment of order-sorted Horn clause logic with equality specifications J: $(\Sigma,\Pi,C)\subseteq(\Sigma',\Pi',C')$, i.e., $\Sigma\subseteq\Sigma'$, $\Pi\subseteq\Pi'$, and $C\subseteq C'$. Then any Σ',Π',C'-model M' can be regarded as a Σ,Π,C-model just by forgetting the operations in Σ-Σ' and the predicates in Π-Π'; of course, this process of "forgetting" is a functor $\mathbf{Mod}_{\Sigma',\Pi',C'}\rightarrow\mathbf{Mod}_{\Sigma,\Pi,C}$. Intuitively, by an "extension" of a Σ,Π,C-model M we probably understand a Σ',Π',C'-model M' such that M is a Σ,Π,C-submodel of M'. However, if we insist on the submodel relation, such an M' in general may not exist, due to the fact that C' (having more axioms than C) may force identifying different elements of M. Thus, it is better to generalize our intuitive notion and just require that M and M' are linked by a Σ,Π-homomorphism f: M→M', i.e., that M' contain an *image* of M. In this way we obtain a category $\mathbf{Ext}_J(M)$ with objects all such extensions f: M→M' and with morphisms h: (f: M→M')→(f': M→M'') those Σ',Π'-homomorphisms h that preserve the image of M, i.e., such that f'=h∘f. The existence problem for free extensions can then be made precise by asking the following question:

Does $\mathbf{Ext}_J(M)$ *have an initial object?*

This is exactly the same question as whether the forgetful functor $\mathbf{Mod}_{\Sigma',\Pi',C'}\rightarrow\mathbf{Mod}_{\Sigma,\Pi,C}$ has a left adjoint [21]. The answer is *Yes*, and we denote such an initial object by $F_J(M)$. We will actually show that $\mathbf{Ext}_J(M)$ can be axiomatized as a class of models definable by Horn clauses, and since we have already proved that those classes have initial models the result then follows directly. We need only construct the signature $\Sigma'(M)$ that adds the elements of M disjointly as new constants, and introduce the notion of the **positive diagram** of the model M, denoted $\mathrm{Diag}^+(M)$, which is just the set of $\Sigma(M),\Pi$-sentences of the form $(\forall\emptyset)\ \sigma(a1,...,an)=M^w_\sigma(a1,...,an)$ for $(a1,...,an)\in M_w$ and σ: w→s in Σ, or of the form $(\forall\emptyset)$ P(a1,...,an) for $(a1,...,an)\in M^w_P$ and P:w in Π.

Lemma 27: For J: $(\Sigma,\Pi,C)\subseteq(\Sigma',\Pi',C')$ an inclusion of order-sorted Horn clause logic with equality specifications and M a Σ,Π,C-model, the categories $\mathbf{Ext}_J(M)$ and $\mathbf{Mod}_{\Sigma'(M),\Pi',C'\cup\mathrm{Diag}^+(M)}$ are isomorphic.

Proof: Giving a $\Sigma'(M),\Pi',C'$-model is the same as giving a $\Sigma',\Pi'C'$-model M' together with an S-sorted function f: M→M' that gives an interpretation in M' for each constant in M (S is the set of sorts for Σ). Similarly, a $\Sigma'(M),\Pi'$-homomorphism is just a Σ',Π'-homomorphism h: M'→M'' that "preserves the constants" in M, i.e., such that $f'=h\circ f$ for f and f' the functions interpreting the M-constants in M' an M''. So, we just need to check that a $\Sigma'(M),\Pi',C'$-model f: $M\rightarrow M'$ satisfies $Diag^+(M)$ iff f is a Σ,Π-homomorphism, and this is trivial by construction. □

Corollary 28: For Σ,Π an order-sorted signature with predicates and M a Σ,Π-model, we have
$M \simeq \mathcal{T}_{\Sigma(M),\Pi,Diag^+(M)}$.

Proof: Pick J to be the identity inclusion $(\Sigma,\Pi,\emptyset)\subseteq(\Sigma,\Pi,\emptyset)$ and notice that then the identity homomorphism 1_M: $M\rightarrow M$ is obviously the initial model of $\mathbf{Ext}_J(M)$. □

We can now discuss a particular kind of free extension where the Σ,Π-model M is considered to be "built-in" and no new sorts or function symbols are added, but only new predicate symbols, yielding a new predicate signature Π' with a new "program" C' axiomatizing the new predicate symbols, which i a set of Horn clauses with only predicates in Π'-Π in their heads. This is also the approach taken by [19], but our free extension construction obtains by general principles what they describe as the "least fixpoint" of a somewhat complicated continuous operator.

Corollary 29: For J: $(\Sigma,\Pi,\emptyset)\subseteq(\Sigma,\Pi',C')$ an inclusion of order-sorted Horn clause logic with equality specifications, with C' a set of Σ,Π'-Horn clauses such that all the heads are in Π'-Π, and M a Σ,Π-model, the extension map $M\rightarrow F_J(M)$ is a Σ,Π-isomorphism.

Proof: $F_J(M)=\mathcal{T}_{\Sigma(M),\Pi,C'\cup Diag^+(M)}$ but, considering the rules of order-sorted deduction, it is clear that the clauses in C' do not contribute any new Σ,Π-sentences to those obtainable from $Diag^+(M)$. Since the function symbols are the same, this just means that, after forgetting about the predicate symbols in Π'-Π, $\mathcal{T}_{\Sigma(M),\Pi,C'\cup Diag^+(M)}$ becomes $\mathcal{T}_{\Sigma(M),\Pi,Diag^+(M)}$ and we have already seen that this las model is isomorphic to M. □

3.6 Built-Ins and Constraint Languages

A Σ,Π-model M can alway be axiomatized by its diagram. However, such an axiomatization is not in general finite. Even if there is a finite axiomatization satisfying the requirements for correctness of th operational semantics (e.g., that the equations are confluent and terminating rewrite rules, etc.) and one could rely on it to solve queries using the standard operational semantics for order-sorted algebra with equality, one would still prefer to have more efficient "built-in" special-purpose algorithms to solve such queries. Such algorithms are available for many widely used models, such as numbers, infinite trees, etc. Simplifying the picture a bit, we are assuming an algorithm Sol_M that when given a query (i.e., an existential formula $\exists B_1,...,B_n$) provides a solution iff the formula is satisfied by M. Such an algorithm is *complete* iff it enumerates a **complete set of solutions**, i.e., a set $Sol_M(B_1,...,B_n)$ of substitutions θ such that every witness f: $X\rightarrow M$ solving $\exists B_1,...,B_n$ factors as $f=f'\circ\theta$ for some θ in the set, and conversely, every composition of one such θ with *any* assignment to M is a witness. In other words, every "concrete" solution f is described by some member of a family of "generic" solutions.

Suppose now that we want to build in the Σ,Π-model M using an algorithm Sol_M and that we also want to freely extend M by some additional predicates and clauses[8] in such a way that the map

[8] This is the case treated by [19] using least fixpoint techniques, and is actually rather restrictive. In general, one might want to extend M by additional sorts and functions, as well as predicates and clauses, in such a way that the free extension $F_J(M)$ **protects** the built-in model M, i.e., such that when $F_J(M)$ is resticted to the signature of the built-in, one gets a model isomorphic to M. If the additional function symbols involved are all *constructors*, what we say here generalizes easily. However, the most general case needs further study.

$M \to F_J(M)$ is an isomorphism. The last subsection already proved that it is an isomorphism when the heads of the new clauses only involve new predicate symbols, and this subsection will assume that condition throughout.

How can we combine a solution algorithm Sol_M with the standard order-sorted operational semantics for the non built-in part of the extension in order to get a complete algorithm to solve queries? An answer can be gathered from the description of the free extension $F_J(M)$ as the initial model $\mathcal{T}_{\Sigma(M),\Pi',C' \cup Diag^+(M)}$ where (Σ,Π',C') is the specification (with nonempty sorts) containing the old function symbols and both the old and new predicates, and the new Horn clauses. Now, any query to be solved is necessarily of the form $\exists\ C_1,...,C_j,B_1,...,B_k$, where the $C_1,...,C_j$ are Σ,Π-atoms (i.e., only use the syntax of the built-in) and the B_i are all atoms whose predicate symbol is in Π'-Π. By Herbrand's Theorem, the query has a solution iff there is a witness f: $X \to F_J(M)$. Such a witness is *a fortiori* a witness for the query $\exists\ C_1,...,C_j$ so that there is a substitution $\theta \in Sol_M(C_1,...,C_j)$ such that f factors through θ. This means that the query $\exists\ C_1,...,C_j,B_1,...,B_k$ will have a solution iff for some $\theta \in Sol_M(C_1,...,C_j)$ the query $\exists\ \theta B_1,...,\theta B_k$ has a solution. Now, remember that $F_J(M) \simeq \mathcal{T}_{\Sigma(M),\Pi',C' \cup Diag^+(M)}$. Thus, after choosing to explore a particular θ in $Sol_M(C_1,...,C_j)$, an additional step in the search for a possible solution is, of course, resolution. This can only take place with the clauses in C', since the positive diagram only involves the old predicate symbols. Specifically, if $\theta B_i = P(t_1,...,t_n)$ and C' contains a clause of the form $P(t_1',...,t_n') \Leftarrow C'_1,...,C'_p,B'_1,...,B'_q$ then we can create a new subgoal by replacing θB_1 by $t_1 = t'_1,...,t_n = t'_n,C'_1,...,C'_p,B'_1,...,B'_q$. An additional next step can then be to choose a substitution θ' in $Sol_M(t_1 = t'_1,...,t_n = t'_n,C'_1,...,C'_p)$, thus yielding the overall subgoal $\theta' B'_1,...,\theta' B'_q,\theta' \circ \theta B_2,...,\theta' \circ \theta B_k$. Proceeding in this way, that is, by alternating calls to Sol_M with resolution steps using the clauses in C', gives a complete strategy for solving our original query.

However, this strategy may be too costly if calls to Sol_M are expensive. And it may be impracticable if our simplifying assumption that Sol_M applies to any conjunction of the Σ,Π-sentences does not hold, in a case where the acceptable sentences for some algorithm have a more restricted form that can ony be reached after being sufficient instantiated by substitutions. Thus, an alternative, and equaly complete strategy, is to *delay* calls to Sol_M until after all the atoms involving new predicates have been removed from the goal by resolution steps. This means "giving the benefit of the doubt" to atoms involving the built-in predicates, so that the search space, although it can be explored faster as far as the non-built-in predicates are concerned, is nevertheless broadened. It is also possible to have a "mixed" strategy, in which Sol_M is called immediately for certain predicates for which it happens to be efficient (such as perhaps equality, which might reduce to unification when only constructors are involved, or to unification without the occur check when M consists of infinite trees), whereas calls to Sol_M could be delayed for predicates where it is inefficient or where certain instantiations of the arguments are required by the algorithm. All these alternatives remain complete, since all are equivalent to satisfaction in the model $\mathcal{T}_{\Sigma(M),\Pi',C' \cup Diag^+(M)}$ which is our standard for correctness.

The above sketches an approach to constraint langauges based upon order-sorted Horn clause logic with equality. Denotational semantics is given by any model which is initial among all those having some fixed sorts, functions, and relations interpretated into a fixed order-sorted model (a "built-in"); and operational semantics is given by a combination of resolution and built-in algorithms. The main reason for taking this approach is to implement such a language efficienly, and we have discussed some of the more delicate issues that arise in this regard.

4 Logical Programming

This section discusses our broad perspective on logic programming, based on the notion of "institution" [10], which combines formal syntax with model theory and deduction at a very high leve of generality. At the present stage of development, we can only claim that institutions provide a useful general framework and viewpoint, rather than a formal foundation for all aspects of our research on programming paradigms and their combinations. However, what we have so far actually supports most of our research, and also provides much broader perspective toward what might be the proper concern of "logic programming" than any other available foundation. Moreover, the areas tha are not yet fully formalized represent some interesting opportunities for further research.

The abstractness and generality of the material treated here makes it very appropriate to use categor theory as a language for expressing the concepts and developing their properties. Since a paper of thi length cannot develop from scratch the category theory that will be needed, we assume that the reade is already familiar with the basics; for some introduction to these concepts, see [21, 1].

4.1 Institutions and Logical Programming Languages

Today's computer science is undergoing enormous growth, in both its artifacts and its theories. This creates an equally enormous need for conceptual unification, since otherwise we will drown in the floo of undigested information. In particular, there is a population explosion among the logical systems that are being used by computer scientists, including first order logic, equational logic, modal logic, higher order logic, temporal logic, intuitionistic logic, dynamic logic, order-sorted Horn clause logic, and the many specialized logics used in various verification systems and theorem provers.
Institutions [10, 6] formalize the notion of a logical system, and seem useful in capturing programming and specification language paradigms and features independently of any specific language or logic, as well as in unifying programming paradigms. Institutions avoid commitment to any particular logical system by doing constructions once and for all at a higher level of generality. In addition to the sentences, models and satisfaction already mentioned, institutions also encompass homomorphisms of models and proofs between sentences. One view is that institutions generalize classical model theory by *relativizing* it over signatures. This intuition is stated in the following slogan:

Truth is invariant under change of notation.

This subject is closely related to "abstract model theory" as studied by logicians, e.g., [3]. The forma definition will use the following notation: categories are underlined, and $|\underline{C}|$ denotes the class of object of $\underline{C}$.

Definition 30: An **institution** I consists of:

- a category $\underline{\mathrm{Sign}}$ of **signatures**
- a functor $\underline{\mathrm{Mod}}$: $\underline{\mathrm{Sign}} \rightarrow \underline{\mathrm{Cat}}^{\mathrm{op}}$ giving **Σ-models** and **Σ-morphisms**
- a functor $\underline{\mathrm{Sen}}$: $\underline{\mathrm{Sign}} \rightarrow \underline{\mathrm{Cat}}$ giving **Σ-sentences** and **Σ-proofs**
- a **satisfaction** relation $\models_\Sigma \subseteq |\underline{\mathrm{Mod}}(\Sigma)| \times |\underline{\mathrm{Sen}}(\Sigma)|$ for each $\Sigma \in |\underline{\mathrm{Sign}}|$

such that

- **satisfaction**: $m' \models_{\Sigma'} \mathrm{Sen}(\phi)s$ iff $\mathrm{Mod}(\phi)m' \models_\Sigma s$ for each $m' \in |\underline{\mathrm{Mod}}(\Sigma')|$, $s \in |\underline{\mathrm{Sen}}(\Sigma)|$, ϕ: $\Sigma \rightarrow \Sigma'$ in $\underline{\mathrm{Sign}}$, and
- **soundness**: $m \models_\Sigma s$ and $s \rightarrow s' \in \mathrm{Sen}(\Sigma)$ imply $m \models_\Sigma s'$ for $m \in |\underline{\mathrm{Mod}}(\Sigma)|$.

□

We now give a somewhat informal explication of the notion of logical programming.

Definition 31: A logical programming language $\mathcal{L}$ has an associated institution I such that:

- a **program** P of $\mathcal{L}$ consists of a signature Σ from I and a finite set of Σ-sentences[9];
- the **operational semantics** of an $\mathcal{L}$-program P is given by proofs in I, from some given query to an answer in some normal form[10]; and
- the **denotational semantics** of an $\mathcal{L}$-program P with signature Σ is given by a class of Σ-models in I[11].

□

Functional programming takes some institution of equational logic as its basis, perhaps unsorted, many-sorted, or order-sorted, perhaps first order or higher order, and then computation reduces a given sentence to a normal form. FP [2] uses a fixed higher order program P, and computation reduces user-supplied expressions to their normal form. OBJ [9] is based on first order order-sorted equational logic; the user first supplies the program P, perhaps only implicitly as a combination of smaller programs (i.e., "modules"); computation is again reduction of a well-formed expression to a normal form. Pure logic programming takes some institution of first order Horn clause logic as its basis, perhaps unsorted, many-sorted, or even order-sorted. The user supplies a program P and a "query" Q containing some variables; the operational semantics then tries to prove some substitution instance of Q from P, and returns the substitution if it succeeds. Eqlog [11] does much the same, but is based on the order-sorted Horn clause logic with equality institution, so that its sentences are much more general than in ordinary logic programming. Eqlog returns both the substitution and the substitution instance of the query, so that functional programming in the general style of OBJ is also a special case. FOOPS [12] is a combination functional and object-oriented programming language, based upon a "reflective" first order, order-sorted equational logic, and not only the user-supplied expression, but also the program, are modified by computation. Although we know the sentences and rules of deduction for this logic, we do not yet know what models are appropriate, so it is not yet an institution.

Actually, Definition 31 is even more general than we have led you to believe, since it also includes specification languages. The difference between a logical programming language and a specification language is the *efficiency* of deduction. Since this is partly subjective, and partly a matter of technology, we have not put it in a formal definition. Rather, we can just say that a **specification language** is an *inefficient* logical programming language. Some specification languages are "loose", in the sense that they take the class of *all* models that satisfy the given sentences as their denotation; for example, Clear [5]. In this case, the language needs some rather fancy sentences, such as the "data constraints" [10], to define abstract data types. Other specification languages take just the initial models for the denotation for a program, such as ACT ONE (see [8]), and some are even restricted to a fixed set of data structures, such S-expressions or numbers; for example, the original Boyer-Moore

---

[9] In practice, some sort of modularization mechanism, perhaps based on colimits as in [6], may be provided to facilitate constructing a new program by combining old programs.

[10] In general, the answer will consist not only of some I-sentence which has been proven, but also some information obtained during the proof, such as a substitution.

[11] In many cases, this class will be the class of initial models satisfying P.

theorem prover [4]. Instead of giving an expression to be reduced or a query to be answered, the user of a specification language can usually pose quite general hypotheses about the properties of a program; therefore, computation is rather general theorem proving. Also, the mode of user interaction is generally much freer than for a programming language, with the user directly participating in some aspects of the proof process. In this context, OBJ and Eqlog are "wide spectrum" languages, in that they have subsets which are quite efficient, other subsets that are tollerably efficient and would be useful for rapid prototyping (e.g., associative commutative matching), and still other subsets (e.g., the verification of theories) that are really only suitable for specification and design.

5 Conclusions

This paper has suggested that techniques somewhat more model-theoretic than those usually used in the logic programming literature may have some advantages, for example, in giving the semantics of constraint languages, as well as in combining logic and functional programming, and in reaping the various benefits of order-sorted logic that we have tried to make clear. We have also argued that order-sorted Horn clause logic with equality, especially in connection with built-ins, provides about as expressive and general a logical programming language as one might want, provided one is willing to do without states and objects. Moreover, we have given further details of the semantics of Eqlog that complete the picture given in [11]; in particular, we have given two sets of rules of deduction for order-sorted Horn clause logic with equality, one fully general, and the other for the case where all sorts are non-empty, and we have also proven completeness, initiality, Herbrand and free extension theorems. It is the latter which serves as a semantic foundation for constraint languages, and we argue that this model-theoretic approach is an attractive alternative to more syntactic approaches. One nice point is that abstraction, i.e., representation independence, is an explicit part of the formalism. We have also developed in some detail a very general framework for "logical programming," based upon the institution notion, and we have shown how the various cases discussed in the paper fit into that framework. Finally, a number of new questions have been raised, including various more general free extension theorems, and finding an appropriate model theory for object-oriented programming.

References

1. Michael A. Arbib and Ernest Manes. *Arrows, Structures and Functors*. Academic Press, 1975.

2. John Backus. "Can Programming be Liberated from the von Neumann Style?". *Communications of the Association for Computing Machinery 21*, 8 (1978), 613-641.

3. Jon Barwise. "Axioms for Abstract Model Theory". *Annals of Mathematical Logic* 7 (1974), 221-265.

4. Robert Boyer and Moore, J. *A Computational Logic*. Academic Press, 1980.

5. Rod Burstall and Joseph Goguen. "Putting Theories together to Make Specifications". *Proceedings, Fifth International Joint Conference on Artificial Intelligence 5* (1977), 1045-1058.

6. Rod Burstall and Joseph Goguen. *Lecture Notes in Computer Science*. Volume 86: The Semantics of Clear, a Specification Language. In *Proceedings of the 1979 Copenhagen Winter School on Abstract Software Specification*, Springer-Verlag, 1980, pp. 292-332.

7. Rod Burstall and Joseph Goguen. Algebras, Theories and Freeness: An Introduction for Computer Scientists. In *Proceedings, 1981 Marktoberdorf NATO Summer School*,
Reidel, 1982.

8. Hartmut Ehrig and Bernd Mahr. *Fundamentals of Algebraic Specification 1: Equations and Initial Semantics*. Springer-Verlag, 1985.

9. Kokichi Futatsugi, Joseph Goguen, Jean-Pierre Jouannaud and José Meseguer. Principles of OBJ2. In *Proceedings, Symposium on Principles of Programming Languages*,
Association for Computing Machinery, 1985, pp. 52-66.

10. Joseph Goguen and Rod Burstall. Institutions: Abstract Model Theory for Computer Science. CSLI-85-30, Center for the Study of Language and Information, Stanford University, 1985. Also submitted for publication; a preliminary version appears in *Proceedings, Logics of Programming Workshop*, edited by Edward Clarke and Dexter Kozen, Volume 164, Springer-Verlag Lecture Notes in Computer Science, pages 221-256, 1984.

11. Joseph Goguen and José Meseguer. Eqlog: Equality, Types, and Generic Modules for Logic Programming. In *Functional and Logic Programming*, Douglas DeGroot and Gary Lindstrom, Eds., Prentice-Hall, 1986, pp. 295-363. An earlier version appears in *Journal of Logic Programming*, Volume 1, Number 2, pages 179-210, September 1984.

12. Joseph Goguen and José Meseguer. Extensions and Foundations for Object-Oriented Programming. In preparation for *Research Directions in Object-Oriented Programming*, edited by Bruce Shriver and Peter Wegner. Preliminary version in *SIGPLAN Notices*, Volume 21, Number 10, pages 153-162, October 1986.

13. Joseph Goguen and José Meseguer. "Remarks on Remarks on Many-Sorted Equational Logic". *Bulletin of the European Association for Theoretical Computer Science 30* (October 1986), 66-73. Also to appear in *SIGPLAN Notices*..

14. Joseph Goguen and José Meseguer. Order-Sorted Algebra I: Partial and Overloaded Operations, Errors and Inheritance. To appear, SRI International, Computer Science Lab, 1987. Given as lecture at Seminar on Types, Carnegie-Mellon University, June 1983.

15. Joseph Goguen and José Meseguer. Order-Sorted Algebra Solves the Constructor-Selector Problem. In preparation.

16. Joseph Goguen, Jean-Pierre Jouannaud and José Meseguer. Operational Semantics of Order-Sorted Algebra. In *Proceedings, 1985 International Conference on Automata, Languages and Programming*,
Springer-Verlag, 1985. Summary presented at IFIP WG2.2 (Boston MA) June 1984.

17. Joseph Goguen, James Thatcher and Eric Wagner. An Initial Algebra Approach to the Specification, Correctness and Implementation of Abstract Data Types. RC 6487, IBM T. J. Watson Research Center, October, 1976. Appears in *Current Trends in Programming Methodology, IV*, edited by Raymond Yeh, Prentice-Hall, 1978, pages 80-149.

18. Joseph Y. Halpern, John H. Williams, Edward L. Wimmers and Timothy Winkler. Denotational Semantics and Rewrite Rules for FP. In *Proceedings, Symposium on Principles of Programming Languages*,
Association for Computing Machinery, 1985, pp. 108-120.

19. Joxan Jaffar and Jean-Louis Lassez. Constraint Logic Programming. Monash University, Australia, 1986. Draft.

20. Joxan Jaffar and Spiro Michaylov. Methodology and Implementation of a Constraint Logic Programming System. Monash University, Australia, 1986. Draft.

21. Saunders Mac Lane. *Categories for the Working Mathematician.* Springer-Verlag, 1971.

22. José Meseguer and Joseph Goguen. Initiality, Induction and Computability. In *Algebraic Methods in Semantics*, Maurice Nivat and John C. Reynolds, Eds., Cambridge University Press, 198 pp. 459-541. Also SRI CSL Technical Report 140, December 1983.

23. José Meseguer, Joseph Goguen and Gert Smolka. Order-Sorted Unification. SRI International, 1987. In preparation.

24. Michael O'Donnell. *Equational Logic as a Programming Language.* MIT Press, 1985.

25. J. Alan Robinson. "A Machine-oriented Logic Based on the Resolution Principle". *Journal of the Association for Computing Machinery 12* (1965).

26. Gert Smolka, Joseph Goguen and José Meseguer. Order-Sorted Equational Computation. SRI International, 1987. In preparation.

27. C. Walther. Unification in Many-sorted Theories. In *Advances in Artificial Intelligence - Proceedings, Sixth European Conference on Artificial Intelligence*, North-Holland, 1984, pp. .

FIFTH GENERATION COMPUTER PROJECT: CURRENT RESEARCH ACTIVITY AND FUTURE PLANS

Koichi Furukawa

Institute For New Generation Computer Technology
1-4-28, Mita, Minato-ku, Tokyo 108 Japan

1. Introduction

The FGCS project, aiming at developing a new generation of general purpose computers, began in 1982 and is now almost half way through the ten years of the project. The project was established to explore a qualitatively new approach to computer science in order to solve many difficult problems which have accumulated in the field. We considered that the two single most important and difficult problems are opening up a new market for computers to keep the computer industry growing, and overcoming the low productivity of software compared with hardware. We spent three years developing the target of a new broad market for next generation computers, and concluded that knowledge information processing will be the answer.

At the same time, we attempted to design a computer system adequate for the new application area, i.e. knowledge information processing, and produced the rough sketch of the system shown in Fig. 1. The system has two significant features: one is a highly parallel architecture deviating from the traditional von Neumann architecture, and the other is the

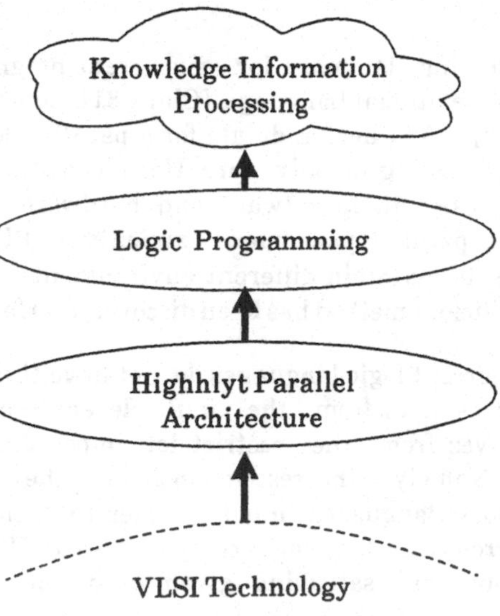

Fig.1 The role of logic programming in the FGCS project

bridge of logic programming to span the chasm between knowledge information processing and the parallel architecture.

Logic programming has been functioning as a strong guideline and as a vehicle to promote research in the project. As a result of our research so far, we have succeeded in developing a more detailed framework providing a clearer perspective on how the bridge must be constructed, the chasm spanned. It consists of a set of programming languages layered in a hierarchy and a set of program transformation methods forming the links between them.

We have designed two new logic programming languages. Guarded Horn Clauses (GHC) is an abstract machine language for parallel execution, and Complex Indeterminate Language (CIL) is an extended version of Prolog suited for writing knowledge information processing application programs. We have also worked up meta programming techniques for introducing user languages by defining their interpreters along with a general method for compiling programs written in those new languages into Prolog. The method is based on the idea of applying partial evaluation to meta programs.

Program transformation is the key to achieving both expressiveness and efficiency of programming languages. One of the new program transformation methods we developed is designed to handle the transformation of some kinds of CIL programs into normal Prolog programs, and the other transforms normal Prolog programs into GHC programs. By successively applying the transformation methods, the CIL programs can be transformed into GHC programs. These are the tentative steps we have taken so far toward establishing the link between knowledge programming and parallel architecture.

In Section 2 an informal explanation of GHC will be given using examples. Meta programming techniques and their optimization by partial evaluation will be presented in Section 3. Two program transformation methods will be described in Section 4, followed by the conclusion in Section 5.

2. Guarded Horn Clauses

GHC is a logic programming language for concurrent programming and parallel execution. It is a successor of Relational Language [Clark 81], Concurrent Prolog [Shapiro 83a] and PARLOG [Clark 84]. Another candidate for a parallel logic language is Horn logic itself, i.e. a language consisting of only pure Horn Clauses (PHC, for short). PHC has, however, serious drawbacks both in software and hardware. The software problem is that you cannot describe parallel phenomena explicitly in PHC, and the hardware problem is that you have to maintain different environments for each or-branch of computations, for which no efficient method has been discovered so far.

On the other hand, concurrent logic languages do not have these two problems (to be precise, Concurrent Prolog suffers from the multiple environment problem). This favorable characteristic derives from the restrict ion imposed on PHC to obtain "guarded" Horn clauses. Namely the restriction makes the underlining execution mechanism of concurrent logic languages much simpler than that of PHC. The only apparent drawback of concurrent logic languages compared with PHC is that they loose the capability to find all solutions satisfying given conditions based on don't know nondeterminism. But we succeeded in removing this drawback by program transformation [Ueda 86]. The details will be discussed below in Section 4.

GHC is a language consisting of a set of guarded Horn clauses, as the name suggests. We use a vertical bar "|" called commit operator to designate the guard part of each clause: the guard part is to the left of the commit, and the body part is on the right. The guard part specifies the condition for the body to be selected for successive computation. The important features of GHC are the following suspension rules [Ueda 85]:

(a) The guard of a clause cannot export any bindings to (or, make any bindings observable from) the caller of that clause, and

(b) the body of a clause cannot export any bindings to (or, make any bindings observable from) the guard of that clause before commitment.

Rule (a) determines synchronization and rule (b) execution of bodies. Let us take a simple example of service at a counter with two queues. We need to merge these two queues into one in order to make a single queue for service. Let us define a procedure `merge(Xs,Ys,Zs)`, in which two queues `Xs` and `Ys` will be merged into a single queue `Zs`, in terms of GHC:

```
(m1) merge([X|Xs],Ys,Zs) :-  true  | Zs=[X|Us],merge(Xs,Ys,Us).
(m2) merge(Xs,[Y|Ys],Zs) :-  true  | Zs=[Y|Us],merge(Xs,Ys,Us).
(m3) merge([],Ys,Zs) :-  true  | Zs=Ys.
(m4) merge(Xs,[],Zs) :-  true  | Zs=Xs.
```

The fact that the clause (m1) waits for people arriving at the first queue is represented by its first argument `[X|Xs]`. The usual situation using the merge program is something like

```
?- queue1(As),queue2(Bs),merge(As,Bs,Cs),serve(Cs).
```

where `queue1(As)` and `queue2(Bs)` are processes generating a sequence of people joining the queues. Suppose that the processes `queue1` and `queue2` do not generate any instances. Then, `As` (and `Bs` also) will remain as a variable and the execution of the merge process will be suspended due to the necessary unification `As=[X|Xs]` and the rule of suspension. What this mean is since the expression `[X|Xs]` asserts that it has at least one element, the unification will force the conclusion that the same fact is true for `As`, and this means the unification would give a binding to the variable appearing in the caller. When `queue1` instantiates the variable `As` to, say, `[john|Rest]`, the above unification will become `[john|Rest]=[X|Xs]` and this can be solved without giving any new binding to variables in the caller. Therefore, the guard part of the clause (m1) can be successfully solved and it can be committed for successive computation. The body of (m1) consists of a unification which will give a binding to the variable `Zs` representing the merged queue, and a recursive call to the merge process. When there are people in both queues, clauses (m1) and (m2) can both solve the guard parts. In such a case, one of the clauses is chosen nondeterministically for successive computation.

It is very easy to represent assembly line-like parallel processing in GHC. In an assembly line program, a shared variable between processes will represent a sequence of unfinished products. Programming in GHC corresponds to designing such an assembly

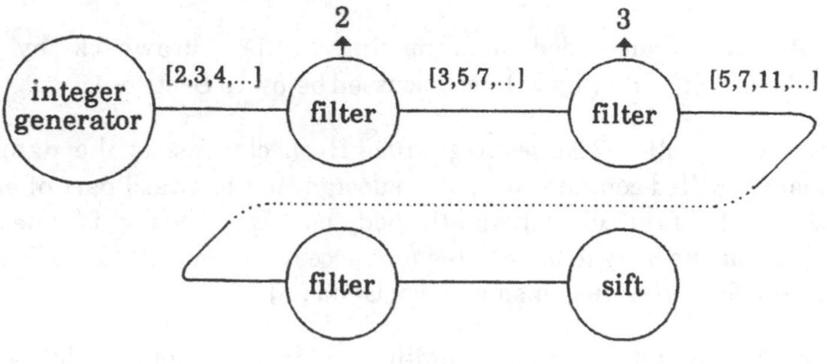

Fig.2 The process structure of a prime generation program by Aristotle's sieve

line, and its execution corresponds to building and operating it to manufacture products. Since new processes are created during execution of the GHC program, it is possible to modify the assembly line while operating it. A prime generation program by Aristotle's sieve is an example of dynamic creation of processes. The system consists of an integer generator, a sequence of dynamically created filter processes corresponding to each prime to remove multiples of the prime, and a sift process to continue creation of filter processes as shown in Fig. 2.

Shared variables among processes can be regarded as communication channels and the entire channels form a communication network defining a process structure. It is expected that the process structure will reflect the target problem's structure: in other words, in parallel programs, the process structure will play the role of a data structure in sequential programs. Furthermore, since each process is an active object, the entire process structure's function is much richer and stronger than that of a data structure.

Let us consider the problem of finding all possible paths from some point to a fixed goal. A typical programming technique in writing a Prolog or LISP program is to use a stack or queue to maintain all partial paths traversed (we do not consider using backtrack in Prolog here). The program is shown in Fig. 3. The first argument of the predicate "paths" is the stack. The same problem is easily written in GHC, as shown in Fig. 4, where no stack appears explicitly. A process structure corresponding to the control stack is created dynamically as shown in Fig. 5. Note that the structure is no more a stack than a collection of possible partial paths. Also, the GHC program is simpler and easier to understand. This comes from the fact that you can capture the program in an object-oriented way; that is, a process represents an object.

3. Knowledge Programming Methodology

A knowledge programming system is a system for building various kinds of knowledge based application systems and requires many programming paradigms such as object-oriented programming, meta programming, constraint programming, and so on to describe a wide range of application systems.

Concurrent logic languages are known to be well suited to realizing object-oriented programming [Shapiro 83b]. Several research efforts are underway aimed at designing an

```
start_paths(Start,Goal,Paths) :- paths([[Start]],Goal,Paths).

paths([],_,[]) :- !.
paths([First|Rest],Goal,[Path|Paths]) :-
         First = [Goal|_],
        reverse(First,Path),
        paths(Rest,Goal,Paths).
paths([First|Rest],Goal,Paths) :-
         expand(First,Add),
        append(Add,Rest,Next),
        paths(Next,Goal,Paths).

expand([Last|Rest],Ts) :-
         neighbors(Last,Nodes),
        removeIf(Nodes,[Last|Rest],Ts).

removeIf([],_,Z) :- !, Z=[].
removeIf([N|Ns],Path,Ts) :-
        member(N,Path),!,removeIf(Ns,Path,Ts).
removeIf([N|Ns],Path,Ts) :-
          Ts=[[N|Path]|Ts1],removeIf(Ns,Path,Ts1).

member(X,[X|_]) :- !.
member(X,[Z|Y]) :- member(X,Y).

append([],X,X).
append([U|X],Y,[U|Z]):-append(X,Y,Z).

reverse(X,Y) :- appendReverse(X,[],Y).

appendReverse([],X,X).
appendReverse([U|X],V,Y) :- appendReverse(X,[U|V],Y).

neighbors(start,Z) :- Z=[a,d].
neighbors(a,    Z) :- Z=[start,b].
neighbors(b,    Z) :- Z=[a,c,goal].
neighbors(c,    Z) :- Z=[b,d,goal].
neighbors(d,    Z) :- Z=[start,c,e].
neighbors(e,    Z) :- Z=[d,goal].
neighbors(goal, Z) :- Z=[b,c,e].
```

Fig.3 A path finding program using stack in Prolog

object-oriented programming language or system based on concurrent logic languages [Furukawa 84], [Kahn 86]. But they are not well developed yet, and we need further research to obtain significant results.

```
start_paths(Start,Paths) :- true | pathFinder(Start,[],Paths).

pathFinder(goal,History,Paths) :- true | Paths=[[goal|History]].
pathFinder(Node,History,Paths) :- Node\=goal |
      (Node -> Nexts), pathFinder1(Node,Nexts,History,Paths).

pathFinder1(Node,[],History,Paths) :- true | Paths=[].
pathFinder1(Node,[N|Ns],History,Paths) :- true |
      member(N,History,Result),
      childPathFinder(Result,N,[Node|History],P1),
      pathFinder1(Node,Ns,History,P2),
      merge(P1,P2,Paths).

childPathFinder(true,_,_,Paths) :- true | Paths=[].
childPathFinder(false,Node,History,Paths) :- true |
      pathFinder(Node,History,Paths).

member(_,[],R) :- true | R=false.
member(X,[X|_],R) :- true | R=true.
member(X,[A|Y],R) :- X\=A | member(X,Y,R).

merge([X|Xs],Ys,Zs) :- true | Zs=[X|Us],merge(Xs,Ys,Us).
merge(Xs,[Y|Ys],Zs) :- true | Zs=[Y|Us],merge(Xs,Ys,Us).
merge([],Ys,Zs) :- true | Ys=Zs.
merge(Xs,[],Zs) :- true | Xs=Zs.

start->Next :- true | Next=[a,d].
a->Next :- true | Next=[start,b].
b->Next :- true | Next=[a,c,goal].
c->Next :- true | Next=[b,d,goal].
d->Next :- true | Next=[start,c,e].
e->Next :- true | Next=[d,goal].
```

Fig. 4 A path finding program in GHC

In this section, we concentrate rather on the topics of meta programming and constraint programming.

3.1 Meta Programming

Although Prolog can deduce goals from rules and facts, its built-in fixed control structure (i.e., the top down and left-to-right strategy) has been the object of considerable criticism. Recently a methodology called meta programming has emerged and its usefulness has been shown in realizing various inference systems with different control structures than the built-in one[Sterling 84]. Examples are Production System, a bottom-up parser, a parallel parser, a symbolic computation system, and a backward reasoning system with certainty factor handling.

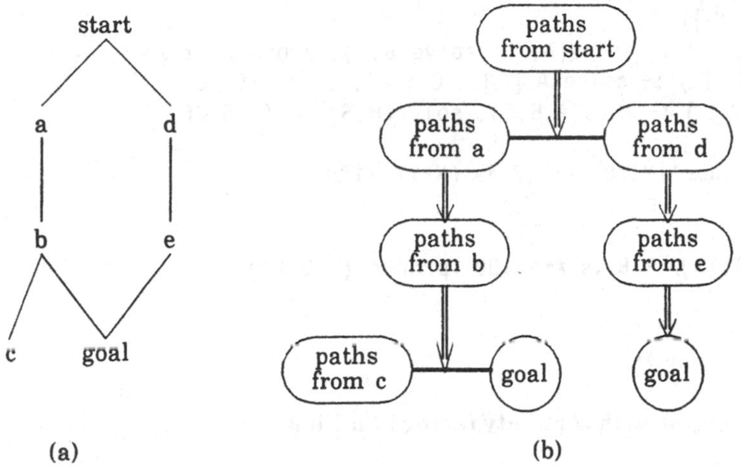

Fig. 5 A map and its corresponding process structure

These examples show that the addition of meta programming features can make Prolog into a good knowledge programming language. However, meta programming has a serious drawback concerning efficiency, because of its interpretive mode of execution. To remedy this defect, we developed a very powerful compiling method based on partial evaluation [Futamura 71,83], [Takeuchi 86].

Fig. 6 shows a simple example of rule compilation by partial execution in Fig. 6. Fig. 6 (b) is a set of rules of which the inference engine is given in Fig. 6 (a). The result obtained by partial execution of the inference engine together with the given set of rules is shown in Fig. 6 (c).

For intuitive understanding of the above transformation process, we try "symbolical" execution of the goal

```
?- solve(should_take(A,aspirin),[B]).      (1)
```

Note that this execution is symbolic because we do not have sufficient information for actual execution. By applying the fourth definition of "solve" clauses to the goal (1), we obtain the following sequence of goals:

```
?- rule(should_take(A,aspirin),B,F),
   solve(B,S), cf(F,S,B).                  (2)
```

Next, we apply the first definition of the "rule" clauses to the first goal of (2) and execute the body of the clause. Then, we find the values of B and F and obtain a new sequence of goals:

```
?- solve((complains_of(A,Symptom),
          suppresses(aspirin,Symptom),
```

```
solve(true   ,[100]).
solve((A,B) ,Z     ) :- solve(A,X), solve(B,Y), append(X,Y,Z).
solve(not(A),[CF] ) :- solve(A,[C]), C < 20, CF is 100-C.
solve(A      ,[CF] ) :- rule(A,B,F), solve(B,S), cf(F,S,CF).

cf(X,Y,Z) :- product(Y,100,YY),Z is (X*YY)/100.

product([],A,A).
product([X|Y],A,XX) :- B is X*A/100, product(Y,B,XX).

rule(A,B,F) :- ((A:-B)<>F).
rule(A,true,F) :- (A<>F).
```

(a) An inference engine with certainty factor handling

```
should_take(Person,Drug) :-
        complains_of(Person,Symptom),
        suppresses(Drug,Symptom),
        not(unsuitable(Drug,Person)) <> 70.

suppresses(aspirin,pain) <> 60.
suppresses(lomotil,diarrhoea) <> 65.

unsuitable(Drug,Person) :-
        aggravates(Drug,Condition),
        suffers_from(Person,Condition) <> 80.

aggravates(aspirin,peptic_ulcer) <> 70.
aggravates(lomotil,impaired_liver_function) <> 70.
```

(b) A set of rules with certainty factor

```
solve(should_take(A,aspirin),[B]) :-
        solve(complains_of(A,pain),C),
        solve(suffers_from(A,peptic_ulcer),D),
        cf(80,[70|D],E),E<20,F is 100-E,
        append(C,[60,F],G),cf(70,G,B).
solve(should_take(A,lomotil),[B]) :-
        solve(complains_of(A,diarrhoea),C),
        solve(suffers_from(A,impaired_liver_function),D),
        cf(80,[70|D],E),E<20,F is 100-E,
        append(C,[65,F],G),cf(70,G,B).
```

(c) A result of partial execution of the inference engine (a) together with a set of rules (b)

Fig. 6 An example of rule compilation by partial execution

```
        not(unsuitable(Drug,A))),S),          (3)
   cf(70,S,B).
```

The next execution step is the application of the second definition of the "solve" clauses, which results in the following goal sequence:

```
?- solve(complains_of(A,Symptom),S1),
   solve((suppresses(aspirin,Symptom),
        not(unsuitable(aspirin,A))),S2),      (4)
   append(S1,S2,S),          cf(70,S,B).
```

The normal Prolog processor would now proceed to the execution of the first goal of (4). But in this case we cannot execute the goal "solve(complains__of(A,Symptom))" because this goal is only solved by the input from the user when the system is actually used. Therefore, symbolic execution proceeds to execute the next goal and produces the goals:

```
?- solve(complains_of(A,Symptom),S1),
   solve(suppresses(aspirin,Symptom),S21),
   solve(not(unsuitable(aspirin,A)),S22),     (5)
   append(S21,S22,S2),
   append(S1,S2,S),cf(70,S,B).
```

Now, we try to execute the second goal "solve(suppresses(...))" of (5). Note that this goal can be completely solved by applying the first definition of the suppresses clauses, which unifies the variable "Symptom" to the constant "pain" and "S21" to 70. The resulting goal sequence is as follows:

```
?- solve(complains_of(A,pain),S1),
   solve(not(unsuitable(aspirin,A)),S22),
    append(60,S22,S2),                        (6)
   append(S1,S2,S),cf(70,S,B).
```

Note that the variable Symptom in the first predicate "solve(complains_of(A,Symptom),S1)" is also instantiated. Continuing the symbolic execution process, we finally obtain the result given in Fig. 6 (c).

We succeeded in speeding up the original interpretive program by about three times for the above example. We also examined another example of an algebraic manipulation system which was five times faster. These numbers suggest that partial evaluation is a very promising technique for optimization of meta programs. Another merit of the approach is that meta programming enforces a clear separation of object knowledge from control, which makes the programs far easier to understand than the mixed approach. Goebel et al. [Goebel 86] described a MYCIN-like diagnosis system in terms of the combination of a meta interpreter and a set of logical formulas connecting malfunctions and symptoms. In his system the connection is represented in such a way that *"If X has a malfunction A, then it has a set of symptoms B"*, instead of *"If X has a set of symptoms B, then you can conclude that X has a malfunction A"*, which is the representation style in MYCIN. The behaviour of a meta interpreter is described by something like *"If you want to identify that X has some malfunction A, then you need to show that X has all symptoms that A gives rise to."* By partially executing the meta interpreter together with logical formulas describing the relationship between malfunctions and symptoms, we managed to obtain a set of "compiled" rules which are similar to those in MYCIN.

3.2 Constraint Programming

Constraint Programming is another important paradigm in knowledge programming. There have been many efforts to incorporate it into the logic programming framework [Colmerauer 82,86], [Mukai 85], [Dincbus 86], [Jaffar 86]. They are roughly divided into two groups: one is Colmerauer's and Mukai's work dealing with only passive constraints based on a freeze mechanism, and the other is Dincbus's and Lassez's work dealing with not only passive constraints but also active constraints.

We developed a language called CIL (Complex Indeterminate Language), a version of Prolog with passive constraints, and with the addition of the "complex indeterminate" concept from situation semantics. It possesses not only a freeze mechanism, but also "indefinite terms" to represent frame structures. Indefinite terms are used to represent semantic structures in the experimental discourse understanding system called DUALS [Mukai 85], [Yokoi 86].

Besides the natural language understanding system, we tried to use CIL to build a VLSI CAD system for solving layout problems and it was shown that constraint programming is useful for representing building block layout problems.

4. Program Transformation

The layers of logic languages we have described, that is, the concurrent logic languages like GHC and knowledge programming logic languages such as CIL are good stepping stones toward dividing the original problem of bridging the gap between knowledge information processing and highly parallel computer architecture into three smaller problems: 1. Developing knowledge information processing application systems in knowledge programming languages such as CIL; 2. Transforming programs in knowledge programming logic languages (such as CIL) into those in GHC; and 3. Developing an efficient highly parallel computer on which programs in GHC run very fast.

Here, we focus on the second problem. The general compilation method of meta programs described in Section 2 is regarded as one of the very promising techniques to partial solution of the problem. It transforms two layer programs consisting of a meta interpreter and object programs into single layer programs.

In this section, we present two other program transformation methods. One is for removing freeze from passive constraints programs, and the other is for removing backtrack. The latter method is applied to transform Prolog programs into GHC programs.

4.1 Program transformation for removing freeze

We developed several methods to transform programs with passive constraints into those without them using unfold/fold transformation method [Burstall 77].

Let us explain one of the ideas of the transformation methods briefly. We consider a problem of finding all paths between two points in a given map, possibly including cycles.

Fig. 7 shows an elegant program using passive constraints to check cycles in possible solutions to avoid wasteful search efforts. The reason why we need constraints is that the check goal must be in front of the path generation goal to protect the program from falling into an infinite loop.

The constraints are a set of inequalities for all pairs of nodes in each possible path. We need the freeze mechanism to delay the evaluation of each of these inequalities appearing as constraints until both of the variables in it are instantiated.

By shuffling the set of inequalities and rearranging properly between other goals, it becomes possible to evaluate all inequalities immediately after they are called. We found a way of shuffling analogous to the exchange of the summation order by structural commutativity such as

$$\sum_{j=1}^{n}\sum_{i=j+1}^{n} X_{ij} = \sum_{i=2}^{n}\sum_{j=1}^{i-1} X_{ij}$$ [Seki 86].

4.2 Program Transformation for removing backtrack

To remedy an apparent drawback of GHC compared with Prolog, Ueda [Ueda 86] proposed a transformation method from "all solutions search" Prolog programs to

```
good_path(X,Y,Path) :-
       good_list(Path), path(X,Y,Path).

good_list(L) :- freeze(L,good_list1(L)).

good_list1([]). good_list1([X|L]) :-
        out_of(X,L), good_list(L).
out_of(X,L) :- freeze(L,out_of1(X,L)). out_of1(X,[]).
out_of1(X,[Y|L]) :- dif(X,Y), out_of(X,L).

path(X,X,[X]).
path(X,Y,[X|Path]) :-
       neighbor(X,Z), path(Z,Y,Path).

neighbor(X,Y) :- neighbor1(X,Y).
neighbor(X,Y) :- neighbor1(Y,X).

neighbor1(a,b).
neighbor1(a,c).
neighbor1(b,d).
neighbor1(b,c).
neighbor1(c,e).
neighbor1(d,e).
```

Fig. 7 An elegant path finding program using passive constraint in Prolog II

equivalent GHC programs. His method has two phases: the first phase involves performing of mode analysis to determine, for each variable, whether it is an input or an output variable, and, given the analyzed program, the transformation is performed in the second.

We will briefly explain the method using the following example:

```
(g0)   ?- append(U,V,[1,2,3]).
(a1)   append([],Z,Z).
(a2)   append([A|X],Y,[A|Z]) :- append(X,Y,Z).
```

When execution starts, we first obtain a partial answer [1|X] from (a2), and, after the successive recursions and backtracks, we get three values for X; namely X=[], X=[2] and X=[2,3].

The problem here is that we need to copy the structure [1|X] for all three different computations of X, which would cause a serious problem in an actual parallel execution environment due to the undecidability of the "var" check included in the copy operation [Ueda 86].

To avoid the copy problem, we rewrite the clause (a2) into the following:

```
(a2)'   append(X1,Y,[A|Z]) :- append(X,Y,Z),X1=[A|X].
```

The recursive call in (a2)' does not require any copy operations since the variable X1 does not change during the recursion. But in this case we need an extra job after the recursion: namely, to cons A to X to obtain X1. The and-or graph for the goal (g0) is shown if Fig. 8.

Now let us design an appropriate process structure of GHC to compute all possible solutions of (X,Y). By mapping or-branches in the original Prolog program to and-forks in the target GHC program, we obtain a process structure and its corresponding recursive program schema in GHC as shown in Fig. 9.

Let us consider the behaviour of a particular process, say, the process P3 in the Fig. 9. Since this process corresponds to the computation following the path (a2)' (a2)' (a1), we obtain the following equations:

```
(g1)   ?- X3=[],Y=[3],X2=[2|X3],X=[1|X2].
```

as a result of unfolding the original goal according to the given path. These equations for building solutions constitute the process Q3 in Fig. 9. To realize this final computation, necessary information such as "1", "2", and "3" is stacked during the P's recursions, and it is used in building the solution in the "cont" program. The name "cont" comes from the fact that the final computation (g1) can be interpreted as a collection of continuation tasks after the recursions in the clause (a2)'.

The transformed program is shown in Fig. 10, where ap corresponds to P, ap1 to Q and ap2 to P', respectively. Note that the computation for building solutions such as (g1) is included in ap1 as a call to the "cont" program.

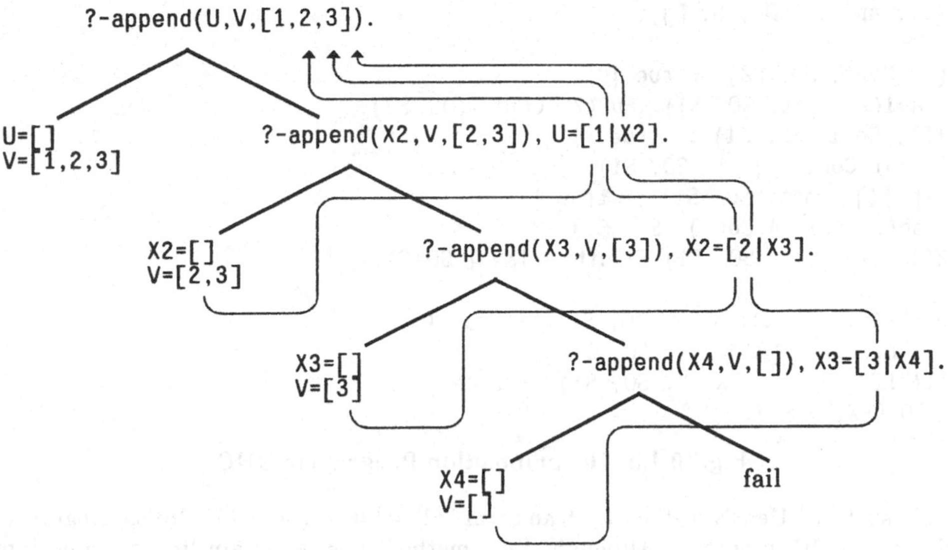

Fig. 8 An and-or tree of the goal `?-append(U,V,[1,2,3])`

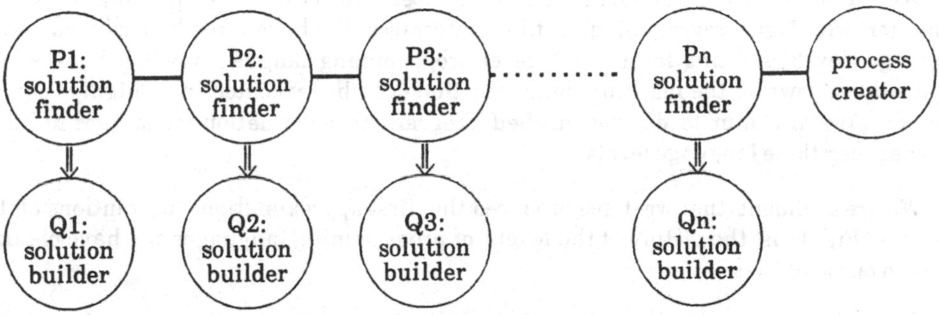

(a) A process structure of the list decomposition program in GHC

```
<process_creator> :- <termination-condition> | <finalizer>.
<process_creator> :- otherwize |
        <solution_finder>,<process_creator>.

<solution_finder> :- true | <solution_builder>.
```

(b) A program schema for the process structure (a).

Fig. 9 GHC process structure and its program schema for the list decomposition problem.

```
:-..., ap(Z, 'LO', S, []), ...

ap(Z, Cont, SO, S2) :-true |
    ap1(Z, Cont, SO, S1), ap2(Z, Cont, S1, S2).
ap1(Z, Cont, SO, S1) :- true  |
    cont(Cont, [], Z, SO, S1).
ap2([A|Z], Cont, SO, S1) :- true |
    ap(Z, 'L1'(A,Cont), SO, S1).
ap2(Z,     _,     SO, S1) :- otherwise | SO=S1.

cont('L1'(A,Cont), X, Y, SO, S1) :- true |
    cont(Cont, [A|X], Y, SO, S1).
cont('LO',         X, Y, SO, S1) :- true |
    SO=[(X,Y)|S1].
```

Fig. 10 List Decomposition Program in GHC

We sketched Ueda's method to transform "all solutions search" Prolog programs to equivalent GHC programs. Although this method has a certain limitation on input programs, it is known that it covers a wide range of application programs.

5. Conclusion

We set out in the Fifth Generation Computer project to develop a highly parallel computer with logic programming as the centerpiece. We have already designed several language levels, starting from high level programming languages which handle large applications, down to the machine language that can be executed in a highly parallel manner. We also aim to develop unified program transformation techniques to fill the gaps between these language levels.

We are confident that we have produced the first approximations to solutions of this problem. Fig. 11 is the picture of the levels of programming languages we have obtained through our activities so far.

We can now see the basic outline of the path from applications to parallel execution, although the path has not taken concrete shape yet. Application programs are written in a powerful knowledge programming language equipped with meta programming facilities. These are transformed to more efficient programs written in a general purpose user language. Then these programs are further translated into the more primitive parallel logic programming language FGHC, which can be executed by Multi-PSI and/or PIM.

What remains is to give this path concrete shape. Our approach is to isolate the component problems and solve them one by one and put the results together to achieve the target.

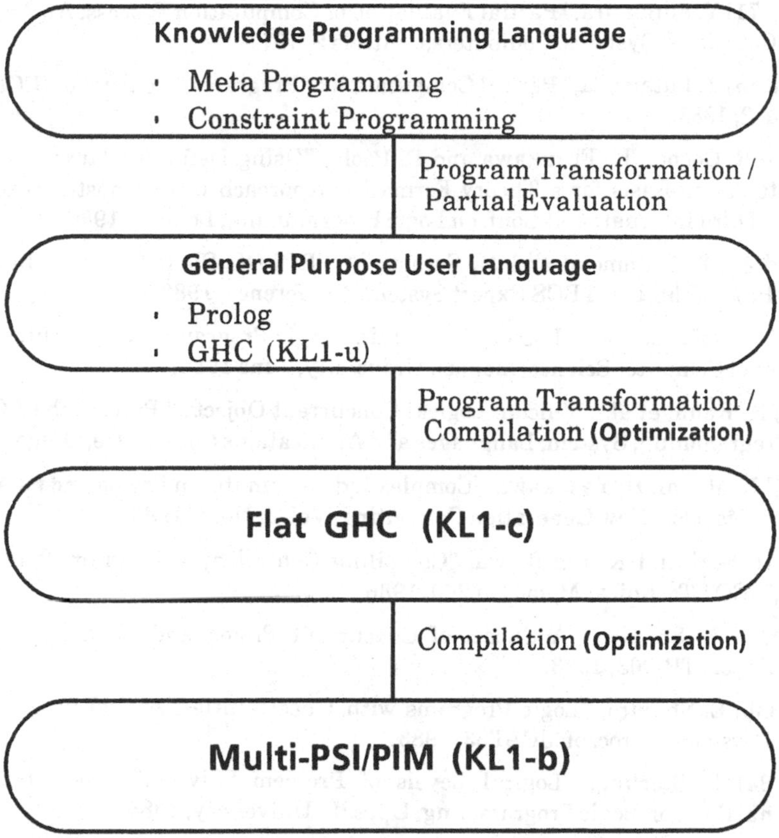

Fig. 11 Levels of programming languages and transformation methods among them

References

[Burstall 77] R. Burstall and J. Darlington, "A Transformation System for Developing Recursive Programs," JACM Vol. 24,No. 1, 1977.

[Clark 84] K. Clark and S. Gregory, "PARLOG: Parallel Programming in Logic," Research Report DOC 84/4, Imperial College, April, 1984.

[Colmerauer 82] A. Colmerauer, "Prolog and Infinite Trees," In Logic Programming, K. L. Clark and S. A. Tarnlund (eds.), Academic Press, 1982.

[Colmerauer 86] A. Colmerauer, "Theoretical Model of Prolog II," in Logic Programming and Its Applications, M. Van Caneghem and D. H. D. Warren (eds.), Albex Publishing Corp., 1986.

[Dincbus 86] M. Dincbus and P. Vanhentenryck, "Constraints and Logic Programming," Technical Report TR-LP-9, ECRC, Munich, 1986.

[Furukawa 84] K. Furukawa, A. Takeuchi, S. Kunifuji, H. Yasukawa, M. Ohki, K. Ueda, "Mandala: A Logic Based Knowledge Programming System," Proc. of the FGCS'84, 1984.

[Futamura 71] Y. Futamura, "Partial Evaluation of Computation Process: An Approach to a Compiler-Compiler," Systems, Computers,Controls 2, 1971.

[Futamura 83] Y. Futamura, "Partial Computation of Programs," Journal of IECE of Japan, Vol. 66, No. 2, 1983.

[Goebel 86] R. Goebel, K. Furukawa and D. Poole, "Using Definite Clauses and Integrity Constraints as the Basis for a Theory Formation Approach to Diagnostic Reasoning," in Proc. of the Third International Conf. on Logic Programming, London, 1986.

[Hammond 83] P. Hammond and M. Sergot, "A PROLOG Shell for Logic Based Expert Systems," Proc. of the Third BCS Expert Systems Conference, 1983.

[Jaffar 86] J. Jaffar and J-L. Lassez, "Constraint Logic Programming," Technical Report, Department of Computer Science, Monash University, June 1986.

[Kahn 86] K. Kahn, et al., "Vulcan: Logical Concurrent Objects," Proc. of the ACM Object-oriented Programming, System, Languages and Applications Conference, Oregon, 1986.

[Mukai 85] K. Mukai, H. Yasukawa, "Complex Indeterminates in Prolog and its Application to Discourse Models," New Generation Computing, Vol. 3, No. 4, 1985.

[Seki 86] H. Seki and K. Furukawa, "Compiling Control by a Program Transformation Approach," ICOT Technical Memo No.240, 1986.

[Shapiro 83a] E. Shapiro, "A Subset of Concurrent Prolog and Its Interpreter," ICOT Technical Report TR-003, 1983.

[Shapiro 83b] E. Shapiro, "Logic Programs with Uncertainties: A Tool for Implementing Rule-based Systems," Proc. of IJCAI'83, 1983.

[Sterling 84] L. Sterling, "Logical Levels of Problem Solving," Proc. of the Second International Conf. on Logic Programming, Uppsala University, 1984.

[Takeuchi 86] A. Takeuchi and K. Furukawa, "Partial Evaluation of Prolog Programs and its Application to Meta Programming," in Proc. of the IFIP Congress 86, 1986.

[Ueda 85] K. Ueda, "Guarded Horn Clauses," ICOT Technical Report TR-103, 1985, also in Logic Programming '85, Lecture Notes in Computer Science, 221, Springer-Verlag, 1986.

[Ueda 86] K. Ueda, "Making Exhaustive Search Programs Deterministic,"

A COMPOSITIVE ABSTRACTION ALGORITHM FOR COMBINATORY LOGIC*

Adolfo PIPERNO

Dipartimento di Matematica
Istituto "G.Castelnuovo"
Universita' degli Studi di Roma "La Sapienza"
P.le Aldo Moro 5, I-00185 ROMA, Italy.**

Abstract.

The problem of the translation of λ-terms into combinators (bracket abstraction) is of great importance for the implementation of functional languages. In the literature there exist a lot of algorithms concerning this topic, each of which is based on a particular choice of a combinatory basis, of its cardinality, of an abstraction technique.

The algorithm presented here originated from a modification of the definition of abstraction given by Curry in 1930, and has the following interesting properties:

i) it employs a potentially infinite basis of combinators, each of which depends on at most two parameters and is, therefore, directly implementable;

ii) it gives compact code, introducing a number of basic combinators which is proportional to the size of the expression to be abstracted and invariant for one and multi-sweep abstraction techniques;

iii) it gives the result in the form $\mathbf{R}\,\mathbf{I}\,M_1 \ldots M_n$, where **R** is a regular combinator expressed as a composition of basic combinators, **I** is the identity combinator, and $M_1, \ldots, M_n$ are the constant terms appearing into the expression subjected to the translation process.

It comes out that a slight modification of the algorithm yields a combinatory equivalent of Hughes' supercombinators.

Keywords: Functional programming, Compiler design, Evaluation techniques.

0. Introduction.

We assume the reader to be familiar with the basic definitions and properties of λ-calculus and theory of combinators not explicitly cited in this paper; for a complete treatment of them see e.g. [Bar] and [CurFe].

In particular:

- λ-terms will be untyped λ-β-η-terms, possibly containing constants;
- the word combinator will indicate a closed λ-term, which will be denoted by a boldface character; we will assume that the correspondence between λ-calculus and combinatory logic has already been defined and adopt λ-notation

*) This research has been supported by grants of the Ministry of Public Instruction, Italy.
**) This work originated as the author's thesis in Mathematics (supervisor Prof. C.Böhm) by such an affiliation.

to indicate the functional behaviour of a combinator;

- the problem of abstraction in combinatory logic (CL), which is the central issue of the process of translation from λ-calculus to CL, is introduced in the following way:

let be given any CL-term U and the variables $x_1,...,x_n$ ($n \geq 1$); the *abstract* of U with respect to $x_1,...,x_n$ (denoted $[x_1,...,x_n]$ U) is a CL-term F such that:

i) x_i does not occur in F ($1 \leq i \leq n$);

ii) $Fx_1...x_n \geq U$. ($Fx_1...x_n$ *reduces to* U).

The abstraction is a correspondence between CL-terms; it is constructively defined by means of an algorithm, which can be viewed as a proof for combinatory completeness; related algorithms can be classified in two branches:

- *multi-sweep* algorithms, which repeatedly operate on one variable at a time, in the following way: $[x_1,...,x_n]\ U =_{def} [x_1]([x_2](...([x_n]\ U)...))$;

- *one-sweep* algorithms, which operate simultaneously on all the variables $x_1,...,x_n$; we will use the notation $[\vec{x}_n]$ U to indicate that the operation $[x_1,...,x_n]$ U has to be performed by such an algorithm.

The interest in the abstraction algorithms of combinatory logic comes from computer science: in the last few years many so-called functional languages have been proposed, together with special techniques for their implementation. Some of these, starting with the one by Turner [Tur79a,b], make use of an algorithm of translation from λ-calculus to combinatory logic in order to achieve the compilation of a program. Functional languages are in effect enriched versions of λ-calculus, and the combinatory code obtained from the translation process is more easily executable by a computer than performing β-reductions.

Such an approach is of practical interest if the size of the resulting code is not too large; an exhaustive treatment about the complexity of the algorithms existing in the literature can be found in [Mul].

A different implementation technique for functional languages is the one suggested by Hughes [Hug]; the compilation process makes use of the so-called *supercombinators;* these are introduced as a generalisation of Turner's combinators avoiding the growth of the compiled code; however they need to be interpreted somehow, while Turner's ones are directly implementable.

The main inspiration for the present research comes from the comparison between the two schemes described above, the motivation being to find a combinatory equivalent of supercombinators, i.e. a combinatory basis and an abstraction algorithm operating on it in order to give a combinatory interpretation of them.

The resulting algorithm derives from the sources of combinatory logic; in fact the required basis comes from a modification of the one introduced by Curry in 1930-32 [Cur30,Cur32], and the algorithm comes from a modification of the definition of abstraction given by Curry in 1933 [Cur33].

In sections 1,2 we will introduce the set of combinators employed by the algorithm as a compositive basis for regular combinators; in section 3 we will give an intuitive description of the abstraction process; this will be modified and formalized in sections 4 and 5.1,2, with the definitions of two versions of the final algorithm, corresponding to one and multi-sweep techniques; complexity problems will be analysed in section 6.

1. Basic combinators.

We will first recall the definitions of some fundamental combinators:

$\mathbf{I} \equiv \lambda x.x$ the elementary identificator;

$\mathbf{K} \equiv \lambda fx.f$ the elementary cancellator;

$\mathbf{W} \equiv \lambda fx.fxx$ the elementary duplicator;

$\mathbf{C} \equiv \lambda fxy.fyx$ the elementary permutator;

$\mathbf{B} \equiv \lambda fgx.f(gx)$ the elementary compositor (infix: $f \circ g \equiv \mathbf{B}fg$).

We will now give a classification of CL-terms which is useful to introduce the combinatory basis employed in the abstraction algorithm (see [Sta] for an interesting treatment about basis problems in CL):

Definition 1.1:

A CL-term T is said to be *pure* if it is a combination of variables only.

Definition 1.2:

A combinator $\mathbf{T}$ is said to be *proper* if $\mathbf{T} \equiv \lambda x_0 \ldots x_n.T$, where T is a pure combination of the variables $x_0,\ldots,x_n$.

Definition 1.3:

A proper combinator $\mathbf{U}$ is said to be *regular* if $\mathbf{U} \equiv \lambda x_0 \ldots x_n.x_0 U_1 \ldots U_m$, where $U_1,\ldots,U_m$ are pure combinations of $x_1,\ldots,x_n$.

Let us consider the set $\mathbf{R}$ of all regular combinators; it is easy to verify that:

(i) $\mathbf{R}$ constitutes a monoid with respect to the operation ($\circ$) of composition;

(ii) considering the elements of $\mathbf{R}$ as operators acting on variables, $\mathbf{R}_1 \circ \mathbf{R}_2$ is obtained operating first with $\mathbf{R}_1$ and secondly with $\mathbf{R}_2$ ($\mathbf{R}_1$, $\mathbf{R}_2 \in \mathbf{R}$).

We describe some sequences of regular combinators, i.e. parametric subsets of $\mathbf{R}$, in order to specify a subset $\mathbf{B} \subset \mathbf{R}$ such that every $\mathbf{Z} \in \mathbf{R}$ can be expressed as a composition of elements belonging to $\mathbf{B}$.

$\mathbf{B}$ will be called *compositive basis* for regular combinators.

The sequences are given together with their inductive definition:

Identificators: $\mathbf{I}_n \equiv \lambda x_0 x_1 \ldots x_n . x_0 x_1 \ldots x_n$ $(n \geq 0)$;

Def. I1: $\mathbf{I}_0 = \mathbf{I}$; $\mathbf{I}_{t+1} = \mathbf{B}\mathbf{I}_t$;

Cancellators: $\mathbf{K}_n \equiv \lambda x_0 x_1 \ldots x_n . x_0 x_1 \ldots x_{n-1}$ $(n \geq 1)$;

Def. K1: $\mathbf{K}_1 = \mathbf{K}$; $\mathbf{K}_{t+1} = \mathbf{B}\mathbf{K}_t$;

Multiplicators: $\mathbf{W}_{n,r} \equiv \lambda x_0 x_1 \ldots x_n . x_0 x_1 \ldots x_{n-1} x_n \ldots$ (r+1 times) $\ldots x_n$ $(n \geq 1, r \geq 0)$;

Def. W1: $\mathbf{W}_1 = \mathbf{W}$; $\mathbf{W}_{t+1} = \mathbf{B}\mathbf{W}_t$;

Def. W2: $\mathbf{W}_{n,1} = \mathbf{W}_n$; $\mathbf{W}_{n,s+1} = \mathbf{W}_n \circ \mathbf{W}_{n,s}$;

Def. W3: $\mathbf{W}_{n,0} = \mathbf{I}_n$;

<u>Permutators:</u> $\mathbf{C}_{m+n,m} \equiv \lambda x_0 x_1 \ldots x_m \ldots x_{m+n-1} x_{m+n} \cdot x_0 x_1 \ldots x_{m+n} x_m \ldots x_{m+n-1}$ $(m \geq 1,\ n \geq 0)$;

Def. C1: $\mathbf{C}_1 = \mathbf{C}$; $\mathbf{C}_{t+1} = \mathbf{BC}_t$;

Def. C2: $\mathbf{C}_{n,1} = \mathbf{C}_n$; $\mathbf{C}_{n+k+1,n} = \mathbf{C}_{n+k+1,n+k} \circ \mathbf{C}_{n+k,n}$;

Def. C3: $\mathbf{C}_{n,n} = \mathbf{I}_n$;

<u>Compositors:</u> $\mathbf{B}_n\mathbf{B}_m \equiv \lambda x_0 x_1 \ldots x_m \ldots x_{m+n+1} \cdot x_0 x_1 \ldots x_m (x_{m+1} \ldots x_{m+n+1})$ $(m \geq 0,\ n > 0)$;

Def. B1: $\mathbf{B}_0 = \mathbf{I}$; $\mathbf{B}_{t+1} = \mathbf{B} \circ \mathbf{B}_t$;

Def. B2: $\mathbf{B}_0\mathbf{B}_t = \mathbf{B}_t$; $\mathbf{B}_{s+1}\mathbf{B}_t = \mathbf{B}(\mathbf{B}_s\mathbf{B}_t)$.

Note that the permutators cited above are different from those introduced by Curry in [Cur30] and [Cur32]; this choice is due to complexity reasons, and will be motivated in section 6.

In the next section we will give a theorem of existence and uniqueness to prove that the sequences of combinators introduced above effectively constitute a compositive basis for **R**; the theorem was proved by Curry in [Cur30], [Cur32]; the complete proof involving the different permutators can be found in [Ptes].

2. Compositive normal form.

Notation: from this point onwards we will use Gothic characters to indicate compositions of basic combinators; in particular:

$\mathfrak{K}$: any composition of cancellators or identificators;

$\mathfrak{W}$: any composition of multiplicators;

$\mathfrak{C}$: any composition of permutators;

$\mathfrak{B}$: any composition of compositors or identificators.

<u>Definition 2.1:</u> (Compositive form of regular combinators)

A regular combinator **R** is said to be in *compositive form* (CF) if it is expressed as a composition of regular combinators (called *atoms* of **R**).

<u>Definition 2.2:</u> (Compositive normal form of regular combinators)

A regular combinator **R** is said to be in *compositive normal form* (CNF) if it is expressed in the form (2.2.0) $\mathfrak{K} \circ \mathfrak{W} \circ \mathfrak{C} \circ \mathfrak{B}$,

where $\mathfrak{K}$, $\mathfrak{W}$, $\mathfrak{C}$, $\mathfrak{B}$ (called *components* of **R**) are respectively:

2.2.1 $\mathfrak{K} \equiv \mathbf{I}_h$ (h=1,2...) or $\mathfrak{K} \equiv \mathbf{K}_{h_r} \circ \mathbf{K}_{h_{r-1}} \circ \ldots \circ \mathbf{K}_{h_1}$, where $h_1 < h_2 < \ldots < h_r$;

2.2.2 $\mathfrak{W} \equiv \mathbf{W}_{h_r,k_r} \circ \mathbf{W}_{h_{r-1},k_{r-1}} \circ \ldots \circ \mathbf{W}_{h_1,k_1}$, where $h_1 < h_2 < \ldots < h_r$;

2.2.3 $\mathfrak{C} \equiv \mathbf{C}_{1+a_1,1} \circ \mathbf{C}_{2+a_2,2} \circ \ldots \circ \mathbf{C}_{n+a_n,n}$, where $a_i \geq 0$, $1 \leq i \leq n$;

2.2.4 $\mathfrak{B} \equiv \mathbf{I}_h$ (h=1,2...) or $\mathfrak{B} \equiv \mathbf{B}_{m_q}\mathbf{B}_{n_q} \circ \mathbf{B}_{m_{q-1}}\mathbf{B}_{n_{q-1}} \circ \ldots \circ \mathbf{B}_{m_1}\mathbf{B}_{n_1}$,

where $m_k \geq 0$, $n_k > 0$, $1 \leq k \leq q$, and $m_q > m_{q-1} > \ldots > m_1$.

Convention: we will omit the combinators $\mathbf{I}_h$ (h=1,2...) in a compositive form different from an identificator.

Definition 2.3: (Principal CNF of regular combinators)
A regular combinator **R** is said to be in *principal compositive normal form* (PCNF) if it is in CNF and $\mathfrak{C}$ corresponds to a permutation which does not interchange variables having the same name.

Example: We consider the combinators:
$\mathfrak{X} \equiv \mathbf{W}_{2,1} \circ \mathbf{C}_{2,1} \circ \mathbf{B}_1\mathbf{B}_1$ and $\mathfrak{Z} \equiv \mathbf{W}_{2,1} \circ \mathbf{C}_{3,1} \circ \mathbf{B}_1\mathbf{B}_1$; it is easy to verify that both $\mathfrak{X}$ and $\mathfrak{Z}$ represent the combinator **S** ($\equiv \lambda xyz.xz(yz)$), but only $\mathfrak{X}$ is in PCNF.

Theorem 2.4: (Existence and uniqueness theorem)
Let **R** be a regular combinator; there exists one and only one combinator $\mathfrak{R}$ in PCNF such that $\mathfrak{R}$ is extensionally equal to **R**; we will call $\mathfrak{R}$ the PNCF of **R**.

Corollary 2.5: (PCNF of proper combinators)
Let **P** be a proper combinator; there exists one and only one regular combinator $\mathfrak{R}$ in PCNF such that $\mathfrak{R}\,\mathbf{I}$ is extensionally equal to **P**.

The difference between the known concept of normal form of a combinator (i.e. a term constituted only by constants and not containing any redex as a subterm) and the one described above will become more evident in the next section, where we will define the notion of normal representation of a CL-term. In the world of regular combinators however the concept of PCNF shares some similarity with that of strong normal form, and it is possible to define an algorithm which, given a regular combinator $\mathfrak{R}$ expressed as a composition of basic combinators, yields the PCNF of $\mathfrak{R}$, repeatedly applying some schemes of tranformation rules [Ptes]; by corollary 2.5 this algorithm can be extended to the set of proper combinators.

3. Normal representation of a CL-term.

In this section we will extend the notion of PCNF to the whole set of CL-terms, in order to express any term as a function of a predetermined sequence of variables $x_1,\ldots,x_n$ (even not occurring in the considered term). A *normal representation* will be defined also for terms not possessing normal form in the usual sense.[1]

The definition of *normal representation* of a CL-term X is given in three steps [CurFe]:

3.1) Reduction to the case where X is a pure term: let X be a combination of the variables $x_1,\ldots,x_n$ (possibly not occurring in X) and the atomic constants $a_1,\ldots,a_p$, appearing in X exactly in the specified order (free variables, i.e.

(1) Obviously in such a case uniqueness is lost; note that the uniqueness of the normal representation is lost also for not proper terms possessing normal form.

variables different from $x_1,\ldots,x_n$, are treated as constants); let X' be the term obtained replacing $a_1,\ldots,a_p$ with the variables $y_1,\ldots,y_p$, not occurring in X; if the combinator **H'** represents X' as a function of $y_1,\ldots,y_p,x_1,\ldots,x_n$, then $\mathbf{H'}a_1\ldots a_p$ represents X as a function of $x_1,\ldots,x_n$.

3.2) <u>Reduction to a regular term</u>: let Y be a pure combination of the variables $x_1,\ldots,x_n$ (possibly not occurring in Y) and let y be a variable not occurring in Y; it follows that $Y' \equiv yY$ is a regular combination of $y,x_1,\ldots,x_n$; if the combinator **U'** represents Y' as a function of $y,x_1,\ldots,x_n$, then $\mathbf{U} \equiv \mathbf{U'I}$ represents Y as a function of $x_1,\ldots,x_n$.

3.3) <u>Analysis of a regular term</u>: see definitions 2.2, 2.3 and theorem 2.4.

The notion of normal representation of a CL-term actually defines an abstraction algorithm, which is constituted by:

a) a preliminary phasis, corresponding to step 3.1 of the above given definition;

b) a properly abstraction phasis, which yields the PCNF of the proper combinator corresponding to the pure combination resulting from the preliminary phasis. This is done by a Markov algorithm in which the rewriting rules generate the components of the PCNF of a regular combinator; the intuitive meaning of the abstraction process is the following:

let M be a pure combination of the variables $x_1,\ldots,x_n$ (possibly not occurring in M); the combinator $\mathfrak{R}$ such that $\mathfrak{R}\mathbf{I}x_1\ldots x_n \geq M$ is obtained, starting from M, in four steps:

(i) elimination of parentheses appearing in M, in the order specified in 2.2.4;

(ii) reordering of variables (2.2.3);

(iii) elimination of multiplicities of variables (2.2.2);

(iv) elimination of cancellations of variables (2.2.1).

4. Introducing the compositive abstraction algorithm.

The sketch of algorithm described in the previous section, given by Curry in [Cur33], is complicated by the substitution process attending the preliminary phasis. However we observe that the new variables introduced in 3.1 are not involved in the steps (ii), (iii) and (iv) of the abstraction algorithm (note that this was not true with Curry's choice of permutators); in addition to this, we will modify the substitution rule of 3.1 in order to 'neutralize' the new variables also with respect to step (i); after this, we will define the final version of the abstraction algorithm.

<u>Definition 4.1:</u>

Let M be a CL-term and $\mathbf{A}$ the set of the *atoms* (variables and atomic constants) of M; the binary tree bT(M) associated to M is inductively defined as follows:

$bT(a) = a \quad$ if $\quad M \equiv a \in \mathbf{A}$;

$bT(AB) = {}_{bT(A)}\!\wedge_{bT(B)} \quad$ if $\quad M \equiv AB$.

Definition 4.2: (Constant components of a CL-term)

Let bT(M) be the binary tree associated to the term M containing in this order the (not necessarily distinct) atomic constants $a_1,\dots,a_p$; we will call *constant components* of M the subterms of M associated to those subtrees of bT(M) whose leaves are labelled by constants ($\in \{a_1,\dots,a_p\}$) only.

Definition 4.3: (Maximal constant components of a CL-term)

Let $\mathbf{C_C}(M)$ be the multiset of the constant component of the term M; a term $A \in \mathbf{C_C}(M)$ is said to be *maximal* if there does not exist a term $B \in \mathbf{C_C}(M)$ such that bT(A) is a son of bT(B) in bT(M).

We will write $\mathbf{C_{MC}}(M)$ to indicate the set of maximal costant components of M.

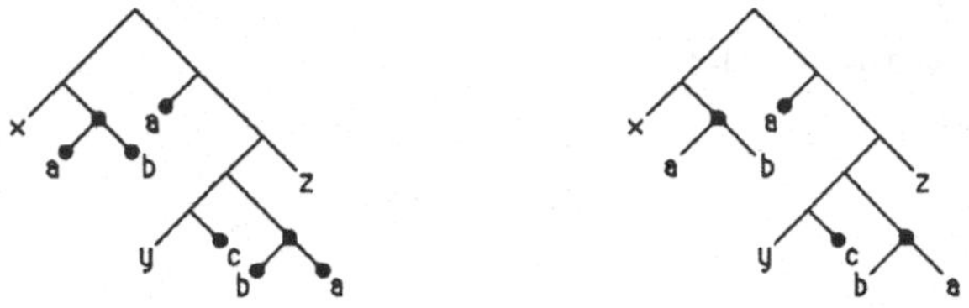

(*a*) Fig. 4.4 (*b*)

Fig.4.4 shows (*a*) the constant components and (*b*) the maximal constant components of the term $M \equiv x(ab)(a(yc(ba)z))$.

Hence $\mathbf{C_{MC}}(M) \equiv \{(ab), a, c, (ba)\}$

5.1. Compositive abstraction algorithm (one-sweep).

Initial position: Let be given the problem $[\vec{x}_n]T$.

Let $\mathbf{C_{MC}}(T) \equiv \{M_1,\dots,M_q\}$ be the set of maximal constant components of T, and $\mathbf{V} \equiv \{x_1,\dots,x_n\}$.

If $T \equiv h_1T_2\dots T_m$, where $h_1 \in \mathbf{C_{MC}}(T) \cup \mathbf{V}$, we make the following position:

$$[\vec{x}_n]T \rightarrow [\vec{x}_n]\mathbf{I}\,h_1T_2\dots T_m.$$

Abstraction:

(Notation: $\mathbf{H}$ will indicate a combinator: at the beginning $\mathbf{H} \equiv \mathbf{I}$ by initial position).

Termination:

$$[\vec{x}_n]\mathbf{H}\,M_1\dots M_q x_1\dots x_n \rightarrow \mathbf{H}\,M_1\dots M_q,$$ where x_i does not occur in M_j, for any $x_i \in \mathbf{V}$ and $1 \le j \le q$.

Elimination of parentheses:

$$[\vec{x}_n]\mathbf{H}\,h_{0,1}\dots h_{0,j_0}(h_{1,1}M_{1,2}\dots M_{1,j_1})\dots(h_{p,1}M_{p,2}\dots M_{p,j_p}) \rightarrow$$

$$\rightarrow [\vec{x}_n]\mathbf{B}_{j_0}\mathbf{B}_{j_1-1}\mathbf{H}\,h_{0,1}\dots h_{0,j_0}h_{1,1}M_{1,2}\dots M_{1,j_1}\dots(h_{p,1}M_{p,2}\dots M_{p,j_p}),$$

where $h_{i,j} \in \mathbf{C_{MC}}(T) \cup \mathbf{V}$ ($0 \le i \le p$; $1 \le j \le j_i$), $M_{h,k}$ is any term, and for all t ($1 \le t \le p$) there exists an r_t ($1 \le r_t \le n$) such that in $M_{t,2}$ there is at least an occurrence of x_{r_t}.

Permutation:

$[\vec{x}_n]\,\mathbf{H}\,h_1 \ldots h_{r-1} h_r h_{r+1} \ldots h_j h_{j+1} \ldots h_p \rightarrow$

$\rightarrow [\vec{x}_n]\,\mathbf{C}_{j,r}\,\mathbf{H}\,h_1 \ldots h_{r-1} h_{r+1} \ldots h_j h_r h_{j+1} \ldots h_p,$

where $h_k \in \mathbf{C}_{MC}(T) \cup \mathbf{V}$ $(1 \le k \le p)$, $h_r \equiv x_s \in \mathbf{V}$, and:

if there exists a z $(r+1 \le z \le p-1)$ such that $h_z \equiv x_v \in \mathbf{V}$,

then $h_{z+1} \equiv x_u \in \mathbf{V}$ and $v \le u$;

if $h_j \equiv x_t$ $(x_t \in \mathbf{V})$ then $t < s$;

if $h_{j+1} \equiv x_t$ $(x_t \in \mathbf{V})$ then $t \ge s$.

Elimination of multiplications:

$[\vec{x}_n]\,\mathbf{H}\,M_1 \ldots M_q x_{j_1} \ldots x_{j_k} x_{j_{k+1}} \ldots x_{j_{k+r}} \ldots x_{j_s} \rightarrow$

$\rightarrow [\vec{x}_n]\,\mathbf{W}_{q+k,r}\,\mathbf{H}\,M_1 \ldots M_q x_{j_1} \ldots x_{j_k} x_{j_{k+r+1}} \ldots x_{j_s},$

where $j_i \in \mathbf{V}$ $(1 \le i \le s)$, and:

$j_{k+t} = j_k$ $(1 \le t \le r)$;

$j_i < j_{i+1}$ $(1 \le i \le k-1)$;

$j_i \le j_{i+1}$ $(k+r+1 \le i \le s-1)$.

Elimination of cancellations:

$[\vec{x}_n]\,\mathbf{H}\,M_1 \ldots M_q x_1 x_2 \ldots x_{i-1} x_{j_1} \ldots x_{j_s} \rightarrow$

$\rightarrow [\vec{x}_n]\,\mathbf{K}_{i+q}\,\mathbf{H}\,M_1 \ldots M_q x_1 x_2 \ldots x_{i-1} x_i x_{j_1} \ldots x_{j_s},$

where $j_s \le n$; $j_1 > i$; $j_r < j_{r+1}$ $(1 \le r \le s-1)$.

5.2. Compositive abstraction algorithm (multi-sweep).

Initial position:

Let be given the problem $[x_1, \ldots, x_n]\,T$.

Let $\mathbf{C}_{MC}(T) \equiv \{M_1, \ldots, M_q\}$ be the set of maximal constant components of T, and $\mathbf{V} \equiv \{x_1, \ldots, x_n\}$.

If $T \equiv h_1 T_2 \ldots T_m$, where $h_1 \in \mathbf{C}_{MC}(T) \cup \mathbf{V}$, we make the following position:

$$[x_1, \ldots, x_n]\,T \rightarrow [x_1]([x_2](\ldots([x_n]\,h_1 T_2 \ldots T_m)\ldots)).$$

Abstraction:

For every $x \in \mathbf{V}$:

Termination:

$[x]\,\mathbf{H}\,V_1 \ldots V_s x \rightarrow \mathbf{H}\,V_1 \ldots V_s$, if x does not occur in V_j, for $1 \le j \le s$.

Elimination of parentheses:

$[x]\,\mathbf{H}\,h_{0,1} \ldots h_{0,j_0} (h_{1,1} M_{1,2} \ldots M_{1,j_1}) \ldots (h_{p,1} M_{p,2} \ldots M_{p,j_p}) \rightarrow$

$\rightarrow [x]\,\mathbf{B}_{j_0} \mathbf{B}_{j_1-1}\,\mathbf{H}\,h_{0,1} \ldots h_{0,j_0} h_{1,1} M_{1,2} \ldots M_{1,j_1} \ldots (h_{p,1} M_{p,2} \ldots M_{p,j_p}),$

where $h_{i,1} \in \mathbf{C}_{MC}(T) \cup \mathbf{V}$ $(0 \le i \le p)$, and

- for $2 \le j \le j_0$, $h_{0,j} \equiv x$ or x does not occur in $h_{0,j}$
- there is at least an occurrence of x in $(h_{1,1} M_{1,2} \ldots M_{1,j_1})$.

Permutation:

$[x]\ \mathbf{H}\ h_1 \ldots h_{r-1} h_r h_{r+1} \ldots h_j h_{j+1} \ldots h_p \rightarrow$

$\rightarrow\ [x]\ \mathbf{C}_{j,r}\ \mathbf{H}\ h_1 \ldots h_{r-1} h_{r+1} \ldots h_j h_r h_{j+1} \ldots h_p,$ where:

- for $1 \le k \le r-1$, $h_k \equiv x$ or x does not occur in h_k ;
- $h_r \equiv x$;
- for $r+1 \le k \le j$, x does not occur in h_k ;
- for $j+1 \le k \le p$, $h_k \equiv x$.

Elimination of multiplications:

$[x]\ \mathbf{H}\ V_1 \ldots V_s x \ldots (r \text{ times}) \ldots x \rightarrow$

$\rightarrow\ [x]\ \mathbf{W}_{s+1,r}\ \mathbf{H}\ V_1 \ldots V_s x,$

where x does not occur in V_k $(1 \le k \le s)$.

Elimination of cancellations:

$[x]\ \mathbf{H}\ V_1 \ldots V_s \rightarrow$

$\rightarrow\ [x]\ \mathbf{K}_{s+1}\ \mathbf{H}\ V_1 \ldots V_s x,$

where x does not occur in V_k $(1 \le k \le s)$.

We now give an example of the application of the compositive abstraction algorithm, for both one and multi-sweep techniques. Note that the result of the one-sweep version of the algorithm is a regular combinator in PCNF, while the result of the multi-sweep version is a composition of regular combinators in PCNF, not on its whole in PCNF.

Let us consider the problem $[\vec{x}_4]\ x(ab)(a(ydz(baz)))(c(bx))$,
with $x_1 \equiv x$, $x_2 \equiv y$, $x_3 \equiv z$, $x_4 \equiv t$:

Initial position:

$[\vec{x}_4]\ x(ab)(a(ydz(baz)))(c(bx)) \rightarrow [\vec{x}_4]\ \mathbf{I}x(ab)(a(ydz(baz)))(c(bx)) \rightarrow$

Elimination of parentheses:

$\rightarrow [\vec{x}_4]\ \mathbf{B}_2\mathbf{B}_1\mathbf{I}x(ab)a(ydz(baz))(c(bx)) \rightarrow$

$\rightarrow [\vec{x}_4]\ \mathbf{B}_3\mathbf{B}_3(\mathbf{B}_2\mathbf{B}_1\mathbf{I})x(ab)aydz(baz)(c(bx)) \rightarrow$

$\rightarrow [\vec{x}_4]\ \mathbf{B}_6\mathbf{B}_1(\mathbf{B}_3\mathbf{B}_3(\mathbf{B}_2\mathbf{B}_1\mathbf{I}))x(ab)aydz(ba)z(c(bx)) \rightarrow$

$\rightarrow [\vec{x}_4]\ \mathbf{B}_8\mathbf{B}_1(\mathbf{B}_6\mathbf{B}_1(\mathbf{B}_3\mathbf{B}_3(\mathbf{B}_2\mathbf{B}_1\mathbf{I})))x(ab)aydz(ba)zc(bx) \rightarrow$

$\rightarrow [\vec{x}_4]\ \mathbf{B}_9\mathbf{B}_1(\mathbf{B}_8\mathbf{B}_1(\mathbf{B}_6\mathbf{B}_1(\mathbf{B}_3\mathbf{B}_3(\mathbf{B}_2\mathbf{B}_1\mathbf{I}))))x(ab)aydz(ba)zcbx \rightarrow$

Permutation: (We put $\mathfrak{B} \equiv \mathbf{B}_9\mathbf{B}_1 \circ \mathbf{B}_8\mathbf{B}_1 \circ \mathbf{B}_6\mathbf{B}_1 \circ \mathbf{B}_3\mathbf{B}_3 \circ \mathbf{B}_2\mathbf{B}_1$)

$\rightarrow [\vec{x}_4]\ \mathbf{C}_{11,8}(\mathfrak{B}\mathbf{I})x(ab)aydz(ba)cbxz \rightarrow$

$\rightarrow [\vec{x}_4]\ \mathbf{C}_{10,6}(\mathbf{C}_{11,8}(\mathfrak{B}\mathbf{I}))x(ab)ayd(ba)cbxzz \rightarrow$

$\rightarrow [\vec{x}_4]\ \mathbf{C}_{9,4}(\mathbf{C}_{10,6}(\mathbf{C}_{11,8}(\mathfrak{B}\mathbf{I})))x(ab)ad(ba)cbxyzz \rightarrow$

$\rightarrow [\vec{x}_4]\ \mathbf{C}_{7,1}(\mathbf{C}_{9,4}(\mathbf{C}_{10,6}(\mathbf{C}_{11,8}(\mathfrak{B}\mathbf{I}))))(ab)ad(ba)cbxxyzz \rightarrow$

Elimination of multiplications: (We put $\mathfrak{C} \equiv \mathbf{C}_{7,1} \circ \mathbf{C}_{9,4} \circ \mathbf{C}_{10,6} \circ \mathbf{C}_{11,8}$)

$\rightarrow [\vec{x}_4]\ \mathbf{W}_{7,1}(\mathfrak{C}(\mathfrak{B}\mathbf{I}))(ab)ad(ba)cbxyzz \rightarrow$

$\rightarrow [\vec{x}_4]\ \mathbf{W}_{9,1}(\mathbf{W}_{7,1}(\mathfrak{C}(\mathfrak{B}\mathbf{I})))(ab)ad(ba)cbxyz \rightarrow$

Elimination of cancellations: (We put $\mathfrak{W} \equiv \mathbf{W}_{9,1} \circ \mathbf{W}_{7,1}$)

$\rightarrow [\vec{x}_4]\ \mathbf{K}_{10}(\mathfrak{W}(\mathfrak{C}(\mathfrak{B}\mathbf{I})))(ab)ad(ba)cbxyzt \rightarrow$

Termination: (We put $\mathfrak{K} \equiv \mathbf{K}_{10}$) $\to$ $\mathfrak{K}(\mathfrak{W}(\mathfrak{C}(\mathfrak{B}\mathbf{I})))$ (ab) ad (ba) cb.

Thus $[\vec{x}_4]$ x(ab)(a(ydz(baz)))(c(bx)) $\to$ $(\mathfrak{K} \circ \mathfrak{W} \circ \mathfrak{C} \circ \mathfrak{B})\,\mathbf{I}$ (ab) a d (ba) c b.

Let us now consider the problem [x,y,z,t] x(ab)(a(ydz(baz)))(c(bx)):

Initial position: [x,y,z,t]x(ab)(a(ydz(baz)))(c(bx)) $\to$

[x]([y]([z]([t] $\mathbf{I}$ x(ab)(a(ydz(baz)))(c(bx))))) $\to$

Abstraction with respect to the variable t:

$\to$ [x]([y]([z]([t] $\mathbf{K}_5\mathbf{I}$ x(ab)(a(ydz(baz)))(c(bx))t))) $\to$ (We put $\mathfrak{R}_4 \equiv \mathbf{K}_5$)

$\to$ [x]([y]([z] $\mathfrak{R}_4\mathbf{I}$ x(ab)(a(ydz(baz)))(c(bx)))) $\to$

Abstraction with respect to the variable z:

$\to$ [x]([y]([z] $\mathbf{B}_2\mathbf{B}_1(\mathfrak{R}_4\mathbf{I})$ x(ab)a(ydz(baz))(c(bx)))) $\to$

$\to$ [x]([y]([z] $\mathbf{B}_3\mathbf{B}_3(\mathbf{B}_2\mathbf{B}_1(\mathfrak{R}_4\mathbf{I}))$ x(ab)aydz(baz)(c(bx)))) $\to$

$\to$ [x]([y]([z] $\mathbf{B}_6\mathbf{B}_1(\mathbf{B}_3\mathbf{B}_3(\mathbf{B}_2\mathbf{B}_1(\mathfrak{R}_4\mathbf{I})))$ x(ab)aydz(ba)z(c(bx)))) $\to$

$\to$ [x]([y]([z] $\mathbf{C}_{9,8}(\mathbf{B}_6\mathbf{B}_1(\mathbf{B}_3\mathbf{B}_3(\mathbf{B}_2\mathbf{B}_1(\mathfrak{R}_4\mathbf{I}))))$ x(ab)aydz(ba)(c(bx))z)) $\to$

$\to$ [x]([y]([z] $\mathbf{C}_{8,6}(\mathbf{C}_{9,8}(\mathbf{B}_6\mathbf{B}_1(\mathbf{B}_3\mathbf{B}_3(\mathbf{B}_2\mathbf{B}_1(\mathfrak{R}_4\mathbf{I})))))$ x(ab)ayd(ba)(c(bx))zz)) $\to$

$\to$ [x]([y]([z]$\mathbf{W}_{8,1}(\mathbf{C}_{8,6}(\mathbf{C}_{9,8}(\mathbf{B}_6\mathbf{B}_1(\mathbf{B}_3\mathbf{B}_3(\mathbf{B}_2\mathbf{B}_1(\mathfrak{R}_4\mathbf{I}))))))$x(ab)ayd(ba)(c(bx))z)) $\to$

(We put $\mathfrak{R}_3 \equiv \mathbf{W}_{8,1} \circ \mathbf{C}_{8,6} \circ \mathbf{C}_{9,8} \circ \mathbf{B}_6\mathbf{B}_1 \circ \mathbf{B}_3\mathbf{B}_3 \circ \mathbf{B}_2\mathbf{B}_1$)

$\to$ [x]([y] $\mathfrak{R}_3(\mathfrak{R}_4\mathbf{I})$ x(ab)ayd(ba)(c(bx))) $\to$

Abstraction with respect to the variable y:

$\to$ [x]([y] $\mathbf{C}_{7,4}(\mathfrak{R}_3(\mathfrak{R}_4\mathbf{I}))$ x(ab)ad(ba)(c(bx))y) $\to$ (We put $\mathfrak{R}_2 \equiv \mathbf{C}_{7,4}$)

$\to$ [x] $\mathfrak{R}_2(\mathfrak{R}_3(\mathfrak{R}_4\mathbf{I}))$ x(ab)ad(ba)(c(bx)) $\to$

Abstraction with respect to the variable x:

$\to$ [x] $\mathbf{B}_5\mathbf{B}_1(\mathfrak{R}_2(\mathfrak{R}_3(\mathfrak{R}_4\mathbf{I})))$ x(ab)ad(ba)c(bx) $\to$

$\to$ [x] $\mathbf{B}_6\mathbf{B}_1(\mathbf{B}_5\mathbf{B}_1(\mathfrak{R}_2(\mathfrak{R}_3(\mathfrak{R}_4\mathbf{I}))))$ x(ab)ad(ba)cbx $\to$

$\to$ [x] $\mathbf{C}_{7,1}(\mathbf{B}_6\mathbf{B}_1(\mathbf{B}_5\mathbf{B}_1(\mathfrak{R}_2(\mathfrak{R}_3(\mathfrak{R}_4\mathbf{I})))))$ (ab)ad(ba)cbxx $\to$

$\to$ [x] $\mathbf{W}_{7,1}(\mathbf{C}_{7,1}(\mathbf{B}_6\mathbf{B}_1(\mathbf{B}_5\mathbf{B}_1(\mathfrak{R}_2(\mathfrak{R}_3(\mathfrak{R}_4\mathbf{I}))))))$ (ab)ad(ba)cbx $\to$

(We put $\mathfrak{R}_1 \equiv \mathbf{W}_{7,1} \circ \mathbf{C}_{7,1} \circ \mathbf{B}_6\mathbf{B}_1 \circ \mathbf{B}_5\mathbf{B}_1$)

$\to$ [x] $\mathfrak{R}_1(\mathfrak{R}_2(\mathfrak{R}_3(\mathfrak{R}_4\mathbf{I})))$ (ab)ad(ba)cb.

Thus [x,y,z,t]x(ab)(a(ydz(baz)))(c(bx)) $\equiv$ $(\mathfrak{R}_1 \circ \mathfrak{R}_2 \circ \mathfrak{R}_3 \circ \mathfrak{R}_4)\mathbf{I}$ (ab) a d (ba) c b.

6. Complexity.

In the analysis of complexity of the algorithms described in sections 5.1,2 we shall adopt the following conventions:

- the *length* of a CL-term T (denoted by $\mathcal{L}(T)$) is the number of atoms occurring in it, i.e. the number of leaves of bT(T);
- the *length* of a regular combinator $\mathfrak{R}$ expressed in compositive form (denoted by $\ell(\mathfrak{R})$) is the number of basic combinators involved in the representation of $\mathfrak{R}$;
- the *length of an abstraction problem* is the sum of the length of the term to be abstracted and the number of abstracted variables;
- the *complexity* of the algorithm is the order of magnitude of the length of the result as a function of the length of the abstraction problem, in the worst case.

Note that the compositive algorithm makes use of a parametric set of basic combinators; as observed by Mulder [Mul], in such a case we must multiply the complexity of the algorithm by a factor which can be:

(i) 1, if we count each combinator as an item;

(ii) proportional to the size of parameters, if we consider the representation of the introduced combinators into a computer.

We will use the notation $\lfloor h \rfloor$ to indicate the greatest integer $\leq h$ ($\in \mathbf{Q}$).

Complexity measurement will be made for pure CL-terms; in fact, constant subterms occurring in a combination are never handled by the abstraction process of the algorithms.

<u>Theorem 6.1:</u>

Let be given the problem $[\vec{x}_n]$ X, where X is a pure combination of the variables $x_1,\ldots,x_n$ (each of them possibly not occurring in X; $n \geq 1$), and let $\mathfrak{R}$ be the regular combinator resulting from the application of the compositive one-sweep algorithm; then, assuming $\mathcal{L}(X) > 1$:

$$(6.1.1) \qquad \ell(\mathfrak{R}) \leq \lfloor {}^5/_2\, \mathcal{L}(X) \rfloor - 3 + t,$$

where t (< n) is the number of variables, between $x_1,\ldots,x_n$, not occurring in X.

<u>Proof:</u> $\mathfrak{R} \equiv \mathfrak{K} \circ \mathfrak{W} \circ \mathfrak{C} \circ \mathfrak{B}$; hence $\ell(\mathfrak{R}) = \ell(\mathfrak{K}) + \ell(\mathfrak{W}) + \ell(\mathfrak{C}) + \ell(\mathfrak{B})$, with:

(6.1.2) $\ell(\mathfrak{K}) = t$;

(6.1.3) $\ell(\mathfrak{W}) \leq \lfloor \mathcal{L}(X)/_2 \rfloor$, the maximum number of duplications that may appear in X;

(6.1.4) $\ell(\mathfrak{C}) \leq \mathcal{L}(X) - 1$, the maximum number of permutators needed to represent a permutation of $\mathcal{L}(X)$ items;

(6.1.5) $\ell(\mathfrak{B}) \leq \mathcal{L}(X) - 2$, the maximum number of parentheses that may appear in X.

The 6.1.1 follows immediately from 6.1.2-5.

Let us now consider the problem $[x_1,\ldots,x_n]$ X, in order to analyse the complexity of the multi-sweep version of the compositive algorithm with respect to the one-sweep one.

<u>Theorem 6.2:</u>

For every pure combination X of the variables $x_1,\ldots,x_n$ (possibly not occurring in X), let $\mathfrak{R}$ be the regular combinator, in PCNF, such that $\mathfrak{R}\,\mathbf{I} \equiv [\vec{x}_n]$ X, and $\mathfrak{R}_1,\ldots,\mathfrak{R}_n$ the regular combinators, in PCNF, such that $(\mathfrak{R}_1 \circ\ldots\circ \mathfrak{R}_n)\,\mathbf{I} \equiv$ $\equiv [x_1,\ldots,x_n]$ X; the following property holds: $\ell(\mathfrak{R}) = \ell(\mathfrak{R}_1 \circ\ldots\circ \mathfrak{R}_n)$.

<u>Sketch of the proof:</u> We have:

- $\mathfrak{R}_i \equiv \mathfrak{K}_i \circ \mathfrak{W}_i \circ \mathfrak{C}_i \circ \mathfrak{B}_i$ $(1 \leq i \leq n)$;
- $\mathfrak{R} \equiv \mathfrak{K} \circ \mathfrak{W} \circ \mathfrak{C} \circ \mathfrak{B}$.

The theorem follows from proving:

(6.2.1) $\ell(\mathfrak{K}) = \Sigma_{i=1,\ldots,n}\, \ell(\mathfrak{K}_i)$; (6.2.2) $\ell(\mathfrak{W}) = \Sigma_{i=1,\ldots,n}\, \ell(\mathfrak{W}_i)$;

(6.2.3) $\ell(\mathfrak{C}) = \Sigma_{i=1,\ldots,n}\, \ell(\mathfrak{C}_i)$; (6.2.4) $\ell(\mathfrak{B}) = \Sigma_{i=1,\ldots,n}\, \ell(\mathfrak{B}_i)$.

The complete proof, here omitted, can be found in [Ptes].

Note that theorem 6.2 is not valid with Curry's permutators; this point can be intuitively explained as follows: during the permutation phasis of the abstraction process, variables are moved from left to right; it is easy to verify that this operation can be done in one step by the new permutators, but not by the old ones.

7. Conclusion.

To summarize, we showed a new (old) abstraction algorithm which seems to be interesting for the following reasons:

- it is compositive: the resulting code has a 'structured' look, i.e. it may be viewed as a succession of procedure callings, hence it is quite readable;
- it is efficient: the worst case mentioned above concerns pure combinations; in the general case, the complexity rate is a function of the number of variables occurring in the term to be abstracted, not of its whole length; this fact makes the algorithm suitable for the compilation of a functional program;
- it can be defined in both one and multi-sweep techniques, preserving the length of the resulting code: this 'invariance property' is not valid for any other abstraction algorithm;
- it gives a combinatory equivalent of Hughes' supercombinators: in effect supercombinators are proper combinators; their interpretation can be achieved adding to the abstraction rules of the multi-sweep version of the compositive algorithm a clause of belonging to the set of *maximal free expressions* (see [Hug]). This point will be better explained in the appendix.

Acknowledgement.

The author is grateful to Prof.Corrado Böhm for helpful suggestions and discussions about the subject of this paper.

References.

[Bar] - H.P.Barendregt, The Lambda Calculus, its Syntax and Semantics, Studies in Logic, Vol.103, North-Holland, Amsterdam (1984).

[Cur30] - H.B.Curry, Grundlagen der kombinatorischen Logik, American Journal of Mathematics, Vol.52 (1930).

[Cur32] - H.B.Curry, Some additions to the theory of combinators, American Journal of Mathematics, Vol.54 (1932).

[Cur33] - H.B.Curry, Apparent variables from the standpoint of Combinatory Logic, Annals of Mathematics, Vol.34 (1933).

[CurFe] - H.B.Curry & R.Feys, Combinatory logic, Vol.1, North-Holland, Amsterdam (1958).

[Hug] - R.J.M.Hughes, SuperCombinators: a new implementation method for Applicative Languages, Symp.on LISP and Funct.Progr.,ACM (Aug 1982).

[Mul] - J.C.Mulder, Complexity of combinatory code, University of Utrecht (int.rep., 1985).

[Ptes] - A.Piperno, Metodi di astrazione in logica combinatoria: analisi, proposte, applicazioni, Tesi di laurea, 1986.

[Sta] - R.Statman, On translating lambda terms into combinators: the basis problem, LICS, Boston, 1986.

[Tur79a] - D.A.Turner, Another algorithm for bracket abstraction, The Journal of Symbolic Logic, Vol.44 n.2 (1979).

[Tur79b] - D.A.Turner, A new implementation technique for applicative languages, Software Practice and Experience, n.9 (1979).

APPENDIX: Compositive algorithm and supercombinators.

We suppose the reader to be familiar with the notions of *supercombinators* and *fully lazy evaluation* ; we will show in an intuitive way how the compositive abstraction algorithm can be modified in order to yield a purely combinatory interpretation of supercombinators.

Supercombinators were introduced by Hughes [Hug] with the purpose of giving an efficient implementation technique of full laziness; they are built up, starting from an arbitrary λ-expression E, in the following way:

1) find the innermost λ-expression λt.H appearing in E;

2) let $F_1,\ldots,F_n$ be the non-constant maximal free expressions(1) (MFE) of H, ordered as stated by some optimisation rules: replace $F_1,\ldots,F_n$ with the variables $x_1,\ldots,x_n$, not occurring in E, and let H^* be the term obtained after this substitution;

3) give a name (τ) to $\lambda x_1\ldots x_n t.H^*$;

4) replace λt.H with $\tau F_1\ldots F_n$ in E;

5) repeat steps 1-4 until there are no more λ-expressions.

The method described above can be considered as an algorithm of translation from λ-calculus to CL, working with the infinite basis constituted by the whole set of proper combinators; the resulting supercombinators, however, are not directly implementable, and need an extra level of interpretation.

Let us now consider the multi-sweep version of the compositive abstraction algorithm, where the conditions that rule the steps of the algorithm are enriched in an opportune way with some clauses of belonging to the set of MFE of the expression subjected to the abstraction process.

It comes out that the result of the operation [x] T, when subjected to the final algorithm, is of the form $\mathfrak{R}|C_1\ldots C_k F_1\ldots F_n$, where $\mathfrak{R}$ is a regular combinator (in PCNF), $C_1,\ldots,C_k$ are constant subexpressions of T, and $F_1,\ldots,F_n$ are the MFEs of λx.T. Thus $\mathfrak{R}|C_1\ldots C_k$ is the combinatory interpretation, via the compositive abstraction algorithm, of the supercombinator resulting from the application of Hughes' method to λx.T.

In addition to this, the optimisation rules, introduced by Hughes to improve the efficiency of supercombinators, can be enclosed into the permutation step of the final algorithm.

Summarizing, it is possible to modify the multi-sweep version of the compositive abstraction algorithm, in order to have a purely combinatory equivalent of Hughes' method, which has the following properties:

- it preserves the linearity property of the native algorithm;
- it makes use of a directly implementable set of combinators: no extra level of interpretation is needed.

---

(1) recall that a *free expression* of λx.T is a subexpression of T which does not depend on the bound variable x, and that a free expression is called *maximal* if it is not a proper subexpression of a free expression.

Linear Logic and Lazy Computation

J.Y. Girard
Equipe de Logique, UA753 du CNRS
Mathématiques, Tour 45-55, 5e étage
2 place Jussieu, 75251 Paris CEDEX 05 FRANCE

Y. Lafont
INRIA, Projet Formel
Domaine de Voluceau, Rocquencourt
BP105 78153 Le Chesnay CEDEX
FRANCE

Abstract

Recently, J.Y. Girard discovered that usual logical connectors such as $\Rightarrow$ (implication) could be broken up into more elementary *linear* connectors. This provided a new *linear* logic [Girard86] where hypothesis are (in some sense) used *once* and *only once*. The most surprising is that all the power of the usual logic can be recovered by means of recursive logical operators (connector "of course").

There are two versions of the *linear logic*: the *intuitionistic* one and the *classical* one. It seems that the second provides a appropriate formalism for *parallelism* and *communication*. This approach is entirely new and requires a further development. Here we restrict our attention to the *intuitionistic* version and to the consequences of the *linear* constraint to the computation process.

We give two equivalent presentations of the (propositional part of) *linear* logic: a sequent calculus and a (categorical) combinator system.

Then we introduce *inductive* and *projective* connectors, in particular the connector ! (read "of course"). It plays a fundamental role in the encoding of usual intuitionistic logic into *linear* logic.

There is a *cut elimination theorem* for the sequent calculus that corresponds to an *evaluation mechanism* for the combinator system. We present a very simple (abstract) machine that performs *linear* computations with the following features:

- A *very natural* lazy evaluation mechanism.
- No need of *garbage collector*.

Finally, we discuss the relevance of *linear* logic to implement functional languages.

1 A sequent calculus for the linear intuitionistic logic

First, we present the *elementary* part of the *linear intuitionistic logic* in a 'Gentzen like' formalism [Gentzen].

The connectors are **1** (tensor unit), $\otimes$ (tensor product), **t** (direct unit), & (direct product), **0** (direct zero), $\oplus$ (direct sum) and $\multimap$ (linear implication). Thus there are two different conjunctions (the tensor product and the direct product).

In the following rules A, B, C denote formulas and Γ, Δ denote sequences $A_1, ..., A_n$ of formulas. A *sequent* $A_1, ..., A_n \vdash A$ means that A is a consequent of $A_1 \otimes ... \otimes A_n$.

1.1 Structural rules

$$\frac{}{A \vdash A}\ (\text{identity}) \qquad \frac{\Gamma \vdash A \quad \Delta, A \vdash B}{\Gamma, \Delta \vdash B}\ (\text{cut}) \qquad \frac{\Gamma, A, B, \Delta \vdash C}{\Gamma, B, A, \Delta \vdash C}\ (\text{exchange})$$

1.2 Logical rules

$$\frac{}{\vdash \mathbf{1}} \qquad \frac{\Gamma \vdash A}{\Gamma, \mathbf{1} \vdash A} \qquad \frac{\Gamma \vdash A \quad \Delta \vdash B}{\Gamma, \Delta \vdash A \otimes B} \qquad \frac{\Gamma, A, B \vdash C}{\Gamma, A \otimes B \vdash C}$$

$$\frac{}{\Gamma \vdash \mathbf{t}} \qquad \frac{\Gamma \vdash A \quad \Gamma \vdash B}{\Gamma \vdash A \& B} \qquad \frac{\Gamma, A \vdash C}{\Gamma, A \& B \vdash C} \qquad \frac{\Gamma, B \vdash C}{\Gamma, A \& B \vdash C}$$

$$\frac{}{\Gamma, \mathbf{0} \vdash A} \qquad \frac{\Gamma \vdash A}{\Gamma \vdash A \oplus B} \qquad \frac{\Gamma \vdash B}{\Gamma \vdash A \oplus B} \qquad \frac{\Gamma, A \vdash C \quad \Gamma, B \vdash C}{\Gamma, A \oplus B \vdash C}$$

$$\frac{\Gamma, A \vdash B}{\Gamma \vdash A \multimap B} \qquad \frac{\Gamma \vdash A \quad \Delta, B \vdash C}{\Gamma, \Delta, A \multimap B \vdash C}$$

The essential difference with the usual intuitionistic calculus is the *absence* of two *essentially non linear* structural rules:

$$\frac{\Gamma \vdash B}{\Gamma, A \vdash B}\ (\text{weakening}) \qquad \frac{\Gamma, A, A \vdash B}{\Gamma, A \vdash B}\ (\text{contraction})$$

See appendix A for comparison.

Theorem 1 *This calculus admits cut elimination: "every proof without hypothesis can be transformed into a cut free proof".*

The proof is essentially the same as Gentzen's one (for usual intuitionistic logic). It is even simpler because of the absence of weakening and contraction.

Let us remind that the *cut elimination* property has very pleasant consequences: the *consistency*[1] of the system and the *subformula* property (a cut free proof contains only subformulas of the sequent that it proves).

1.3 Examples of proofs

From now on, *Heyting* (logic, formula, proof) means *usual intuitionistic*.

A first (very crude) interpretation of the system is to see **1** and **t** as the *true* proposition, $\otimes$ and & as a conjunction, **0** as the *false* proposition, $\oplus$ as a disjunction and $-\!\!\bullet$ as an implication. With this translation, every provable *linear* formula becomes obviously a provable *Heyting* formula.

For example, the *linear* formula $(A\&B)-\!\!\bullet A$ (here A and B are atomic formulas) has the following (*linear*) proof:

$$\dfrac{\dfrac{A \vdash A}{A\&B \vdash A}}{\vdash (A\&B)-\!\!\bullet A}$$

Of course, the corresponding *Heyting* formula $(A \wedge B) \Rightarrow A$ is also provable.

But the converse is absolutely false: The *linear* formula $(A \otimes B)-\!\!\bullet A$ is not (*linearly*) provable. Yet the corresponding *Heyting* formula $(A \wedge B) \Rightarrow A$ is still provable.

Let us show that $(A \otimes B)-\!\!\bullet A$ is not provable: Take a *cut free* proof of $\vdash (A \otimes B)-\!\!\bullet A$. The end of your proof *has to be*:

$$\dfrac{\dfrac{A, B \vdash A}{A \otimes B \vdash A}}{\vdash (A \otimes B)-\!\!\bullet A}$$

In *linear* logic, it is impossible to prove $A, B \vdash A$ (in a cut free proof, the last rule has to be an exchange ... and you cannot find a beginning for this proof).

One of the notable features of the *linear* logic is the following distributivity property ($A \equiv B$ means that $A \vdash B$ and $B \vdash A$ are both provable):

$$A \otimes (B \oplus C) \equiv (A \otimes B) \oplus (A \otimes C)$$

Of course it is not true if you replace $\otimes$ by &.

A *cut* free proof for the left to right sense is:

$$\dfrac{\dfrac{\dfrac{\dfrac{}{A \vdash A} \quad \dfrac{}{B \vdash B}}{A, B \vdash A \otimes B}}{A, B \vdash (A \otimes B) \oplus (A \otimes C)} \quad \dfrac{\dfrac{\dfrac{}{A \vdash A} \quad \dfrac{}{C \vdash C}}{A, C \vdash A \otimes C}}{A, C \vdash (A \otimes B) \oplus (A \otimes C)}}{\dfrac{A, B \oplus C \vdash (A \otimes B) \oplus (A \otimes C)}{A \otimes (B \oplus C) \vdash (A \otimes B) \oplus (A \otimes C)}}$$

Such a *cut free* proof is easy to find in a bottom up fashion.

---

[1] In our case, the consistency is obvious (it is just a propositional calculus). Moreover there is a very simple translation of the linear logic into the usual one that preserves provability (see section 1.3).

2 Combinators for the linear logic

Linear combinators are an alternative presentation for the linear logic[2].

A combinator is a "name" for an assertion $A \to B$ (B is consequent of A), where A, B are *formulas*. In some sense, combinators are more elementary than sequent rules. Sequent proofs are better for the human, but combinators are closer to the machine.

2.1 Sequential combinators

$$\frac{}{\mathbf{id} : A \to A} \qquad \frac{x : A \to B \quad y : B \to C}{y \circ x : A \to C}$$

2.2 Parallel and arrange combinators

$$\frac{}{\mathbf{1} : \mathbf{1} \to \mathbf{1}} \qquad \frac{x : A \to B \quad y : C \to D}{x \otimes y : A \otimes C \to B \otimes D}$$

$$\frac{}{\mathbf{ol} : A \leftrightarrow \mathbf{1} \otimes A : \mathbf{cl}} \qquad \frac{}{\mathbf{or} : A \leftrightarrow A \otimes \mathbf{1} : \mathbf{cr}}$$

$$\frac{}{\mathbf{ex} : A \otimes B \leftrightarrow B \otimes A : \mathbf{ex}} \qquad \frac{}{\mathbf{al} : A \otimes (B \otimes C) \leftrightarrow (A \otimes B) \otimes C : \mathbf{ar}}$$

2.3 Logical combinators

$$\frac{}{\langle\rangle : X \to \mathbf{t}} \qquad \frac{x : X \to A \quad y : X \to B}{\langle x, y\rangle : X \to A \& B} \qquad \frac{}{\mathbf{fst} : A \& B \to A} \qquad \frac{}{\mathbf{snd} : A \& B \to B}$$

$$\frac{}{\{\} : \mathbf{0} \to X} \qquad \frac{}{\mathbf{inl} : A \to A \oplus B} \qquad \frac{}{\mathbf{inr} : B \to A \oplus B} \qquad \frac{x : A \to X \quad y : B \to X}{\{x, y\} : A \oplus B \to X}$$

$$\frac{x : X \otimes A \to B}{\mathbf{lcur}\ x : X \to A {-\!\!\bullet} B} \qquad \frac{}{\mathbf{lapp} : (A {-\!\!\bullet} B) \otimes A \to B}$$

For comparison see appendix B.

Proposition 1 *The two formalisms (sequents and combinators) are equivalent:*

Every combinator $\varphi : A \to B$ gives a proof of $A \vdash B$, and every proof of a sequent $A_1, ..., A_n \vdash B$ gives a combinator $\varphi : A_1 \otimes ... \otimes A_n \to B$.

---

[2]They are the exact analogues of what are *categorical combinators* for *Heyting* logic (see appendix B) [Lambek80,Curien85,Curien86]. For a category theoretical view, see appendix C.

The proof is straigthforward. In the following rules, Γ is cumbersome, but you can push it to the right side using the connector $\multimap$:

$$\frac{}{\Gamma, 0 \vdash A} \qquad \frac{\Gamma, A \vdash C \quad \Gamma, B \vdash C}{\Gamma, A \oplus B \vdash C}$$

3 The connector "of course"

The *linear* constraint is very strong. To recover the expressiveness of *Heyting* logic, it is necessary to introduce a new connector: ! (read *"of course"*).

More generally, we can enrich the *linear* logic with *inductive* and *projective* connectors, two dual notions that we illustrate in the following sections:

3.1 Inductive connectors

Let us construct a "type" of natural numbers in our *linear* logic.

The first solution is a recursive definition (a natural number is *zero* or the *successor* of a natural number):

$$\mathbf{Nat} = \mathbf{1} \oplus \mathbf{Nat}$$

However, this definition does not capture the fact that **Nat** is the "best" solution of this "equation". In particular, you need recursive definitions to construct usual functions over integers.

A more adequate solution is to introduce explicit combinators:

$$\frac{}{\mathbf{zero} : \mathbf{1} \to \mathbf{Nat}} \qquad \frac{}{\mathbf{succ} : \mathbf{Nat} \to \mathbf{Nat}} \qquad \frac{x : \mathbf{1} \to X \quad y : X \to X}{\mathbf{nrec}\, x\, y : \mathbf{Nat} \to X}$$

Let us give, for example, a (non recursive) definition of the addition:

$$\frac{\overline{\mathbf{cl} : \mathbf{1} \otimes \mathbf{Nat} \to \mathbf{Nat}}}{\mathbf{lcur}\,\mathbf{cl} : \mathbf{1} \to \mathbf{Nat} \multimap \mathbf{Nat}}$$

$$\frac{\dfrac{\overline{\mathbf{lapp} : (\mathbf{Nat} \multimap \mathbf{Nat}) \otimes \mathbf{Nat} \to \mathbf{Nat}} \quad \overline{\mathbf{succ} : \mathbf{Nat} \to \mathbf{Nat}}}{\mathbf{succ} \circ \mathbf{lapp} : (\mathbf{Nat} \multimap \mathbf{Nat}) \otimes \mathbf{Nat} \to \mathbf{Nat}}}{\mathbf{lcur}(\mathbf{succ} \circ \mathbf{lapp}) : \mathbf{Nat} \multimap \mathbf{Nat} \to \mathbf{Nat} \multimap \mathbf{Nat}}$$

$$\mathbf{add} = \mathbf{lapp} \circ ((\mathbf{nrec}(\mathbf{lcurcl})(\mathbf{lcur}(\mathbf{succ} \circ \mathbf{lapp}))) \otimes \mathbf{id}) : \mathbf{Nat} \otimes \mathbf{Nat} \to \mathbf{Nat}$$

Other *inductive connectors* can be introduced, for example the connector **List** with the following recursive definition:

$$A\,\mathbf{List} = \mathbf{1} \oplus (A \otimes (A\,\mathbf{List}))$$

The reader may find the corresponding combinators ...

3.2 Projective connectors

If you replace $\oplus$ by $\&$, you obtain the dual notion of *projective connector*.

For example the connector ! has the following recursive definition:

$$!A = A\&\mathbf{1}\&(!A\otimes !A)$$

As for **Nat**, we introduce new combinators:

$$\frac{x : X \to A \quad y : X \to \mathbf{1} \quad z : X \to X \otimes X}{\mathbf{make}\, x\, y\, z : X \to !A}$$

$$\frac{}{\mathbf{read} : !A \to A} \qquad \frac{}{\mathbf{kill} : !A \to \mathbf{1}} \qquad \frac{}{\mathbf{dupl} : !A \to !A\otimes !A}$$

The connector ! is a "trick" to eliminate the *linear* constraint.

First, $!A$ is a "universal coalgebra" over A:

Proposition 2 *The following combinator can be constructed:*

$$\frac{x : !A \to B}{\mathbf{lift}\, x : !A \to !B}$$

! is also a sort of "exponential" operator (it links together the two conjunctions $\&$ and $\otimes$):

Proposition 3 $!\mathbf{t} \equiv \mathbf{1}$ *and* $!(A\&B) \equiv !A\otimes !B$
In other words, the following combinators can be constructed:

$$\mathbf{subl} : !\mathbf{t} \leftrightarrow \mathbf{1} : \mathbf{crys} \qquad \mathbf{crac} : !(A\&B) \leftrightarrow !A\otimes !B : \mathbf{glue}$$

See appendix D for detailed constructions.

3.3 Encoding of Heyting logic into linear logic

We saw in section 1.3 a translation of *linear* logic into Heyting logic. Conversely, Heyting logic can be *merged* into *linear* logic (with the connector !).

First we give a translation of *Heyting* formulas into *linear* ones:

- $|A| = A$ (A is an atomic formula)
- $|t| = \mathbf{t}$ and $|A \wedge B| = |A|\&|B|$
- $|f| = \mathbf{0}$ and $|A \vee B| = !|A|\oplus !|B|$
- $|A \Rightarrow B| = !|A| \multimap |B|$

Proposition 4 *A Heyting formula A is provable if and only if $|A|$ is (linearly) provable.*

The proof uses the following lemma[3]:

Lemma 1 *Let A,B be two* Heyting *formulas. Every categorical combinator* $x : A \to B$ *gives a linear combinator:* $|x| :!|A| \to |B|$.

For example, if $x : A \wedge B \to C$ gives $|x| :!(|A|\&|B|) \to C$, then $\mathbf{cur}\, x : A \to B \Rightarrow C$ gives $\mathbf{lcur}(|x| \circ \mathbf{glue}) :!|A| \to !|B| \multimap C$.

In fact, the necessary combinators are exactly those introduced by propositions 2 and 3.

4 Computation

4.1 The evaluation mechanism

Our purpose is to show that the *linear* logic is well-suited for *lazy* evaluation (following the philosophy of [Lafont86]).

Lazy types are:

$$\mathbf{t} \quad A\&B \quad \mathbf{0} \quad A \oplus B \quad A \multimap B$$

Values of *lazy* types are not *computed* but *frozen.* A frozen value is made of a *constructor* and another value, and it is unfrozen by a *destructor.*

Constructors are:

$$\langle\rangle \quad \langle\varphi, \psi\rangle \quad \mathbf{inl} \quad \mathbf{inr} \quad \mathbf{lcur}\, \varphi$$

Destructors are:

$$\mathbf{fst} \quad \mathbf{snd} \quad \{\} \quad \{\varphi, \psi\} \quad \mathbf{lapp}$$

Values are terms:

- $()$
- (u, v) where u, v are values
- $\gamma \cdot u$ where γ is a *constructor* and u a value

We inductively define a relation $u : A$ (u "is a value" of A) for a value u and a *linear* formula A:

$$\frac{}{() : \mathbf{1}} \qquad \frac{u : A \quad v : B}{(u, v) : A \otimes B} \qquad \frac{\gamma : A \to B \quad u : A}{\gamma \cdot u : B}$$

We define an operation: $\dfrac{\varphi : A \to B \quad u : A}{\varphi\, u : B}$

[3] Note that a *Heyting* formula A is provable when there exists a categorical combinator $t \to A$, and a *linear* formula A is (linearly) provable when there exists a *linear* combinator $\mathbf{1} \to A$.

- $\mathbf{id}\, u = u \quad (\varphi \circ \psi)\, u = \varphi(\psi\, u)$
- $\mathbf{1}() = () \quad (\varphi \otimes \psi)(u, v) = (\varphi\, u, \psi\, v)$
- $\mathbf{ol}\, u = ((), u) \quad \mathbf{cl}((), u) = u \quad \mathbf{or}\, u = (u, ()) \quad \mathbf{cr}(u, ()) = u$
  $\mathbf{ex}(u, v) = (v, u) \quad \mathbf{al}(u, (v, w)) = ((u, v), w) \quad \mathbf{ar}((u, v), w) = (u, (v, w))$
- $\langle\rangle\, u = \langle\rangle \cdot u \quad \langle \varphi, \psi \rangle\, u = \langle \varphi, \psi \rangle \cdot u$
  $\mathbf{fst}(\langle \varphi, \psi \rangle \cdot u) = \varphi\, u \quad \mathbf{snd}(\langle \varphi, \psi \rangle \cdot u) = \psi\, u$
- $\mathbf{inl}\, u = \mathbf{inl} \cdot u \quad \mathbf{inr}\, u = \mathbf{inr} \cdot u$
  $\{\varphi, \psi\}(\mathbf{inl} \cdot u) = \varphi\, u \quad \{\varphi, \psi\}(\mathbf{inr} \cdot u) = \psi\, u$
- $(\mathbf{lcur}\, \varphi)\, u = (\mathbf{lcur}\, \varphi) \cdot u \quad \mathbf{lapp}((\mathbf{lcur}\, \varphi) \cdot u, v) = \varphi(u, v)$

Theorem 2 *The previous definition is well founded: Computations using these rules always terminate.*

The proof uses induction over combinators, values and formulas.

The theorem extends to inductive and projective connectors. For example for the connector !:

- $(\mathbf{make}\, \varphi\, \psi\, \rho)\, u = (\mathbf{make}\, \varphi\, \psi\, \rho) \cdot u$
  $\mathbf{read}((\mathbf{make}\, \varphi\, \psi\, \rho) \cdot u) = \varphi\, u$
  $\mathbf{kill}((\mathbf{make}\, \varphi\, \psi\, \rho) \cdot u) = \psi\, u$
  $\mathbf{dupl}((\mathbf{make}\, \varphi\, \psi\, \rho) \cdot u) = ((\mathbf{make}\, \varphi\, \psi\, \rho) \otimes (\mathbf{make}\, \varphi\, \psi\, \rho))(\rho\, u)$

Finally, we may add primitive types with primitive values and primitive combinators, for example a type **Num** with:

- $0 : \mathbf{Num} \quad 1 : \mathbf{Num} \quad 2 : \mathbf{Num} \ldots$
  $\mathbf{minus} : \mathbf{Num} \to \mathbf{Num} \quad \mathbf{sum} : \mathbf{Num} \otimes \mathbf{Num} \to \mathbf{Num} \ldots$

4.2 The Linear Abstract Machine

The *Linear Abstract Machine* is a cousin of the *Categorical Abstract Machine* [CAM]. But the *linear* constraint allows a radically different allocation of the memory space.

The memory space is divided into three areas:

- The *code* area is *static* (the code doesn't change during the execution) and is organized as a graph.
- The *environment* area is *dynamic* with two part: the *current tree* (or actual environment) and the *free list* (or memory heap).
- The *dump* (or stack) is *dynamic* and *linear*.

The main point is that the actual environment is organized as a tree[4], and the space allocation is completely provided (no need of *garbage collector*, see section 5).

As usual, the code is a list of elementary instructions (notations: $c :: C$ denotes the list whose head is c and whose tail is C, $[]$ denotes the empty list and γ denotes a constructor).

Linear Abstract Machine					
Before			After		
code	environment	dump	code	environment	dump
$pushl :: C$	(u, v)	D	C	u	$v :: D$
$consl :: C$	u	$v :: D$	C	(u, v)	D
$pushr :: C$	(u, v)	D	C	v	$u :: D$
$consr :: C$	v	$u :: D$	C	(u, v)	D
$ol :: C$	u	D	C	$((), u)$	D
$cl :: C$	$((), u)$	D	C	u	D
$or :: C$	u	D	C	$(u, ())$	D
$cr :: C$	$(u, ())$	D	C	u	D
$ex :: C$	(u, v)	D	C	(v, u)	D
$al :: C$	$(u, (v, w))$	D	C	$((u, v), w)$	D
$ar :: C$	$((u, v), w)$	D	C	$(u, (v, w))$	D
$\gamma :: C$	u	D	C	$\gamma \cdot u$	D
$fst :: C$	$(pair(C', C'')) \cdot u$	D	C'	u	$C :: D$
$snd :: C$	$(pair(C', C'')) \cdot u$	D	C''	u	$C :: D$
$altv(C', C'') :: C$	$inl \cdot u$	D	C'	u	$C :: D$
$altv(C', C'') :: C$	$inr \cdot u$	D	C''	u	$C :: D$
$lapp :: C$	$((lcurC') \cdot u, v)$	D	C'	(u, v)	$C :: D$
$[]$	u	$C :: D$	C	u	D
$[]$	u	$[]$		Return u	

Every *linear* combinator φ gives code $\|\varphi\|$ for the LAM (notation: @ denotes the concatenation of lists):

- $\|\mathbf{id}\| = []$ $\quad \|\varphi \circ \psi\| = \|\psi\| @ \|\varphi\|$
- $\|\mathbf{1}\| = \|\mathbf{id}\| = []$
  $\|\varphi \otimes \psi\| = \|(\mathbf{id} \otimes \psi) \circ (\varphi \otimes \mathbf{id})\| = [pushl] @ \|\varphi\| @ [consl; pushr] @ \|\psi\| @ [consr]$

For the other connectors, the translation is obvious:

- $\|\langle \varphi, \psi \rangle\| = [pair(\|\varphi\|, \|\psi\|)]$ $\quad \|\mathbf{fst}\| = [fst] \ldots$

4.3 Compilation of inductive and projective combinators

There is no specific LAM instruction for inductive and projective combinators. In fact they can be compiled into looping code.

Let us consider for example the connector !, with its recursive definition:

[4]In a strong sense, that means a connected graph without cycle and without shared nodes.

$$!A = A\&\mathbf{1}\&(!A \otimes !A)$$

!A is a direct product with three projections (Here, trd denotes the third projection):

$$\mathbf{read} = \mathbf{fst} : !A \to A \qquad \mathbf{kill} = \mathbf{snd} : !A \to \mathbf{1} \qquad \mathbf{dupl} = \mathbf{trd} : !A \to !A \otimes !A$$

The combinator **make** is compiled into the following *looping* combinator:
make $x\ y\ z = m$ where $m = \langle x, y, (m \otimes m) \circ z \rangle$

5 Relevance of linear logic for computation

5.1 Lazyness

We have to clarify the difference between *Heyting* logic and *linear* logic, and the simplification *linear* logic gives.

In *Heyting* logic, there is only one conjunction $\wedge$:
A *strict* value of $A \wedge B$ is a pair (u, v) where u is a value of A and v a value of B. Such a value may be too "evaluated" if you apply the destructor fst or snd.

A *lazy* value of $A \wedge B$ is a frozen value $\langle \varphi, \psi \rangle \cdot u$ where u is a value of a type X and φ, ψ are combinators, $\varphi : X \to A$ and $\psi : X \to B$. Such a value may be too little "evaluated" if you apply the destructor app.

Of course, it is possible to *unfreeze* frozen values when necessary, but this mechanism seems rather complicated and unnatural, compared to the strict evaluation mechanism [CAM,MaSu].

The problem is that two essentially different kinds of destructors (the *projections* and the *application*) may operate over values of type $(A \Rightarrow B) \wedge A$.

In *linear* logic, the dilemma disappears:
Values of $A \otimes B$ are *strict* values, and the two components are necessary: There is no projection $A \otimes B \to A$ or $A \otimes B \to B$.

Values of $A\&B$ are *lazy* values, and the only possible destructors for such a value are fst and snd.

5.2 Memory allocation

Implementations of symbolic (LISP) or functional (ML) languages need a separate mechanism (the *garbage collector*) to recover the memory space used by abandoned pieces of data. Garbage collecting takes time and sometimes place. Moreover, it complicates the implementation ...

In *linear* logic, the connector corresponding to the management of environment is $\otimes$ (& is *lazy*). Thus, *projections* and *pairing* don't act on the environment. This allows the environment to be kept in a tree whose nodes are never *abandoned* or *shared.*

More precisely, the transitions of the *Linear Abstract Machine* are *left* and *right* linear with respect to the environment (but not to the code). *Left* linearity is expected for an abstract machine, but *right* linearity is rather surprising.

In our "implementation", we add a fourth register (the *free list*) to the *Linear Abstract Machine*. Some instructions (*consl*, *consr*, *ol*, *or* and the constructors) *take* a free location from the *free list*. Other instructions (*pushl*, *pushr*, *cl*, *cr*, *fst*, *snd*, *altv*, *lapp*) return a location to the *free list* (this is legitimate because nodes are not shared). The other instructions (like *ex*) act as physical modifications.

Of course, we don't need a *garbage collector* because nodes are never abandoned.

5.3 Compilation of functional languages

We saw in section 3.3 a translation of categorical combinators into linear combinators. But there is a classical translation of functional programs into categorical combinators [CAM,MaSu]. That gives a compilation of functional programs into the *Linear Abstract Machine*.

Unfortunately, this compilation is not realistic. In fact, a very simple program gives a big piece of code. For example, the categorical combinator $\varphi \circ \psi$ is translated into the linear combinator $|\varphi| \circ$ (**lift** $|\psi|$), and **lift** is not a primitive combinator (see appendix D), and **make** is not a primitive instruction (see section 4.3) ...

Of course, this translation is too brutish. The problem is to understand how the *linearity* that occurs in a program (and there is a lot of linearity in classical algorithms) can be recognized (by the machine or by the programmer) for our *linear* implementation.

A possible continuation for this article should be the elaboration of a realistic optimized translation, or rather the development of a new programming style, in a new high level language adapted to our *linear* implementation. This new language should hold simultaneously elegance of functional languages and efficiency of procedural languages.

Appendix

A The sequent calculus for the usual intuitionistic logic

A.1 Structural rules

$$\frac{}{A \vdash A}\ \text{(identity)} \qquad \frac{\Gamma \vdash A \quad \Delta, A \vdash B}{\Gamma, \Delta \vdash B}\ \text{(cut)} \qquad \frac{\Gamma, A, B, \Delta \vdash C}{\Gamma, B, A, \Delta \vdash C}\ \text{(exchange)}$$

$$\frac{\Gamma \vdash B}{\Gamma, A \vdash B}\ \text{(weakening)} \qquad \frac{\Gamma, A, A \vdash B}{\Gamma, A \vdash B}\ \text{(contraction)}$$

A.2 Logical rules

$$\frac{}{\vdash t} \qquad \frac{\Gamma \vdash A \quad \Delta \vdash B}{\Gamma, \Delta \vdash A \wedge B} \qquad \frac{\Gamma, A \vdash C}{\Gamma, A \wedge B \vdash C} \qquad \frac{\Gamma, B \vdash C}{\Gamma, A \wedge B \vdash C}$$

$$\frac{}{f \vdash A} \qquad \frac{\Gamma \vdash A}{\Gamma \vdash A \vee B} \qquad \frac{\Gamma \vdash B}{\Gamma \vdash A \vee B} \qquad \frac{\Gamma, A \vdash C \quad \Delta, B \vdash C}{\Gamma, \Delta, A \vee B \vdash C}$$

$$\frac{\Gamma, A \vdash B}{\Gamma \vdash A \Rightarrow B} \qquad \frac{\Gamma \vdash A \quad \Delta, B \vdash C}{\Gamma, \Delta, A \Rightarrow B \vdash C}$$

B Categorical combinators

B.1 Sequential combinators

$$\frac{}{\mathbf{id} : A \to A} \qquad \frac{x : A \to B \quad y : B \to C}{y \circ x : A \to C}$$

B.2 Logical combinators

$$\frac{}{\langle\rangle : X \to t} \qquad \frac{x : X \to A \quad y : X \to B}{\langle x, y\rangle : X \to A \wedge B} \qquad \frac{}{\mathbf{fst} : A \wedge B \to A} \qquad \frac{}{\mathbf{snd} : A \wedge B \to B}$$

$$\frac{}{\{\} : f \to X} \qquad \frac{}{\mathbf{inl} : A \to A \vee B} \qquad \frac{}{\mathbf{inr} : B \to A \vee B} \qquad \frac{x : A \to X \quad y : B \to X}{\{x, y\} : A \vee B \to X}$$

$$\frac{x : X \wedge A \to B}{\mathbf{cur}\, x : X \to A \Rightarrow B} \qquad \frac{}{\mathbf{app} : (A \Rightarrow B) \wedge A \to B}$$

C Linear categories

C.1 Terminology

A *symmetric monoidal* category is a category $\mathcal{C}$ with a bifunctor $\otimes : \mathcal{C} \times \mathcal{C} \to \mathcal{C}$ and an object $\mathbf{1} \in \mathcal{C}$ such that:

$$\mathbf{1} \otimes X \overset{\nu}{\cong} X \qquad X \otimes Y \overset{\sigma}{\cong} Y \otimes X \qquad (X \otimes Y) \otimes Z \overset{\alpha}{\cong} X \otimes (Y \otimes Z)$$

Here $\cong$ denotes a *natural isomorphism*. In addition, there are several *coherence* axioms that constrain those natural isomorphims (for example: $\sigma \circ \sigma = \mathbf{id}$, $\nu \circ \alpha = \nu \otimes \mathbf{id}$).

A *symmetric monoidal closed* category is a symmetric monoidal category $\mathcal{C}$ such that, for every $A \in \mathcal{C}$, the functor $X \mapsto X \otimes A$ has a right adjoint $Y \mapsto A \multimap Y$. That means:

$$\mathbf{Hom}(X \otimes A, Y) \cong \mathbf{Hom}(X, A \multimap Y)$$

Finally, a *linear* category is a symmetric monoidal closed category with finite products and coproducts[5].

C.2 Examples

Of course, a category with finite products (or coproducts) is a monoidal category. Therefore a category with finite products, finite coproducts and exponentials is a linear category[6]. For example **SET** is a linear category: $\otimes$ and & are the cartesian product, $\oplus$ is the disjoint union, and $I \multimap J = J^I$.

A more interesting model is the category of modules over a ring: $\otimes$ is the tensor product, & the direct product, $\oplus$ the direct sum, and $A \multimap B = \mathbf{Hom}(A, B)$. Of course, & and $\oplus$ are identical.

Another example is the category **TOP** of topological spaces. **TOP** is not cartesian closed but it is a linear category: & is the cartesian product and $\oplus$ is the disjoint union. $E \otimes F$ is $E \times F$ with the finest topology that makes sections $x \mapsto (x, y)$ and $y \mapsto (x, y)$ continuous. $E \multimap F$ is the space of continuous maps $E \to F$ with the pointwise convergence topology.

D Some useful linear combinators

$$\mathbf{trans} = \mathbf{ar} \circ ((\mathbf{al} \circ (\mathbf{id} \otimes \mathbf{ex}) \circ \mathbf{ar}) \otimes \mathbf{id}) \circ \mathbf{al} : (A \otimes B) \otimes (C \otimes D) \to (A \otimes C) \otimes (B \otimes D)$$

$$\frac{x : !A \to B \quad \overline{\mathbf{kill} : !A \to \mathbf{1}} \quad \overline{\mathbf{dupl} : !A \to !A \otimes !A}}{\mathbf{lift}\ x = \mathbf{make}\ x\ \mathbf{kill}\ \mathbf{dupl} : !A \to !B}$$

[5]The categorical notion corresponding to "!" is more complex. It makes use of the notion of *internal comonoïd*.

[6]This justifies the translation of section 1.3. Moreover, in such a category, "!" exists (it's the identity functor).

$$\frac{}{\mathbf{subl} = \mathbf{kill} :!\mathbf{t} \to \mathbf{1}}$$

$$\frac{\dfrac{}{\langle\rangle : \mathbf{1} \to \mathbf{t}} \quad \dfrac{}{\mathbf{id} : \mathbf{1} \to \mathbf{1}} \quad \dfrac{}{\mathbf{ol} : \mathbf{1} \to (\mathbf{1} \otimes \mathbf{1})}}{\mathbf{crys} = \mathbf{make}\ \langle\rangle\ \mathbf{id}\ \mathbf{ol} : \mathbf{1} \to !\mathbf{t}}$$

$$\frac{\dfrac{\dfrac{}{\mathbf{fst} : A\&B \to A}}{!\mathbf{fst} :!(A\&B) \to !A} \quad \dfrac{\dfrac{}{\mathbf{snd} : A\&B \to B}}{!\mathbf{snd} :!(A\&B) \to !B}}{!\mathbf{fst} \otimes !\mathbf{snd} :!(A\&B) \otimes !(A\&B) \to !A \otimes !B}$$

$$\mathbf{crac} = (!\mathbf{fst} \otimes !\mathbf{snd}) \circ \mathbf{dupl} :!(A\&B) \to !A \otimes !B$$

$$\frac{\dfrac{\dfrac{}{\mathbf{read} :!A \to A} \quad \dfrac{}{\mathbf{kill} :!B \to \mathbf{1}}}{\mathbf{read} \otimes \mathbf{kill} :!A \otimes !B \to A \otimes \mathbf{1}} \quad \dfrac{}{\mathbf{cr} : A \otimes \mathbf{1} \to A}}{\mathbf{cr} \circ (\mathbf{read} \otimes \mathbf{kill}) :!A \otimes !B \to A}$$

$$\frac{\dfrac{\dfrac{}{\mathbf{kill} :!A \to \mathbf{1}} \quad \dfrac{}{\mathbf{read} :!B \to B}}{\mathbf{kill} \otimes \mathbf{read} :!A \otimes !B \to \mathbf{1} \otimes B} \quad \dfrac{}{\mathbf{cl} : \mathbf{1} \otimes B \to B}}{\mathbf{cl} \circ (\mathbf{kill} \otimes \mathbf{read}) :!A \otimes !B \to B}$$

$$\frac{\dfrac{\dfrac{}{\mathbf{kill} :!A \to \mathbf{1}} \quad \dfrac{}{\mathbf{kill} :!B \to \mathbf{1}}}{\mathbf{kill} \otimes \mathbf{kill} :!A \otimes !B \to \mathbf{1} \otimes \mathbf{1}} \quad \dfrac{}{\mathbf{cl} : \mathbf{1} \otimes \mathbf{1} \to \mathbf{1}}}{\mathbf{cl} \circ (\mathbf{kill} \otimes \mathbf{kill}) :!A \otimes !B \to \mathbf{1}}$$

$$\frac{\dfrac{}{\mathbf{dupl} :!A \to !A \otimes !A} \quad \dfrac{}{\mathbf{dupl} :!B \to !B \otimes !B}}{\mathbf{dupl} \otimes \mathbf{dupl} :!A \otimes !B \to (!A \otimes !A) \otimes (!B \otimes !B)}$$

$\mathbf{glue} = \mathbf{make}\ \langle \mathbf{cr} \circ (\mathbf{read} \otimes \mathbf{kill}), \mathbf{cl} \circ (\mathbf{kill} \otimes \mathbf{read}) \rangle\ (\mathbf{cl} \circ (\mathbf{kill} \otimes \mathbf{kill}))\ (\mathbf{trans} \circ (\mathbf{dupl} \otimes \mathbf{dupl})) :!A \otimes !B \to !(A\&B)$

References

[CAM] G. Cousineau, P.L. Curien and M. Mauny. "The Categorical Abstract Machine." In Functional Programming Languages and Computer Architecture, Ed. J. P. Jouannaud, Springer-Verlag LNCS 201 (1985) 50–64.

[Curien85] P. L. Curien. "Categorical Combinatory Logic." ICALP 85, Nafplion, Springer-Verlag LNCS 194 (1985).

[Curien86] P. L. Curien. "Categorical Combinators, Sequential Algorithms and Functional Programming." Pitman (1986).

[Gentzen] G. Gentzen. "The Collected Papers of Gerhard Gentzen." Ed. E. Szabo, North-Holland, Amsterdam (1969).

[Girard86] J.Y. Girard "Linear Logic" to appear in TCS.

[Lafont86] Y. Lafont "De la Déduction Naturelle à Machine Catégorique" to appear.

[Lambek80] J. Lambek. "From Lambda-calculus to Cartesian Closed Categories." in To H. B. Curry: Essays on Combinatory Logic, Lambda-calculus and Formalism, Eds. J. P. Seldin and J. R. Hindley, Academic Press (1980).

[MaSu] M. Mauny and A. Suarez. "Implementing Functional Languages in the Categorical Abstract Machine." in Proceedings of the 1986 ACM Conference on Lisp and Functional Programming.

The Natural Dynamic Semantics of Mini-Standard ML

Dominique Clément

SEMA-METRA

INRIA SOPHIA-ANTIPOLIS

Rue Emile Hugues, 06560 Valbonne/France

Abstract

We describe how to express the dynamic semantics of a small subset of the Standard ML language in Natural Semantics. The present specification is based on a communication of R.Milner that describes the dynamic semantics of Standard ML in a structural style, and can be viewed as an example of the "programming effort" that is necessary to obtain an executable version of such a specification. The main aspects of Natural Semantics covered concern its relationships with typed inference systems and with some properties of natural deduction. The description has been tested on a computer but we do not give here details on the compilation techniques.

1. Introduction

The use of inference systems to specify the static and dynamic semantics of programming languages has its origin in the presentation of semantics in a structural axiomatic style in Plotkin[15]. For example, to express that a "phrase P evaluates to a value α in an environment e" we can write a formal sentence of the form:

$$e \vdash P : \alpha$$

where the evaluation predicate ":" is defined by a set of axioms and inference rules. Such a system formally defines the sound phrases (with respect to dynamic semantics) of a programming language as those that can be inferred from the system. In other words, the *evaluation* of a phrase P to a value α is defined by the existence of a derivation tree for $e \vdash P : \alpha$.

Natural Semantics is a specification formalism originating in Plotkin's structural semantics but with flavors of Gentzen's natural deduction[3], [10]. A specification in Natural Semantics is defined by inference rules involving several *judgements*. For dynamic semantics judgements are generally of the form $e \vdash P : \alpha$, meaning that the term P has value α in context e. Then it is possible to prove formal properties of these specifications: Natural Semantics has be used to prove the correctness of translations[6] for the central part of the ML language.

But beside this purely descriptive aspect, a key question of interest is the use of logical systems as *executable specification* formalisms. Natural semantics is one such executable specification formalism. Specifications are written in Typol[7], a language that implements Natural Semantics, and compiled to produce typecheckers, interpreters, and translators[4].

In this paper we present the natural dynamic semantics of Standard ML, or more exactly of a subset of Standard ML. As pointed out by Milner[12] the design of Standard ML is based on simple and well understood ideas that have been experimented with in previous versions of ML or in other functional languages. Furthermore Milner gives a formal definition of the dynamic semantics of core Standard ML[13]

This work is partially supported under ESPRIT, Project 348

in a structural axiomatic style. Hence we have the opportunity to use Natural Semantics on a completely specified language.

In the next section we present the main aspects of Natural Semantics that we use to specify the dynamic semantics of ML. Then we describe the subset of Standard ML used in the sequel of this paper together with the relevant semantic domains. In the following two sections we discuss two aspects of ML, namely exceptions and pattern matching, that need special attention. The first one is a direct application of the notion of judgements, while the second one is also related to the specification of *negation* within inference rules. Finally we give the semantics of expressions, followed by all rules that are necessary to complete the specification of the dynamic semantics of our subset of Standard ML.

2. Natural Semantics

A specification in Natural Semantics is an inference system, i.e. a collection of inference rules that have the following form:

$$\frac{\textit{hypotheses}}{\textit{conclusion}}$$

where both *hypotheses* and *conclusion* are of the form $\Gamma \vdash \textit{term} : \alpha$, where Γ is a set of hypothesis on, at least, the variables of *term*. In such a formula, which is called a *sequent*, the context Γ, the subject *term*, and the value α are *abstract trees* that belong to a finite system of types called an abstract syntax definition. The identification of Natural Semantics objects with abstract syntax trees is a central aspect of this formalism.

First this identification implies that the tree terms used within Natural Semantics act as *type constructors*. Next this identification implies that every variable in Natural Semantics, also called meta-variable, stands for values that belong to some abstract syntax definition. In other words the meta-variables of a specification in Natural Semantics are *typed*. We illustrate these two aspects on simple examples.

2.1. Terms are type constructors

An abstract syntax is defined by a system of types with *sorts*, *subsorts*, and *functions*. The notion of subsorts is used to express containment relations between sorts.

Consider the system of types with two sorts VAR and EXP, with the relation VAR $\prec$ EXP to express that a variable is also an expression, and with two functions: $\textit{var} :\rightarrow \text{VAR}$ and $\textit{application} : \text{EXP} \times \text{EXP} \rightarrow \text{EXP}$. In this system of types a tree term such as $\textit{application}(\textit{var}F, \textit{var}X)$ is of type EXP, while the two subtrees $\textit{var}F$ and $\textit{var}X$ are of type VAR. Hence in a sequent of the form $\Gamma \vdash \textit{application}(\textit{var}F, \textit{var}X) : \alpha$, the subject stands for applications where the operator and the operand are both restricted to be object language variables.

Now consider the term $\textit{application}(\text{OPERATOR}, \text{OPERAND})$, where OPERATOR and OPERAND are meta-variables. This term is of type EXP if and only if the two variables OPERATOR and OPERAND are of type EXP. In the sequent $\Gamma \vdash \textit{application}(\text{OPERATOR}, \text{OPERAND}) : \alpha$, the subject now stands for applications where both the operator and the operand are general expressions. This means in particular that the values of these two variables must be tree terms that belong to the sort EXP (or to subsorts of EXP, such as the sort VAR).

Hence the abstract syntax tree terms used within Natural Semantics act as type constructors. Furthermore the meta-variables that occur strictly within a tree term are implicitely *typed* by an abstract syntax definition. In fact every meta-variable within a specification in Natural Semantics is typed, and this typing is of primary importance for the style of Natural Semantics specifications, as we explain now.

2.2. Variables are typed

As in other first order logic languages, a variable in Natural Semantics is used to impose equality constraints among subterms or to share information between different objects. But a variable occurrence in a Natural Semantic inference rule also expresses a *constraint* on the values that can be substituted to that variable.

Consider the following rule that could be used to specify the evaluation of an ML expression when it is reduced to an ML variable:

$$e \vdash x : \alpha \qquad (e(x) = \alpha)$$

Assume that the variable e denotes an environment that is a mapping of ML variables to ML values, and that the variable α denotes an ML value. Now to express that this rule is restricted to ML variables, i.e. on tree terms of the form *var* X, the meta-variable x must be declared of type VAR. Without such a containment on the values of the meta-variable x, any ML expression could be substituted to x.

Hence a meta-variable in Natural Semantics can be used as an *instantiation filter* to restrict the domain of validity of an inference rule. But this filtering on the values of meta-variables is directly computed from the abstract syntax definitions. Define the *phylum* associated to a sort as the set of functions obtained from the partial order defined by the subsort relations. With our example of system of types with two sorts VAR and EXP, the phylum associated to the sort VAR is reduced to the set $\{var\}$, while the phylum associated to the sort EXP is the set $\{var, application\}$. Then a meta-variable of type S denotes a variable that can only be substituted by a term whose root symbol belongs to the phylum P identified with type S, i.e. it is equivalent to an untyped variable v that satisfies a boolean predicate of the form $v \in$ P.

The typing of meta-variables presented here provides a nice modularization mechanism for Natural Semantics specifications. In particular the type information on meta-variables can be used to distinguish rules that express different evaluations of the same construct of a programming language. As we shall see later, this situation is central in the specification of the dynamic semantics of Standard ML because of the ML exception mechanism. Note that this typing is essentially a matter of style. For instance in the example above, it is possible to use the tree term *var* X instead of the meta-variable x to restrict the use of the inference rule to ML variables. More generally any inference rule with type information can also be expressed as an inference rule without type information but with auxiliary boolean predicates.

3. Abstract Syntaxes

The Standard ML language defined in [12] is a quite complete functional programming language, even without Input/Output primitives nor Modules for separate compilation. For the purpose of this paper we only consider a subset of the Core language that includes the most relevant features of Standard ML in the context of their specification in Natural Semantics. A complete specification of the dynamic semantics of the full Standard ML language has also been done[5].

From Standard ML we keep the following constructs:

+ Declarations: value and exception declarations using value bindings and exception bindings,

+ Expressions: application, raising and handling exceptions, and function abstraction,

+ Patterns: to create value bindings by pattern matching.

but we omit the following:

- type, datatype, abstract datatype declarations, and type expressions (all of them are relevant of static semantics),
- local declarations, both in declarations (using **local**) and in expressions (using **let**),
- sequences in value bindings and exception bindings,
- recursive value bindings,
- labelled records and the layered pattern construct,
- side-effect constructs, i.e. references and assignment.

3.1. Abstract Syntax of Core Mini-ML

The principal syntax classes of our Mini-Standard ML language are defined in terms of the three disjoint primitive classes given in Figure 1.

sorts VAR, CON, EXN
functions

var	:	→	VAR	value variables
con	:	→	CON	value constructors
exn	:	→	EXN	exception names

Figure 1. Primitive Classes

An exception name is always completely determined by its occurrence in abstract syntax trees. But this is not true for value variables and value constructors for which the scope of datatype bindings must be taken into account. We assume that any ambiguity on the class of an identifier has been solved (by a type-checker for example), i.e. we assume in the following that ML abstract syntax trees are always well formed. Examples of value constructors are: booleans *true* and *false*, list constant *nil* and list constructor "::". Value variables occur in value bindings such as "$x = 1$".

The abstract syntax of declarations, value and exception bindings, patterns, and expressions is given in Figure 2.

The purpose of declarations is to bind identifiers to values. Value bindings are used to declare value variables while exception bindings are used to declare exceptions. An exception binding is either a simple exception binding or an exception name: the sort EXN is a subsort of the sort EXCBIND.

Patterns are linear terms containing only variables and value constructors. In our subset of Standard ML the unique compound pattern is the *construction* of the form "*con pat*". Finally, atomic expressions are value variables and value constructors (see the subsort section). Compound expressions are the function abstraction **fun**, the application *exp exp'*, raising exceptions with **raise**, and handling exceptions with **handle**.

"Declarations"

sorts DEC

functions

val	:	VALBIND	→	DEC	**val** *valbind*
exception	:	EXCBIND	→	DEC	**exception** *excbind*

"Value Bindings"

sorts VALBIND

functions

simple_value	:	PAT×EXP	→	VALBIND	*pat* = *exp*

"Exception Bindings"

sorts EXCBIND

subsorts EXN ≺ EXCBIND

functions

simple_excbind	:	EXN×EXN	→	EXCBIND	*exn*=*exn'*

"Patterns"

sorts PAT

subsorts (VAR, CON) ≺ PAT

functions

construction	:	CON×PAT	→	PAT	*con pat*

"Expressions"

sorts EXP, MATCH, MRULE, HANDLER, HRULE

subsorts (VAR, CON) ≺ EXP

functions

fun	:	MATCH	→	EXP	**fun** *match*
application	:	EXP×EXP	→	EXP	*exp exp'*
raise	:	EXN×EXP	→	EXP	**raise** *exn* **with** *exp*
handle	:	EXP×HANDLER	→	EXP	*exp* **handle** *handler*
match	:	MRULE^+	→	MATCH	$mrule_1 \mid \cdots \mid mrule_n$
mrule	:	PAT×EXP	→	MRULE	*pat* ⇒ *exp*
handler	:	HRULE^+	→	HANDLER	$hrule_1 \parallel \cdots \parallel hrule_n$
with	:	EXN×MATCH	→	HRULE	*exn* **with** *match*

Figure 2. Abstract Syntax of ML

3.2. Abstract Syntaxes of Semantic domains

Now we need to define semantic domains such as the domain of values VAL and the environment domain ENV. To define the abstract syntaxes of these domains we will need four sorts of the abstract syntax definition of Mini Standard ML: the sort MATCH, the sort CON, the sort VAR, and the sort EXN. All these sorts are *imported*. This means that we import the language defined by the reflexive closure of each one of these four sorts.

The abstract syntax of values is given in Figure 3. A function value is a partial function represented as a **closure**. A closure is a pair of a function body, i.e. an ML match *match*, and of an environment *e*.

The value of a constructor is that value constructor, the sort CON is a subsort of VAL, and a construction value is a product of a value constructor and of an ML value. Following Milner, basic functions such as "+" and "−" are defined as members of the sort BASFUN, which is a subsort of VAL. But for each basic function f in BASFUN, **apply**(f, α) denotes the result of applying f to a value α. Such partial functions are members of the sort APPLY.

sorts VAL, BASFUN, APPLY

subsorts (CON, BASFUN, APPLY) $\prec$ VAL

functions

closure	:	MATCH×ENV	→	VAL	$[\![match, e]\!]$
prod	:	CON×VAL	→	VAL	(con, val)
apply	:	BASFUN×VAL	→	APPLY	$f(val)$

Figure 3. Values

To associate values to ML variables and exceptions to ML exception names we use an **environment** defined by the abstract syntax given in figure 4. This environment is a *list* of pairs.

sorts ENV, PAIR, VAR_PAIR, EXN_PAIR

subsorts (VAR_PAIR, EXN_PAIR) $\prec$ PAIR

functions

var_pair	:	VAR×VAL	→	VAR_PAIR	$var \mapsto val$
exn_pair	:	EXN×EXC	→	EXN_PAIR	$exn \mapsto exc$
env	:	PAIR*	→	ENV	environment e

Figure 4. Environments

An **exception** is an object that belongs to the sort EXC and to which an exception name *exn* may be associated. The nature of an exception is immaterial. A **packet** is a pair of an exception and an "excepted" value, and it is the unique operator of the sort PACK. Neither exceptions nor packets are values. Finally the singleton sort FAIL denotes failure (Figure 5).

sorts EXC, PACK, FAIL

functions

pack	:	EXC×VAL	→	PACK	packet *pack* or $<exc, val>$
exc	:		→	EXC	exception *exc*
fail	:		→	FAIL	failure *fail*

Figure 5. Packets, Exceptions, and Fail

3.3. Environment as context

Finally we need to define the manipulation primitives on the environment domain ENV. A first possibility is to give a functional definition of these environment manipulation primitives, as Milner does in [13]. First the environment is defined as the product of a value environment *ve* and of an exception environment *ee*. Each component of an environment is considered as a member of $MAP(S, S')$, the set of finite partial functions from a set S to a set S′. The basic operations on mappings are defined as follows:

Primitives on mappings.

i) If m belongs to MAP(X,Y) then

$$m(x) = y \quad \Leftrightarrow \quad (x,y) \in m$$

ii) For two maps m and m', the map m + m' is defined by:

$$m + m'(x) = \begin{cases} m'(x) & \text{if } m'(x) \text{ is defined,} \\ m(x) & \text{otherwise.} \end{cases}$$

Then environment primitives are defined in terms of these basic operations with the help of some notations: if $e = (ve, ee)$ and $e' = (ve', ee')$ then $e + e'$ denotes $(ve + ve', ee + ee')$; furthermore $e + ve'$ denotes $(ve + ve', ee)$ and $e + ee'$ denotes $(ve, ee + ee')$.

Although such a functional definition of environment manipulations is perfectly meaningful, it is possible to give another definition that is more in the style of Natural Semantics. First the environment e is considered as a list of ***propositions*** of the form $x : \alpha$ or $exn : exc$, where the meta-variables x, α, exn, and exc denote respectively an ML variable, an ML value, an ML exception name, and an exception. PAIR* is the set of finite sequences of such propositions. We write an empty sequence "[]" (the empty environment) and $e[x : \alpha]$ the sequence obtained from the sequence e by adding one more assumption [10]. Then to look for the value associated to an ML variable x in an environment e, we define the sequent $\overset{\text{val\_of}}{\vdash}$ as follows:

set VAL_OF is

$$e[x : \alpha] \vdash x : \alpha \tag{1}$$

$$\frac{e \vdash x : \alpha}{e[y : \beta] \vdash x : \alpha} \quad (y \neq x) \tag{2}$$

$$\frac{e \vdash x : \alpha}{e[exn : exc] \vdash x : \alpha} \tag{3}$$

end VAL_OF;

Rule 1 is very similar to the tautology $x : \alpha \vdash x : \alpha$, while rule 2 is akin of the thinning rule in Natural Deduction. The third rule is necessary to skip assumptions on exception names. To look for the exception associated to an exception name exn, we use the sequent $\overset{\text{exc\_of}}{\vdash}$, that is defined with the same kind of rules. The role of the environment in natural semantics is now quite explicit: it is the *context*, i.e. a set of hypothesises on identifiers, necessary to derive the value of a phrase. Note that we assume here that the environment contains at least one assumption on all free identifiers, ML variables and ML exception names, of the ML term that is evaluated. This consistency property should be proved as a lemma satisfied by well typed ML programs.

4. Specification of Exceptions

The principle followed by Milner[13] to specify the dynamic semantics of Standard ML is to define an *evaluation* relation "$\Rightarrow$" with inference rules, called *evaluation rules*, of the form:

$$\frac{e_1 \vdash \mathrm{P}_1 \Rightarrow r_1 \cdots e_n \vdash \mathrm{P}_n \Rightarrow r_n}{e \vdash \mathrm{P} \Rightarrow r}$$

A formal sentence such as $e \vdash \mathrm{P} \Rightarrow r$ expresses that, in a given environment e, the phrase P evaluates to a result r. Of course the nature of r depends on the syntax class of P. For example the result r is an environment when P is an ML declaration, but it is an ML value when P is an ML expression. So the evaluation of Standard ML is formally defined by an inference system, from which sentences may be inferred.

Then it is necessary to specify the exception mechanism of Standard ML, which is defined by the following principle of exception propagation[12]: whenever a sub-phrase evaluates to a packet then no further sub-evaluations occur and the exception is propagated, i.e. the packet is also the result of the main phrase. This is achieve by adding, for every evaluation rule, n further rules, one for each k with $1 \leq k \leq n$, called packet propagation rules. Generally packet propagation rules for a term P are of the form:

$$\frac{e_1 \vdash P_1 \Rightarrow r_1 \quad \cdots \quad e_k \vdash P_k \Rightarrow pack}{e \vdash P \Rightarrow pack}$$

where the variables r_i, with $1 \leq i \leq k-1$, are not packets.

In Natural Semantics we follow the same kind of approach, but we consider that the dynamic semantics of Standard ML is defined with different *judgements* on ML terms. First, we define the evaluation of ML phrases with judgements of the form $e \vdash \mathrm{P} : r$ where the result r is not a packet. Then we specify exceptions of Standard ML with judgements of the form $e \vdash \mathrm{P} : p$ where p can only be a packet.

For example the dynamic semantics of Mini-ML declarations is defined by the judgement:

$$e \vdash \mathrm{DEC} : e'$$

where both e and e' are of type ENV. Then, because a declaration may evaluate to a packet, we define another judgement:

$$e \vdash \mathrm{DEC} : pack$$

where the variable *pack* is of type PACK. Now the exception propagation mechanism of Standard ML can be defined as *transition rules* between these different kinds of judgements.

As a small digression, we would like to indicate how the type constructor interpretation of abstract terms is used to make our specification executable. Consider our judgements as ternary predicates "$\_ \vdash \_ : \_$", one for each form of judgements, that belong to a meta-system: such predicates can be evaluated within the meta-system in a Prolog like manner. Now the operator "$\_ \vdash \_ : \_$" is heavily overloaded, and to execute these predicates in the meta-system it is necessary to solve this overloading (this is one of the purposes of the compiler of Natural Semantics specifications). This is achieved by computing the type of each predicate from the abstract syntax definitions of the object terms. Note that, to avoid such an overloading, we could have defined two syntacticaly different judgements, one of the form $e \vdash \mathrm{P} : r$, the other of the form $e \vdash \mathrm{P} :: pack$. With this approach exception propagation rules are *coercion* rules between these judgements. But we prefer to use the type information on meta-variables to distinguish judgements on terms that belong to the same sort, but on disjoint semantic domains.

We return now to the specification of exceptions. For Mini-Standard ML we have the following types for our judgements, classified according to the syntactic nature of the subject P:

1) **declarations:** $e \vdash \text{DEC} : e$ of type ENV × DEC × ENV and $e \vdash \text{DEC} : pack$ of type ENV × DEC × PACK,
2) **value bindings:** $e \vdash \text{VALBIND} : e'$ of type ENV × VALBIND × ENV and $e \vdash \text{VALBIND} : pack$ of type ENV × VALBIND × PACK,
3) **exception bindings:** $e \vdash \text{EXCBIND} : e'$ of type ENV × EXCBIND × ENV,
4) **expressions:** $e \vdash \text{EXP} : \alpha$ of type ENV × EXP × VAL and $e \vdash \text{EXP} : pack$ of type ENV × EXP × PACK.

To illustrate our approach, consider Mini-Standard ML declarations. First we define the judgement $e \vdash \text{DEC} : e'$, Figure 6. This judgement corresponds to the normal evaluation of an ML declaration.

$$\frac{e \vdash \text{VALBIND} : e'}{e \vdash \mathbf{val}\ \text{VALBIND} : e'} \quad (1)$$

$$\frac{e \vdash \text{EXCBIND} : e'}{e \vdash \mathbf{exception}\ \text{EXCBIND} : e'} \quad (2)$$

Figure 6. Evaluating a Declaration

The evaluation of a value declaration and of an exception declaration, rules 1 and 2, are expressed in terms of the evaluation of their bindings, respectively value binding and exception binding. They both evaluates to an environment e'. Then we define the judgement $e \vdash \text{DEC} : pack$ of type ENV × DEC × PACK for exceptions, Figure 7. It is only necessary to add a rule because ML exception declarations never evaluate to a packet.

$$\frac{e \vdash \text{VALBIND} : pack}{e \vdash \mathbf{val}\ \text{VALBIND} : pack} \quad (3)$$

Figure 7. Exception in Declarations

5. Specification of Pattern-matching

Another interesting aspect of the dynamic semantics of Standard ML is the use of the same mechanism for value bindings in value declarations, **val** $x = 1$, parameter bindings in applications, (**fun** *match*) e, and exception handlings, *exn* **with** *match*. This is achieved with a pattern-matching mechanism between ML patterns and ML values. For example a conditional expression **if** e_1 **then** e_2 **else** e_3 is equivalent to the following application:

$$\begin{pmatrix} \mathbf{fun} & true \Rightarrow e_2 \\ & false \Rightarrow e_3 \end{pmatrix} e_1$$

where $true \Rightarrow e_2$ and $false \Rightarrow e_3$ are the so-called *mrules* of the match.

Given a pattern PAT and an ML value α the first purpose of ML matching is to act as a filter between the structure of the pattern and the structure of the value. The second purpose of ML matching is to bind the ML variables that occur in the pattern with ML values. Furthermore ML pattern matching is independent of the environment. Hence it is possible to describe the ML pattern-matching mechanism with a judgement $\vdash \text{PAT}, \alpha : e$ of type PAT × VAL × ENV. For our subset of Standard ML, this judgement is defined by the rules given in Figure 8.

$$\vdash x, \alpha : [x : \alpha] \tag{1}$$

$$\vdash con, con : \emptyset \tag{2}$$

$$\frac{\vdash \text{PAT}, \text{VAL} : e}{\vdash \text{CON PAT}, (\text{CON}, \text{VAL}) : e} \tag{3}$$

Figure 8. Matching a Pattern to a Value

The rule 1 shows the binding facet of ML pattern matching: an ML variable matches any value and the environment $[x : \alpha]$ is built. A value constructor matches only with the *same* value constructor, and no environment is built, rule 2. Finally the rule 3 specifies the matching of a construction with a product value. Both must have the same constructor as first component, then pattern-matching is recursively applied to their second components.

But this judgement only describes valid pattern matchings, i.e. matchings that do not *fail*. Indeed as a filter the matching fails for some pairs of patterns and values. Rather informally the ML pattern-matching fails when no proof tree can be obtained from the previous system. In some sense we are faced with the well known problem of negation in inference rules. To solve the difficulty we propose a solution based on rules conditioned by boolean predicates.

We define another form of judgement $\vdash \text{PAT}, \alpha : \textit{fail}$, of type PAT × VAL × FAIL, by the rules of Figure 9. Basicaly the ML pattern-matching only fails for incompatible pairs of ML pattern and of ML value. Note that an ML variable matches with any value: this matching never fails. For an ML constructor, the matching fails for every ML value that is not "equal" to this constructor, rule 4. Rule 5 expresses the same kind of condition for an ML construction. But there is another case of failure for ML constructions because the matching of the pattern PAT and of the value VAL may fails, rule 6.

$$\vdash con, val : fail \qquad (val \neq con) \tag{4}$$

$$\vdash \text{CON PAT}, val : fail \qquad (val \neq (\text{CON}, \text{VAL})) \tag{5}$$

$$\frac{\vdash \text{PAT}, \text{VAL} : fail}{\vdash \text{CON PAT}, (\text{CON}, \text{VAL}) : fail} \tag{6}$$

Figure 9. Failure of ML Matching

Remark: the rules that describe normal evaluation and exception propagation are sometimes rather similar. Consider the two rules 1 and 3 for declarations, figures 6 and 7, and the two rules 3 and 6 for expressions, figures 8 and 9. With some loss in modularity, it is possible to merge these rules as follows:

$$\frac{e \vdash \text{VALBIND} : e_p}{e \vdash \text{val VALBIND} : e_p} \qquad \frac{\vdash \text{PAT}, \text{VAL} : e_f}{\vdash \text{CON PAT}, (\text{CON}, \text{VAL}) : e_f}$$

where the meta-variables e_p and e_f are respectively of type ENV ∪ PACK and ENV ∪ FAIL. But now we have two new judgements of type ENV × DEC × (ENV ∪ PACK) and PAT × VAL × (ENV ∪ FAIL). This technique can be used for the purpose of concision.

6. Specification of Expressions and other classes

To complete the specification of the dynamic semantics of our subset of Standard ML we have to define judgements on matches, handlers, value bindings, exception bindings, and expressions. But all these specifications are done with the approach presented on ML declarations, and they are rather similar. Hence we will only give details on the dynamic semantics of Mini-Standard ML expressions.

6.1. *Expressions*

First consider the judgement $e \vdash \text{EXP} : \alpha$ on variables, value constructors, functions, and applications, Figure 10, but without considering exceptions.

$$\frac{e \overset{\text{val\_of}}{\vdash} x : \alpha}{e \vdash x : \alpha} \tag{1}$$

$$e \vdash \text{con} : \text{con} \tag{2}$$

$$e \vdash \text{fun MATCH} : [\![\text{MATCH}, e]\!] \tag{3}$$

$$\frac{e \vdash \text{EXP} : \text{con} \qquad e \vdash \text{EXP}' : \alpha'}{e \vdash (\text{EXP EXP}') : (\text{con}, \alpha')} \tag{4}$$

$$\frac{e \vdash \text{EXP} : f \qquad e \vdash \text{EXP}' : \alpha \qquad \overset{\text{apply}}{\vdash} f, \alpha : \alpha'}{e \vdash (\text{EXP EXP}') : \alpha'} \tag{5}$$

$$\frac{e \vdash \text{EXP} : [\![match, e']\!] \qquad e \vdash \text{EXP}' : \alpha' \qquad e' \vdash match, \alpha' : \alpha}{e \vdash (\text{EXP EXP}') : \alpha} \tag{6}$$

Figure 10. Evaluating an expression

The set of rules called **val_of**, rule 1, is used to look for the value α associated to the value variable x (this set is decribed in section 3.3). Rules 4, 5, and 6 describe the evaluation of an application according to the result of the evaluation of its operator. Note that the type information on meta-variables *con* and f is used to distinguish rules, rules 4 and 5, that have the same object term, but different premises, $e \vdash \text{EXP} : \text{con}$ and $e \vdash \text{EXP} : f$. In rule 5 the meta-variable f is of type BASFUN ∪ APPLY: this rule specifies the evaluation of basic functions. The set **apply** is defined as follows, where the meta-variable b is of type BASFUN:

set APPLY is

$$\vdash b, \alpha : b(\alpha) \tag{1}$$

$$\frac{\alpha'' = \text{eval}(b, \alpha, \alpha')}{\vdash b(\alpha), \alpha' : \alpha''} \tag{2}$$

end APPLY;

The **eval** function is considered as predefined evaluator that is capable of applying a basic function b to values α and α' and to return a value α''. Here the result depends only on the function b, which is for example addition on integers.

Then we define our judgements on expressions that deal with exceptions, i.e. the *raise* expression and the *handle* expression, Figure 11.

$$\frac{e \overset{\textbf{exc\_of}}{\vdash} \text{EXN} : exc \qquad e \vdash \text{EXP} : \alpha}{e \vdash \text{raise EXN with EXP} : \langle exc, \alpha \rangle} \tag{7}$$

$$\frac{e \overset{\textbf{exc\_of}}{\vdash} \text{EXN} : exc \qquad e \vdash \text{EXP} : pack}{e \vdash \text{raise EXN with EXP} : pack} \tag{8}$$

$$\frac{e \vdash \text{EXP} : \alpha}{e \vdash \text{EXP handle HANDLER} : \alpha} \tag{9}$$

$$\frac{e \vdash \text{EXP} : pack \qquad e \vdash \text{HANDLER}, pack : \alpha}{e \vdash \text{EXP handle HANDLER} : \alpha} \tag{10}$$

Figure 11. Expressions with exceptions

A raise expression always evaluates to a packet, which is generated by the raise, rule 7, or which is the result of the evaluation of the expression, rule 8. The set **exc_of** is used to look for the exception exc associated to the exception name EXN (see section 3.3). The handler part of an handle expression is only used when the expression part of the handle evaluates to a packet, rule 10. The application of the handler to the packet is described with the judgement $e \vdash$ HANDLER, PACK : VAL.

Finally the judgements $e \vdash$ EXP : α and $e \vdash$ EXP : $pack$ are used to specify the exception propagation mechanism in expressions, Figure 12.

$$\frac{e \vdash \text{EXP} : \alpha \qquad e \vdash \text{EXP}' : pack}{e \vdash (\text{EXP EXP}') : pack} \tag{11}$$

$$\frac{e \vdash \text{EXP} : pack}{e \vdash (\text{EXP EXP}') : pack} \tag{12}$$

$$\frac{e \vdash \text{EXP} : f \qquad e \vdash \text{EXP}' : \alpha \qquad \overset{\textbf{apply}}{\vdash} f, \alpha : pack}{e \vdash (\text{EXP EXP}') : pack} \tag{13}$$

$$\frac{e \vdash \text{EXP} : [\![match, e']\!] \qquad e \vdash \text{EXP}' : \alpha' \qquad e' \vdash match, \alpha' : pack}{e \vdash (\text{EXP EXP}') : pack} \tag{14}$$

$$\frac{e \vdash \text{EXP} : pack \qquad e \vdash \text{HANDLER}, pack : pack}{e \vdash \text{EXP handle HANDLER} : pack} \tag{15}$$

Figure 12. Exception propagation for expressions

The rule 13 is necessary because some basic functions, such as "+" may raise so-called standard exceptions. This implies that a new rule must be added to the set **apply**:

$$\frac{pack = eval(b, \alpha, \alpha')}{\vdash b(\alpha), \alpha' : pack}$$

In the last two rules 14 and 15, both the application of a match to a value and the application of a handler to a packet may evaluate to a packet. Note that a packet which is not trapped by a handler is propagated as it is, rule 15.

6.2. *Applying a match*

In the application of a match $\text{PAT}_1 \Rightarrow \text{EXP}_1 \mid \cdots \mid \text{PAT}_n \Rightarrow \text{EXP}_n$ to a value α, each component of the match, the so-called ***mrule*** $\text{PAT}_i \Rightarrow \text{EXP}_i$, is applied to the value α from left to right until one succeeds. This is described by the rules 1 and 2 of Figure 13. If none succeeds, then the packet $<ematch, ()>$ is returned, rule 3, where ***ematch*** is a predefined exception bound to the exception identifier "match". The application of an ***mrule*** to a value α is described by the rules 4 and 5. When the pattern PAT matches with the value α, the mrule evaluates as the expression EXP, rule 4. But the application fails when the pattern and the value do not match, rule 5.

$$\frac{e \vdash \text{MRULE}, \alpha : \alpha_p}{e \vdash \text{MRULE} \mid \text{MRULE\_S}, \alpha : \alpha_p} \tag{1}$$

$$\frac{e \vdash \text{MRULE}, \alpha : fail \qquad e \vdash \text{MRULE\_S}, \alpha : \alpha_p}{e \vdash \text{MRULE} \mid \text{MRULE\_S}, \alpha : \alpha_p} \tag{2}$$

$$e \vdash \text{match}[], \alpha : <ematch, ()> \tag{3}$$

$$\frac{\vdash \text{PAT}, \alpha : e' \qquad e ; e' \vdash \text{EXP} : \alpha_p}{e \vdash \text{PAT} \Rightarrow \text{EXP}, \alpha : \alpha_p} \tag{4}$$

$$\frac{\vdash \text{PAT}, \alpha : fail}{e \vdash \text{PAT} \Rightarrow \text{EXP}, \alpha : fail} \tag{5}$$

Figure 13. Applying a match

6.3. *Applying a handler*

The application of a handler, ***hrule***$_1$ $\|$ $\cdots$ $\|$ ***hrule***$_n$, to a packet ***pack*** evaluates in a rather similar manner than the application of a match to a value. But the packet is propagated when none of the hrules matches with that packet, rule 3. To apply a **with** to a packet, the exception exc' associated to the exception name EXN in the environment e must be "equal" to the first component exc of the packet, rule 4. Hotherwise the application fails, rule 5. The boolean predicates ***eqexc*** and ***neqexc*** are used to test equality on exceptions.

6.4. *Evaluating a value binding*

We give in figure 15 the rules for value bindings. In rule 1 the environment e' is obtained by pattern-matching between the pattern and the value α of the expression. When this matching fails the packet $<ebind, ()>$ is returned, where ***ebind*** is a predefined exception bound to the exception identifier "ebind". The last rule, rule 3, describes packet propagation.

6.5. *Evaluating an exception binding*

The rules for exception binding are given in Figure 16. In rule 1 the exception identifier exn X is associated to a ***new*** exception ***exc***. But in rule 2 the exception ***exc*** was already associated to the exception name EXN$'$.

$$\frac{e \vdash \text{HRULE}, pack : \alpha_p}{e \vdash \text{HRULE} \parallel \text{HRULE\_S}, pack : \alpha_p} \tag{1}$$

$$\frac{e \vdash \text{HRULE}, pack : fail \qquad e \vdash \text{HRULE\_S}, pack : \alpha_p}{e \vdash \text{HRULE} \parallel \text{HRULE\_S}, pack : \alpha_p} \tag{2}$$

$$e \vdash \text{handler}[], pack : pack \tag{3}$$

$$\frac{e \overset{\text{exc\_of}}{\vdash} \text{EXN} : exc' \qquad e \vdash \text{MATCH}, \alpha : \alpha_p}{e \vdash \text{EXN with MATCH}, <exc, \alpha> : \alpha_p} \quad (eqexc(exc', exc)) \tag{4}$$

$$\frac{e \overset{\text{exc\_of}}{\vdash} \text{EXN} : exc'}{e \vdash \text{EXN with MATCH}, <exc, \alpha> : fail} \quad (neqexc(exc', exc)) \tag{5}$$

Figure 14. Applying a handler

$$\frac{e \vdash \text{EXP} : \alpha \qquad \vdash \text{PAT}, \alpha : e'}{e \vdash \text{PAT} = \text{EXP} : e'} \tag{1}$$

$$\frac{e \vdash \text{EXP} : \alpha \qquad \vdash \text{PAT}, \alpha : fail}{e \vdash \text{PAT} = \text{EXP} : <ebind, ()>} \tag{2}$$

$$\frac{e \vdash \text{EXP} : pack}{e \vdash \text{PAT} = \text{EXP} : pack} \tag{3}$$

Figure 15. Evaluating a value binding

$$e \vdash \text{exn X} : \{\text{exn X} \mapsto exc\} \tag{1}$$

$$\frac{e \overset{\text{exc\_of}}{\vdash} \text{exn X}' \mapsto exc}{e \vdash \text{exn X} = \text{exn X}' : \{\text{exn X} \mapsto exc\}} \tag{2}$$

Figure 16. Evaluating an exception binding

7. Related work and conclusion

The use of type information presented in this paper can be related to the work of Aït-Kaci[1] and of Mycroft[14] on typed logic. The approach proposed in this paper is a more modest effort that does not use all the generality of the typing inclusion mechanism developped by Aït-Kaci[1] in the Login language. But our motivations are slightly different: Login is intended to be a programming language for database applications while Natural Semantics is a formal specification formalism. For instance in Natural Semantics we do not seem to need type inheritance.

We have illustrated the use of Natural Semantics to specify the dynamic semantics of an applicative language with exception and pattern-matching. The most important features of Natural Semantics that have been used are the identification of tree terms with abstract syntax trees, tree terms are used as instantiation filters, together with the use of type information on meta-variables. We found that last aspect the key to produce modular and readable Natural Semantic descriptions.

Although we have not considered the implementation aspect of such a specification, the existence of a compiler for Natural Semantics makes it feasible to execute the specification of the dynamic semantics presented in this paper. Techniques to obtain an efficient implementation, and that have been omitted from this paper, are still under development.

Acknowledgements: I would like to thank to J.Despeyroux for fruitful discussions and G. Kahn for detailed suggestions and corrections.

REFERENCES

[1] H. AÏT-KACI, AND R. NASR "Logic and Inheritance", ACM Journal of Logic Programming, pp 219-228, 1986

[2] H. AÏT-KACI, "A Lattice-Theoretic Approach to Computation Based on a Calculus of Partially-Ordered Type Structures", Ph.D Thesis, University of Pensylvania, 1984.

[3] CLÉMENT D., J. DESPEYROUX, T. DESPEYROUX, L. HASCOET, G.KAHN, "Natural Semantics on the Computer", INRIA Research Report RR 416, INRIA-Sophia-Antipolis, June 1985.

[4] CLÉMENT D., J. DESPEYROUX, T. DESPEYROUX, G. KAHN, "A Simple Applicative Language: Mini-ML", Conference on Lisp and Functional Programming, 1986.

[5] CLÉMENT D. "The Natural Dynamic Semantics of Standard ML", *to appear as Inria report.*

[6] DESPEYROUX J., "Proof of Translation in Natural Semantics", *Logic in Computer Science*, Cambridge, Massachussets, June, 1986.

[7] DESPEYROUX T., "Executable Specification of Static Semantics", *Semantics of Data Types*, Lecture Notes in Computer Science, Vol. 173, June 1984.

[8] GENTZEN G. "The Collected Papers of Gerhard Gentzen", E.Szabo, Noth-Holland, Amsterdam, 1969.

[9] GORDON M., R. MILNER, C. WADSWORTH, G. COUSINEAU, G.HUET, L. PAULSON, "The ML Handbook, Version 5.1", INRIA, October 1984.

[10] HUET G., "Formal Structures for Computation and Deduction", Courses Notes at CMU, May 1986.

[11] KAHN G., "Natural Semantics", Proc. of Symp. on Theoritical Aspects of Computer Science, Passau, Germany, February 1987.

[12] MILNER R., "The Standard ML Core Language", Polymorphism, Volume II, Number 2, October, 1985.

[13] MILNER R., "The Dynamic Operational Semantics of Standard ML", Department of Computer Science, University of Edinburgh, Edinburgh, England, April 1985 *Private communication.*

[14] MYCROFT A. AND O'KEEFE R.A., "A Polymorphic Type System for Prolog", Journal of Artificial Intelligence 23(3), pp 295-307, 1984.

[15] PLOTKIN G.D., "A Structural Approach to Operational Semantics", DAIMI FN-19, Computer Science Department, Aarhus University, Aarhus, Denmark, September 1981.

[16] PRAWITZ D., "Natural Deduction, a Proof-Theoritical Study", Almqvist & Wiksell, Stockholm, 1965.

[17] WATT D. A., "Executable Semantic Descriptions", Software-practice and experience, Vol. 16(1), p.13-43, january 1986.

LISTLOG - A PROLOG EXTENSION FOR LIST PROCESSING

Zsuzsa Farkas

Computer Research and Innovation Center - SZKI

H - 1015 Budapest, Donati utca 35-45, Hungary

Abstract

In this paper an alternative list representation for logic programs is introduced, based on so-called segment variables. These variables represent a whole sublist (segment) of a list, that is, when substituting such a variable by a list, not the list itself, but its elements are considered the elements of the original list. The notion of segment variables was first introduced in the LISP70 pattern matcher [1], and was suggested to be used in PROLOG by Marc Eisenstadt, as a step towards a more human man-machine interface for PROLOG. The original motivation for using these variables was to simplify the definition of some basic list processing predicates, mainly by avoiding recursion.

However, we have shown that this list representation has an even more important advantage: it brings the declarative and the procedural semantics of several list handling predicates nearer to each other, e.g. allowing a more complete set of solutions or avoiding some infinite loops.

LISTLOG is a PROLOG extension, handling these list expressions; it is implemented as a front-end to PROLOG, providing an extended matching algorithm.

1. List expressions with segment variables

A segment variable represents a whole segment (sublist) of a list. For example, in a PROLOG list expression

[a, X , b]   (*)

substituting

X <-- [c , d]

the list will contain [c ,d] as the second element. Intuitively, however, one may want to have

[a , c , d , b]

as the result of such a substitution. To allow this, we introduce a new type of variable, called segment variable, handled in a special way: it can be substituted only by a list expression, and when such a variable is substituted by a list, this list becomes s sublist of the original list. For segment variables we will use a '^' prefix to distinguish them from normal variables. That is,

[a , ^ X, b] will become [a , c , d , b]

when the substitution X <-- [c,d] is applied (cf previous example (*)).

This is a quite natural extension of normal PROLOG lists: in the expression

[a , b | X]

X also represents a whole (final) segment of the list, but here we have the restriction that only the variable after the vertical bar is handled in this way. Our generalization simply means, that we allow such a variable not only at the last position. The above list can be rewritten in LISTLOG as

[a , b , ^ X]

representing the lists beginning with the elements a and b and continuing with any number of any elements. Similarly,

[a , ^ X , b]

can be used to represent the lists beginning with a, ending with b, and containing any number of any elements in between.

In LISTLOG we allow all the normal PROLOG expressions, only the list expressions are different:

The syntax of expressions:

<expression> ::= <list expression> | ...

<list expression> ::= [<list_elem>, ..., <list_elem>]

<list elem> ::= <segment variable> | <expression>

<segment variable> ::= ^ <variable>

2. Defining list handling predicates in LISTLOG vs PROLOG

The main motivation for introducing this list representation was to provide means for defining list handling predicates in a less algorithmic way as it is possible in PROLOG. Though these PROLOG definitions might be understandable to be read, it may cause difficulty for a naive user to formulate e.g. the "between" relation (see below). The main problem with these PROLOG definitions is the use of recursion, and a certain algorithmic approach. An other thing which is not easy to be accustomed to is the assymetry of the PROLOG lists: the first and the last elements of a list are handled in a completely different way.

However, when these problems do exist for the naive users, we are aware that this is not a central topic in logic programming and therefore it is not worthwhile to distract the users' attention from the main points such as declarative approach, backtracking, etc. Defining an alternative list representation and providing a suitable unifying algorithm, we achieve such an extension to PROLOG which might be used easier, though only in the special area of list processing.

In the following you can compare the definition of some basic list handling predicates:

in PROLOG

```
member(X,[X | L]).
member(X,[Y | L]) :-
     member(X,L).

append([],L,L).
append([A|L1],L2,[A|L]) :-
     append(L1,L2,L).

first_elem([X|L],X).
last_elem([X],X).
last_elem([Y|L],X) :-
    last_elem(L,X).

sublist(SL,L):-
     append(PREV,SL,LL),
       append(LL,LATER,L).

between(X,Y,B,[X|L]):-
     until(L,Y,B) .
between(X,Y,B,[Z|L]) :-
     between(X,Y,B,L) .

until([Y|_],Y,[]) .
until([Z|L],Y,[Z|B]) :-
     until(L,Y,B) .

reverse([],[]).
reverse([A|L],RL):-
     reverse(L,LL),
       append(LL,[A],RL).

palindrome([]).
palindrome([A|L]) :-
     palidnrome(L1),
       append(L1,[A],L).
```

in LISTLOG

```
member(X,[^PREV, X , ^LATER]).

append(L1,L2,[^L1, ^L2]).

first_elem([X, ^L],X).
last_elem([^L, X], X).

sublist(SL, [^PREV, ^SL, ^LATER]).

between(X,Y,B,[^L1,X,^B,Y,^L2]).

reverse([],[]).
reverse([A,^L],[^LL,A]) :-
      reverse(L,LL).

palindrome([]).
palindrome([A , ^L, A] ):-
     palindrome(L).
```

3. Advantages of LISTLOG to PROLOG

a. Solutions in a more concise form

A difference between the PROLOG and LISTLOG list representation is that some object sets which in PROLOG may be described only by infinitely many expressions, in LISTLOG can be represented by a single expression. For example, those lists containing the constant '1' as element can be described in PROLOG by the following expressions:

```
[1 | T]
[X1, 1| T]
[X1, X2, 1 | T]
  ...
```

while in LISTLOG by

```
[ ^X , 1, ^T ]
```

As a consequence of this, some goals having an infinite sequence of solutions in PROLOG, will have only a single one in LISTLOG, of course, having the same meaning - representing the same set of objects.

The simplest example illustrating this difference is:

```
? member(1,L).
```

in PROLOG:	in LISTLOG :
L = [1 | T]	L = [^X , 1 , ^T]
= [X1 , 1 | T]	
= [X1,X2,1 | T]	
....	

b. Producing a more complete set of solutions

As it is well known, even in pure PROLOG there are differences between the declarative and procedural semantics. One of the aspects of this is that some of the logically valid solutions are not produced by the PROLOG execution mechanism. The following example illustrates a situation when in LISTLOG a more complete set of solutions is gained:

```
? member(1,L) and member(2,L).

  in PROLOG                          in LISTLOG

L = [1,2|T]                      L = [^X, 1 , ^Y, 2 , ^Z]
  = [1,X1,2 |T]                    = [^X, 2 , ^Y, 1 , ^Z]
  = [1,X1,X2,2|T]
  ....
```

The solution set produced in PROLOG is rather restricted: we can never find a list in which '2' preceeds '1', moreover, '1' is always stuck in the first position. In LISTLOG there are only two solutions, but they describe all the logically possible solutions. Note that this difference is a consequence of the property dealt with in the previous section, that is, of the possibility of describing a larger set of objects by an expression in LISTLOG than in PROLOG. The reason why PROLOG gives only these solutions is that the second subgoal has infinitely many solutions already for the first solution of the first subgoal, and the interpreter would return to the first subgoal only after exhausting all the possible solutions of the second subgoal. In LISTLOG the more concise form of the solutions makes possible to avoid this.

c. Avoiding infinite loops

A third problem with the PROLOG execution mechanism is that in some cases it produces an infinite loop instead of a negative answer, as in the following examples:

```
? member(1,L) and not member(1,L).

? next_to(X,Y,L) and not preceeds(X,Y,L).

? sublist([1],[2]).

? first_elem(L,1) and last_elem(L,2) and palindrom(L).
```

The structure of the infinite loop is that a first subgoal has infinitely many solutions, all of them refused by a second subgoal. These type of goals are answered with 'NO' in LISTLOG, again due to the more concise form of the solutions.

4. Unification in LISTLOG

As we have extended the notion of expressions, an extended unification algorithm must be provided as well. Before presenting such an algorithm, first revisit the general definitions for unification and then those properties different in PROLOG and LISTLOG. (A summary of general unification is found in [3]).

a. General notions of unification

instantiating an expression means substituting simultaneously some of its variables by other expressions and performing the possible simplifications. The expression produced by instantiating is called an instance of the original one.

simplifying an expression means replacing those subexpressions whose arguments become known by the value of the function at the given arguments

an expression E is the **unifier** of two expressions E1 and E2 if it is an instance of both of them, belonging to the same substitutions.

if U1 and U2 are unifiers of two expressions, then U1 is **more general** than U2 if U2 is an instance of U1.

b. Simplification in LISTLOG

In the above definition only the notion of simplification depends on the given formal system: e.g. in PROLOG no simplification is needed since in Herbrand interpretations functions are defined having the function expressions themselves as values.

Simplification in LISTLOG means to flatten the elements of the list substitituted for a segment variable into the elements of the list containing this variable. E.g. the expression

[a , X , ^ [c , Y], b] is simplified to [a , X , c , Y b]

The following expressions e.g. can be unified in LISTLOG :

```
E1 = [1 , ^X]                                   E2 = [^Y, 2]
      |                                               |
      S = { X <- [^Z, 2], Y <- [1, ^Z] }
      ↓                                               ↓
[1, ^[^Z, 2]]                                   [^[1, ^Z], 2]
        \                                           /
         =        after simplification         =
                      \                  /
                         [1, ^Z, 2]
```

c. Maximally general unifiers

As we know, in PROLOG there always exists a most general unifier for any two unifiable expressions, and the PROLOG unification algorithm is a deterministic procedure, giving this unifier. In LISTLOG this is not true: there may be expressions having not comparable unifiers, as it is illustrated by the following example:

```
  E1 = [^X, 1 , ^Y]                              E2 = [^V, 2 , ^Z]
        |                                               |
S1  = {V  <- [^X,  1, ^W],                     S2 = {X <- [^V, 2, ^W],
       Y <- [^W, 2, ^Z] }                            Z <- [^W, 1, ^Y] }
        ↓                                               ↓
U1 = [^X, 1, ^W, 2, ^Z]                        U2 = [^V, 2, ^W, 1, ^Y]
```

that is, U1 and U2 are both unifiers of E1 and E2, and none of them is an instance of the other.

There may be infinitely many incomparable unifiers: these two expressions have the following unifiers:

```
      E1 = [1, ^X]                     E2 = [^X, 1]

                  U1 = []
                  U2 = [1]
                  U3 = [1,1]
                    ...
```

It follows from the above that here we may have only maximally general unfiers instead of most general ones.

5. A unification algorithm

According to the above, our unification algorithm will be nondeterministic, producing each of the maximally general unifiers.

The algorithm presented here is a natural extension of the unfication used in PROLOG. The difference is that in PROLOG the only constructors are 'nil' and '.' , while in LISTLOG also the 'append' function is considered as constructor. (This corresponds to the list of form [^X,...]). We denote the list that results by appending the lists PRE and SUF together by

PRE .. SUF

The unfication algorithm is based on the following properties of lists:

(1) L1 = [] ==> L1 = L2 <==> L2 = []

(2) H1 . T1 = H2 . T2 <==> H1 = H2 and T1 = T2

Properties (1) and (2) are used in PROLOG; further properties, (3) and (4), are added for LISTLOG unification:

(3) P1 .. S1 = P2 .. S2 <==> P1 = P2 and S1 = S2 or

P1 = P2 .. S and S2 = S .. S1 or

P2 = P1 .. S and S1 = S .. S2.

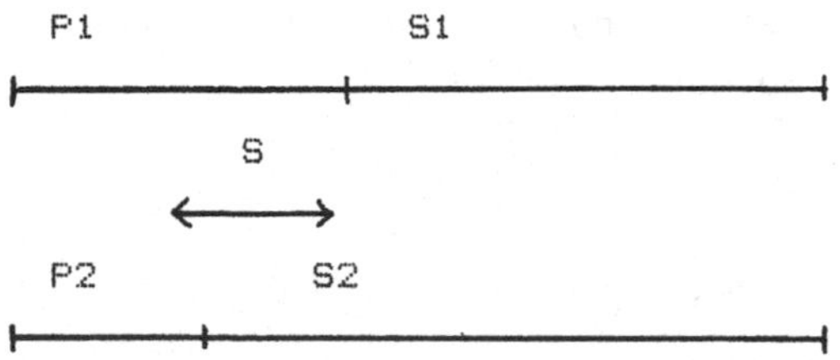

(4) P .. S = H . T <==> P = [] and S = H . T or

P = H . P1 and P1 .. S = T

The unification defined in PROLOG

```
operator(^, fx, 700).

unify(X,Y) :-
  elem(X), !, X=Y .
unify(X,Y) :-
  elem(Y), !, X=Y .
unify(X,Y) :-
  is_list(X), !, unify_lists(X,Y);
  is_list(Y), !, unify_lists(X,Y) .
unify(X,Y) :-
  decomp(X,[N|AL1]),comp([N|AL2],Y),unify_args(Al1,Al2).

unify_args([],[]) .
unify_args([A|L1],[B|L2]) :-
  unify(A,B), unify_args(L1,L2) .


(u1) unify_lists([],[]) .
(u2) unify_lists([S|T],L) :-
       bound_segment(S,SX), !, simplify(SX,S1), app(S1,T,L1),
         unify(L1,L) .
(u3) unify_lists(L,[S|T]) :-
       bound_segment(S,SY), !, simplify(SY,S1), app(S1,T,L1),
         unify(L,L1) .
(u4) unify_lists([S],L) :-
       unbound_segment(S,S1), !, S1=L .
(u5) unify_lists(L,[S]) :-
       unbound_segment(S,S1), !, S1=L .
(u6) unify_lists([S1|T1],[S2|T2]) :-
       unbound_segment(S1,X), unbound_segment(S2,Y), !,
          (X == Y, ! , unify(T1,T2);
           X=[^ Y,^ Z], unify([^ Z|T1],T2);
           Y=[^ X,^ Z], unify(T1,[^ Z|T2])) .
(u7) unify_lists([H|T1],[S|T2]) :-
       unbound_segment(S,X), !,
          (unify(X,[]), unify([H|T1],T2);
           unify(X,[H,^ Z]), unify(T1,[^ Z|T2])) .
(u8) unify_lists([S|T1],[H|T2]) :-
       unbound_segment(S,X), !,
          (unify(X,[]), unify(T1,[H|T2]);
           unify(X,[H,^ Z]), unify([^ Z|T1],T2)) .
```

```
(u9) unify_lists([S|T],[]) :-
       unbound_segment(S,X), !, unify(X,[]), unify(T,[]) .
(u10) unify_lists([],[S|T]) :-
       unbound_segment(S,X), !, unify(X,[]), unify(T,[]) .
(u11) unify_lists([H1|T1],[H2|T2]) :-
       unify(H1,H2), !, unify(T1,T2) .

      elem(X) :-
         X==[], !, fail;
         var(X), !;
         constant(X), !.

      is_list(L) :-
         var(X), ! , fail;
         L=[], !;
         L=[_|_] .

      bound_segment(S,X) :-
         var(S), !, fail;
         S=(^ X), (var(X), !, fail;
                     !) .

      unbound_segment(S,X) :-
          var(S), !, fail;
          S=(^ X), var(X).

      simplify(X,X) :-
          elem(X), !.
      simplify(L1,L2) :-
          is_list(L1), !, simplify_list(L1,L2) .
      simplify(X,Y) :-
          decomp(X,[N|AL1]), simplify_args(AL1,AL2),comp([N|AL2],Y).

      simplify_args([],[]) .
      simplify_args([A|L1],[B|L2]) :-
          simplify(A,B), simplify_args(L1,L2) .

      simplify_list([],[]) :-
          ! .
       simplify_list([E|L],[E1|L1]) :-
          unbound_segment(E,_), !, E1=E, simplify_list(L,L1).
```

```
simplify_list([E|L],EL) :-
   bound_segment(E,X), !, simplify(X,X1),
      simplify_list(L,L1), app(X1,L1,EL).
 simplify_list([E1|L1],[E2|L2]) :-
   simplify(E1,E2), simplify_list(L1,L2) .

 app([],L,L) .
 app([A|L1],L2,[A|L]) :-
   app(L1,L2,L) .
```

An example unification

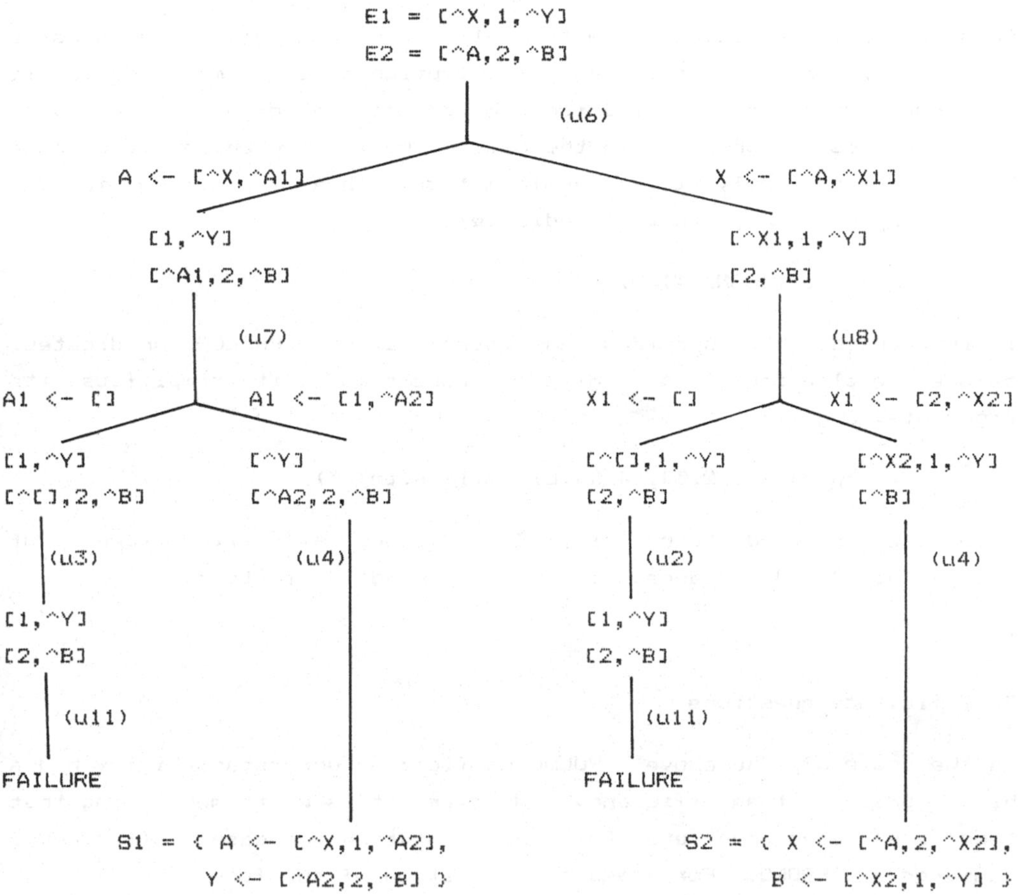

U1 = [^X,1,^A2,2,^B]   **U2 = [^A,2,^X2,1,^Y]**

6. Transforming LISTLOG statements into PROLOG

As the only difference between PROLOG and LISTLOG lies in the data structures they handle, the only necessary transformation is to use our unification algorithm instead of the normal PROLOG one. This is done in such a way that the expressions occurring in the head of a statement are substituted by (new) variables, and the above unification algorithm is called explicitly before executing the body of the statement. E.g.

```
member(X,[^P,X,^S]).          =====>    member(X,Y) :-
                                            unify(Y,[^P,X,^S]).

append(L1,L2,[^L1,^L2]).      =====>    append(L1,L2,L) :-
                                            unify(L,[^L1,^L2]).
```

An additional problem is how to call the PROLOG built-in predicates such as 'write'. In the above execution scheme simplification is performed during the unification when entering a definition. However, this causes a problem in the case of built-in predicates, because here we cannot apply this transformation. This is solved in our system in such a way, that a predicate

```
call(CONDITION)
```

is introduced which provides an interface for PROLOG predicates: before evaluating the given condition it simplifies its arguments. E.g.

```
append([1,2,3],[4,5],L),call(write(L)).
```

gives the expected output [1,2,3,4,5], the simplified form of [^[1,2,4],^[4,5]] produced by the "append" definition.

7. Efficiency questions

In the case of the above PROLOG unification understandability had a higher priority than efficiency. However, it is worth mentioning that there are cases when even this implementation increases efficiency, compared to PROLOG. For example, a question of the form

```
? reverse([1,2,3,4,5,6,...,n] , []).
```

in PROLOG can be answered negatively only by actually reversing the list, while in LISTLOG this answer is produced by a single

```
unify([^X, 1], [] )
```

unification step, independently of the length of the list to be reversed.

8. Conclusions, further plans

We have shown the advantages of an alternative list representation for logic programming. LISTLOG, the resulted PROLOG extension is implemented in PROLOG at the moment, but we are considering a more efficient direct implementation for it. Further directions are to try to generalize this method from lists to other PROLOG structures, or remaining in the list processing area, to refine further the above list representation [4].

References

[1] L.G.Tesler - H.J.Enea - D.S.Smith:
The Lisp70 pattern matching system.

[2] M.Eisenstadt:
An improved man-machine interface for PROLOG.
Imperial College - Open University joint project, 1984.

[3] J.H.Stickman:
Universal unification.
7th International Conference on Automated Deduction, LNCS 170, Springer Verlag, 1984.

[4] Zs. Farkas:
Length restricted segment variables in PROLOG.
(in preparation)

Intensional Negation of Logic Programs:
examples and implementation techniques

Roberto Barbuti, Paolo Mancarella, Dino Pedreschi, Franco Turini

Dipartimento di Informatica
Università di Pisa
Corso Italia, 40
56100 Pisa - Italy

Abstract

Intensional negation is a transformation technique which, given the Horn clause definitions of a set of predicates p_i, synthesizes the definitions of new predicates $p_i\sim$ the meaning of which is the effective part of the complement of p_i's success set. The main advantage with respect to the standard negation as failure rule is the symmetry in handling both positive and negative information, up the ability of computing non ground negative goals as well as producing non ground output as result of negative queries.

1. Introduction

In the field of deductive data bases [8] and expert systems construction [6, 10, 11] logic programming is gaining momentum. On the other hand the expressiveness of logic programming is still too inadequate for addressing such problems in a natural way. In particular, the ability of handling negative knowledge is a recognized weak point of the logic programming approach.

Up to now, the only kind of negation which has been thoroughly studied is the so called *negation as failure* [7]. Negation as failure is a meta inference rule allowing to prove the negation of a ground goal, when the proof of the corresponding positive goal finitely fails.

The rule has been proved sound and complete for a particular transformation of Horn theories (completed Horn theories) [9]. Furthermore, the soundness and completeness has been proved for certain classes of general logic programs, i.e. programs containing negative literals in the body of clauses [3, 5, 7, 14, 15, 19, 20].

The major drawback of the negation as failure inference rule is that it works correctly only if, during the refutation process, each selected negative literal is ground. In [7, 14, 15, 19, 20] classes of logic theories with the above properties are characterized.

The main contribution of this paper consists in allowing the correct computation of non ground negative goals. As a consequence, the correct answer substitutions for negative goals can be computed. This result is obtained by transforming a Horn logic program (not containing negative literals) into the corresponding *negative* one and querying the latter with the negative goal.

The key idea supporting the transformation is the following. A logical term t (with respect to a first order language L which provides constant and constructor symbols) can be viewed as an intensional representation of the set of all its ground instances. If t does not contain multiple occurrences of the same variable then also its set-theoretic complement can be intensionally represented by means of a finite set of terms [13]. For example, given the usual representation of natural numbers (0, s(0), ...), the complement of the term s(0) can be intensionally represented by the set of terms {0, s(s(x))}. This process can be shown correct provided that all the values of each interpretation domain are obtained by the application of constructors to the constants in L. As an example, the above complement of the term s(0) is correct w.r.t. all the domains satisfying the axiom $\forall x\ (x=0 \lor \exists y\ \ x=s(y))$. This kind of axiom will be referred to, in the sequel, as *domain closure axiom* (DCA) as in [14]. Actually, intensional negation is based upon the ability of finitely representing the complement of the terms occurring in the clause heads, and this is possible avoiding multiple occurrences of variables in clause heads [13]. This restriction is met by a suitable transformation which turns logic programs into a left-linear form.

The intensional negation approach can be viewed as an extension of the approach presented in [18] in two main respects. First of all, intensional negation is able to deal with logic programs in the general case. Secondly, the ability of computing non ground answer substitutions to negative queries is an attractive feature of intensional negation which, in general, is not met by the approach in [18].

The transformation technique allows a symmetric representation of positive and negative knowledge. Indeed the negative program is a *general* logic program, i.e. negation as failure can be used in clause bodies. In this respect, the transformation technique leads to a computable (by means of a suitable inference rule), intensional representation of the negative knowledge implicit in a logic program. The possibility of handling an intensional representation of negative knowledge is a powerful knowledge engineering method. Indeed, in many applications of deductive data bases and expert systems, the ability of directly checking the implicit negative information can help in debugging and tuning knowledge bases.

2. Proving negative formulæ in logic programming

This section presents some well known results on gathering negative information in logic programming. A thoroughly presentation of this subject can be found in [16]. As pointed out in the introduction, the most important rule for negation is the so called *negation as failure* rule (*naf*) which approximates in an effective way the *closed world assumption* (CWA) [17]. The CWA inference rule states that if a ground atom A is not a logical consequence of a program P then it is possible to infer $\neg A$.

Using the SLD resolution it is possible to prove $\neg A$ with respect to a program P under the CWA if the goal $\leftarrow A$ has a finitely failed SLD-tree. Obviously, a SLD-tree is not always finitely failed; any proof procedure is semi-decidable and can loop forever. As a consequence, the *naf* rule has been introduced [7], which states that if A is in the SLD finite failure set of a program P, then it is possible to infer $\neg A$ with respect to a *completed* program ***P*** (in [16] the notation comp(P) is used instead of ***P***).

According to [16, 2], the SLD finite failure set of P is defined to be the set of all $A \in B_P$ (the Herbrand base of P) for which there exists a finitely failed SLD-tree for $P \cup \{\leftarrow A\}$. The soundness and completeness results for the *naf* rule are given with respect to the completed program ***P*** [9, 7]. The completeness result for the *naf* rule states that if P is a program and $A \in B_P$, then if $\neg A$ is a logical consequence of ***P*** then A is in F_P, i.e. the finite failure set of P. This result is independent of the implementation of the proof procedure. Using a fair SLD resolution [16, 12], a sound and complete implementation of F_P is obtained, i.e. the SLD finite failure set is equal to F_P.

3. Intensional negation

In this section the approach to the synthesis of negative programs is presented by means of examples of increasing complexity. The approach is based on the *completion* of a logic program which, roughly speaking, corresponds to replace the if connectives ($\leftarrow$) in the program with iff connectives ($\Leftrightarrow$), and the domain closure axiom.

In the sequel, programs with no multiple occurrences of the same variable in clause heads are termed *left-linear*, and a variable occurring in a clause body but not in the corresponding clause head is termed *right-free*. The following subsections present the application of intensional negation to left-linear programs without right-free variables, to left-linear programs with right-free variables and to non left-linear programs respectively.

3.1. Left-linear programs without right-free variables

The following program Even defines the set of even numbers, represented as terms of the Herbrand universe {0, s(0), s(s(0)), . . . }.

even(0) $\leftarrow$

even(s(s(x))) $\leftarrow$ *even*(x)

The completed program ***Even*** corresponding to Even is

Even

$\forall x \; (even(x) \Leftrightarrow x=0 \vee \exists y \, (x=s(s(y)), even(y)) \,)$

We are omitting here the axiomatization of the equality theory on the Herbrand universe, defining predicate =, and the associated DCA [14]. Subformulæ such as $\exists y \; x=s(s(y))$ will be referred in the sequel as *positive guards* (for variable x).

The aim is to synthetize the definition of a new predicate, *even~*, such that *even~*(n) holds iff *even*(n) is provably false or, in other words, the theory ***Even*** $\cup\{even(n)\}$ has no models. The flavor of the transformation can be obtained by the examination of its main steps.

1) Applying logical negation to the axiom for *even* and interpreting occurrences of negative atoms $\neg even(t)$ as occurrences of the positive atom *even~*(t), we obtain the axiom

$\forall x \, (even\sim(x) \Leftrightarrow \neg\,(x=0), \neg\,\exists y \, (x=s(s(y)), even(y)) \,)$

which can be further transformed into

$\forall x \, (even\sim(x) \Leftrightarrow x\neq 0, \forall y \, (x\neq s(s(y)) \vee even\sim(y)) \,)$

2) Let x be an arbitrary term, then the subformula $\forall y \, (x\neq s(s(y)) \vee even\sim(y))$ can be shown equivalent to

$\forall y \, (x\neq s(s(y))) \vee \exists y \, (x=s(s(y)), even\sim(y)).$

Hence, by substituting $\forall y \, (x\neq s(s(y)) \vee even\sim(y))$ with this last formula and by $\wedge$-distribution we obtain

$$\begin{aligned}\forall x \, (even\sim(x) \Leftrightarrow \quad & x\neq 0, \forall y \; x\neq s(s(y)) \quad \vee \\ & x\neq 0, \exists y \, (x=s(s(y)), even\sim(y)) \,).\end{aligned}$$

Subformulæ such as $\forall y \; x\neq s(s(y))$ are termed *negative guards* (for variable x).

3) The next step consists in transforming negative guards into (a disjunction of) positive guards, still preserving their logical meaning, i.e. computing the intensional complement of the term involved in the right hand side of a negative guard. The technique has been introduced for the negation of predicates in the framework of symbolic evaluation [1]. Here the technique is implemented by a transformation, named *Ex*, which will be discussed in section 4. The application of *Ex* to the negative guards in the example yields:

- $Ex(x\neq 0) \equiv \exists y \; x=s(y)$
- $Ex(\forall y \; x\neq s(s(y))) \equiv x=0 \vee \exists z \, (x=s(z), Ex(\forall v \; z\neq s(v))) \equiv x=0 \vee \exists z \, (x=s(z), z=0)$
  $\equiv x=0 \vee x=s(0)$

The definition of *even~* becomes:

$\forall x\ (even\sim(x) \Leftrightarrow\ \exists y\ x=s(y),\ x=0\ \lor$
$\exists y\ x=s(y),\ x=s(0))\ \lor$
$\exists z\ x=s(z),\ \exists y\ (x=s(s(y)), even\sim(y))\ ).$

4) Conjunctions of formulæ with positive guards for the same variable can be turned into a single formula by finding the *most general unifier*, if any, of their guards, and propagating this m.g.u. to the remaining parts. In the example

- $\exists y\ x=s(y),\ x=0\ \Rightarrow$ **ff** — Since the m.g.u. of s(y) and 0 does not exist
- $\exists y\ x=s(y),\ x=s(0))\ \Rightarrow\ x=s(0)$ — m.g.u.(s(y), s(0)) = {<y,0>}
- $\exists y\ x=s(y),\ \exists z\ x=s(s(z))\ \Rightarrow\ \exists z\ x=s(s(z))$ — m.g.u.(s(y),s(s(z))))={<y,s(z)>}

Hence one obtains the completed definition of *even~*

$\forall x\ (even\sim(x) \Leftrightarrow\ x=s(0)\ \lor\ \exists y\ (x=s(s(y)), even\sim(y))\ ).$

5) Finally, the logic program for the new predicate is

even~(s(0)) ←
even~(s(s(x))) ← *even~*(x)

which, as one might expect, defines exactly the set of odd numbers.

Querying such a program with a ground goal such as ← *even~*(s(0)) yields the same answer as querying the original program with a goal ← ***naf*** *even*(s(0)), where ***naf*** stands for the *negation as failure* operator. Indeed, such a goal is nothing but a test (which does not involve computing answer substitutions) and this is the only kind of goal that the query evaluation process based on the *naf* rule is able to handle correctly. More properly, the evaluation of a non ground goal such as ← ***naf*** *even*(x) is simply a way to prove whether $\forall x\ \neg even(x)$ holds or not w.r.t. to the completed program. On the other hand, the goal ← *even~*(x) using intensional negation is a way to prove whether $\exists x\ \neg even(x)$ holds or not and, as usual, to compute the values for x which make the formula true. In the example, the goal ← ***naf*** *even*(x) fails while the goal ← *even~*(x) succeeds enumerating the odd numbers as solutions. This provides a nice notion of symmetry between the use of positive and negative knowledge.

Consider, as a further example, the following program LessOrEqual wich defines the relation "≤" on natural numbers.

LessOrEqual(0, x) ←
LessOrEqual(s(x), s(y)) ← *LessOrEqual*(x, y).

The completed definition of *LessOrEqual* is

$$\forall x\,(\,LessOrEqual(x_1, x_2) \Leftrightarrow \quad x_1{=}0 \;\vee$$
$$\exists y_1 y_2\;(x_1{=}s(y_1),\, x_2{=}s(y_2),\, LessOrEqual(y_1, y_2))\,)$$

The next steps of the transformation yield the following results:

$$\forall x\,(\,LessOrEqual{\sim}(x_1, x_2) \Leftrightarrow$$
$$x_1{\neq}0,\, (\forall y_1\, x_1{\neq}s(y_1) \vee \forall y_2\, x_2{\neq}s(y_2)) \quad \vee$$
$$x_1{\neq}0,\, \exists y_1 y_2\; (x_1{=}s(y_1),\, x_2{=}s(y_2),\, LessOrEqual{\sim}(y_1, y_2))\,)$$

$$\forall x\,(\,LessOrEqual{\sim}(x_1, x_2) \Leftrightarrow$$
$$\exists y_1\, x_1{=}s(y_1),\, x_2{=}0 \quad \vee$$
$$\exists y_1 y_2\; (x_1{=}s(y_1),\, x_2{=}s(y_2),\, LessOrEqual{\sim}(y_1, y_2))\,)$$

The logic program corresponding to the above definition is

LessOrEqual~(s(x), 0) ←
LessOrEqual~(s(x), s(y)) ← *LessOrEqual~*(x, y)

which is the expected definition of the relation ">".

As mentioned before, intensional negation allows querying a logic program with arbitrary goals containing also negative atoms. As an example, the query

← *LessOrEqual~*(x, s(s(0))) (•)

gives the only answer x=s(s(s(y))) which denotes the set of numbers greater than 2, while the corresponding query using the *naf* rule

← ***naf*** *LessOrEqual*(x, s(s(0))) (••)

fails. One might wonder that the behavior of (•) can be simulated using the original program extended with the clauses

nat(0) ←
nat(s(x)) ← *nat*(x)

and rephrasing (••) as

← *nat*(x), ***naf*** *LessOrEqual*(x, s(s(0))) (•••)

In this way *nat* acts as a generator for numbers and the negative atom is selected with ground terms bound to x. Nevertheless, this query is somewhat weaker than (•), since the evaluation of (•) gives the whole solution in one shot, whereas (•••) diverges enumerating all the ground solutions. As this example shows, the symmetry between the treatment of positive and negative knowledge is pervasive up to the ability of producing *non ground output*.

3.2. Left-linear programs with right-free variables

The sample programs which have been considered so far do not contain *right-free* variables, i.e. variables occurring only in the body of a clause. Consider for instance the program

$$p(x) \leftarrow q(x,z)$$
$$q(a,b) \leftarrow$$

Applying the same transformation steps of the previous examples, one would obtain the following intensional negation for predicates p and q

$$p\sim(x) \leftarrow q\sim(x,z) \quad (*)$$
$$q\sim(b,x) \quad \leftarrow$$
$$q\sim(a,a) \quad \leftarrow$$

Then, both p(a) and p~(a) are provable in the whole theory, i.e. the theory is inconsistent since p~ is viewed as an effective counterpart of $\neg p$. The problem is that the right-free variables (such as z in the clause of p) are *unguarded* existentially quantified variables in the completed definition and thus they become unguarded *universally* quantified variables in the negative program. The completed definition of p is

$$\forall x \ \ (p(x) \Leftrightarrow \exists z\, q(x,z)\,)$$

hence

$$\forall x \ \ (\neg p(x) \Leftrightarrow \forall z\, \neg q(x,z)\,)$$

while the actual meaning of (*) is

$$\forall x \ \ (p\sim(x) \Leftrightarrow \exists z\, q\sim(x,z)\,).$$

Although it is possible to replace negative guards (i.e. universally quantified formulæ involving predicate =) with some appropriate existentially quantified construction, this is not the case when arbitrary predicates are involved, as in $\forall z\, \neg q(x,z)$. However, for any substitution of a term t for x, if the proof of q(t,z) finitely fails (resp. succeeds) we obtain a proof of $\forall z\, \neg q(t,z)$ (resp. $\neg\forall z\, \neg q(t,z)$) [9]. This means that the *naf* rule is appropriate to compute formulæ of such kind, since there is no need to gather output substitutions for the free variables as z in the example. Thus, in the program obtained by intensional negation, a formula like $\forall z\, \neg q(x,z)$ can be implemented by

$$q\sim(x,w),\ \textbf{\textit{naf}}\ q(x,z) \qquad (\bullet)$$

where ***naf*** q(x,z) is called a *naf literal*. The evaluation of ***naf*** q(x, z) succeeds if and only if the goal $\leftarrow q(x,z)$ finitely fails. From a computational point of view, the evaluation of q~(x,w) in (•) provides candidate substitutions $t_1, t_2,\ldots$ for x, such that $\exists w\, \neg q(t_i,w)$ holds, and the computation of ***naf*** $q(t_i,z)$ filters those substitutions t_i such that $\forall z\, \neg q(t_i,z)$ holds too. It is worth noting that the use of different variable names for right-free variables avoids undesired interferences between the computations of the two subformulæ. The appropriate refutation procedure (SLDIN resolution [4]) for programs with intensional negation has to cope with non ground *naf* literals which, as shown above, act as filters for correct solutions. To accomplish this task, the SLDIN refutation procedure uses a computation rule which selects a *naf* literal if the whole goal is composed of *naf* literals only, and applies the negation as failure rule to *naf* literals. Thus, SLDIN guarantees that *naf* literals are selected after the non-naf literals have provided the candidate solutions.

It is worth noting that SLDIN resolution deals with queries which are *non allowed queries* for SLDNF resolution [16]. Nevertheless, when a *naf* literal is selected the SLDIN resolution never *flounders* [15] since the negation as failure rule is actually used only to prove a universally quantified theorem.

Concluding the example, the intensional negation is

p~(x) ← q~(x,w), ***naf*** q(x,z)	p(x) ← q(x,w)
q~(b,x) ←	q(a,b) ←
q~(a,a) ←	

Again, a non ground query such as ← p~(x) succeeds with the answer x=b while ←***naf*** p(x) fails. Moreover the inconsistency pointed out above does not hold anymore since ← p~(a) fails under SLDIN resolution.

In the case of clauses with right-free variables occurring in more than one literal in its body, as in

p(x,y) ← q(x,w), r(w,y)

intensional negation is carried out in two steps. First, the clause is replaced by an equivalent one with only one literal in its body, introducing a new predicate symbol. In the example

p(x,y) ← s(x,y,w)
s(x,y,w) ← q(x,w), r(w,y).

Second, intensional negation of the transformed program is computed as in the previous example and a *naf* literal is introduced for each definition with right-free variables. In the example

p~(x,y) ← s~(x,y,w), ***naf*** s(x,y,z)
s~(x,y,w) ← q~(x,w)
s~(x,y,w) ← r~(w,y).

Whenever a clause contains only right-free variables, as in

p(a) ← q(x)

the definitions computed by intensional negation only contain *naf* literals. In the example this leads to the definition

p~(a) ← ***naf*** q(x).

Notice that in the body of the clause defining p~(a) there is no need to introduce the conjunction q~(x), ***naf*** q(y) since no candidate solution has to be computed. In fact, from the completed definition of p we obtain

$p(a) \Leftrightarrow \exists y\, q(y) \quad \text{i.e.} \quad \neg p(a) \Leftrightarrow \forall y\, \neg q(y).$

Thus, in order to prove p~(a) is sufficient to test whether ∀y¬q(y) holds or not, which is just accomplished by means of the *naf* literal ***naf*** q(y).

As a final example, consider the intensional negation of a program for the ancestor relation, where *Parent*(x,y) means y is a parent of x, *Ancestor*(x,y) means y is an ancestor of x.

Parent(John, Mary) ←
Parent(John, Bill) ←
Parent(Mary, Paul) ←
Parent(Bill, Anne) ←
Ancestor (x,y) ← *Parent*(x,y)
Ancestor (x,y) ← *Ancestor*(x,z), *Parent*(z,y).

First of all, since the last clause contains right-free variables in more than one literal, it is replaced by a new clause which makes use of a new predicate symbol, say *ProperAncestor*. This transformation yields the following program

Parent(John, Mary) ←
Parent(John, Bill) ←
Parent(Mary, Paul) ←
Parent(Bill, Anne) ←
Ancestor (x,y) ← *Parent*(x,y)
Ancestor (x,y) ← *ProperAncestor*(x,y,z)
ProperAncestor(x,y,z) ←*Ancestor*(x,z), *Parent*(z,y).

The definitions computed by intensional negation are

Parent~(John, John) ←
Parent~(John, Paul) ←

.

.

.

Parent~(Paul, Mary) ←
Ancestor~(x,y) ← *Parent~*(x,y), *ProperAncestor~*(x,y,z), ***naf*** *ProperAncestor*(x,y,w)
ProperAncestor~(x,y,z) ← *Ancestor~*(x,z)
ProperAncestor~(x,y,z) ← *Parent~*(z,y)

Notice that the clause defining *Ancestor~* states that y is not an ancestor of x if neither y is a parent of x nor y is a proper ancestor of x through any z. Under SLDIN-resolution the query ←*Ancestor~*(Mary,y) succeeds enumerating the solutions Mary, Bill, John, Anne.

3.3. Non left-linear programs

A final issue concerns intensional negation of *non left-linear* programs, i.e. programs with clauses containing multiple occurrences of the same variable in their heads. Consider the following program which states the relation between a number and its successor:

$plus1(x, s(x)) \leftarrow$

The first step is to apply a ***linearization algorithm*** which turns each program into an equivalent left-linear form, thus turning back to the previous cases. The linearization of *plus1* is:

$plus1(x,s(y)) \quad \leftarrow \quad eq(x,y)$

where *eq* is the equality predicate defined by the clause

$eq(x, x) \quad \leftarrow.$

Furthermore, the completion of *plus1* over which intensional negation acts is:

$$\forall x_1\, x_2\ (plus1(x_1, x_2) \Leftrightarrow \exists y\ (x_2{=}s(y),\ eq(x_1, y)\,)\qquad (1)$$

Notice that we have distinguished = from *eq*: The former is introduced when the completion is carried out, while the latter is introduced by the linearization algorithm in order to turn the program into a left-linear form. From a semantic point of view both = and *eq* are the identity relation over the Herbrand universe, but they are handled differently by intensional negation. Consider the intensional negation of (1):

$$\forall x_1\, x_2\ (plus1{\sim}(x_1, x_2) \Leftrightarrow \forall y\ (x_2{=}s(y) \vee eq{\sim}(x_1, y)\,)$$

As before, we distinguish between ≠ and *eq~*: In particular ≠ appears only in negative guards which can be further transformed into a disjunction of positive guards, while *eq~* is handled like an ordinary predicate symbol. In the case of our running example:

$$\forall x_1\, x_2\ (plus1{\sim}(x_1, x_2) \Leftrightarrow x_2{=}0 \vee\ \exists y\ \ (x_2{=}s(y) \vee eq{\sim}(x_1, y)\,)$$

Putting the above definition into its Horn clause form one gets:

$plus1{\sim}(x_1, 0) \quad \leftarrow$

$plus1{\sim}(x_1, s(y)) \quad \leftarrow eq{\sim}(x_1, y)$

which defines exactly the set of pairs of naturals <n, m> such that m≠n+1, provided that *eq~* defines the set of pairs <n, m> such that m≠n. This is achieved providing the following *ad hoc* intensional negation of the predicate *eq*:

$eq{\sim}(0, s(x)) \quad \leftarrow$

$eq{\sim}(s(x), 0) \quad \leftarrow$

$eq{\sim}(s(x), s(y)) \quad \leftarrow eq{\sim}(x, y).$

Indeed, = and *eq* make explicit two different roles played by unification in logic programming. In fact the latter makes explicit the use of unification to state constraints of the kind ***the same (unspecified) object must occur in different positions within the terms of a clause head.*** In the previous example, *plus*(x, s(x)) ← means that the relation *plus1* holds between a generic natural number n and the natural number obtained applying the constructor s to n itself.

Now, consider the definition p(x, x) ← , which means that each object is related via p with itself and with no other object. Answering the question *which objects are not related via* p*?* one can just say *objects which are not identical.* Hence, the definition p~(x, y) ← is incorrect, since it would imply also that an object is *not* related via p with itself, and this is unconsistent with respect to the definition of p. A correct definition of p~ can be achieved using the *eq~* predicate: $p\sim(x, y) \leftarrow eq\sim(x, y)$, which means *if objects x and y are not identical, then they are not related via* p.

On the other hand, the = predicate makes explicit the use of unification to describe the structure that objects should exhibit in order to be candidate components of a tuple satisfying some relation. This is what is done by positive guards. Take for instance the definition $p(s(x)) \leftarrow q(x)$, which means *a number is in the set denoted by* p *if* i) *it is the successor of some other number* n, *and* ii) n *satisfies* q. With the *if and only if* interpretation one can safely say that a number which is not the successor of any other number is in the complement of p. This is exactly the meaning of the definition $p\sim(x) \leftarrow \forall y\ x{\neq}s(y)$ i.e. $p\sim(0) \leftarrow$. Furthermore one has to state that a number is in the complement of p if it satisfies the condition i) above but it does not satisfiy the condition ii). This is exactly the meaning of the definition $p\sim(s(x)) \leftarrow q\sim(x)$. The use of predicate = makes explicit the role of conditions analogous to condition i) above.

It is important to notice that the predicate *eq~* is not computationally equivalent to, say, *non-unification* : for instance, the unification of the terms x and s(x) fails because of the occur check, while the refutation of $\leftarrow eq\sim(x, s(x))$ diverges, even if any ground instance of such a goal succeeds. This suggests that intensional negation is not equivalent to non-unification: The results in [4] characterize the behavior of intensional negation in terms of a suitable theory. But the use of predicate *eq* (and hence *eq~*) guarantees that all programs that are to be intensionally negated can be brought into a left-linear form, and this makes possible to translate systematically negative guards into finite disjunctions of positive guards [13]. Looking at the clausal program resulting from intensional negation, it is worth noting that guards (involving predicate =) are absorbed again into unification, while the occurrences of predicate *eq~* are not, since *eq* is handled like any other predicate symbol. As a consequence, intensional negation yields always left-linear programs, apart from the predicate *eq* which is handled in a special way.

4. Computing transformations of negative guards

A central issue in the intensional negation approach is the transformation of negative guards into their existential form. As mentioned in the introduction, a (positive or negative) guard can be viewed as an intensional definition of a subset of the Herbrand universe [1]. For instance, referring to the Herbrand universe of naturals, the positive guard $\exists y\ x{=}s(y)$ denotes the set $\{x \mid x{\geq}1\}$, while the negative guard $\forall y\ x{\neq}s(s(y))$ denotes the set $\{0,1\}$. Under *DCA*, a set S described by a negative guard can always be described by a disjunction of positive guards, corresponding to an intensional constructive definition of S, since each universally quantified variable occurs exactly once in a negative guard [13]. Thus, a transformation *Ex* which, given a negative guard $\forall y\ x{\neq}t$ builds the equivalent disjunction of positive guards, can be defined by structural induction on the term t. The general definition of *Ex* can be found in [4], while an instance of *Ex* is shown below with respect to the Herbrand universe of naturals.

(1) $Ex\,(\forall y\ x \neq y) \equiv \mathrm{ff}$

(2) $Ex\,(x \neq 0) \equiv \exists y\ x=s(y)$

(3) $Ex\,(\forall y\ x \neq s(t)) \equiv x=0 \vee \exists z\ x=s(z),\ Ex\,(\forall y\ z \neq t)$.

For instance,

$$Ex\,(\forall y\ x \neq s(s(y))) \equiv x=0 \vee x=s(0)$$

$$Ex\,(x \neq s(0)) \equiv x=0 \vee \exists z\ x=s(z),\ Ex\,(z \neq 0) \equiv x=0 \vee \exists z\ x=s(z), \exists y\ z=s(y) \equiv x=0 \vee \exists y\ x=s(s(y))$$

The last step uses the obvious reduction

$$\exists z\ x=t, \exists y\ z=t' \equiv \exists y\ x=t\,[t'/z]$$

A simple way to implement *Ex* is achieved using the Horn clause definition of the inequality predicate *eq~* and querying it with appropriate goals. This technique is shown by the following example. Consider the Herbrand universe over constants a and b and the binary constructor f. The predicate*eq~* is defined by

eq~ (a,b) ←
eq~ (a, f(x,y)) ←
eq~ (b,a) ←
eq~ (b, f(x,y)) ←
eq~ (f(x,y), a) ←
eq~ (f(x,y), b) ←
eq~ (f(x,y), f(v,w)) ← *eq~* (x,v)
eq~ (f(x,y), f(v,w)) ← *eq~* (y,w).

Next, consider the negative guard $\forall y\ x \neq f(a,y)$. The solutions for x satisfying this guard can be obtained querying the above program with the goal ← *eq~* (x, f(a,*any*)) where *any* is a new constant symbol which acts as a *universal Skolem constant*. These solutions are x=a, x=b, x=f(b,y), x=f(f(y,z),w). The use of the constant *any* forces the failure of recursive calls like *eq~* (z,*any*), as in case (1) of the definition of *Ex*. Interpreting a solution like x=f(b,y) as $\exists y\ x=f(b,y)$ and taking the disjunction of all the solutions we obtain the formula $(x=a \vee x=b \vee \exists y\ x=f(b,y) \vee \exists yzw\ x=f(f(y,z),w))$ which is exactly $Ex\,(\forall y\ x \neq f(a,y))$.

The use of this implementation technique is twofold. Of course, it can be viewed as an implementation of the *Ex* transformation, as mentioned above. On the other hand, it can be used as the basis for a slight variant of intensional negation which directly replaces negative guards with appropriate calls of predicate *eq~* , possibly involving the *any* constant.

Referring back to the predicate *even~* of sec. 3.1., after step 2) of the transformation, i.e.

$$\forall x\ (\mathit{even\sim}(x) \Leftrightarrow \quad x{\neq}0, \forall y\ x{\neq}s(s(y)) \quad \vee$$
$$x{\neq}0, \exists y\ (x{=}s(s(y)), \mathit{even\sim}(y))\ )$$

the guards can be replaced by appropriate calls to predicates *eq* and *eq~* as follows

$$\forall x\ (\mathit{even\sim}(x) \Leftrightarrow \quad \mathit{eq\sim}(x,0), \mathit{eq\sim}(x, s(s(\mathit{any}))) \quad \vee$$
$$\mathit{eq\sim}(x,0), \mathit{eq}(x,s(s(y))), \mathit{even\sim}(y))\ ).$$

At last, the clausal definition of *even~* is

even~ (x) $\leftarrow$ *eq~* (x,0), *eq~* (x, s(s(*any*)))
even~ (x) $\leftarrow$ *eq~* (x,0), *eq* (x, s(s(y))), *even~* (y).

Finally, notice that this implementation technique is particularly useful in some application area of logic programming, such as deductive databases and expert systems, where the knowledge domain is likely to change dynamically. In such cases, using the standard form of intensional negation one is compelled to recompute the negative predicates whenever the knowledge domain changes, since the clauses for negative predicates embed the transformation of negative guards. On the other hand, the explicit use of predicates *eq* and *eq~* avoids this overall recomputation, since the redefinition of *eq* and *eq~* is only needed.

5. Conclusions

In [4] the formalization of intensional negation is carried out. The main results concern the soundness and completeness of SLDIN-resolution. The soundness theorem states that if the proof of *p~*(t) succeeds under SLDIN-resolution with answer substitution λ, then $\neg p(t\,\lambda)$ can be inferred under the negation as failure rule. This result implicitly gives the semantic equivalence between intensional negation and the negation as failure rule. On the other hand, if λ is a substitution such that $\neg p(t\lambda)$ can be inferred under the negation as failure rule, than the proof of *p~*(t) under SLDIN-resolution succeeds with a (possibly infinite) collection of answer substitutions $\{\lambda_i\}$such that each instance of $t\lambda$ can be obtained as an instance of $t\lambda_i$, for some i. If only left-linear programs are taken into account, this completeness result can be strenghtened, in the sense that the finiteness of the collection $\{\lambda_i\}$ is guaranteed. Roughly speaking, if non left-linear programs are the matter of concern, intensional negation makes use explicitly of the predicate *eq~* which in some cases gives an infinite set of solutions. As an example, consider the program

p(x, x) $\leftarrow$

defined over natural numbers. In order to compute its intensional negation, the clause is transformed into its semantically equivalent left-linear form

$p(x,y) \leftarrow eq(x,y)$

and than the computed definition for $p\sim$ is

$p\sim(x,y) \leftarrow eq\sim(x,y)$.

As shown in a previous example, the definition of $eq\sim$ in this case is

$eq\sim(0, s(x)) \leftarrow$

$eq\sim(s(x), 0) \leftarrow$

$eq\sim(s(x), s(y)) \leftarrow eq\sim(x, y)$.

Now, the proof of $\leftarrow p(x,s(x))$ finitely fails under standard SLD-resolution because of *occur checking*. On the other hand, the proof of $\leftarrow p\sim(x,s(x))$ under SLDIN-resolution diverges with answer substitutions x=0, x=s(0), x=s(s(0)),... since these are the substitutions computed by the derived goal $\leftarrow eq\sim(x, s(x))$.

The work described in the paper is only a first step of a larger and more ambitious research effort. The general aim of this effort could be summarized by the motto *putting logic theories together as a knowledge engineering tool*. This means providing a number of operators on logic theories capable, for example, of joining them, negating them and so forth. Such a set of operators along with constructs for composing them would provide a sound, formal tool for manipulating chunks of knowledge represented as logic programs.

The intensional negation we have proposed is only a small part of this overall construction. Indeed, the most needed extension is the possibility of writing general programs, in the sense of using the negation of the paper freely in building logic programs. This further extension, besides providing a fully usable operator for manipulating theories (for example with such an extension $p\sim\sim \equiv p$ can be proved) has some advantages *per se*. Indeed, as discussed in the paper, the evaluation of a goal p~(t) where t is a non-ground term leads to the computation of all the instances t' of t such that the proof of p(t') finitely fails. This possibility seems a notable extension to the expressive power of logic programming in that it allows queries of the form *all elements for which a certain property does not hold*. The extension seems to be of importance especially in deductive data bases applications and expert systems where the negative knowledge is essentially finite. Work done so far in this direction seems to point out that the computation rule SLDIN extends smoothly to the case of general programs.

Another drawback of intensional negation seems to be the inefficiency of the resulting programs. An open problem is the study of optimization techniques able to improve this situation.

References

[1] Ambriola,V., Giannotti,F., Pedreschi,D., Turini,F. "Symbolic Semantics and Program Reduction". **IEEE Trans. on Soft. Eng.** SE-11,8 (Aug.85) 784-794.

[2] Apt,K.R., Van Emden, M.H. "Contribution to the Theory of Logic Programming". **J.ACM**, 29, 3, (1982) 841-862.

[3] Aquilano,C., Barbuti,R., Bocchetti,P., Martelli,M. "Negation as Failure: Completeness of the Query Evaluation Process for Horn Clause Programs with Recursive Definitions".**Journal of Automated Reasoning**, 2 (1986) 155-170.

[4] Barbuti,R., Mancarella,P., Pedreschi,D., Turini,F. "Intensional Negation of Logic Programs". submitted for publication to the **Journal of Logic Programming** (1986).

[5] Barbuti,R., Martelli,M. "Completeness of the SLDNF-Resolution for a Class of Logic Programs". Proc. of 3rd Int. Conf. on Logic Programming, London, July 14-18 (1986).

[6] Barr,A., Feigenbaum,E.A. (Eds.) **The Handbook of Artificial Intelligence**. Vol.1, Pitman, London (1981).

[7] Clark,K.L. "Negation as Failure". in **Logic and Data Bases** (Gallaire, H. and Minker,J. Eds.) Plenum, New York (1978) 293-322.

[8] Gallaire,H., Minker,J., Nicolas,J.M. "Logic and Databases: a Deductive Approach". **ACM Comp.Surv.** 16,2 (June 1984) 153-186.

[9] Jaffar,J., Lassez,J.-L., Lloyd,J.W. "Completeness of the Negation-as-Failure Rule". Proc. 8th Int. Joint Conf. on Art. Int., Karlsruhe (1983) 500-506.

[10] Kowalski, R.A. **Logic for Problem Solving**. Elsevier North Holland, New York (1979).

[11] Kowalski, R.A. "Logic Programming". Proc. IFIP 83, Paris (1983) 133-145.

[12] Lassez,J.-L., Maher,M. "Closures and Fairness in the Semantics of Logic Programming". **TCS**, 29 (1984)

[13] Lassez,J.-L., Marriot,K. "Explicit and Implicit Representation of Terms Defined by Counter Examples". to appear in **Journal of Automated Reasoning**.

[14] Lloyd,J.W., Topor,R.W. "A Basis for Deductive Data Base Systems". **Journal of Logic Programming**, 2,2 (1985) 93-103.

[15] Lloyd,J.W., Topor,R.W. "A Basis for Deductive Data Base Systems II". **Journal of Logic Programming**, 1 (1986) 55-67.

[16] Lloyd,J.W. **Foundations of Logic Programming**. Springer Symbolic Computation Series, Berlin (1984).

[17] Reiter,R. "On Closed World Data Bases". in **Logic and Data Bases** (Gallaire, H. and Minker,J. Eds.) Plenum, New York (1978) 55-76.

[18] Sato,T., Tamaki,H. "Transformational Logic Program Synthesis". Proc. Conf. on Fifth Generation Computer Systems, (1984).

[19] Shepherdson,J.C. "Negation as Failure: a Comparison of Clark's Completed Data Bases and Reiter's Closed World Assumption". **Journal of Logic Programming**, 1,1 (1984) 51-79.

[20] Shepherdson,J.C. "Negation as Failure II". **Journal of Logic Programming**, 2,3 (1985) 185-202.

Improving the execution speed of compiled Prolog with modes, clause selection, and determinism

Peter Van Roy †

Katholieke Universiteit Leuven
Departement Computerwetenschappen
Celestijnenlaan 200A
B-3030 Heverlee
Belgium

Bart Demoen

BIM
Kwikstraat 4
B-3078 Everberg
Belgium

Yves D. Willems

Katholieke Universiteit Leuven
Departement Computerwetenschappen
Celestijnenlaan 200A
B-3030 Heverlee
Belgium

1. Introduction

Much Prolog code is deterministic or almost so. The searching capabilities of Prolog are only used in special situations. Many Prolog procedures consist of a number of clauses of which only one (or a few) can succeed at any call. In fact, some are in effect case statements. Too often this code is executed by the general mechanism of backtracking which has much overhead [Mellish 85]. But the backtracking performed in most cases is but a special case. It is usually called *shallow* backtracking because it stays with the parent's choice point.

We describe a novel method of compiling Prolog which avoids the general backtracking mechanism whenever possible. In particular, it increases the speed of shallow backtracking and avoids the creation of choice points. It is developed with the BIM-Prolog system [Demoen 86] in mind, but any Prolog based on the 'Warren Abstract Machine' described in [Warren 83], can benefit from it. In this report a familiarity with the so called WAM is assumed.

The method is based on three concepts: modes, deterministic clauses, and improved clause indexing. Our goal is to make shallow backtracking as cheap as possible without hindering the programmer. Creating choice points and selecting clauses by unification and failure are replaced, as much as possible, by completely deterministic testing and selection of clauses. The aim is to achieve an efficiency comparable to that of simple tests and indexed jumps in conventional languages. This is realised by:

(1) A new scheme for *clause indexing* which is efficient and smart. It avoids creating choice points whenever possible. It gives the programmer the freedom to define predicates in any way without loss of efficiency. The compiler determines how to use the procedure's arguments for selection of clauses.

(2) Taking advantage of *determinism* in clauses. Clause indexing not always narrows the possibilities down to a single clause. In that case, the combination of unification and general backtracking is replaced by simple tests, jumps and a quick restoration of

---

† presently at the Computer Science Division, Department of EECS, University of California at Berkeley, Berkeley, CA 94720.

state. We introduce a class of clauses for which this technique is extremely fast. A definition of deterministic clauses, covering much Prolog code, is given.

(3) Taking advantage of *mode* declarations of procedures. The Prolog programmer should add mode declarations wherever maximal execution speed is needed. Our mode definitions combine flexibility for the programmer with usefulness for the compiler. Note that we obtain improvements even whithout mode declarations.

(4) An extension of the abstract machine's instruction set to support the above three optimizations. The instruction set of [Warren 83] is extended in a logical way to gain the maximum advantage from indexing, determinism, and modes. Keeping an intermediate code rather than moving straight to assembly makes the operation of the abstract machine much clearer. A translation to assembly should give no problems because the new instructions are simpler than existing instructions.

(5) A modified compilation scheme for clauses and procedures. The existing compiler serves as a base to implement the improved scheme. The new clause and procedure are compilers largely independent. The main disadvantage of the scheme is the increase in the size of the generated code.

(6) The optimization was developed with the concept of *graceful degradation* in mind. As fewer and fewer of the conditions for an optimal compilation are fulfilled, the performance improvement decreases gracefully. But it remains significant. The maximum speedup is obtained for a procedure consisting only of deterministic clauses, with distinct head arguments and annotated with modes. But the speedups obtained when one or more of these three conditions are missing from some clauses is still significant.

The use of modes to increase performance is well known [Warren 77]. But the net performance improvement due only to the resulting speedup of unification is difficult to measure. This is because modes allow for other optimizations. According to several Prolog implementors the net improvement is in the neighborhood of 10%, but for nrev/2, the effect of modes is a factor of 3 in BIM-Prolog.

The performance improvement due to efficient clause indexing depends greatly on the particular procedure tested. Tests show that it reaches peaks of orders of magnitude for some search tasks.

Measurements were done to determine the performance improvements due to determinism alone. For a small procedure which can exploit it, a decrease in execution time of about 30% can be expected. This is the case for the procedure split/4 in Warren's quicksort benchmark [Warren 77]. An upper limit on the speed improvement is about a factor of 3. It is therefore clear that this optimization is promising.

The optimization of Prolog compilation has also been studied by Mellish [Mellish 85]. Especially the recognition of determinate predicates and the automatic generation of modes. Recognition of determinism is also addressed in [Sawamura & Takeshima 85] and generalised to the notion of functionality in [Debray & Warren 86a]. A better approach to automatic mode generation is in [Debray & Warren 86b] and is further improved upon in [Bruynooghe et al. 86]. The latter discusses some other optimizations based on information derived by abstract interpretation. That information on determinism and modes can help in closing the performance gap between Prolog and conventional languages is illustrated with a prototype of a very restricted language in [Bruynooghe & Weemeeuw 86]; a broader discussion is in [Bruynooghe 86].

This paper is a shortened and improved version of [Van Roy & Demoen 86]

2. Definitions

2.1. Definition of a try-block

A try-block is an ordered set of clauses which must be tried in sequence. It is usually implemented as a block of code starting with a try instruction, followed by retry instructions, and ending with a trust instruction:

```
try clause1
retry clause2
...
retry clauseM
trust clauseN
```

A try-block is a subset of the clauses of a procedure. The indexing algorithm of the compiler (section 4) attempts to reduce the set of clauses to be tried and passes control between clauses in a try-block by means of fast sequences of tests.

2.2. Definitions and notations for modes

In this section the rationale for the different modes is explained. Our goal is to obtain code consisting of a simple sequence of selections. Modes help in two ways: they tell which head arguments can be used to select against, and they help to determine if a clause is deterministic. We classify head arguments into four basic types. Either the programmer can tell the compiler the type of each argument, or the types can be inferenced automatically [Debray & Warren 86b]. Our modes are inspired by [Warren 77] and [Mellish 81]. The most important difference is the introduction of structured modes. These mode definitions can be compiled easily.

2.2.1. The basic modes

Our basic modes are listed in table 1.

Table 1: Notation for the basic modes

Mode	Synonyms			Characterization
Input	i	in	+	Main functor instantiated.
Output	o	out	-	Unbound variable which does not share.
Ground	g		++	Contains no variables.
Input-output	io	inout	?	All other cases.

2.2.2. Structured modes

To pinpoint more complex cases, structured modes are introduced. They are refinements of the input mode because they tell more about the main functor than mode input does. There are two structured modes.

s(M1, M2, ..., Mn)

where Mi is any mode, and n is the arity. This mode is only used for clauses where the head argument is any structure (except a list) of arity n. This mode says that the argument is instantiated at run time to an n-ary structure whose ith component has mode Mi.

l(M1, M2)

where M1 and M2 are any modes. The actual argument must be a list, with the modes M1 and M2 for its head and tail.

2.3. Definition of a test

A procedure call Q in a procedure P :- ... , Q , ... is a test if execution of Q

(1) does not cause side-effects

(2) does not create choicepoints

(3) only binds variables local to clause P and Q

(4) does not create structures on the heap.

In a similar spirit, unifications in the head of the procedure P can be classified into test or non-tests, depending on whether they satisfy conditions (3) and (4). Q being a test is a dynamic notion because it depends on the instantiation pattern of the call to P. The class of tests can be extended in various ways by relaxing (3) and (4). In our current system, only calls to certain built-ins are recognised as tests.

2.4. Definition of a deterministic clause

If, by executing only tests, control can reach a point in a clause - the commit point - such that all following, yet untried clauses can be discarded without affecting the outcome of the computation (they will fail without side-effects) then that clause is a deterministic clause. Our notion of deterministic clause is very pragmatic, for a more principled one see [Debray & Warren 86a]. Whether a clause is deterministic or not can depend on different factors:

(1) The clause itself. A cut in the body of the clause, preceded only by tests, makes the clause deterministic.

(2) On the procedure of which the clause is a part and its mode. If it is possible to show that the form of the *input* or *ground* arguments and the tests of a clause C are such that none of the following clauses can be entered beyond their tests, then inserting a cut after the tests of C does not alter in any way the meaning of the procedure. So C is a deterministic clause. The *input-output* and *output* arguments' values do not have any influence.

(3) The actual arguments of a call. They can be such that the following clauses cannot unify with them. For example, if an input argument is a constant, and all following clauses have a structure in the head, then the clause is deterministic for constants.

Example:

```
:-mode(i,i).
h(a, _x) :- test(_x), !, ...
h(a, _x) :- ...
h(b, _x) :- ...
h(b, f(3)) :- ...
```

The first clause is deterministic because of the cut (1).

The second clause is deterministic because of (2): if the input argument matches 'a', it cannot match 'b'. The second clause can be replaced by:

```
h(a, _x) :- !, ...
```

The third clause is deterministic if the second argument at the call is a constant or a list (3). If the second argument is a structure then the third clause is not deterministic.

The fourth clause is deterministic because it is the last clause (2).

2.5. Definition of the head of a deterministic clause

If there exists a (real or imaginary) *cut* operator preceded by tests only, then the *head* of a deterministic clause is considered to include all tests up to the cut operation.

3. Compilation of a single clause

The method sketched in this section is an extension of the code generation for WAM in [Van Roy 84].

3.1. The entry points

We take advantage of deterministic clauses and delay the creation of a choice point. This requires extra entry points: a single clause can have up to four entry points.

Determinism and nondeterminism of the clause

A clause can be contained in many try-blocks. Whether or not a clause is deterministic depends on the particular try-block. Some clauses are always deterministic, for example those with a cut as first goal and only input arguments. Other clauses are only deterministic in some try-blocks. Being deterministic or not depends on different factors: the clause itself, all clauses in the procedure, the modes, and the try-block considered. See section 2.

Different actions are necessary in the two cases. A nondeterministic clause may need to create a choice point, whereas a deterministic clause never needs to do this. A clause therefore needs two entries: one where it is considered as deterministic, and one where it is nondeterministic.

The existence of a choice point

At the entry of a clause, there may or may not be a choice point created by a previous clause of the same procedure. Different actions are necessary in these two cases as well. A comitted deterministic clause must remove the choice point if it exists. A nondeterministic clause has to change the retry address of the choice point if it exists. Otherwise it must set up the choice point itself. Therefore the two entries, deterministic and nondeterministic, must each be split into two parts: with or without a choice point.

The four entry points

(1) A deterministic entry with choice point *(det-cp)*,
(2) A deterministic entry without choice point *(det-nocp)*,
(3) A nondeterministic entry with choice point *(nondet-cp)*,
(4) A nondeterministic entry without choice point *(nondet-nocp)*.

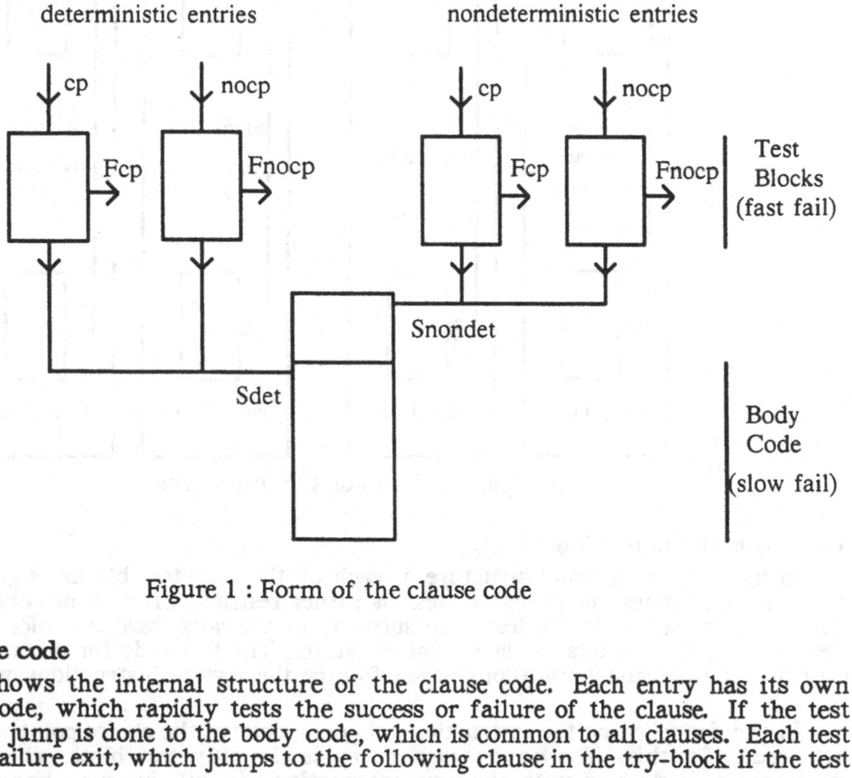

Figure 1 : Form of the clause code

3.2. The clause code

Figure 1 shows the internal structure of the clause code. Each entry has its own block of test code, which rapidly tests the success or failure of the clause. If the test succeeds then a jump is done to the body code, which is common to all clauses. Each test block has one failure exit, which jumps to the following clause in the try-block if the test fails.

Kinds of failure

As can be seen from figure 1, there are three kinds of failure. There are two basic kinds of failure:

(1) Fnocp: fast failure, no choice point: failure consists of restoring some registers and jumping to the *nocp* entry of the next clause (if there is no next clause, a special label initiates a slow failure).

(2) Fcp : fast fail, choice point exists: failure consists of restoring some registers and jumping to the *cp* entry of the next clause.

In the nondeterministic case, no registers need to be restored because of a peculiarity of the *nondet* test blocks. This, as well as the Sdet and Snondet entries in the body, will be clarified in section 3.3 and 3.4.

(3) Slow failure : if the body fails, then the slow standard backtracking is initiated. The retry address is the *cp* entry of the next clause.

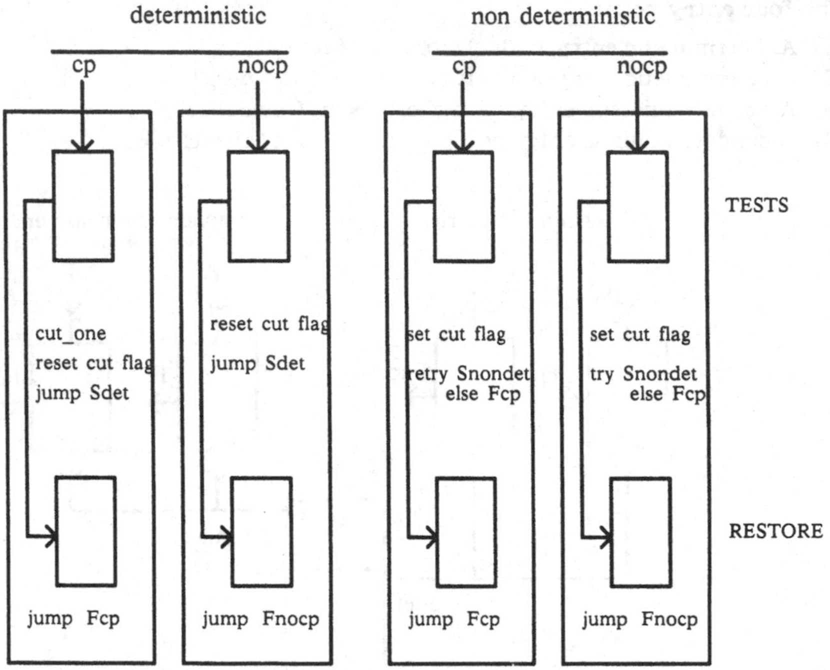

Figure 2 : Form of the test blocks

3.3. Form of the test blocks

In figure 2 the internal structure of each of the four test blocks is given. For non-deterministic entries, the notion of 'test' is rather restricted: it may not change any registers. This is because if the test code succeeds in the *nocp* case, a choice point must be created with all registers in their *original* state. The test code for deterministic entries may do bindings and unifications: upon failure the restore instructions will restore the state.

In the *det-cp* entry the instruction cut_one removes the choice point. The cut flag is not needed for this. The *nondet-nocp* entry is the only test block which can create a choice point. It does so with the 'try' instruction. It will jump to *Fcp* if it created a choicepoint, otherwise to *Fnocp*. In the *nondet-cp* entry the 'retry' instruction updates the retry address of the existing choice point.

The cut flag is not needed in the test blocks since the presence or absence of the choice point is known upon entry. The cut flag is needed only for cuts in the body. If the body contains no cuts then it is not needed at all. If needed, it can be set or reset in the test blocks just before the body code is entered.

3.4. Form of the body code

Consider the body code in figure 1. It has two entries from the *det* and *nondet* test blocks, denoted by the labels *Snondet* and *Sdet*. The reason for this is the difference in the tests which can be done by the *det* and *nondet* test blocks.

A *nondet* test block may not alter any registers. Therefore only a small part of the head is allowed in the test block. The other part of the head is included in the body code from *Snondet* to *Sdet*.

A *det* test block can contain all code of the head, including any bindings. If the tests succeed, only the code in the body which comes after the head needs to be done. Therefore a jump to *Sdet* is done,to avoid executing the same code twice.

3.5. More details about the clause code

The interaction of clause and procedure compilation is minimal. The procedure compiler only needs to know whether the clause occurs in one or more try-blocks, because this has an effect on the method of determining the failure addresses Fnocp and Fcp.

In ordinary WAM code, it is necessary to set up an environment with the *allocate* instruction before accessing permanent variables. A simple modification of the instruction set makes it possible to use permanent variables in the head of a clause without having to execute *allocate* first. Permanent variables are normally accessed from the E register, which points to the current environment. If E is not available (*allocate* has not yet been executed), then it is still possible to access permanent variables by using the A register if it points correctly to the top of stack. This idea can be used to delay *allocate* until after the test blocks.

All registers and arguments of structures have a mode. The mode of a variable depends on the instruction in which it first occurs. The mode can change during execution of the head code, as the variable becomes more instantiated. This means that each instruction exists in several versions, annotated with the arguments' mode(s).

3.6. An example of clause compilation

To illustrate the above considerations, consider the clause:

```
:-mode(i,i,o).
diff(_u+_v, _x, _du+_dv) :-
      atom(_x), !,
      diff(_u, _x, _du),
      diff(_v, _x, _dv).
```

The final code generated (which corresponds to figures 1 and 2) is given in an instruction set which is a variation of [Warren 83]. It is self-explanatory in most cases. The *save* and *restore* instructions will save and restore registers. The *calltest* and *get_struc_in* instructions execute a test, but instead of doing a general fail operation they simply jump to a label upon failure.

```
{*** Deterministic entry cp ***}
det_cp:
      get_struc_in          +/2, X1, label3
      unify_var_in          X4
      unify_var_in_A        Y3
      get_var_in_A          Y2, X2
      save                  X1  {<- save instruction inserted}
      put_val               X2, X1
      calltest              atom/1, label2 {<- label added to test}
      get_struc_out         +/2, X3
      unify_var_out         X3
      unify_var_out_A       Y1
      cut_one                                  {Remove one choice point}
      jump                  Sdet

label2:
      restore               X1
label1:
      jump                  Fcp

{*** Deterministic entry nocp ***}
det_nocp:
      (code identical to deterministic entry cp, except no cut_one)
label4:
      restore               X1
label1:
      jump                  Fnocp

{*** Nondeterministic entry cp ***}
nondet_cp:
      get_struc_in     +/2, X1, label5
      retry            Snondet else Fcp
label5:
      jump             Fcp

{*** Nondeterministic entry nocp ***}
nondet_nocp:
      (code analogous to nondet_cp)

{*** Body code nondet entry ***}
Snondet:
      unify_var_in          X4
      unify_var_in_A        Y3
      get_var_in_A          Y2, X2
      put_val               X2, X1
      call                  atom/1
      get_struc_out         +/2, X3
      unify_var_out         X3
      unify_var_out_A       Y1
      cut_first
```

```
{*** Body code det entry ***}
Sdet:
        put_val         X4, X1
        put_val_A       Y2, X2
        allocate
        call            diff/3, 3
        put_val         Y3, X1
        put_val         Y2, X2
        put_val         Y1, X3
        deallocate
        execute         diff/3
```

This example shows the kind of code explosion which is possible. Often a significant code reduction can be done by removing superfluous code. Such is the case here. For example, since this clause is deterministic the two *nondet* entries along with the *nondet* part of the body code can be removed.

4. Compilation of a procedure

The compilation of a procedure is done in two steps: (1) generation of the selection code and (2) generation of the try-blocks.

4.1. The selection tree

Information (e.g. mode) and assumptions about the actual arguments can be used to reduce the set of clauses to be tried. Different assumptions lead to different sets. Each set gives rise to a try-block. Selection of the proper try-block is done by the selection code which checks which assumptions are valid. Three kinds of information are used:

(1) The types (tags) and values of the actual arguments.

(2) The modes of the procedure.

(3) The head arguments of all the clauses.

The code which does the selection has the form of an n-ary tree: the *selection tree*. The tree has two kinds of nodes and one kind of leaf. The nodes do the selection. Both kinds of nodes will do a selection based on the contents of an argument register. The leaves try sequentially the sets of clauses which remain. Each branch of the tree has two attributes: the set of clauses still possible, and the set of argument registers yet to be considered.

(1) The *switch node* does a four-way branch depending on the type of an argument (variable, list, constant, or structure).

(2) The *hash node* does a multi-way branch depending on the value of an argument. The possible arguments are a series of constants or structures. The selection is done according to a hash table.

(3) Each *leaf* has one attribute: the set of clauses remaining after the selection.

The execution of a procedure call begins at the root of the selection tree. The root node does the first selection. Execution continues down the tree with further selection at the nodes until a leave is reached.

4.1.1. A simple example of selection

Consider the procedure:

```
:-mode(i,i).
h(a, _x) :- test, !, ...
h(a, _x) :- ...
h(b, _x) :- ...
h(b, f(3)) :- ...
```

The resulting code is:

```
        switch_on_argument 1
        var:        fail
        const:      c_lbl
        list:       fail
        struc:      fail

c_lbl:
        hash_on_constant 1
        a           a_lbl
        b           b_lbl

a_lbl:                      {try clauses 1 and 2}
        try_block           {C1,C2}   {code for try-block explained later}
b_lbl:
        switch_on_argument 2
        var:        fail
        const:      clause3
        list:       clause3
        struc:      s_lbl

s_lbl:                      {try clauses 3 and 4}
        try_block           {C3,C4}
```

4.2. The try-block

4.2.1. The structure of a try-block

An entry of a clause can be a member of one or more try-blocks. If it occurs in only one try-block (a *single* occurrence clause) then fixed failure addresses *Fcp* and *Fnocp* can be compiled in the clause to try the next clause. If it occurs in more than one try-block (a *multiple* occurrence entry) then indirect jumps via a new global register (called *T*) must be compiled. The T register points to a table of *Fnocp-Fcp* address pairs. Each try-block has its own table. A correct, but not optimal, place to increment T, is in the beginning of each clause.

A try-block may contain a mixture of single or multiple occurrence clauses. This gives no problems. The address table only needs entries for the multiple occurrence clauses. If most clauses are single occurrence then the address tables will be short.

A try-block may contain a mixture of deterministic and nondeterministic clauses. This also is easily handled: for deterministic clauses use the *det* entries of the clause and for nondeterministic clauses use the *nondet* entries.

The execution of a try-block starts with the *nocp* entry of the first clause. If it fails then a jump is done to the *cp* or *nocp* entries of the following clause, depending on whether the choice point was created or not. The goal is to avoid creating the choice point as long as possible, by testing and failing in a simple way. As long as the choice point is not needed execution will jump from *nocp* entry to *nocp* entry. When a simple test and fail is not possible the choice point will be created. From then on the following clauses are entered through the *cp* entries. This pattern of execution is shown in figure 3. Execution starts at the *nocp* entry of clause 1, which is nondeterministic. Clause 3 is deterministic. All other clauses are nondeterministic.

A deterministic clause cannot create a choice point. If it is entered at the *nocp* entry, then the next clause will also be tried at the *nocp* entry. Therefore the goal of delaying the creation of a choice point as long as possible will be achieved better if there are many deterministic clauses in the try-block, and if the first clauses are deterministic.

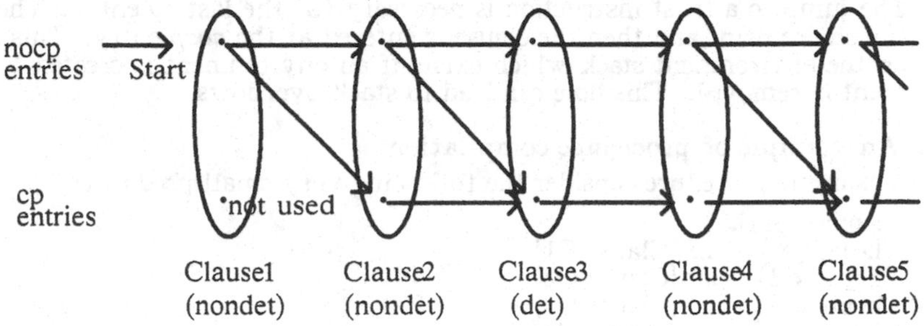

Figure 3 : Execution of a try-block

4.2.2. Compilation scheme of the try-block

The code for all try-blocks is generated together. This is necessary because clauses can be single or multiple occurrence. The existence of multiple occurrence clauses means that the try-blocks influence each other.

(1) Determine for each clause the number of try-blocks its *nondet* and *det* entries are in. This results in counts for *nondet* and *det* entries which must be kept separate.

(2) Generate code for each clause according to the scheme in section 3. If the *det* entries are used in only one try-block then they are compiled with fixed failure addresses *Fcp* and *Fnocp*. If they occur in more than one try-block then indirect jumps via the T register are compiled. The same is done for the *nondet* entries. This is the only interaction between procedure and clause compilation.

(3) For each try-block create a table of *Fcp-Fnocp* address pairs of all the multiple occurrence clauses in the try-block. The single occurrence clauses do not occur in the table.

(4) Generate code to load the T register with the address of the table, and to jump to the first *nocp* entry in the table. For each try-block this results in code of the form:

```
start_try:      {Start of try-block's code}
      move      #table_try, T
      jump      nocp_clause1

table_try:      {Table of address pairs}
      nocp_clause2,  cp_clause2
      ...
      nocp_clauseN,  last_clause
      fail,          trust_fail

last_clause:    {Remove choice point for last clause}
      trust     det_nocp_clauseN
```

The table starts with the second clause. The address of the first clause is in the jump instruction. The two special labels *fail* and *trust_fail* have the following actions: *fail* will perform a general fail operation, *trust_fail* will remove the choice point and then perform a general fail operation.

The jump to a trust instruction is necessary for the last *cp* entry. The trust removes the choice point and then the clause is entered at the *nocp* entry. This avoids the hole on the environment stack which exists if an environment is created before the choice point is removed. This hole can lead to stack overflows.

4.3. An example of procedure compilation

As an example procedure consider the following very small predicate:

```
:-mode(i, i).
h(aa, _y)  :- ...  {Clause C1}
h(_x, dd) :- ...  {Clause C2}
h(bb, ee)  :- ...  {Clause C3}
h(_x, _y) :- ...  {Clause C4}
h(cc, _y)  :- ...  {Clause C5}
```

The procedure compilation of this predicate is done in two steps. The first step will give the selection tree which reduces the number of clauses to be tried. The second step compiles the try-blocks which try only those clauses. The selection code for this procedure is:

```
        switch_on_argument 1
        var:      fail          {because input mode}
        const:    lbl_C1        {clauses left to try: all clauses}
        list:     lbl_L1        {clauses left to try: C2, C4}
        struc:    lbl_S1        {clauses left to try: C2, C4}

{*** Constant Label ***}
lbl_C1:
        hash_on_constant 1
        aa        lbl_aa        {clauses left to try: C1, C2, C4}
        bb        lbl_bb        {clauses left to try: C2, C3, C4}
        cc        lbl_cc        {clauses left to try: C2, C4, C5}
        else      lbl_L1        {clauses left to try: C2, C4}

        ....

{*** List Label ***}
lbl_L1:
        switch_on_argument 2
        var:      fail          {because input mode}
        const:    try_24        {clauses left to try: C2, C4}
        list:     try_4         {clause left to try: C4}
        struc:    try_4         {clause left to try: C4}

{*** Structure Label ***}
lbl_S1:
        (code identical to list label)
```

Only label lbl_bb is worth expanding further, we leave it as an exercise. After the selection what remains are the following try-blocks:

```
{C4}
{C1, C4}
{C2, C4}
{C3, C4}
{C4, C5}
{C1, C2, C4}
{C2, C4, C5}
```

Now we must determine for each clause the number of try-blocks its *det* and *nondet* entries are in. This is easily found by inspection, giving:

Clause C1: *nondet* entry occurs twice, as first clause.
Clause C2: *nondet* entry occurs twice as first and once as second clause.
Clause C3: *nondet* entry occurs once, as first clause.
Clause C4: *nondet* entry occurs twice, *det* entry five times.
Clause C5: *det* entry occurs twice, as last clause.

All the clauses' other *det* or *nondet* entries are not needed. Only clause C3 will be compiled with fixed failure addresses because it is the only single occurrence clause. All other clauses are compiled with indirection. Now we can combine what we know to generate the code for the try-blocks:

```
try_4:
      move            #table_4, T
      jump            det_nocp_C4
table_4:
      fail,           nop (trust_fail not needed)

      .... (code for try_14)
      .... (code for try_24)

try_34:
      move            #table_34, T
      jump            nondet_nocp_C3       {C3 will jump to C4}
table_34:
      fail,           trust_fail

      .... (code for try_45, try_124)

try_245:
      move            #table_245, T
      jump            nondet_nocp_C2
table_245:
      nondet_nocp_C4,    nondet_cp_C4
      det_nocp_C5,    lastclause_245
      fail,           nop (trust_fail not needed)
lastclause_245:
      trust           det_nocp_C5
```

The code for the whole procedure consists of the selection code, the try-block code, and the clause code. This example shows a code multiplication similar to that of clause code. To reduce the amount of code it is possible to combine overlapping code segments in many places, for example the code segments which start with lbl_L1 and lbl_S1. Try-blocks which overlap in their last parts can also be combined.

5. Evaluation of the optimizations

In this section a number of simulated benchmark results are presented. The measurements are rough, but useful enough to decide whether the optimizations are worth the effort. The timings show that when the optimizations are applicable they can give significant performance improvements. We were not able to measure the speed improvement of all three optimizations taken together.

5.1. Effects of determinism

The speed improvement due only to the exploitation of deterministic clauses is measured. The main improvements of deterministic clauses are the elimination of choice point creation and general fail operations.

Total execution time is measured using the average times for each instruction. These times are taken from the PLM performance article [Dobry 85]. This gives a rough but useful indication of the speedup to be expected.

5.1.1. Results on the split/4 benchmark

Measured was the total execution time of the procedure split/4 in Warren's quicksort benchmark [Warren 77]. The results are:

Speedup (unoptimized code has no environment): x 1.35
Speedup (unoptimized code has an environment): x 1.43

Number of machine cycles:

30260 for the old split (with environment),
28610 for the old split (without environment),
21230 for the new split.

The distinction between having or not having an environment is a consequence of the fact that in split/4 the cut flag has not been altered before the cut is encountered. Therefore no environment is needed for the cut. A smart compiler could recognize this and compile a special cut instruction which looks at the global cut flag instead of at the cut flag in the environment.

5.1.2. Results on the minimum/3 benchmark

Using the following definition:

```
min_list([_x], _x).
min_list([_x|_l], _m) :-
        min_list(_l, _y),
        minimum(_x, _y, _m).

:-mode(i,i,o).
minimum(_a, _b, _a) :- _a<_b, !.
minimum(_a, _b, _b).
```

find the minimum of the 50-element list used in Warren's quicksort benchmark. The total execution time of minimum/3 is measured using the same method as for split/4. The result is a speedup of a factor of 2.6.

Number of machine cycles:

3790 for the old minimum,
1470 for the new minimum.

No environment is needed for minimum/3. This is an extreme case in the sense that the bodies of the clauses are very small, so the elimination of try and fail will have a proportionally large effect. Therefore it gives an idea of the upper bound of the speedup.

5.2. Effects of clause indexing

The procedure *borders* from the Chat80 program [Warren 82] is improved by two orders of magnitude when clause selection is done on more arguments than just the first. Further measurements were not done for lack of time.

5.3. Effects of modes

The speed improvement due to modes alone (the speedup of unification), disregarding any other optimization made possible by modes is in the neighborhood of 10%. This is an intuitive figure cited by the implementors of BIM-Prolog. More exact measurements were not done because of lack of time to disentangle the influence of modes on other optimizations.

6. Acknowledgements

We would like to thank all the members of the Prolog research group at the university of Leuven for the congenial atmosphere. We thank especially Andre Marien and Alain Callebaut for many fruitful discussions and Maurice Bruynooghe for numerous suggestions to improve the final version of this paper.

This research was sponsored by grant KBAR/SOFT/1 from the Belgian 'Dienst voor Programmatie van het Wetenschapsbeleid' and by Defense Advanced Research Projects Agency (DOD) Arpa Order No. 4871, monitored by Space & Naval Systems Warfare Command under Contract No. N00039-84-C-0089.

7. References

Bruynooghe M., *Is logic programming real programming*, in Proc. AIMSA86, eds. Ph. Jourrand, V. Sgurev, Varna, sept. 1986, North Holland, in print

Bruynooghe M., Weemeeuw P., *Towards more efficiency of Prolog on conventional hardware*, Report CW 45, Dept. of Computer Science, K.U.Leuven.

Bruynooghe M., Demoen B., Callebaut A. and Janssens G., *Abstract interpretation at work*, Draft report, Dept. of Computer Science, K.U.Leuven.

Debray S.K., Warren D.S., *Detection and optimization of functional computations in Prolog*, Proc. 3th Int. Conf. on Logic Programming., London, july 1986, 490-504.

Debray S.K., Warren D.S., *Automatic mode inference for Prolog programs*, Proc. 1986 Symposium on Logic Programming, Salt Lake City, sept 1986, 78-88.

Demoen, B., *BIM-Prolog Manual*, BIM, Kwikstraat 4, B-3078 Everberg Belgium, 1986.

Dobry, T. et al, *Performance Studies of a Prolog Machine Architecture*, Proc. 12th Int. Symp. Comp. Arch., June 1985.

Mellish, C.S., *The Automatic Generation of Mode Declarations for Prolog Programs*, Research Report 163, Dept. of Artificial Intelligence, Univ. of Edinburgh, 1981.

Mellish, C.S., *Some Global Optimizations for a Prolog compiler*, J. Logic Programming, pp. 43-66, Vol. 1, 1985.

Sawamura H., Takeshima T., *Recursive unsolvability of determinacy, solvable cases of determinacy and their applications to Prolog optimization*, Proc. 1985 Symposium on Logic Programming, Boston, july 1985, 200-207.

Van Roy, P., *A Prolog Compiler for the PLM*, Report No. UCB/CSD 84/203, Univ. of California, Berkeley, Nov. 1984.

Van Roy, P., Demoen, B., *Improving the execution speed of compiled Prolog with modes, clause selection, and determinism.* CW Report No. 51, K.U.Leuven, Dept. of Comp. Sc., nov. 1986.

Warren, D.H.D., *Applied Logic - Its use and implementation as a programming tool*, Ph.D. Thesis, Univ. of Edinburgh, 1977. Reprinted as Technical Note 290, SRI International, 1983.

Warren, D.H.D., *An Efficient Easily Adaptable System for Interpreting Natural Language Queries*, American Journal of Computational Linguistics, pp. 110-122, Vol. 8, 1982.

Warren, D.H.D., *An Abstract Prolog Instruction Set*, AI Center, SRI International, Menlo Park CA 94025, 1983.

SIMULATION RESULTS OF A MULTIPROCESSOR PROLOG ARCHITECTURE BASED ON A DISTRIBUTED AND/OR GRAPH

C. Percebois, I. Futó, I. Durand, C. Simon, B. Bonhoure
Laboratoire "Langages et Systèmes Informatiques"
Université Paul Sabatier
118, route de Narbonne - 31062 Toulouse Cedex - France

ABSTRACT

This paper summarizes the principal results of the simulation of the COALA (Calculateur Orienté Acteurs pour la Logique et ses Applications) machine : an Actor-Oriented Computer for Logic and its Applications.

The simulation was supported by two basic software systems : a functional simulator simulating the functional aspects of the distributed interpreter written in PASCAL and a system simulator written in T-PROLOG, a simulation language based on PROLOG.

The system simulator enabled us to obtain the duration of execution of PROLOG programs executed on the COALA machine and to compare the effects of various numbers of processing elements and various network topologies on the overall performance of COALA.

1 - THE AND/OR CONNECTION GRAPH MODEL

Several execution models for parallel inference processing have been proposed such as data-flow models [AMA 84], AND-OR process models [CON 85] and reduction models [ONA 85]. In models which handle AND-parallelism, the consistency of solutions poses certain problems : most of these models rely upon the sequential AND/OR tree and handle the tree in a parallel fashion. A constraining and difficult process management technique is required to synchronize processes associated with the nodes of the AND/OR tree. As a result of this process management, a hierarchical tree structure, where process communication is based on data sharing, is necessary.

Inspired by R. Kowalski's connection graph [KOW 79], our model represents a new perspective on the parallel interpretation of PROLOG. This connection graph includes one arc for each pair of matching atoms on opposite sides of the implication symbol in different clauses. Associated with each arc is the resolvent obtained by resolving the atom connected by the arc.

In the sequential model [KOW 79], the selection of an arc connected to a goal and the generation of the associated resolvent form together what is called a resolution step. In such a step, the selected arc is deleted and new arcs are added connecting atoms of the resolvent to the rest of the graph.

Clearly, in a parallel model [PER 86], both AND and OR parallelisms are related to the simultaneous treatment of several arcs : OR-parallelism is obtained by the parallel selection and resolution of the arcs descending from the same literal ; AND-parallelism arises from the simultaneous unification on the arcs descending from all the literals of the clauses connected by the arc chosen for the resolution.

Example : Let us consider the following graph :

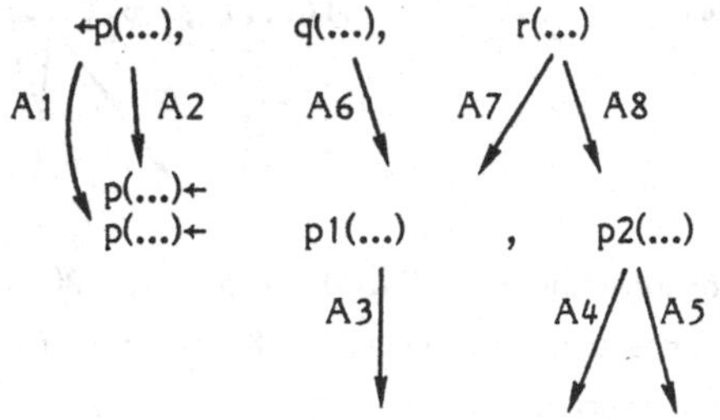

If the leftmost literal p is chosen for the resolution, arcs A1 and A2 are activated and each one produces a resolvent. For the resolvent of arc A1, the new arcs are built from arcs A3, A4, A5, A6, A7 and A8 ; for arc A2, from arcs A6, A7 and A8.

Resolvent of arc A1 :

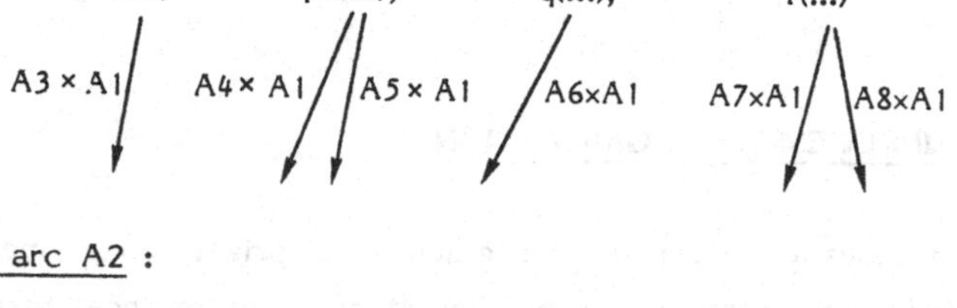

Resolvent of arc A2 :

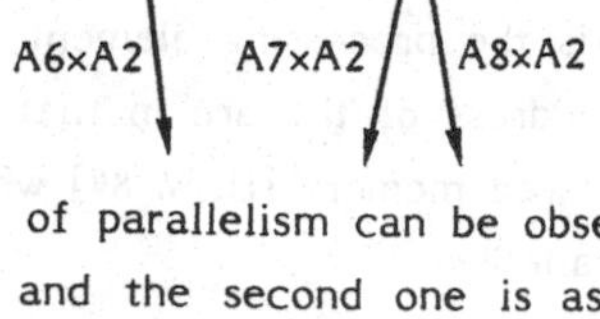

Two levels of parallelism can be observed : the first one appears when building different resolvents and the second one is associated with the creation of different arcs for each resolvent. These two levels correspond respectively to OR and AND parallelisms ; however, in our model, they are processed in the same way.

A precompilation of the source PROLOG program generates the initial connection graph. To represent the graph, we have simply to represent each of its arcs. An arc connects two parent clauses, the "origin clause" and the "extremity clause", and knows its unification environment and the list of the arcs descending from the extremity clause called "son arcs". Arcs descending from other literals in the origin clause, called "brother arcs", will be communicated to the literal chosen for the resolution, when latter is selected.

Thus, in the graph :

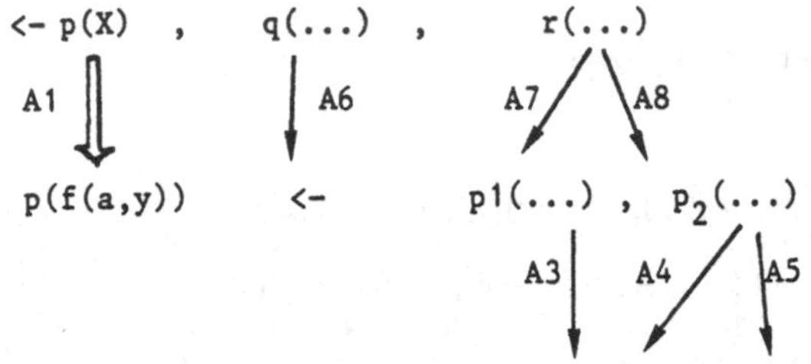

<- p(X), q(...), r(...) is the origin clause, p(f(a,y)) <- p1(...), p2(...) is the extremity one ; A3, A4 and A5 are the son arcs and A6, A7 and A8 are the brother arcs. Arc A1 is implemented by the following structure :

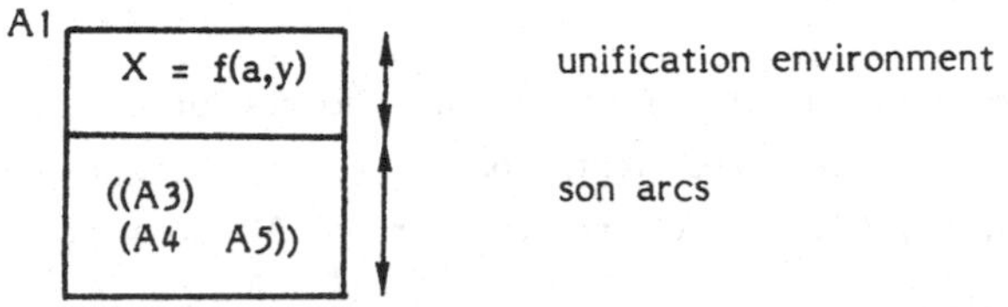

In this very simple data structure, it is no longer necessary to store the literal names.

2 - THE COALA MULTIPROCESSOR ORGANIZATION

Each processor possesses one part of the graph in a private local memory called "Graph Memory". Globally, the memory can be viewed as a set of local memories [KEL 79, MAG 80]. An arc of the graph can reference other distant arcs. This reference must be a tuple of the form (PE, address) where "PE" is the processing element whose memory contains the referenced arc and "address" is the address of the arc in that local memory. This solution suppresses the bottleneck due to a shared memory [HEW 84] where contention effectively swamps the benefits obtained from parallelism.

In the same way, the task queue from which processors seek eventual processing is distributed among the processing elements, like the graph. This avoids the bottleneck encountered when using a centralized task queue. If a processor needs to access an arc residing in another memory, it forms a request packet containing the address of the arc, the type of operation sought, and various parameters if required [KEL 79]. The general structure of a request packet is given by the following figure :

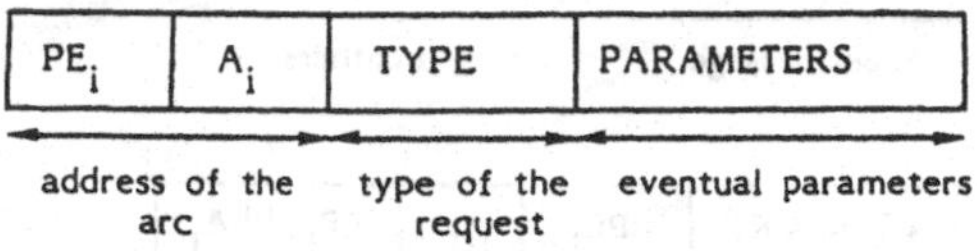

An incoming message is interpreted by the processing element specified in the address of the arc. The dialogue between processing elements is taken into account by switches which deal with the routing of packets.

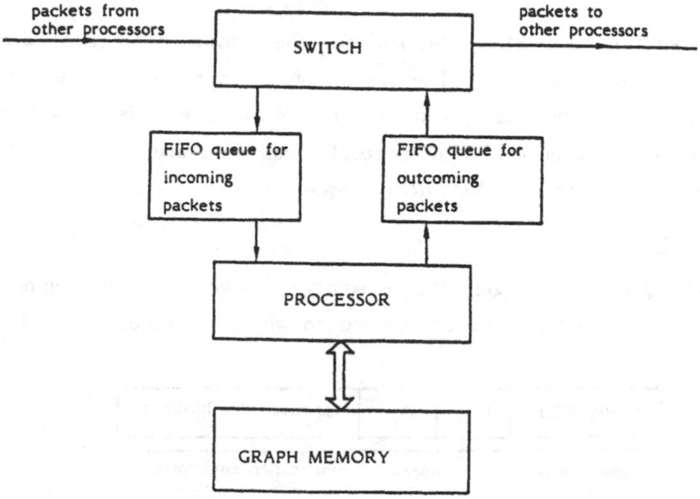

Figure 1 - General organization of the COALA machine

Conceptually, the topology of the communication network can be arbitrary, but must obviously ensure the reliable transmission of messages from one processor to another.

3 - COMMUNICATION BETWEEN PROCESSING ELEMENTS

The messages of the model are directly related to the basic operations of a PROLOG interpreter : resolution and unification.

3.1 - Resolution

At every step of the resolution, a literal is selected for resolution. A RESOLVE-REQ request is sent to each arc descending from this literal. This request contains the identification of all brother arcs of the selected literal, so as the ensure the upkeep of the graph. The arc receiving this request sends its unification environment to each of its sons and brothers through UNIFY-REQ requests. The replies corresponding to the UNIFY-REQ requests are either UNIFY-ACK in case of success, or UNIFY-NACK in case of failure.

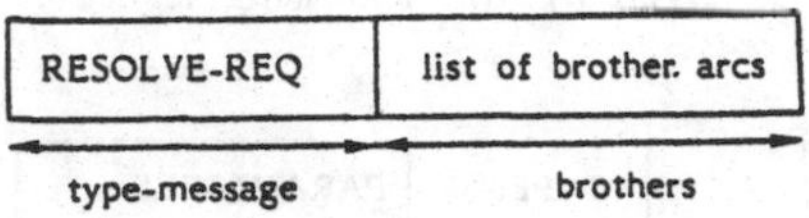

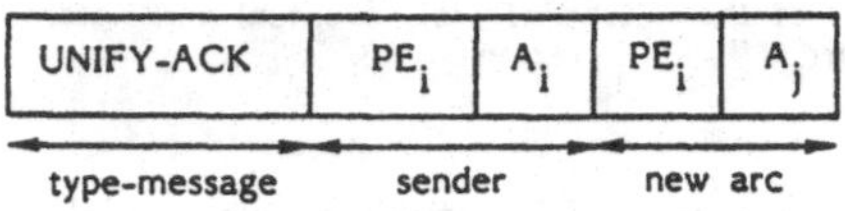

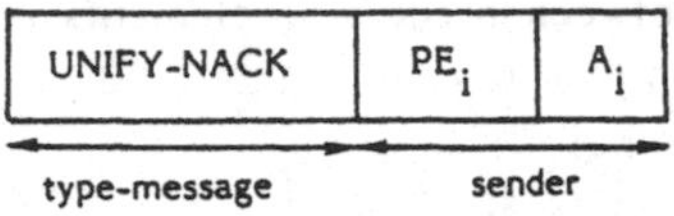

When a resolvent is successfully determined, the resolution proceeds with the selection of a new literal to be resolved. The resolution of an arc having neither brother nor son corresponds to the empty clause. Thus an arc's environment is a solution to the initial problem. The arcs created for an unsuccessful resolvent are garbage collected by use of a third request type called DESTROY-REQ request.

3.2 - Unification

The UNIFY-REQ request triggers the unification between two environments : the environment in the request and the one of the arc to which the request is addressed.

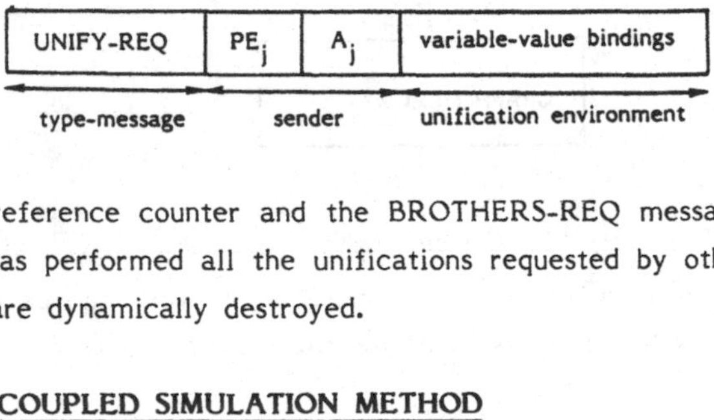

By use of a reference counter and the BROTHERS-REQ message, an arc is garbage collected once it has performed all the unifications requested by other arcs. Thus, all the arcs of the graph are dynamically destroyed.

4 - A STRONGLY COUPLED SIMULATION METHOD

The first step of the simulation process was the realization of a functional simulator which simulates the functional aspects of the distributed interpreter. During this step, neither the impact of inter-processor communication nor network topology were taken into account. Written in PASCAL, the functional simulator executes program statements sequentially. This simulator enables one to obtain the duration of execution of messages on a MC68000 (10 MHz) microprocessor. The duration of execution of a message is the number of MC68000 cycles required to handle the message, where the base cycle time is 10^{-7} s.

In order to validate the COALA machine, it was necessary to compare the impact of different numbers of processors (supposed here to be MC68000) and different network topologies on the machine's overall performance. Thus, the second step of the simulation process was the production of a system simulator. Written in T-PROLOG [FUT 84], a simulation language based on PROLOG, the system simulator assigns a process to each of the processors and executes the PROLOG program taking into account the duration of execution of messages, the state of the communication channels (busy/free) and the state of the processors (busy/free).

The T-PROLOG primitives such as new (create a process), send (send a message), wait-for (wait for a message) and hold (suspend a process) are used for communicating messages between processors and to simulate the elapsed time.

Finally, the general scheme of the simulation of COALA is given in Figure 2. Both simulators are running on a VAX 11/780. The functional simulator, in addition, runs on an SM-90 computer for MC68000 measurements.

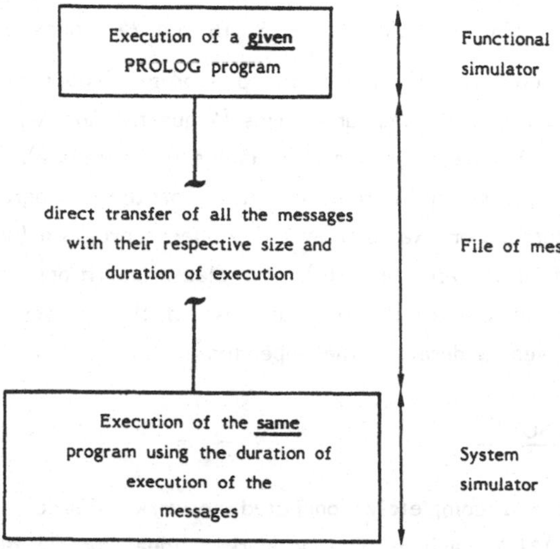

Figure 2 - The COALA system simulation

Contrary to most existing simulations which use a loosely coupled method [ONA 85], our simulation used a strongly coupled simulation method [FUT 86] because it was noticed that the transfer of statistical results from the functional simulator to the system simulator introduced a certain bias in our measurements. To illustrate this particularity, Table 1 gives a few execution time values, in µs, corresponding to the RESOLVE-REQ and UNIFY-REQ messages.

Measurements show that the average processing time for a message is about 1000 µs. The longest message is 170 bytes. Supposing a 10 Mbps communication channel, the transfer time of the longest message is 136 µs. This means that the transfer time cannot be neglected.

message / program	RESOLVE-REQ			max. / min.	UNIFY-REQ			max. / min.
	min.	max.	ave.		min.	max.	ave.	
4-QUEENS	239	7761	2209	32	1198	7330	3006	6
COLOR	2661	3288	1236	1.2	1037	3288	1977	3
REVERSE	769	3989	2535	5	1239	5517	3337	4

Table 1 - Variation of processing times

Finally, the simulation process considers that the network is not ideal (i.e. conflicts may occur), that the communication channel has a 10 Mbps transfer rate with full-duplex links and that each processor has a buffer of sufficient size. The results of this strongly coupled simulation method describe quite exactly the behaviour of the COALA machine using MC68000 and using the same PASCAL procedures as the distributed interpreter. As for the network topology, we have envisaged the completely connected, near-neighbour mesh, cube and hypercube networks with 4, 9, 16 and 25 processors.

For purposes of comparison, we introduced a program operating on large data structures such as lists, n-uplets and compound terms (4-queens) and a program operating on simple data structures such as constants and variables (pc database). Due to the difference in data structure handling, the duration of execution of these programs is largely dependent on these data structures. For example, in the 4-queens program (used in general to measure multiprocessor PROLOG architectures), the clause partitions are small but the search space becomes large because of the recursive use of the clauses. The corresponding PROLOG programs are given in detail in the appendix.

5 - SIMULATION RESULTS

Firstly, we chose a completely connected network in order to define the number of processors of the COALA machine. This network is ideal for our distributed interpreter but the number of switching elements required for a large number of processors renders the topology unrealizable. Figure 3 shows the overall performance of COALA for the 4-queens problem when increasing the number of processors.

As additional processors are used (up to 18), duration of execution decreases. Then it levels off : between 9 and 18 processors, execution time is nearly the same. However, this result shows that the COALA machine is able to support the parallelism in PROLOG programs.

As for the pc database program, the future behaviour of our machine has been simulated by increasing the number of assertions. Thus, pc database (n) indicates the pc database program with n assertions for two partitions. For each program, measurements show that duration of execution decreases and that saturation occurs. However, this saturation is

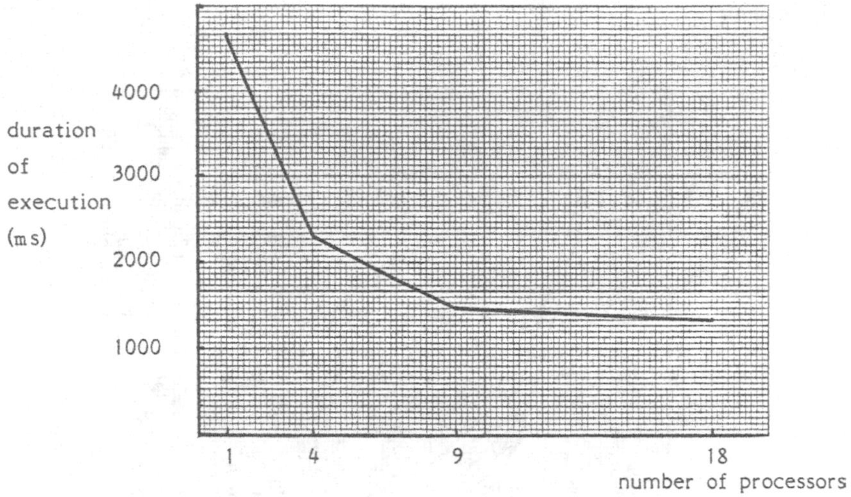

Figure 3 - Effect of the number of processors for the 4-queens problem

only bound to the application size and we assume that the number of processors does not entail a bottleneck situation in the performance of COALA. Figure 4 resumes this property.

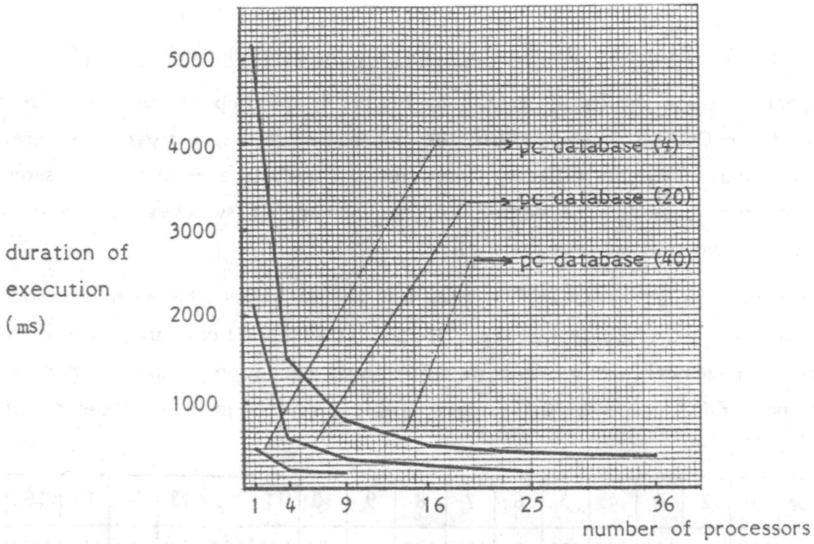

Figure 4 - Effect of the number of processors for the pc database problem

Some topologies have been simulated taking communication time into account. In addition to duration of execution, many other parameters have been used to define the topology of COALA. In particular, among these parameters is the diameter i.e. the longest path between two nodes in the network. Figure 5 shows the simulation results for the pc database (20) problem.

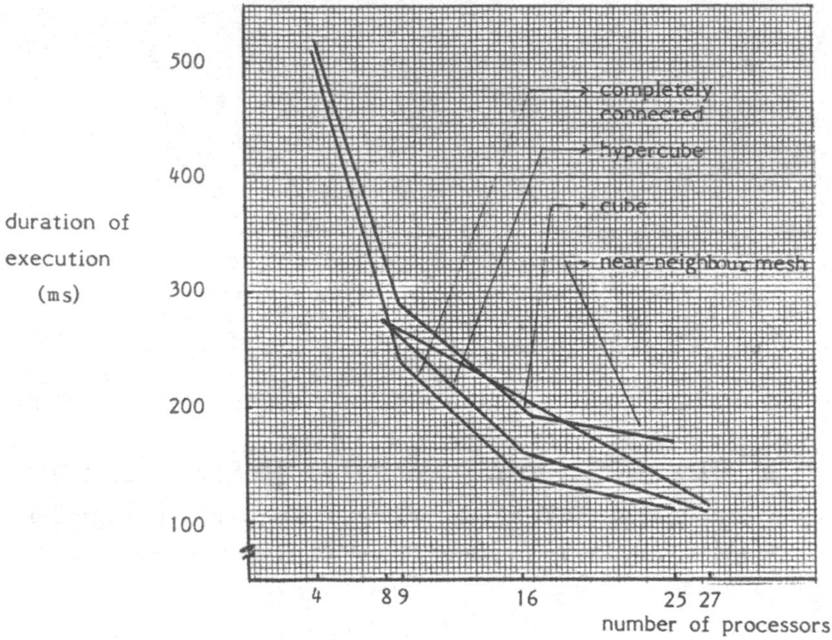

Figure 5 - Effect of the topology for the pc database (20) problem

With respect to these results illustrated in Figure 5, we propose the hypercube as the basic topology of the COALA machine. With the hypercube, messages traverse several numbers of channels and so exhibit different latencies but results are nearly the same as a completely connected topology. The degree i.e. the number of switches associated with a node permits an implementation with hundreds of processors.

When executing the pc database (20) program on the hypercube with 16 processors, only 2.2 channels are traversed on average. In the same conditions, the load average of each communication channel with respect to duration of execution is about 2 per cent and the maximum input FIFO queue is 70 messages. Table 2 relates in detail these results.

processor	1	2	3	4	5	6	7	8	9	10	11	12	13	14	15	16
total	188	188	188	188	188	186	186	186	186	170	186	180	120	147	147	147
max.	63	70	68	65	63	55	58	56	55	67	61	50	38	42	46	37
ave.	18	20.3	19.4	18.9	17.7	16.1	17.7	15.7	15.2	17.2	16.5	14	7.4	7.3	7.9	6.4

Table 2 - Distribution of messages in FIFO queues

These results correlate with an acceptable FIFO queue load balancing. In the same way, processor load balancing does not need dynamic process allocation as in other approachs [KEL 84]. In our model, the distribution of the arcs is equivalent to the distribution of the tasks among the processors. Figure 6 shows processor load balancing for the pc database (20) problem using 9 processors.

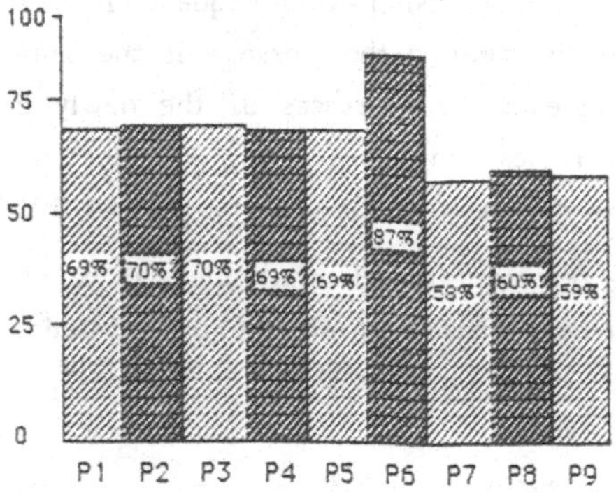

Figure 6 - Processor load balancing for the pc database (20) problem

Unfortunately, for programs operating on large data structures, results are not as good as for programs operating on simple data structures. This behaviour is related to the small partitions of clauses and to the use of recursivity. Figure 7 shows processor load balancing for the 4-queens problem using 9 processors. Results are similar with programs such as quicksort, reverse ...

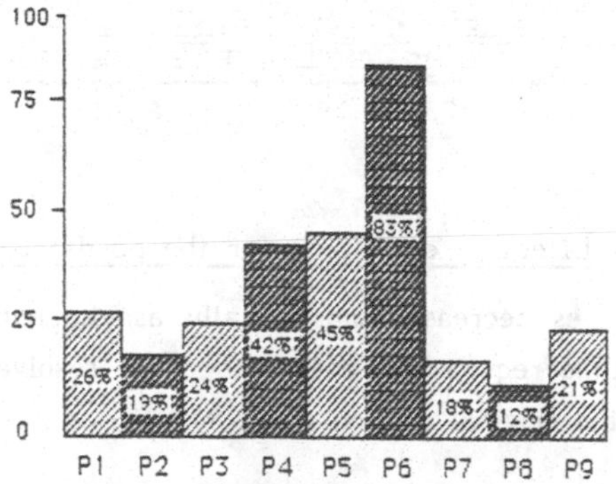

Figure 7 - Processor load balancing for the 4-queens problem

We are currently investigating various mechanisms intented to improve the model and to define a knowledge base machine [MUR 84]. In particular we seek to take advantage of dynamic results of programs operating on simple data structures.

When a PROLOG program uses a large number of assertions, the basic model builds lists of sons and therefore lists of brothers which are for too lengthy Consequently, the processing time required to define the next resolvent is proportional to the number of UNIFY-ACK and UNIFY-NACK messages waited for by this resolvent. It is quite easy to modify the original representation by representing all the arcs of the same partition stored on the same processor by an extra-arc containing the list of real addresses of the original arcs.

When such an arc receives a UNIFY-REQ request, it distributes this request among its arcs. The algorithm used in treating the message is the same as before, except that no message is sent directly. Instead, the addresses of the newly created arcs update the old ones. If the new list of addresses contains at least one element, a UNIFY-ACK message is sent to the resolvent ; if the list is empty, a UNIFY-NACK message is sent.

An advantage of this representation is that the list of sons of an arc contains only one arc per processing element instead of all the arcs defining the literal. This property greatly reduces the number of messages as shown in Figure 8.

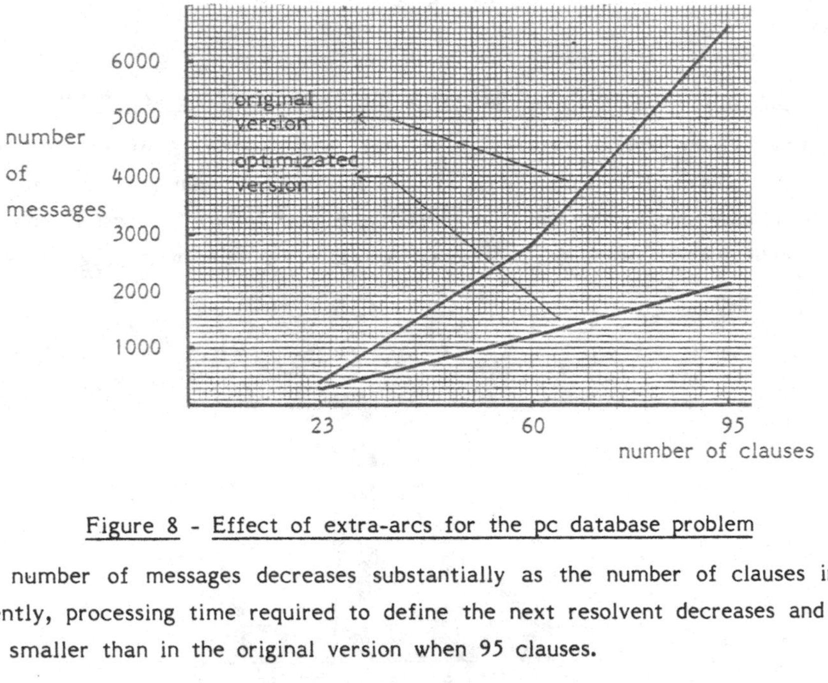

Figure 8 - Effect of extra-arcs for the pc database problem

The number of messages decreases substantially as the number of clauses increases. Consequently, processing time required to define the next resolvent decreases and is about 12 times smaller than in the original version when 95 clauses.

CONCLUSION

The AND/OR connection graph model represents a new perspective on the parallel interpretation of PROLOG. The graph is distributed, without duplication, among the processing elements ; consequently, accessing the graph entails no bottleneck situation . In particular, control is not based on a hierarchical structure.

The simulation system allows us to obtain dynamic measurements. Simulation conditions closely reflect the behaviour of the distributed interpreter running on the future COALA machine with MC68000 microprocessors as processing elements. A strongly coupled simulation method was used in order to simulate large PROLOG programs and large network topologies. This method does not introduce any approximation for measurements.

It appears that an acceptable performance may be achieved using somewhere near 100 processors. The hypercube topology seems to be the best compromise for the COALA network. Each processing element is connected through bidirectional full-duplex, point-to-point communication channels to its near-neighbours forming a small diameter network.

An important result is that programs operating on simple data structures do not require dynamic process allocation. The architecture is well-suited for knowledge base applications. For this purpose, we have defined mechanisms to improve efficiency of the AND/OR connection graph model and, in the future, we will investigate the adequacy of a knowledge base architecture to the COALA machine. For programs operating on large data structures, a better distribution of tasks among the processing elements must be define.

ACKNOWLEDGEMENTS

This work has been realized within Professor R. Beaufils's team and is supported by the "Gréco de Programmation" of the "Centre National de la Recherche Scientifique".

REFERENCES

[AMA 84] M. Amamiya, R. Hasegawa - A Logic Program Execution based on Data-Flow Control - Proc. Logic Programming Conference 84, November 1984, pp. 507-516.

[CON 85] J.S. Conery, D.F. Kibler - AND Parallelism and Nondeterminism in Logic Programs - New Generation Computing - 1985, Vol. 3, pp. 43-70.

[FUT 84] I. Futó, J. Szeredi - System Simulation and Co-operative Problem-Solving on a PROLOG basis - Implementations of PROLOG - ed. J. Campbell, Ellis Hortwood Ltd., England - 1984, pp. 164-174.

[FUT 86] I.Futó, C. Percebois, I. Durand, C. Simon, B. Bonhoure - Simulation Study of a Multiprocessor PROLOG Architecture - First Italian Conference on Logic Programming, Genova, Italy, March 1986 (invited paper).

[HEW 84] C. Hewitt, H. Lieberman - Design Issues in Parallel Architectures for Artificial Intelligence - COMPCON Spring 1984, February 1984, pp. 418-423.

[KEL 79] R.M. Keller, G. Lindstrom, S. Patil - A Loosely Coupled Applicative Multi-Processing System - AFIPS Press, 1979, pp. 613-622.

[KEL 84] R.M. Keller, F.C.H. Lin, J. Tanaka - Rediflow Multiprocessing - COMPCON Spring 1984, February 1984, pp. 410-417.

[KOW 79] R. Kowalski - Logic for Problem Solving - The Computer Science Library, Elsevier, 1979.

[MUR 84] K. Murakami, T. Kakuta, R. Onai - Architecture and Hardware Systems : Parallel Inference Machine and Knowledge Base Machine - Proc. International Conference on Fifth Generation Computer Systems 1984, November 1984, pp. 18-36.

[ONA 85] R. Onai, M. Aso, M. Shimizu, K. Masuda - Architecture of a Reduction-Based Parallel Machine : PIM-R - New Generation Computing - 1985, Vol. 3, pp. 197-228.

[PER 86] C. Percebois, I. Futó, I. Durand, C. Simon, B. Bonhoure - An Actor-Oriented Multiprocessor Architecture for PROLOG : COALA - First Italian Conference on Logic Programming, Genova, Italy, March 1986 (invited paper).

APPENDIX

4-queens program

```
queens(nil,Y,Y).
queens(c(X1,X2),Y,Z) :- select(U,c(X1,X2),V),
                        safe(U,Y,1),queens(V,c(U,Y),Z).
select(X,c(X,Y),Y).
select(U,c(X,Y),c(X,V)) :- select(U,Y,V).
safe(U,nil,W).
safe(U,c(P,Q),N) :- nodiag(U,P,N),plus(N,1,M),safe(U,Q,M).
nodiag(U,P,N) :- plus(P,N,T1),moins(P,N,T2),diff(U,T1),diff(U,T2).

:- queens(c(1,c(2,c(3,c(4,nil)))),nil,Q).
```

pc database (40) program

```
ibm_comp(PNAME,CPU,OS):-pnps(PN,PNAME,X,Y),pco(PN,CPU,OS),
                        bit_16(CPU),os_simil(OS).

bit_16(8086).
bit_16(8088).
bit_16(m8088).
bit_16(i8088_2).
bit_16(82286).
bit_16(82086).

os_simil(ms_dos).
os_simil(dos_10).
os_simil(z_dos).
os_simil(dos_211).
os_simil(dos_20).
os_simil(msdos_21).
os_simil(dos_30).
os_simil(prop_30).
os_simil(prop_20).
os_simil(dos_11).
```

```
pnps(p1,agil,3000,s1).                 pco(p1,8088,ms_dos).
pnps(p2,corona_p,2700,s2).             pco(p2,8088,ms_dos).
pnps(p3,corona_p,2500,s3).             pco(p3,8088,ms_dos).
pnps(p4,mbc_555,1100,s4).              pco(p4,8086,dos_11).
pnps(p5,zenith_1,3000,s6).             pco(p5,z80,cp_m).
pnps(p6,genie_16,2000,s6).             pco(p5,8086,z_dos).
pnps(p7,rainbow,2500,s7).              pco(p6,8088,ms_dos).
pnps(p8,osborne,2000,s6).              pco(p7,8088,cp_m_86).
pnps(p9,dasher_1,3400,s8).             pco(p7,z80,cp_m).
pnps(p10,z_158,5100,s5).               pco(p8,z80,cp_m).
pnps(p11,turbo_pc,4000,s11).           pco(p9,8088,dos_211).
pnps(p12,kay_16,2500,s10).             pco(p10,8088,ms_dos).
pnps(p13,copam_pc,2000,s11).           pco(p11,i8088_2,ms_dos).
pnps(p14,don_pc,2000,s12).             pco(p12,82286,dos_20).
pnps(p15,dyn_xt,2000,s13).             pco(p13,8086,dos_20).
pnps(p16,laser_pc,2000,s14).           pco(p14,8088,ms_dos).
pnps(p17,ap_pc,2600,s15).              pco(p15,8086,dos_20).
pnps(p18,m24_sp,3000,s16).             pco(p16,8088,dos_20).
pnps(p19,micral,6000,s17).             pco(p17,8086,msdos_21).
pnps(p20,prop_16,4000,s18).            pco(p18,8086,ms_dos).
pnps(p21,com_64,500,s19).              pco(p19,82086,dos_30).
pnps(p22,proper_8,2000,s18).           pco(p20,8088,prop_30).
pnps(p23,vt_16,4000,s20).              pco(p21,z80,cp_m).
pnps(p24,ncr_pc,3000,s21).             pco(p22,z80,cp_m).
pnps(p25,oplite,3000,s22).             pco(p23,m8088,prop_20).
pnps(p26,pap_c,2500,s23).              pco(p24,8088,ms_dos).
pnps(p27,p_1600,2700,s24).             pco(p25,8088,ms_dos).
pnps(p28,ph_p3100,3000,s25).           pco(p26,8088,ms_dos).
pnps(p29,s_9001,2500,s4).              pco(p27,8088,ms_dos).
pnps(p30,sil_216,4000,s26).            pco(p28,8088,ms_dos).
pnps(p31,s_pc50,6500,s27).             pco(p29,8088,ms_dos).
pnps(p32,tandy,1500,s28).              pco(p30,8088,ms_dos).
pnps(p33,tele_pc,4000,s29).            pco(p31,8088,ms_dos).
pnps(p34,ti_pc,2500,s30).              pco(p32,8088,ms_dos).
pnps(p35,wang_pc,3000,s31).            pco(p33,8088,ms_dos).
pnps(p36,axel_20,2000,s32).            pco(p34,8088,ms_dos).
pnps(p37,caf_bip,2200,s32).            pco(p35,8088,ms_dos).
pnps(p38,ericsson,2800,s34).           pco(p38,8088,ms_dos).
pnps(p39,logical,6000,s35).            pco(p39,8088,ms_dos).

:- ibm_comp(PNAME,CPU,OS).
```

Generating Efficient Code from Strictness Annotations

by

Gary Lindstrom
Lal George
Dowming Yeh

Department of Computer Science
University of Utah
Salt Lake City, UT 84112

ABSTRACT

Normal order functional languages (NOFLs) offer conceptual simplicity, expressive power, and attractiveness for parallel execution. However, current implementations of NOFLs on conventional von Neumann machines are not competitive with those of imperative languages. The central reasons for this poor performance include the high control overhead (e.g. demand evaluation) and fine object code granularity (e.g. SKI combinators) used in most NOFL implementations. Strictness analysis gathers information that helps to overcome these inefficiencies through optimized compilation. We propose here a rule-based strategy for such compilation, working from a new textual representation for strictness analyzed source programs. This representation offers readability and ease of manipulation, while expressing all essential strictness information, including basic block structure and block dominance and disjunction relationships. The rules presented here show how to compile this intermediate form into optimized single processor G-machine code. In addition, this representation appears to be useful for a number of other execution methods, including interpretation, compilation into conventional Lisp with "promises", and mapping into "supercombinators" for parallel architectures.[1]

1. NOFLs and Strictness Analysis

1.1. Basic Concepts

Most modern functional languages are based on *normal order* semantics, where divergence of a program occurs only if the program's overall result directly depends on a divergent subexpression. Customary implementations of NOFLs ensure this property by individually operationalizing the normal order characteristics of *each operator*, e.g. through demand evaluation or combinator reduction.

NOFLs offer many advantages in programming practice, including clean treatment of I/O streams, overlapped production and consumption of large data objects, and the facile representation of feedback systems. For example, functional modeling of non-trivial hardware systems seems to require normal order evaluation in a fundamental sense [15].

Another appeal of NOFLs is their suitability for distributed evaluation on innovative architectures, e.g. via graph reduction. However, a more pressing need exists for efficient NOFL implementations on *today's* machines, to gain (i) experience with large-scale software engineering in NOFLs, and (ii) a better understanding of what is *familiar* about their implementation, as well as what is *exotic*. In comparison, one must be impressed with the rapid acceptance that has greeted Prolog, and acknowledge that this has been greatly aided by the early availability of efficient implementations on conventional computers [17].

One of the most promising avenues currently under investigation for improving the efficiency of NOFLs is *strictness analysis* [14]. Under this technique *strict subsets* of operators, i.e. groups unconditionally executable together, are determined at compile time. The major strictness analysis research areas at the moment include:

- "non-flat" domains [6, 8, 16], and
- higher-order functions [1, 4, 11].

While strictness analysis *theory* appears to be developing apace, its *application* to actual code

---

[1] This material is based upon work supported by the National Science Foundation under Grant No. DCR-8506000.

generation seems to be lagging. An exception is the recent paper [3], which uses a finite domain. We attempt here to fill this gap, by showing a method which relates well to existing compiler technology, and sheds light on the similarities and differences in compiling NOFLs for single- and multi-processor machines.

1.2. Overview of Method

Our method involves four processing steps, from source program to optimized object code:

1. The source program is converted to function graph form, after exhaustive common sub-expression (CSE) detection and elimination. CSEs are represented via binary output, single input **fork** operators, e.g. $(\mu, \nu) = \mathbf{fork}(\upsilon)$.
2. Strictness analysis is performed on the function graph representation, using abstract interpretation on a "non-flat" infinite domain of predicted patterns of evaluation.
3. The resulting annotated graph is converted to textual form, which may be viewed as a semantically attributed abstract syntax tree.
4. Finally, the textual form is translated to object code, optimized by observance of the block structure, predicted prior evaluation, and type information conveyed by the semantic attributes.

1.3. Analysis Method

The first two steps of our method are reported in [12] and [13]. We briefly summarize their essentials here, by way of background for our new results involving steps 3 and 4 above.

1.3.1. Simplified Domain

It is useful to describe our method first via a *simplified* abstract interpretation domain, and then an *augmented* domain. The former represents the effects of a *single source* of hypothesized demand, while the latter analyzes the effect of *all sources* of demand throughout the program, on a "wholesale" basis.

The primitive elements of our simplified domain are as follows:

- $\perp$ expresses a total lack of compile time information as to whether an expression will be evaluated, and if it is, what datatype wil result.
- **d** represents a compile-time hypothesis or inference that an expression will be subjected to *at least* one level of evaluation, ie, to an atom or tuple (possibly with suspended components).
- $\mathbf{d}^*$ conveys the information that an expression will be subjected to an *exhaustive* evaluation attempt, i.e. to an atom, or a finite or infinite composition of tuples of atoms or error indicators, (but with no *a priori* expectation of which case, if any, will result).
- **a** generically designates all atomic values, including functions. However, **a** can also be interpreted as "demand with atomic result required.
- T indicates conflicting information on the value of an expression, i.e. values which are constrained simultaneously to be atomic and nonatomic. This indicates a rudimentary type error.

This primitive element set is closed with binary Cartesian cross products, representing *pairs* produced by the **cons** operator. The resulting set, constitutes the domain D used in [12]. The operators receiving non-$\perp$ annotations as a result of a non_$\perp$ hypothesis on a particular arc is termed a *strictness subset* of the graph.

1.3.2. Augmented Domain

Reference [13] presents an augmentation of this simplified domain, supporting "wholesale" strictness analysis on an entire function graph. In comparison to the former approach, the analysis method is extended in two respects:

1. $\perp$ has been removed from the domain. This reflects the fact that, although prediction of evaluation causality at compile time is imperfect,

   a. code must be compiled for *every* operator in a function, and

   b. when that code is executed, it will *certainly* be executed under at least simple demand.

Hence the role of $\bot$ in the domain is played by d.

2. However, the fact that a d is placed where a $\bot$ would previously have appeared on an arc must not be construed as necessarily *extending* a strictness subset. Rather, it must indicate the introduction of a *new* strictness subset, which might have arisen from an *independent* application of the previous method with d asserted instead of $\bot$ on the arc in question.

   To establish such a subset boundary, we augment D to include natural number *subscripts* on each denoted level of evaluation. In anticipation of their ultimate use for code generation, we term such subscripts *block numbers*.

   - Initially, all block numbers are considered to be distinct. As the analysis proceeds, some block numbers become *equivalenced*, and their associated strictness subsets are thereby merged.
   - There are also the important notions of block *dominance* and *disjunction*, discussed in section 1.3.3.

In referring to an element of D, it is important at certain times to refer to its outermost block number; other times, that number is irrelevant. To help make this distinction clear, we adopt the following notation:

- When the outermost block number of an element of D must be mentioned, that element will be denoted by a subscripted early alphabet Greek letter, e.g. α_i, β_j, γ_k.
- When the outermost block number of an element of D is irrelevant, that element will be denoted by a non-subscripted late alphabet roman letter, e.g. x, y, z.

Our domain D is as follows:

Domain:

$$D = \{d_i,\ d^e_i,\ a_i,\ T_i\} \cup [u,\ v]_i \qquad i = 0,\ 1,\ \ldots,\ \text{and } u,\ v \in D$$

Equality:

$$\alpha_i = \alpha_j \quad (\alpha \text{ not a pair}) \qquad \Leftrightarrow i \equiv j$$
$$[u,\ v]_i = [x,\ y]_j \qquad \Leftrightarrow i \equiv j \wedge u = x \wedge v = y$$

Partial Ordering:

$$d_i < d^e_j \qquad \Leftrightarrow i \equiv j$$
$$d^e_i < a_j \qquad \Leftrightarrow i \equiv j$$
$$d_i < [x,\ y]_j \qquad \Leftrightarrow i \equiv j$$
$$d^e_i < [x,\ y]_j \qquad \Leftrightarrow i \equiv j \wedge d^e_i \le x \wedge d^e_i \le y$$
$$[u,\ v]_i \le [x,\ y]_j \qquad \Leftrightarrow i \equiv j \wedge u \le x \wedge v \le y$$
$$\alpha_i \le T_j \qquad \Leftrightarrow i \equiv j$$

Note that these rules imply:

1. d^e_i is never a lower bound on any element of D in which an α_j appears for some j not equivalent to i.

2. Similarly, d^e_i is never a lower bound on any element of D in which d_k appears for any k.

Failure of either of these properties to hold would indicate a decrease in "commitment" to evaluate *fully* the denoted expression within block i, once the eager evaluation indicated by d^e_i has begun.

1.3.3. Dominance and Disjunction

A principal result of the strictness analysis method outlined in [13] is the final equivalence relation derived among block numbers. However, another important relationship exists among blocks, reflecting necessary evaluation order.

Definition. A block i *dominates* a block j, denoted $i \angle j$, if whenever block j is executed, that execution is a consequence of block i also being executed.

Dominance among blocks is an important concept that facilitates the generation of efficient object code. For example, if a CSE is shared between two blocks bearing a dominance relationship, then evaluation of that CSE can be moved into the dominating block.

Four axioms govern the dominance relationship:

a. $(\forall i,\ j)\ i \angle j \Rightarrow$
$(\forall m,\ n)\ m \equiv i \wedge n \equiv j \Rightarrow m \angle n$ *(equivalence consistency)*

b. $(\forall i)\ i \angle i$ *(reflexivity)*

c. $(\forall i, j, k)\ i \angle j \wedge j \angle k \Rightarrow i \angle k$ *(transitivity)*

d. $(\forall i, j)\ i \angle j \wedge j \angle i \Rightarrow i \equiv j$ *(antisymmetry).*

Lastly, a disjunction relationship among block numbers, denoted $i = j \vee k$, is also determined by our analysis. This too is made consistent over equivalence classes, e.g. if $m \equiv i$, $n \equiv j$, and $p \equiv k$, then $m = n \vee p$ in the example above. Disjunctions are used to associate blocks that are related through `cond` operators. If, for example, a CSE is shared by both arms (`then/else` parts) of a conditional, then that expression can be "hoisted" to the surrounding unconditional block.

1.3.4. Sample rules

We denote the strictness annotations of an arc v by $\chi(v)$. The analysis method proceeds by the application of *strictness rules*, expressed in terms of *precondition* - *postcondition* pairs. These should be interpreted as "if the *precondition* is true, make the *postcondition* true". Notice from the partial ordering specified in section 1.3.2 that "making a postcondition true" can mandate block number equivalencing. For example, suppose $v = \texttt{ident}(\mu)$, with $\chi(v) = \alpha_i$ and $\chi(\mu) = \beta_j$. Then the postcondition $\alpha_i \le \chi(\mu)$ ensures that i is equivalenced to j. This captures the idea that `ident` is strict in its argument, and should not constitute a boundary between strictness subsets. Hence block i is merged with block j.

Our strictness analysis rules are designed to be *monotonic* in the sense that:

- If a value in D is changed, it is always to a *greater* value in the partial order.
- If the equivalence relation is changed, it is always through equivalencing two block numbers, thereby *coarsening* it.
- The dominance and disjunction relations are changed only through extension by equivalence consistency.

Our method terminates when no further annotation changes result from rule application, or when it is deemed that sufficient information has been obtained for compilation needs. There is evidence that uniform termination of our method, and others involving infinite domains, cannot be guaranteed [10].

A representative sample of our strictness analysis rules are enumerated in [13]. To suggest their flavor, we exhibit here the "backward" or "demand flow" rules for a (lazy) tuple constructor and selector.

$v_0 = \texttt{cons}(v_1, v_2)$, where $\chi(v_0) = \alpha_i \wedge \chi(v_1) = \beta_j \wedge \chi(v_2) = \delta_k$

Precondition 1:

$[u, v]_i \le \alpha_i$

Postcondition 1: *(laziness; j and k not made $\equiv i$)*

$u \le \chi(v_1) \wedge v \le \chi(v_2)$

Precondition 2:

$d^e{}_i \le \alpha_i$

Postcondition 2: *(eagerness; j and k made $\equiv i$)*

$d^e{}_i \le \chi(v_1) \wedge d^e{}_i \le \chi(v_2)$

$v_0 = \texttt{car}(v_1)$, where $\chi(v_0) = \alpha_i$

Precondition:

(none)

Postcondition:

$[\alpha_i, d_k]_i \le \chi(v_1)$ *(new k, cf. $\perp$)*

2. Resulting Graph Structure

Given a function graph with final annotations and their associated equivalence relation, basic blocks can be formed. We collect together all operators $v = \textbf{OP}(\ \ldots\ )$, where $\chi(v) = \alpha_i$ for equivalent i. Four varieties of basic blocks result:

- Function bodies.
- Conditional arms.
- Actual parameters.
- Tuple components.

The first two syntactic occurrences always cause block boundaries to be formed. The last two may or may not occur at block boundaries, depending on the strength of the strictness analysis results. To illustrate, we show an annotated graph taken from [13].

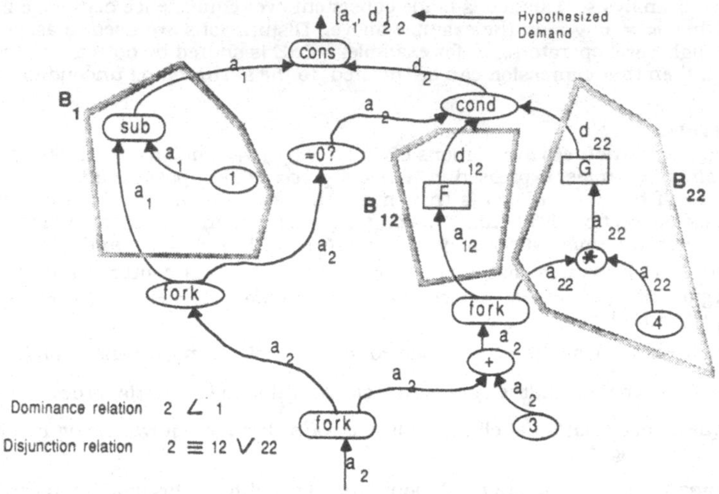

Figure 2-1: Sample annotated function graph.

2.1. Basic Block Structure

The basic blocks that result have several important properties:

1. They nest in a manner consistent with the dominance relation previously obtained.
2. Within a block, the arc annotations convey only datatype information (i.e. atomic vs. pair value predictions). Hence the subscripts used to accomplish block partitioning may now be discarded.
3. The arcs crossing block boundaries represent values produced in one block and consumed in another.

We categorize arcs crossing block boundaries into three kinds, depending on the transition in block level that each represents (see figure 2-2):

1. *Ascending:* arguments to nonstrict operators, e.g. **cons**, **cond** and **apply**.
2. *Descending:* a CSE usage, e.g. (v_0, v_1) = **fork**(v_2), where $\chi(v_0) = \alpha_i$, $\chi(v_1) = \beta_j$, and $\chi(v_2) = \gamma_k$, with $i \angle j$ or $k = i \vee j$.
3. *Lateral:* a CSE as above, but with i and j incomparable.

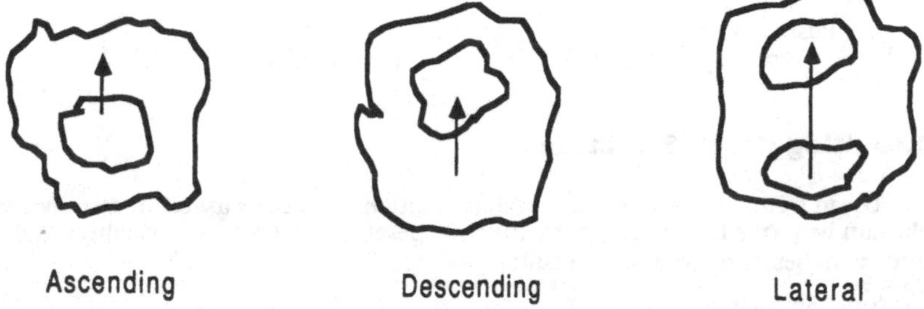

Figure 2-2: Arcs between basic blocks.

2.2. Applicative Order Interpretation of Basic Blocks

As remarked in section 2.1, the outcome of our strictness analysis method has two components: (i) determination of basic blocks, and (ii) atom/list type annotation of the result value denoted by each arc. This information is used in compilation for two distinct purposes: (i) conversion to applicative order evaluation, and (ii) generation of code in which redundant expression evaluation and type checking operations are omitted. We first consider conversion to applicative order, and return to redundant operation suppression in section 2.3.

In fact, once isolation of basic blocks in a NOFL program has been accomplished, the program has in a sense already been converted to applicative order form. This statement will be given sharper meaning in section 3, where a textual representation for a derived applicative order language is specified. However, intuitive support for this claim can be offered as follows:

1. We informally define *applicative order* evaluation on this "blocked" graph representation as follows:

   - Whenever the result of a block is needed at run time, all the operators local to the block are evaluated in bottom up manner. This can be done by unconditional code executing in any order that observes data dependencies, i.e. systematically left to right, in some other order optimizing register usage, or even in parallel.

   - The need for the result of an inner block is a run time event not predictable by the compile time analysis. As noted in section 2, there are four types of blocks, but only three can occur as inner blocks. We consider each in turn.

     - *Conditional arms:* The predicate and any CSE's shared across sibling conditional arms are evaluated in the surrounding block. Once the predicate is evaluated, the **then** or **else** part is selected as appropriate, and its block is evaluated in applicative order.

     - *Actual parameters:* Isolation of an actual parameter into a separate block indicates compile time uncertainty of the need for its evaluation. In our applicative order interpretation, we view such a block as evaluating at function call time to a *suspension*, encapsulating the block's code and values entering through descending arcs.

     - *Tuple components:* Tuple components appearing as separate blocks indicate similar evaluation uncertainty at compile time. These are also compiled into suspensions, for subsequent evaluation as needed by an appropriate selector.

2. This applicative interpretation has many advantages:

   - Evaluation order is outermost-first with respect to block nesting. This, together with our data dependency based evaluation order within blocks, means that all arcs descending into an inner block carry values which are necessarily pre-evaluated when accessed from within.

   - Since inner block nesting is static, these values will be located in known registers or stack locations when compiled code is used. Such values are used directly within conditional arms; for actual parameters and tuples, the values are speedily accessed at suspension creation time, as follows.

     - Formal parameter accesses may trigger the evaluation of an actual parameter, existing as a suspension. These can be represented as function applications, closed with a full parameter set conveying environment values (i.e. those on descending arcs entering the corresponding actual parameter block). Hence normal **apply** operator semantics and implementation techniques can be employed.

     - Selector accesses behave similarly.

2.3. Datatyping Information

The datatype information in arc annotations provides reliable datatype information, in the sense that if an arc is annotated with a datatype indicator **t**, we may be sure that (i) any value **v** conveyed by that arc at run time will be consistent with **t**, and (ii) all usages of **v** will be consistent with **t**, or will check the type more specifically.

This means that many operators, e.g. **car**, can be applied to values without run time type testing if the value's type annotation, e.g. $[d_i, d_j]_k$, so indicates. If the type annotation is simply d_i, then we know the value will be prior evaluated, but to an unknown type. In this case the **car** can be compiled *with* type testing, but *without* an internal **eval** providing for the case when the value is a suspension.

Even more important are guarantees of prior evaluation as shown by equivalence of subscripts across type descriptor levels. For example, $[d_i, _j]_i$ indicates that when the pair is computed in block **i**, its first component will *also* be computed, to at least an atom or pair (possibly of suspensions). The exhaustive demand indicator d^*, signalling full applicative order, is particularly useful since call by value implementation may be used in thoroughly this case.

2.4. Soundness

Formal proof of the soundness of our applicative order interpretation is beyond the scope of this paper. However, it can be informally argued as follows:

- *Will we evaluate enough?* Yes, because all assumptions of prior evaluation are validated by our method observing outermost-first evaluation order among blocks (observing dominance) and bottom up evaluation order within blocks (observing data dependencies).
- *Will we evaluate too much?* No, because the only dangers are infinite data construction (protected by tuple suspensions), and non data producing runaway recursions (which, in keeping with [14], can only occur *earlier* in our method).

3. Textual Representation

We now turn to the new program representation developed since the preparation of our previous two papers.

3.1. Why a Textual Representation?

The graphical representation of strictness information is conceptually pleasing, but poses some practical difficulties. These include awkwardness of transmission through input and output devices, and unfamiliarity as a programming notation. As an alternative, we have developed a textual notation which captures all the essential information in an annotated graph, while facilitating subsequent processing, especially code generation.

3.2. Intermediate Representation

We require an intermediate representation that captures both the annotations placed on the arcs of the graph and the dominance relation between basic blocks. Typically function application will be represented by the intermediate form **(expr (f ℜ(e1)..ℜ(em)) sr)** where **f** is the function being applied to arguments also represented in our intermediate form. **ℜ(ei)** is the intermediate representation of the ith argument and **sr** is the strictness pattern expected from the function application. **sr** is expressed as a list structure representing values in our *simplified* domain (see sec. 1.3.1). Often, **sr** will be stronger than the pattern to which the function in the expression has been compiled to produce, so appropriate **eval** and type checking instructions will be compiled on the result. The dominance relation between blocks derived by our strictness analysis is used to place the **susp** form defined in section 3.3.

The individual varieties of expressions are represented as follows.

Constants: Unstructured literals are represented directly, since no strictness information is required, e.g. **1, 2.34, nil, true, false** etc.

CSEs: Common subexpressions are introduced via a **let** construct. Each newly introduced variable names a CSE represented in our intermediate form. The let is placed local to the *expr* forming the basic block ℜ(en) local to which the CSE appears.

```
(expr (let ((var1     ℜ(e1))
             ...
             (varm     ℜ(em)))
        ℜ(en))
      sr)
```

Local variables and formal parameters:

These are represented as (*var* **x sr sx**), where **x** is the formal parameter or local variable, and **sr** is as explained above. **sx** is the degree to which the formal parameter **x** has currently been evaluated. Again, **sr** may be stronger than **sx**, if for example a CSE is used in a conditional context that is stronger than its unconditional prior evaluation.

User defined function application:
When all arguments are present in a function application, the representation is as explained above, namely (*expr* (**f** $\Re$(**e1**) .. $\Re$(**en**)) **sr**).

Functional argument and higher order functions:
A full treatment regarding functions as first class objects would be beyond the space limits of this paper. However, our an intermediate representation and compilation techniques aim at *full laziness* as defined by Hughes [5], and thus avoid recomputation as much as possible.

Suspended Results: This is represented as (*susp* (**f** $x_1..x_n$) **sr**); see section 3.3.

3.3. Suspended results

In this paper only suspended results for function applications with all arguments will be considered. On the G-machine as presented by Johnsson [7], the creation of a graph for a function application is extremely costly, both in execution time and heap space. We shall see how to optimise this here. A suspended result for a function application (**f e1..en**) with all arguments present is represented through our analysis as a block boundary enclosing this application. All the arcs *into* the block represent *imports* required to build the suspension ie. the descending arcs as per figure 2-2. We then construct a suspension for a new function **g**, whose actual parameters are these very imports. Thus the new function **g** is defined as **g x1..xm = f e1..en**, where **x1..xm** correspond to the imported variables. Creating a suspension in this case now simply involves building a graph for a much simpler application. The **sr** in the **susp** expression represents the result produced when the suspension is demanded. This information is not utilized in this paper.

3.4. Example

We illustrate our representation on the familiar **append** function. In figure 3-1, we assume that the strictness signature of **append** is (**d, d**) → **d**, indicating that **append** is a function of two arguments, both of which will be prior evaluated to either an atom or a (possibly suspended) tuple. Similarly, the result of **append** is to be delivered already evaluated as an atom or tuple.

```
(fun append (x y)
   (expr (if (expr (null (var x d d)) a)
             (var y d d)
             (expr (cons
                         (expr (hd (var x [⊥, ⊥] [⊥, ⊥])) ⊥)
                         (susp (append1 x y) d))
                      [⊥, ⊥]))
         d))
```

Figure 3-1: Textual representation of annotated append.

Notes:

- The definition for **append1** is **append1 x y = append (tl x) y**, and its strictness signature is **append1: ([⊥,⊥] d) → d**.
- With the strictness information available for **x**, it is not necessary to create a suspension for the expression (**hd x**).

4. Compilation Rules

In [13], hand generated code for figure 2-1 is given to suggest the quality of code that might be generated using the strictness information our method gathers. Our prototype compiler is being written in Prolog [2] mainly for the power of pattern matching provided by unification, and the ease of adding optimisations as new clauses to the compiler. We now formalize the G-code generation as a set of Prolog clauses.

4.1. Major Rule Groups

The major clauses are defined below.

`f(AST, G_CODE)` Generates `G_CODE` for a *function definition* from the intermediate form, `AST`. The clause assumes that actual parameters will have been pre-evaluated to the degree predicted by our analysis before a call to the function is made.

`t(AST, MAP, SDEPTH, G_CODE)`
This clause attempts to perform tail recursion optimisation, for the expression represented in `AST`. `MAP` and `SDEPTH` are the mapping of parameters and local variables to positions on the stack, and the current depth of the evaluation stack respectively.

`e(AST, MAP, SDEPTH, G_CODE)`
This clause will evaluate the expression represented by `AST` and leave a pointer to the result on top of the evaluation stack - the s_stack.

`b(AST, MAP, SDEPTH, G_CODE)`
Generates code for arithmetic operations. This scheme is an optimization to conserve on the utilization of heap space during the generation of intermediate results. The result of evaluating `AST` is left on top of an arithmetic stack - the *a-stack*.

`susp(AST, MAP, SDEPTH, G_CODE)`
Create a graph. `AST` represents an instance of our `susp` intermediate form.

`s(PAT1, PAT2, G_CODE)`
Generates code to raise the strictness pattern of a result from `PAT1` to be `PAT2`. This is typically required when the result produced by a function application is weaker than that required.

4.2. Language Subset

For expository reasons and to demonstrate the use of strictness information during code generation, we shall restrict ourselves to a very small language defined below.

D (*Definitions*) ::=	Fun $x_1..x_n$ = E
E (*Expressions*) ::=	Constants I IntOp E E I RelOp E E
	cons E E I ListOp E I Fun E..E I if E E E
Constants ::=	Integers I Booleans I nil
IntOp ::=	add I sub I mult I div
RelOp ::=	gt I ge I lt I le I eq I ne
ListOp ::=	hd I tl I null
Fun ::=	Identifier

Functions are applied with all arguments present. We now present each of the rule groups in turn. All the clauses have been extracted from our existing compiler. However they are presented here in a simplified form omitting parameters required for later phases of the code generation. Also, most of the error checking clauses and clauses to terminate recursion have been omitted for brevity. The clauses below are written in the DEC10 Prolog syntax [2]. $\perp$ is denoted by ? in the clauses.

4.3. F-scheme: Function Compilation

```
F-1. f([fun, Fname, Parm, Body], GCode) :-
        length(Parm, Lp), Lp1 is L + 1,      /* Compute stack depth */
        args_map(Parm, PMap, Lp1),           /* mapping of params onto stack */
        t(Body, PMap, Lp1, GCode).           /* try Tail Recursion Optimisation */
```

Given a function definition we attempt to perform tail recursion optimisation via the `t-scheme`. `args_map` returns the mapping of formal parameters to positions on the stack. The default is handled by rule T-3.

4.4. T-scheme: Tail Recursion Optimization

```
T-1. t([expr, [F|Args], Sr], Map, Depth, GCode) :-
        type(F, FormalPrm, Sf),                     /* database lookup */
        length(Args, L), length(FormalPrm, L),      /* sufficient args? */
        reverse(Args, RArgs),                       /* not relevant here */
        eArgs(RArgs, Map, Depth, EArgs),            /* evaluate args */
        s(Sf, Sr, Strict),                          /* refine result pattern*/
```

```
        (Strict == [] ->
            append(EArgs, [[move,M], [jfun,F]], GCode);
            flatten1([EArgs, [[move,M], [fcall,F]], Strict], GCode))

T-2. t([expr, [if, E1, E2, E3], Sr], Map, Depth, GCode) :-
        b(E1, Map, Depth, E1Code),                  /* result on a-stack*/
        t(E2, Map, Depth, E2Code),                  /* then part */
        t(E3, Map, Depth, E3Code),                  /* else part */
        (flatten1([E1Code, [[jtrue,L1]], E3Code,
                            [[label,L1]], E2Code],
                GCode)).

T-3. t(E, Map, Depth, GCode) :-                     /* default case */
        e(E, Map, Depth, ECode),                    /* evaluate and update */
        flaten1([ECode, [[update], [ret]]], GCode).

T-4. eArgs([A| Args], Map, Depth, GCode) :-
        e(A, Map, Depth, E1Code),                 /* evaluate arg */
        Depth1 is Depth + 1,                      /* position for next arg*/
        eArgs(Args, Map, Depth1, ArgsCode),       /* rest of args */
        append(E1Code, ArgsCode, GCode).
```

When a user defined function culminates in a call to another user defined function, tail recursion optimisation is possible. In Rule T.1 we check that the function has been supplied with sufficient arguments, and evaluate them via the **eArgs** clause. The **eArgs** evaluates each of the arguments using the **e-scheme**. Note that the degree to which each of the arguments is to be evaluated is contained in our abstract representation. The **s-scheme** is used to raise the pattern produced by the function, namely **Sf**, to the level **Sr**. Tail recursion optimisation (via the ***jfun*** instruction) is only possible if this refinement code is absent. The newly created arguments are moved in place of the old via the [***move***, M] instruction. Rule T.2 propagates the recursion scheme into the branches of the conditional, with the default rule being T.3. The **t-scheme** is extended naturally to the **let** construct by evaluating the common subexpressions to the degree required, and propagating the **t-scheme** into the expression to be evaluated. The default rule evaluates the expression and updates the result application node.

4.5. E-scheme: Evaluate Expression

```
E-1. e(I, _, _, [[pushint, I]]) :- integer(I).  /* no evaluation required*/
                likewise for boolean constants and nil.

E-2. e([var, X, Sr, Sx], Map, Depth, [[push, OFFSET]| STRICT]) :-
        assoc(X, Map, [X, OFFSET]),
        s(Sx, Sr, STRICT).                          /* refinement possible*/

E-3. e([expr,[add,E1,E2],Sr], Map, Depth, GCode) :-   /* arithmetic */
        (Sr==d; Sr==a; Sr==de),
        b([expr,[add,E1,E2],a], Map, Depth, BCode),
        append(BCode, [[mkint]], GCode).
                likewise for sub, div, mult.

E-4. e([expr,[eq,E1,E2],Sr], Map, Depth, GCode) :-    /* relational */
        (Sr==d; Sr==a; Sr==de),
        b([expr,[eq,E1,E2],Sr], Map, Depth, BCode),
        append(BCode, [[mkbool]], GCode).

E-5. e([expr,[if,E1,E2,E3],Sr], Map, Depth, GCode) :- /* conditional */
        b(E1, Map, Depth, E1Code),
        e(E2, Map, Depth, E2Code),
        e(E3, Map, Depth, E3Code),
        flatten1([E1Code, [[jtrue,L1]], E3Code, [[jmp,L2]],
                          [[label,L1]], E2Code, [[label,L2]]],
               GCode).

E-6. e([expr,[null,E],Sr], Map, Depth, GCode) :-            /* null operator */
        e(E, Map, Depth, ECode),
        append(ECode, [[null]], GCode).
```

```
E-7. e([expr,[hd,[var,X,_,[B,_]]],A], Map, Depth,           /* (hd x) */
                              [[push,OFF],[hd]| STRICT]) :-
        assoc(X, M, [X, OFF]),
        s(B, A, STRICT).                          /* refinement possible */
               Likewise for tl function     /* after direct access */

E-8. e([expr,[hd,[var,X,_,d]],A], Map, Depth,
                              [[push,OFF],[hd_check]| STRICT]) :-
        assoc(X, M, [X, OFF]),                   /* test required */
        s(?, A, STRICT).                          /* refinement possible */
               Likewise for tl

E-9. e([expr,[hd,[var,X,_,de]],A], Map, Depth,
                              [[push,OFF],[hd_check]| STRICT]) :-
        assoc(X, M, [X, OFF]),                 /* test required */
        s(de, A, STRICT).                      /* further tests possible */
               Likewise for tl

E-10. e([expr,[hd,[expr,[F|Args],_]],A], Map, Depth, GCode) :-
        type(F, P, [B,_]),
        length(P, L), length(Args, L),           /* sufficient args */
        e([expr,[F|Args],[B,?]], Map, Depth, FCode),  /* call function */
        s(B, A, STRICT),                           /* refine result */
        flatten1([FCode, [hd], STRICT], GCode).
               Likewise for tl
```

E-11. Rule 8 is extended to handle function application in a fashion similar to rule 10.

E-12. Rule 9 extended to handle function application in a fashion similar to rule 10.

```
E-13. e([expr,[hd,E],_], Map, Depth, GCode) :-     /* default case*/
        e(E, Map, Depth, ECode),
        append(ECode, [[hd_check]], GCode).

E-14. e([expr,[cons,E1,E2],_], Map, Depth, GCode) :-
        e(E1, Map, Sd, Vd, E1Code),                 /* head part */
        Sd1 is Sd +1,
        e(E2, Map, Sd1, Vd, E2Code),                /* tail part */
        flatten1([E1Code, E2Code, [[cons]]], Code).

E-15. e([susp|S], Map, Depth, GCode) :-             /* graph creation */
        susp([susp|S], Map, Depth, GCode).

E-16. e([expr,[F|Args],Sr], Map, Depth, GCode) :    /* function application */
        type(F, P, Sf),
        length(P, M), length(Args, M),              /* sufficient args */
        reverse(Args, RArgs),
        Depth1 is Depth + 1,
        eArgs(RArgs, Map, Depth1, EArgs),           /* evaluate args*/
        s(Sf, Sr, STRICT),                          /* refine result */
        flatten1([[[mkhole]], EArgs, [[fcall,F]], STRICT], GCode).

E-17. e(E, _, _, _, [[error]]) :-
        error("Cannot compile expression").
```

The **e-scheme** leaves a pointer to a result on top of the evaluation stack. Rule E-2 refines a formal parameter to the degree required. Rules E-3 and E-4 transfer the code generation task to the B-scheme which computes all temporaries on the arithmetic stack, until the result is to be finally transferred to the s-stack via the ***mkbool*** or ***mkint*** instructions. In Rule E-6, the instruction ***null*** leaves a boolean result on the a-stack. Rules E-7 to E-13 are optimisations on the head and tail functions, which take advantage of the specific situation to generate better code. The default rule is E-13. The instruction ***hd_check*** accesses the *head* component of the list after a type *check* has been performed. In Rule E-14 we handle function application. The degree of evaluation required by each of the arguments will be manifest in our intermediate representation. The ***mkhole*** instruction makes space for the result on the heap, and the ***fcall*** instruction performs the context switch. This rule under fully strict conditions generates code that follow the *call-by-value* semantics of parameter passing.

4.6. B-scheme: Compute Basic Value

```
B-1. b(I, _, _, [[pushbasic,I]]) :- integer(I).
                Likewise for boolean constants.

B-2. b([var,X,Sr,a], Map, Depth, [[getv,OFF]]) :-
        (Sr==d; Sr==a),
        assoc(X, Map, [X, OFF]).

B-3. b([expr,[add,E1,E2],Sr], Map, Depth, GCode) :-
        b(E1, Map, Depth, B1Code),
        b(E2, Map, Depth, B2Code),
        flatten1([B1Code, B2Code,[[add]]], GCode).
                Likewise for sub, mult, div, eq, ne, gt, ge, lt, le

B-4. b([expr, [if, E1, E2, E3], Sr], Map, Depth, Code) :-
        (Sr == d ; Sr == a),
        b(E1, Map, Depth, E1Code),
        b(E2, Map, Depth, E2Code),
        b(E3, Map, Depth, E3Code),
        flatten1([E1Code, [[jtrue,L1]], E3Code, [[jmp, L2],
                       [label, L1]], E2Code, [[label, L2]]],
             Code).

B-5. b(E, Map, Depth, GCode) :-
        e(E, Map, Depth, Vd, ECode),
        append(ECode, [[get]], GCode).
```

The B-scheme rule does the standard bottom up evaluation of entirely strict expressions on the arithmetic stack. Rule B-5, needs to resort to the **e-scheme** to compute the value of the expression **E**, and get its result on the a-stack.

4.7. Susp-scheme: Create Graph

```
susp([susp,[F|Free],_], Map, Depth, [[pushfun,F]| FreeC]) :-
        Depth1 is Depth + 1,
        susp_param(Free, Map, Depth1, FreeC).

susp_param([X| Free], Map, Depth, [[push,OFF],[mkap]| FreeC]) :-
        assoc(X, Map, [X, OFF]),
        Depth1 is Depth + 1,
        susp_param(Free, Map, Depth1, FreeC).
```

This scheme constructs the graph for the **susp** intermediate form. We merely need to determine the offset of the free variables required in the graph and connect them together via the ***mkap*** instruction.

4.8. S-scheme: Strictness Pattern Refinement

```
S-1. s(X, X, []).

S-2. s(?, d, [[eval]]).

S-3. s(?, a, [[eval],[atomicp]]).

S-4. s(?, [A,B], [[eval],[listp]| GCode]) :- s([?,?], [A,B], GCode).

S-5. s(d, a, [[atomicp]]).

S-6. s(d, [A,B], [[listp]| Code]) :- s([?, ?], [A, B], Code).
```

```
S-7. s(a, [A, B], [[error]]) :- error("Atomic value where list expected").

S-8. s(de, a, [[atomicp]]).

S-9. s(de, [A,B], [[listp]| Code]) :-
        s([de,de], [A,B], Code).

S-10. s([A,B], [C,D], Code) :-
        s(A, C,  Code1),
        s_head(Code1, Code1_head),
        s(B, D, Code2),
        s_tail(Code2, Code2_tail),
        append(Code1_head, Code2_tail, Code).

S-11. s(_, _, []).

S-12. s_head([], []).
S-13. s_head(Code, Code_head) :-
        flatten1([[[push_top],[hd]], Code, [[pop]]],  Code_head).

S-14. s_tail([], []).
S-15. s_tail(Code, Code_tail) :-
        flatten1([[[push_top],[tl]], Code, [[pop]]], Code_tail).
```

s(Pat1, Pat2, GCode) generates code to refine Pat1 to be Pat2.

4.9. Peephole Optimisations

Direct short cuts are made when updating the application node with the result. Instead of forming the result structure on top of the stack and then copying the result into the application node to be updated, we directly create the result on the application node. Thus the following optimisations result:

```
[cons][update] → [update_cons]
[mkint][update] → [update_int]
[mkbool][update] → [update_bool]
[mkap][update] → [update_appl]
```

In the same spirit there is no need to create a boolean value on the a-stack if it is going to be immediately tested and removed in the next instruction. Therefore we get the following optimisation:

```
[eq][jtrue,Label] → [jeq, Label]
[lt][jtrue,Label] → [jlt, Label]
[null][jtrue,Label] → [jnull, Label]     etc.
```

5. Sample Code Generated

Below we give the code generated for the from function defined below.

```
from x y = if x > y then nil else cons x (from (x + 1) y);
```

The intermediate representation assuming a strictness signature of (a a) → de is shown below. This was used to generate the first column in figure 5-1. The second column in figure 5-1 was generated assuming a strictness signature of (⊥ ⊥) → d. This is a convenient example to hand test the rules given in this paper.

```
(fun from (x y) (expr (if E1 E2 E3) de))
where
        E1 = (expr (gt2 (var x a a) (var y a a)) a)
        E2 = nil
        E3 = (expr (cons (var x de a)
                         (expr (from (expr (add2 (var x a a) 1) a)
                                     (var y a a))
                               de)
                   (de de)))
```

Several differences should be noted when comparing the code generated in the two cases, referred to as the strict version (SV) and the non strict version (NSV).

```
 1.  getv(3)         /* a_stack := x */        1.  push(3)        /* s_stack := x */
 2.  getv(2)         /* a_stack := y */        2.  eval          /* evaluate */
 3.  jgt2(g0001)     /* test */                3.  atomicp       /* atom test */
                                               4.  get           /* a_stack := x */
 4.  push(3)         /* s_stack := x */        5.  push(2)       /* s_stack := y */
 5.  mkhole          /* result node */         6.  eval          /* evaluate */
 6.  push(2)         /* s_stack := y */        7.  atomicp       /* atom test */
 7.  getv(3)         /* a_stack := x */        8.  get           /* a_stack := y */
 8.  pushbasic(1)    /* a_stack := 1 */        9.  jgt2(g0002)   /* test */
 9.  add2
10.  mkint           /* s_stack := x+1 */     10.  push(3)       /* param x */
11.  fcall(from)     /* call from */          11.  pushfun(from1)/* new function*/
12.  update_cons     /* make result */        12.  push(3)       /* s_stack:= x */
13.  ret                                      13.  mkap          /* make graph */
                                              14.  push          /* s_stack:= y */
14.  label(g0001)                            15.  mkap          /* make graph */
15.  pushnil          /* s_stack := nil */    16.  update_cons   /* make result */
16.  update                                   17.  ret
17.  ret

                                              18.  label(g0002)
                                              19.  pushnil
                                              20.  update
                                              21.  ret
```

Figure 5-1: Sample Code For Function from

- In the SV, the parameters are directly accessed and moved to the arithmetic stack whereas in the NSV, evaluation and type checking is performed.

- The SV implements *call-by-value* parameter passing semantics whereas the NSV creates a suspended result to be later evaluated upon demand.

One would expect that in a fully strict version of a function, the G-code generated would be comparable to that produced by any LISP compiler. Indeed our preliminary timing tests seem to confirm this notion.

Our analysis method is currently under development. To be able to test our compiler we have developed an annotated user language, with type declarations, where the type information is propagated into the subexpressions of a function definition. The resulting intermediate form is not as rich as the one we expect from the analysis due to the simple nature of the pattern propagation. The resulting G-code is macro expanded to form a C program [9]. This has enabled us to perform some valuable comparisons, the results of which are summarized below. All timings were measured on a VAX 8600 running UNIX™.

	SV	NSV[2]	ML[3]	Miranda	PSL[4]	C	Pascal
fib 20	0.7	1.4	1	26.3	0.7	0.1	0.1
tak 18 12 6	2.1	7.2	11	87.0	1.4	0.3	0.8
sieve 2..500 (10 times)	3.2	7.0	13	43.0	3.2	-	-
insertion sort[5]	4.3	13.0	23	51.0[6]	2.8	-	-

References

[1] Burn, G. L., C. L. Hankin, and S. Abramsky.
     Theory and practice of strictness analysis for higher order functions.
     April 1985.
     Dept. of Computing, Imperial College of Science and Technology.

[2] Clocksin, W.F. and Mellish, C.S.
     Programming in Prolog.
     Springer-Verlag, 1984.
     2nd Edition.

---

[2]A small amount of strictness information was used in defining some of the functions to avoid the tedium involved in our annotated source language

[3]Standard ML, Timing Resolution = 1 sec

[4]Compiled Portable Standard LISP without fast integers

[5]Sorted a list of 500 elements in reverse order

[6]Sorted a list of 250 elements in reverse order

[3] Fairbairn, Jon, and Stuart C. Wray.
Code generation techniques for functional languages.
In *Proc. Symp. on Lisp and Func. Pgmming.*, pages 94-104. ACM, 1986.

[4] Hudak, P., and J. Young.
A set-theoretic characterization of function strictness in the lambda calculus.
In *Proc. Workshop on Implementations of Functional Languages.* Chalmers Univ., Aspenas, Sweden, February, 1985.

[5] Hughes, R. J. M.
Super Combinators.
In *Lisp and Functional Programming Conference*, pages 1-10. ACM, 1982.

[6] Hughes, J.
Strictness detection in non-flat domains.
Programming Research Group, Oxford.

[7] Johnsson, T.
Efficient compilation of lazy evaluation.
In *Proc. Symp. on Compiler Const.* ACM SIGPLAN, Montreal, 1984.

[8] Kieburtz, R. B., and M. Napierala.
A studied laziness -- strictness analysis with structured data types.
1985.
Extended abstract, Oregon Graduate Center.

[9] Kernighan, B.W. and Ritchie, D.M.
Software Series: The C Programming Language.
Prentice-Hall, Englewood Cliffs, New Jersey 07632, 1978.

[10] Kieburtz, R. B.
Abstract interpretations over infinite domains cannot terminate uniformly.
February 17, 1986.
Unpublished note, Dept. of Computer Science, Oregon Graduate Center.

[11] Kuo, T.-M., and P. Mishra.
On Strictness and its Analysis.
In *Proc. Symp. on Princ. of Pgmming. Lang.*. ACM, Munich, West Germany, March, 1987.
To appear.

[12] Lindstrom, Gary.
Static evaluation of functional programs.
In *Proc. Symposium on Compiler Construction*, pages 196-206. ACM SIGPLAN, Palo Alto, CA, June, 1986.

[13] Lindstrom, Gary, Lal George and Dowming Yeh.
Optimized compilation of functional programs through strictness analysis.
August 4, 1986.
Technical summary.

[14] Mycroft, A.
The theory and practice of transforming call-by-need into call-by-value.
In *Int. Symp. on Prgmming.* Springer, April, 1980.
Lecture Notes in Computer Science, vol. 83.

[15] Sheeran, Mary.
Designing regular array architectures using higher order functions.
In *Proc. Conf. on Functional Programming Languages and Computer Architectures*, pages 220-237. Springer Verlag, 1985.
Lecture Notes in Computer Science, vol. 201.

[16] Wadler, Phil.
Strictness analysis on non-flat domains (by abstract interpretation over finite domains).
November 10, 1985.
Unpublished note, Programming Research Group, Oxford Univ.

[17] Warren, David H. D.
Applied logic: its use and implementation as a programming tool.
Technical Report, SRI, Inc., 1983.
Note 290.

Hoisting: Lazy Evaluation in a Cold Climate

Simon Finn

Department of Computing Science
University of Stirling
Stirling FK9 4LA

1 Introduction

There has been much work recently aimed at combining the formalisms of functional and logic programming; some, such as the original work on LOGLISP [Robinson and Sibert 82], treat reduction and deduction as two separate mechanisms, while others, such as [Goguen and Meseguer 84] and [Darlington et al. 86] attempt a more comprehensive unification based on narrowing. The author's language, Simplex, follows the LOGLISP approach of having two separate sublanguages (and consequently two implementation mechanisms). The implementation of Simplex differs from that of LOGLISP in two ways: the functional sublanguage is lazy (not applicative order) but the implementation of the logic language uses only depth-first (not breadth-first) search. (So Simplex has a 'good' implementation of functional programming allied with a 'bad' implementation of logic programming, while LOGLISP has the reverse.)

The unfortunate interaction of lazy evaluation and logic programming produces an implementation problem which is examined in this paper. Lazy evaluation is a strategy that delays performing work in the hope that the work will ultimately prove to be unnecessary. The basic assumption is that there is no penalty for the delay - the postponement should not increase the total amount of work required. In a purely functional setting, the chief challenge to the validity of this assumption is posed by beta-reduction. Beta-reduction requires the copying of expressions; if an expression is not already in normal form, this seems to imply a duplication of the work required to normalise it. Fortunately, this problem has been solved by the development of techniques such as graph-reduction; rather than physically copying an expression, an indirection is used instead, so that when (if) the original expression is reduced, the benefit is shared by all of its instances.

The addition of logic programming introduces another, more subtle, way in which an unreduced expression may be copied. The difficulty arises from the branching of the search tree - whenever a disjunction is processed, each possibility must be examined independently (either sequentially or in parallel) and each path explored requires its own copy of every extant expression. The copying that this implies also poses a problem for lazy evaluation, but one that is not addressed by graph-reduction or suchlike techniques. The difficulty is that delaying the reduction of an expression may lead to the duplication of work since the same reduction may need to be performed on several different search paths. The total amount of work performed on any one search path is not increased by this (so with a processor-per-path machine there might be no difficulty) but the increase in total workload will reduce the overall performance where the number of processors is limited. Some mechanism to allow the results of reductions to be shared between separate search paths is needed to avoid this overhead.

Unfortunately, there is more to the problem than this: sharing the result of a reduction between two different search paths may not be safe. For example, the result of reducing the expression 'x+1' depends on 'x'; if two different search paths instantiate this variable to different values then each must perform the reduction independently. On the other hand, if 'x' has the same value, it may be possible to save a reduction by storing and then reusing the result.

The subject of this paper is a technique - hoisting - which is designed to detect whether (and how widely) the result of a reduction may be shared, and to implement its sharing. (The name 'hoisting' derives from the way that a long-delayed reduction may be 'hoisted' up the search tree so that its result may be shared by many search paths.) In a sense, hoisting is a generalisation of lazy evaluation; for purely functional programs, a lazy reducer performs no more (and possible fewer) reductions than an applicative-order one. The addition of the branching occasioned by logic programming destroys this pleasant property: for any given program, lazy evaluation may or may not require fewer reductions. Whatever the program, a system employing hoisting will do at least as well (in terms of the number of reductions performed) as a comparable lazy or applicative-order system. The implementation of hoisting will necessitate some additional run-time overheads; the amount required will depend on the particular search strategy employed. The combination of hoisting with parallel or breadth-first searching does not seem attractive - the overheads required are too great - but for depth-first sequential search hoisting can be implemented as a combination of graph-reduction and backtracking.

2 Hoisting

Let us ignore for a moment the mechanics by which reductions are to be shared and concentrate on the problem of deciding when a reduction is sharable. What we require is a characterisation of those parts of the search tree where the work involved in performing a reduction may be safely shared. The key to finding such a characterisation is the following important property of graph-reduction: once a redex appears in the graph, reducing it will always produce the same result (interpreted as meaning the effect on the local structure of the graph) no matter how long the reduction is delayed or what other reductions are performed in the meantime. (This observation is just a rather strong Church-Rosser result; its strength derives from the ability to consider part of the graph in isolation and ignore changes wrought by other reductions to the rest of it.) The addition of 'logical variables' appears to spoil the situation since, as we have seen, the same expression may be reduced in different ways depending on how these variables become instantiated. For example:

```
          /\
         /  \
        /    \
       /\     1        ==>        2
      /  \             x=1
     /    \
   Add     x
```

```
          /\
         /  \
        /    \
       /\     1        ==>        3
      /  \             x=2
     /    \
   Add     x
```

The property can be saved if we insist that a redex has not actually 'appeared' in the graph until all the variables that its reduction will dereference have been instantiated. (Or, put more simply, its not a redex until it can actually be reduced.) The, on any one search path, the previous result still holds since no instantiated variable can later change its value. (The problems caused by variables which 'change value' only occur when the system jumps from one search path to another.) In summary, once a redex has appeared in the program graph, nothing that happens lower in the search tree, whether the instantiation of further variables or reductions elsewhere in the graph, can ever change the effect of reducing it.

It was observed in the introduction that the problem of the interaction of lazy evaluation and logic programming is that delaying the reduction of an expression may require the same reduction sequence to be performed many times at different point in the search tree. The result of the previous paragraph guarantees that if the expression in question is a redex, then every attempt to reduce it will produce exactly the same change to the graph structure. It should now be obvious that any redex is a prime candidate for 'hoisting' - once it appears in the graph, the result of its eventual reduction is fixed. This being so, it should be safe to delay the reduction, perform it just once, and then share the result over some subtree of the search space.

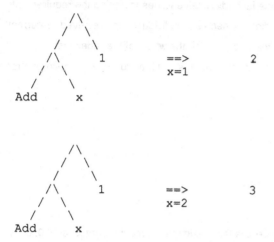

A problem now appears: how can the system econnomically determine, when it performs a reduction, the point in the search tree at which that redex first appeared (i.e. the first point at which the reduction could have been performed) ? This question needs to be answered in order to determine the largest subtree of the seach space that can safely share the result of each reduction step. The solution is to associate an extra integer field - the tag - with each graph node. The tag of a node will be used to record the depth of the search tree when that node acquired its current value. When a node is first created, its tag will be initialised to the then current tree depth; whenever the node is updated , its tag is updated too. A redex appears in the graph (precisely) when all nodes which constitute its body receive values matching the requirements of some reduction rule. Since the tags indicate when each individual node received its current value, it is trivial to calculate the level of the tree at which the whole of the redex first appeared. For example, using brackets to indicate the tags attached to node, the following redex:

```
          /\(0)
         /  \
        /    \
      /\(0)   1(1)
     /  \
    /    \
 Add(2)  2(1)
```

first appeared at level 2 of the graph (since 2 is the maximum i.e. most recent level of 0, 0, 1, 1 and 2). Here we have to include all five tags in the calculation; it is not enough to know that the arguments are 2 and 1, we also have to know that the operator is 'Add' and that it is applied to these two operands.

Deciding which tags to use in the calculation can be a rather subtle business; for example, the following redex first appeared at level 3 (not level 5) of the graph:

```
            /\(0)
           /  \
          /    \
        /\(3)   z(4)
       /  \
      /    \
    /\(2)   y(1)
   /  \
  /    \
S(0)    x(5)
```

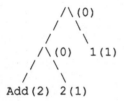

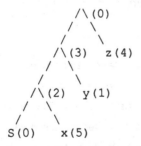

The reason for this is that to perform an S reduction, the system only needs to know that the S combinator is applied to three arguments (so level 3 is calculated as the maximum of 0, 2, 3 and 0). It doesn't need the actual values of the arguments to perform the reduction, so their tags are not included in the calculation. If the value of one of the arguments were to change, the reduction would still be correct - the new graph would simply contain the new value in the same place that the old graph had the old value. In operational terms, the value of a tag must be included in the calculation if (and only if) the graph-reducer has to examine the value of the corresponding cell to perform the reduction.

It might seem that we have completely solved the problem posed at the beginning of the section: the result of reduction is sharable from the moment that the redex appears in the graph, which in turn can be determined by using the tags of the body of the redex. It would indeed be possible to implement a system on the above lines, and the system would perform some measure of hoisting, but it would be suboptimal. The problem is that not only can lazy evaluation delay the reduction of an expression once it has appeared in the program graph, it can also delay the moment at which the expression first appears at all (by delaying the reduction which gives rise to it). The key to getting the full benefit of hoisting is to realise that not only is it safe to share the result of performing a reduction from the point in the search tree at which the redex actually appeared but that sharing is also safe from the highest point at which the redex could (by using a different reduction strategy) have been made to appear. The advantage of this is that the higher in the search tree the result can be hoisted, the more widely it can be shared and the fewer times the reduction must be repeated.

The justification of 'full' hoisting again relies on the Church-Rosser property mentioned earlier. So far as the effect on the program graph is concerned, it doesn't matter whether a sequence of reductions is performed as soon as each is possible or only when the final result is required. Delaying reductions (as with lazy evaluation) may delay the appearance of the hoistable redex but can't alter its form and so can have no effect on the result of its eventual reduction.

One previously solved problem now returns: how does the system, when performing a reduction, determine the highest point in the search tree at which a redex could have been produced ? The previous scheme won't do - it will only say when a redex was actually produced. What is needed is a subtle adjustment in the meaning of the tags: rather than record the point in the search tree at which each cell received its current value, each tag will now indicate the highest point in the tree at which the corresponding cell could possibly have been reduced to its current value. The highest point in the tree at which a redex 'could have appeared' can than be calculated from the tags of the nodes which constitute its value. Since a redex 'could have been reduced' as soon as it 'could have appeared', the same calculation will also give the correct tag for the result of the reduction. The simultaneous calculation of the new result and it tag, 'tagged reduction', is described in more detail in the next section.

3 An Implementation of Hoisting

This section describes the author's implementation of a hoisting system based on the combination of combinator graph-reduction [Turner 79] with depth-first sequential search. The particular choice of reduction system is not essential (for example, using supercombinators [Hughes 82] would be a straightforward extension); what is important is the way the system uses tags to calculate the highest point of the search tree at which each reduction could have been performed (section 3.1). The restriction to depth-first search is also important; this means that there is no need to copy the entire program graph when a choice-point is encountered. Instead, changes to the graph structure are logged and reversed on backtracking; the tags are used to decide which changes should be logged and when they should be reversed (section 3.2). Finally, a small change to the tagging scheme is introduced which result in a decrease in the number of store updates (but not reductions) required; this is described in section 3.3.

3.1 Tagged Combinator Reduction

For each reduction that it performs, the graph-reducer has to calculate how widely the result may be shared i.e. how high in the search tree it may be hoisted. This section describes this calculation; the description is only concerned with what happens on one particular search path; the actions taken on backtracking are described in the next subsection. Provided we only consider one search path at a time, a single integer (the tag) will be enough to indicate unambiguously the highest point of the search tree to which any particular result may be hoisted. The tag used is the depth in the search tree; any two edges on the same search path will correspond to different tags.

```
              |
              | (0)
              |
             / \
        (1) /   \ (1)
           /     \
          /\     /\
     (2) /  \ (2)   \ (2)
        /    \
             /\
        (3) /  \ (3)
           /    \
```

```
Search Tree with edges labeled with tree-depth
     (number of choice-points encountered)
```

Every graph node has a corresponding tag which indicates the highest point of the tree at which its current value could have been computed. When the program is first loaded, all the tags are set to zero (the original program is valid over the whole search space). When new graph nodes are created, or existing graph nodes are overwritten, as the result of a reduction, the new tag is calculated in a manner to be described shortly. Any graph node created by the system for any other reason (for example as the consequence of standardising clauses apart) is tagged with the then current depth in the search tree.

Whenever the system performs a reduction, it overwrites the root node of the redex with a new value; tagged reduction must calculate an appropriate tag to go with this value. The old and new tags will be compared to discover whether the old value should be saved and, if so, when it should be subsequently restored; this is described more fully in the next subsection. The rule used to calculate the new tag is very simple: the new tag should be the maximum of the tags of all the nodes whose values are examined to perform the reduction. This is a reflection of the fact that the reduction could have been performed (precisely) when all the values used to match the reduction rule could have become available. For example, the rule for the S combinator is:

```
           /\(s)                              /\(t)
          /   \                              /   \
         /     \                            /     \
       /\(r)   z(k)        ==>          /\(t)   /\(t)
      /   \                             /       /   \
     /     \                           /       /     \
   /\(q)   y(j)                      x(i)    y(j)    z(k)
  /   \
 /     \
S(p)   x(i)

                    t = max(p,q,r,s)
```

Note that it is important to include the tags of the internal application nodes in this calculation - its no use S being available for reduction if it has not been applied to three arguments. In contrast, the tags of the arguments themselves are not used in the calculation. This is because the precise values of x, y, and z are not needed to perform this reduction - it is valid so long as each of them is the same after the reduction as before it. The new tag is the maximum of the tag of the combinator itself and of the tags of the application nodes; the tags of the actual arguments are disregarded. This treatment of tags is typical of a combinator that simply embeds its arguments in a new applicative structure. The new tag is used to update the root node of the subgraph and to label any new graph nodes that are introduced (here the applications of x and y to z).

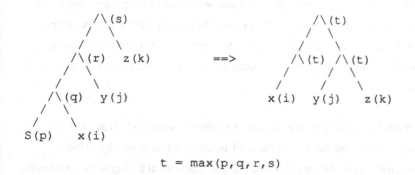

The treatment of combinators that examine the values of their arguments is different; here the tags of the arguments must be taken into consideration. For example, the rule for 'Add' (assuming the arguments are already in normal form) is:

```
        /\(r)
       /  \
      /    \
    /\(q)  y(t)          ==>          x+y(u)
   /  \
  /    \
Add(p) x(s)

                  u = max(p,q,r,s,t)
```

The reason for the difference is that the actual values of the arguments are used in the reduction; if either were to change then the result of the reductions would becone incorrect. (If the arguments are not already in normal form but have to be forced fisrt then it is important to use the post-forcing tags for the arguments rather than the pre-forcing ones as the tags may have been increased by the intervening reductions.) The general rule is that a tag is included in the calculation if (and only if) the'graph-reducer has to examine the contents of the corresponding cell to perform the reduction. (Less operationally, this means that the tag of an argument is included in the calculation precisely when the reduction rule constrains the argument to be in some normal form.)

Dereferencing a 'logical variable' may be treated as if it were a special kind of reduction (in particular, it is analogous to I reduction). The result of 'reducing' a bound variable is the expression to which it is bound; the tag of the result is the maximum of the tag of the expression and the tree level at which the variable was bound (stored as the tag of the variable).

```
x ---> e        ===>        e
(p)    (q)                 (r)

           r = max(p,q)
```

Actually, this account is a little too simple, since if the expression (e) is not in head-normal form, then copying it may require it to be normalised several times, losing lazy evaluation. A similar problem arises with the reduction of an application of the I combinator; the soultion in each case is to force the expression before copying it.

3.2 Backtracking

The previous subsection described how tagged reduction maintains a tag for each graph node which specifies how 'sharable' its value is. The mechanism described there dealt with only one search path at a time; the problem is more general than this (if the system only had to try one search path, there would be no point in bothering with tags at all). The purpose of having tags is to determine when a result can be safely shared between different search paths; in terms of a depth-first implementation, this means that the tags will be used to decide which store updates must be trailed and when each such update must be reversed.

The graph structure is not duplicated when a choice-point is encountered, although a separate copy of it is logically required for each branch. Instead, a strategy is used that is similar to the treament of variable bindings in Prolog; changes are logged on a 'trail' and reversed on backtracking (e.g. see Warren 77). The new trail (keeping this name for want of a better one) will store address / value / tag triples in a number of pools, with one pool for each level of the search tree. Each pool will contain a set of triples; when a update which needs trailing is performed, the address / old value / old tag triple is added to the pool indexed by the new tag. Later, when the system backtracks from level n+1 to level n, the n+1th pool is emptied and its contents used to roll back those changes to the graph structure that are no longer valid. (In general the system may have to backtrack by more than one level at a time. This is handled by processing each pool in turn, starting with the highest numbered.)

The algorithm for deciding when the old value of a cell should be saved is simple: compare the new tag with the old tag. If the new tag is greater, then the old value should be saved before the update is performed; if the two tags are equal (by construction, the new tag will never be the lesser) then no special action is required. The justification of this rule is that when the two tags are equal, both the old and new values of the node are valid in the same subtree of the search space, so that when backtracking invalidates the new value, there will be no point in reverting to the old one. By contrast, if the old tag is smaller, then the old value is valid in a larger (containing) subtree, so restoration will be worthwhile.

This doesn't mean that the old value should necessarily be restored when the system returns to the immediately previous choice-point; the entire purpose of maintaining the tags is to avoid this. A little thought will show when the old value should be restored - when the system backtracks out of the subtree in which the new value is valid. The new tag defines the subtree in which the new value is valid, so there is a simple test for this circumstance: the system should restore the old value when backtracking reduces the then current depth in the search tree to less than the new tag. In effect, the trail is used as a stack of sets; any of the sets may be enlarged at any time, but they are discharged using a strictly last-in / first-out discipline.

We now have an implementation of hoisting for a sequential depth-first search strategy; only one refinement remains unexplained. By taking further advantage of the particular search strategy used (subtrees are explored left-to-right), the size of the trail (though not the number of reductions performed) can be reduced.

3.3 A Last-Call Optimisation

The tagging scheme based on tree-depth works well except in one respect. When the system returns to a choice-point after exploring the last alternative branch, it restores the program graph ot its state when the choice-point was first encountered. This is wasteful, since the next thing the system will do is backtrack further, which may discard or further restore the just-altered graph nodes. The purpose of saving the old values on the trail is so that they may be later reused; if there is no further use for a node, then there is no point in saving and later restoring it. This will be the case precisely when there are no unexplored alternatives to try between the choice-point indexed by the old tag and the choice-point indicated by the new tag. In this situation, backtracking past the latter choice-point (invalidating the new value of the node) will be followed, inexorably and immediately, by backtracking past the former (invalidating the old value of the node). It would be possible, but rather expensive, to check this condition whenever an update is attempted; a better solution is to alter the tagging scheme slightly:

```
              |
              | (0)
              |
             / \
       (1) /     \ (0)
          /       \
         /\       /\
  (2) /   \ (1)     \ (0)
     /     \
           /\
     (2) /   \ (1)
        /     \
```

New Tagging Scheme

The rule generating the new tags is that the tag is the depth in the search tree, excluding rightmost branches. In operational terms, the old scheme used the number of choice-points encountered along a path from the root while the new scheme uses the number of choice-points with unexplored alternatives. The effect of this change is to perform a kind of last-call optimisation; the value of a node will not be trailed if it will never be needed again. (There is no change in the number of reductions required - both tagging schemes are equally good in this respect - the difference is in the number of store updates required.) This optimisation is particulary important in systems such as the author's which only permit binary disjunctions since the natural way to simulate multi-way choice on such a system (tail-nesting alternatives) would otherwise lead to an unnecessary proliferation of different tags and consequent waste of trail space.

4 Limitations

The scheme for hoisting described in the body of this paper has two important limitations which restrict its applicability. The first problem is that the particular tagging scheme described is only sufficient for a depth-first sequential system. A parallel system would require a more elaborate tag to indicate the subtree in which each reduction is valid. Also, a graph node would no longer be a simple memory cell; since its value may depend on which part of the search space is being explored, it must appear to have different values to different processes. (This can be acheived, for example, by using the tag of the subtree currently being explored to determine which value is appropriate.) These considerations do not make the use of hoisting impossible with a parallel implementation; they do, however, make it unduly expensive.

The second limitation is that the whole idea of hoisting assumes that the processes of reducing the program graph and exploring the search tree are distinct. In systems based on narrowing this is not the case; reduction, unification and search interact. A narrowing in one part of the program graph may (by instantiating a non-local variable) render impossible a potential narrowing in a completely different part of the program graph. This non-local interaction appears to prevent hoisting, since a potential narrowing may not, unlike a reduction, be valid in a whole subtree of the search space. The situation may not be as simple as this, however; for a language such as Darlington's [Darlington et al. 86], it may be expected that most narrowings are simply reductions (i.e. they are deterministic and instantiate no non-local variables). Moreover these reductions behave in just the way needed to make hoisting work; they can be implemented by graph-rewriting (since they are deterministic) and are valid in a whole subtree of the search space (since no non-local variables are instantiated). The 'genuine' narrowings (where an expression matches more than one rewrite rule) are responsible for the branching of the search space; these could be treated as the combination of a disjunction (forming a choice-point) and a reduction.

5 References

[Darlington et al. 86]
The Unification of Functional and Logic Languages
J. Darlington, A.J. Field and H. Pull
in 'Logic Programming: Functions, Relations and Equations'
ed. D. DeGroot and G. Lindstrom
Prentice-Hall 1986

[Goguen and Meseguer 84]
EQLOG: Equality, Types and Generic Modules for Logic Programming
J. Goguen and J. Meseguer
Journal of Logic Programming, 1984, Vol 1, No 2, pp 179-209

[Hughes 82]
Super-Combinators: A New Implementation Method for Applicative Languages
R. J. M. Hughes
1982 ACM Symposium on LISP and Functional Programming, Pittsburgh 1982

[Robinson and Sibert 82]
LOGLISP: Motivation, Design and Implementation
J.A. Robinson and E.E. Sibert
ed. K.L. Clark and S.-A. Tarnlund,
Academic Press 1982

[Turner 79]
A New Implementation Technique for Applicative Languages
D.A. Turner
Software Practice and Experience, 1979, Vol 9

[Warren 77]
Implementing PROLOG - Compiling Logic Programs
D.H.D. Warren
DAI Research Reports No 39,40, Edinburgh University 1977

INDUCTIVE ASSERTION METHOD FOR LOGIC PROGRAMS

Włodzimierz Drabent† and Jan Małuszyński

Department of Computer and Information Science
Linköping University, 581 83 Linköping, Sweden
computer mail: jmz@liuida.uucp

ABSTRACT

Certain properties of logic programs are inexpressible in terms of their declarative semantics. One example of such properties would be the actual form of procedure calls and successes which occur during computations of a program. They are often used by programmers in their informal reasoning. In this paper, the inductive assertion method for proving partial correctness of logic programs is introduced and proved sound. The method makes it possible to formulate and prove properties which are inexpressible in terms of the declarative semantics. An execution mechanism using the Prolog computation rule and arbitrary search strategy (eg. OR-parallelism or Prolog backtracking) is assumed. The method may be also used to specify the semantics of some extra-logical built-in procedures for which the declarative semantics is not applicable.

1. INTRODUCTION

One of the most attractive features of logic programs is their declarative semantics [Apt, van Emden][Lloyd]. It describes program meaning in terms of least Herbrand models and logical consequence. It states, informally speaking, that whatever is computed by a logic program is its logical consequence and whatever its logical consequence is may be computed (unless the interpreter gets into an infinite loop due to an imperfect search strategy). More precisely, if a goal $\leftarrow A$ succeeds with a substitution θ as an answer then $\forall A\theta$ is a logical consequence of the program. If $\forall A\theta$ is a logical consequence of the program then there exists a computation for $\leftarrow A$ giving an answer substitution σ which is more general then θ (there exists γ such that $\theta = \sigma\gamma$). The least Herbrand model of a program is equal to the set of all ground atomic formulas A for which there exists a successful computation for the goal $\leftarrow A$.

In most cases the declarative semantics is sufficient for dealing with logic programs. For instance it may form a basis for formal program synthesis [Hogger]. However, there are some important properties of logic programs which are inexpressible in terms of the declarative semantics. An example of such a property is the correctness of a mode declaration. It is also often the case that a Prolog procedure is written under the assumption that all its invocations are of a certain form (and does not work properly when called in another way). Consider, for example, the procedure

append(X–Y, Y–Z, X–Z).

which appends difference lists. When used with the two first arguments being variables it produces incorrect results (they are not difference lists). Another example is the procedure

---

† present address: Institute of Computer Science, Polish Academy of Sciences, P.O.Box 22, 00-901 Warszawa PKiN, Poland

This research has been partially supported by the National Swedish Board for Technical Development, projekt nr STUF 85-3166 and STU 86-3372.

permute:

```
permute( [ ], [ ] ).
permute( T, [E|P] ) :- remove( T, E, T1 ), permute( T1, P ).
remove( [H|T], H, T ).
remove( [H|T], E, [H|T1] ) :- remove( T, E, T1 ).
```

which loops (after producing one answer) when invoked with a variable as the first argument. In every day reasoning about logic programs it is often necessary to discuss the actual form of procedure calls and answers. Features of this kind will be called here run-time properties as they concern not only a program's answer but also its execution process. Of course they cannot be dealt with in terms of the declarative semantics.

The declarative semantics is also insufficient in that it cannot predict the actual form of an answer. Knowing that $\forall A\theta$ is a logical consequence of a program we cannot say which substitutions are the answers to the goal $\leftarrow A$ (we only know that there is *an* answer more general than θ). Consider two programs:

```
p(f(a)).                                p(f(X)).
p(f(X)).                                q(a).
q(a).
```

The declarative semantics of both programs is the same, but for a goal $\leftarrow p(Y)$ they give different sets of answers. Proving what the actual answers are is possible in our approach.

This paper describes an inductive assertion method for proving run time properties of logic programs. In this work we are inspired by the well-known results of [Floyd] and [Hoare] for imperative programs but, due to the rather different nature of logic programs, direct application of these results is not possible. Our assertions refer to the bindings of the arguments of a procedure at each possible call of this procedure and upon its completion. Our notion of correctness relies on such assertions; a program is correct iff the conditions expressed by the assertions of a procedure are satisfied whenever this procedure is called, and whenever it achieves a success. We deal only with partial correctness: a procedure may loop or fail but if the program is correct we still know that the arguments of every subsequent call have the properties expressed by the corresponding assertion. A similar problem is tackled in [Mellish] but the approach is different, based on abstract interpretation. An attempt to treat termination of logic programs in a formal way is presented in [Francez et al].

The rest of the paper is organized as follows. Section 2 introduces the notion of the asserted logic program. Section 3 contains an informal explanation of the method with some example proofs. Its purpose is to introduce intuitions facilitating understanding of Section 4 which presents the method in a formal way. This section also contains some comparisons with the abstract interpretation method. A proof of the main theorem of this section is presented separately in Section 5. Section 6 contains conclusions. This paper is a slightly modified version of [Drabent, Małuszyński].

2. LOGIC PROGRAMS WITH ASSERTIONS

In this section we introduce the notion of an asserted logic program. We assume familiarity with foundations of logic programming, as presented for instance in [Lloyd].

By a logic program we mean a set of Horn clauses of the form

$$a_0 :- a_1, \ldots, a_n. \qquad n \geq 0,$$

including a goal clause of the form

$$:- a_1, \ldots, a_n. \qquad n \geq 0$$

where each a_i is an atomic formula of the form $p(t_1,\ldots,t_m)$ $(m \geq 0)$ consisting of a m-ary predicate symbol p and terms $t_1,\ldots,t_m$. The terms have the standard syntax: they are either variables or are constructed from functors and variables (constants are zero-argument functors).

By an n-ary procedure q of a logic program we mean the set of all clauses of the program whose left-hand sides begin with the n-ary predicate letter q.

In the examples we will use the syntax of Edinburgh Prolog [Bowen et al] including the list notation (functors including constants beginning with a small letter, variables beginning with a capital letter, [ ] standing for the empty list, $[Head|Tail]$ for the list consisting of $Head$ and $Tail$, $[t_1,\ldots,t_n]$ for an n-element list).

In this paper the form of procedure calls and answers during execution of logic programs is treated formally in the framework of SLD-derivations. Nothing about search strategy is assumed; it may be, for instance, OR-parallelism or the backtracking of Prolog. But in order to be able to obtain nontrivial results, some limitations on the computation rule are needed. In this paper the Prolog computation rule is used (the leftmost atomic formula in a current goal is always selected).

Our intention is to describe the form of procedure arguments at every possible call and upon its completion, and to prove correctness of such descriptions. This resembles the idea of introducing assertions for imperative programs [Floyd, Hoare]. Assertions are logic formulas that characterize states (variable valuations) of imperative programs. These formulas are to be interpreted on the data domain referred to by the program. The assertions can be seen as a specification of a program. They facilitate understanding of programs and are used as a basis for program verification. For each statement S of a program two assertions, a precondition and a postcondition, are given. They describe, respectively, states before the execution of S and states after this execution.

Experience has shown that it is often more convenient to use *binary* assertions [Tarlecki] which involve two states. For example a postcondition for a statement may describe the relation between the input and output states of this statement (while a "normal", unary assertion describes a set of states). In our approach, in order to describe a logic program a unary precondition and a binary postcondition are associated with every predicate symbol p of the program. The precondition characterizes the arguments of every call of the procedure p, and the postcondition describes relations between these arguments and their final instances when a call succeeds. The pair of pre- and postcondition will be called here an *assertion*. A program with an assertion for every its predicate symbol is called an *asserted program*.

An asserted program is said to be *correct* iff, during its execution, for any procedure call the precondition of the procedure is satisfied, and upon a success of the call the postcondition is satisfied. Note that this is partial correctness. It does not say whether a success actually occurs. A formal definition of program correctness is given in Section 4.

Now we introduce a metalanguage for writing assertions for logic programs. The language of clauses (the logic programming language) will be referred to as the object language. The domain of interpretation for the metalanguage are (not necessarily ground) terms of the object language. This is because the metalanguage is intended to describe relations on (object language) terms. The functors and the predicate symbols of the metalanguage given in the definition below refer only to some basic operations and relations. We do not intend to give an exhaustive list of such symbols, nor to restrict ourselves to some minimal set.

DEFINITION 2.1 (of the metalanguage of assertions)

1. Variables:

   a. ${}^\bullet p_i$, $p_i^\bullet$ $(i = 1,\ldots,n)$ where p is an n-ary predicate of the object language.

   b. T, U, V, ...

Comment: ${}^\bullet p_i$ stands for the value of i-th argument of p at invocation of the procedure p. $p_i^\bullet$ stands for the value of this argument at success. T, U, V,... stand for any terms.

2. n-ary functors $(n \geq 0)$:

   a. n-ary functors of the object language.

   b. variables of the object language: $X, Y, Z, \ldots$ $(n = 0)$.

   c. ...

For the functors from the cases a. and b. the interpretation of a functor is the functor itself.

3. Terms: standard definition.

4. Predicate symbols: $=$, var, ground, $\prec$, $\cong$, ...

Interpretation:

$=$ – term equality,

var(T) iff T is an (object language) variable,

ground(T) iff T is an (object language) ground term,

T $\prec$ U iff T is a subterm of U,

T $\cong$ U iff the terms T and U are variants of each other (they differ at most in the names of their variables),

disconnected($\mathtt{V}_1,\ldots,\mathtt{V}_n$) iff no variable occurs in more than one of the terms $\mathtt{V}_1,\ldots,\mathtt{V}_n$,

subterm(T, U, I) iff T $\prec$ U and I is the corresponding selector (assuming any fixed way of assigning selectors to subterm occurrences).

5. Logical connectives and quantifiers: **true**, **false**, $\vee$, &, $\Rightarrow$, ...

6. Formulas: standard definition.

7. An *assertion* for the predicate p is an expression

$$p : \mathbf{pre}\ F_1; \mathbf{post}\ F_2$$

where F_1, F_2 are formulas which do not contain the variables ${}^\bullet q_i$, $q_i^\bullet$ for $q \neq p$ and $p_i^\bullet$ does not occur in F_1. F_1, F_2 are called the precondition and the postcondition for p. □

Sometimes it is necessary to add integer arithmetic to the metalanguage. In this case we add numbers, arithmetical functors and predicates with the obvious interpretation.

Let a be an (object language) atomic formula of the form $p(t_1,\ldots,t_n)$. We will often say "pre-(post-)condition for a" instead of "pre-(post-)condition for p".

DEFINITION 2.2

Let $a = p(t_1,\ldots,t_n)$.

1. *a satisfies its precondition* F_1 iff F_1 is true w.r.t. (any) interpretation in which the values of ${}^\bullet p_1,\ldots,{}^\bullet p_n$ are, respectively, $t_1,\ldots,t_n$.

2. Let σ be a substitution. $(a, a\sigma)$ *satisfies its postcondition* F_2 iff F_2 is true w.r.t. (any) interpretation in which the values of ${}^\bullet p_1,\ldots,{}^\bullet p_n$ are, respectively, $t_1,\ldots,t_n$ and the values of $p_1^\bullet,\ldots,p_n^\bullet$ are, respectively, $t_1\sigma,\ldots,t_n\sigma$. □

EXAMPLE 2.1

Let p be a three argument predicate symbol. This is an assertion for p:

p : **pre** var(${}^\bullet p_2$) & var(${}^\bullet p_3$) & ${}^\bullet p_2 \not\prec {}^\bullet p_1$ & ${}^\bullet p_3 \not\prec {}^\bullet p_1$;

post $p_2^\bullet = p_3^\bullet = [\,]$ $\vee$

$\neg$ground($p_2^\bullet$) & ((var(V) & V $\prec p_2^\bullet$) $\Rightarrow$ V $\prec p_3^\bullet$)

The precondition means that the second and the third arguments of p are variables which do not occur in the first argument. The postcondition means that either the second and the third arguments are empty lists or the second one is nonground and every variable occurring in it also occurs in the third argument. Note that this is actually a unary postcondition (since it is independent of the arguments of the call of p).

The atomic formula $p([1,2],X,Y)$ satisfies its precondition and $p([1,X],X,Y)$ does not. The postcondition is satisfied by $(p([1,2],X,Y),\ p([1,2],[\,],[\,]))$ and by $(p([1,2],X,Y),\ p([1,2],[V,Z],[pair(1,V),pair(2,Z)]))$.

The program below is a part of the program *serialise* [Bowen et al].

$$:-\ p(\mathtt{T},X,Y). \qquad \text{where } X \not\prec \mathtt{T}, Y \not\prec \mathtt{T} \tag{0}$$

$$p([\,],[\,],[\,]). \tag{1}$$

$$p([A|LA],\ [B|LB],\ [pair(A,B)|LC]) :-\ p(LA,LB,LC). \tag{2}$$

This program together with the assertion is an asserted program. (Note that formally it is a class of programs as a class of goal statements is specified. X and Y are object language variables while T stands for any term not containing these variables.) □

EXAMPLE 2.2 (of an asserted program)

The program from Example 2.1 (but without any conditions for T in (0)) and with the following assertion for p:

pre true ;
post $p_2^\bullet = p_3^\bullet = [\,]$ ∨
$\mathrm{var}({}^\bullet p_2)$ & $\mathrm{var}({}^\bullet p_3)$ & ${}^\bullet p_2 \not\prec {}^\bullet p_1$ & ${}^\bullet p_3 \not\prec {}^\bullet p_1 \Longrightarrow$
$\neg\mathrm{ground}(p_2^\bullet)$ & $((\mathrm{var}(\mathtt{V})$ & $\mathtt{V} \prec p_2^\bullet) \Rightarrow \mathtt{V} \prec p_3^\bullet)$ □

EXAMPLE 2.3 (of an asserted program)

The program from Example 2.1 with the following assertion for p:

pre $\mathrm{var}({}^\bullet p_2)$ & $\mathrm{var}({}^\bullet p_3)$ & ${}^\bullet p_2 \not\prec {}^\bullet p_1$ & ${}^\bullet p_3 \not\prec {}^\bullet p_1$;
post $p_2^\bullet = [\mathtt{V}_1,\ldots,\mathtt{V}_n],\ n \geq 0$ & $\forall_{i,j}\ \mathrm{var}(\mathtt{V}_i)$ & $(i \neq j \Rightarrow \mathtt{V}_i \neq \mathtt{V}_j)$.

The postcondition means that the second argument of p (at a success of p) is a list of different variables. □

3. INFORMAL INTRODUCTION TO THE PROOF METHOD

The section contains an informal and intuitive presentation of the content of Section 4. Some readers may prefer to skip it and refer directly to that section.

Let us discuss computations of a program P relating to its clause

$$a_0 :-\ a_1, \ldots, a_n. \tag{*}$$

The clause may be invoked only when a current subgoal, say b, is unifiable with a_0. As a result of the unification some of the variables occurring in a_0 will be instantiated to terms, not necessarily ground. Let V denote a variable occurring in (*) or in b. The value of V after the unification will be denoted by $\mathtt{V}_0$. The value of an unbound variable is the variable itself. So $\mathtt{V}_0 = \mathtt{V}$ for example if V does not occur in a_0.

Let a_1' be a_1 with every variable V substituted by $\mathtt{V}_0$. After the unification, a_1' becomes the current subgoal. Upon a success of a_1' the variable bindings are updated: the value of each V is denoted by $\mathtt{V}_1$, and a_1' with the new bindings is denoted by a_1''.

Note that the difference between $\mathtt{V}_0$ and $\mathtt{V}_1$ is due to binding some of the variables which occur both in $\mathtt{V}_0$ and in a_1'. The variables are being bound to terms which replace them in $\mathtt{V}_0$ giving $\mathtt{V}_1$. If there are no such variables then $\mathtt{V}_0 = \mathtt{V}_1$. Further, $\mathtt{V}_0$ and $\mathtt{V}_1$ may differ even if V does not occur in a_1.

EXAMPLE 3.1

1. Let $V_0 = V$, $a_1 = p(V,b) = a_1'$. Suppose that $a_1'' = p(f(c),b)$, then $V_1 = f(c)$.

2. Let $V_0 = f(X,Y)$, $U_0 = X$, $a_1 = q(U)$ then $a_1' = q(X)$. Suppose that $a_1'' = q(g(Z))$. Then $U_1 = g(Z)$, $V_1 = f(g(Z),Y)$. V does not occur in a_1 but $V_1 \neq V_0$ □

In the sequel of the computation, each a_i may become a current subgoal with current values of its variables. The current value of a variable $\mathtt{V}$ at this moment is denoted by $\mathtt{V}_{i-1}$ and a_i' is a_i with every variable $\mathtt{V}$ substituted by $\mathtt{V}_{i-1}$. Upon a success of a_i' the variable bindings are updated; a_i with these new bindings is denoted by a_i'' and the value of $\mathtt{V}$ at this moment is denoted by $\mathtt{V}_i$. The dependencies between $\mathtt{V}_{i-1}$ and $\mathtt{V}_i$ are of the same kind as discussed above for $i = 1$.

Now we are ready to present an informal definition of a *valuation sequence* for the clause (*) and the (sub-) goal b. This is a sequence $\rho_0, \ldots, \rho_n$ of substitutions such that there exists a program P (containing (*)) and a computation of P for which

$$\rho_i = \{\mathtt{V} \mapsto \mathtt{V}_i \mid \mathtt{V} \text{ is a variable occurring in (*) or } b\}.$$

Thus $a_i' = a_i\rho_{i-1}$ and $a_i'' = a_i\rho_i$. Note that the definition takes into account only what is implied by the very clause (*) and b. It does not depend on any other clauses. Every computation of any program where the subgoal b invokes the clause (*) has a corresponding valuation sequence for (*) and b. This is true also in the case of failures and backtracking. If a_i' fails then, in the corresponding valuation sequence, $\mathtt{V}_0, \ldots, \mathtt{V}_{i-1}$ are the values of $\mathtt{V}$ which actually occurred in the computation. Backtracking is understood here as an attempt to construct another computation. Note that a valuation sequence exists iff b is unifiable with a_0.

A formal definition of a valuation sequence is presented in the next section and is based on the following properties. Firstly, ρ_0 is a most general unifier of b and a_0. Then, the difference between ρ_{i-1} and ρ_i is such that there exists a substitution σ_i and $\rho_i = \rho_{i-1}\sigma_i$ (σ_i is actually a computed answer substitution for a_i'). Furthermore, σ_i may change only the values of those variables which occur in a_i' and it may not introduce variables which have already occurred in the computation but do not occur in a_i'.

EXAMPLE 3.2

Let $b = p(c, Z)$. Consider the clause

$$p(A, C) :- q(A, B), r(B, C), s.$$

One of the possible valuation sequences is

$A_0 = c,\ B_0 = B,\ C_0 = Z,$

$A_1 = c,\ B_1 = f(Y),\ C_1 = Z,$

$A_2 = A_3 = c,\ B_2 = B_3 = f(d),\ C_2 = C_3 = e.$

The reader may construct a corresponding program. For all valuation sequences $B_0 = B$, $A_0 = c = A_1 = A_2 = A_3$ and $B_2 = B_3$, $C_2 = C_3$. The other possible C_0 is $C_0 = C$. □

Let a_0'' be a_0 in which every variable $\mathtt{V}$ is substituted by $\mathtt{V}_n$. If P is a correct program, then $a_1', \ldots, a_n'$ must satisfy their preconditions and $(a_1', a_1''), \ldots, (a_n', a_n'')$ must satisfy their postconditions. The precondition for b and the postcondition for (b, a_0'') must hold as well.

The following verification criterion (cf. also Fig. 1) is proved in the next section and is a basis for our proof method. (For simplicity a goal clause $:- a_1, \ldots, a_n$ is represented as $\mathbf{goal} :- a_1, \ldots, a_n$ where both the precondition and postcondition for goal are true).

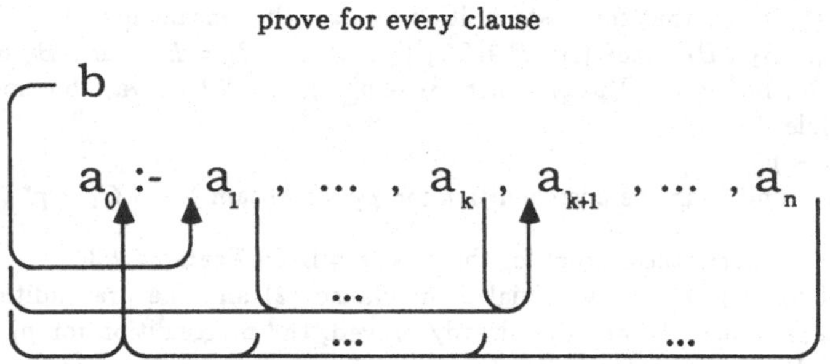

Figure 1. Verification condition, a diagram. Arrows stand for implications.

To prove that the program is correct, it is enough to prove for every clause $a_0 :- a_1, \ldots, a_n$ in the program ($n \geq 0$) that, for any goal b satisfying its precondition and any valuation sequence (for the clause and b),

1. the precondition for a'_1 holds,
2. for $k = 1, \ldots, n-1$, the precondition for a'_{k+1} is implied by the postconditions for $(a'_1, a''_1), \ldots, (a'_k, a''_k)$,
3. the postcondition for (b, a''_0) is implied by the postconditions for $(a'_1, a''_1), \ldots, (a'_n, a''_n)$.

An explanation for the above may be as follows. The correctness proof is divided into local proofs dealing with single clauses. For each clause $a_0 :- a_1, \ldots, a_n$ we can assume that the subgoal b invoking it satisfies its precondition. This should follow from the proofs related to the clauses involved in the computation leading to b as the current subgoal. But we have to prove that the precondition for a'_1 holds. Further, a'_1 may either fail or succeed giving a''_1. Since we already know that the precondition for a'_1 holds, it follows from the proofs for appropriate clauses that the postcondition for (a'_1, a''_1) holds. We can use this fact to prove the precondition for a'_2. Generally, to prove the precondition for a'_{k+1} it can be assumed that the postconditions for $(a'_1, a''_1), \ldots, (a'_k, a''_k)$ hold (because the preconditions for $a'_1, \ldots, a'_k$ are already proved). The same assumption, for $k = n$, can be used to prove the postcondition for (b, a''_0).

Note that for $n = 0$ it is enough to prove the postconditions for (b, a''_0) (the conditions 1. and 2. and the premises in 3. disappear). For $n = 1$ the case 2. disappears.

In our proofs we will use some abbreviations and notational conventions. Let (*) be the clause under consideration. When it does not lead to ambiguity, we will say that a precondition is satisfied by a_i (instead of the appropriate instance of a_i). The same for postconditions. If the predicate symbol of a_i is p, we will also say that the pre-(post-)condition for p is satisfied (or "... for p_i" if p occurs more than once in the clause). For example, in a proof for the clause $test(X) :- testa(cond1, X, Y), testb(Y), test(Y)$ we usually say "the postcondition for $testb$ is satisfied" instead of "the postcondition for (a'_2, a''_2) is satisfied" where a'_2 and a''_2 are appropriate instances of $testb(Y)$ (that means $a'_2 = testb(Y_1)$, $a''_2 = testb(Y_2)$).

By ${}^{\bullet}p_{i,j}$ and $p^{\bullet}_{i,j}$ we denote the value of the j-th argument of p_i at the moment of its invocation and its success respectively. The index i may be skipped when p occurs only once in the clause. So in the example above, ${}^{\bullet}test_{3,1} = Y_2$, $test^{\bullet}_{3,1} = Y_3$, ${}^{\bullet}testa_1 = testa^{\bullet}_1 = cond1$.

EXAMPLE 3.3 A correctness proof for the program from Example 2.1.

The proof for clauses (0) and (1) is immediate. Consider (2):

$$p([A|LA], [B|LB], [pair(A, B)|LC]) :- p(LA, LB, LC).$$

Let the head of (2) be unified with b satisfying its precondition; then $b = p(\mathtt{T}, \mathtt{X}, \mathtt{Y})$ where $\mathtt{X} \neq \mathtt{Y}$ (because of the occur check). Then B_0, LB_0, LC_0 are distinct variables and none of them occurs in LA_0. So the precondition for p_1 (strictly speaking, for $p(LA_0, LB_0, LC_0)$) holds.

It remains to prove that the postcondition for p_0 (that means for $(b,\ p([A_1|LA_1],\ [B_1|LB_1],\ [pair(A_1,B_1)|LC_1]))$) holds. $B_1 = B_0$ since B_0 does not occur in LA_0, LB_0, LC_0. So $\neg$ground$(p^\bullet_{0,2})$ (since $B_1 \prec p^\bullet_{0,2}$). Let V be a variable and $V \prec p^\bullet_{0,2}$. Two cases are possible:

1. $V = B_1 \prec p^\bullet_{0,3}$,
2. $V \prec LB_1$ and from the postcondition for p_1 we obtain $V \prec LC_1 \prec p^\bullet_{0,3}$. Q.E.D.

EXAMPLE 3.4 A correctness proof for the program from Example 2.3.

The proof for (0) and (1) is trivial. The clause (2) and the precondition for p are the same as in Example 3.3. As we have already proved, the precondition for p_1 holds and $B_1 = B_0$ & var(B_1). From the postcondition for p_1

$LB_1 = [V_1,\ldots,V_n]$, $n \geq 0$ & $\forall_{i,j}$ var(V_i) & $(i \neq j \Rightarrow V_i \neq V_j)$.

So $p^\bullet_{0,2} = [B_1, V_1,\ldots,V_n]$. We have also $\forall_i\ B_1 \neq V_i$ because B_1 does not occur in the invocation of p_1 (see also section 4, the definition of valuation sequence, condition 4). Hence the postcondition for p_0 holds. Q.E.D.

4. THE METHOD

The main part of this section is a definition of program correctness and the verification theorem. These are preceded by a few necessary definitions and followed by examples. The section concludes with some comparisons between our method and abstract interpretation.

Let t be a term and $\theta = \{V_1 \mapsto t_1,\ldots,V_n \mapsto t_n\}$ a substitution. The following notation will be used:

variables(t) is the set of (object language) variables occurring in t,
variables$(t_1,\ldots,t_n)$ = variables$(t_1) \cup \ldots \cup$ variables(t_n),
dom$(\theta) = \{V_1,\ldots,V_n\}$,
variables(θ) = variables$(t_1,\ldots,t_n)$. □

We use the traditional definition of SLD-derivation as presented in [Lloyd] restricting it to the fixed computation rule of Prolog. We must make explicit some assumptions which are stated there, but not precisely enough. For a most general unifier (mgu) θ of t_1 and t_2 we require that it does not introduce new variables:

variables$(\theta) \subseteq$ variables$(t_1) \cup$ variables(t_2).

Note that θ does not use unnecessary variables:

dom$(\theta) \subseteq$ variables$(t_1) \cup$ variables(t_2).

For an SLD-derivation we require that variables are standardized apart. That is, if

$G_0, G_1,\ldots; C_1, C_2,\ldots; \theta_1, \theta_2,\ldots$ is an SLD-derivation then for every $i < j$
variables$(C_i) \cap$ variables$(C_j) = \emptyset$ and
variables$(G_i) \cap$ variables$(C_j) = \emptyset$

(where $G_0, G_1,\ldots$ is the goal sequence, $C_1, C_2,\ldots$ is the clause variant sequence and $\theta_1,\theta_2,\ldots$ is the unification sequence of the derivation; the sequences may be finite or infinite).

DEFINITION 4.1

An asserted program P is *correct* iff for every SLD-derivation of P where $G_0, G_1,\ldots$ is the sequence of goal clauses and $\theta_1, \theta_2,\ldots$ is the sequence of substitutions and for every i if

$$G_i = :\!-a_1,\ldots,a_m, \qquad m \geq 0$$

then

1. a_1 satisfies its precondition,
2. if there exists $j > i$ such that

$$G_j = :\!-(a_2,\ldots,a_m)\theta_{i+1}\ldots\theta_j$$

then $(a_1, a_1\theta_{i+1}\ldots\theta_j)$ satisfies its postcondition for the least such j. □

Informally, a_i is a procedure call, $\theta_{i+1}\dots\theta_j$ the corresponding computed answer substitution, $a_1\theta_{i+1}\dots\theta_j$ the instantiation of a_1 at the moment of its success. The part of the SLD-derivation between i and j is, intuitively, the computation corresponding to procedure call a_1.

To facilitate formulation of the main theorem we introduce the notion of a valuation sequence.

DEFINITION 4.2

A sequence of substitutions $\rho_0,\dots,\rho_n$ $(n \geq 0)$ is a *valuation sequence* for a clause $a_0 :- a_1,\dots,a_n$ and for an atomic formula (a goal) b iff

0. $\mathrm{variables}(b) \cap \mathrm{variables}(a_0, a_1,\dots,a_n) = \emptyset$
1. ρ_0 is an mgu of b and a_0

and there exist $\sigma_1,\dots,\sigma_n$ (called an *answer sequence*) such that for $i = 1,\dots,n$

2. $\rho_i = \rho_{i-1}\sigma_i$
3. $\mathrm{dom}(\sigma_i) \subseteq \mathrm{variables}(a_i\rho_{i-1})$
4. $\mathrm{variables}(\sigma_i) \cap \mathrm{variables}((a_0 :- a_1,\dots,a_n)\rho_{i-1}) \subseteq \mathrm{variables}(a_i\rho_{i-1})$. □

ρ_i can be understood as a valuation of clause variables upon a success of $a_i\rho_{i-1}$ (provided it succeeded). σ_i is the corresponding computed answer substitution. Using the notation from the previous section, $\mathtt{V}\rho_i = \mathtt{V}_i$ for any variable $\mathtt{V}$ occurring in the clause.

The theorem below is the main result of this paper and the basis of our proof method. In the theorem we assume that $a_0 =$ **goal** for a goal clause where **goal** is a special predicate symbol which does not occur elsewhere. The assertion for **goal** is **pre true; post true.**

THEOREM 4.1 (verification condition)

Let P be an asserted program. A sufficient condition for P to be correct is:

for every $a_0 :- a_1,\dots,a_n$ being a clause of P $(n \geq 0)$,
for every b which satisfies its precondition,
for every their valuation sequence $\rho_0,\dots,\rho_n$

1. the precondition for $a_1\rho_0$ is satisfied,
2. for every $k = 1,\dots,n-1$, if $(a_1\rho_0, a_1\rho_1),\dots,(a_k\rho_{k-1}, a_k\rho_k)$ satisfy their postconditions then the precondition for $a_{k+1}\rho_k$ is satisfied,
3. if $(a_1\rho_0, a_1\rho_1),\dots,(a_n\rho_{n-1}, a_n\rho_n)$ satisfy their postconditions then the postcondition for $(b, a_0\rho_n)$ is satisfied. □

Note that for a unary clause $(n = 0)$ the conditions 1., 2., 3. above reduce to

3. the postcondition for $(b, a_0\rho_0)$ is satisfied.

For $n = 1$ they reduce to

1. the precondition for $a_1\rho_0$ is satisfied,
3. if $(a_1\rho_0, a_1\rho_1)$ satisfy its postcondition then the postcondition for $(b, a_0\rho_1)$ is satisfied.

The verification condition is expressed in semantic terms. While proving implications 2. and 3. one has to refer to properties of substitution composition, substitution application and unification. An interesting problem is finding a set of proof rules which would correspond to theorem 4.1 and would allow to perform proofs in a syntactic way, like in the axiomatic semantics. This could make possible automatization of the method.

Two example proofs of program correctness are given at the end of the previous section. Here we present another two examples relating to mode declarations.

EXAMPLE 4.1

Consider the following program

$$:- q(\mathtt{T}). \tag{0}$$
$$q(L) :- p(L, M, N),\ s(N, L1, L2). \tag{1}$$
$$p([\,],[\,],[\,]). \tag{2}$$
$$p([A|LA],\ [B|LB],\ [pair(A,B)|LC]) :- p(LA, LB, LC). \tag{3}$$
$$s([\,],[\,],[\,]). \tag{4}$$
$$s([X|L],[X|L1],L2) :- s(L, L1, L2). \tag{5}$$
$$s([X|L],L1,[X|L2]) :- s(L, L1, L2). \tag{6}$$

(where the procedure p is the same as in the previous examples) with the assertions

q : **pre true; post true**

p : **pre true; post** $p_3^\bullet = [\mathtt{T}_1,\ldots,\mathtt{T}_n],\ n \geq 0\ \&\ \forall_i \neg\mathrm{var}(\mathtt{T}_i)$

s : **pre** ${}^\bullet s_1 = [\mathtt{T}_1,\ldots,\mathtt{T}_n],\ n \geq 0\ \&\ \forall_i \neg\mathrm{var}(\mathtt{T}_i)\ \&\ \mathrm{var}({}^\bullet s_2)\ \&\ \mathrm{var}({}^\bullet s_3)$; **post true**

As the correctness proof for the program is easy, we present here proofs for clauses (1) and (5) only.

A proof for (1): Let the head of (1) be unified with b satisfying its precondition. As the precondition is **true**, $b = q(\mathtt{S})$ (where S is any term) and $\rho_0 = \{L \mapsto \mathtt{S}\}$ or, if S is a variable, $\rho_0 = \{\mathtt{S} \mapsto L\}$. Let $a_1 = p(L, M, N)$ and $a_2 = s(N, L1, L2)$. Then $a_1\rho_0$ satisfies its precondition. Assume that $(a_1\rho_0, a_1\rho_1)$ satisfies its postcondition. This means that $N\rho_1 = [\mathtt{T}_1,\ldots,\mathtt{T}_n]$, $n \geq 0\ \&\ \forall_i \neg\mathrm{var}(\mathtt{T}_i)$ and the precondition for $a_2\rho_1 = s((N\rho_1), L1, L2)$ holds. This completes the proof for (1) since the postcondition for q is **true**.

A proof for (5): Let $b = s([\mathtt{T}_1,\ldots,\mathtt{T}_n],\mathtt{U},\mathtt{V})$ satisfies its precondition (this means $n \geq 0$, $\mathtt{U},\mathtt{V}$ are variables, $\mathtt{T}_1,\ldots,\mathtt{T}_n$ are not variables). Let b be unified with the head of (5) by mgu ρ_0. Then $n \geq 1$,

$$b\rho_0 = s([X|L],[X|L1],L2)\rho_0 = s([\mathtt{T}_1|[\mathtt{T}_2,\ldots,\mathtt{T}_n]],[\mathtt{T}_1|\mathtt{W}],\mathtt{X})$$

(where $\mathtt{W},\mathtt{X}$ are variables) and

$$s(L, L1, L2)\rho_0 = s([\mathtt{T}_2,\ldots,\mathtt{T}_n],\mathtt{W},\mathtt{X})$$

which satisfies its precondition. This completes the proof for (5) since the postcondition for s is **true**.

From the precondition for s it follows that the procedure s may be given a mode declaration $s(+,-,-)$ (since at every call of s the first argument is not a variable and the remaining arguments are variables). □

EXAMPLE 4.2

Consider the program fragment

$$p :- q(f(a), X),\ r(X). \tag{1}$$
$$s(Y) :- q(Y, X),\ t(X). \tag{2}$$
$$q(f(X), X). \tag{3}$$

with the assertions

p : **pre true; post true**

q : **pre true; post** $\mathrm{ground}({}^\bullet q_1) \Rightarrow \mathrm{ground}(q_2^\bullet)$

r : **pre** $\mathrm{ground}({}^\bullet r_1)$; **post true**

Let all the remaining assertions be **pre true; post true**. It is easy to prove that this asserted program is correct (under the assumption that the procedure q consists only of (3) and that the only invocation of r occurs in (1)). So the procedure r may be given a mode declaration $r(+)$. □

Neither of the mode declarations that are shown to be correct in these examples can be found using the abstract interpretation method of [Mellish]. In Example 4.1 this is because of too restricted domains of abstract interpretation. To find the mode declaration for s it is necessary to know that p_3^* is a list of non-variable elements, but the abstract interpreter supports no description between "ground term" and "term whose arguments are variables". (Actually, this shows why the abstract interpreter is not able to find an adequate mode declaration for the procedure *split* in the program *serialize* [Bowen et al], since the procedure s is a simplified version of *split*). To find the mode declaration from Example 4.2 it is necessary to treat the calls of q in (1) and (2) in a different way. This is possible in our approach (implications in a binary postcondition can be used for this purpose) but impossible in the abstract interpretation method mentioned above.

This weakness of abstract interpretation is due to its automaticity: the same apparatus is applied to every program while a proof method like ours can use assertions tailored to the problem on hand (cf. Examples 2.1, 2.2, 2,3, 4.1 where four distinct assertions are given to the same procedure).

5. PROOF OF THE VERIFICATION THEOREM

This section proves the soundness of our method. To facilitate the proof we introduce some definitions. Let $G_0, G_1, \ldots; C_1, C_2, \ldots; \theta_1, \theta_2, \ldots$ be an SLD-derivation (the reader is referred to [Lloyd] for standard definitions and theorems).

DEFINITION

A *k, l-subrefutation* (of this derivation) is $G_{k-1}, \ldots, G_l; C_k, \ldots, C_l;\ \theta_k, \ldots, \theta_l$ such that

$G_{k-1} = :\!-b, b_1, \ldots, b_m, \qquad m \geq 0$

$G_l = :\!-(b_1, \ldots, b_m)\theta_k \ldots \theta_l$

and l is the least such number. □

DEFINITION

A *k, j-subderivation* (of this derivation) is $G_{k-1}, \ldots, G_j; C_k, \ldots, C_j;\ \theta_k, \ldots, \theta_j$ such that

$G_{k-1} = :\!-b, b_1, \ldots, b_m, \qquad m \geq 0$

and for $k \leq i \leq j$ G_i is not of the form $:\!-(b_1, \ldots, b_m)\theta_k \ldots \theta_i$. □

A subrefutation beginning with $:\!-b, \ldots$ is a fragment of an SLD-derivation related to a successful procedure call b. A subderivation beginning with the same goal may be treated as a not yet completed computation associated with b.

The sufficient condition from the Theorem 4.1 will often be referred to as (SC).

LEMMA 5.1

Let $G_{k-1}, \ldots, G_l; C_k, \ldots, C_l; \theta_k, \ldots, \theta_l$ be a subrefutation of an SLD-derivation of a program P for which (SC) is satisfied. Let $k \leq i \leq l$ and

$G_{k-1} = :\!-b, b_1, \ldots, b_m,$

$\sigma_i = \theta_k, \ldots, \theta_i,$

$G_i = :\!-(A_i, b_1, \ldots, b_m)\sigma_i$, where A_i is a sequence of atomic formulas.

Then

dom$(\sigma_i) \subseteq$ variables$(b, C_k, \ldots, C_i)$,

variables$(\sigma_i) \subseteq$ variables$(b, C_k, \ldots, C_i)$ and

variables$(A_i\sigma_i) \subseteq$ variables$(b, C_k, \ldots, C_i)$. □

COROLLARY

Let $G_0, G_1, \ldots; C_1, C_2, \ldots; \theta_1, \theta_2, \ldots$ be an SLD-derivation of a program for which (SC) is satisfied. Let there exist a k,l-subrefutation of the derivation. Let $G_{k-1} = :\!-b, b_1, \ldots, b_m$. Then

$G_{k-1}\theta_k \ldots \theta_l = G_{k-1}\sigma$

where

$\sigma = \theta_k \ldots \theta_l|\text{variables}(b)$ (and $|$ is defined by $\theta|X = \{V \mapsto t \in \theta \mid V \in X\}$).

More generally, for every $s \leq k$

$$G_{s-1}\theta_s \ldots \theta_l = G_{s-1}\theta_s \ldots \theta_{k-1}\sigma \quad \Box$$

LEMMA 5.2

Let $G_0, G_1, \ldots; C_1, C_2, \ldots; \theta_1, \theta_2, \ldots$ be an SLD-derivation of a program for which (SC) is satisfied. Let a k,l-subrefutation of the derivation exist. Let $G_{k-1} = :\!-b, b_1, \ldots, b_m$ where b satisfies its precondition. Then $(b, b\theta_k \ldots \theta_l)$ satisfies its postcondition. $\Box$

PROOF by induction on l.

Let the premises of the lemma hold.

$l = k$:

Let G_k be derived from G_{k-1} and a unary clause a_0 using an mgu θ_k. Then from (SC) follows the postcondition for $(b, a_0\theta_k)$.

$l > k$:

Let the lemma hold for every number less than l. Then

$$G_k = :\!-(a_1, \ldots, a_n, b_1, \ldots, b_m)\theta_k$$

is derived from G_{k-1} and a clause $C_k = a_0{:}\!-a_1, \ldots, a_n$, $n > 0$. The substitution θ_k is an mgu of b and a_0.

There exist $r_0, \ldots, r_n$ such that $r_0 = k$, $r_n = l$ and, for $i = 1, \ldots, n$,

$$G_{r_i} = :\!-(a_{i+1}, \ldots, a_n, b_1, \ldots, b_m)\theta_k \ldots \theta_{r_i},$$

the derivation has a $(r_{i-1}{+}1), r_i$-subrefutation, and r_i is the least index for which it holds. The $(r_{i-1}{+}1), r_i$-subrefutation can be understood as a successful execution of the procedure call $a_i\theta_k \ldots \theta_{r_{i-1}}$.

Let $\rho_0 = \theta_k$ and for $i = 1, \ldots, n$

$$\sigma_i = \theta_{r_{i-1}+1} \ldots \theta_{r_i}|\text{variables}(a_i\theta_k \ldots \theta_{r_{i-1}}),$$

and $\rho_i = \rho_{i-1}\sigma_i$ (σ_i may be treated as a computed answer substitution for goal $a_i\theta_k \ldots \theta_{r_{i-1}}$). We want to prove that $\rho_0, \ldots, \rho_n$ is a valuation sequence for b and C_k. It remains to show that conditions 3 and 4 of Definition 4.2 hold.

Let $G = G_k$ or $G = G_{k-1}\theta_k$. From the Corollary it follows that for $i = 0, \ldots, n-1$ if

$$G\theta_{k+1} \ldots \theta_{r_i} = G\sigma_1 \ldots \sigma_i$$

then

$$G\theta_{k+1} \ldots \theta_{r_{i+1}} = G\sigma_1 \ldots \sigma_{i+1}.$$

By induction $G\theta_{k+1} \ldots \theta_{r_i} = G\sigma_1 \ldots \sigma_i$ for $i = 0, \ldots, n$. Hence

$$b\rho_n = b\theta_k \ldots \theta_l,$$

$$a_i\rho_{i-1} = a_i\theta_k \ldots \theta_{r_{i-1}} \qquad (*)$$

(and $\text{dom}(\sigma_i) \subseteq \text{variables}(a_i\rho_{i-1})$ which is condition 3 of Definition 4.2),

$$a_i\rho_i = a_i\theta_k \ldots \theta_{r_i}.$$

By Lemma 5.1 applied to the $(r_{i-1}{+}1), r_i$-subrefutation (where $G_{r_{i-1}} = :\!-a_i\rho_{i-1}, \ldots$ by (*)) $\text{variables}(\sigma_i) \subseteq \text{variables}(\theta_{r_{i-1}+1} \ldots \theta_{r_i}) \subseteq \text{variables}(a_i\rho_{i-1}, C_{r_{i-1}+1}, \ldots, C_{r_i})$. Hence $\text{variables}(\sigma_i) \cap \text{variables}((a_0, \ldots, a_n)\rho_{i-1}) \subseteq \text{variables}(a_i\rho_{i-1})$ (since variables in the derivation are standardized apart and variables$((a_0,\ldots,a_n)\rho_{i-1}) \cap$ variables$(C_j) = \emptyset$ for $j > r_{i-1}$). We have proved that $\rho_0,\ldots,\rho_n$ is a valuation sequence for b and C_k.

Now, by (SC1), the precondition for $a_1\rho_0$ is satisfied.

If the precondition for $a_i\rho_{i-1}$ is satisfied then the postcondition for $(a_i\rho_{i-1}, a_i\rho_i)$ is satisfied (for every $i = 1,\ldots,n$, by the inductive assumption).

The preconditions for $a_2\rho_1,\ldots,a_n\rho_{n-1}$ hold (by (SC2)).

The postcondition for $(b, b\rho_n)$ holds (by (SC3)).

But $b\rho_n = b\theta_k\ldots\theta_l$ which completes the proof. □

LEMMA 5.3

Let $G_0, G_1,\ldots; C_1, C_2,\ldots; \theta_1, \theta_2,\ldots$ be an SLD-derivation of a program for which (SC) is satisfied. Then for every s the first atomic formula of G_s satisfies its precondition. □

PROOF by induction on s.

If $s = 0$ then the thesis follows immediately from (SC1). Let the lemma hold for every number less than s. Two cases are possible.

1.

$$\begin{aligned} G_s &= \text{:-}(a_1,\ldots,a_n,b_1,\ldots,b_m)\theta_s, \qquad n > 0 \\ G_{s-1} &= \text{:-}b, b_1,\ldots,b_m \end{aligned}$$

The precondition for b is satisfied and G_s is derived from G_{s-1} and a clause a_0:$-a_1,\ldots,a_n$. θ_s is an mgu of b and a_0. From (SC1) it follows that the precondition for $a_1\theta_s$ is satisfied.

2. (n in the previous case is 0)

There exists $k < s$ ($k \geq 0$) such that

$$\begin{aligned} G_s &= \text{:-}(b_1,\ldots,b_m)\theta_k\ldots\theta_s \\ G_{s-1} &= \text{:-}(b_0,b_1,\ldots,b_m)\theta_k\ldots\theta_{s-1} \\ G_k &= \text{:-}(a_1,\ldots,a_t,b_1,\ldots,b_u,\ldots b_m)\theta_k \\ G_{k-1} &= \text{:-}b, b_{u+1},\ldots,b_m. \end{aligned}$$

Let k be the greatest such number (when $k = 0$ then let G_{-1} = :–goal, $\theta_0 = \epsilon$ and C_0 be the goal clause **goal**:– ...). Repeating the construction from the proof of Lemma 5.2 using $a_1,\ldots,a_t,b_1,\ldots,b_u$ instead of $a_1,\ldots,a_n$ and introducing r_v only for $v \leq t$ ($r_0 = k$, $r_t = s$) we prove that the precondition for b_1 is satisfied. The evaluation sequence under consideration (for b and C_k) is $\rho_0,\ldots,\rho_{t+u}$ where $\rho_i = \rho_{i-1}\sigma_i$. σ_i is as in the previous proof for $i = 1,\ldots,t$. For $i = t+1,\ldots,t+u$, $\sigma_i = \epsilon$. We omit details of the proof. □

Theorem 4.1 follows immediately from lemmas 5.3 and 5.2.

6.CONCLUSIONS

In this paper, the inductive assertion method for logic programs was introduced and proved sound. The metalanguage of assertions was defined. The assertions can describe properties that are inexpressible in terms of the declarative semantics. The verification theorem makes it possible to prove the partial correctness of programs with respect to their assertions.

We think that the ability of stating and proving assertions is important for the following reasons:

1. Assertions may improve the legibility of some logic programs. They may be treated as formalized comments specifying the actual form of procedure calls and successes.

2. Prolog programmers quite often reason about their programs in terms of execution (this is reflected by comments, mode declarations, etc.). By introducing assertions one makes explicit some facts upon which this reasoning is based.

3. Intuitive principles of reasoning about logic programs can be formulated as a systematic method for proving the correctness of a logic program.

4. The declarative semantics gives no formal explanation of the concept of the "logical variable" essential in many applications. The introduction of a metalanguage that refers to non-ground terms should make it possible to handle this concept in a more rigorous way.

5. It may be conceivable to use a metalanguage similar to the one presented here in logic programming systems. A debugging tool might use assertions to perform additional checking. A compiler might use them to guide optimizations.

Our approach can easily be extended to deal with some extra-logical built-in procedures. It can provide their formal semantics and also the absence of some run-time errors can be proved. The declarative semantics is inapplicable to this kind of procedures.

EXAMPLE Axiomatic semantics of the Prolog [Bowen et al] built-in procedure *var*

The meaning of the procedure may be described by the assertion

var : **pre true** ;

post var($^{\bullet}var_1$) & $^{\bullet}var_1 = var_1^{\bullet}$. □

EXAMPLE Correctness of use of the Prolog built-in procedure *is*

Consider the assertion

is : **pre** intexpr($^{\bullet}is_2$) ;

post true

where intexpr(T) iff T is an expression built out of integers and arithmetical functors. If an asserted program with the above assertion is correct then no run-time error connected with wrong arguments of *is* occurs. □

Our method is valid for the Prolog computation rule and for every search strategy (thus including OR-parallelism). It is also valid for Prolog programs containing the cut and negation-as-failure (although it is not able to exploit specific properties of the cut and *not*, cf. the assertion for *not*: **pre true; post** $not_1^{\bullet} = {}^{\bullet}not_1$).

ACKNOWLEDGEMENTS

Thanks are due to Henryk Jan Komorowski for his critical comments. Ivan Rankin helped to improve the English of the previous version of this paper.

REFERENCES

[Apt, van Emden] Apt, K.R. and van Emden, M.H., "Contributions to the Theory of Logic Programming", J.ACM. 29, 3 (July 1982), 841-862

[Bowen et al] D.L. Bowen, L. Byrd, F.C.N. Pereira, L.M. Pereira and D.H.D. Warren, "Prolog-20 user's manual", 1984

[Drabent, Małuszyński] W.Drabent and J. Małuszyński , Proving runtime properties of logic programs, Research Report LITH-IDA-R-86-23, Linköping University, July 1986

[Floyd] Floyd, R.W., "Assigning Meanings to Programs", Proc.Symp.Appl.Math., Vol. 19: Mathematical Aspects of Computer Science (J.T.Schwartz, ed.), pp. 19–32, American Mathematical Society, Providence, Rhode Island, 1967

[Francez et al] Francez,N., Grumberg,O., Katz,S., Pnuelli,A., "Proving Termination of Prolog Programs" in "Logics of Programs. Proceedings, 1985", ed. by R.Parikh, Springer Lecture Notes in Computer Science 193, 89–105

[Hoare] Hoare,C.A.R. "An Axiomatic Basis for Computer Programming", Comm. ACM 12, 10 (Oct. 1969), 576–580,583

[Hogger] Hogger,C.J. "Derivation of Logic Programs", J.ACM 28, 2 (April 1981), 372–392

[Lloyd] Lloyd,J.W. "Foundations of Logic Programming", Springer-Verlag 1984

[Mellish] Mellish,C.S. "Abstract Interpretation of Prolog Programs", Third International Conference on Logic Programming, London, July 1986 and "The Automatic Generation of Mode Declarations for Prolog Programs", DAI Reaserch Paper 163, Dept of Artificial Intelligence, University of Edinburgh, 1981

[Tarlecki] Tarlecki,A., "A Language of Specified Programs", Science of Computer Programming 5 (1985) 59–81

HIGHER ORDER GENERALIZATION IN PROGRAM DERIVATION

Alberto Pettorossi
IASI - CNR
Viale Manzoni 30
00185 Roma (Italy)

Andrzej Skowron
Institute of Mathematics
Warsaw University
00-901 Warsaw (Poland)

ABSTRACT

We define and study a particular kind of generalization strategy for deriving efficient functional programs. It is called *higher order generalization* because it consists in generalizing variables or expressions into functions. That strategy allows us to derive efficient one-pass algorithms with low time×space complexity.

Through some examples we show the power of our generalization strategy and its use together with the tupling strategy. Applying those strategies one may avoid the introduction of circular programs [Bir84].

1. INTRODUCTION

A major problem in the derivation of programs by transformation is the lack of a general theory which guarantees the improvements of program performances when applying the basic transformation rules.

In some cases, however, it is possible to realize those improvements by using powerful strategies. Some of them have been defined and studied in the past, as for instance, the composition strategy, the tupling strategy, and the generalization strategy. For a recent survey in this area the reader may refer to [Fea86].

We will define a new kind of generalization strategy and we will study its properties through a couple of examples. That strategy, together with the composition and the tupling strategy, avoids the multiple traversal of data structures and it saves time and space resources. Related work can be found in [Bir84].

We consider recursive equation programs, like the ones presented in the classical work by Burstall and Darlington [BuD77]. We will not give their formal definition here, but we hope that the reader will have no difficulties in understanding them. The actual language we use is a variant of HOPE [BMS80].

Obviously, the generalization strategy we propose is independent from the language chosen, and it can also be applied when one derives programs using different formalisms.

The basic transformation rules for recursive equation programs include:

- the **unfolding rule**. It is the replacement of a left hand side of a recursion equation by its corresponding rigth hand side.
  For instance, given the equations:
  f(x)=E1[g(a)],   g(x)=E2[x],
  where E[e] denotes the expression E with the occurrence of the subexpression e, the unfolding of g(a) in E1 produces the following new program version:
  f(x)=E1[E2[a/x]],   g(x)=E2[x].
- the **folding rule**. It is the inverse of the folding rule by interchanging the l.h.s. and the r.h.s.
- the **definition rule**. It is the introduction of a new recursive equation whose r.h.s. is not an instance of already existing equations.

Those basic rules have been often described in the literature (see, for instance, [Fea86]). We will not go into the details here. Let us only remark that we need to use some strategies, because a naive sequence of applications of the unfolding and folding rules may take us back to the initial program version.

In what follows we will apply the higher order generalization strategy for solving two problems: the first one is a *compilation problem* due to Swierstra [Swi85] and the second one is a *tree transformation problem* due to Bird [Bir84]. We think that the programs we will derive have good merits with respect to efficiency and clarity of derivation. (Their correctness will be given us for free, as usual in the transformation approach).

2. HIGHER ORDER GENERALIZATION FOR A COMPILATION PROBLEM

We consider a compilation problem for transforming lists of letters denoting declarations and uses of identifiers into new lists, where for each use of an identifier we indicate the corresponding declaration.

In order to formally specify our problem, let us introduce the following data structures atom and prog (short for program):

<u>data</u> atom == decl(letter) ++ use(letter)

<u>data</u> prog == list atom

where letter is a given set, which we may consider to be {a,b,…,z}. decl, use, and list are type constructors. list atom denotes the type of *nested lists* of atoms.

We also assume that together with a data definition we are given the corresponding *discriminators*. For instance, in our case we are given "isuse" and "isdecl". isuse satisfies the following axiom: isuse(y)=true iff y=use(x) for any x∈letter, and analogously for isdecl.

For simplicity, we also adopt the convention of writing x instead of use(x) and X instead of decl(x). We hope that no confusion will arise between the letter x and the atom use(x), both written as x.

Thus, the set of atoms is {A,a,B,b,…,Z,z}.

Here are two examples of lists of type prog:

[A a c [B b a] C a] and [[A b] a B]. Another one is the list:

p1=[A a b [a c A D b C] B b], which we will use as a running example.

We assume that the declarations in the lists of type prog obey the familiar block discipline, where blocks are identified by square brackets. For instance, if we have the following prog:

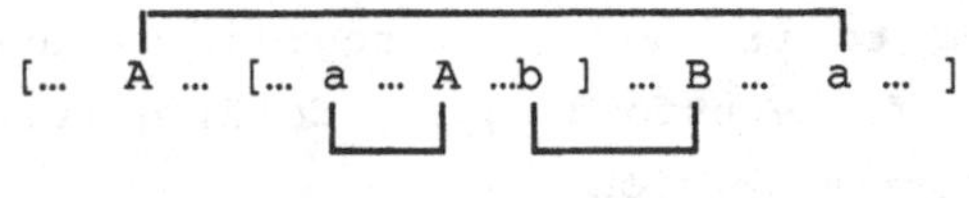

with no other occurrences of A's and B's, the declaration-use correspondences are denoted by the arcs we have drawn.

Notice that for any letter x its declaration X may occur *after* (that is, to the rigth of) its first use x. Indeed in p1 the declaration C occurs after c.

We also assume that in any given prog, each use of a letter has a unique corresponding declaration, which occurs in its block or in one of its enclosing blocks.

In the Appendix we provide the function OK:prog → bool, which checks that condition.

For instance, OK([A a a [B b]])=true, OK([A B [b a]])=true, and OK([A a a b [a A] B])=true, while OK([A A a])=false (because there are two A declarations within the same block) and OK([a B [b A]]) = false (because there is no an "active" declaration A for a).

We would like to compile a given nested list of atoms into a nested list of pairs of numbers, where each pair corresponds to a use-occurrence of an atom in the given list. The first number of each pair gives us the *level of nesting* of the block where the corresponding declaration occurs, while the second number gives us the *sequence order* of that declaration within the block where it occurs. For instance, for p1 we want to obtain the list:

l1 = [(0,0) (0,1) [(1,0) (1,2) (0,1)] (0,1)],

which encodes the use-declaration correspondence shown by the following arcs:

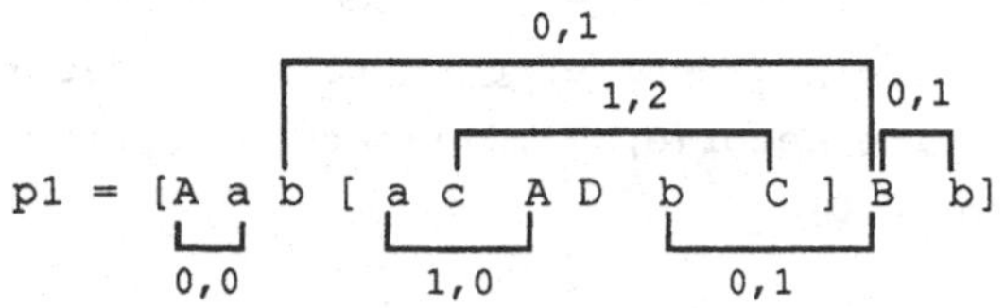
0,1
1,2
0,1
p1 = [A a b [a c A D b C] B b]
0,0
1,0
0,1

The pair (0,0) which is for the first a from the left, tells us that the corresponding declaration A is at level of nesting 0 and it is the first declaration (from the left) in that level. Analogously, the pair (1,2) for c tells us that the corresponding declaration C is at level of nesting 1 and it is the third declaration in it (after A and D).

For obtaining the list l1 from p1 a possible first step is to derive the "decorated list" dp1=[A00 a b [a c A10 D11 b C12] B01 b], where we have attached to each declaration the corresponding <level-of-nesting, sequence-order> pair. (For simplicity, we wrote Xnm instead of X<n,m>).

Having dp1, it will be easier to compute the list l1, because we have available for each declaration the relevant pair of numbers. Unfortunately, we have to pay that advantage, because we are forced to traverse the list dp1, after the first traversal of the given list p1 (which was necessary to derive dp1).

However, the application of the tupling strategy and the higher order generalization strategy will avoid that drawback, and it will allow us to obtain an efficient one-pass algorithm. The main contribution of this paper consists exactly in this point.

We also show the power of those strategies when we use them together, because we obtain the same efficiency results which are possible at the expenses of extending our language by allowing circular programs [Bir84].

Therefore, for representing the list dp1 we need the following data structures, where level and order are natural numbers:

```
data decoratom == decl(letter) ×level ×order  ++  use(letter)
data decorprog == list decoratom
```

with the discriminators: isddecl and isuse.

The following function **decor** produces the decorprog dp1 from p1:

```
dec decor: prog ×level ×order → decorprog
--- decor(nil,n,r)=nil
--- decor(e::l,n,r)=if isuse(e) then e::decor(l,n,r)
                    elseif isdecl(e) then <e,n,r>::decor(l,n,r+1)
                    else decor(e,n+1,0)::decor(l,n,r)                •
```

We have: dp1=decor(p1,0,0).

Now we present the function **nad** which computes the **n**ew **a**ctive **d**eclarations (represented as functions from letters to <level,order> pairs) *at the top level* of a block in a given decorprog.
nad works by taking as a second argument the active declarations in the enclosing blocks. As an example, consider the following decorprog dp1:

```
       dp1    dp2      dp3       dp4
        ↘      ↘        ↘         ↘
         [ ...  [  ~~~  [  ]  ~~~  [  ] ~~~ ]  ...]    .
```

nad(dp2,d) computes the declarations valid in the sections with tildes, for a given d representing the declarations valid in the sections with dots. The declarations valid in dp3 and dp4 can be computed by a recursive call of nad.

```
dec nad: decorprog × (letter → level×order)
         → (letter → level × order)
--- nad(nil,d)=d
--- nad(e::l,d)=if isuse(e) then nad(l,d)
                elseif isddecl(e) then update(e,nad(l,d))
                else nad(l,d)                                        •
```

Given a function f, update(<x,n,r>,f) produces the new function g s.t. g(x)=<n,r> and g(y)=f(y) for y≠x.

The active declarations at the top level of a given dp1 are computed by nad(dp1,emptyfunction), because there are no enclosing blocks.

Given dp1 and the active declarations at the top level of dp1, the following function **comp** (short for compile) computes the desired list l1.

```
dec comp: decorprog × (letter → level × order) → list level × order
--- comp(nil,d)=nil
--- comp(e::l,d)=if e=use(x) then d(x)::comp(l,d)
                 elseif isddecl(e) then comp(l,d)
                 else comp(e,nad(e,d))::comp(l,d)                    •
```

Therefore:
l1=comp(dp1,nad(dp1,emptyfunction)) where dp1=decor(p1,0,0), because we have first to decorate the list p1, and then we have to compute the new active declarations in dp1 for an empty enclosing block. Finally we have to compile dp1.

The compiling program we have constructed makes multiple traversals of the data structures involved. It seems very difficult to produce in this case a one-pass algorithm, because the declaration of the identifiers may occur after their use. However, we will show that the higher order generalization strategy, together with the tupling strategy, allows us to solve that problem.

We do not present here a formal characterization of the power of those strategies and their synergism, but we hope that the reader may convince himself that the proposed strategies do work in a large number of cases.

3. THE TRANSFORMATION PROCESS TOWARDS THE ONE-PASS COMPILATION

A first step towards the derivation of the one pass algorithm we have specified in the previous Section is the application of the *composition strategy* [Pet84a] for the initial expression comp(dp1,nad(dp1,emptyfunction)), because both comp and nad visit the same data structure, and the latter is an argument of the former.

That is a standard case for applying that strategy, which usually avoids the generation of intermediate data (see also [Wad85]).
The incorporation into the one-pass algorithm of the function decor(p1,0,0) which constructs dp1, will be done later.

By composition we define the function:
f(l,d)=comp(l,nad(l,d)). After a few folding/unfolding steps we get the following explicit definition:

```
dec f: decorprog × (letter → level × order) → list level × order
```

```
--- f(nil,d)=nil
--- f(e::l,d)=if e=use(x) then nad(l,d)(x)::f(l,d)
              elseif isddecl(e) then comp(l,update(e,nad(l,d)))
              else f(e,nad(l,d))::f(l,d)                          •
```

From the above definition of f we notice that:
i) the functions nad(l,d) and f(l,d) both visit the same data structure l, and
ii) it is impossible to fold into a recursive call of f the expression comp(l,update(e,nad(l,d))), because it does not match the expression comp(l,nad(l,d)).

As indicated in [Pet84b] the fact i) suggests us to apply the *tupling strategy*, while for point ii) we need to use the *higher order generalization strategy*, which consists in generalizing an expression into a function. In our case it works as follows.

We define the function compile(l,g(e1,l,d)) defined as:
comp(l,update(e1,nad(l,d))) if g=λxyz.update(x,nad(y,z)), and
comp(l,nad(l,d)) if g=λxyz.nad(y,z).

Now the folding step required in point ii) is possible, and we can use a recursive call of compile with the suitable higher order argument g. The idea of the higher order generalization is related to the one in [Dar81], where the author uses the *mismatch* information deriving from a forced folding, to find a suitable generalization step.

We define the function:
H(e1,l,d,g)=<nad(l,d), compile(l,g(e1,l,d))>.
The functionality of H can be obtained from those of nad and compile. The latter one is:

(decorprog × (atom × level × order) × decorprog × (letter→(level × order))
→ (letter→(level×order))) → list level × order.

After a few folding/unfolding steps we get the recursive equations for the function H, where we used the following notations:
H(e1:e2,l,d,g1) = <nad(l,d), comp(l,update(e1,update(e2,nad(l,d))))>,
g1=λxyz.update(x,nad(y,z)), g2=λxyz.nad(y,z), and
πi <a1,…,an> = ai for i=1,…,n.

```
H(e1,nil,d,g)=<d,nil>
H(e1,e::l,d,g)=if e=use(x) then
                <u, (if g=g1 then update(e1,u)(x) else u(x)) :: v>
                        where <u,v> = H(e1,l,d,g)
                elseif isddecl(e) then <update(e,u),v>
```

```
                    where <u,v> = if g=g1 then H(e1:e,l,d,g1)
                                              else H(e,l,d,g1)
           else <u, (if g=g1 then π2 H(e1,e,update(e1,u),g2)
                                  else π2 H(e1,e,u,g2)) :: v>
                    where <u,v> = H(e1,l,d,g)                    •
```

Therefore, for producing the list l1 from dp1 we compute:

π2 H(◊,dp1,emptyfunction,g2) = comp(dp1,nad(dp1,emptyfunction)) (by definition), where ◊ satisfies this equality: update(◊,d)=d.

Notice that during the computation, the function H visits its second argument e::l only once. Indeed, H(…,e::l,…) is computed in terms of H(…,e,…) and H(…,l,…).

Therefore, by using the tupling strategy and the higher order generalization strategy we avoided the multiple traversals of e::l. On the contrary, they would have been necessary if we used the functions nad and comp. We will come back to this point later.

Testing the equality of functions when computing H is easy, because it amounts to check syntactical identities only. (Indeed one could simply code g1 and g2 using the numbers 1 and 2.)

A final step remains to be done. We need to avoid the visit of the given prog p1 for producing the corresponding decorated prog dp1.

In order to do so, we have to redo the steps we have presented above for the derivation of H from comp(l,nad(l,d)).

We will replay that derivation using as a starting point suitable variants of the functions nad and comp. We call those variants Nad and Comp. They are produced by applying again the composition strategy. Their inputs are prog's, not decorprog's. By that process we realize the promised incorporation of the function decor into nad and comp.

We have: Nad(p,d,n,r)=nad(decor(p,n,r),d). Its definition is:

```
dec Nad: prog × (letter → level × order) × level × order
                      → (letter → level × order)
--- Nad(nil,d,n,r)=d
--- Nad(e::l,d,n,r)=if isuse(e) then Nad(l,d,n,r)
          elseif isddecl(e) then update(<e,n,r>,Nad(l,d,n,r+1))
          else Nad(l,d,n,r)                                       •
```

The call nad(decor(p1,0,0),emptyfunction) is replaced by:
Nad(p1,emptyfunction,0,0).

We also have: Comp(p,d,n)=comp(decor(p,n,0),d). Its definition is:

```
dec Comp: prog × (letter → level × order) × level
                         → list level × order
--- Comp(nil,d,n)=nil
--- Comp(e::l,d,n)=if e=use(x) then d(x)::Comp(l,d,n)
              elseif isdecl(e) then Comp(l,d,n)
              else Comp(e,Nad(e,d,n+1,0),n+1)::Comp(l,d,n)     •
```

Notice that, in analogy to Nad, we could have defined the function Comp(p,d,n,r)=comp(decor(p,n,r),d), but a simple analysis of the resulting equations would have shown that the argument r is not necessary.
The call comp(decor(p1,0,0),emptyfunction) is replaced by:
Comp(p1,emptyfunction,0).

Now, as for nad and comp, the tupling and generalization strategies suggest us the definition of the following function L (analogous to H):

```
L(e1,l,d,g,n,r)=<Nad(l,d,n,r), Compile(l,g(e1,l,d,n,r),n)>, where:
Compile(l,g(e1,l,d,n,r),n)=Comp(l,update(e1,Nad(l,d,n,r)),n) if g=g1,
                          =Comp(l,Nad(l,d,n,r),n) if g=g2.
```

The types of the arguments of L are:

e1:atom×level×order, l:prog, d:letter→level×order,

g:(atom×level×order)×prog×(letter→ level×order)×level×order →(letter→level×order), n:level, r:order, and the type of the output of L is: (letter→ level×order)×(list level×order).

As we did for H, we then derive the equations for L, where L(b:c,…,g1,…) stands for <…, Comp(…,update(b,update(c,…)),…)>:

```
L(e1,nil,d,g,n,r)=<d,nil>
L(e1,e::l,d,g,n,r)=if e=use(x) then
          <u, (if g=g1 then update(e1,u)(x) else u(x)) :: v>
            where <u,v> = L(e1,l,d,g,n,r)
          elseif isdecl(e) then <update(<e,n,r>,u),v>
            where <u,v>= if g=g1 then L(e1:<e,n,r>,l,d,g1,n,r+1)
                                 else L(<e,n,r>,l,d,g1,n,r+1)
          else <u, (if g=g1 then π2 L(e1,e,update(e1,u),g2,n+1,0)
                            else π2 L(e1,e,u,g2,n+1,0)) :: v>
            where <u,v> = L(e1,l,d,g,n,r)                        •
```

Thus the required list l1 is equal to $\pi2$ L(◊,p1,emptyfunction,g2,0,0), which is equal to Comp(p1,emptyfunction,0).
As usual, for ◊ we have: update(◊,d)=d.

The derivation process is now completed and we derived a one-pass algorithm as required.

Let us clarify the notion of *one-pass* in our context. It is a notion relative to a particular argument of the function being defined. In our case it is the second argument of L, which is the given list of atoms to be "compiled". We say that L is one-pass because for each branch of its conditional definition, the recursive calls of L have as arguments disjoint substructures of the relevant argument. Indeed, L(…,e::l,…) is defined in terms of L(…,e,…) and L(…,l,…) only.

One could doubt whether it is actually convenient to use one-pass algorithms at the expenses of having functions with higher order parameters. For that respect let us remark that: i) the initial versions of our programs may already have higher order parameters (like nad, in our case) and ii) the higher order generalization may result in the use of a *low order* parameter only (g = 1 or 2, in our case).

For our derivation computer experiments showed that for progs of length 40 or more, the one-pass algorithm is indeed faster than the initial multi-pass version. (Obviously, those performances depend also on how fast parameters are passed among recursive calls in the available machine.)

The transformation steps we have shown, are quite tedious to be made by hand. A transformation system like the one described in [BaP77, Fea79] can be of great help.

A final remark concerns the readability of the derived versions. Indeed, it is difficult to understand the definition of the function L. That fact should not be regarded as a drawback of the transformation method. One only need to understand the initial program versions. The application of the basic rules and strategies will guarantee that correctness is preserved and performances are improved.

An alternative solution to our compilation problem is presented in [Swi85]. Also in that case higher order functions are used, and the solution is found by applying a method based on attribute grammars evaluation.

4. A TREE TRANSFORMATION PROBLEM

Let us consider a second example of application of the higher order generalization strategy. It is taken from a problem described in [Bir84]. We are asked to replace the value of all leaves in a given tree by their minimal value. For instance:

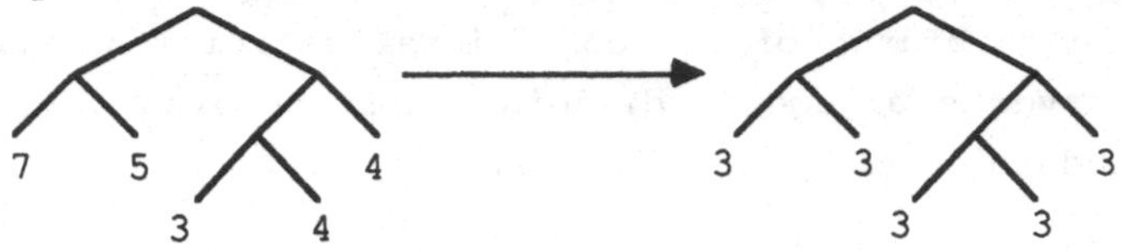

The obvious solution of the problem requires two traversals of the tree: the first one for computing the minimal leaf value and the second one for performing the replacement. We get the program:

```
data tree(num) == niltree ++ tip(num) ++ tree(num) Δ tree(num)
dec transform: tree(num) → tree(num)
--- transform(t) = replace(t,minv(t))
dec minv: tree(num) → num
--- minv(niltree) = +∞
--- minv(tip(n)) = n
--- minv(t1 Δ t2) = min(minv(t1),minv(t2))
dec replace: tree(num) × num → tree(num)
--- replace(niltree,m) = niltree
--- replace(tip(n),m) = tip(m)
--- replace(t1 Δ t2,m) = replace(t1,m) Δ replace(t2,m)            •
```

A way of avoiding a second traversal of the given tree is to remember its structure when computing the minimum leaf value. If one does so, a second visit for replacing the leaf values is not necessary. Remembering the tree structure and finding the minimum leaf can be done at the same time by defining a higher order function and using the tupling strategy as follows.

```
dec struct_min: tree(num) → ((num → tree(num)) × num)
--- struct_min(niltree)=<λx.niltree,+∞>
--- struct_min(tip(n))=<λx.tip(x),n>
--- struct_min(t1Δt2)=<λx.str1 Δ str2, min(m1,m2)>
      where <λx.str1,m1>=struct_min(t1), <λx.str2,m2>=struct_min(t2) •
```

Thus, transform(t) becomes: a1(a2) <u>where</u> <a1,a2>=struct_min(t).

One may object that in the above program the given tree has been copied when constructing the first component of the output of struct_min, and therefore the program is not space efficient.

However, since struct_min visits the tree only once, one may discard the leaves of the tree after their visit. A *destructiveness analysis* can be helpful in this case [Pet84c]. Thus, given a tree t, for constructing the first component of struct_min(t) we can reuse the memory cells which were needed for storing t.

The computation evoked by struct_min(t) when producing the output <a1,a2> and the subsequent application of a1 to a2 can be seen as follows: first, the given tree is visited to find the minimum leaf and pointers to the leaf positions are recorded, and then, the pointed positions are filled with the value which has been found.

Thus, the generalization strategy can be applied also for avoiding the use of pointers. They will be represented by parameters of suitable functions, and then function applications, that is, passing actual parameters, realize the required manipulations.

The higher order generalization strategy is used in this example for generalizing a *data structure* into a *function which manipulates it* (not for allowing a folding step, as in the previous compilation problem). From a tree t we indeed obtained the tree transformer: π1(struct_min(t)).

The use of a higher order object, like the first component of struct_min, allows us to achieve in our tree transformation problem the same performances obtained by using circular programs and lazy evaluation in [Bir84].

5. CONCLUSIONS

We defined a higher order generalization strategy, and we illustrated through examples its important role in the derivation of efficient programs by transformations. That role has been already recognized in the area of automated deduction and theorem proving for the invention of suitable lemmas [Aub76, BoM75, Cha76].

We want to stress that the *mismatch* information for a forced folding was crucial for suggesting our generalization steps. Related work has been done by [AbV84, HuH82, MaW79] for proving properties of recursively defined functions and various approaches to program synthesis.

A point for further investigation is the generalization technique for obtaining data structure transformers, which we presented in the previous Section. It can be viewed as realizing *communications among agents* [Pet84a].

A final point to be underlined is the synergism between the generalization strategy and the tupling strategy. Neither of them, if used separately, could have been powerful enough to solve with the required efficiency the transformation problems we considered. Their joint use was essential for our derivations.

6. ACKNOWLEDGEMENTS

Many thanks to the members of the IFIP WG.2.1 for their stimulating conversations. R.Bird, R.Paige, D.Swierstra, and the referees made valuable suggestions.

This work was supported by the IASI Institute of the National Research Council in Rome (Italy) and the Institute of Mathematics of Warsaw University (Poland).

7. REFERENCES

[AbV84] Abdali, K.S. and Vytopil, J.: "Generalization Heuristics for Theorems Related to Recursively Defined Functions" Report Buro Voor Systeemontwikkeling. Postbus 8348, Utrecht, Netherlands (1984).

[Aub76] Aubin, R.: "Mechanizing Structural Induction" Ph.D. Thesis, Dept. of Artificial Intelligence, University of Edinburgh (1976).

[BaP77] Bauer, F.L., Partsch, H., Pepper, P. and Wössner, H.: "Notes on the Project CIP: Outline of a Transformation System" TUM-INFO-7729 Tech. Report Institut für Informatik, der Technischen Universität München, Germany (1977).

[Bir84] Bird,R.S.: "Using Circular Programs to Eliminate Multiple Traversal of Data" Acta Informatica 21 (1984), 239-250.

[BMS80] Burstall, R.M., MacQueen, D.B., and Sannella, D.T.: "HOPE: An Experimental Applicative Language" Proc. LISP Conference 1980 Stanford USA (1980), 136-143.

[BoM75] Boyer, R.S. and Moore, J.S.: "Proving Theorems About LISP Functions" J.A.C.M. 22, 1 (1975), 129-144.

[BuD77] Burstall, R.M. and Darligton, J.: "A Transformation System for Developing Recursive Programs" J.A.C.M. Vol.24, 1 (1977) 44-67.

[Cha76] Chatelin, P.: "Program Manipulation: to Duplicate is not to Complicate" Report Université de Grenoble, CNRS Laboratoire d'Informatique (1976).

[Dar81] Darligton, J.: "An Experimental Program Transformation and Synthesis System" Artificial Intelligence 16, (1981), 1-46.

[Fea79] Feather, M.S.: "A System for Developing Programs by Transformations" Ph.D. Thesis, Dept. of Artificial Intelligence, University of Edinburgh (1979).

[Fea86] Feather, M.S.: "A Survey and Classification of Some Program Transformation Techniques" Proc. TC2 IFIP Working Conference on Program Specification and Transformation. Bad Tölz, Germany (ed.

L. Meertens) (1986).

[HuH82] Huet, G. and Hullot, J.M.: "Proofs by Induction in Equational Theories with Constructors" JCSS 25, 2 (1982), 239-266.

[MaW79] Manna, Z. and Waldinger, R.: "Synthesis: Dreams → Programs" IEEE Transactions of Software Engineering SE-5, 4 (1979), 294-328.

[Pet84a] Pettorossi, A.: "Methodologies for Transformation and Memoing in Applicative Languages" Ph. D. Thesis, Computer Science Department, Edinburgh University, Edinburgh (Scotland) (1984).

[Pet84b] Pettorossi, A.: "A Powerful Strategy for Deriving Efficient Programs by Transformation" ACM Symposium on Lisp and Functional Programming, Austin, Texas (1984), 273-281.

[Pet84c] Pettorossi, A.: "Constructing Recursive Programs which are Space Efficient" in: Computer Program Synthesis Methodologies (Biermann, Guiho, and Kodratoff, eds.) Macmillan Publ. Co., New York (1984), 289-303.

[Swi85] Swierstra, D.: "Communication 513 SAU-15". IFIP WG.2.1, Suasalito, California, USA (1985).

[Wad85] Wadler, P.L.: "Listlessness is Better than Laziness" Ph. D. Thesis, Computer Science Department, CMU-CS-85-171, Carnegie Mellon University, Pittsburgh, USA (1985)

8. APPENDIX

The following function OK tests whether or not a given prog has exactly one declaration occurrence for each letter.

```
dec OK: prog → bool
--- OK(p) = let <b,v> = activedecl(p,ϕ) in
            if b then OKdecl(p,v) else false          •
```

OK calls the function OKdecl(p,v) tests whether or not in a given context there is *at least* one declaration for each use of a letter. OKdecl takes as a second argument a set v of letters, which includes: i) the definitions occurring in the blocks enclosing the prog p, and ii) the definitions which are active at the top level of p (not in subblocks, i.e. sublists of p). It is defined as follows:

```
dec OKdecl: prog × set letter → bool
--- OKdecl(nil,v) =true
--- OKdecl(e::l,v)=if e=use(x) then (decl(x)∈v and OKdecl(l,v))
                   elseif isdecl(e) then OKdecl(l,v)
                   else let <b,u> = activedecl(e,ϕ) in
                     if b then (OKdecl(e, u ∪ v) and OKdecl(l,v))
                     else false                                  •
```

OK and OKdecl call the following function activedecl which given a prog p, tests the existence of *at most* one declaration for each letter. In the case of a positive answer, that is the first component of the answer is true, the second component gives us the active declarations for the top level of p. (The second argument for activedecl is used only for collecting the declarations encountered so far while visiting p.)

```
dec activedecl: prog × set letter → bool × set letter
--- activedecl(nil,v)=<true,v>
--- activedecl(e::l,v)=if isdecl(e) then
                (if e∈v then <false,ϕ> else activedecl(l, v ∪ {e}))
                else activedecl(l,v)
```

The function OK requires multiple visits of the prog p. We leave to the reader the task of deriving a one-pass algorithm as we did in Sections 2. and 3. That derivation requires again the application of the strategies we have described in the paper.

It will not be difficult (although a bit cumbersome to do by hand) to incorporate also that program into the compilation algorithm of Section 3.

Implementing Algebraically Specified Abstract Data Types in an Imperative Programming Language

Muffy Thomas,
Dept. of Computing Science,
University of Stirling,
Stirling, Scotland.

Abstract

We consider one aspect of the implementation of algebraically specified ADTs: choosing data structures for an efficient implementation. The class of hierarchical ADTs which insert and access data without key is considered. The *storage relations* and *storage graphs* (relations with additional efficiency information) of an ADT are defined and we discuss how implementation decisions can be made according to their properties.

1. Introduction

The algebraic specification of abstract data types, *ADTs*, [ADJ] [EhM], encourages the construction of correct and efficient programs by separating the two concerns of *specification* and *implementation*. The specifier concentrates on problem solving and capturing the intended behaviour of the data objects. When the specifier is satisfied that the specification is in some sense good (perhaps consistent, complete and satisfies some required properties), then the specification may be implemented.

The implementer concentrates on the problems of efficient representation and storage management in the implementing language whilst ensuring correctness. The degree of difficulty of implementation is inversely related to the similarity between the specification language and the implemententation language.

There has been considerable research into methodologies and techniques for algebraic specification [Geh] [PeV], and into the implementation of ADTs by functional programs, [Moi] [Pro] [Sub]. Although students and programmers have been implementing ADTS in imperative languages for some time according to intuition and informal rules, there is little methodology and there are few software tools available to aid the implementation of ADTs correctly and efficiently.

Here we consider some of the problems of implementing ADTs in a language such as Pascal.The aim of the paper is twofold. The first is to formalise some aspects of the problems of choosing the implementing data structures; we consider choosing linked data structures for the class of hierarchical ADTs which do not insert or access data by key. The second is to discuss how an efficient implementation can be constructed using the chosen data structures .

1.1 Outline of Paper

First, we shall formalise, for a class of ADTs, the notion of *storage graphs.* A storage graph is a graph representation of an element of an ADT. Each storage graph is a directed graph with some nodes designated as *access nodes.*The edges are labelled by a *storage relation* and the nodes are labelled by a *contents set*. Given an ADT, a class of storage relations is defined. They are derived from the specification and describe the order in which the data items held in an element of an ADT may be traversed, or reached. The class of contents sets is derived from the class of storage relations. The access nodes are deduced from the implementation of the operations of the ADT as operations on storage relations.

Second, we discuss how to choose the implementing data structures according to the properties of the storage graphs of an ADT. As an example we show how to choose the data structures for a linked implementation of a Queue specification. Finally, we briefly discuss how to construct an implementation of the operators of an ADT using the chosen data structures.

2. Related Work

Most related work is concerned with either imperative implementations for model-based specifications [Kan] [Low] [Row] [Set], or functional implementations for equational specifications [Ape] [Moi] [Sub]. There is little related work on the problem of imperative implementations for equational specifications. The [Ape] project analyses equational specifications for a singly-linked list and doubly-linked list implementation; but because the system is knowledge-based and without a formal methodology, there are problems with the integrity of the system. The idea of representing data structures by directed graphs was first suggested in the early seventies by both [Ear] and [Ros] (the latter with a restriction to connected digraphs). One aim of the present paper is to reconsider these digraph approaches within the framework of algebraic specification and high level imperative programming languages with user defined data types.

3. Keyless Abstract Data Types

In this section we define some notation for the class of hierarchical ADTs without key and we discuss the reasons for restricting attention to this class.

Some familiarity with equational algebraic specification is assumed; for example, see [EhM] and [ADJ]. A specification consists of a signature Σ and a set E of equations. Specifications are hierarchical [Bro] and include two designated sorts, the *derived sort* and the *primitive sort.*

The figure below displays a taxonomy of ADTs: we shall consider the class of ADTs which we call *keyless ADTs.*

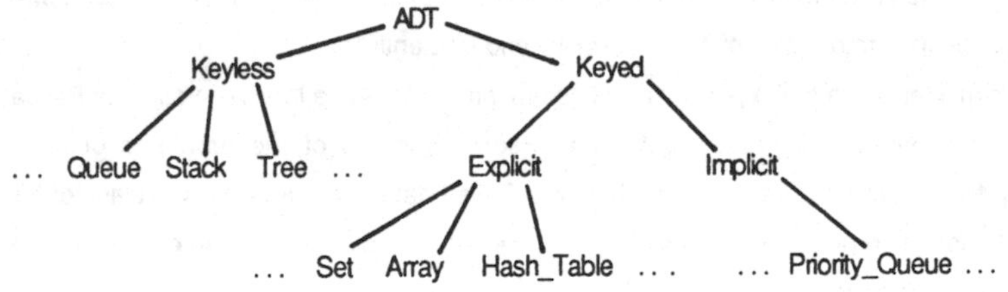

A keyless ADT imposes a structure on the elements of the primitive sort which is *independent* of any existing relationship between the elements. Storage and retrieval are specified by reference to some chronological ordering.

A keyed ADT imposes a structure on the elements of the primitive sort which is *dependent* on some property of the elements. If the key is explicit, the storage and retrieval are specified by reference to some relation between indices and primitive elements. If the key is implicit, then storage and retrieval is specified by reference to some ordering relation between primitive elements.

Clearly, the way in which an ADT is implemented depends on whether and how the ADT uses keys. Moreover, whereas the implementation of keyless ADTs may, in general, be constructed without reference to an algorithm or program using the ADT, the implementation of keyed ADTs is much more dependent upon the dynamic use of the ADT. In the following, we shall consider only keyless ADTs.

Definition: A **hierarchical ADT** is a specification (Σ,E) containing at least two distinguished sorts, a **derived** sort τ and a **primitive** sort δ. The **primitive specification** [Bro] is denoted (Σ_p,E_p).

Definition: Let (Σ,E) be a hierarchical specification. (Σ,E) is **keyless** iff

i) $\forall\, \Sigma_{w,\tau}$: if $\Sigma_{w,\tau}$ is inhabited then $w \in \{\delta,\tau\}^*$,

ii) $\forall\, \Sigma_{w,\delta}$: if $\Sigma_{w,\delta}$ is inhabited then $w = \tau$,

iii) the equations in $E \backslash E_p$, where \ is set difference, do not contain operators from Σ_p.

3.1 Partitioned Specifications

In order to discuss arbitrary specifications, an operator classification is necessary. Our classification extends the [KaS] classification of generators and defined functions.

The set of generators of a signature Σ is denoted Σ_g. We make a further subdivision of the defined operators. For example, some operators, such as **pop** in the usual **Stack** specification can be defined as "eliminators", and some, such as **top**, as "selectors". We formalise this distinction by designating disjoint sets of operators in a hierarchical specification.

Definition: A **partitioned** specification (Σ,E) is a hierarchical, keyless specification in which the operators of Σ are partitioned into 6 classes: Σ_{gd}, Σ_{gp}, Σ_e, Σ_r, Σ_s, and Σ_o. The arities of the operators in each class are constrained as follows:

$\Sigma_{gd} \subseteq \Sigma_{w,\tau}$ where $w \in \{\delta,\tau\}$ $\qquad$ Σ_{gp} = generators of Σ_p

$\Sigma_s = \Sigma_{\tau,\delta}$ $\qquad$ $\Sigma_e \subseteq \Sigma_{\tau,\tau}$

$\Sigma_r \subseteq \Sigma_{\tau,\tau}$ $\qquad$ $\Sigma_g = \Sigma_{gd} \cup \Sigma_{gp}$.

The partition classes denote the **generator** (derived), **generator** (primitive), **eliminator**, **rearranging**, **selector** and any **other** operators resp. The partition is given by the user; we now explain the ideas behind the definition. Generators define all the values of the specification, terms containing only generators and variables are called **generator terms.** A **selector** is an operator which returns elements of the primitive type. An **eliminator** is an operator which eliminates, or removes, elements of the primitive type contained in a generator term of the derived type. For example, the operator **tail** is an eliminator in the usual specification of lists; the result of an application of **tail** to a list generator term is always another list which contains fewer terms of the primitive sort. A **rearranging operator** is an operator which preserves the primitive type elements contained in a generator term of the derived type. For example, the operator **reverse** is a rearranging operator in the usual specification of lists; the result of an application of **reverse** to a list generator term is always another list containing exactly the same primitive terms.The remaining operators are in the "others" partition. This may include predicates and any operators which add primitive type elements to derived type elements but which are not designated as generators.

3.2 Semantic Requirements

In order to prove the classifications given in later sections, it will be necessary to ensure that there is at least one ground generator term in each equivalence class induced by the equations. Therefore specifications should be consistent and complete [KaS]. Completeness means that every term that is the application of a defined function to a ground generator term can be shown to be equivalent to a ground generator term. Errors are allowed, but do not propogate. The constant *err* is included in all primitive signatures, it is an *improper* element; all other elements are *proper*. In the following, specifications are partitioned, keyless, consistent and complete.

The following specification of **Queue** will be used to illustrate the subsequent definitions. We omit mention of the primitive operations on **Nat**.

spec **Queue**
basedon Nat
sorts queue
opns
eq: queue
add: queue,nat-> queue
front: queue -> nat
dequeue: queue -> queue
isempty: queue -> bool

eqns ∀ q:queue, d,d':nat.

front(eq)	=	*err*
dequeue(eq)	=	eq
dequeue(add(eq,d))	=	eq
dequeue(add(add(q,d),d'))	=	add(dequeue(add(q,d)),d')
front(add(eq,d))	=	d
front(add(add(q,d),d'))	=	front(add(q,d))
isempty(eq)	=	true
isempty(add(q,d))	=	false

partition $\Sigma_{gd} = \{eq,add\}$ $\Sigma_e = \{dequeue\}$ $\Sigma_s = \{front\}$ $\Sigma_r = \{\}$ $\Sigma_o = \{isempty\}$

4. Linked Data Structures

Data structures in languages such as Pascal are classified by storage allocation mechanism, namely static or dynamic. Implementation methods are classified accordingly. Array based implementation , or *sequential* allocation, exploits the fact that the index type is ordered. If arithmetic operations are also available in the index type, then related items may be stored at positions whose difference is defined by an arithmetic expression. In contrast, direct implementation, or *linked* allocation, links cells together explicitly. Because the positions of free cells are not related, (they are removed one at a time from the heap at runtime), cells containing related items must be explicitly linked together. Linked implementations use only as much space as is needed (apart from the overhead of links) whereas sequential implementations may waste space. However, sequential allocation may be preferable when specifications are bounded, or when keyed (random) access to stored items is required. Because our specifications are not bounded and specify keyless ADTs, only linked implementations are considered.

A linked implementation requires the definition of a **data cell** data structure and a **head cell** data structure.

Data cells contain the "data", ie. elements of the primitive sort; together they form an *implementation structure* (for example, a singly-linked list). The implementer must be able to deduce from the axioms which data cells should be linked together; namely, which primitive type elements should be related. For example, we must decide, for a binary tree, whether we should be able to retrieve the child of a node, or the parent of a node, or both, efficiently. A methodology for deriving implementation structures is required.

Data cells are only accessed through a head cell. The head cell represents the element of the derived type by holding the address, or index, of one or more positions in the implementation structure. The nature and number of positions held in a head cell can affect program efficiency; an additional location in the head cell can reduce the time complexity of several procedures. There are no fixed rules for determining which positions the head cell must refer to and we just rely on experience and reasoning. [Mar] calls such positions "naturally designated positions". For example, we would include the top position in a stack head cell, or the root, and possibly the leaves, in a tree head cell. Clearly the choice of designated, or *access*, positions depends on both the underlying implementation structure and the operations of the ADT; a methodology for deriving access positions from implementation structures and operations is required.

5. Storage Relations

In this section we define the storage relations of an ADT. A storage relation describes the way in which primitive sorted terms, the "data", are removed and selected from a term of the derived sort, the "data structure". The relation incorporates some implementation decisions because, in general, there are several ways of deriving a particular term of the primitive sort from a term of the derived sort. We define some properties of storage relations which are useful from an implementation point of view and show how an ADT can be classified according to its storage relations.

Given a term t, of the derived sort, a particular term d, of the primitive sort, may be retrieved by applying various permutations of rearrangers, eliminators, and a selector. Rearrangers and eliminators may be arbitrarily interleaved; the application of the selector must of course be last. In general, d may be described (if possible) by a term of the form: $\sigma_s(\sigma_n(\ldots(\sigma_1(t)\ldots))$ where $\forall i: 0 \leq i \leq n: \sigma_i \, \varepsilon \, (\Sigma_r \cup \Sigma_e)$, $\sigma_s \, \varepsilon \, \Sigma_s$. In many specifications there will be several possible choices for $\sigma_1,\ldots,\sigma_n$. We will restrict our attention to the following possibilities: $\sigma_1 \, \varepsilon \, (\Sigma_r \cup \Sigma_e)$ and $\forall i: 1<i \leq n: \sigma_i \, \varepsilon \, \Sigma_e$.

The motivation for this restriction is as follows. The storage relations reflect a view of how data is stored and retrieved in an element of the ADT; we look for the simplest structure which allows efficient retrieval of the stored data. We therefore consider, for every t of the derived sort, how the data it contains may be retrieved (by elimination and selection), and how, after the rearrangement of t, the data is retrieved (by elimination and selection). For each term of the primitive sort there may be one, many, or no terms describing its retrieval from a term of the derived sort. The storage relation defines the order in which primitive terms are retrieved given these restrictions. The relation ensures that the efficiency of selection, (repeated) elimination and rearrangement are taken into account; the efficiency of repeated rearrangement is not ensured, if it is intended then the user should define a new operator.

5.1 Terms with Variables

We are not concerned with the *values* of the terms of the primitive sort as such, but with their *positions* in ground generator terms of the derived sort. We define a new signature for each specification; the signature contains δ-sorted variables in place of the primitive signature.

Definition: Let (Σ,E) be a specification with primitive signature Σ_p. Let X be an infinite set of δ-sorted variables distinct from those occurring in E. Let Σ^* denote $(\Sigma \setminus \Sigma_p \cup X \cup err)$; the elements of X are now considered as constants of sort δ. The partition of Σ is given by taking $(\Sigma^*)_g$ to be $(\Sigma_{gp} \cup X \cup err)$; the other partition classes are as before.

The equations in E may be regarded as Σ^*-equations, since no operators from Σ_p occur in E [section 3]. We may therefore consider the quotient term algebra $T(\Sigma^*)/\equiv_E$ as a (Σ,E)-algebra.

Because we want the δ-sorted constants to denote positions in τ-sorted ground generator terms, we will consider only those congruence classes which contain ground generator terms with at most one occurrence of each δ-sorted constant.

Definition: Let (Σ,E) be a specification.

$T^*(\Sigma,E) =_{def} \{ C \in T(\Sigma^*)/\equiv_E \mid$ if $t \in C$ and $t \in T((\Sigma^*)_g)$ then t contains at most one occurrence of each δ-sorted constant$\}$

Some examples will illustrate this definition. If (Σ,E) is the **Queue** specification and **X={x1,x2,...}**, then $T^*(\Sigma,E)$ contains classes such as: **[add(eq,x1)]** and **[dequeue(add(add(eq,x2),x2))]**. It does not contain the class **[add(add(eq,x1),x1)]**. If (Σ,E) is the sequence specification **Seq** given in [Bro], then $T^*(\Sigma,E)$ contains classes such as:

[conc(m(x1),m(x2))], **[conc(m(x3),m(x4))]**, and **[conc(conc(m(x1),m(x2)),conc(m(x3),m(x4)))]**.

It does not contain the class **[conc(conc(m(x1),m(x2)),conc(m(x1),m(x2)))]**; the function defined by **conc** is partially defined on $T^*(\Sigma,E)$.

5.2 Relations

Given a term t, we define the *storage relation* at t; we begin by defining $\downarrow t$, a subset of $T^*(\Sigma,E)_\tau$.

Definition: Let (Σ,E) be a specification and let $t \in T(\Sigma^*)_\tau$.

$$\downarrow t =_{def} \{ C \in T^*(\Sigma,E)_\tau \mid \exists n \geq 0: \exists \sigma_1,\ldots,\sigma_n \in \Sigma_e : \exists t' \in T(\Sigma^*)_\tau : (([t] = [t']) \vee (\exists \sigma_r \in \Sigma_r: [t'] = [\sigma_r(t)])) \wedge (\sigma_n(\ldots\sigma_1(t')\ldots) \in C) \}.$$

In the Queue example, given t = **[add(add(eq,x1),x2)]**, $\downarrow t$ = { **[add(add(eq,x1),x2)]**, **[add(eq,x2)]**, **[eq]** } ; $\downarrow t$ consists of the classes containing the subqueues of t.

Definition: Let (Σ,E) be a specification , and let $t \in T(\Sigma^*)_\tau$. The **elimination** relation --> on $\downarrow t$ is defined by

$$C \rightarrow C' =_{def} \exists \sigma \in \Sigma_e : \sigma(C) = C', \quad \text{for} \quad C,C' \in \downarrow t .$$

It is important to note that --> does not denote the (syntactic) sub-term relation, although it may coincide with it in some specifications such as **Stack**. In the **Queue** example,

[add(add(eq,x1),x2)] --> [add(eq,x2)]

because **dequeue ([(add(add(eq,x1),x2))]) = [add(eq,x2)].**

We now use the selectors and --> to construct a family of relations on $T^*(\Sigma,E)_\delta$.

Definition: Let (Σ,E) be a specification, and let $t \in T^*(\Sigma)_\tau$. The **storage relation** at t, $\Rightarrow_t$, is the following binary relation:

$D \Rightarrow_t D' =_{def} \exists \sigma \in \Sigma_s: \exists C,C' \in \Downarrow t:$

$$((C \text{-->} C') \wedge (\sigma(C) = D) \wedge (\sigma(C') = D')) \quad \text{for } D, D' \in T^*(\Sigma,E)_\delta.$$

The interpretation of $\Rightarrow_t$ depends on the specification. For example, in the usual **Stack** specification $\Rightarrow_t$ denotes "after"; $x \Rightarrow_t y$ means that x was put on the stack after y and is therefore more accessible. In the **Queue** specification, $\Rightarrow_t$ denotes the converse, ie. "before"; $x \Rightarrow_t y$ means that x was put on the queue before y and is therefore more accessible. In the **Queue** example, given t = **add(add(eq,x1),x2)**, there is only one proper pair in $\Rightarrow_t$, namely **[x1]** $\Rightarrow_t$ **[x2]**.

We will restrict the domain of $\Rightarrow_t$ to the proper "contents" of [t]. Recall the notation $f^{\to}(S)$ for the image of S under f.

Definition: Let (Σ,E) be a specification and $t \in T(\Sigma^*)_\tau$. The **contents set** of t, $\Downarrow t$, is defined as follows:

$\Downarrow t =_{def} \cup \{ \sigma^{\to}(\Downarrow t) \mid \sigma \in \Sigma_s \wedge \forall c \in C.\ c \text{ is proper}\}.$

As an example, consider the specification of **Stack** with **pop2**, an operator which removes two items at a time. Given t = **push(push(push(push(create,x1),x2),x3),x4)**, then $\Downarrow t = \{ [x4], [x2] \}$.

5.3 Properties of Relations

We will, in the following sections, make implementation decisions based on properties of the structures defined by storage relations on contents sets. The implementer must use his or her imagination to decide which properties might be useful for the implementation; we define some such properties below.

Various conditions may be imposed on a relation on a set and its elements; the following conditions from [End] are standard: **reflexive**, **transitive**, **symmetric**, **antisymmetric**, **comparable**, **minimal**, and **maximal**. We define some further conditions.

Definition:

1. R^* is the reflexive, transitive closure of R.
2. A relation R on set S is **down-directed** iff $\forall x,y: \exists w: (x\ R^*\ w \wedge y\ R^*\ w)$.
3. A relation R on set S is **upwards-directed** iff $\forall x,y: \exists w: (w\ R^*\ x \wedge w\ R^*\ y)$.
4. A relation R on set S is **n-regular** iff every element is related to no elements, or to exactly n distinct elements.

5. A relation R on set S is **(n:m)-regular** iff it is not p-regular, for some p, $n \le p \le m$, and every element is related to no elements, or to no more than m elements and no less than n elements.

6. A relation R on set S is **singly-linked linear** iff R^* on S is antisymmetric, all pairs in R^* are comparable and when S is non-empty, minimal and maximal elements exist.

7. A relation R on set S is **singly-linked circular** iff R on S is antisymmetric and 1-regular, and R^* on S is symmetric.

8. A relation R on set S is **doubly-linked linear** iff R on S is symmetric, R^* on S is symmetric, all pairs in R^* are comparable, and R on S i s (1:2)- regular.

9. A relation R on set S is **singly-linked down-directed** iff R^* on S is antisymmetric and R on S is down-directed.

10. A relation R on set S is **doubly-linked circular** iff R on S is symmetric, all pairs in R^* are comparable, and R on S is 2-regular.

We use the properties of storage relations to classify ADTs:

> **Definition**: Let (Σ,E) be a specification. When for every $t \in T(\Sigma^*)_\tau$, $(\Downarrow t, \Rightarrow_t)$ has the property X (of being singly-linked linear etc.), we say that (Σ,E) has **storage type** X.

For example, we can show that **Queue** has a singly-linked linear storage type; the usual specification of **Stack** also has this storage type. As further examples, consider the sequence specification **Seq**, the usual specification for **Binary_Tree** and the usual specification for **List**; these types have doubly-linked linear, 2-regular singly-linked down-directed and singly-linked linear storage types resp. If we add a circular **shift** operator to **List** ,the storage type becomes singly-linked circular ; if we add a **reverse** operator (either using an append operator or using an auxiliary binary operator) then we have a doubly-linked linear storage type. These results are not suprising; we would expect to implement stacks and ordinary lists by similar data structures but we would not expect to implement reversible lists efficiently with the same data structure. The proofs of these classifications have been done manually; mechanisation of these proofs is planned [Sti].

6. Storage Graphs

In this section the *storage graphs* of an ADT are defined. A storage graph is a *representation* of an element of an ADT; it is a directed graph with some additional information about which nodes should be accessed efficiently at any time.

> **Definition: A storage graph** is a triple (N,E,A) where (N,E) is a directed graph with **nodes** N and **edges** E , and A is a non-empty subset of N whose elements are calles **access nodes** .

Storage graphs will be defined for all classes $[t] \varepsilon T^*(\Sigma,E)_\tau$. The nodes and edges are given by the storage relations and contents sets; it remains for us to define the access nodes.

6.1 Access Nodes

The function of the set of access nodes is twofold. First, it defines the access to nodes in the digraph by indicating which nodes are immediately accessible at all times. Clearly all nodes should be reachable; namely, for each node in a storage graph, there should be an access node such that there is a path from the access node to that node. (This is similar to the notion of a root ,or countable basis [Har] except that the set is not required to be minimal.) Second, the set defines the space-time trade-off; namely, membership of this set may be allocated to a position which is not necessary to ensure reachability but would enable (time) efficient implementations of certain operations. We proceed to define the access nodes according to these two principles.

6.1.1 Accessibility

The most "natural" access to the nodes of the digraph is that which is defined by the selectors. Clearly designating selected nodes as access nodes ensures that selectors can be implemented in constant time. However, these nodes alone do not ensure that all nodes are reachable, the nodes selected after one application of rearrangement must be included. Together, these nodes are referred to as the *selected positions*, or SP(t) given $t \varepsilon T(\Sigma^*)_\tau$.

Definition: Let (Σ,E) be a specification with selectors $s_1, \ldots ,s_n$ and rearrangers $r_1, \ldots, r_m$. Let $t \varepsilon T(\Sigma^*)_\tau$, the **selected positions** of t, **SP(t)**, are defined by
$SP(t) =_{def} \{ s_1(t), \ldots, s_n(t), s_1(r_1(t)), \ldots, s_n(r_1(t)), \ldots\ s_1(r_m(t)), \ldots, s_n(r_m(t)) \}$.

The selected positions ensure that all nodes are reachable.

Lemma: Let (Σ,E) be a specification . $\forall\ t \varepsilon T(\Sigma^*)_\tau : \forall x\ \varepsilon \Downarrow t : \exists\, p \varepsilon\ SP(t): (p \overset{*}{\Rightarrow}_t x)$.
Proof: By defn. of $\Downarrow t$, there is a σ_s in Σ_s and C in $\downarrow t$ st. $\sigma_s(C)=x$. By defn. of $\downarrow t$, there is an $n \geq 0$, $\sigma_1, \ldots, \sigma_n$ in Σ_e, and t' in $\downarrow t$ st. $\sigma_n(\ldots\sigma_1(t')\ldots)$ is in C . Either $[t] = [t']$, or there is a σ_r in Σ_r st. $[t']=[\sigma_r(t)]$. By defn. of --> on $\downarrow t$, $[\sigma_{n-1}(\ldots\sigma_1(t')\ldots)]$ --> C, $[\sigma_{n-2}(\ldots\sigma_1(t')\ldots)]$ --> $[\sigma_{n-1}(\ldots\sigma_1(t')\ldots)]$, ... , $[t']$ --> $[\sigma_1(t')]$; by transitivity, $[t'] \overset{*}{\dashrightarrow}$ C. By the (transitive) defn. of $\overset{*}{\Rightarrow}_t$, $[\sigma_s(t')] \overset{*}{\Rightarrow}_t \sigma_s(C)$. $\sigma_s(C)=x$, and so $[\sigma_s(t')] \overset{*}{\Rightarrow}_t x$.
$SP(t)=\{ [\sigma_s(t)], [\sigma_s(\sigma_r(t))] \}$; if $[t']=[t]$ then $p= [\sigma_s(t)]$ otherwise $p= [\sigma_s(\sigma_r(t'))]$.

6.1.2 Space-Time Tradeoff

The selected positions define the nodes which can be designated as access nodes; which other positions, in general, should be added for efficient implementations? The answer depends on the structure of the storage relation *and* the operations of the ADT. For example, both **Stack** and **Queue** have singly-linked linear storage type. The selected positions, in both cases, are the maximal positions, given by **top(t) and front(t)** resp., for some t. After inspecting the operations of these ADTs, we would expect, in the **Queue** example, to include the minimal position as an additional access node; we would not expect to include this position among the access nodes of **Stack**. Additional access nodes will be defined by the (additional) selectors which must be synthesised in order to implement the specification by storage relations. The set of such selectors will called **ST(t)**, for some $t \varepsilon T(\Sigma^*)_\tau$

A hierarchical, algebraic notion of implementation is adopted [Gog] [Nou]. Implementation is essentially the process of imposing the structure of the (initial) algebra of the *implemented* ADT onto the (initial) algebra of the *implementing* ADT. The operators of the implemented ADT may be implemented by *derived* operators in the implementing ADT; techniques such as those in [KaS] allow us, under certain circumstances, to synthesise derived operators automatically.

An algebraic specification of storage relations and an abstraction mapping between the storage relations and the τ-sorted elements is required. The specification depends on the specification of sets and relations, and also on the partition of the object specification. For the purposes of this paper we do not consider how to give a parameterised specification of storage relations, nor do we give the entire specification for the **Queue** example. Instead, the relevant signatures are given; the set theoretic equations are obvious and the others can be derived from the definitions in section 5.2. Specifications are parameterised using a notation like that of **Clear** [San]; comments follow after "!".

```
meta  U = sorts elem end

meta  Spec = sorts  τ, δ end

proc  Set ( D:U ) = enrich  D + Bool by
data sorts  set
opns
∅     :     set                          ! empty
{_}   :     elem         -> set          ! singleton
_∪_   :     set,set      -> set          ! union
_\_   :     set,set      -> set          ! difference
_ε_   :     elem,set     -> bool         ! membership
_==_  :     elem,elem    -> bool         ! equality
eqns        {omitted}
end         ! Set

proc  Pair ( D:U )  = enrich  D by
data sorts  pair
opns
( _ , _ ):  elem,elem    -> pair         ! mk pair
s     :     pair         -> elem         ! source element
t     :     pair         -> elem         ! target element
eqns        {omitted}
end         ! Pair

Proc  Edges ( D:U )  = enrich  derive from Set( D )   by nset is set, ∅n  is ∅, [_]i s {_}   end
                         +     derive from Set ( Pair( D ) [ elem is pair ])
                                                      by eset is set, U  is ∪, \\ is \, ∅e is  ∅end
                         by
opns
sce   :  eset,elem -> eset               ! only pairs with elem as source
tgt   :  eset,elem -> eset               ! only pairs with elem as target
maps:    eset      -> nset               ! map s
mapt :   eset      -> nset               ! map t
eqns
all S:eset, x:pair, y:elem.     sce(S U {x}, y)     = sce(S,y) U {x}        if  (s(x) == y)
all S:eset, x:pair, y:elem.     sce(S U {x}, y)     = sce(S,y)              if  (¬(s(x) == y))
all S:eset, y:elem.     sce(∅,y)                    = ∅
        {rest omitted}
end     ! Edges
```

proc Graph (S:Spec) = ***enrich*** Edges (S [elem ***is*** δ])
+ ***derive from*** Set (S [elem is τ]) ***by*** tset is set, ... ***end***
by

data sorts graph
opns

$\Downarrow$	:	τ	->	nset
$\Rightarrow$	:	τ	->	eset
(_ , _)	:	nset,eset	->	graph
$\downarrow$	:	τ	->	tset
_==_	:	τ,τ	->	bool
_==_	:	δ,δ	->	bool

{rest of signature omitted}
eqns {omitted, equations depend on partition of S}
end ! Graph

Note that storage relations are now defined on all elements of $T(\Sigma,E)/\equiv_E$. Because the Graph specification contains the object specification, the generator terms of S are subterms of the generator terms of Graph(S), and the abstraction mapping comes for "free":

$$\textbf{abs}: \text{Graph(s)} \to S \qquad \textbf{abs}\,(\Downarrow t, \Rightarrow_t) =_{def} t.$$

A small constraint is imposed on the form of the specification of the derived operators (the implementations of the operators of the object specification). In every equation of the form:

$$F(\Downarrow t, \Rightarrow_t) = \text{r.h.s.}$$

r.h.s. may not contain an occurrence of a subterm of t. The motivation for this restriction is that ultimately, τ-sorted terms will be implemented by variables of type head cell (in a given environment and store); therefore definitions should not depend of the syntactic form of termsof the given ADT.

Consider, as an example, the implementation of **Queue** by **Graph(Queue).** The abstraction mapping **abs** is given by the two equations:

abs ($\Downarrow$eq ,$\Rightarrow$eq) = eq, and **abs**($\Rightarrow$add(q,d),$\Downarrow$add(q,d)) = add(q,d).

The operators of **Queue** are implemented by the following derived operators (in bold upper case) in **Graph(Queue).**

$\forall \tau$:queue,D:nat.

EQ	=	$(\emptyset,\emptyset)$	
ADD (($\Downarrow$t ,$\Rightarrow$t), D)	=	($\Downarrow$t $\cup$ { D }, $\Rightarrow$t)	if (isempty(t))
ADD (($\Downarrow$t ,$\Rightarrow$t) ,D)	=	($\Downarrow$t $\cup$ { D }, $\Rightarrow$t $\cup$ { (last(t), D) })	if $\neg$(isempty(t))
DEQUEUE ($\Downarrow$t ,$\Rightarrow$t)	=	($\Downarrow$t \ { front(t) }, $\Rightarrow$t \\ sce($\Rightarrow$t, front(t)))	
FRONT ($\Downarrow$t ,$\Rightarrow$t)	=	front(t)	
ISEMPTY ($\Downarrow$t ,$\Rightarrow$t)	=	isempty	

where last is a derived operator in **Queue** with equations last(eq) = *err* and last (add(q,d)) = d .

In this example, SP(t) = { front(t) } , and ST(t) = { last(t) }.

Definition: Let (Σ,E) be a specification and let $t \in T(\Sigma^*)_\tau$. The **storage graph** at t is defined by the tuple: ($\Downarrow$t , $\Rightarrow_t$, A(t)), where A(t) = SP(t) $\cup$ ST(t).

7. Implementing Abstract Data Types

In this section we discuss how the storage type and storage graphs of an ADT can determine the choice of implementing data structures . We briefly discuss how implementations are constructed .

7.1 Choosing Data Structures

In the absence of further information concerning the dynamic use of the ADT, the motivation for the choice of (linked) data structures is that each τ-sorted element is represented by a storage graph . The nodes of the graph are represented by data cells, the edges by pointers between data cells, and the access nodes by a head cell.

The *data type* of head cells is chosen according to the storage graphs of the ADT. The data type is a product, or Pascal ***record*** of pointers of type data cell. The number of pointer fields is defined according to the cardinality of the access node sets in the storage graphs. Namely, for each term t, there will be a one-one correspondence between the elements of A(t) and the fields of the head cell. (Note that in Pascal a record type containing exactly one field whose type is ^T, where T is some data type, is equivalent to the type ^T.)

The *data type* of data cells is chosen according to the storage type of the ADT. The data type is a **record** consisting of one field whose type is the (representation) of the primitive sort, and when the storage type is m- or (n:m)-regular, it contains m pointers of type data cell. (If the storage type is not regular then another record type is necessary in order to link together data cell pointers. We do not pursue this as we believe that ADTs with non-regular storage types cannot be specified as keyless ADTs.)

Consider the data structures for **Stack** and **Queue**. Both specifications have the same storage type, singly-linked linear; therefore for both the data cell is

data_cell = **record** contents: integer; next: ^data_cell; **end**

In **Stack**, the cardinality of the access node sets is at most 1 and in **Queue** it is at most 2.The head cell for **Stack** is ^data_cell and for **Queue** it is **record** first:^data_cell; last:^data_cell; **end.**

Consider the **Seq** example; it has doubly-linked linear storage type and the cardinality of the access nodes sets is at most 2, (there are no synthesised selectors in the Graph implementation and for all t , ST(t) = { first(t), last(t) } . The implementing data structures are:

data _cell = **record** contents: integer; succ: ^data_cell; pred: ^data_cell; **end;**

head_cell = **record** first: ^data_cell; last: ^data_cell; **end;**

7.2 Constructing an Imperative Implementation

The details of implementation cannot be presented here and so only a brief outline follows. It is not difficult to see that the data structures given in the previous section allow time-efficient implementations to be constructed. Of course the data structures alone do not ensure correct implementation, many properties of the storage relations, for example antisymmetry, are not ensured by the pointer types of Pascal.

The programming language, with the appropriate definitions of head_cell and data_cell, must be specified as an ADT; assume the specification is called **ProgLang**. For a given ADT **S**, the operations of **Graph(S)** must be implemented (in the usual way) by derived operators in **ProgLang**. These operators may be regarded as procedures. Elements of **ProgLang** are triples (v,ρ,σ) where v is a (head cell) identifier, ρ is an environment, and σ a store. Implementation can be summarised by the following (commutative) diagram; assume $[t] \varepsilon T(\Sigma)/\equiv_E$ and $\sigma[t] = [t']$.

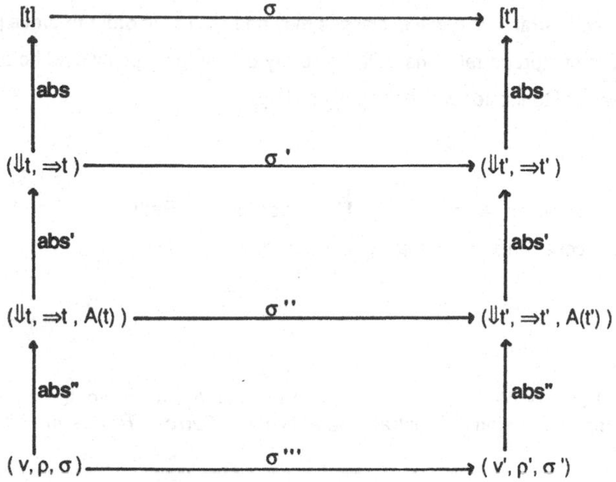

In the **Queue** example, if σ is **add**, then σ' is the **ADD** given in section 6.1.2. σ'', **ADD"** , is defined by

$$\mathbf{ADD''}((\Downarrow t, \Rightarrow t, A(t)), D) = (\mathbf{ADD}(\Downarrow t, \Rightarrow t), \{ front(t) \} \cup \{ D \}) \quad \text{if } \neg (isempty(t))$$

$$\mathbf{ADD''}((\Downarrow t, \Rightarrow t, A(t)), D) = (\mathbf{ADD}(\Downarrow t, \Rightarrow t), \{ D \}) \quad \text{if } (isempty(t))$$

The definition of **abs"** is not as straightforward as **abs** and **abs'**. The domain of **abs"** has to be defined by giving a representation invariant [KaS] to ensure that head cells point to valid queues; the mapping itself is quite complicated because of the nature of imperative languages with pointers.

Finally, a brief note on efficiency. First, transformations in the programming language may further improve the efficiency of the implementation. For example, the head cell of a reversible list may also contain information about how the storage relation is represented by the fields of the data cells. Second, we may wish, in some circumstances, to "trade" back some space for time; namely, to make the access node set a countable basis. In the implementation, there is a time overhead associated with each access node; namely, the head cell has to be adjusted according to changes to the implementation structure. In some cases this overhead may outweigh the benefits of constant time access to some position(s); then it would be preferable to remove the position(s) from the access node set (thus making access to them linear).

8. Conclusions and Future Work

We have formalised some aspects of the efficient implementation of ADTs using imperative data structures. Our approach agrees with intuition; when it is applied to familiar examples it produces expected results. The approach is influenced by two factors: the properties which the implementer uses to classify ADTs, and the partitioning of signatures. The properties should be useful from the point of view and the partitioning must be sensible.

The investigation into a methodology for imperative implementations of ADTs has only begun and much work remains to be done. Several topics require further formalisation and the application of the definitions must be considered; it is hoped that the classification of ADTs by storage type may be proved/disproved with the help of an equational reasoning laboratory such as ERIL [Dic]. Some additional properties of the eliminator and rearranging partition classes may be required in order to prove properties such as the well-foundedness of storage relations. A large library of storage types would be useful, and the approach should be extended to include other classes of ADTs.

Acknowledgements

I would like to thank Roy Dyckhoff, Alan Hamilton, Moira Norrie, Chic Rattray and Don Sannella for many discussions and helpful comments on the topic of this paper.

References

[ADJ] Goguen J.A.,Thatcher J.W.,Wagner E.G., "ADJ: An Initial Approach to the Specification, Correctness and Implementation of Abstract Data Types", *Current Trends in Programming Methodology*, Chapter 5, 1978.

[Ape] Bartels U.,Olthoff W.,Raulefs P., "APE: An Expert System for Automatic Programming from Abstract Specifications of Data Types and Algorithms." MEMO SEKI-BN-81-01, Institut fur Informatik, Universitat Kaiserslautern, 1981.

[Bro] Broy M., "Algebraic Methods for Program Construction:The Project CIP", pg. 199-222, *Nato ASI Series vol. F8,* Program Transformation and Programming Environments, Springer-Verlag 1984.

[Dic] Dick, A.J.J. , "Equational Reasoning and Rewrite Sysytems on a Lattice of Types," PhD. Thesis, Dept. of Computing, Imperial College, London,1986.

[Ear] Earley J., "Toward and Understanding of Data Structures",*C.A.C.M.* vol. 14, no.10, 1971.

[EhM] Ehrig H.,Mahr B., *Fundamentals of Algebraic Specification 1,* EATCS Monographs on Theoretical Computer Science, Springer-Verlag 1985.

[End] Enderton H.B., *Elements of Set Theory*, Academic Press 1977.

[Geh] Gehani N., McGettrick A.D (Eds.), Software Specification Techniques, Addison-Wesley 1986.

[Har] Harary F., *Graph Theory* , Addison-Wesley, Reading, Mass.,1969.

[Kan] Kant E., Barstow D.R.,"The Refinement Paradigm:The Interaction of Coding and Efficiency Knowledge in Program Synthesis", *IEEE Trans. on Soft. Eng.*,vol SE-7, no.5, Sept. 1981.

[KaS] Kapur D.,Srivas M., "A Rewrite Rule Based Approach for Synthesising Abstract Data Types, *CAAP'85"*, Lecture Notes in Computer Science ,vol. 185,Springer-Verlag.

[Low] Low J.R., "Automatic Data Structure Selection:An Example and Overview" ,*CACM* ,vol. 21 no. 5, May 1978.

[Mar] Martin J., *Data Types and Data Structures*, Prentice Hall 1986.

[Moi] Moitra A., "Direct Implementation of Algebraic Specification of Abstract Data Types", *IEEE Trans. on Soft. Eng.*, vol SE-8, no. 1, Jan. 1982.

[Nou] Nourani C.F., "Abstract Implementations and Their Correctness Proofs", *J.A.C.M.*, vol. 30, no.2, 1983.

[PeV] Pequeno T.H.C., Veloso P.A.S., "Do Not Write More Axioms Than You Have To", Proceedings of International Computer Symposium, Vol 1., 1978.

[Pro] Prospectra Project Summary, ESPRIT Project no. 390.

[Ros] Rosenberg, A.L., "Symmetries in data graphs", *SIAM J.Comput.* 1, 1972.

[Row] Rowe L.A., Tong F.M., "Automating the Selection of Implementation Structures", *IEEE Trans. onSoft. Eng.*, vol SE-4, no. 6, Nov 1978.

[San] Sannella D., "A Set-Theoretic Semantics for Clear", Acta Informatica, No. 21, 1984.

[Set] Freudenberger S.M.,Schwartz J.T., Sharir M., "Experience with the SETL Optimizer," *ACM ToPLaS,* vol. 5, No. 1, Jan. 1983.

[Sti] Alvey Project No. 007, Dept. of Computing Stirling,Stirling University, Stirling Scotland.

[Sub] Subrahmanyam P.A., "A Basis for a Theory of Program Synthesis", Phd. Thesis extract, USC Information Sciences Inst. and Dept of Computer Science, Univ. of Utah, 1980.

A Declarative Environment
for Concurrent Logic Programming*

Keith L. Clark and Ian T. Foster
Dept of Computing, Imperial College
180 Queen's Gate, South Kensington
London SW7 2BZ
janet: klc/itf@uk.ac.ic.doc
uucp: ...!mcvax!ukc!icdoc!klc/itf

Abstract

A logic programming environment should provide users with declarative control of program development and execution and resource access and allocation. It is argued that the concurrent logic language PARLOG is well suited to the implementation of such environments. The essential features of the PARLOG Programming System (PPS) are presented. The PPS is a multiprocessing programming environment that supports PARLOG (and is intended to support Prolog). Users interact with the PPS by querying and updating collections of logic clauses termed data bases. The PPS understands certain clauses as describing system configuration, the status of user deductions and the rules determining access to resources. Other clauses are understood as describing meta relationships such as inheritance between data bases. The paper introduces the facilities of the PPS and explains the essential structure of its implementation in PARLOG by a top down development of a PARLOG program which reads as a specification of a multiprocessing operating system.

1. Introduction

Language-based operating systems and programming environments have demonstrated the advantages of defining systems in a high-level language [Joseph et al, 1978], [Wulf, 1981], [Sandewall, 1978]. Such systems are most effective when the high-level language's computational model is capable of representing operational aspects of the underlying computer system and at the same time is close in spirit to that of the languages to be supported by the system. It must also be efficiently implementable.

This paper describes a logic programming environment implemented in a concurrent logic language. This is the PARLOG Programming System, or PPS [Foster, 1986a]. This programming environment aims to provide low-level support for declarative programming in logic languages by providing simple and expressive environment structures that are accessible as logic clauses with a declarative reading.

The PPS is implemented in PARLOG [Clark and Gregory, 1984a]. This language has been found to be particularly well-suited to the implementation of logic progamming environments. Of particular importance is its powerful control meta call, which permits a PARLOG program to initiate and control execution of other programs. A second aim of this paper is therefore to introduce and illustrate the use of PARLOG and its meta call for implementing programming environments. In this respect the paper is a sequel to [Clark and Gregory, 1984b]

The user views the PPS as a set of data bases. This set includes data bases that he defines himself and others defining system and program structure or containing libraries of useful program components. The PPS also maintains data bases representing more volatile information such as the history of user interaction, data structures constructed by query evaluations and currently active program evaluations. All information is available in declarative form and can be accessed both by the user and by other logic programs.

The user interacts with this set of data bases using a single mechanism: the *query*. The user initiates evaluation of a query in a PPS data base (in other words, inititates execution of a program) using the following syntax:

```
<data base> : <query>
```

This requests that <query> be evaluated in <data base>. For example:

```
utilities: analyse(my_db, A)
```

The user can use this mechanism to run any program defined in a PPS data base.

The PPS, which runs on Sun workstations, provides a window interface to facilitate user interaction. The user enters queries in the *console window*. Each valid query that is entered is allocated a unique identifier and a *query interface window*. The user is subsequently able to interact with a query using its interface window.

The paper introduces the facilities of the PPS and explains the essential structure of its implementation in PARLOG by a top down development of a PARLOG program which reads as a specification of a multiprocessing operating system. Even so, the PARLOG program presented is only a slight simplification of the actual PPS implementation.

The paper assumes familiarity with the general concepts of logic programming and Prolog, but it does briefly introduce PARLOG in section 2. Section 3 describes the basic structure of the PPS and presents the core of its implementation. Sections 4 and 5 introduce the PPS's meta programming and program structuring tools, presenting the extensions to the core implementation that they require. Section 6 describes how the PPS handles resource access. Finally, related work is surveyed and conclusions presented.

2. PARLOG

PARLOG differs from Prolog in three important respects: concurrent evaluation, 'don't-care non-determinism' and its use of mode declarations to specify communication constraints on shared variables. Each relation call in a PARLOG conjunction can be evaluated concurrently as a separate process. Shared variables act as communication channels along which messages are sent.

2.1 Don't-Care Non-Determinism

A PARLOG clause is a Horn clause optionally augmented with a commit operator, ':', which is used to separate the right hand side of the clause into a conjunction of guard conditions and a conjunction of body conditions:

$$r(t_1, \ldots, t_k) \text{ <- <guard conditions> : <body conditions>}$$

where $t_1, \ldots, t_k$ are argument terms.

Both the <guard conditions> and the <body conditions> are conjunctions of relation calls. There are two types of conjunction: the parallel '//' (C1 // C2) in which the conjuncts C1 and C2 are evaluated concurrently and the sequential '&' (C1 & C2) where C2 will only be evaluated when C1 has successfully terminated.

In the evaluation of a relation call $r(t_1', \ldots, t_k')$, all of the clauses for the relation r will be searched in parallel for a candidate clause. The above clause is a candidate clause if the head $r(t_1, \ldots, t_k)$ matches the call $r(t_1', \ldots, t_k')$ *and* the guard succeeds. It is a non-candidate if the match or the guard fail. If all clauses are non-candidates the call fails, otherwise one of the candidate clauses is selected and the call is reduced to the substitution instance of the body of that clause. There is no backtracking on the choice of candidate clause. We 'don't care' which candidate clause is selected. In practice, the first one (chronologically) to be found is chosen.

The search for a candidate clause can be controlled by using either the parallel clause search operator '\\' or the sequential clause search operator ';' between clauses. If a relation is defined by the clauses:

```
Clause1 \\
Clause2 ;
Clause3.
```

Clause3 will not be tried for candidacy until both Clause1 and Clause2 have been found to be non-candidate clauses.

Often the programmer will not care whether clauses and calls are evaluated sequentially or concurrently. PARLOG therefore supports a neutral conjunction operator ',' and a neutral clause search operator '..'. These are compiled to either parallel or sequential operators, depending on the granularity of the parallelism supported by the target machine.

2.2 Modes

Every PARLOG relation definition has a mode declaration associated with it, which states whether each argument is input (?) or output (^). For example, the relation merge(X,Y,Z) has the mode (?, ?, ^) to merge lists X and Y to list Z:

```
mode merge( X?, Y?, Z^ ).
merge( [ E | X ], Y, [ E | Z ] ) <- merge( X, Y, Z ) \\
merge( X, [ E | Y ], [ E | Z ] ) <- merge( X, Y, Z ) \\
merge( [ ], Y, Y ) \\
merge( X, [ ], X ).
```

(Dec-10 Prolog syntax [Clocksin and Mellish, 1981] is used throughout this paper. Upper-case letters denote variables. Lower-case letters, integers and strings enclosed in single quotes denote constants.)

Concurrently evaluating relation calls communicate via shared variables: the modes impose a direction on this communication. Non-variable terms that appear in input argument positions in the head of a clause can only be used for input matching. If an argument of the call is not sufficiently instantiated for an input match to succeed, the attempt to use the clause suspends until some other process further instantiates the input argument of the call. For example, the first clause for merge has [E | X] in its first input argument position. Until the call has a list or partial list structure of the form [E | X] in the first argument position the first clause is suspended.

If all clauses for a call are suspended, the call suspends. A candidate clause can be selected even if there are other, suspended, clauses.

2.3 PARLOG's Process Interpretation

A logic program can generally be given both a *declarative* and a *procedural* interpretation. Its declarative interpretation indicates how it represents knowledge, whilst its procedural interpretation indicates how it can be used to solve problems. Concurrent logic languages permit a third interpretation, a *process* interpretation, which is useful when explaining the operational behaviour of certain programs in these languages. This interpretation appears particularly relevant to systems programs written in these languages.

The process interpretation of logic was first described in [van Emden and Lucena, 1982]. When applied to concurrent logic languages, it allows programs to be viewed as defining networks of communicating processes. Reduction modifies this network. A PARLOG relation:

```
P <- A // B
```

thus describes the replacing of a process P by two new processes, A and B. Tail-recursive relations define long-lived (or *perpetual*) processes. Non-shared argument terms can be regarded as describing local state. Variables that are shared between two or more processes define communication channels. For example, in a conjunction:

```
user( Requests ) // server( Database, Requests )
```

the user process may pass messages of the form query(Query, Result) to server by appending them to the Requests stream. Result is assumed to be a variable. server receives these messages and processes Query relative to its local state, Database. It can then instantiate the Result variable to true or false to indicate to user the result of the query. The passing of the Result variable to server and its subsequent instantiation is an example of a programming technique first illustrated in [Shapiro, 1984], who termed it *incomplete messages*. This paper uses the alternative description, *back communication*, introduced in [Clark and Gregory, 1984a]. It is a very powerful feature of concurrent logic languages.

The process interpretation, though operational in nature, is thus a useful descriptive tool. In particular, it indicates how PARLOG can be used to represent changing state without side-effecting data base operations: perpetual processes can iterate with a different local argument. server can for example also process update messages, which generate a new local state NewDatabase:

```
mode server( Database?, Requests? ).

server( Database, [ query( Query, Result ) | Requests ] ) <-
        process_query( Database, Query, Result ),
        server( Database, Requests) ..
server( Database, [ update( Update, Result ) | Requests ] ) <-
        process_update( Database, Query, Result, NewDatabase ),
        server( NewDatabase, Requests ).
```

The implementation of the PPS, described in the next section, makes extensive use of perpetual processes to represent entities whose state may be subject to change over time.

2.4 The PARLOG Control meta call

The use of PARLOG for systems programming and other applications where one PARLOG program must control the execution of another is greatly facilitated if a control meta call is available. Clark and Gregory originally proposed a three-argument control meta call primitive [Clark and Gregory, 1984b] and showed how it could be used both for systems programming and to reduce or-parallel evaluation of guards of alternative clauses to and-parallel evaluation. Foster has proposed an extended five-argument meta call primitive for general systems programming work [Foster, 1986b] and it is this form of the call that is used in the PPS implementation of PARLOG.

The PARLOG control meta call is a sophisticated meta control mechanism that enables PARLOG meta programs to invoke the PARLOG machine on arbitrary goals and then interface to the monitoring and control functions of the machine with streams. A call to this primitive has the general form:

```
call( Module?, Resources?, Goal?, Status^, Control?)
```

The primitive initiates an attempt to evaluate Goal using the code in Module with bounded resources Resources. The call only fails if its arguments are invalid. Otherwise it generates a Status stream of messages about the evaluation and it consumes a stream of Control messages. The meta program that initiated execution of Goal can use these streams to monitor and control the execution of Goal. call can also be invoked without the Resources or Module arguments, or, as in Prolog with only the Goal argument.

The meta call accepts Control stream messages **stop, suspend, continue** and **resources**. The first three cause the goal evaluation to be stopped, suspended and resumed respectively. The fourth modifies the resources allocated to the goal evaluation.

The meta call may generate Status stream messages **failed, succeeded, stopped, suspend, continue, exception(_)** and **exception(_,_,_)**. The first three of these represent termination states of the Goal evaluation and are produced as the meta call succeeds. (Note that the meta call succeeds even when Goal fails.) **suspend** and **continue** are echoed when the corresponding Control stream messages are received. The single-argument exception message is generated when various sorts of exceptions occur, such as deadlock or excessive use of resources. Its argument is bound to the type of exception that occurred and the goal evaluation is suspended. The three-argument exception message is generated when what are termed *pseudo-exceptions* [Foster, 1986b] occur. This message has the general form exception(Type, Goal, NewGoal). Type indicates the sort of exception that occurred, for example, a call to a relation not defined in Module. Goal is the goal that caused the pseudo-exception. This goal is replaced with the new goal call(NewGoal), which then suspends waiting for the variable NewGoal to be bound.

The pseudo-exception message allows a monitoring meta program to process pseudo-exceptions in a number of ways. It may instantiate NewGoal to false, which has the effect of failing the call that caused the exception. Alternatively, for an undefined relation exception, signalled by a Type value undefined, the monitor program may instantiate NewGoal to a meta call that attempts to solve Goal in another data base: eval(OtherModule, Goal), where OtherModule names some other object code module. Subsequent sections of this paper will indicate how this meta call feature is exploited in the implementation of the PPS.

3. The Implementation of the PPS

The PPS is a network of communicating PARLOG processes. The system is booted by a call to the relation pps with a top level definition:

```
pps <-  console_manager( Terms ) //
        user_manager( Terms, Requests ) //
        database_managers( Requests).
```

which sets up the initial network:

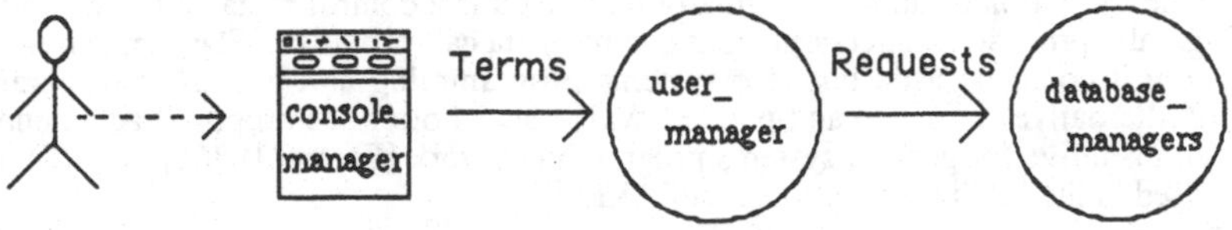

The console_manager accepts user input entered in a special console window. The console window has the layout:

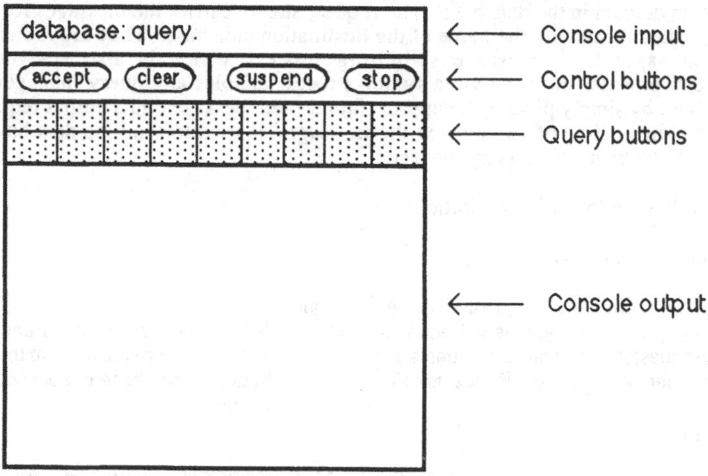

The user enters queries in the console input sub-window or selects query buttons which encode certain common queries. Recall that a query has the form database: query. A query can be a request to evaluate some conjunction of calls or a *meta query* request to access or update a definition in a data base. The console manager thus generates a stream of PARLOG terms representing queries to named data bases. The user_manager processes these terms, spawning a *query manager* for each query it receives. The query manager will send an initial request on the Requests stream for permission to evaluate the query in the named data base. It then monitors the evaluation of the query, passing out on the Requests stream subsidiary queries to other data bases that may be generated by the evaluating query. It sends out a query termination signal when the query finally terminates. The query manager also creates a new query interface window through which the user can interact with the evaluating query. This has the layout:

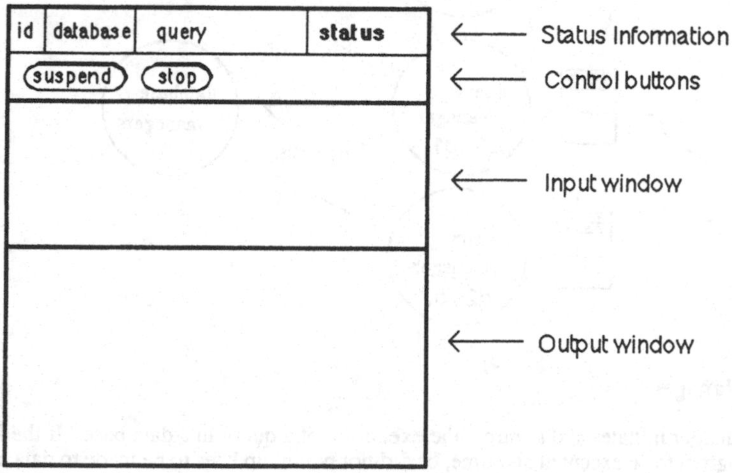

The database_managers process will spawn a manager for each data base currently defined in the PPS. The request stream from the user_manager (and the individual query managers that is spawns) carries all the access and update messages to the individual data base managers. Access to a data base is controlled by a data base manager in order to prevent the data base being updated whilst a query is using a relation defined in the data base. The request stream carries the messages for every data base, so the messages are tagged with the name of the destination data base. They are routed to the the correct data base manager by a message switching process which is also spawned by the database_managers process. Routing via a switch process enables any query manager to send a message to any data base by simply placing the appropriate tagged message on its output request stream. Back communication - the binding of variables in the message - is used to send the data base manager response directly back to the requesting query manager.

user_manager has the following definition:

```
mode user_manager( Terms?, Requests^ ).

user_manager( [ ':'( Database, Query ) | MoreQueries ], Requests ) <-
        query_manager( Database, Query, Requests1) //       % spawn query manager and
        merge( Requests1, Requests2, Requests ) //          % merge the requests from this
        user_manager( MoreQueries, Requests2 ) ..           % query with those of subsequent
                                                            % queries
user_manager( [ ], [ ] ).
```

Note that the processing of subsequent queries by the user_manager is executed in parallel with the evaluation of the first query. The user can therefore have several concurrently evaluating queries. Each query manager spawned will generate a stream of requests to access or update a particular data base. The various request streams generated are merged to give the single Requests stream that is passed to the message switching process created by the database_managers process. If two queries are entered by the user, two query managers will be spawned. Note that the user can independently interact with the console_manager and the two queries via their respective interface windows. The process communication network will be:

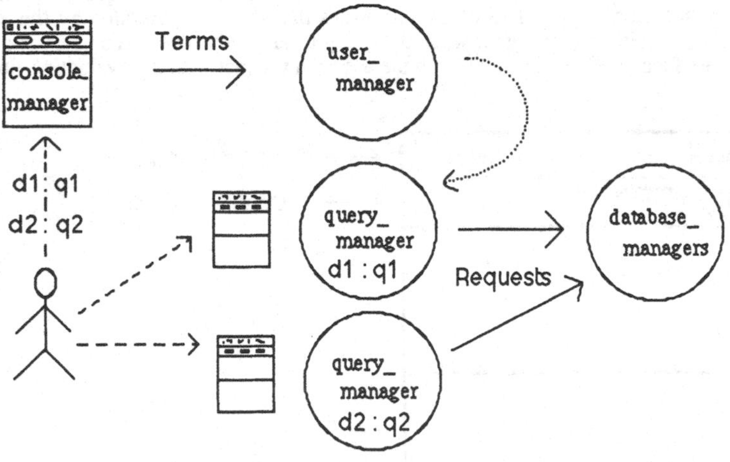

3.1 The Query Manager

The query manager initiates and controls the execution of a query in a data base. If the PPS only allowed a single program to be executed at a time, or did not permit updates to be made to data bases, the query manager could handle normal queries by simply looking up the name of the loaded module containing the compiled defintions for the data base and then executing the query via a meta call. No output request stream to a collection of data base managers would be needed and the query manager could have a definition of the form:

```
mode query_manager( Database?, Query? ).

query_manager( Database, Query ) <-
        lookup( Database, Module ) ,
        query_panel( Panelin, Panelout, Database, Query ) //
        q_m( Panelin, Panelout, Database, Query, Status, Control ) //
        call( Module, Query, Status, Control ).
```

query_panel is a process which sets up and interacts with the query interface window and q_m is a query monitor process that interfaces between the meta call query evaluation and the query_panel control process using the meta call Status and Control streams and the Panelin, Panelout input and output streams of query_panel. It handles all the status and exception messages sent out on the Status stream of the meta call, reporting to the user where necessary via a message sent on Panelout. It also handles user input, such as button commands to suspend or stop the query, by reflecting these messages it receives from query_panel on the Panelout stream onto the meta call Control stream. A query manager of this form is just a slight generalisation of the shell programs presented in [Clark & Gregory, 1984b].

However, in a multiprocessing system which also allows users to update data bases the above query manager is too simple. It would be possible to initiate a second query that modified a relation definition currently being used in a previously initiated query. Though this is unlikely in a single-user system, the PPS design is intended to form the basis for a multi-user system in which update/use contention is much more likely. It is also logically incorrect to allow programs to be modified whilst they are being used. It is far better to cleanly separate the meta level operation of update from the object level operation of evaluation.

The PPS prevents update/use contention by requiring all requests to execute or modify progams in a data base to pass via a manager for the data base. The requests sent to the data base manager are of the form:

```
message( Database, Request, Result )
```

where Database is the destination data base, Request is the request and Result is a back communication variable. In the case of a normal request to evaluate a query the message term is of the form:

```
message( Database, query( Query, Done ), Result ).
```

and Result will generally be bound by the database manager for Database to the response term:

```
eval( Module, Query )
```

indicating that the unmodified query is to be evaluated using the compiled definitions in Module, the module corresponding to Database. More generally, the response could be a modified query to be evaluated relative to some other module, thus allowing for query transformation and virtual program structures. Such possibilites have not yet been explored in the PPS.

The Done component of the communicated message is initially an unbound variable which will serve to carry the query termination signal to the manager for Database. This variable, and the corresponding termination signal variables for all other concurrent queries to Database, are retained by its data base manager. The Done signal variable is bound to the constant done by the query manager of Query. The data base manager will only allow an update to precede if all the signal variables of the concurrent queries have been bound by their query managers. This is the lockout mechanism that prevents update during use.

The PPS query_manager relation is actually defined as follows:

```
mode query_manager( Database?, Query?, Requests^ ).

query_manager( Database, Query, [ message(Database, query(Query, Done), Result) | Reqs ] ) <-
        query_panel(Panelin, Panelout, Database, Query ) //
        q_m( Done, Panelin, Panelout, Database, Reqs, Status, Control ) //
        call( Result, Status, Control ).
```

This relation defines a process network that can be represented as follows:

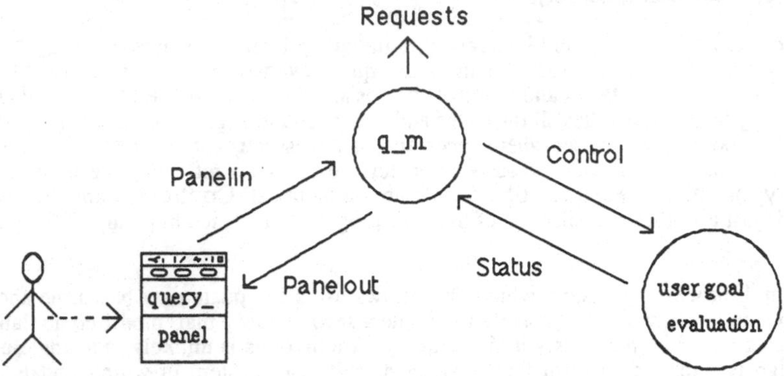

The query monitor q_m is defined as:

```
mode q_m( Done^, Panelin?, Panelout^, Database?, Requests^, Status?, Control^ ).

q_m( Done, Panelin, Panelout, Database, Requests, Status, Control ) <-
        data( Panelin ) :
        user( Done, Panelin, Panelout, Database, Requests, Status, Control ) \\
q_m( Done, Panelin, Panelout, Database, Requests, Status, Control ) <-
        data( Status ) :
        status( Done, Panelin, Panelout, Database, Requests, Status, Control ).
```

Note the use of the data primitive in the above program. This is a PARLOG primitive which suspends if its argument is an unbound variable, and succeeds for any other argument. In the above program it delays the branch to either the user or the status subprograms until a message is received on either the user input stream Panelin or the meta call Status output stream.

3.1.1 Handling User Input

On the query interface window monitored by the query_panel process the user may select buttons to *suspend* or *stop* the evaluation of the query. Another button is created when the query is suspended that allows the user to *continue* evaluation. When one of these buttons is selected the query_panel process sends out a corresponding message on its Panelin stream. The suspended q_m process therefore reduces to a call to the user relation. This echoes the message received on Panelin onto its Control stream, which is the control input stream of the meta call call(Result,Status,Control) of the query_manager. This causes the query to suspend, continue or stop as required. user is defined as:

```
mode user( Done^, Panelin?, Panelout^, Db?, Requests^, Status?, Control^ ).

user( done, [ stop | Panelin ], Panelout, Db, Requests, Status, [ stop | Control ] ) ..
user (Done, [ suspend | Panelin ], Panelout, Db, Requests, Status, [ suspend | Control ] ) <-
        q_m( Done, Panelin, Panelout, Db, Requests, Status, Control ) ..
```

```
user( Done, [ continue | Panelin ], Panelout, Db, Requests, Status, [ continue | Control ] ) <-
        q_m( Done, Panelin, Panelout, Db, Requests, Status, Control ).
```

Note that the Done variable is instantiated if the query is stopped so that data base manager for the Db data base knows that this query has terminated.

3.1.2 Status Messages

The query monitor may receive status messages from the evaluating meta call informing it that the user query has succeeded, failed, or is suspended due to an exception. Status messages suspend and continue may also be received. These are echoed by the meta call onto its status stream when these control messages are received on its control stream. They can be ignored by the status stream monitor. Status messages are processed by the status relation:

```
mode status( Done^, Panelin?, Panelout^, Db?, Requests^, Status?, Control^ ).

status( done, Panelin, [ succeeded ], Db, [ ], [ succeeded | Status ], Control ) ..
status( done, Panelin, [ failed ], Db, [ ], [ failed | Status ], Control ) ..
status( done, Panelin, [ Type ], Db, [ ], [exception( Type ) | Status ], [ stop | Control ] ) ..

status( Done, Pin, Pout, Db, Req, [exception( Type, Goal, NewGoal ) |Status], Control ) <-
        exception(Done, Pout, Db, Req, Type, Goal, NewGoal, NewPout, NewReq ) ,
        q_m(Done, Pin, NewPout, Db, NewReq, Status, Control) ;

status( Done, Panelin, Panelout, Db, Requests, [ Other | Status ], Control ) <-
        q_m( Done, Panelin, Panelout, Db, Requests, Status, Control ).
```

The first three clauses handle status messages that announce termination of the query for one reason or another. On receiving the message the status process binds the Done signal variable to the constant done so that the data base manager for the Db data base knows that this query has terminated. The message is echoed on the Panelout message stream to be reported to the user in the query interface window. In the case of the single argument exception message, which remember signals that the query is suspended due to such conditions as deadlock and memory limitation, a stop message is appended to the control stream to terminate evaluation. Note that the output Request stream to the data base managers is also terminated.

The fourth clause calls a relation exception to process pseudo-exception messages before recursively calling q_m with potentially modified Panelout and Requests arguments. This allows the exception handler to send messages to the user or some data base manager whilst handling the exception.

The fifth clause is a default clause which ignores the other status messages. Note the essential use of the sequential clause-search operator between clauses 4 and 5 to ensure that the last clause is treated as a default clause.

3.2 Simple Exception Handling

Recall that the three argument exception message is used to report conditions such as an attempt to evaluate a relation not defined in the current module. A very simple exception handler would just report the exception to the user and then cause the query to terminate as though the user had entered a **stop** command. A slightly more sophisticated exception handler might instead display the call to the user and allow the user to enter an alternative call. The user could then enter false, to force failure of the call to the undefined relation, or he could select the stop button to abort the evaluation.

An exception handler that passes calls to undefined relations to the query_panel process to allow for such a response from the user can be defined as follows:

```
mode exception( Done?, Panelout^, Db?, Requests^, Type?, Goal?, NewGoal^, NewP?, NewR?).

exception( Done, [ input(Goal, NewGoal) | Panelout ], Db, Requests, undefined, Goal,
                                                NewGoal, Panelout, Requests) ;
exception( Done, [ output( [exception,Type, in,Goal] ) | Panelout ], Db, Requests, Type, Goal,
                                                false, Panelout, Requests) .
```

The first clause processes calls to undefined relations by passing an *input* message to the query_panel process. On receiving the message input(Goal,NewGoal), query_panel will display Goal in the query interface window and bind NewGoal to the input entered by the user. The second clause is a catch-all clause that processes all other pseudo-exceptions by instantiating NewGoal to false and sending an *output* message to the query control panel to inform the user of the exception.

Recall tbat the PARLOG exception handling mechanism which generates the exception messages exception(Type, Goal, NewGoal) also replaces the goal Goal with the variable NewGoal in the user program. Instantiating NewGoal immediately causes the user program to resume execution by evaluating NewGoal. Suppose that NewGoal is instantiated to false. This situation can be represented as follows:

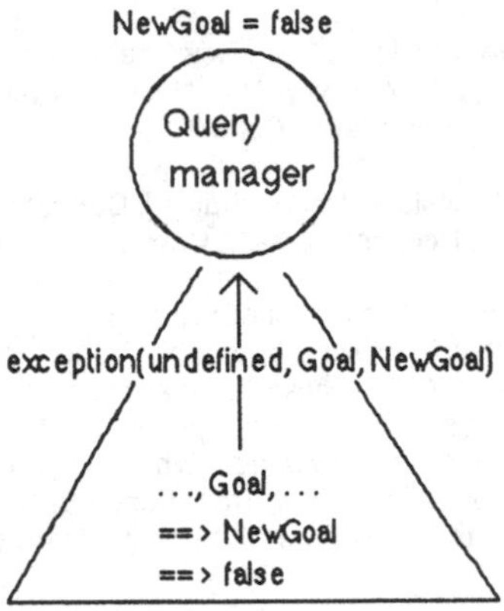

The query manager monitoring the user computation receives the exception message, determines that Goal should be failed, and instantiates NewGoal to false. The user process evaluating Goal is thus replaced with a call to false.

Section 5 presents a much more sophisticated exception handler that allows calls to relations undefined in a module to be evaluated relative to another module. This exception handler uses the special PPS program structuring data which links program modules.

3.3 Database Managers

The source and compiled code for the current PPS data bases are stored on a *logical disk* [Foster and Kusalik, 1986]. This is essentially an indexed term storage device. Access to the logical disk is controlled by a disk server, which processes the *retrieve* and *store* messages that are used to retrieve and store information on the disk. The term with index 0 on the logical disk is always a list of terms of the form db(Database, SourceId, ObjectId) giving the names of all current PPS data bases as well as the logical disk indexes of the source and object code for these data bases.

The call database_manager in the pps intialisation program invokes the disk server and sends it the message retrieve(0, DbList) to access term 0 to retrieve the list of db terms. It then calls an auxilary relation db_ms to spawn one data base manager process per data base. It also spawns the switch process to route the messages received from query managers to the appropriate data base managers:

```
database_managers( Requests ) <-
        disk_server( [ retrieve(0, DbList) | Disk ] ) //      % Retrieve list of data bases.
        db_ms( DbList, Disk, SwitchList ) //                  % Spawn data base managers.
        switch( Requests, SwitchList ).                       % Spawn switch (described below).
```

The process db_ms recurses down the DbList returned by the disk server, spawning a data base manager, a call to db_mgr, for each data base on the list.

```
mode db_ms( DbList?, Disk^, SwitchList^ ).

db_ms( [ db( Db,SrcId, ObjId ) | DbList ], [ retrieve( SrcId, Source ), retrieve( ObjId, Object ) | Disk ],
                                                        [sw( Db, ReqStream ) | RestofSwitchList ] ) <-
        ( load( Object, Module ) &
        db_mgr( ReqStream, Db, Source, Module, [ ] ) ) //
        db_ms( DbList, Disk, RestofSwitchList ) ..
db_ms( [ ], [ ], [ ] ).
```

Each db_mgr spawned has an input request stream ReqStream which is initially an unbound variable. The switch process will send messages to this data base manager by routing them from its input Requests stream to the ReqStream for the Db named in the message. The db_ms process therefore also contructs a switch list of terms of the form sw(Db,ReqStream) which is output to the switch process. db_mgr also has as arguments the name of the data base it is managing, the Source code for the data base returned by the retrieve(SrcId,Source) message sent to the disk_server, and the name of the in-core Module into which the object code has been loaded by the load call. Notice that the sequential connective after the load call delays the spawning of db_mgr until the load has terminated. This prevents the manager allowing a query to start evaluating before the object code has been fully loaded.

Assume disk term 0 is a list of two db terms. Then the process network created by data base_manager is as follows:

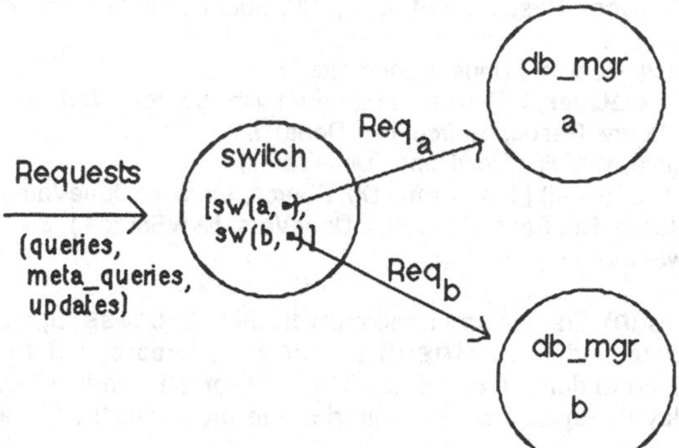

A data base manager receives messages in the form message(Request, Result), where Request may be a query, meta_query or update request.

Normal query requests are of the form:

```
query( Query, Done )
```

and will usually be handled by binding the Result variable to the term:

```
eval( Module, Query ).
```

which is then evaluated by the meta call of the query manager that sent the message. Alternatively, if some form of access control needs to be supported, messages can be augmented with user passwords and Result could be instantiated to a call to the primitive raise_exception to inform the user that access to this data base is denied.

Remember that the Done variable will be bound by the query manager when the query terminates. The list of all the Done variables for the active queries is held as the last argument of the db_mgr process. Hence the argument is initialised to the empty list when the manager is invoked.

Meta queries are sent to a data base manager when a user program calls one of the special meta relations described in the next section. They allow the user to access and analyse source programs. A meta query message has the form meta_query(MetaQuery) and is processed by the data base manager by invoking the auxiliary relation:

```
process_meta_query( MetaQuery, Result, Source, NewDone )
```

This is passed the Result variable of the incoming message and the Source for the data base. It processes the MetaQuery relative to the Source data base, binding Result to true or false depending on whether the meta query succeeds or fails. (In addition it may also bind variables in the MetaQuery term of the message.) NewDone is a fresh synchonisation variable which process_meta_query will bind to the constant done when the meta query has terminated in exactly the same way that the Done variables of normal queries are bound on termination by the query managers. It will prevent an update to the source before the meta query has terminated.

Updates are processed similarly, but in addition they lead to changes to the local Source argument of the manager process. The in-core module Module containing the data base's compiled code is also modified. Updates are only allowed if there are no currently active queries using the compiled code or accessing the source of the data base.

```
mode db_mgr ( InStream?, Db?, Source?, Module?, DoneVars? ).

db_mgr( [ message(query(Query, Done), Result) | InStream ], Db, Source, Module, DoneVars ) <-
        Result = eval( Module, Query )  //
        db_mgr( InStream, Db, Source, Module, [ Done  | DoneVars ] ) ..
db_mgr( [ message(meta_query(MetaQuery), Result) | InStream ], Db, Source, Module, DoneVars ) <-
        process_meta_query( MetaQuery, Result, Source, NewDone)  //
        db_mgr ( InStream, Db, Source, Module, [NewDone | DoneVars] ) ..
db_mgr( [ message(update(Update), Result) | InStream ], Db, Source, Module, DoneVars )  <-
        process_update( Update, Result, Db, Source, Module, DoneVars, NewSource )  &
        db_mgr( InStream, Db, NewSource, Module, [ ] ).
```

If there any active queries, that is, if DoneVars has any unbound variable, process_update can either delay the update or refuse the update and bind Result to false. A guard call to the relation active_queries(DoneVars) can be used to delay the update. This relation suspends if any variable on DoneVars is unbound. This will delay the update until all queries and meta queries that are accessing this database have terminated.

```
mode active_queries( DoneVars? ).

active_queries( [ Done | DoneVars ] )  <-
        data( Done )  &
        active_queries( DoneVars )  ..
active_queries( [ ] ).
```

3.4 Message Passing in the PPS

The switch process is defined in PARLOG as follows:

```
mode switch( InStream?, OutStreams^ ).

switch( [ message( To, Message, Result ) | InStream ], SwList ) <-
        perform_switch( To, Message, Result, SwList, NewSwList ) ,
        switch( InStream, NewSwList ).

mode perform_switch( To?, Message?, Result^, SwLIst?, NewSwList^ ).

perform_switch( To, Message, Result, [ sw( To,Stream ) | SwList], [ sw(To, NewStream ) | SwList ] ) <-
        Stream = [ message( Message, Result ) | NewStream ] ;
perform_switch( To, Message, Result, [ Other | SwList ], [ Other  | NewSwList ] ) <-
        perform_switch(To, Message, Result, SwList, NewSwList ) ..
perform_switch( To, Message, false, [ ], [ ] ) .
```

Each time a message message(To, Message, Result) is received from a query manager, perform_switch is called to recurse down the list of sw(DatabaseName, Stream) terms. If it finds the data base named To it appends the message message(Message, Result) to its stream. Otherwise it instantiates Result to the constant false to indicate failure to route the message.

This use of a switch process provides very flexible communications. Query managers (and hence users) can communicate with any data base without possessing an explicit stream to that data base. A simple extension of the above switch program will allow new data bases to be created easily at run-time. On receiving a create_new_database message, a new data base manager process can be invoked and its request stream added to the switch list of sw(data baseName, Stream) pairs held by the switch process.

The switch process may appear to be a potential bottleneck. However, the table lookup implemented in the above program by a recursion down the switch list can be implemented as a special language primitive. Moreover, the merges required to concentrate the requestsstreams from the different query managers passed into the switch can also be efficiently implemented as language primitives [Shapiro and Safra, 1986]. They do not need to be implemented by the merge program given in section 2.

4. Meta Relations

An important aspect of the PPS is the support it provides for meta programs: programs that reason about other programs. This support is provided by *meta relations*. These are relations which, when encountered in a user program, are dispatched by the query manager to the database that they want to access. They permit a program to access other programs as data.

Logic can be used to represent knowledge in two ways: as terms and as relations [Kowalski, 1979]. A meta program that analyses another program can thus either work on a term representing that program, perhaps structured as follows:

```
database( my_db, [ ( 'f/1', . . . ), ( 'g/1', . . . ) , . . . ] )
```

or by accessing a data base of relations:

```
definition( my_db, 'f/1', . . .).
definition( my_db, 'g/1', . . .).
. . .
```

The PPS adopts the latter approach, providing meta relations that can be viewed as extending a user program in one data base with (implicit) sets of clauses describing other data bases. Meta relations supported by the PPS include:

databases(Databases^)
: retrieves a list of all data bases defined in the PPS.

dict(Database?, Dict^)
: succeeds if Database is a data base, retrieving a list Dict of defined relations.

definition(Database?, Relation?, Definition^)
: succeeds if Relation is defined in Database, retrieving its Definition.

definition(Database?, Relation?, Time?, Definition^)
: succeeds if Relation is defined in Database at or prior to Time, retrieving its Definition at Time.

history(Database?, Relation?, History^)
: succeeds if Relation is defined in Database, retrieving a list History of timestamped definitions.

Note that meta relations such as definition retrieve a PARLOG term representing the parsed definition, not the source text of the definition. Thus if a PPS data base rectangle included the relation:

```
area(A) <- height(H) // width(W) // mul(H, W, A).
```

then the meta relation call

```
definition( rectangle, 'area/1', Definition )
```

would bind the variable Definition to the term:

```
relation( area, 1, [?], clause( [A], [ ], calls( parallel, [ height(H), width(W), mul(H, W, A) ] ) ) )
```

This is a term giving the essential structure of the definition.

4.1 The Implementation of Meta Relations

All calls to meta relations are recognised by the PARLOG compiler and converted into calls to the raise_exception primitive with arguments **primitive** and the meta relation call, so that they will be reported by the meta call as a **primitive** exception. The call is then handled by the exception handler, which needs to be redefined as:

```
mode exception( Done?, Panelout^, Db?, Requests^, Type?, Goal?, NewGoal^, NewP?, NewR? ).

exception( Done, Pout, Db, [ message( To, meta_query( Goal ), NewGoal ) | Requests ], primitive,
                                                  Goal, NewGoal, Pout, Req uests) <-
        is_meta( Goal ) :
        decode_destination( Goal, To ) ..
exception( Done, Pout, Db, [ message( To, update( Goal ), NewGoal ) | Requests ], primitive,
                                                  Goal, NewGoal, Pout, Requests ) <-
        is_update( Goal ) :
        decode_destination( Goal, To ) ..
exception( Done, [ input( Goal, NewGoal) | Pout ] , Db, Req, undefined, Goal, NewGoal, Pout, Req ) ;
exception( Done,  [ output( [exception, Type, in, Goal] ) | Pout ], Db, Req, Type, Goal, false, Pout, Req ) .
```

The first two clauses identify calls to meta relations and updates and generate meta query or update messages to the appropriate data base. decode_destination looks at the meta relation arguments to determine which data base the message should be sent to. The third clause passes other undefined calls to the query's interface window as before, whilst the fourth default clause fails all other exceptions.

4.2 The Application of Meta Relations

Meta relations facilitate the construction of programs such as static analysers, meta interpreters and debuggers. Programs which would be hard to write in conventional language systems are easy to write in the PPS. For example, a program that analyses a data base, reporting relations defined but not called, relations called but not defined and meta relations called is given here. Calls to meta relations are in bold.

```
mode analyse( Database?, Analysis^ ).

analyse( Database, Analysis ) <-
        dict( Database, Dict ) ,
        calls( Database, Dict, [ ], Calls ) ,
        separate( Dict, Calls, Analysis ).

mode calls( Database?, Dict?, CallsIn?, CallsOut^ ).

calls( Database, [ ], Calls, Calls) ..
calls( Database, [Relation | Dict], Calls, Calls2 ) <-
        definition( Database, Relation, Definition ) ,
        calls_relation( Relation, Definition, Calls, Calls1 ) ,
        calls( Database, Dict, Calls1, Calls2 ).
```

The relation calls_relation walks over a relation definition, outputing all relation calls on a difference list. separate compares lists of defined and called relations and outputs lists of relations defined but not called, relations called but not defined and meta relations called.

A number of meta programs (such as analyse) are included in the PPS. These can be both called by the user directly and incorporated in user programs either by run-time import or by compile-time copying. The way in which this is done is described in the next section. New tools can thus be constructed from old. For example, the user could combine the analyse tool listed above with a program of his own to generate a new tool that performs the same job for a set of data bases:

```
mode user_analyse( Databases?, Analysis^ ).

user_analyse( [ Database | Databases ], Analysis ) <-
        analyse( Database, Analysis1 ) ,
        user_analyse( Databases, Analysis2 ) ,
        merge_analyses( Analysis1, Analysis2, Analysis ).
```

This use of tools can be compared with both Unix shell-scripts (which allow Unix tools to be combined to give new programs) and compile-time linking of standard Unix libraries. The inheritance of code from system objects in SmallTalk is a related mechanism.

5. Describing Program Structure: Meta Clauses

It has been shown how the PPS allows users to execute programs located in data bases and write programs that manipulate other programs as data. The utility of the data base would be very limited however if it were not possible to construct new programs from program fragments located in various data bases and to use the data base as a program structuring tool.

The ability to construct programs from several data bases implies also the ability to partition large programs into fragments located in distinct data bases. This allows the user to:

- separate static and dynamic (changeable at run-time) program fragments.
- structure programs to make them easier to understand and maintain.
- reuse old code.

Some mechanism is required to represent the linking of data bases. The mechanism used in the PPS is the *meta clause*: a logic clause describing where a relation that is called but not defined in a data base should be evaluated. Like module import lists, meta clauses can be used to stitch together program components from various sources. However, meta clauses are a much more declarative representation of program structure than module import lists. PPS meta clauses are located in data bases and can thus be accessed and modified using the same mechanisms used to access and modify other programs.

5.1 Meta Clauses: Location and Application

Meta clauses are located in data bases termed *meta data bases.* These do not differ syntactically or structurally from other data bases but are distinguished as such by clauses defining the relation meta_database, located in the data base system. For example, when developing the analysis program user_analyse listed in section 4 in a data base my_db, the user might associate a meta data base my_meta with the data base. This association can be represented by an explicit clause in the data base system:

```
meta_database( my_db, my_meta )
```

my_meta might then contain the following definition of the specially recognised refer relation:

```
my_meta:
        mode refer( Relation?, Database^ ).

        refer( X, utilities )  <-  defined( X, utilities )  :  true;
        refer( X, library )    <-  defined( X, library ).
```

where defined uses the meta relation dict to determine whether a relation is defined in a data base:

```
defined( Relation, Database ) <-
        dict( Database, Dict ) ,  on( Relation, Dict ).
```

refer(Relation, Database) is a meta clause that states that Relation should be referred to Database for evaluation. Such a meta data base has defined the program structure:

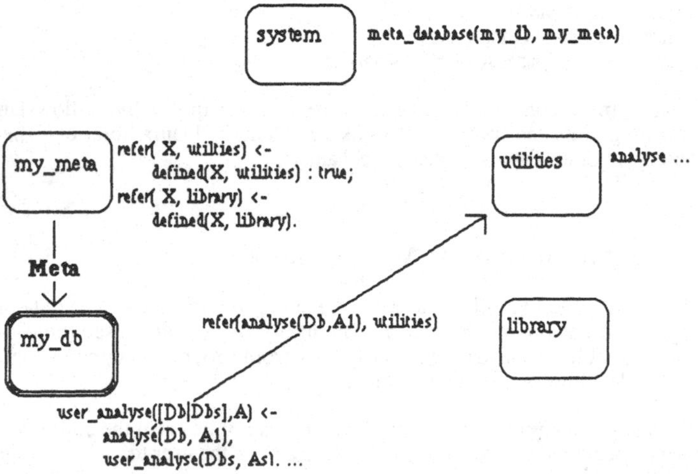

A user query such as:

```
my_db: user_analyse( [ database1, database2 ], A )
```

leads to calls to the relation analyse. The PPS refers to the meta data located in my_meta at this point and determines that these calls should be referred to the data base utilities.

Alternatively, the user might wish to link in his own version of analyse, located in the data base my_db1. This can be done by adding a new first clause:

```
refer( analyse(X, Y), my_db1 ) ;
```

to the above refer definition.

5.2 Meta Clauses: Implementation

The implementation of meta clauses requires an extension to the exception handler described in section 4. Rather than referring all calls to undefined relations to the user, the exception handler must access the meta clauses associated with the data base in which the query is being evaluated in order to determine whether the calls can be referred to another data base. If done naively, this would require a message to system to query the meta_database relation, followed by a message to the appropriate meta data base to query the refer clauses, for each call to an undefined relation. This overhead can be avoided if the system data base is queried initially to find the name of the meta data base which is then queried to find the name of its compiled code module. The meta data base module name is passed as an extra argument to the query monitor and exception handler.

The third clause in the exception program given in section 4.1 above must be replaced with the following three clauses. Note the extra MetaModule argument which is the cached name of the meta data base's compiled code module:

```
exception( Done, [ input( Goal, NewGoal ) | Panelout ], Db, MetaModule, Requests, undefined,
                         Goal, NewGoal, Panelout, Requests) <-
      call( MetaModule, refer( Goal, user ) ) : true ;
exception( Done, Panelout, Db, MetaModule,
                         [ message( ReferDb, query(Goal, Done), NewGoal ) | Requests],
                         undefined, Goal, NewGoal, Panelout, Requests) <-
      call( MetaModule, refer( Goal, ReferDb ) ) : true ;
exception( Done, Pout, Db, MetaModule, Requests, undefined, Goal, false, Pout, Requests) ;
```

The first clause has a guard which succeeds if Goal is to be referred to the user. If so, an input message to the query control panel is generated. The second clause determines whether Goal can be referred to another data base for evaluation. If it can, a query message is generated and the goal that led to the exception is replaced with the goal returned by the data base manager to which the query message is directed. This is done by passing the NewGoal variable to the data base manager in the query message. The third clause deals with goals that cannot be referred elsewhere. These are failed.

Note that the Done variable sent to the ReferDb database manager is the Done variable associated with the query when its query manager is spawned, not a new variable. The same variable is sent to the meta data base when it is initially queried to retrieve MetaModule. Update to any database referenced by a query evaluation is thus prevented during the course of the query evaluation. The only exception to this rule is the database system, which can be updated at any time that it is not being directly queried.

5.3 Query-the-User

Examples above have shown how meta clauses can specify that calls to undefined relations are to be referred both to other data bases and to the user for evaluation. Referring calls to the user implements a programming technique known in logic programming as *query-the-user* [Sergot, 1982]. This can be used both for interactive, top-down program development and for implementing declarative interactive systems.

In the PPS, calls to undefined relations that are referred to the user are displayed in the 'input' window in the query's control panel. For example, consider the query:

```
benefit : entitled( john )
```

where the data base benefit contains the single relation:

```
mode entitled( Person? ).

entitled( Person ) <-
        aged(Person, Age), lesseq( 60, Age ) : true \\
entitled( Person ) <-
        earns(Person, Salary ), lesseq( Salary, 2000 ) : true \\
entitled( Person ) <-
        disabled( Person ) : true.
```

which states that a person is entitled to a benefit if they are more than 60 years old, *or* they earn less than 2000, *or* they are disabled. Assume that the single meta clause refer(X, user) is linked to benefit. The query interface panel that would result from evaluating this query is:

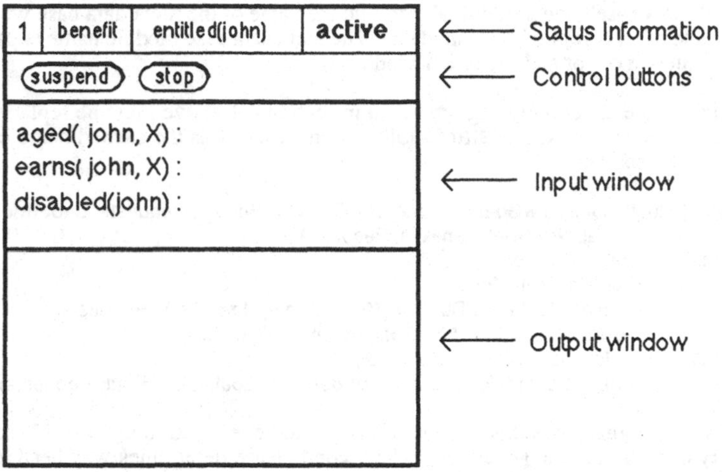

The input window presents three queries to the user:

```
aged( john, X) ? :
earns( john, X) ? :
disabled( john) ? :
```

The user can provide answers to any of these queries by typing a new goal after the query. In the example, providing the answer true to the third query (that is, indicating that John is disabled) suffices to succeed the original query. John's age and earnings do not need to be specified. Other more powerful goals can be provided as answers. The goal X = 35, provided as an answer to the first query, indicates that John is aged 35. The user can also invoke debuggers or meta interpreters. For example, the goal evaluate_in(john_info, earns(john, X)), provided as an answer to the second query, replaces the goal with a call to a meta interpreter that attempts to solve the goal earns(john, X) using definitions located in the data base john_info.

5.4 Efficient Use of Meta Clauses

When prototyping an application it is clearly very convenient to be able to link together components of existing programs. Meta clauses allow the user to do this very easily. The overhead of evaluating meta clauses at run-time may however be excessive in a production system, particularly if imported relations are frequently used. In this case, meta clauses can be transformed or applied at compile-time to transform an inefficient prototype into a more efficient program. This can be done at several levels.

Firstly, the meta clauses themselves can be transformed. If they define a search-path, they can be partially evaluated with respect to the current contents of the data bases in that path to give a bulkier but more efficient set of meta clauses. For example, the contents of the meta data base my_meta listed in section 5.1 above can be transformed to a set of unit clauses:

```
refer( analyse(X,Y), utilities ) ..
refer( ..., ... ) ..
etc ...
```

If the underlying implementation supports indexing, access to such a set of meta clauses will be very rapid indeed. This transformation can be compared with the use made in Berkeley Unix of hash tables to speed up directory searches.

A more powerful transformation can be applied to the object program by using the meta clauses as instructions to a compiler. This can copy imported program components to generate a new data base in which goals can be executed directly without run-time evaluation of meta clauses. This is effectively what a linker does in conventional language systems. This approach will generate an extremely efficient program, but is liable to be expensive.

A third approach recognises that programs are frequently constructed from sets of data bases that are only modified between runs, rather than at run-time. If these *data base families* are defined as such by the user and the PPS ensures that no data base in a family can be modified whilst any data base in that family is being queried, then query messages are not required within the family and can be replaced with direct calls to relations in other data bases within the family. This gives the efficiency of copying without the space overheads. Direct calls can be generated by adding linking clauses to data bases within a data base family. For example, consider the example programs in section 4.3. If the databases my_db and utilities form a family, the user_analyse program requires the addition of the linking clause:

```
analyse(Database, Analysis) <- eval(util_module, analyse( Database, Analysis) ) ,
```

to the database my_db, where **util_module** is the name of the compiled code module associated with utilities.

Direct calls to relations within a family can be combined with referral to data bases outside the family.

5.5 Other Meta Clauses

The application and implementation of the refer meta clause has been presented and it has been shown that this meta clause allows certain program structures to be described in logic. Other meta clauses are required to describe more complex program structures.

Evaluation of a call to an undefined relation that is referred to another data base may in turn lead to calls to other relations undefined in the referred-to data base. When refer clauses are used, as in the examples above, the original data base and its meta clauses are referenced to at this point. The refer meta clause thus addresses similiar problems to the 'self' message in object-oriented programming systems.

An alternative meta clause is refer_remote. This specifies that when a call to an undefined relation occurs in a referred-to data base, the meta clauses associated with the referred-to data base should be consulted. These may in turn lead to calls to other data bases which the user need not be aware of. refer_remote thus permits the modularisation of programs and the description of data base hierarchies.

6. Resource Access

A programming environment must provide user programs with access to resources such as secondary storage, i/o devices and data bases. This should be done using abstractions that enable programs to perform this access simply and elegantly. Previous sections have shown how meta relations and meta clauses allow users to access PPS data bases as source and program. This section describes how the PPS supports input and output, secondary storage and data base update.

6.1 Input/Output

Every query evaluating in the PPS has a query interface window associated with it. This has input and output sub-windows and is effectively a virtual terminal for the query evaluation. The user program can access this resource in several ways. Input and output *meta relations* can be used to access the window directly. Alternatively, *request streams* can be allocated and used to provide more controlled access to the window: the user program appends requests to streams rather than calling meta relations directly. Lastly, meta clauses can be used to refer undefined relations to the user and hence initiate *query-the-user* interactions, as described in the previous section.

6.1.1 I/O Meta Relations

Providing access to input and output resources poses problems in logic languages because the side-effecting primitives usually used to provide this access do not have a declarative reading. Concurrent logic languages provide a partial solution to this problem: a concurrent logic program can be regarded as co-operating with a user, viewed as a process, to construct a stream of i/o request terms.

One way of representing this view of i/o in a concurrent logic language is to augment the original goal with an extra argument representing the request stream. This approach has the disadvantage that every relation that could conceivably perform i/o, and the relations that call these relations, must also have this extra argument. Furthermore, the various request streams generated must be merged. This obscures the meaning of programs and introduces possible sources of programmer error. For example, a program that walks over a tree represented as a recursively defined structure tree(Node, LeftTree, RightTree), displaying all nodes:

```
mode show_tree( Requests^, Tree? ).

show_tree( Requests, tree( Root, LeftTree, RightTree ) ) <-
        show_tree( Requests1,LeftTree ) //
        show_tree( Requests2, RightTree ) //
        merge( [output( Root ) ], Requests1, Requests2, Requests ) ..
show_tree( [ ], [ ] ).
```

where merge is a fair three-way merge. The clumsiness of this approach motivated the designers of Logix [Silvermann et al, 1986] to provide syntactic sugar for appending a request to the request stream. For example:

kb # request

This is expanded to the appropriate stream operations by a precompiler. The above example can be represented as follows using this notation:

```
mode show_tree(Tree?).

show_tree( tree( Root, LeftTree, RightTree ) ) <-
        kb#output( Root ),
        show_tree( LeftTree ),
        show_tree( RightTree ) ..
show_tree( [ ] ).
```

which is easier to understand and precludes the possibility of programmer error.

The PPS takes a different approach. It is sematically equivalent to this syntactic sugar (and thus to streams and merges), however it avoids the need for streams and merges altogether by exploiting the PARLOG control meta call's exception handling mechanism. Certain i/o relations are defined to be meta relations and are thus trapped by the PPS when called in user programs. The exception handler then sends them to the query_panel process. I/o meta relations include input_term and output_term. The above program can be written as follows in the PPS:

```
mode show_tree( Tree? ).

show_tree( tree( Root, LeftTree, RightTree ) ) <-
        output_term( Root ),
        show_tree( LeftTree ),
        show_tree( RightTree ) ..
show_tree( [ ] ).
```

A call to input_term has as arguments a prompt string and a variable which is bound to the user response. The call suspends waiting for the response. If several input requests are made at about the same time, the user may respond to them in an order different from the display order in the query window. For example, the user could write:

```
. . .// input_term( 'Prompt A', A ) // input_term( 'Prompt B', B ) // undefined( X ) // . . .
```

where undefined(X) is a call to an undefined relation. All three of these calls would thus be trapped by the PPS. Assuming that a meta clause said that the undefined call was to be referred to the user, the PPS would display three input requests in the input sub-window of the query's interface window:

```
Prompt A  :
Prompt B :
undefined( X ) :
```

The user can select to provide input to any (or none) of these requests.

An input_term request can be regarded as a query to a remote database in the same way as a query-the-user interaction. The prompt represents the query.

6.1.2 Explicit Sequencing of Input and Output

A disadvantage of using meta relations (or annotations such as kb#request) is that the only way to explicitly sequence input and output requests is to sequence the reduction of goals in a program. This may sometimes place unacceptable constraints on parallelism. For example, given a program:

```
mode compiler( Tokens?, Code^ ).

compiler( Tokens, Code ) <-
        parser( Tokens, ParseTree ) //
        code_generator( ParseTree, Code ).
```

it may be desired to sequence output so that diagnostics generated by parser are displayed before those generated by code_generator. If meta relations or annotations are used for output, this requires rewriting the program using a sequential conjunction operator:

```
mode compiler( Tokens?, Code^ ).

compiler( Tokens, Code ) <-
        parser( Tokens, ParseTree ) &
        code_generator( ParseTree, Code ).
```

This severely reduces the potential for parallelism in the program.

This example can be used to illustrate the advantages of explicit request streams, which can be *appended* to sequence i/o independently of the computation strategy specified for associated goals. Using explicit request streams, the example can be rewritten as:

```
mode compiler( Requests^, Tokens?, Code^ ).

compiler( Requests, Tokens, Code ) <-
      parser( Requests1, Tokens, ParseTree ) //
      code_generator( Requests2, ParseTree, Code ) //
      append( Requests1, Requests2, Requests ).
```

Explicit request streams can thus sometimes be very useful. Yet using such streams for all i/o is clumsy. The PPS therefore introduces another meta relation, io_request, which returns an i/o stream to which i/o requests can subsequently be appended. This enables a program to use stream-based i/o when it needs to. For example, the compiler program given here could be called in the context of another program as follows:

```
. . ., io_request( Stream ), compiler( Stream, Tokens, Code ), . . .
```

The io_request relation creates a sub-window within the query interface window, to which i/o requests placed on the stream are sent. Request streams created using io_request can thus be used concurrently with i/o meta relations such as output_term. Request streams might typically be used for normal program output, whilst meta relations are used for diagnostic output, a combination which can be compared with Unix's standard output and standard error streams.

6.2 Data Base Update

As has been seen, PPS data bases can be modified by means of update messages. A suitable abstraction is required to allow user programs to generate these message in meaningful ways. The simplest approach (and that currently implemented in the PPS) is to support a meta relation that asserts a new definition for a PARLOG relation:

```
new_definition( Database, Relation, Definition )
```

When called in a program, this is trapped by the PPS (using the PARLOG meta call's exception handling mechanism) and translated into an update message to the appropriate data base. The use of this meta relation can be illustrated with an example: a program that copies a relation from one data base to another:

```
copy( Relation, FromDatabase, ToDatabase ) <-
      definition( FromDatabase, Relation, Definition ) ,
      new_definition( ToDatabase, Relation, Definition ).
```

where definition is the meta relation that retrieves the definition of Relation in FromDatabase and new_definition is the updating meta relation. Such a meta relation can also be used to implement more sophisticated editors and program transformation tools.

Asserting a new version of a relation in a data base extends the relation history, which is maintained as a list of (time, definition) pairs, where time is a timestamp. Subsequent queries and meta queries will access the new definition. Previous versions can still be accessed using meta relations such as:

```
definition( Database, Relation, Time, Definition )
```

which retrieves the definition of Relation which applies at Time. This meta relation can be used to write a meta program that restores an earlier version of a relation:

```
restore( Database, Relation, Time ) <-
      definition ( Database, Relation, Time, Definition ) &
```

```
new_definition( Database, Relation, Definition ).
```

Programs that execute queries with respect to earlier versions of a data base or generate new data bases containing previous states are also easy to write.

6.3 Persistent data bases

Secondary storage devices allow users to store data for long periods of time. They normally support file systems, which provide structure for user data and allow users to experiment with changes to programs, maintain alternative versions and restore previous versions. They may also serve as a mechanism for transporting data, both between applications and between physical systems. The PPS provides a storage abstraction that subsumes many of these functions. This is the data base, which is implemented as a persistent history. Data bases provide for the persistence of user data, provide a structuring mechanism and provide backups of old versions. They also provide a common format for all data in the PPS. The term *persistence* indicates that the user can refer to data without concern for its location or longevity [Atkinson et al, 1983].

Section 3.3 described how a PPS data base is implemented using a perpetual process that maintains the definitions of the relations in the data base as a PARLOG term. Meta queries are evaluated with respect to this term, as are updates which if successful generate a new term representing a modified data base. If the PPS were implemented on hardware that guaranteed the persistence of PARLOG computation, this representation of data bases would be sufficient. In general, however, the PPS must access secondary storage to load data bases and record modifications.

The program db_ms in section 3.3 showed data base source and object code being loaded in its entirety by queries to the disk server. In practice, the PPS may contain many data bases, many of which may not referenced in any one session. Furthermore, the source history in particular may be large and seldom referenced. The overhead, both in memory and processing time, of always transferring all data bases into memory is unacceptably high. Mechanisms to permit the incremental loading of object and source code are therefore introduced.

6.3.1 Virtualising Object Code

The object code for a data base is only loaded when the data base is queried. Though a suitable exception handler could load the object code for individual relations as required, the object code for the entire data base is currently loaded as a unit for greater efficiency. The program db_ms that spawns the data base managers must thus be rewritten to spawn *data base initiators*:

```
mode db_ms( DbList?, Disk^, SwitchList^ ).

db_ms( [ db( Db, SourceId, ObjectId ) | DbList ], Disk, [ sw( Db, ReqStream ) | RestofSwitchList ] ) <-
        db_initiator( ReqStream, Db, SourceId, ObjectId, Disk1 ) //
        merge( Disk1, Disk2, Disk) //                          % merge Disk streams.
        db_ms( DbList, Disk2, RestofSwitchList ) ..
db_ms( [ ], [ ], [ ] ).
```

The data base initiator simply waits for an access to the data base and then loads the data base's object code before initiating the database manager:

```
mode db_initiator( InStream?, Db?, SourceId?, ObjectId?, Disk^ ).

db_initiator( InStream, Db, SourceId, ObjectId, [ retrieve( ObjectId, Object ) | Disk ] ) <-
        data( InStream ) :
        load( Object, Module ) &
        db_mgr( InStream, Db, SourceId, Module, [ ], Disk ).
```

Note that the data base manager has an extra argument which is a disk request stream and that it now carries the source index number as its source argument, instead of retrieved source. The process network illustrated in section 3.3 is thus as follows:

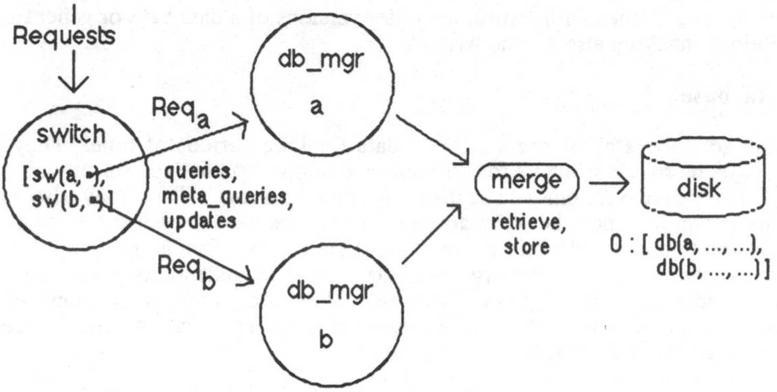

6.3.2 Persistent Binary Trees

The source code, which is generally much larger and less frequently referenced than the object code, is maintained as a *persistent binary tree* [Foster, 1986c]. This is a binary tree ordered on relation name (for rapid access to a particular relation) in which each node contains disk identifiers for a relation history and two offspring nodes. The initial Source argument of the data base manager is the disk identifier of the first node in this tree. This and other nodes are accessed when the relations process_meta_query or process_update (which process meta queries and updates respectively) use the relation pb_dereference to dereference links in the persisent binary tree. This recognises disk identifiers (represented as integers) and generates retrieve messages to the disk server to retrieve nodes. In-memory sections of the tree are represented as PARLOG terms instead of disk identifiers. Repeated retrievals lead to the tree being gradually copied into memory.

```
mode pb_dereference( Node?, Term^, DiskOut^, DiskIn? ).

pb_dereference( Node, Term , [ retrieve( Node, Term ) | Disk], Disk ) <-
    integer( Node ) : true ;
pb_dereference( Node, Node, Disk, Disk ).
```

As pb_dereference can copy nodes into memory, both process_meta_query and process_update now generate a new Source term representing a possibly modified in-memory component of the tree. The data base manager is therefore as follows:

```
mode db_mgr( InStream?, Db?, Source?, Module?, DoneVars?, DIsk^ ).

db_mgr( [message(query(Query, Done), Result) | InS], Db, Source, Module, DoneVars, Disk) <-
    Result = eval( Module, Query ) //                % // : concurrent evaluation of queries
    db_mgr (InS, Db, Source, Module, [ Done | DoneVars ], Disk ) ..
db_mgr( [ message(meta_query(MetaQuery), Result) | InStream], Db, Source, Module,
                                                                    DoneVars, Disk) <-
    process_meta_query( MetaQuery, Result, Source, Disk1, NewDone, NewSource ) //
    merge(Disk1, Disk2, Disk) //                     % //, merge : concurrent meta queries
    db_mgr( InStream, Db, NewSource, Module, [ NewDone | DoneVars ], Disk2 ) ..
db_mgr( [ message(update(Update), Result ) | InStream ], Db, Srce, Module, DoneVars, Disk) <-
    process_update( Update, Result, Db, Srce, Module, DoneVars, Disk, NewSrce, NewDisk) &
    db_mgr( InStream, Db, NewSrce, Module, DoneVars, NewDisk).
```

6.3.3 Releasing Memory and Recording Updates

The previous sections showed how the PPS implements a form of virtual memory by copying source and object code into memory only as required. For these techniques to be useful, mechanisms are required to free memory when it is no longer needed. These mechanisms must ensure that modifications to source and object code are recorded on disk.

The PPS records modifications to object code on disk as they are performed. The memory occupied by object code modules can therefore be freed without further processing (using the primitive unload), with the proviso that data base managers must ensure that object code is not deleted whilst in use. A change to source, on the other hand, is recorded as modifications to the in-memory component of a persistent binary tree. A mechanism to free memory used to hold source must copy modified branches of the tree back to disk before allowing the source term to be garbage collected. The implementation of this mechanism in PARLOG is not difficult if in-memory persistent binary tree nodes are represented as 5-tuples:

```
node( RelationName, Value, LeftTree, RightTree, Modified )
```

where Modified is either the disk identifier of the node, if the node has not been modified, or true if it has. A recursive commit can then be defined, which writes modified nodes of a sub-tree with Root back to disk (by generating store messages to the disk server) and returns the disk identifier of the root of a new tree:

```
mode commit( Root?, DiskId^, Disk^, NewDisk? ).

commit( node( Name, Value, Left, Right, true ), DiskId, Disk, NewDisk ) <-
        commit( Left, CLeft, Disk, Disk1) ,
        commit( Right, CRight, Disk1, Disk2) ,
        Disk2 = [ store( node( Name, Value, CLeft, CRight ), DiskId ) | NewDisk ] ;
commit( node( Name, Value, Left, Right, DiskId ), DiskId, Disk, Disk ).
```

unload and commit thus provide the means to release memory. These mechanisms can be activated by special 'release' messages sent to the data base manager. A data base manager clause to process a release_source message is as follows:

```
db_mgr( [ message( release_source, Result) | InStream ], Name, Source, Disk ) <-
        commit( Source, NewSource, Disk, NewDisk ) ,
        db_mgr( InStream, Name, NewSource, NewDisk ) ..
```

Release messages can be generated by a central memory server, either periodically or when memory runs short. The first approach can be compared with the Unix 'sync' command, which is called periodically to flush buffered i/o to disk. The implementation of the second approach can exploit the resource control provided by the PARLOG meta call. All PPS entities can be run inside a meta call and allocated limited memory resources. If these resources are consumed, a **resources** exception message is generated. This is effectively a request for more resources. When the central server receives such a message it can generate release messages to selected data bases. The memory freed in this way can then be allocated to the entity that has exhausted its resources.

6.4 Other Resources

Previous sections have described how data bases are implemented in the PPS using data base managers that process query, meta_query and update messages relative to data bases maintained as both source and object code. Other resources can be modelled as managers which process the same messages in different ways. For example, a PPS entity termed the *name server* processes queries of the form unique_name(X) by unifying the argument X with a name that is unique in the sense that every query to the name server is unified with a different value. The *editor server* processes queries of the form run_editor(Definition, NewDefinition) by creating an edit window containing Definition and unifying NewDefinition with a structure representing the contents of the window when the user finishes editing. The editor server can be understood as solving the relation run_editor by querying the user. Its use can be illustrated with an example: a program that edits Relation in Database:

```
edit( Relation, Database ) <-
    definition( Database, Relation, Definition) ,
    run_editor( Definition, NewDefinition ) ,
    new_definition( Database, Relation, NewDefinition ).
```

This program retrieves the definition of Relation in Database using the definition meta relation, uses the relation run_editor to query the user for a new definition and then stores the new version of Relation using the new_definition meta relation described in section 6.2.

Another form of PPS resource is the *term data base*. These are data bases that are maintained purely as PARLOG terms representing PARLOG programs. Queries are evaluated with respect to these terms by a process of interpretation. Interpretation is slower than execution, but update of source is faster than recompilation. The PPS history data base and a number of other seldom-accessed but volatile data bases representing system state are therefore implemented in this way. The history data base records its contents as a list of tuples:

```
query( Identifier, Database, Query, Variables, State )
```

(representing a Query assigned Identifier executed in Database, generating variable bindings Variables and currently in State) and processes queries by performing a lookup on this list. Similar techniques can be used to incorporate Prolog (or other languages) into the PPS.

7. Comparison with Related Work

The PPS is a logic programming environment implemented in a logic programming language. It is characterised by its declarative architecture in which user and system progams and system state and structure are represented as logic clauses. These clauses are both executable as programs and accessible as data. This dual nature of PPS entities facilitates tool construction and allows program transformations to be described in logic. At a lower level, implementation of the PPS is characterised by a message-passing architecture which provides fundamental support for multiprocessing and conflict resolution.

Programming environments for Lisp [Sandewall, 1978] and Prolog (notably micro-Prolog [McCabe and Clark, 1980], with its Lisp-like internal syntax) commonly provide primitives that allow both programs to be accessed as data and data to be treated as program. The primitives that construct or modify programs at run-time are typically non-logical (but see [Bowen, 1986]). Mechanisms to prevent concurrent update and execution of programs are not generally provided.

Syntax-based editors allow users of certain procedural languags to interact with programs as data structures [Teitelbaum and Reps, 1981]. The identity of source and executable program is commonly lost in these systems, however. SmallTalk browsers [Goldberg, 1983] and MacProlog windows [French, 1985] maintain this identity. MacProlog, for example, automatically recompiles the contents of a window that has been edited prior to running programs in it.

Because the PPS represents both programs and their structure as logic clauses, it is easy to represent and retrieve information about programs. Programming environments for more procedural languages achieve this functionality by a data base approach [Linton, 1984], [Ramamoorthy, 1985]. Information about programs and their specifications is stored in a data base and can be reasoned about. Certain Lisp systems adopt a similar approach [Teitelman and Masinter, 1981], [CLP Project, 1986]. The user reasons about a data base rather than about the actual programs, however. This can complicate updates, as the data base and the entities it describes must be kept consistent.

The implementation of the PPS can be understood in terms of a message-passing process model that can be compared with Actor and object-oriented systems [Hewitt et al, 1973], [Goldberg, 1983]. The logic variable and the back communication that this allows leads to somewhat different programming techniques, however. A programming environment that can be compared with the PPS in many respects is Logix [Silvermann et al, 1986], implemented in the concurrent logic language FCP [Mierowsky et al, 1985]. Logix provides a Unix-like user environment but does not appear to be structured as declaratively as the PPS. The use of concurrent logic languages for systems programming has also been considered by Kusalik [Kusalik, 1986].

The construction of operating systems and programming environments as entities connected by streams is not new: the message-passing paradigm is well-known and this use of streams has been proposed for functional operating systems [Henderson, 1982], [Jones, 1984]. Problems with stream 'spaghetti' has motivated proposals very similar to the PPS switch for functional languages [Stoye, 1986].

The meta programming facilities of the PPS have parallels in other logic programming systems. For example, Multilog [Kauffmann and Grumbach, 1986] incorporates *worlds* and allows users to define inheritance relationships between worlds. These relationships are not defined in logic, however. Mandala [Furukawa et al, 1984] and Prolog/KR [Nakashima, 1984] incorporate similiar concepts. Bowen proposes a meta-level extension to Prolog that enables data bases to be manipulated as first class objects in a Prolog-like language [Bowen, 1986]. PPS data bases, though akin to Bowen's theories (in that they are collections of definitions manipulable by a meta program) are named entities rather than language objects. PPS data bases can also be compared with the entities in Kowalski's logic-based open system [Kowalski, 1986]. This models complex systems as collections of knowledge bases that communicate their beliefs by assertions. Entities receiving assertions may modify their beliefs. The PPS supports knowledge bases which can assimilate knowledge, but requires that computation occur in query managers. In object-oriented programming terms, these can be viewed as *instances* of the entities described by data bases. The PPS is thus a somewhat more sophisticated (though less general) structure.

8. Conclusions and Further Work

This paper has combined a description of essential features of a logic progrmaming environment with a presentation of the use of the concurrent logic language PARLOG for systems programming. This combination was possible because the declarative nature of PARLOG allows PARLOG programs to be read as specifications.

PARLOG is well-suited to the implementation of programming environments. Because it is a high-level, declarative language, complex systems can be specified succinctly and elegantly. Its concurrent constructs and process interpretation allow it to describe concurrent activity. Its control meta call allows it to control computation effectively.

The logic programming environment described is the PARLOG Programming System, which is characterised by its declarative architecture in which user and system progams and system state and structure are represented as logic clauses. These clauses are both executable as programs and accessible as data. This facilitates tool construction and allows program transformations to be described in logic. At a lower level, implementation of the PPS is characterised by a message-passing architecture which provides fundamental support for multiprocessing and conflict resolution.

The PPS is currently implemented on the PARLOG system implemented at Imperial College [Foster et al, 1986]. This is an emulator for an abstract machine, the Sequential PARLOG Machine [Gregory et al, 1986] and runs on Unix machines. A version for Sun workstations incorporates an interface to the Sun window system, which is exploited by the PPS. Certain limitations of this implementation have restricted the PPS's development. Firstly, object code cannot be represented as PARLOG terms. This complicates the implementation of persistent databases, as separate mechanisms must be used to manipulate object and source code. Secondly, the resource-bounded deduction described by the five argument meta call is not supported. This prevents the PPS from tackling interesting resource allocation problems. Both these limitations should be resolved in a new PARLOG implementation currently being designed. As the target machine for this implementation is a multiprocessor, the PPS will become a multiprocessor programming environment without further modification.

Further work aims to extend the PPS to multi-user operation. This will require the introduction of additional system structures termed *contexts* that define both name spaces (mapping user names for data bases to global names) and access permissions. More complex mechanisms to prevent contention may also be required. Another extension to the PPS aims to allow properties (such as 'created by', 'description', 'analysis data') to be associated with relations. Relations are currently stored in the PPS as simple (timestamp, definition) pairs. The ability to associate arbitrary properties with relations will facilitate the implementation of 'knowledge-based' tools. It is also hoped to develop the user interface to the PPS by introducing browsers and other interactive tools. The range of meta clauses supported by the PPS will also be extended and efficient implementation of these clauses using compilation and transformation techniques investigated. The PPS will also be extended to support Prolog data bases. This will allow investigation of techniques for combining PARLOG and other logic languages.

Acknowledgements

This work was supported by the Science and Engineering Research Council. The authors are grateful to current and visiting members of the PARLOG research group at Imperial College, Alistair Burt, Andrew Davison, Steve Gregory, Tony Kusalik, Melissa Lam and Graem Ringwood for their contributions to PARLOG implementation, for valuable discussions on a variety of topics and generally for providing an agreeable research environment. The authors are also grateful to Martyn Cutcher from ICL, who has shown a continued interest in the research.

References

Atkinson, M.P., Bailey, P.J., Chisholm, K.J., Cockshott, W.P. and Morrison, R. (1982), "An Approach to Persistent Programming", *The Computer Journal*, 26(4), pp 360-365.

Bowen, K.A. (1986), "Meta-level Programming and Knowledge Representation". In *New Generation Computing*, 3, pp 359-383.

CLP Project (1986), "Introduction to the CLF Environment", USC Information Sciences Institute.

Clark, K.L., and Gregory, S. (1984a), "PARLOG: Parallel Programming in Logic", Research Report DoC 84/4, Department of Computing, Imperial College, London, and in *ACM Trans. on P rogramming Languages and Systems*, 8 (1), pp. 1-49, 1986.

Clark, K.L., and Gregory, S. (1984b), "Notes on Systems Programming in PARLOG". In *Proc. Intl. Conf. on 5th Generation Computer Systems* (Tokyo, November 1984), ed Aiso. H., Elsevier North Holland, pp. 299-306.

Clocksin, W.F. and Mellish, C.S. (1981). *Programming in Prolog*, Springer-Verlag, New York.

van Emden, M.H., and de Lucena, G.J. (1982), "Predicate Logic as a Language for Parallel Processing". In *Logic Programming*, eds Clark, K.L and Tarnlund, S-A., Academic Press, London, pp 189-198.

Foster, I.T., Gregory, S., Ringwood, G. A., and Satoh, K. (1986). "A Sequential Implementation of PARLOG". In *Proc. of the 3rd Intl. Logic Programming Conf.*, London, 1986.

Foster, I.T. (1986a). "The PARLOG Programming System: Reference Manual". Dept of Computing, Imperial College, London.

Foster, I.T. (1986b), "Logic Operating Systems: Design Issues", Research Report, Dept. of Computing, Imperial College, London. Submitted for publication.

Foster, I.T. (1986c), "Persistent Parallel Logic", Research Report (in preparation), Dept. of Computing, Imperial College, London.

Foster, I.T. and Kusalik, A.J. (1986), "A Logical Treatment of Secondary Storage". In *Proc. Symp. on Logic Programming*, Salt Lake City, pp 58-69.

French, P. (1985), *MacProlog User Guide*, Logic Programming Associates Ltd.

Furukawa, K., Takeuchi, A., Kunifuji, S., Yasukawa, H., Ohki, M., and Ueda, K. (1984), "Mandala, a Logic Based Knowledge Programming System". In *Proc. Intl. Conf. on 5th Generation Computer Systems* (Tokyo, November 1984), ed Aiso. H., Elsevier North Holland, pp 613-622.

Gregory, S., Foster, I.T., Ringwood, G.A. and Burt, A.D. (1986), "The Sequential PARLOG Machine", Research Report (in preparation), Dept. of Computing, Imperial College, London.

Goldberg, A. (1983), *Smalltalk-80: The Language and its Implementation*, Addison Wesley.

Henderson, P. (1982), "Purely Functional Operating Systems". In *Functional Programming and its Applications*, Eds Darlington, Henderson and Turner, CUP.

Hewitt, C. et al (1973), "A Universal Modular Actor Mechanism for Artificial Intelligence". In *Proc. I JCAI*, 1973.

Jones, S.B. (1984), "A Range of Operating Systems Written in a Purely Functional Style", Technical Monograph PRG-42, Oxford University Computing Laboratory, 1984.

Joseph, M., Prasad, V.R., Narayana, K.T., Ramakrishna, I.V. and Desai, S. (1978), "Language and Structure in an Operating System". In *Proc. 2nd Intl Conf. on Operating System Theory and Practice.*

Kauffmann, H., and Grumbach, A. (1986), "MULTILOG: Multiple Worlds in Logic". In *Proc. 7th ECAI*, Brighton, UK, pp 291-305.

Kowalski, R.A. (1979), *Logic for Problem Solving*, North Holland.

Kowalski, R.A. (1986), "Logic-Based Open Systems", Research Report, Dept. of Computing, Imperial College, London.

Kusalik, A.J. (1986), "Specification and Initialisation of a Logic Computer System", in *New Generation Computing*, 4, pp. 189-209, 1986.

Linton, M. (1984), "Implementing Relational Views of Programs", *Proc ACM SIGSOFT/SIGPLAN Software Engineering Symp. Practical Software Development Environments.*

McCabe, F.G. and Clark, K.L., (1980), *Micro-Prolog 3.0 Programmer's Reference Manual,* Logic Programming Associates Ltd.

Mierowsky, C., Taylor, S., Shapiro, E., Levy, J., and Safra, M. (1985), "The Design and Implementation of Flat Concurrent Prolog", Technical Report CS85-09, Weizmann Institute, Rehovot.

Nakashima, H. (1984), "Knowledge Representation in Prolog/KR". In *Proc. Intl. Symp. on Logic P rogramming*, IEEE Computer Society, pp 126-130.

Ramamoorthy, C.V. et al (1985), "GENESIS: An Interactive Environment for Development and Evolution of Software". In *Proc. COMPSAC*, 1985.

Sandewall, E. (1978), "Programming in an Interactive Environment: The Lisp Experience". In *Computing Surveys*, 10(1), pp 35-71.

Sergot, M.J. (1982), "A Query-the-user Facility for Logic Programming". DoC Report 82/18, Dept. of Computing, Imperial College. In *New Horizons in Educational Computing*, Yazdani, M., ed, Ellis Horwood.

Shapiro, E.Y. (1984), "Systems Programming in Concurrent Prolog", in *Proc. 11th ACM POPL Symp.*, Salt Lake City, Utah.

Shapiro, E.Y. and Safra, S. (1986), "Multiway Merge with Constant Delay in Concurrent Prolog". In *New Generation Computing*, 4(2), pp 211-216.

Silverman, W., Hirsch, M., Houri, A., and Shapiro, E.Y. (1986), "The Logix User Manual, Version 1.21", Technical Report CS-21, Weizmann Institute, Rehovot.

Stoye, W. (1986), "A New Scheme for Writing Functional Operating Systems", Research Report, University of Cambridge Computing Laboratory, Cambridge, 1986.

Teitelbaum, T., and Reps, T. (1981), "The Cornell Program Synthesiser: A Syntax-Directed Programming Environment". In *CACM*, 24(9).

Teitelman, W. and Masinter, L. (1981), "The Interlisp Programming Environment". In *IEEE Computer* 14(4), pp 25-33.

Wulf, W.A. (1981), *HYDRA/C.mmp: An Experimental Computer System*, McGraw-Hill, N.Y.

Or-Parallel Execution Models of Prolog

David H.D. Warren
Department of Computer Science
University of Manchester, Manchester M13 9PL

Introduction

Iultiprocessor machines based on state-of-the-art microprocessors hold promise for elivering much higher computing power at a reasonable cost. However, such mahines will not gain wide acceptance unless they can be viewed essentially as "black oxes" that simply run software faster. There are enough complexities in software evelopment without burdening the programmer with the further problem of exlicitly managing parallelism. The challenge, therefore, is to exploit parallelism in pplication programs in a way that is *invisible* to the programmer, and that does ot incur major overheads.

ı general, this is an extraordinarily difficult problem, since most programming ınguages are based on von Neumann constructs that are inherently sequential. It therefore natural to turn to non von Neumann languages. In this context, Prolog ands out as being uniquely qualified to unlock the potential of multiprocessors. is one of the few, if not the only, non von Neumann language that is already in ide use for serious applications. Indeed, its popularity is based predominantly on s suitability for programming advanced applications. The basic language (Horn auses, annotated with goal ordering plus cut) does not include any von Neumann onstructs, yet is sufficiently powerful that it represents the bulk of applications ode.

hus, the general goal, towards which this paper is directed, is how to exploit ırallelism transparently in Prolog. Prolog offers two main kinds of parallelism: -parallelism and and-parallelism. In this paper, we focus on or-parallelism. We ill examine different models for executing Prolog in or-parallel on shared memory ultiprocessors. We focus on or-parallelism in particular, since it seems to offer od potential for large-scale, large-granularity parallelism across a wide range of plications. Or-parallelism typically manifests itself in the form of "generate and st" or "iterate and compute". Examples are querying a deductive database, parsg a natural language sentence, searching for a string in a document, or compiling set of objects. Often, as in the last example, the or-parallelism is "wrapped up" a 'setof' construct.

ıe main problem with implementing or-parallelism is how to represent different ndings of the same variable corresponding to different branches of the search space.

We will discuss a progression of possible implementations, starting from a simple abstract model, and moving to more complex models that aim to be more efficient. In this way, we intend to illuminate what the implementation choices are [6].

The models to be discussed are: (1) the Abstract Model of classical resolution theory which involves copying all inherited structure; (2) the Naïve Model, where bindings are stored in a simple chronological list; (3) the SRI Model, originally proposed by Warren at SRI, where each processor has its own binding array; (4) the Argonne Model, designed and implemented by Lusk and Overbeek at Argonne [4,1], where there is a hash array recording the bindings on each arc of the or-parallel tree; (5) the Manchester-Argonne Model, a variant of the Argonne model proposed by Warren, where hash arrays are only created as arcs become actually shared; (6) the Argonne-SRI Model, a variant of the SRI Model which uses the "favoured" binding approach of the Argonne Model.

Of particular concern, in comparing these models, are the costs of creating and accessing variable bindings. In standard Prolog implementations, these are both very fast operations that can be performed in constant time. Creating a binding is essentially just a write to memory (an assignment to the variable value cell), plus in general, a "trailing" of the variable's address by pushing it onto a pushdown list called the "trail". Accessing a binding is nothing more than a memory read of the variable's value cell. It is vital to maintain comparable efficiency for these operations in an or-parallel implementation.

It is also vital to keep down the cost of creating multiple tasks at an or-parallel branch point. Ideally this overhead should be no greater than the cost, in a standard Prolog implementation, of backtracking through these alternative tasks. In standard Prolog implementation such as the WAM [8,7,2], this creation of multiple tasks corresponds to the 'try', 'retry', 'trust' operations which create and restore choice points. All these are constant-time operations which can be implemented in, typically, 15 or 20 machine instructions. (There is also the cost of "untrailing" variable bindings, but this is probably better viewed as a (delayed) part of the cost of creating a variable binding).

In general, we want to keep the cost of all operations in a parallel implementation very close to what they would be in a sequential implementation. Otherwise, what we gain through parallelism can easily be lost in extra overheads.

2 The Abstract Model

A basic reference point in comparing or-parallel models is the classical "Abstract Model" of resolution theory (specialised to Horn clauses and Prolog control). We will describe it in some detail, mainly to "set the scene" for the other models.

he computation is viewed as a tree, where each node is labelled with a "task" onsisting of a list of goals. For the root node, the task is just the initial query. ther nodes are labelled with derived tasks, the derivation process being resolution. ach node corresponds to one possible way of matching the leftmost goal of the arent node's task with a program clause. The derived task can be viewed as a copy the parent task, with the leftmost goal replaced by (a copy of) the body of the atching clause, and with variable instantiations being made as required for the atch.

andard sequential Prolog explores the computation tree in a depth-first, left-to-ght manner. At any point in time, the processor is "at" a particular node, working 1 the task at that node. The processor keeps a record of the branch of the tree ove it. In an actual Prolog implementation, such as the WAM, the representation the task tree is rather indirect. We will discuss the details a bit more later. owever one can imagine a Prolog implementation which follows very directly the ostract model. The main difference between such an implementation and a "real" nplementation is that it would keep an actual copy of the tasks on the branch ove the current node, whereas the real implementation does not, but is able to construct the earlier tasks as needed on backtracking.

hus our abstract model has the (rather serious) overhead at each step of having to ake a physical copy of the goals inherited from the parent task. However, if one ccepts this, then it is rather easy to support or-parallelism.

ultiple processors can be simultaneously exploring different branches of the tree. ne processor can start exploring the tree in the standard depth-first left-to-right anner. As soon as it creates a node with unexplored arcs remaining to the right, nother processor can "steal" one of these arcs and start exploring the subtree be-eath it, again in the standard manner. This process can continue until all the ailable processors are busy. When processors backtrack, they will of course avoid xploring arcs that have been "stolen" by other processors. When a processor back-acks to the point it started from, it becomes idle and available to explore any nexplored arc that currently exists. In general, we shall assume (in this and sub-quent models) that it will never pick an arc if there is an ancestral node with nexplored arcs.

is not strictly necessary for the processors to follow the standard Prolog search ocedure. At any point they could relinquish the node they are currently at, and ck some other unexplored arc. However by following the standard search procedure far as possible, each processor will for the most part act just like a sequential olog processor, and standard implementation techniques and optimisations can applied. Ideally, the computation tree will be such that each processor will get ge subtrees to explore, and only rarely will a processor have to "switch tasks" d jump to a different part of the tree. Thus the aim is to achieve very coarse-ained or-parallelism, where each chunk of work is very much like a standard Prolog computation.

The disadvantage of the abstract model as a basis for a practical implementatio is, as we have mentioned, the massive copying that would be necessary at eacl (parallel) branch point. This drawback would appear to rule it out as a practica approach. However, leaving this drawback aside, the model has some nice prop erties: the processors can work completely independently on physically separat data, and the implementation could in all other respects be the same as a sequentia implementation.

3 The Naïve Model

There is a rather simple modification of the Abstract Model that is useful for un derstanding the later, more elaborate models. We will call this the "Naïve Model"

In this model, a task is represented as a list of goals together with a list of variabl bindings. When we derive a new task by resolution, variable bindings are onl applied to the new variables. Variables in the old goals are left unchanged. Instea corresponding bindings are added to the front of the bindings list. Thus the bindin list records bindings in reverse order of their creation, i.e. most recent bindin first, oldest binding last. Because there is no alteration of the old goals, the sam physical copy can be shared between the parent and its offspring. Likewise, th offspring binding lists are simply extensions of the parent binding list. Thus th model takes good advantage of the kind of sharing of substructures that is familia in Lisp and other symbolic languages.

There is a very close correspondence between the Naïve Model and a standard Pr log implementation. The binding list is analogous to the trail. Because a sequenti Prolog implementation is only exploring one branch at a time, it can afford to insta tiate the variables in the inherited goals, provided it "undoes" these instantiatio before backtracking to an alternative branch. It uses the trail to perform this und ing. The trail can be thought of as a binding list where one records just the variab name, rather than a name/value pair, since the value is stored separately in t variable value cell. It would in fact add very little to the overall cost of making binding to store the value as well as the address in the trail, although there wou normally be no point in this.

A binding of a variable is said to be unconditional if the variable was created sin the last parallel branch point. Such a binding will be the same for all processo having access to the variable. Bindings which are unconditional do not need to recorded in the binding list. Instead, the binding is simply applied to the variab value cell. This is analogous to the way the trail is optimised in a standard Prol implementation. A similar optimisation can be applied to all the models we sh discuss.

n the Naïve Model, one cannot look up a variable's value simply by referring to he value cell. Instead, one has to search through the binding list. The access ime is therefore, on average, proportional to the number of bindings in the current inding list, (or, with a simple refinement, to the number of bindings that are more ecent than the variable in question). Either way, the access time is not bounded. 'his is the Naïve Model's major drawback. To offset this it has some considerable dvantages: it is conceptually simple, there is no overhead on setting up a parallel ranch point, and processors can switch tasks easily without any task initialisation verheads.

The SRI Model

'he "SRI Model", was first proposed by D.H.D. Warren at SRI in 1983, in private iscussions and unpublished documents. It has much in common with a scheme roposed independently by D.S. Warren [9], and contains elements of the indepenently conceived "shallow binding" scheme of Miyazaki et al [3]. The SRI Model an be viewed as a modification of the Naïve Model, in which each processor has s own private binding array. The binding array can be considered to be a local emory attached to the individual processor. In this binding array, the processor hadows" the bindings from the binding list it is currently working with. That , the binding array contains essentially the same information as the binding list, ored in a form that gives constant-time access to the value of any variable. The nding array could be implemented simply as an ordinary array; the variables on a anch would be numbered in chronological order, and that number would be used a simple index into the binding array. Alternatively, the binding array could be nplemented as a hash table accessed by hashing on the variable address.

indings are added to the binding array at each resolution step, and are removed 1 backtracking. When a processor runs out of work and wants to switch tasks to me new node, it has to change the state of its binding array to reflect the state of e binding list at the new node. It could simply reinitialise its binding array from ratch. However, normally the new state will have a lot in common with the old ate, and there is a more efficient way to achieve the required new state.

onceptually, the processor backtracks to the common ancestral node, removing ndings from its binding array in the normal way. It then "skims" forward to the w node, installing the bindings that have already been found by the processor r processors) that explored that path. Thus the bindings that correspond to the mmon portion of the old and new binding lists are left intact in the binding array. hat is, any binding created before the common ancestral node is left untouched the binding array. All that is happening is that bindings from the old binding t that are more recent than the common ancestral node are removed from the nding array, and bindings from the new binding list that are more recent than the common ancestral node are copied into the binding array. In this way, the cost of switching nodes is proportional to the "distance" between them, or more precisely to the number of bindings on the path between them.

The advantage of the SRI model is that most operations are very similar to what they would be in a sequential implementation. In particular, variable access and binding are both constant-time operations, and do not cost much more than they would in, say, the WAM. [1]

The main disadvantage of the model is the cost of switching between tasks. In the worst case, a processor might switch back and forth between nodes on two long branches, duplicating work by continually removing and reinstating the same bindings. Thus the model is unsuitable for fine-grained parallelism, but should perform well if the processors can always pick large chunks of work to do.

5 The Argonne Model

The "Argonne Model", which Lusk and Overbeek have designed and actually implemented, was partly influenced by the SRI model. It can be viewed as taking an alternative, and very ingenious, approach to improving on the Naïve Model. The model has been implemented in C as an extension of the WAM, and the implementation has been designed to be easily portable across a range of shared memory multiprocessors: it currently runs on HEP, Sequent and Encore machines.

A key idea is the concept of a "favoured" binding. Each shared variable can be considered to "belong" to one of the processors, generally the one that created it. This processor is the "favoured" processor for that variable, and is allowed to actually bind the variable value cell. The cell is marked with a special bit to show that this binding is only relevant to the favoured processor.

The other, non-favoured, processors view the shared variable as being an "alien" variable, belonging to another processor. They have to look elsewhere than the value cell to find out whether the variable is bound as far as they are concerned. The mechanism used is a chain of hash tables. This can be viewed as an optimisation of the binding list of the Naïve Model. There is a hash table for each arc of the or-parallel tree, recording the bindings of shared variables made on that arc. The hash tables on a branch are kept in a chain. A binding can be looked up in this hash table chain in much the same way as in the Naïve Model's binding list, but faster, depending on the hash table size. As an optimisation, each processor keeps a private chain of those hash tables that are "relevant" to that processor. A hash

[1] In an idealised implementation with infinite processors where each processor is shadowed by another processor recording the same bindings, the execution time for a problem would be proportional to the length of the longest branch. In this rather unrealistic sense, the model can approach the best conceivable exploitation of or-parallelism.

able is relevant if it contains a binding of an "unfavoured" or "alien" variable, i.e. ne not "belonging" to the processor concerned.

ariables that are not shared with other processors are said to be "private", and indings can be implemented by unconditionally binding the variable value cell, s in the standard WAM. The variable may subsequently become shared, but all rocessors will see the same unconditional binding.

orresponding to this classification of variables into "unfavoured", "favoured" and private", the branch a processor is working on is divided into an "unfavoured" ection, a "favoured" section, and a "private" section. The private section is the art beneath the last potential parallel branch point. The favoured section is the st of the branch beneath the node at which the processor started when it last witched tasks, i.e. those arcs for which this processor is the "leftmost" processor orking on that arc. The unfavoured section is everything above up to the root.

et us now sum up what is entailed in the key operations. To access a variable: if ne variable is private or favoured, we simply extract the value from the value cell, xactly as in the WAM; if the variable is unfavoured, we search for a binding in the hain of relevant hash tables (and we only need to search as far as the point where ne variable was created, c.f. the Naïve Model). To bind a variable: if the variable private, we simply assign to the value cell; if the variable is favoured, we assign to ne value cell with a special mark, and enter the binding in the current hash table; if e variable is unfavoured, we just enter the binding in the hash table, and make the ash table relevant by entering it in the chain of relevant hash tables if this has not ready been marked as done. To switch tasks is extremely simple: the processor ist initialises its relevant hash table chain to be the general chain existing at the ew node. (If the chains are implemented as linked lists, this is just a question of itialising a pointer).

he advantages of the Argonne Model are that there is a very low overhead on vitching tasks, and there is quick, constant-time, access to most variables, except r those that are unfavoured. It is hoped that the proportion of variable references at are unfavoured will be small, provided the processors can pick relatively large sks high up the tree. There is some evidence that this can be achieved in practice, it we will discuss this point further in the concluding section.

he main disadvantage of the Argonne Model is that the access time for an unvoured variable is not bounded, but is proportional to the number of unfavoured ndings made so far on the branch. This is a rather worrying feature, since the num-r of such unfavoured bindings could grow indefinitely. The hash table mechanism duces the cost of access, but does not cure the basic basic complexity problem. the current Argonne implementation, the hash table size is fixed at 16, and the ble is not expanded if it becomes "overfull"; instead, entries simply build up in e of 16 linked lists. This means that the hash table mechanism is only gaining constant factor speedup of around 16 over a simple binding list as in the Naïve

Model. Even if hash tables were expanded dynamically, variable access would still be proportional to the number of relevant hash tables, and this number can alsc grow indefinitely.

A more minor disadvantage is that quite a lot of work is done building hash tables which are not really needed, since the arcs corresponding to these hash tables never become shared. However, this is of less concern, since it does not introduce any nor constant-time overheads.

6 The Manchester-Argonne Model

A variant of the Argonne Model has been proposed by Warren. We will call thi the "Manchester-Argonne Model". The aim of this model is to make access to unfavoured variables a bounded cost operation, while preserving the main feature and advantages of the Argonne Model.

A key observation about the Argonne Model is that the hash tables are largel superfluous on arcs that are not actually shared. The Manchester-Argonne Mode therefore does not create the hash table for an arc unless, and until, another pro cessor wants to share that arc. The processor that creates the arc merely insert the bindings in a binding list, as in the Naïve Model. Doing this is just a mino extension of the "trailing" operation in sequential Prolog. The second processor which wants to share the arc, then creates the hash table it requires from the in formation in the binding list. It simply copies the bindings corresponding to th about-to-be-shared arc into a new hash table. At this point, the number of binding is known, so the size of the hash table can be chosen to fit the number of entries i must contain, in contrast to the standard Argonne model. The cost of looking up binding in a hash table can therefore be kept a constant-time operation, assumin a good hashing function. Each processor also needs a private binding array, simila to that of the SRI Model, to store the unfavoured bindings it itself makes.

When a node ceases to be a parallel branch point, because all but one of the subtree beneath the node have been completely explored, the node can be discarded, an hash tables above and below the node merged. Bindings below are checked to se whether they are now private, in which case they can be applied to the variabl value cell (and removed from the binding list); otherwise they are inserted in th hash table above. The size of the hash table above may be increased if necessar Probably, hash table sizes should be a power of 2, so that the number of times a element is copied is kept logarithmic in the size of the array. The reason for doin this merging of hash tables is to keep bounded the number in existence at any tim and thereby to keep bounded the cost of variable lookup.

To look up an unfavoured binding, the processor first looks in its private bindir array and then accesses the chain of hash tables corresponding to the shared ar above it. The cost is proportional to the number of shared arcs above it plus one. The number of such arcs cannot be greater than the number of processors [2], and is more likely to be of the order of the logarithm of the number of processors. Thus he cost of access is bounded (for a given machine) and likely to be relatively small. The operations of accessing other variables and creating bindings are very close to what they would be in sequential Prolog. The operation of switching tasks may nvolve some overhead, but it is less than in the SRI Model. On switching tasks, new hash array may have to be created, at a cost proportional to the number of bindings on the about to be shared arc. Note that this is work that the Argonne Model would have to do anyway at the time the bindings were originally created. One can think of the Manchester-Argonne Model as a "lazy creation of hash tables" ersion of the Argonne Model. Note also that there will be no significant overhead n switching tasks if the arc to which we are moving is already shared.

here is also the overhead on deleting a branch point of coalescing hash tables. This ost is generally proportional to the number of bindings on the arc below. There ay also be the subsidiary cost of enlarging the hash table above, if necessary. n the worst case, this could make the cost of maintaining an unfavoured binding e logarithmic in the number of unfavoured bindings, but it seems unlikely the ehaviour in practice would approach the worst case.

n balance, therefore, we feel the Manchester-Argonne Model is likely to perform gnificantly better than the Argonne Model.

The Argonne-SRI Model

is possible to modify the SRI Model by introducing a treatment of favoured ariables as in the Argonne Model. We will call this variant the "Argonne-SRI Model". In this model, each processor has a private binding array just as in the SRI Model. However, the binding array only contains unfavoured bindings. Favoured indings are implemented as in the Argonne Model, by assigning to the variable alue cell with a special mark.

n switching of tasks, the binding array is changed in exactly the same way as in the RI Model. This will result in a set of unfavoured bindings being removed from the nding array, and a new set of unfavoured bindings being installed. No favoured ndings will be involved, since we assume a processor doesn't switch tasks until it as backtracked to the node from which it started its current task, by which point will have undone any favoured bindings it has made.

hen the favoured processor at a node backtracks past the node leaving other ocessors still working beneath the node, it is in principle possible for one of the

[2]This follows from our assumption that idle processors pick nodes as high up the tree as possible.

other processors to be promoted to be the favoured processor at that node. The promoted processor needs to check all the bindings in its private binding array and remove any which have become favoured, transferring the binding to the variable value cell. A similar possibility is available in the Manchester-Argonne Model. For either model, it seems doubtful whether the cost of performing the promotion is worthwhile.

The Argonne-SRI Model's operational behaviour is very similar to the SRI Model in that it takes constant time to access or bind a variable, but switching tasks is relatively expensive. The cost of switching tasks is proportional to the number of variable bindings on the path between the nodes (as in the SRI Model).

In implementation terms, what the Argonne-SRI Model does within a task is remarkably close to the standard sequential model. It is only in the accessing and binding of unfavoured variables that significant extra time or space is required. The SRI Model, on the other hand, incurs overheads on most variable accesses. There will be an extra memory access to the binding array, and the binding array needs to be large enough to store the majority of variable bindings, rather than just those that are unfavoured. For these reasons, the Argonne-SRI Model is probably preferable to the SRI Model.

8 Conclusion

Which of these models is best? We feel it is very difficult to reach a firm conclusion until we are in a position to do a detailed experimental comparison of the models on large-scale programs. A lot depends on the strategy used for selecting which branches to execute in or-parallel, and the user annotation which guides this.

Our current feeling of the order of merit as practical models is:

```
                      Argonne < Manchester-Argonne
Abstract < Naive <
                      SRI < Argonne-SRI
```

Thus our choice would be between the Argonne-SRI and Manchester-Argonne models. Both models have the advantage of being virtually identical to a standard sequential model except for the treatment of unfavoured variables.

Of the two, the Argonne-SRI Model is somewhat simpler, and guarantees that all variable accesses (even unfavoured) are very fast, constant-time operations. Its main disadvantage is the cost of switching tasks. Thus it requires a selection strategy that voids generating very small tasks. If such a strategy can be achieved, it should erform very well. [3]

f more fine-grained parallelism is unavoidable, then the Manchester-Argonne Model eems the best choice. It offers a good compromise between speed of access to ariables and speed of switching tasks. Although access to unfavoured variables is elatively expensive, the cost is kept bounded. In this respect it seems to offer a ignificant improvement over the Argonne Model.

esults by Kish Shen [5], on simulating relatively small-scale examples, show that he percentage of variable reference that are unfavoured can often be uncomfortably igh. Greater than 20% is common and greater than 50% is not unusual. [4] A ood selection strategy can usually keep the percentage low, but such a strategy ill generally favour an SRI-like model in any case. If we cannot rely on a good election strategy, and need an Argonne-like model, then it seems vital to keep down he cost of unfavoured variable accesses, which is what the Manchester-Argonne Iodel achieves.

Acknowledgements

he ideas described in this paper owe much to interactions with colleagues at Argonne ational Laboratory, the Swedish Institute of Computer Science, and Manchester University. he presentation benefitted particularly from comments by Mats Carlsson, Ross Overbeek nd Kish Shen.

he work was supported by the UK Science and Engineering Research Council.

References

] R. Butler, E. L. Lusk, R. Olson, and R. A. Overbeek. *ANLWAM: A Parallel Implementation of the Warren Abstract Machine.* Internal Report, Argonne National Laboratory, U.S.A, 1986.

] J. Gabriel, T. Lindholm, E. L. Lusk, and R. A. Overbeek. *A Tutorial on the Warren Abstract Machine.* Technical Report ANL-84-84, Argonne National Laboratory, Argonne, Illinois, Oct. 1984.

] T. Miyazaki, A. Takeuchi, and T. Chikayama. A sequential implementation of Concurrent Prolog based on the shallow binding scheme. In *The 1985 International Symposium on Logic Programming*, pages 110–118, IEEE, 1985.

[3] A possible way to achieve this, suggested by Kish Shen, is to prevent an or-parallel node from ing shared until the processor that generated it has performed some critical number of further ps beneath that node.

[4] These figures typically refer to cases where there are no restrictions on which nodes can be ecuted in parallel. A more restrictive annotation generally brings the percentages down.

[4] R. A. Overbeek, J. Gabriel, T. Lindholm, and E. L. Lusk. *Prolog on Multipro cessors.* Internal Report, Argonne National Laboratory, U.S.A., 1985.

[5] K. Shen. *An Investigation of the Argonne Model of Or-Parallel Prolog.* Master's thesis, University of Manchester, 1986.

[6] J. Syre and H. Westphal. *A Review of Parallel Models for Logic Programmin Languages.* Technical Report CA-07, ECRC, 1985.

[7] E. Tick and D. H. D. Warren. Towards a pipelined Prolog processor. *Ne Generation Computing*, 2(4):323–345, 1984.

[8] D. H. D. Warren. *An Abstract Prolog Instruction Set.* Technical Note 309, SR International, 1983.

[9] D. S. Warren. Efficient Prolog memory management for flexible control strate gies. In *The 1984 International Symposium on Logic Programming*, pages 198 202, IEEE, 1984.

A Appendix

In this appendix, we illustrate some of the main features of the different models. The following program is used as an example.

A.1 Example Program

```
relation(X,Z) :- ancestor(X,Y), descendant(Y,Z).

ancestor(X,X).
ancestor(X,Z) :- parent(X,Y), ancestor(Y,Z).

descendant(X,X).
descendant(X,Z) :- parent(Y,X), descendant(Y,Z).

parent(amy,david). age(amy,7).
parent(ben,david). age(ben,9).
parent(david,hugh). age(david,39).
parent(david,winifred). ...
...

?- relation(david,X), age(X,W), W < 40.
```

A.2 Search Tree

This is a particular state of the search tree for the query given in the exampl program. Five processors are active, and the tasks they are currently working o are shown below the tree. Each node of the tree is marked with the new goal introduced that were introduced at that node; the new bindings introduced ar shown on the arc above. Bindings that are favoured in the Argonne-style model are marked with an asterisk. Unexplored alternatives are indicated with a shor horizontal arc.

```
     relation(david,X),
     age(X,W), W<40
   @
   |
   | ancestor(david,Y),
   | descendant(Y,X)
   @______________________________________________
   |                                              |
*Y=david                                          | parent(david,Z),
   |                                              | ancestor(Z,Y)
   @__________                                    @__
   |           |                                  |
*X=david       | parent(Z,david),               *Z=hugh
   |           | descendant(Z,X)                  |
   @           @_____________________             @__
   |           |                      |           |
*W=39        *Z=ben                 Z=amy       Y=hugh
   |           |                      |           |
   @           @__________            @__         @__
   P1          |           P3         |           |
              X=ben                 X=amy       X=hugh
               |                      |           |
               @                      @           @
               P2                     P4          P5
```

```
Tasks

39<40       age(ben,W), desc(ben,X), age(amy,W), age(hugh,W),
            W<40        age(X,W),    W<40        W<40
```

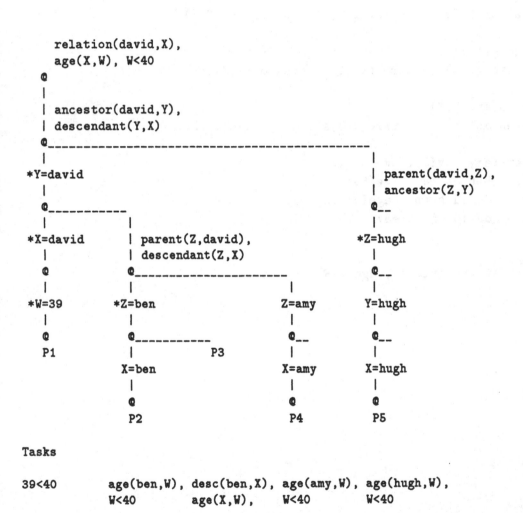

This is how the different models record the binding information for each of the five processors. A box denotes an element of the binding list in the Naive Model, or a hash table in the other models. Chains of hash tables are indicated in an obvious way, with the first table to be searched topmost.

```
Naive Model : Binding List

---------   ---------   ---------   ---------   ---------
_W=39    _| |_X=ben___| |_Z=ben___| |_X=amy___| |_X=hugh__|
_X=david_| |_Z=ben___| |_Y=david_| |_Z=amy___| |_Y=hugh__|
_Y=david_| |_Y=david_|             |_Y=david_| |_Z=hugh__|

SRI Model : Binding Array

---------   ---------   ---------   ---------   ---------
 W=39     | | X=ben    | | Y=david | | X=amy    | | X=hugh   |
 X=david  | | Y=david  | | Z=ben    | | Y=david  | | Y=hugh   |
_Y=david_| |_Z=ben___| |_________| |_Z=amy___| |_Z=hugh__|

Argonne-SRI Model : Binding Array

---------   ---------   ---------   ---------   ---------
          | | X=ben    | | Y=david | | X=amy    | | X=hugh   |
          | | Y=david  | | Z=ben    | | Y=david  | | Y=hugh   |
_________| |_________| |_________| |_Z=amy___| |_________|

Argonne Model : Relevant Hash Table Chain

   ---      ---------   ---------   ---------   ---------
            |_X=ben___| |_Z=ben___| |_X=amy___| |_X=hugh__|
             __:______   __:______   __:______   _ :______
            |_Y=david_| |_Y=david_| |_Z=amy___| | Y=hugh__|
                                     __:______
                                    | Y=david_|

Manchester-Argonne Model : Binding Array + Hash Table Chain

---------   ---------   ---------   ---------   ---------
          | | X=ben    | |          | | X=amy    | | X=hugh   |
_________| |_________| |_________| |_Z=amy___| |_Y=hugh__|
             __:______   __:______   __:______
            |_Y=david_| |_Z=ben___| |_Y=david_|
                         __:______
                        |_Y=david_|
```

A.3 Second Search Tree

Here is another search tree, for a somewhat different query. Four processors are active.

```
    relation(david,X), parent(W,X),
    age(W,V), V<40
  @
  |
  | ancestor(david,Y),
  | descendant(Y,X)
  @
  |
  | parent(david,Z),
  | ancestor(Z,Y)
  @___________________________________
  |                                   |
*Z=hugh                              Z=win
  |                                   |
  @                                   @
  |                                   |
*Y=hugh                              Y=win
  |                                   |
  @____________                       @____________
  |            |                      |            |
*X=hugh        | parent(A,hugh),     X=win         | parent(A,win),
  |            | descendant(A,X)      |            | descendant(A,X)
  @__          @__                    @__          @__
  |            |                      |            |
*W=david     *A=david                W=david     *A=david
  |            |                      |            |
  @            @__                    @            @__
  |            |                      |            |
*V=39         X=david                V=39         X=david
  |            |                      |            |
  @            @__                    @            @__
  P1           |                      P3           |
              W=ben                               W=ben
               |                                   |
               @                                   @
               |                                   |
              V=9                                 V=9
               |                                   |
               @                                   @
               P2                                  P4
```

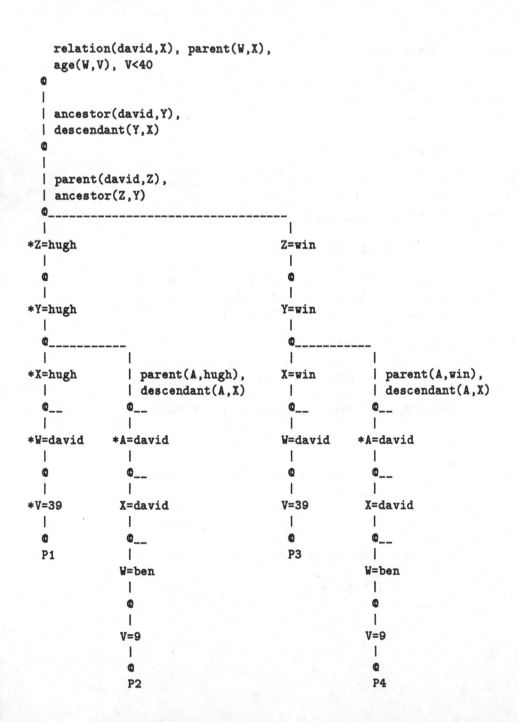

Here is the binding information for the Argonne Model versus the Manchester-Argonne Model.

Argonne Model : Relevant Hash Table Chain

```
   ---      ---------               ---------  ---------
           | V=9     |             | V=39    || V=39    |
           |_W=ben___|             |_W=david_||_W=ben___|
            __:______               __:______  _ :______
           |_X=david_|             |_X=win___|| X=david_|
            __:______               __:______  __:______
           |_Y=hugh__|             |_Y=win___||_Y=win___|
            __:______               __:______  __:______
           |_Z=hugh__|             |_Z=win___||_Z=win___|
```

Manchester-Argonne Model : Binding Array + Hash Table Chain

```
---------   ---------               ---------  ---------
         | | V=9     |             | V=39    || V=39    |
         | | W=ben   |             | W=david || W=ben   |
         | | X=david |             | X=win   || X=david |
         | |         |             | Y=win   ||         |
---------| |_________|             |_Z=win___||_________|
            __:______                           __:______
           | Y=hugh  |                         | Y=win   |
           |_Z=hugh__|                         |_Z=win___|
```

RETRACTIONS: A FUNCTIONAL PARADIGM FOR LOGIC PROGRAMMING

M. Bellia

Dipartimento di Informatica, Università di Pisa

Corso Italia, 40 - 56100 Pisa - Italy

ABSTRACT. Computable relations are expressed as set *retractions*. This class of functions is here discussed in a set theory which is built according to the structure of the Herbrand Universe in clausal logic. The approach provides a functional programming paradigm with almost all the features of the logic programming paradigm.

Keywords: Predicative and functional languages, symbolic expressions, relations, retractions, lambda_calculus, Horn clause theories, Herbrand terms, computable sets.

1. INTRODUCTION

Several proposals are currently pursuing the integration of predicative and functional languages to obtain a super-language with the features of both **[Bellia86]** which, on one hand is adequate to the need of intelligent applications and, on the other hand can efficiently be executed by a special-purpose machine **[Moto-Oka82]**. In spite of the different mechanisms and constructs, predicative and functional languages have some features in common: both are applicatives, i.e. the language main construct is *application* and computations are manipulations of values, and adequate for symbolic computations, i.e. *symbolic data* can be expressed and manipulated as values. Though substantially different in the techniques **[Bellia86]**, all the current proposals are based on extensions and/or on merges of the mechanisms on which the two classes of languages are based. The resulting mechanisms provide the super-language with a programming paradigm which copes with almost all the features of both logic and functional programming. However, logic and functional features, even if present in the resulting super-language, cannot be equally made in use, and sometimes, combinations of them are obscure or meaningless. Moreover, the resulting language is not as simple, semantically clean and well machine supported as the original languages are.

Common to the above mentioned proposals is that in order to combine logic with functional programming features, logical variables (i.e. existentially quantified variables) and functional expressions have to live together. We claim that logic programming features can be equally *expressed* in a purely functional programming paradigm, without changes on the basic mechanisms of functional languages, and without the introduction of any additional construct or mechanism, e.g. logical variables and, narrowing or unification. Inside this functional paradigm, logic programming as well as functional programming can be formulated by combinatory formulas for which promising realizations of reduction machines are in progress **[Berkling75, Clarke80, Darlington81, Kluge80, Mago80]**, and they could be the natural machine support for our super-language. Functional languages are potential super-languages in which logic and functional programming features can be combined in a natural and semantically clean way.

The approach is based on a combination of the computable function theory and of a set theory suitable for computations on sets of symbolic data. To each predicate, defined by a logic program (Horn clause theory), we univocally associate exactly one function of a class of retractions. The elements of the domain and image sets of the retractions are elements of a set theory (of symbolic data) which is build according to the structure of the terms of the Herbrand Universe. To each query in a logic program, we associate a purely functional expression. The expression is an application of the retractions which are associated to the predicates in the logic program, and its evaluation corresponds to the *success set* of the query in the logic program (i.e. set of all the instances of the query which can be deduced from the logic program). The nature of the correspondence between resolution of queries and computation of applications of retractions, the features and properties of the class of retractions, which is here, associated to the set of predicates, the structure of the set theory, which models domain and image sets of retractions, are the main topics of the present parer. Other related topics are functional programming with sets and the combination of logic and functional programming by using retractions to express

This work was partially supported by the European Community under ESPRIT Project 415

predicates and queries.
Section 2 introduces the concept of retraction, relates it to the concept of relation (Definition 2.1) in the theory of computability and then, to the concept of predicate in logic programming. The features and properties of the retractions are formally stated by Propositions 2.1-2.6 and their relevance to the logic programming concepts of program invertibility and of partially evaluated data structures is briefly outlined and exemplified. In particular, Proposition 2.4 states a one-to-one correspondence between a subclass of the retractions on the computable parts of a domain D and the class of computable relations on D, or equally, when D is the Herbrand Universe and relations are expressed by Horn clause theories, the class of predicates. Section 3 concerns the treatment of logic programming predicates as retractions in functional programming and, the structure of the set theory whose elements form the domain and image sets of the retractions. To make the treatment more concrete, Section 3 introduces a functional language to express retractions, and the structure of the set theory is then, discused as the data domain of the language. The language is essentially Church's lambda calculus. Emphasis is placed on the language data domain operators, which are set operators: formal definitions and examples of the use are included. Sections 4 and 5 concern the relations between logical variables and herbrand terms of logic programming, on one side, and functional expressions, on the other. Then, Propositon 4.1 states the existence of a function which maps (tuples of possibly non-ground) Herbrand terms into *constant expressions* , i.e. the class of the language expressions which only contain data and applications of the data domain operators. Section 4 introduces the concept of *most general instance* of a pair of (tuples of) Herbrand terms and relates it to the concept of unification. Then, Proposition 5.1 states a one-to-one correspondence between the computation of the *most general instance* of a pair of (tuples of) Herbrand terms and the application of set intersection to the corresponding constant expressions. Section 6 compares logic programming with functional programming. It shows that, when retractions are used to characterize predicates, almost all the (programming) features of the logic paradigm are preserved in the functional programming paradigm and are straightforwardly combined with the functional ones. Section 7 contains concluding remarks and a brief comparison of our approach with some other proposals for the integration of logic and functional programming.
Exception for Proposition 4.1, proofs are omitted, however they can be found in **[Bellia86b]**.

2. RELATIONS AS SET RETRACTIONS.

As is well known to each *computable relation*, R_D, on a (non empty) space $D = D_1 x ... x D_n$, we can associate a (computable) boolean function $f_R: D \rightarrow \{0,1\}$, such that:

(1) $\forall\, x \in D, \quad x \in R_D \Leftrightarrow f_R(x) = 1$

The function f_R is the *characteristic function* of the set denoted by R_D. Note that, f_R is a partially defined function, hence if x is not in R_D, f_R results 0 or is undefined. Furthermore, if n = 1, D is not a product, and R_D is *degenerate.*
In a sense, f_R reminds us of the concept of *predicate*, and it behaves as a predicate if {0,1} is interpreted as the truth domain. In order to extend functional with logic programming, some authors **[Hsiang83, Dershowitz84, Dershowitz85]**, use a generalization of (1) which could be formulated by

(2) $\forall\, [X] \in P(D), \quad X \subseteq R_D \Leftrightarrow f_R([X]) = \text{true}$

where P(D) is the *power set* of D, [X] is the element of P(D) which denotes the subset $X \subseteq D$, and f_R is a function from P(D) to {true,false}. Then, in order to deal with f_R, the functional language has to be extended to handle sets and functions from sets into values. Anyway, (2) is not all the functional language needs in order to have all the logic programming features. Extensions on the language mechanisms (notably, narrowing and logical variables) have been added in order to give it the multi mode use of relations, i.e. to "answer" questions like: for which x, $f_R(x)$=true holds?
We show that such additional mechanisms can be avoided by using a different characterization of relations. We introduce the following.

<u>Definiton 2.1</u>
Given a space D, let $\{F_R\}$ be the set of all the functions, F_R, which (3) associates to the set of all computable relations R_D on D:

(3) $\forall\, [X] \in P(D), \quad F_R([X]) = [X \cap R_D]$

$F_R : P(D) \rightarrow P(D)$ is a *set function*, mapping sets into sets. ◇

Note that, given R_D, (3) uniquely determines one F_R. We say that F_R is the *representative* (according to (3)) of R_D. To characterize relations on D in terms of functions, (3) uses a class of functions defined in the more complex space P(D).
$\{F_R\}$ is a class of well known functions. It is a class of *retractions* , or idempotent functions.

<u>Proposition 2.1</u>
$\forall\; F_R: P(D) \rightarrow P(D) \in \{F_R\}, \quad F_R$ is a retraction of P(D). ◇

Retractions on sets are widely used in topology, and were used in **[Scott76]** to model data types in programming languages. The image set of a retraction is called its *retract*. A retraction with retract U is called a retract on U.

Proposition 2.2

$\forall F_R : P(D) \rightarrow P(D) \in \{F_R\}$, $\quad F_R$ is a retract on $P([R_D])$. ◇

Note that, the elements of P(D) are partially ordered by set inclusion, $\subseteq$, on D. Later on, we will use $\subseteq$ to denote both the set inclusion on the subsets of D and the ordering relation on the elements of P(D), i.e. if $X \subseteq Y$ then, $[X] \subseteq [Y]$ in P(D).

$\{F_R\}$ is a *proper* subclass of the retractions, as immediately follows from Proposition 2.3.

Proposition 2.3

$\forall F_R : P(D) \rightarrow P(D) \in \{F_R\}, \quad \forall [X] \in P(D), \quad F_R([X]) \subseteq [X]$ ◇

Constant functions are examples of retractions which are not in $\{F_R\}$ (unless D has cardinality 1). For example, let D be the cartesian product D1xD2, where D1={a,b} and D2={c,d}, then P(D) contains 2^4 elements, for instance [{<a,c>}], [{<b,c>,<b,d>}] are elements of P(D). The function f such that:

$\forall X \in P(D), \quad f(X) = [\{\langle a,c\rangle\}]$

is a retraction of P(D) but does not satisfy Proposition 2.3, and is not a member of $\{F_R\}$. Thus, we say that there are no relations on D for which f is the representative. In contrast, the function g such that:

$$g([X]) = \begin{cases} [\{\langle a,c\rangle\}] \text{ if X contains } \langle a,c\rangle \text{ but does not contain } \langle a,d\rangle \\ [\{\langle a,d\rangle\}] \text{ if X contains } \langle a,d\rangle \text{ but does not contain } \langle a,c\rangle \\ [\{\langle a,c\rangle,\langle a,d\rangle\}] \text{ if X contains both } \langle a,c\rangle \text{ and } \langle a,d\rangle \\ [\{\}] \text{ otherwise (i.e. X neither contains } \langle a,c\rangle \text{ nor } \langle a,d\rangle) \end{cases}$$

is a retraction of P(D). g satisfies Proposition 2.3 and is the member of $\{F_R\}$ that (3) associates to the relation R={<a,c>,<a,d>}. Furthermore, according to Proposition 2.2, g is a retraction on P(R). Note that, though each function f in $\{F_R\}$ satisfies both Propositions 2.1 and 2.3, the converse does not hold, i.e. a function which satisfies both the above propositions is not necessarily the representative of some relation. For example, consider the following function g':

$$g'([X]) = \begin{cases} [\{\langle a,c\rangle\}] \text{ if X contains } \langle a,c\rangle \\ [\{\langle a,d\rangle\}] \text{ if } X = \{\langle a,d\rangle\} \\ [\{\}] \text{ otherwise} \end{cases}$$

g' is a retraction of P(D) and satisfies Proposition 2.3. However, Proposition 2.2 does not hold for any R_D. In particular, note that for R above,

$g'([X]) \neq [X \cap R]$ for each X which has {<a,d>} as a proper subset.

A comparison of g' and g shows that g' is *less defined* than g, i.e. $g' = g' \circ g = g \circ g'$ [Scott76] ($\circ$ is function composition), or: $\forall X \in P(D)$, $g'(X)$ defined on X implies $g'(X) \subseteq g(X)$.

Definition 2.2

Given a retraction F_R with retract $U \subseteq P(D)$, we define as *union set* of F_R the subset R of D such that: $R = \{x \in u \mid [u] \in U\}$ ◇

Note that the union set of each retraction, $F_R \in \{F_R\}$, is (the set of points of) the relation R_D of which the retraction is the representative.

Proposition 2.4

$\forall f : P(D) \rightarrow P(D)$

$f \in \{F_{\Re}\}$ iff f is the *greatest* retraction which has union set R, for a subset R of D, and satisfies Proposition 2.3. ◇

Proposition 2.4 completely characterizes the class $\{F_{\Re}\}$ of retractions of P(D). Moreover, it shows how to formulate questions about the behaviour of a relation, in terms of function applications. As an example, let us consider the function f_{app} which (3) associates to the relation **app**, defined as the least relation which satisfies the following axioms (expressed in Horn clause logic):

(4) **app (NIL,y,y) ←.** **app(p.x, y, p.z) ← app(x, y, z).**

f_{app} is a function of $P(D) \rightarrow P(D)$, where D is the cartesian product List x List x List for some space List. We can assume List to be the space of all the lists of naturals, p to be a variable on naturals and x,y,z to be variables on List. Let ListxK.ListxH.K.List be the element of P(D) which denotes the subset of List x List x List which contains all the triples <u,v,w> such that u is any list, v is any list whose *car* is the natural K and w is any list whose car is the natural H and whose *cadr* is the natural K, i.e. ListxK.ListxH.K.List=[{<u,v,w>|v=K.v',w=H.K.w', u,v,w∈List}]. Then the application:

(5) f_{app} (ListxK.ListxH.K.List)

computes the element of P(D) which denotes the subset of List x List x List which is the greatest subset of ListxK.ListxH.K.List and contains all the triples which make valid in (4) the following query:

(6) **app(x, K.y, H.K.z)**
where x, y, and z are logical variables which range over List, and H and K are the above defined constants.
A comparison of (5) and (6) shows that the application in (5) corresponds to the query in (6) and, the value ListxK.ListxH.K.List in (5) corresponds to the triple of *Herbrand terms* in (6). However, ListxK.ListxH.K.List is merely notation, we will define in Section 3 a structure of sets which allows us to constructively express such values. Moreover, in Section 4 to each tuple of Herbrand terms, T, we associate a value (a constant expression), E, such that if f is the retraction that (3) associates to the relation which is the minimal model of a predicate R in a (Horn clause) logic theory, then f(E) computes the element of P(D) which denotes the set of all the values in D which make valid R(T) in the theory.
Finally, if our sets are equipped with suitable operators for product and projection, Proposition 2.4 models in a functional programming paradigm the *program invertibility* feature of predicative languages. For instance, the set of lists to which the variable x in (6) can be instantiated to make valid (6) in (4), can be obtained from (5) by the projection of f_{app} (ListxK.ListxH.K.List) on the first component of the cartesian product List x List x List.
Though $\{F_R\}$ is only a sub-class of the retracts, it is closed under function composition. Thus, the following propositions hold.
Proposition 2.5
$\forall\ f, g : P(D) \rightarrow P(D) \in \{F_R\}, \qquad f \circ g,\ g \circ f \in \{F_R\}$ ◇

Proposition 2.6
$\forall\ f, g : P(D) \rightarrow P(D) \in \{F_R\}, \qquad f \circ g = g \circ f$ ◇

In contrast to Proposition2.5, Proposition 2.6 does not hold for the entire class of the retractions. It says that, from a denotational point of view, the ordering on the composition of functions in $\{F_R\}$ is unessential. Obviously, that is not true when operational semantics is considered. Operationally, Proposition 2.6 allows to model in a functional paradigm the *declarative* (absence of control) feature of predicative languages.

3. A FUNCTIONAL LANGUAGE TO EXPRESS $\{F_R\}$.

Our treatment will be discussed in a first order functional language. The language is essentially Lambda calculus restricted to first order. Lambda calculus is here used as the*abstract functional language* where the concepts of set and of retraction are stated in a clean and simple way.
The language alphabet is a quadruple $A=<D,V_D,P,V_p>$ where D is the set of the language data, P is the set of the language primitive operators, V_D and V_p are denumerable set of variables ranging over D and first order functions on D, respectively. The language expressions are all the closed forms which can be built starting from D plus P, and by λ–abstraction and application of the fixed point operator, Y **[Milner72]** . Each expression has meaning according to α, β, Y reductions, and to the semantics of the primitive operators. Programs are expressions.
The formal definition of the language syntax and semantics is deferred to Apendix I, while an example of the definition and of the evaluation of a program is reported below. Next Section is devoted to the definition of the structure of the language domain, i.e. D+P. In principle, the quadruple A could be arbitrarily set giving origin to several (first order) languages which essentially differ in the language data domain. The structure of the data domain is a relevant point of our construction because it characterizes the structure of the sets which we use to compute with retractions.

EXAMPLE 3.1.
Let us consider the following program in the extended syntax

f1(x)= x+y where 1=y ;
f2(x,y)= f1(x)+y ;
7 * x where f2(2,3)= x.

It corresponds to the expression:

((λx.7 * x)((λx y.((λx.((λy. x+y) 1)) x) + y) 2 3))

which is a closed form and evaluates to

7 * ((λx y.((λx.((λy. x+y) 1)) x) + y) 2 3)
7 * ((λx y.((λy. x+y) 1) + y) 2 3)
7 * ((λx y. (x+1)+ y) 2 3)
7 * ((2+1)+ 3)

3.1. THE VALUES DOMAIN: HU_c^* .

Because of the complete separation between values domain and functions domain, we can freely enrich the language with the definition of its set of values, D, and of the set of operators on them, P. As

pointed out in the language definition, these operators will be primitive operators for the language, and expressions which contain occurrences of these operators will be reduced by α, β, and Y reductions and, if needs, according to the semantics of the operators.
To model predicates (of Horn clause logic) by retractions, in the choice of D we can limit ourselves to relations on D's which are (cartesian) powers of the Herbrand Universe, HU_c.
We briefly recall that HU_c, the Herbrand Universe built from $C = \{\underline{Ci}_k\}$ (finite set of constructors $\underline{Ci}$ of arity k, such that C includes at least one constructor of arity 0), is the minimum set of terms which satisfies both:

- $\forall\ \underline{Ci}_0 \in C,\quad \underline{Ci}_0 \in HU_c$
- $\forall\ \underline{Ci}_k \in C,\ \forall\ t_1,\dots,t_k \in HU_c,\quad \underline{Ci}_k(t_1,\dots,t_k) \in HU_c$

Given HU_c, we define HU_c^* be the (infinite) union of the parts of the (finite cartesian) powers of HU_c, i.e. $HU_c^* = \cup_{i\in N} P(HU_c^i)$.

Definition 3.1 (HU_c^*)
$\forall\, i \in N^+$, let $HUT_i = \{<t_1,\dots,t_i> \mid t_1,\dots,t_i \in HU_c \cup \{\varnothing\}\}$ (i-tuples),
then HU_c^* is the minimal set of values which satisfies both:
- let $HUF = \cup_{i\in N} HUF_i,\ HUF \subset HU_c^*$ (finite sets of i-tuples),
- let $HU\omega = \cup_{i\in N} HU\omega_i,\ HU\omega \subset HU_c^*$ (infinite sets of i-tuples),

where:
+ $HUF_i = \cup_{j\in N} (HUT_i)_\bullet^j$
+ $(HUT_i)_\bullet^0 = \{\varnothing\}$
$(HUT_i)_\bullet^j = (HUT_i)\ _\bullet X\ (HUT_i)_\bullet^{j-1} = \{t_1 \bullet t_2 \mid t_1 \in HUT_i,\ t_2 \in (HUT_i)_\bullet^{j-1}\}$
+ $HU\omega_i = \{\ Sup\{t^j\}\ \}$, being $\{t^j\}$ a set of members of HUF_i, such that:
- $\forall\, j \in N,\ t^j \in (HUT_i)_\bullet^j$ and,
- $\exists\, t \in HUT_i$ such that $t^j = t \bullet t^{j-1}$
+ <_> and • are the tupling and set-constructor operator, respectively. ◇

Though the structure of HU_c^* depends on the properties of <_> and •, we can see that HU_c^* is a family, $\{HU_i^*\}$, indexed by the classes of tupling, HUT_i. Moreover, each HU_i^* contains:
- all the i-tuples of elements of HU_c, i.e. HUT_i,
- all the values obtained by finitely many applications of • to i-tuples, i.e. HUF_i, and
- all the values which are computed by infinitely many applications of • to i-tuples and can be obtained as limit of values of HUF_i, i.e. $HU\omega_i$.

EXAMPLE 3.2.
Let $\underline{0}$ and $\underline{S}$ in $C=\{\underline{0},\underline{S}\}$ be constructors of arity 0 and 1 respectively, then:
- $\underline{0}$, $\underline{S}(\underline{0})$, $\underline{S}(\underline{S}(\underline{0})) \in HU_c$
- $<\underline{0},\underline{0}>$, $<\underline{0},\underline{S}(\underline{0})>$, $<\underline{0},\underline{S}(\underline{S}(\underline{0}))> \in HUT_2$
- $<\underline{0},\underline{0}>$, $<\underline{0},\underline{0}> \bullet <\underline{0},\underline{S}(\underline{0})>$, $(<\underline{0},\underline{0}> \bullet <\underline{0},\underline{S}(\underline{0})>) \bullet <\underline{0},\underline{S}(\underline{S}(\underline{0}))> \in HUF_2$
- the infinite sequence $(\dots((<\underline{0},\underline{0}> \bullet <\underline{0},\underline{S}(\underline{0})>) \bullet <\underline{0},\underline{S}(\underline{S}(\underline{0}))>) \bullet \dots \bullet <\underline{0}, S^k(0)>) \bullet \dots$ computes an element of $HU\omega_2$ ($S^i(0)$ stands for k $\underline{S}$'s followed by $\underline{0}$).

Definition 3.2 (<_>)
Technically, <_> is a family of operators, each one indexed by its arity (any positive integer). It is a function $HU_c \times\dots\times HU_c \rightarrow HUT_i$, it computes the minimal congruence on HU_c^* which satisfies the following axiom:

$\forall\ t_1,\dots,t_k,\ t_1',\dots,t_k' \in HU,$
$<t_1,\dots,t_k> = <t_1',\dots,t_k'>$ iff $\forall\, i \in [1,k],\ t_i = t_i'$
or $t_n = \varnothing,\ t_m' = \varnothing$ for some pair n, m in [1,k] ◇

Notational remark (bottom element, <∅,...,∅>, 1-tuple element,<t>)
In the following, we will use the notation ∅ for $<t_1,\dots,\varnothing,\dots,t_k>$. Though this use is not technically correct (because ∅ is an element of HUT_1, and we should use $<\varnothing,\dots,\varnothing> \in HUT_K$), it equally expresses the theoretical meaning of the above axiom.
Another notational freedom is the use of t for the 1-tuple <t>.

Definition 3.3 (• , set-constructor)
It is a function $HU_c^* \times\dots\times HU_c^* \rightarrow HU_c^*$, it computes the minimal congruence on HU_c^* which satisfies the following axioms:

(1-idempotent) $t \bullet t = t$
(2-commutative) $t_1 \bullet t_2 = t_2 \bullet t_1$
(3-associative) $(t_1 \bullet t_2) \bullet t_3 = t_1 \bullet (t_2 \bullet t_3)$
(4-zero) $t \bullet \varnothing = t$
(5-continuous) $t \bullet Sup\{t^j\} = Sup\{t \bullet t^j\}$ ◇

The definition of $\bullet$ completes the definition of the structure of the language values domain. The elements of HU_c^* result to be a model for subsets of the powers of HU_c: $\varnothing$ represents the empty set, $\bullet$ represents (possibly infinite but computable) set union, and finally, elements of HUT_i, HUF_i, $HU\omega_i$ represent singleton, finite and infinite (computable) sets of i-tuples of values in HU_c, respectively. The elements of HU_c^* are partially ordered by the relation $\subseteq$, defined as follows.

<u>Definition 3.4</u> ($\subseteq$)
Let x and y be elements of HU_c^*, then

$x \subseteq y$ iff $x,y \in HU_i^*$ for some $i \in N$ and,
either: both are elements of HUF_i and $\exists\, w \in HUF_i$ such that $y = w \bullet x$,
or: y is element of $HU\omega_i$ and, assumed $x = \mathrm{Sup}\{x^i\}$ and $y = \mathrm{Sup}\{y^j\}$, $\forall\, x^i \in \{x^i\}, \exists\, y^j \in \{y^j\}$ such that $x^i \subseteq y^j$ ◇

EXAMPLE 3.3.
Let us consider the C of Example 3.2, and let us define: $f(x) = x \bullet f(\underline{S}(x))$. It is easy to note that f is not in $\{F_R\}$ and is not a retraction. However it is a computable function and can be expressed in our language. In particular, $f(\underline{0})$ computes the sequence $\underline{0} \bullet \underline{S(0)} \bullet \underline{S(S(0))} \bullet ... \bullet S^k(0) \bullet ...$ which is an element of $HU\omega_1$.

Note that $\forall\, x \in HU_c^*$, $\varnothing \subseteq x$. Furthermore, $\subseteq$ is a *well-founded* ordering on the elements of HUF.

3.2. OPERATORS ON HU_c^*.

Although the values domain is completely defined, we need some additional operators. Actually, the elements of $HU\omega$ can be expressed in the language by expressions which enumerate all the finite approximations (as was the case for $f(\underline{0})$ in the example 3.3). $HU\omega$ contains a class of elements which can be expressed without the use of limit operations. This class is sub-class of the recursive sets of tuples of HU_c. Moreover, we will see that elements of this class are in correspondence with tuples of Herbrand terms. We enrich the set of operators on HU_c^* in order to express the elements of this class in a way suitable to define this correspondence.

3.2.1. Constructors and inverses.

We associate to each k-arity constructor $\underline{Ci_k}$, a 2-arity function (operator) ci_k which, applied to an index i and a tuple u of HU_c^*, behaves like $\underline{Ci_k}$, if i=1 and u is an element of HUT_k, i.e. u denotes a singleton of HU_c^k, otherwise it computes the element which denotes the set obtained by applying $\underline{Ci_k}$ to the k-subtuple at the position i of each member of the set denoted by u. Formally, ci_k is defined by the following:

<u>Definition 3.5</u> (ci_k , extension of constructors).
Let $\underline{Ci_k}$ be a constructor of arity $k \neq 0$. Then ci_k is a function $N^+ \times HU_c^* \to HU_c^*$. It computes the minimal congruence which satisfies the following axioms:

- $ci_k\,(j,<t_1,...,t_n>) = \varnothing$ iff $n \geq k+j-1$ and $t_h = \varnothing$ for some $h \in [1, n]$
- $ci_k\,(j, <t_1,...,t_{j-1},t_1',..., t_k',t_{j+1},...,t_n>) = <t_1,...,t_{j-1}, \underline{Ci_k}\,(t_1',..., t_k'),t_{j+1},...,t_n>$
- $ci_k\,(j, t_1 \bullet t_2) = ci_k\,(j, t_1) \bullet ci_k\,(j, t_2)$
- $ci_k\,(j, \mathrm{Sup}\{t^i\}) = \mathrm{Sup}\,\{ci_k\,(j, t^i)\}$ ◇

Thus, for each $u \in HU_{k+h}^*$ (i.e. for each set of elements of the power of order k+h), $ci_k\,(j,u)$, such that $h \geq j-1$, computes the element of HU_{h+1}^* (i.e. the set of elements of the power of order h+1) obtained by applying $\underline{Ci_k}$ to the projection on HU_k^* of the j,...,j+k-1 components of each member in the set denoted by u. Though not explicitely given by the above axioms, $ci_k(j,u)$ will be considered *undefined*, if u is such that for no $h \geq j-1$, $u \in HU_{k+h}^*$ (i.e $\#u < k+j-1$).

<u>Property 3.1</u>
- For each constructor function: $ci_k\!\downarrow \circ\, ci_k \neq ci_k \circ ci_k\!\downarrow$.
- Moreover, for each u, $ci_k\!\downarrow (j,u) \ll u$. ◇

The functions ci_k and $ci_k\!\downarrow$ extend to (sets of) tuples of terms the operations of term construction and subterm selection.

<u>Notational remark</u>. ($ci_k(u)$)
$ci_k(1,u)$ (resp. $ci_k\!\downarrow (1,u)$) will also be denoted by $ci_k(u)$ (resp. $ci_k\!\downarrow (u)$) if $\#u = k$.

3.2.2. Cartesian product $\otimes$ $\underline{\otimes}$.

The cartesian product allows to compute the product of elements of HU_c^*. Technically, it is a family of operators, indexed by the arity (any natural). It is a function

$HU_{i1}^* \times ... \times HU_{in}^* \to HU_{i1+...+in}^*$,

it computes the minimal congruence which satisfies the following axioms:

(1-associative) $\otimes t_1,...,t_{j-1}, \otimes t_1',..., t_k'\otimes, t_{j+1},...,t_n\otimes = \otimes t_1,...,t_{j-1},t_1',..., t_k',t_{j+1},...,t_n\otimes$
(2-singleton) $\otimes t_1,...,t_n\otimes = < t_1,...,t_n >$ iff $\forall i \in [1,n], t_i \in HUT_1$
(3-finite set) $\otimes t_1,...,t_i' \bullet t_i'',...,t_n\otimes = \otimes t_1,...,t_i',...,t_n\otimes \bullet \otimes t_1,...,t_i'',...,t_n\otimes$
(4-continuous) $\otimes t_1,...,\mathbf{Sup}\{t^j\}_i,...,t_n\otimes = \mathbf{Sup}\{\otimes t_1,...,t^j,...,t_n\otimes\}$ ◇

Cartesian product is powerful enough to express the element of HU_c^* which denotes the set (containing all the terms of) HU_c. As a matter of fact, let C be the following set of constructors
$C = \{\underline{C1_0},..., \underline{Cn_0}, \underline{C1_1},..., \underline{Cn_1},..., \underline{C1_k},..., \underline{Cn_k}\}$ then
π: $\mathbf{Y}\bar{\pi}.\ \mathbf{c1_0 \bullet ... \bullet cn_0 \bullet c1_1(\bar{\pi}) \bullet ... \bullet cn_1(\pi) \bullet ... \bullet c1_k(\otimes\pi,...,\pi\otimes) \bullet ... \bullet cn_k(\otimes\pi,...,\pi\otimes)}$
π is a constant function. Since Y is the fixed-point operator, π computes the element of HU_1^* which contains all the terms in HU_c. In expressing predicates and queries through retractions and functional applications, π will be used as a constant expression which models unbound (logical) variables. π is the *top_element* of the elements of HU_1^*, hence the following property holds.

<u>Property 3.2</u>

- $\forall \underline{Ci_k} \in C$, $ci_k\downarrow(\pi) = \pi$
- $\forall n \in N^+$, $\otimes\pi,..., \pi\otimes \in HU_n^*$ (where $\otimes\_\otimes$ has arity n)
- $\forall n \in N^+, \forall u \in HU_n^*$, $u \subseteq \otimes\pi,..., \pi\otimes$ ◇

Finally, note that to each function f_n of arity n which maps from $HU_{k1}^* x...x\ HU_{kn}^*$ onto HU_k^*, we can associate a function g_1 of arity 1 which maps $HU_{k1+...+kn}^*$ onto HU_k^* such that:

$$\forall\ x1,...,xn,\quad f_n(x1,...,xn) = g_1(\otimes x1,...,xn\otimes).$$

3.2.3 Projection Pr.

The projection operator allows us to move from (elements of) cartesian products to (elements of) subproducts. It is a function $N^+ \times N^+ \times HU_c^* \rightarrow HU_c^*$, it computes the minimal congruence which satisfies the following axioms:

(1-singleton) $\mathbf{Pr}\ (j,k, <t_1,...,t_j,...,t_{k+j-1},...,t_n>) = <t_j,...,t_{k+j-1}>$ iff $\forall h \in [1,n],\ t_h \neq \varnothing$
$\mathbf{Pr}\ (j,k, <t_1,..., \varnothing,...,t_n>) = \varnothing$ iff $h \geq k+j-1$
(2-finite set) $\mathbf{Pr}\ (j,k, t_1 \bullet t_2) = \mathbf{Pr}\ (j,k, t_1) \bullet \mathbf{Pr}\ (j,k, t_2)$
(3-continuous) $\mathbf{Pr}\ (j,k, \mathbf{Sup}\{t^i\}) = \mathbf{Sup}\ \{\mathbf{Pr}\ (j,k, t^i)\}$ ◇

As is the case for functions $ci_{k\downarrow}$ in the following **Pr** (j,k, u) will be considered undefined if u is such that for no $h \geq j-1$, $u \in HU_{k+h}$.

EXAMPLE 3.6.

Let $\underline{C1_0}$, $\underline{C2_0}$ be two constructors of arity 0 and $\underline{C1_2}$ be a constructor of arity 2:

$\mathbf{Pr}\ (2,1, c1_2\downarrow (2, \otimes\ \pi\ , c1_2\ (c1_0\ , c2_0) \otimes)\ ) = <\underline{C1_0}, \underline{C2_0}>$.

Pr inherits from set theory the following property.

<u>Property 3.3</u>

$\forall t \in HU_k^*$, $\forall$ t1,...,tk$\in HU_1^*$, such that ti = **Pr**(i,1, t) then $t \subseteq$ **Pr**($\otimes$t1,...,tk$\otimes$). ◇

3.2.4. Injection In.

The injection operator allows us to lift on the order of cartesian products. It is a function $N^+ \times HU_1^* \rightarrow HU_c^*$, it computes the minimal congruence which satisfies the following axioms:

(1-singleton: $t \in HUT_1 = HU_c \cup \{\varnothing\}$)
$\mathbf{In}\ (i, t) = <t_1,...,t_i>$ such that $\forall h \in [1,i],\ t_h = t$
(2-finite set) $\mathbf{In}\ (i, t_1 \bullet t_2) = \mathbf{In}\ (i, t_1) \bullet \mathbf{In}\ (i, t_2)$
(3-continuous) $\mathbf{In}\ (i, \mathbf{Sup}\{t^j\}) = \mathbf{Sup}\ \{\mathbf{In}\ (i, t^j)\}$ ◇

Note that **Injection** is only defined on sets containing 1-tuples. Roughly speaking, this function allows to compute the elements of HU_c^* which denote sets containing only elements of the form <x,...,x>, where x is an element of HU_c.

EXAMPLE 3.7.

Let x.x be the following constant function:

x.x: λ . **In** (2 , π) .

Members of x.x are all the pairs of the form <x , x> such that x is a member of π (i.e. $x \in HU_c$).

In expressing predicates and queries through retractions and functional applications, injection allows to model constraints which in logic programming are expressed by the multiple occurrence of variables in the formulas. For instance in the atomic formula P(x,S(x)), the multiple occurrence of x constrains both the arguments of the predicate P, and S(2,In(2,π)) expresses the set of all the terms (of the Herbrand Universe) which satisfy such constraints (see Section 4).

3.2.5. Permutation Pe.

It is a function of $N_k \times HU_k^* \rightarrow HU_k^*$. Technically, it is an i-indexed family of operators (one for each class of tupling). N_k is the finite space containing all the permutations of the integers in the natural interval [1, k].

Pe computes the minimal congruence which satisfies the following axioms:

(1-singleton) **Pe** $(n_1...n_k, <t_1,...,t_k>) = <tn_1,...,tn_k>$
(2-finite set) **Pe** $(n_1...n_k, t_1 \bullet t_2) =$ **Pe** $(n_1...n_k, t_1) \bullet$ **Pe** $(n_1...n_k, t_2)$
(3-continuous) **Pe** $(n_1...n_k,$ **Sup**$\{t^j\}) =$ **Sup** $\{$ **Pe** $(n_1...n_k, t^j)\}$ ◇

<u>Notation remark</u> (n! , n!(i))
In the following we will denote by n! a permutation of the first n integers, and by n!(i) the i-th integer of that permutation.

EXAMPLE 3.8.
Let x.y.x be the following constant function:
x.y.x: **Pe** (1 3 2, ⊗ **In** (2,π) , π ⊗) .
Members of x.y.x are all the 3-tuples of the form <x,y,x> such that the first and third components are equal (and, possibly, different from the second one), and x, y range over all the elements of HU_c

4. HERBRAND TERMS AS MEMBERS OF HU_c^*.

We interpret (ground and non-ground) Herbrand terms as expressions which denote sets. We recall that Herbrand terms are built exactly as the elements of HU_c, starting from a set $\{\underline{Ci}_k\} \cup \{\underline{x}\}$, where $\{\underline{x}\}$ is a denumerable set of (logical) variable symbols.

A Herbrand term, h, on a Universe HU_c, denotes the subset of HU_c containing all the *ground instances* of h. All these sets are recursive sets and, being the set of all (computable) subsets of HU_c contained in HU_c^* (i.e. $HU_1^* \subset HU_c^*$), Herbrand terms denote elements of HU_c^*. Moreover, being computable the set denoted by a term h, methods to enumerate all the ground instances of h are well known. General algorithms which, given h, enumerates all its ground instances could easily be defined. However, our main interest is to associate to each h its denotation in HU_c^* which, in case of need, enumerates all the ground instances of h.

<u>Definition 4.1</u> (constant expressions)
1- 0-arity constructors and <_> applied to 0-arity constructors, are constant expressions;
2- ∅ and π are constant expressions;
3- If $E_1,...,E_n$ are n constant expressions then $E_1 \bullet ... \bullet E_n$ and $\otimes E_1,...,E_n \otimes$ are constant expressions;
4- If E is a constant expression then **In**(k,E), $\mathbf{ci}_k$(j,E), $\mathbf{ci}_k\downarrow$(j,E), **Pr**(i,j,E), **Pe**(n!,E) are constant expressions;
1-5 are the only *constant expressions*. ◇

Note that, constant expressions are expressions which do not contain variables and are not infinite applications of •.

<u>Proposition 4.1</u>
There exists a function η which associates to each tuple $H= h_1,...,h_n$ of Herbrand Terms a *constant expression* E on HU_n^*, containing only occurrences of the function π and of 0-arity constructors, and applications of the operators ci_k, ⊗_⊗, In, and Pe. H and E denote the same subset of the cartesian product of order n. ◇

A constructive proof is reported in Appendix II: We define a function which maps tuple of Herbrand terms into constant expressions, and we show that it satisfies the proposition. Examples of this fact are the definition of π itself (see Example 3.5) which has the same denotation of the single variable term, e.g. $\underline{x}$, the definition of x.x (see Example 3.7) which has the same denotation of the pair of terms $\underline{x,x}$, and the definition of x.y.x (see Example 3.8) which has the same denotation of the triple $\underline{x.y.x}$.

EXAMPLE 4.1.
If $C=\{\underline{C}_0,\underline{C}_2,\underline{C}_3\}$ is the constructor set in HU_c^* and $\underline{C_3(x,C_0,C_2(x,y))}$, $\underline{x}$ is a pair of Herbrand term, then, according to the definition of the function η, as is given in Appendix I, $\eta(\underline{C_3(x,C_0,C_2(x,y)) , x})$ is computed as follows:

- by B, $c_3(1,\eta(\underline{x,C_0,C_2(x,y) , x}))$
- by B, $c_3(1, c_2(3,\eta(\underline{x,C_0,x,y,x})))$
- by Aii, $c_3(1, c_2(3,$**Pe**$(1\,4\,2\,5\,3 ,$ ⊗**In**$(3,\pi)$, $\underline{C}_0$, π⊗))).

In predicative languages, unification is used to compare two (or more) Herbrand Terms. Unificaton computes the Mgu, if any, or fails. Under our interpretation of Herbrand Terms, the following proposition holds.

<u>Proposition 4.2</u>

Let $H = h_1,...,h_n$ be a tuple of Herbrand terms, for each *instantiation function* ϑ :

$$\eta(H\cdot\vartheta) \subseteq \eta(H) \quad \text{[or simply, } H\cdot\vartheta \subseteq H] \ \diamond$$

EXAMPLE 4.2.

The function ϑ such that $\vartheta(\underline{x}) = \underline{C_0}$ and $\vartheta(\underline{y}) = \underline{C_2(C_0,C_0)}$ is a ground instantiation function for the tuple in Example 4.1: $\underline{(C_3(x,C_0,C_2(x,y)) , x)}\cdot\vartheta = \underline{C_3(C_0,C_0,C_2(C_0,C_2(C_0,C_0))) , C_0}$.

This tuple, under our interpretation of Herbrand terms, denotes the (singleton set) $<c_3(\underline{C_0},\underline{C_0},c_2(\underline{C_0},c_2(\underline{C_0},\underline{C_0}))) , \underline{C_0}>$, and is such that:

$$<c_3(\underline{C_0},\underline{C_0},c_2(\underline{C_0},c_2(\underline{C_0},\underline{C_0}))),\underline{C_0}> \ \subseteq \ c_3(1,c_2(3,\mathbf{Pe}(1\,4\,2\,5\,3, \otimes\mathbf{In}(3,\pi),\underline{C_0}, \pi\otimes))),$$

because $\underline{C_0} \subseteq \pi$ and $c_2(\underline{C_0},\underline{C_0}) \subseteq \pi$.

Proposition 4.2 means that the set of all the terms which are instances of a term H defines a class of subsets of the set denoted by H. Note that, this class does not necessarily coincide with the entire class of all the subsets of the set denoted by the term. As an example, consider the single variable Herbrand term $\underline{x}$ in the Universe of Example 4.2., $\underline{C_0}\bullet c_1(\underline{C_0})$ denotes a subset of $\eta(\underline{x})$, but for no instantiation function ϑ, $\underline{x}\cdot\vartheta=\{\underline{C_0},\underline{C_1(C_0)}\}$. The class of all the subsets obtained by instantiation of a term H is included in the class of all the subsets of the set denoted by H. However, Proposition 4.3 shows that this class is a rich class.

<u>Proposition 4.3</u>

If $H= h_1,...,h_n$ and $H'=h_1',...,h_n'$ are two tuples of Hèrbrand terms, then:

$$\eta\ (H\cdot\vartheta) = \mathbf{Sup}\{t\in HU_c^* \mid t\subseteq\eta\ (H)\ ,\ t\subseteq\eta\ (H')\ \}\ ,$$

assuming ϑ (to exist and) to be the Mgu of $\varphi(h_1,...,h_n)$ and $\varphi(h_1',...,h_n')$, where φ is a dummy constructor (or predicate). $\diamond$

Proposition 4.3 tell us that the *most general instance* , Mgi, of two terms is the **Sup**erior of all the subsets which are obtained by instances of the terms under unification functions. Moreover, this set coincides with the **Sup**erior of all the subsets of both terms. Again, Propositon 4.3 allows us to compute the most general instance of two Herbrand terms as the **Sup**erior of an ascending chain of finite applications of $\bullet$ to the elements of HU_c^* which correspond to instances of the Herbrand terms under the ground unification functions.

Proposition 4.3 is of no use in *resolving* clausal theories, because clauses contain logical variables, and we are mainly interested in the function ϑ which computes also the variable bindings. In contrast, because of our interpretation of Herbrand terms (i.e. expressions which denote sets), variables occurring in a Herbrand term are considered to stand for (possibly different invocations of) π or Injection of π, then only the most general instance is of interest and ϑ can be ignored.

Finally, note that the right hand side of the formula in Proposition 4.3 is a formulation of set intersection suitable for the sets denoted by the elements of HU_c^*. We will use this fact in the following Section 5.

We have seen that to each Herbrand term, η associates a constant expression in our language. Moreover, note that several functions η exist, due to the fact that infinite congruent constant expressions exist. As a matter of fact, note that $\forall u\in HU_k^*, \forall v\in HU_c^*$: $\mathbf{Pr}(1,k, \otimes u,v\otimes) = u$.

5. THE OPERATOR Intset.

The previous Section shows how Herbrand terms can be expressed in a functional way, and suggests the use of a language operator to compare elements of HU_c^* (possibly, constant expressions) and to compute set intersections. With this aim, we introduce the function **Intset**.

It is a function $HU_i^* \times HU_i^* \rightarrow HU_i^*$, it computes the minimal congruence which satisfies the following axioms:

(1-idempotent)	$\mathbf{Intset}\ (t\ , t\ ) = t$
(2-commutative)	$\mathbf{Intset}\ (t_1\ , t_2) = \mathbf{Intset}\ (t_2\ , t_1)$
(3-associative)	$\mathbf{Intset}\ (\mathbf{Intset}\ (t_1\ , t_2)\ , t_3) = \mathbf{Intset}\ (t_1\ , \mathbf{Intset}\ (t_2\ , t_3))$
(4-zero)	$\mathbf{Intset}\ (t\ , \varnothing) = \varnothing$
(5-finite set)	$\mathbf{Intset}\ (t_1\ , t_2) = t$ iff $t_1 = t \bullet t_1'\ ,\ t_2 = t \bullet t_2'$ and $\mathbf{Intset}\ (\ t_1'\ , t_2') = \varnothing$
(6-continuous)	$\mathbf{Intset}\ (t, \mathbf{Sup}\{t^j\}) = \mathbf{Sup}\{\mathbf{Intset}\ (t, t^j)$ $\diamond$

Intset behaves like set-intersection on the elements of HU_c^*. It satisfies Proposition 4.3.

<u>Proposition 5.1</u>

$$\forall\ t_1\ , t_2\in HU_c^*\ ,\quad \mathbf{Intset}\ (t_1\ , t_2) = \mathbf{Sup}\{t\in HU_c^* \mid t\subseteq t_1\ ,\ t\subseteq t_2\}\ \diamond$$

Note that Propositon 5.1 means that the Mgi of Herbrand terms corresponds to set intersection defined by **Intset** on the constant expressions that η associates to Herbrand terms. As in the case of the previous operators, **Intset** (u,v) will be considered undefined if $u \in HU^*_i$ and $v \in HU^*_j$ and $i \neq j$.In all the other cases, **Intset** (u,v) is defined and the following property holds.

Property 5.1

Let H, H' be any pair of i-tuples of Herbrand terms, then

$$\mathbf{Intset}\,(\eta(H),\eta(H')) = \begin{cases} \eta(H \cdot \vartheta) & \text{, if } \vartheta \text{ exists} \\ \varnothing & \text{, otherwise} \end{cases}$$

assuming that ϑ is the Mgu of $\varphi(h_1,\dots,h_n)$ and $\varphi(h_1',\dots,h_n')$, where φ is a dummy constructor (or predicate). ◇

EXAMPLE 5.1.

Let C be the set of constructors $\{\underline{0},\underline{S}\}$, such that $\underline{0}$ has arity 0 and $\underline{S}$ has arity 1, then

- **Intset** $(\eta(\underline{S(0)}), \eta(\underline{S(0)}))$ = **Intset** $(S(\underline{0}), S(\underline{0})) = S(\underline{0})$
- **Intset** $(\eta(\underline{0}), \eta(\underline{S(0)}))$ = **Intset** $(\underline{0}, S(\underline{0})) = \varnothing$
- **Intset** $(\eta(\underline{x,y}), \eta(\underline{x,x}))$ = **Intset** $(\otimes\pi,\pi\otimes$, **In**$(2,\pi)) = \eta(\underline{x,x})$ = **In**$(2,\pi)$

6. LOGIC PROGRAMMING, RELATIONS AND FUNCTIONS.

The Horn clause theory (logic program **[Kowalski74]**)

(7) $\quad ADD(\underline{x,0,x}) \leftarrow. \qquad ADD(\underline{x,S(y),S(z)}) \leftarrow ADD(\underline{x,y,z}).$

has a minimal model, which is the set of all the triples of the relation:

(8) $\quad ADD = \{\langle x,y,z\rangle \mid x \in HU,\ y=\underline{0},\ x=z\} \cup \{\langle x,S(y),S(z)\rangle \mid \langle x,y,z\rangle \in ADD\}$

Thus, reasoning about the minimal model of the theory (7) is the same as reasoning about the relation (expressed by) (8). However, (8) is an axiomatic theory, even if it differs from (7) because it is not in Horn clause form, contains just one axiom, and uses set operators. Apart from syntax, (8) is a SuperLOGLISP [Robinson82] definition of ADD. In both theories, to "compute an instance" of ADD, we have to handle all the variables as logical variables. Now, consider the following expression in our language:

(9)
$$\begin{aligned} F_{ADD}(w) = u \bullet v \text{ where } & \mathbf{Intset}(w, \mathbf{Pe}(1\,3\,2, \otimes\mathbf{In}(2,\pi),\underline{0}\otimes)) = u, \\ & S(2,S(3, F_{ADD}(w'))) = v \\ & \text{where } S{\downarrow}(2,S{\downarrow}(3,z)) = w', \mathbf{Intset}(w,S(2,S(3, \otimes\pi,\pi,\pi\otimes))) = z \end{aligned}$$

It defines a function from HU_3^* to HU_3^* which is a retraction. To see that F_{ADD} is a retraction, note that for each w it computes $u \bullet v$. u is the result of **Intset**(w, **Pe**(1 3 2, ⊗**In**(2, π),$\underline{0}$⊗)) then $u \subseteq w$. Moreover, v is the result of $S(2,S(3,F_{ADD}(S{\downarrow}(2,S{\downarrow}(3,z)))))$, where z is such that $z \subseteq w$ and z denotes the subset of the triples in w which have the form $\langle r,S(p),S(q)\rangle$. Examine that expression. Its sub-expression $S{\downarrow}(2,S{\downarrow}(3,z))$ removes one S from the second and the third component of each triple in (the set denoted by) z, then F_{ADD} is recursively applied to that value (note that, $z \ll w$), and finally one S is put back in the second and third component of each triple. Thus, by structural induction on $\ll$, we see that: $S(2,S(3,F_{ADD}(S{\downarrow}(2,S{\downarrow}(3,z))))) \subseteq w$.

Note also, that F_{ADD} satisfies Proposition 2.4. In fact, for each t_1 and t_2 (since **Intset**$(t_1 \bullet t_2, t)$= **Intset**$(t_1,t) \bullet$ **Intset**(t_2,t)), $F_{ADD}(t_1 \bullet t_2) = F_{ADD}(t_1) \bullet F_{ADD}(t_2)$.

Moreover, we can show that F_{ADD} computes the relation ADD, i.e. its union set (see Definition 2.2) is ADD. In fact, each triple of ground Herbrand terms t_1,t_2,t_3 such that $ADD(t_1,t_2,t_3)$ is an instance of $ADD(\underline{x,0,x})$, is not an instance of $ADD(\underline{x,S(y),S(z)})$ and, because of Proposition 5.1 and **Pe**(1 3 2, ⊗**In**(2, π),0⊗) = $\eta(\underline{x,0,x})$, is such that:

Intset$(\eta(t_1,t_2,t_3)$, **Pe**(1 3 2, ⊗**In**(2, π),0⊗)) = $\eta(t_1,t_2,t_3)$ then, $u=\eta(t_1,t_2,t_3)$ and $v=\varnothing$.

Furthermore, each triple t_1,t_2,t_3 such that $ADD(t_1,t_2,t_3)$ is an instance of $ADD(\underline{x,s(y),s(z)})$, is not an instance of $ADD(\underline{x,0,x})$ and is such that:

Intset$(\eta(t_1,t_2,t_3), S(2,S(3, \otimes\pi,\pi,\pi\otimes))) = \eta(t_1,t_2,t_3)$.

Therefore $u=\varnothing$, and $v=\eta(t_1,t_2,t_3)$ iff $F_{ADD}(S{\downarrow}(2,S{\downarrow}(3, \eta(t_1,t_2,t_3)))) = S{\downarrow}(2,S{\downarrow}(3, \eta(t_1,t_2,t_3)))$, i.e. $ADD(\underline{x,y,z})$ is satisfied for $\underline{x}$ bound to the term t_1, and for $\underline{y}$ and $\underline{z}$, respectively bound to t_2 and t_3, reduced of the first occurrence of S.

All the above considerations allows us to conclude that F_{ADD}, when applied to each element w of HU_3^*, computes the element of HU_3^* which denotes the set of all the triples $\langle x,y,z\rangle$ in w which are also in the relation ADD. Moreover, there is a correspondence between the two members of the set union in (8) and the two clauses in (7) on one side, and the sub-expressions of F_{ADD}:

- **Intset**(w, **Pe**(1 3 2, ⊗**In**(2, π),$\underline{0}$⊗)) = u,
- $S(2,S(3, F_{ADD}(w'))) = v$ where $S{\downarrow}(2,S{\downarrow}(3,z)) = w'$, **Intset**$(w,S(2,S(3, \otimes\pi,\pi,\pi\otimes))) = z$,

respectively, on the other side. According to this correspondence, we can associate to the query:

$\leftarrow ADD(h_1,h_2,h_3)$

where h_1,h_2,h_3 is any triple of (possibly non ground) Herbrand terms, the application:

$F_{ADD}(\eta(h_1,h_2,h_3))$.

It computes the element of HU_3^* which denotes the set of all the ground instances of h_1,h_2,h_3 which makes valid the query in the theory (7). For instance, consider the query $\leftarrow ADD(\underline{0,S(0),z})$, which

corresponds to the application $F_{ADD}(\eta(\underline{0,S(0),z}))$, i.e. $F_{ADD}(\otimes\underline{0},S(\underline{0}),\pi\otimes)$. Then the expression $F_{ADD}(\otimes\underline{0},S(\underline{0}),\pi\otimes)$ evaluates to $<\underline{0,S(0),S(0)}>$.
As is the case for SuperLOGLISP, our expressions are always deterministic. The *nondeterminism* of PROLOG-like logic programs is embodied in the structure of the elements of HU_c^* which denote sets of Herbrand ground terms. Moreover, the program *invertibility* feature which in predicative languages is due to logical variables and is supported by the resolution based evaluation rule, is here embodied in the structure of the constant expression and in the properties of our class of retractions. For instance, consider the query $\leftarrow ADD(\underline{x,y,S(0)})$, which corresponds to the application $F_{ADD}(\eta(\underline{x,y,S(0)}))$, i.e. $F_{ADD}(\otimes\pi,\pi,S(\underline{0})\otimes)$. The expression $F_{ADD}(\otimes\pi,\pi,S(\underline{0})\otimes)$ evaluates to $<\underline{0,S(0),S(0)}> \bullet <\underline{S(0),0,S(0)}>$, and the expression $\mathbf{Pr}(2,1,F_{ADD}(\otimes\pi,\pi,S(\underline{0})\otimes)))$ evaluates to $\underline{S(0)} \bullet \underline{0}$.

As another example, consider the Horn clause theory:

$LE(0,y) \leftarrow.$ $\qquad LE(S(x),S(y)) \leftarrow LE(x,y).$

We can associate to LE, the retraction F_{LE} from HU_2^* to HU_2^*:

$F_{LE}(w) = u \bullet v$ where $\mathbf{Intset}(w, \otimes\, \underline{0},\pi \otimes) = u,$

(10) $\qquad S(1,S(2,F_{LE}(w')) = v$

$\qquad$ where $S{\downarrow}(1,S{\downarrow}(2,z)) = w'$, $\mathbf{Intset}(w,S(1,S(2, \otimes\, \pi,\pi \otimes))) = z$ Now, we can extend the theory with the following clause which introduces the relation INTERVAL.

(11) $\quad INTERVAL(\underline{inf,sup,x}) \leftarrow LE(\underline{inf,sup})\, ,\, LE(\underline{inf,x})\, ,\, LE(\underline{x,sup}).$

(11) contains one of the main appealing feature of logic programming, i.e. the *declarative* feature. From a programming point of view, this means that the language sequence control mechanism allows full freedom in the evaluation ordering of the language forms. This is achieved in predicative languages by the mechanism used in the (inferential) operational semantics, to select predicative forms in a query (or clause right part). Due to the commutative and associative properties, set intersection in set based functional programming has the same declarative flavour. For example, consider the retraction of $HU_3^* \rightarrow HU_3^*$:

$F_{INTERVAL}(w) = \mathbf{Intset}(w,u1,u2,u3)$

$\qquad$ where $u1= \otimes F_{LE}(\mathbf{Pr}(1,2, w)),\pi\otimes,$

$\qquad u2= \mathbf{Pe}(1\,3\,2, \otimes F_{LE}(\mathbf{Pr}(1,2, \mathbf{Pe}(1\,3\,2,w))),\pi\otimes),$

$\qquad u3= \mathbf{Pe}(3\,2\,1, \otimes F_{LE}(\mathbf{Pr}(1,2, \mathbf{Pe}(3\,2\,1,w))),\pi\otimes)$

The computation of $F_{INTERVAL}(w)$ can proceed in different ways in order to reduce $\mathbf{Intset}(w,u1,u2,u3)$. For instance, the computation of $F_{INTERVAL}(\otimes S(\underline{0}),\underline{0},\pi\otimes)$ could first reduce both:

$u2= \mathbf{Pe}(1\,3\,2, \otimes F_{LE}(\mathbf{Pr}(1,2, \mathbf{Pe}(1\,3\,2, \otimes S(\underline{0}),\underline{0},\pi\otimes))),\pi\otimes)$, and

$u3= \mathbf{Pe}(3\,2\,1, \otimes F_{LE}(\mathbf{Pr}(1,2, \mathbf{Pe}(3\,2\,1, \otimes S(\underline{0}),\underline{0},\pi\otimes))),\pi\otimes)$

before realizing that u1 is, in any case, reduced to $\varnothing$.
In predicative languages, flat composition is the standard composition rule and moreover, suitable and efficient sequence control mechanisms are hard to design. That is not true here, since we have functional composition. The following retraction $F1_{INTERVAL}$ has the same union set of $F_{INTERVAL}$, but first checks for the correct definition of the interval limits:

$F1_{INTERVAL}(w) = \mathbf{Intset}(w,u2,u3)$

$\qquad$ where $u2= \mathbf{Pe}(1\,3\,2, \otimes F_{LE}(\mathbf{Pr}(1,2, \mathbf{Pe}(1\,3\,2, w1))),\pi\otimes),$

$\qquad u3= \mathbf{Pe}(3\,2\,1, \otimes F_{LE}(\mathbf{Pr}(1,2, \mathbf{Pe}(3\,2\,1,w1))),\pi\otimes)$

$\qquad$ where $w1 = \mathbf{Intset}(w,u1),$

$\qquad\qquad u1= \otimes F_{LE}(\mathbf{Pr}(1,2, w)),\pi\otimes$

The effort for controlling logic programs (and providing a direction to predicative forms, i.e. annotations to transform logic variables in functional variables **[Bellia83, Reddy84]**) is tightly related to the inability to model functions in logic programming and, has been one of the motivations of the integration of the logic and functional programming paradigms. In our approach, which models predicates with retractions, retractions are a special class of functions. Our language allows to express general functional programmming. Functional programming on (data which denote) sets, is not really innovative. Sets are in fact, basic data in SETL **[Shwartz75]**. However, we admit infinite sets (in SETL only finite sets are allowed) and we do not need any nondeterministic operator to select, for instance, the elements of a set (as is the case for **arb** in SETL).
To express the function SUM on naturals, represented by the ground Herbrand terms of HU_c with $C=\{\underline{0},\underline{S}\}$, we can define:

```
SUM(x,y) = if  #(x)=1 and #(y)=1 and card(x)=1 and card(y)=1
           then if  x=0  then  y
                         else  S(SUM(S↓(x),y))
           else ∅
```

SUM is defined on all the values of HU_c^* and computes x+y for each pair of values in HUT_1 and, ∅ everywhere else. For instance, the expression SUM(0,S(0)) evaluates to S(0), while the expression SUM(0•S(0), S(0)) evaluates to ∅, because 0•S(0) is such that **card**(0•S(0))≠1. 0•S(0) is an element of HUF_1 and denotes the set of naturals {0,S(0)}.

A slightly different expression could be given in order to make SUM to compute a partial function:

SUM(x,y) = **if** #(x)=1 and #(y)=1 and **card**(x)=1 and **card**(y)=1
then if x=0 **then** y
else S(SUM(S↓(x),y))
else SUM(x,y)

SUM now computes x+y for each pair of values of HUT_1 and is undefined everywhere else in HU_c^*. SUM could also be considered as a function from HUT_2 in HUT_1, and expressed by:

SUM1(w) = SUM(x,y) **where** Pr(1,1 w)=x , Pr(2,1 w)=y

Moreover, we can extend SUM to compute, for instance, the set {S(0),S(S(0))}, when applied to the cartesian product of {0,S(0)} and {S(0)}. To express it in our language, we use Projections of retractions. For example

SUM2(w) = Pr(3,1, F_{ADD}(⊗w,π⊗))

defines the function SUM extended on sets. It maps a set of pairs {<x,y>} onto the set {x+y | <x,y>∈ w}.

We conclude by noting that the language supports relations (predicates) as a special class of functions. However, this class has all the nice features of logic programming. Moreover, relations and functions are combined by the conventional function composition mechanism. For instance, the expression

F(x,y) = SUM2(Pr(3,1, ⊗$F_{INTERVAL}$(⊗0,S(S(S(S(0)))),x⊗)) , y⊗)

defines the function F which, due to the restrictions on SUM2, is a mapping from HU_1^*x HU_1^* into HU_1^*. For instance, if k is an element of HUT_1, then F(h,k) computes the set resulting by adding k to each natural, n, which is in the set denoted by h and such that n satisfies the relation INTERVAL(0,S(S(S(S(0)))),n).

7. CONCLUSIONS.

The main contribution of the paper is the identification of a *special class* of set functions, retractions, which perhaps is the most primitive concept which relates logic and functional programming. Retractions are concretely discussed in a first order functional language which has to be considered as a model for a family of functional languages more than another language which integrate logic and functional programming.

There exist two languages **[Berkling82, Darlington85]** which share with us the use of set functions as the basic logic-functional integration mechanism. However, our proposal contains some remarkable differences. In both the above mentioned languages, a predicate is defined by a function which returns a "set" of tuples of Herbrand terms whose instances are all the terms of the Herbrand Universe of the (minimal) relation which is a valid interpretation of the predicate (in the logic theory). Hence, Herbrand terms are the symbolic data of the language. However, Herbrand terms are not completely symbolic data. In fact they contain logical variables and require some language ability to cope with term unification. This ability is achieved in SuperLOGLISP by a new reduction rule, ε-reduction, which captures unification and in Darlington's language by assuming narrowing as the language basic expression evaluation rule.

This is the first point of difference with the present approach. Here, Herbrand terms are modelled by a special class of symbolic data, constant expressions, which do not involve (logical) variables and do not require unification to compute with them. All the derivations which can be obtained by ε-reduction or by narrowing, on expressions which contain logical variables, are reformulated here as manipulation of symbolic data.

A second point of difference is the mechanism used to declare functions and predicates. Both SuperLOGLISP and Darlington's language use Set abstractions, i.e. constructs of the form {X | C}, where X is a set of variables and C contains equations on Herbrand terms or invocations of predicates only. In our approach, predicates are a special class of functions, retractions, and are distinct from ordinary functions from the semantic viewpoint. There is no syntactic distinction between retractions and functions, and they can be freely combined through the (standard) function composition mechanism. This is fundamental to our approach: Retractions allow to combine logic and functional programming, in a pure functional programming paradigm, and treat both predicates and ordinary functions by the same object: a set function. A similar feature can be found in other languages **[Dershowitz84, Dershowitz85, Reddy85, Fribourg85]**, where predicates are represented as boolean functions expressed in equational theories. However, the main difference with these languages is the use of special evaluation rules which combine inferences and rewritings in order to

treat this class of boolean functions as relations, and to interface them with ordinary function evaluations. In contrast, predicates and functions are distinct objects in **[Berkling82, Darlington85, Goguen84, Subrahmanyam84, Barbuti85]**, and can be combined according to some composition rules (through special linguistic constructs). The second approach has clear advantages from the language user viewpoint, since it allow the use of queries to compute with predicates and of (expression) evaluations to compute with functions. However, the main limitation of all these languages is to completely establish complexity and machine realizability of the basic language evaluation rules. Our language is oriented to machine architectures and its realization could be directly supported by the reduction machines which are currently developed for functional languages.
In Section 4 we see that constant expressions are enough to represent all the tuples of Herbrand terms. In the same section we see also that tuples of Herbrand terms are less than constant expressions, for instance we see that to each tuple of Herbrand terms we can associate infinite different but equivalent constant expressions. This equivalence is completely but in an abstract way defined by the axiomatization given in Section 3.1 for our operators. In **[Bellia86b]** we show that constant expressions have *normal form* and we give a system of rewrite rules for our operators which reduce constant expressions to normal form. This set of rewrite rules toghether with the rules for α, β, Y reduction, forms also an operational semantic for our calculus with retractions.
The restriction to first order functions is only motivated by our belief that the mechanisms used to unify logic and functional programming are more easy to understand without working about higher order features. Morever, higher order extensions seem to be rather independent from the present treatment of predicates and functions. They could only require the use of higher order retractions (i.e. retractions as values) and some marginal extensions to our set operators. However, further work is needed to fully capture the nature of the higher order features in logic-functional programming languages.

REFERENCES

Barbuti85] **R. Barbuti, M. Bellia, G. Levi** and **M. Martelli**, LEAF: A language which integrates logic, equations and functions. In *Logic Programming: Functions, Relations and Equations* , D. DeGroot and G. Lindstrom, Eds. (Prentice-Hall, 1985).

Bellia83] **M. Bellia, G. Levi** and **M. Martelli**, On compiling Prolog programs on demand driven architectures. Proc. *Logic Programming Workshop'83* (1983) 518-535.

Bellia86] **M. Bellia** and **G. Levi**, The relation between logic and functional languages: A survey. To appear in *J . Logic Programming* .

[Bellia86b] **M. Bellia**, Logic and functional programming by retractions: Operational semantics.In*Derivable Working Group on Semantics, ESPRIT Project 415* (1986).

Berkling75] **K. Berkling**, Reduction languages for reduction machines. *Proc. 2nd Int. Symp. on Computer Architectures* (IEEE Comp. Society Press, 1975)133-140.

Berkling82] **K. Berkling, J.A. Robinson** and **E.E. Sibert**., A proposal for a fifth generation logic and functional programming system, based on highly parallel reduction machine architecture. Syracuse University (November 1982).

Clarke80] **T.J.W. Clarke, P.J.S. Gladstone, C.D. MacLean** and **A.C. Normal**, SKIM - The S.K.I. reduction machine. *Proc. Lisp 80 Conf.* (1980)128-135.

[Darlington81] **J. Darlington** and **M. Reeve**, ALICE: A multiprocessor reduction machine for the parallel evaluation of applicative languages. *Proc. Int. Symp. Functional Programming Languages and Computer Architectures* (1981) 32-62.

[Darlington85] **J. Darlington, A.J. Field** and **H. Pull**, The unification of functional and logic languages. In *Logic Programming: Functions, Relations and Equations*

[Dershowitz84] **N. Dershowitz** and **N.A. Josephson**, Logic programming by completion. *Proc. 2nd Int. Logic Programming Conf.* (1984),313-320.

[Dershowitz85] **N. Dershowitz** and **D.A. Plaisted**, Logic programming cum applicative programming, *Proc. 1985 Symp. on Logic Programming* (IEEE Comp. Society Press, 1985) 54-66.

[[Goguen84] **J.A. Goguen** and **J. Meseguer**, Equality, types, modules and (why not?) generics for logic programming. *J. Logic Programming 1* (1984) 179-210.

[Hsiang83] **J. Hsiang** and **N. Dershowitz**, Rewrite methods for clausal and non-clausal theorem proving. *Proc 10th ICALP* (1983).

[[Kluge80] **W.E. Kluge** and **H. Schlutter**, An architectutre for the direct execution of reduction languages. *Proc. Int. Workshop High Level Computer architecture* (1980).

[Kowalski79] **R.A. Kowalski**, Algorithms=Logic+Control. *C. ACM*, 22 (1979) 424-436
[Mago80] **G.A. Mago**, A cellular computer architecture for functional programming. *Proc. IEEE-COMPCON 80* (IEEE Comp. Society Press, 1980) 179-187.
[Milner72] **R. Milner**, Implementation and application of Scott's logic for computable functions. *Sigplan Notices*, 7 (1972) 1-6.
[Moto-Oka82] **T. Moto-Oka**, Ed., *Fifth Generation Computer Systems.* North-Holland, 1982.
[Reddy84] **U.S. Reddy**, Transformation of logic programs into functional programs. *Proc. 1984 Int. Symp. on Logic Programming* (IEEE Comp. Society Press, 1984)
[Reddy85] **U.S. Reddy**, On the relationship between logic and functional languages. In *Logic Programming: Functions, Relations and Equations*, D. DeGroot and G. Lindstrom, Eds. (Prentice-Hall, 1985).
[Robinson82] **J.A. Robinson** and **E.E. Sibert**, LOGLISP: An alternative to PROLOG. *Machine Intelligence 10* (Ellis Horwood, 1982).
[Scott76] **D. Scott**, Data types as lattices. *SIAM J. on Computing*, 5 (1976)522-587.
[Shwartz75] **J.T. Shwartz**, Automatic data structure choise in a language of very high level. *C. ACM*, 18 (1975) 772-728.
Subrahmanyam84] **P.A. Subrahmanyam** and **J.-H. You**, FUNLOG = functions + logic: A computational model integrating functional and logic programming. *Proc. 1984 Int. Symp. on Logic Programming* (IEEE Comp. Society Press, 1984) 144-153.

APPENDIX I

Language Syntax

1) The language alphabet is $A = \{D, V_d, P, V_p\}$, where:
   - D is a denumerable set of data defined according to the value domain HU_c^*, defined in Section 3.1. Moreover, it can include values for Integers, Booleans and other suitable domains (as directly representable data).
   - P is a (denumerable) set of primitive operators, which includes the operators <_>,•, ⊗_⊗, ∅, π, c_k, $c_k\downarrow$, **In**, **Pe**, **Pr**, **Intset**, defined in Section 3.1, and, according to D, all the arithmetic and boolean operators, the conditional **if_then_else** operator, and the following operators on sets:
     - The tupling operator #, which, applied to a data in HU_i^*, results i, i.e. the class of tupling of the data (Integers and Booleans have tupling 1);
     - The cardinality operator **card** which, applied to data in HUF results the cardinality of the corresponding finite set (Integers and Booleans have cardinality 1). Moreover, **card** is undefined when applied to data in HUω;
     - The equality operator, =, which results true if the arguments are the same data in HUF (Integer and Boolean). It results false or is undefined if the arguments are different data or are both in HUω, respectively.
   - V_d is a denumerable set of variables which range over D.
   - V_p is a family of denumerable sets of variables which range over the first order functions on D, and are indexed by the function arity. (V_d and V_p are disjoint sets)
2) The language expressions are all the closed forms: $\{E \mid E \in F, ch[E]=\{\}\}$, where F is the set of the language forms, and ch[E] is the set of variables which occur free in E.
3) The set F of the forms is:
   - D_F, set of all the data in HUF (Integer and Boolean): $\forall E \in D_F$, $ch[E]=\{\}$;
   - V_d, set of all the variables on D: $\forall E \in V_d$, $ch[E]=\{E\}$;
   - A_F, set of all the applications of primitive or defined functions:
     $A_F=\{(op_n\ E1...En) \mid op_n \text{ has arity } n, op_n \in P \cup V_p, Ei \in F\}$
     $\forall (op_n\ E1...En) \in A_F$, $ch[(op_n\ E1...En)] = \cup_{i=1,n} ch[Ei]$
   - A_λ, set of all the λ_abstraction applications:
     $A_\lambda=\{((\lambda x1...xn.E)\ E1...En) \mid xi \in V_d, xi \neq xj \text{ for } i \neq j, E, Ei \in F\}$
     $\forall ((\lambda x1...xn.E)\ E1...En) \in A_\lambda$,
     $ch[((\lambda x1...xn.E)\ E1...En)] = (ch[E] - \{x1,...,xn\}) \cup (\cup_{i=1,n} ch[Ei])$
   - A_Y, set of all fixed_point function applications:
     $A_Y=\{((Yop_n\ x1...xn.E)\ E1...En) \mid op_n \text{ has arity } n, op_n \in V_p, xi \in V_d, xi \neq xj \text{ for } i \neq j, E, Ei \in F\}$
     $\forall ((Yop_n\ x1...xn.E)\ E1...En) \in A_F$,

$ch[((Yop_n\ x1...xn.E)\ E1...En)]=(ch[E] - \{x1,...,xn\}) \cup (\cup_{i=1,n} ch[Ei])$

Language Semantics. Each form has meaning according to the semantics of the primitive operators and to the following reduction rules:

α_reduction

$(\lambda x1...xn.E)= (\lambda y1...yn.[y1/x1,...,yn/xn]E)$, where $yi \neq yj$ for $i \neq j$ and $yi \notin ch[E]$

β_reduction

$((\lambda x1...xn.E)\ E1...En)=[E1/x1,...,En/xn]E$

Y_reduction

$((Yop_n\ x1...xn.E)\ E1...En)= ((\lambda x1...xn.[(Yop_n\ x1...xn.E)/op_n]\ E)\ E1...En)$

where:

$\forall E \in D_F,\ [E'/x]E=E;$

$\forall E \in V_c \cup V_p,\ [E'/x]E= \begin{cases} E' & \text{if } x=E \\ E & \text{otherwise} \end{cases}$

$\forall (op_n\ E1...En) \in A_F,\ [E'/x](op_n\ E1...En)= ([E'/x]op_n\ [E'/x]E1...[E'/x]En)$

$\forall ((\lambda x1...xn.E)\ E1...En) \in A_\lambda,\ [E'/x]((\lambda x1...xn.E)\ E1...En)=H\ [E'/x]E1...[E'/x]En$

$\forall ((Yop_n\ x1...xn.E)\ E1...En) \in A_F,\ [E'/x]((Yop_n\ x1...xn.E)\ E1...En)=H\ [E'/x]E1...[E'/x]En$

with: $H= \begin{cases} (\lambda x1...xn.E) \text{ resp. } (Yop_n\ x1...xn.E) & \text{if } x \in \{op_n, x1,...,xn\} \\ (\lambda x1...xn.\ [E'/x]E) \text{ resp. } (Yop_n\ x1...xn.\ [E'/x]E) & \text{if } ch[E'] \cap \{x1,...,xn\}=\{\} \end{cases}$

Syntactic extensions

- Sequence of function declarations. As a syntactic extension, we admit the following two forms

$f1(x_1^1,...,x_{n1}^1)=E1;\ ...\ ;\ fm(x_1^m,...,x_{nm}^m)=Em\ ;\ E$

let $f1(x_1^1,...,x_{n1}^1)=E1;\ ...\ ;\ fm(x_1^m,...,x_{nm}^m)=Em$ **in** E

which correspond to the expression

$[F1/f1](...([Fm/fm]E)...)$

with: $Fi= \begin{cases} (\lambda x_1^i...x_{ni}^i.Ei) & \text{if Ei does not contain occurrences of fi} \\ (Yfi\ x_1^i...x_{ni}^i.Ei) & \text{otherwise.} \end{cases}$

Note that Ei can only contains occurrences of fi itself or of functions defined before in the sequence.

- Sequence of function applications and where expression. As a syntactic extension, we admit the following two forms

E , E1=x1 ,..., En=xn

E **where** E1=x1 ,..., En=xn

which have the same meaning and correspond to the expression

$((\lambda x1...xn.E)\ E1...En)$

APPENDIX II

Proposition 4.1 (proof)

We define a function η which satisfies the proposition. To define it we distinguish two cases:

A) (tuples of constants and variables) Let H be the tuple $v_1,...,v_n$ where each v_i is either a 0-arity constructor or a variable, then:

i) if each variable in H occurs only once:

$\eta\ (v_1,...,v_n) = \otimes e_1,...,e_n \otimes$

where $e_i = v_i$ if v_i is a 0-arity constructor

$e_i = \pi$ if v_i is a variable

ii) otherwise (i.e. H contains multiple occurrences of some variables):

$\eta\ (v_1,...,v_n) = Pe(n!, \otimes\ e_1,...,e_m \otimes)$

where a- $\sum_{i=1,m} \#e_i = n$

b- n! and $e_1,...,e_m$ are such that:

1- for each 0-aity constructor v_i

$\exists\ e_j$ such that: $e_j = v_i$ and $\sum_{p=1,j-1} \#e_p = n!(i)-1$

2- for each variable v_i which occurs only once

$\exists\ e_j$ such that: $e_j = \pi$ and $\sum_{p=1,j-1} \#e_p = n!(i)-1$

3- for each variable v_i which occurs k times (k >1),

let i1,...,ik be its occurrences (i.e. $v_{i_1}=...=v_{i_k}$ and $i \in \{i1,...,ik\}$)

$\exists e_j$ such that: $e_j = \mathbf{In}(k,\pi)$ and $\sum_{p=1,j-1} \#e_p = n!(i1)-1$ and for $q \in [1, k-1]$, $n!(i1+q) = n!(i1)+q$

B) (tuples with constructors of arity greater than 0) Let H be the tuple:

$v_1,\ldots,v_{m-1}, \underline{C}_k(h'_1,\ldots,h'_k), h_{m+1},\ldots,h_n$

where each v_i is either a 0-arity constructor or a variable, then:

$\eta(v_1,\ldots,v_{m-1},\underline{C}_k(h'_1,\ldots,h'_k),h_{m+1},\ldots,h_n) = \mathbf{c}_k(m,\eta(v_1,\ldots,v_{m-1},h'_1,\ldots,h'_k,h_{m+1},\ldots,h_n))$

We prove that η, as defined above, satisfies Proposition 4.1, that is:

$\forall a_1,\ldots,a_n \in HU_c,\ \ a_1,\ldots,a_n \in H \Leftrightarrow \langle a_1,\ldots,a_n\rangle \in \eta(H)$

(Part $\Rightarrow$) We assume $a_1,\ldots,a_n \in H$, i.e.

$\exists \Phi$, instantiation function of variables to ground terms, such that: $H\cdot\Phi = a_1,\ldots,a_n$.

We prove by induction on the structure of the constructors $\underline{C}_k$ that:

$\langle a_1,\ldots,a_n\rangle \in \eta(H)$.

A-(tuples of constant and variables, then $\langle a_1,\ldots,a_n\rangle \in \eta(H) = \mathbf{Pe}(n!, \otimes e_1,\ldots,e_m \otimes))$.

i - obvious because of the definition of π and of the cartesian product $\otimes\_\otimes$.

ii- first note that, since a-, $\mathbf{Pe}(n!,\otimes e_1,\ldots,e_m \otimes) \in HU_n^*$, then denotes sets of n-tuples. Furthermore,

1- if h_i is a 0-arity constructor then $h_i\cdot\Phi = h_i = a_i$ and by definition of **Pe** the i-th component of $\mathbf{Pe}(n!,\otimes e_1,\ldots,e_m \otimes)$ is the $n(i)!$-th component of $\otimes e_1,\ldots,e_m\otimes$, but this is h_i.

2- if h_i is a single occurrence variable then $h_i\cdot\Phi = a_i$ and the $n(i)!$-th component of $\otimes e_1,\ldots,e_m\otimes$ is π.

3- if h_i is a multiple occurrence variable then $h_i\cdot\Phi = a_i$ and also $h_{i1}\cdot\Phi = a_{i1} = \ldots = a_{ik}$, if $i1,\ldots,ik$ are all the occurrences of h_i in H, then the $n(i)!$-th component of $\otimes e_1,\ldots,e_m\otimes$ is $\mathbf{In}(k,\pi)$ and it has the $n(i1)!,\ldots,n(ik)!$ components of $\otimes e_1,\ldots,e_m\otimes$ as its components.

B- (tuples with constructor of arity greater than 0)

By the proof of A above, and assumed, as inductive step, $H' = h_1,\ldots,h_{m-1},h'_1,\ldots,h'_k,h_{m+1},\ldots,h_n$ and $\eta(H')$ to denote the same set, the proof that: $\forall \underline{C}_k$ and $m \in [1,n-k+1]$,

$H = h_1,\ldots,h_{m-1}, \underline{C}_k(h'_1,\ldots,h'_k),h_{m+1},\ldots,h_n$ and $\eta(H)$ denote the same set,

immediately follows from part B) of the definition of η and from the definition of the functions $\mathbf{c}_k$.

(Part $\Leftarrow$) We assume $a_1,\ldots,a_n \in \mathbf{Pe}(n!,\otimes e_1,\ldots,e_m \otimes)$, i.e.

$\forall i \in [1,n],\ \ a_i$ is the $n(i)!$-th component of $\otimes e_1,\ldots,e_m\otimes$.

We prove the existence of an instantiation function of variables to ground terms, Φ, such that:

$H\cdot\Phi = a_1,\ldots,a_n$.

We construct Φ.

1- if a_i is a 0-arity constructor, then by b-1. $h_i = a_i$

2- if a_i is π, then by b-2. h_i is a single occurrence variable and we makes $\Phi(h_i) = a_i$

3- if a_i is component of $\mathbf{In}(k,\pi)$, then by b-3. h_i is a multiple occurrence variable and we makes $\Phi(h_i) = a_i$. ◇

Refined strategies for semantic unification

Pier Giorgio Bosco, Elio Giovannetti and Corrado Moiso
CSELT - Centro Studi E Laboratori Telecomunicazioni
via Reiss Romoli 274 -10148 Torino - Italy

1. Introduction

In the last few years there has been a growing interest on "semantic" unification algorithms based on narrowing or paramodulation, particularly in connection with the attempts to integrate logic and functional programming languages on the basis of first-order-logic with equality. When an equational theory **E** can be put into the form of a canonical rewrite system **R**, the well-known results of [**FA**],[**HU**] ensure that a complete set of E-unifiers of a pair of terms **(t1,t2)**, i.e. a complete set of solutions, in the theory **E**, of the equation **?-t1=t2**, can be found by exhaustively searching the space of all possible R-narrowing sequences of the fictitious term **t1=t2**. The practical interest of this method as a possible basis for logic+functional programming languages has been questioned [**GA**], because of its too wide generality, which translates into the huge amount of redundant search usually involved in it. Some refinements which try to reduce the search space have been proposed, from Hullot's one [**HU**] where only so-called "basic" chains are taken into consideration, to more recent ones, based on innermost strategy [**FR1**],[**FR2**], which require additional conditions on the theory **E** besides canonicity, if completeness is to be preserved.

An alternative approach to equation-solving in a theory can be found in the use, under particular conditions, of resolution instead of narrowing, after transformation of the theory into a set of "flat" Horn clauses, i.e. clauses where functional composition has been replaced by logical conjunction of "flat" literals.

This technique was first developed by Brand [**BR**] in the theorem proving domain, while in logic programming it was introduced mainly by [**BB**] and [**TA**], to achieve integration between logic and functional languages.

In this paper we show how this sort of "flat" or "surface" resolution [**CP**] can be applied to obtain a complete E-unification algorithm for canonical theories which do not necessarily present the distinction between functions and constructors (on which both [**BB**] and [**TA**] are based), and how it allows integration between logic and equational programming by means of a single computational mechanism.

The algorithm is shown to be more efficient than unconstrained (basic) narrowing, owing to the fact that the well-known SLD refinement of resolution (for Horn clauses) can be exploited to reduce the search space without losing completeness.

Moreover, a refined narrowing strategy is derived which is equivalent, in a well defined sense, to the SLD-resolution strategy, and thus has the same advantages in terms of redundancy elimination without requiring, as resolution, a previous flattening of the program.

The argument, based on the correspondence that can be established between narrowing sequences and resolution sequences, is roughly the following. As has been above recalled, narrowing is (the core of) a complete unification algorithm for canonical theories; if the program (i.e. the theory) and the equational goal (i.e. the pair of terms to be unified) are transformed into their flat forms, then for every narrowing chain there is a corresponding resolution chain, so the use of (linear) resolution instead of narrowing preserves completeness; it also preserves soundness, because the flattened program is logically equivalent to the original one. But the flattened program is a set of definite Horn clauses, and therefore SLD strategy - where we recall that S stands for *selection* - can be applied without losing completeness: which means that at each step one literal in the goal is selected, and only the further paths which start from resolution against that literal are explored, unlike in (unrestricted) narrowing, where all the possible choices of the subterm to be narrowed are explored.

Finally, this procedure is translated back into a narrowing algorithm where at each step one subterm is selected, and other subterm choices for the same step are not taken into consideration in the search.

The paper is organized as follows: in section 2 we briefly recall the well-known E-unification algorithm based on narrowing; in section 3 we describe the optimized strategy based on flat resolution; in section 4 we compare it with (unrestricted) narrowing; in section 5 we derive the corrispondingly refined narrowing strategy; in section 6 possible applications to the domain of logic/functional programming are considered; in section 7 we give some non-exhaustive indication of the related work in the field; finally, in section 8 we draw some conclusions.

We will use, among others, the following standard notations:

- occurrences are represented by sequences, possibly empty, of naturals;
- **t/u** is the subterm at the occurrence **u** of **t**;
- **t[u<--r]** is the term **t** with the subterm at the occurrence **u** replaced with **r**.

2. The traditional E-unification algorithm based on narrowing.

Let the equational theory **E** consist of a canonical (i.e. confluent and terminating) rewrite system **R**, and **(t1,t2)** be the pair of terms for which a *complete* set of E-unifiers has to be computed, i.e. **?- t1=t2** is the equation that has to be solved in **E** - recall that a set **S** of E-unifiers of **(t1,t2)** is *complete* iff for every unifier σ there is in **S** a unifier σ' such that $\sigma =_E \alpha\sigma'$, i.e. a unifier σ' E-equal to σ or "more general" than σ ($\sigma' \leq_E \sigma$).

Then the narrowing-based E-unification algorithm is, informally, the following (where **eq** is a functor not occurring in the terms of **R**, which represents the equality symbol "="):

```
unify(t1,t2,R) =
      current-goal := eq(t1,t2)
      current-subst := empty-subst
   1. execute don't-know-non-deterministically 2 or 3
   2. let eq(t1',t2') = current-goal
      if t1' and t2' syntactically unify with mgu σ
      then    (σ current-subst) is a E-unifier of t1 and t2
   3. select don't-know-non-deterministically
     a non-variable subterm current-goal/u of current-goal
      and a rule l-->r
     s.t. current-goal/u and l syntactically unify;
      let   σ   =   mgu (current-goal/u, l)
       current-goal := σ(current-goal[u<--r])
       current-subst := σ(current-subst)
     goto 1.
```

The first refinement, introduced by [**HU**], makes use of the notion of *basic* narrowing, i.e., roughly, a narrowing that may only reduce, at each step, a subterm whose outermost functor is a descendant of (a subterm at) a non-variable occurrence of the initial term.

If **O'(t)** is the set of non-variable occurrences of **t**, and **occ** is the set of the "narrowable" occurrences, the refined algorithm is:

```
unify1(t1,t2,R) =
      current-goal := eq(t1,t2)
      current-subst := empty-subst
      occ:= O'(eq(t1=t2))
   1. execute don't-know-non-deterministically 2 or 3
   2. let eq(t1',t2') = current-goal
      if σ is the mgu of t1' and t2'
      then (σ current-subst)    is a E-unifier of t1 and t2
   3. select don't-know-non-deterministically
     a subterm current-goal/u of current-goal with u belonging to occ
      and a rule l-->r
     s.t. current-goal/u and l syntactically unify;
      let   σ   =   mgu (current-goal/u, l)
       current-goal := σ(current-goal[u<--r])
       current-subst := σ(current-subst)
       occ:=(occ - {v | u≤v, i.e. u is a prefix of v})∪{u.v | v is in O'(r)}
     goto 1.
```

Both algorithms explore all possible choices, respectively, of non-variable subterms and of subterms at basic occurrences.

In the following, narrowing will always be intended as basic narrowing, to which additional refinements will be added.

3. Flat resolution

Narrowing and resolution are two inference rules based on the same sort of mechanism, namely unification between a "piece" of the goal (a subgoal in resolution, a subterm of an equation side in narrowing) and a "piece" of a rule (a clause head in resolution, the lhs of a rewrite rule in narrowing), then application of the unifier both to the whole goal and to the whole rule, and finally creation of a goal by "sticking together" (the instances of) the two "remaining pieces" of the goal and the "rule".

The main difference between narrowing and resolution lies in that the former, to try unification, takes from the goal any subterm of the selected literal, while the latter only takes the whole litteral and so the whole argument-terms.

A transformation of narrowing into resolution is then possible if - both in goal and in rules - terms are "flattened out", i.e. subterms are unnested so that resolution is allowed to apply unification to them; to this end, a new auxiliary variable is introduced for each subterm, and all the new "flat" subterms become conditions, i.e. the body of an equational Horn clause, so that in later steps resolution can apply unification to them too.

Actually, for resolution to be able to mimic narrowing, the lhs's of the rules need not be flattened, because after one of them is unified with the goal's subterm being reduced, its occurrence is replaced, in narrowing, by the respective rhs, and so it is no longer available for reduction in the next steps.

In conclusion, the flattening procedure, unlike the ones described in [**BB**] and [**TA**], on the one hand does not leave constructor-terms unflattened, because the distinction between constructors and functions is not necessarily present, on the other hand, owing to the above remark, does not flatten the lhs's of the rules even if nested functors are present.

The algorithm, for rewrite rules **l-->r** and goals **?-t1=t2** is then, with a sloppy but hopefully self-explaining notation, the following:

flat(l-->r) = if r is a variable (also occurring in l)
then l=r
else l=Z :- flatterm(r,Z) (where Z is a new variable)
flatgoal(t1=t2) = flatterm(t1,Z),flatterm(t2,Z) (where Z is a new variable)
flatterm(f(t1,...,tn),Z) =
let t_{i1},...t_{iq} be the non-variable arguments
let Zi=ti if ti is a variable
Zi=Xk if ti is t_{ik} in
f(Z1,...,Zn)=Z,flatterm(t_{i1},X1),....flatterm(t_{iq},Xq)

If **R** is a (canonical) rewrite system, the corresponding "flat resolution" program $\mathbf{R_{flat}}$ is, of course, the set of Horn clauses obtained by flattening all the rewrite rules of **R**.

Every goal submitted to the system has first to be flattened out; then it can be solved by means of the sole use of SLD-resolution as if the equality symbol were an ordinary predicate, provided that the clause **X=X** is added to the program $\mathbf{R_{flat}}$: resolution against **X=X** corresponds to the final step of the narrowing-based unification algorithm, where the two sides of the goal are syntactically unified.

The transformation is sound because the trasformed program is a logical consequence of the original one and of the equality axioms.

For the proof of completeness of flat resolution, we need the following

Lemma: If $\mathbf{t \dashrightarrow^*_R s}$ through a basic derivation, then there exists a substitution σ, whose domain is the set of the new variables introduced in flattening the term **t**, such that σ**Z=s**, and

$R_{flat} \cup \{X=X\} \models \sigma$ flatterm(t,Z).

The lemma can be proved by induction on the length of the derivation

$t=t0 \dashrightarrow_R t1 \dashrightarrow_R \ldots\ldots\ldots \dashrightarrow_R tn=s$.

We are then able to prove the

Proposition (completeness of flat resolution):

If **R** $\models$ σ**t1**=σ**t2**, then there is an SLD-resolution computation which solves the goal **?-flatgoal(t1=t2)** with respect to the program $\mathbf{R_{flat}} \cup$ **{X=X}** and yields a solution τ such that $\tau \leq_R \sigma$, i.e. **R** $\models$ $\sigma =_R \alpha\tau$, where α is any (possibly empty) substitution.

Proof:

Owing to the canonicity of R, every substitution σ can be normalized to a σ_{nor} = {X:=q | q is the normal form of σ(X)}. From **R** $\models$$\sigma$**t1**=$\sigma$**t2** follows then

R $\models \sigma_{nor}$**t1**$=\sigma_{nor}$**t2**; so there must exist a term **t** such that :

σ_{nor}**t1**$\dashrightarrow^*_R$**t** and σ_{nor}**t2**$\dashrightarrow^*_R$**t**

where the two derivation chains $\dashrightarrow^*_R$ are basic (see [**HU**] lemma 3). Then, by our previous lemma, there are two substitutions ρ**1** and ρ**2** such that:

$\mathbf{R_{flat}} \cup$ **{X=X}** $\models$ ρ**1(flatterm(**σ_{nor}**t1,Z))** with ρ**1(Z)=t** and

$\mathbf{R_{flat}} \cup$ **{X=X}** $\models$ ρ**2(flatterm (**σ_{nor}**t2,Z))** with ρ**2(Z) =t**

putting $\rho = \rho1 \cup \rho2$ we have

$\mathbf{R_{flat}} \cup$ **{X=X}** $\models$ ρ**(flatterm (**σ_{nor}**t1,Z),flatterm (**σ_{nor}**t2,Z))**

Due to the normalization of σ_{nor}, we can write:

$\mathbf{R}_{flat} \cup$ {X=X} $\models \rho\, \sigma_{nor}$(**flatterm (t1,Z),flatterm (t2,Z)**)

i.e. $\mathbf{R}_{flat} \cup$ {X=X} $\models \rho\, \sigma_{nor}$**flatgoal(t1=t2)**

Completeness of SLD-resolution ensures that there is a resolution sequence starting from **?-flatgoal(t1=t2)** which yields a result $\tau' \leq \rho\sigma_{nor}$; then

$$\tau = \tau'/Var(t1=t2) \leq \sigma_{nor} =_R \sigma, \quad \text{i.e.} \quad \tau \leq_R \sigma, \qquad \text{q.e.d.}$$

The lemma completes the proof of the logical equivalence between the transformed and the original program and corresponds to the theorem in [**TA**]; the proposition is the proof of the completeness of the resolution on the flattened program as E-unification algorithm.

As a matter of fact, for every basic narrowing derivation there is a corresponding resolution derivation with the same result: a narrowing step performed, with the application of the rule **l --> r**, on the subterm (at the occurrence) **u** in the goal, translates into the resolution of the flat literal corresponding to the term **u** against the clause **flat(l-->r)**, and into the subsequent resolutions against **X=X** of all the literals corresponding to the subterms of **u** (i.e. to the occurrences **u.v**), because in the narrowing sequence these subterms disappear, the term **u** being replaced by the instance of the rhs of the rewrite rule, or become no longer narrowable; syntactical unification between the two sides of the equation translates in successive resolution against **X=X** of all the literals in the goal.

This translation is possible because at each narrowing step:

- there is a one-to-one correspondence between the elements of the set **occ** of narrowable occurrences in algorithm **unify1**, and the literals in the flattened goal.
- there is a one-to-one correspondence between **current-goal** in the algorithm **unify1**, and the flattened goal; in fact, the goal is always of the form **?-L,t1'=Z,t2'=Z**, where **L** is a set of literals, and there is a substitution σ, such that {X=X} $\models \sigma$**L** and **current-goal=eq(**σ**t1',**σ**t2')**.

Thus every solution found by narrowing is found by flat resolution as well, and that explains again why we were able to extend to the latter the completeness result of [**HU**] holding for the former.

Moreover, the construction - which we will sketch in next section - of an onto-map from the set of all the basic narrowing sequences to the set of all the flat SLD-resolution sequences ensures, among other things, that no unsound solutions can be derived by SLD-resolution (or by generic resolution, due to the completeness of SLD strategy).

4. Narrowing and flat SLD-resolution

It is well known that, in case of Horn clauses, the SLD refinement of resolution preserves completeness, whatever be the rule for selecting the literal to be resolved. Once fixed this rule, there is an onto-map from a subset of the set of all linear resolution derivations, including all successful derivations, to the set of all SLD derivations: the inverse image of an SLD derivation is the set of all the derivations that only differ in the order of selection of the literals.

Let us see now what the meaning of this refinement is with respect to our translation of narrowing into resolution.

We start by mapping the set of successful narrowing sequences onto the set of successful resolution sequences: the inverse image of an SLD-resolution derivation is the set of all the narrowing derivations that satisfy the condition that a narrowing step with the rule **l-->r** is performed at the occurrence **u** of the goal iff the literal corresponding to **u** is resolved against clause **flat(l-->r)**.

Given for example the program

(unflattened)	(flattened)
f(a) --> a	f(a)=X :- a=X
g(X)-->X	g(X)=X

and the goal

?- f(X)=g(Y)	?- f(X)=Z,g(Y)=Z

the SLD-resolution derivation

?- f(X)=Z,g(Y)=Z ?- a=Z,g(Y)=Y ?- g(Y)=a ?-

yielding the solution {X:=a;Y:=a}, is the image of two narrowing sequences:

f(X)=g(Y) -»-> a=g(Y) -»-> a=Y result: {X:=a;Y:=a}

f(X)=g(Y) -»-> f(X)=Y -»-> a=Y result: {X:=a;Y:=a}

So, there are less successful flat SLD-resolutions than successful narrowing chains, without losing completeness.

If the selection rule adopted is the *innermost* rule, this map can be surjectively extended to the set of all the narrowing sequences; of course, in correspondence to failing (finitely or infinitely) narrowing sequences there will be failing resolution sequences.The innermost rule consists in always selecting an *innermost literal* , i.e. a literal of the form f(t1,..,tn)=t , where the ti's are not variables introduced during flattening.

More generally, the above map extension is possible whenever the literals selected are always resolved without variables introduced in the lhs of the literal during flattening being bound; for example, an *outermost* selection rule, like the one used in LEAF [**BB**], would do as well. On the contrary, for an arbitrary selection rule the above extension would not work, because in general there would be failing resolution sequences that do not correspond to any narrowing, as in the following example.

Given the program

(flattened)	(unflattened)
f(a)=Z :- c=Z	f(a)-->c
f(b)=Z :- c=Z	f(b)-->c
a=Z :- b=Z	a --> b

and the goal

?- a=X, f(X)=Z, f(R)=Z	?- f(a)=f(R)

the SLD sequence

?- a=X, f(X)=Z, f(R)=Z

?- b=X, f(X)=Z, f(R)=Z

?- b=a, c=Z, f(R)=Z

failure

does not correspond to any narrowing sequence, because after the step

f(a)=f(R) -»-> f(b)=f(R)

the rule f(a)-->c cannot be applied to f(b) anymore. This kind of failure in resolution is actually the counterpart of a failure in trying unification between the term **f(b)** of the goal and the lhs **f(a)** of the rule **f(a)-->c**.

The comparison between the two algorithms shows that in SLD-resolution the number of successful computations leading to a same solution is smaller than in (unrestricted) narrowing, because all the narrowing derivations that only differ in the selection order of subterms are mapped into one SLD sequence corresponding to one selection order.

For example, given the program

(unflattened)	(flattened)
f(X) --> X	f(X) = X
h(h(X)) --> X	h(h(X))=X
h(a) --> a	h(a)=Z :- a=Z

if the goal is

?-f(h(R))=h(h(a))	?- h(R)=X,f(X)=Z,h(Y)=Z,h(W)=Y,a=W

flat SLD-resolution (with an arbitrary selection rule) and (basic) narrowing compute respectively the following sets of solutions:

Computed value of R	number of successful paths		
	SLD	narrowing	basic-narrowing
a	3	20	11
h(a)	3	19	11
h(h(a))	1	6	2
h(h(h(a)))	1	2	1

The same property holds, in case of an innermost rule, for failing derivations too, as shown in the following example:

given the program

(unflattened)	(flattened)
f(X) --> g(X,X)	f(X) = Z :- g(X,X) = Z
h(a) --> a	h(a) = Z :- a = Z

if the goal is

?- f(h(R))=g(a,h(a))	?- h(R)=X,f(X)=Z,a=Y,a=W,h(W)=T,g(Y,T)=Z

flat SLD-resolution with an innermost selection rule and (basic) narrowing computes the following answers:

	number of successful and failing computations	
	SLD	basic-narrowing
{X:= a}	1	3
failure	7	9

The innermost selection rule can be implemented by means of the leftmost selection rule (selection of the left-most literal, as in Prolog), provided that the "compilation" step puts the flat literals in the right order:

```
flat(l-->r) =  if r is a variable (also occurring in l)
                    then  l=r
                      else   l=Z :-  flatterm(r,Z)   (where Z is a new variable)
```

flatgoal(t1=t2) = flat(t1,Z),flat(t2,Z) (where Z is a new variable)
flatterm(f(t1,...,tn),Z) =
let $t_{i1},...t_{iq}$ be the non-variable arguments
let Zi=ti if ti is a variable
Zi=Xk if ti is t_{ik} in
flatterm(t_{i1},X1),....flatterm(t_{iq},Xq), f(Z1,...,Zn)=Z

5. A complete "selection" narrowing strategy

The above comparison between the two algorithms, which resulted in the estimation of a better efficiency of SLD-resolution with respect to the usual presentations of narrowing, is actually somewhat unfair, because the same "selection" strategy can be applied to narrowing too, so producing a refined, but still complete, algorithm which exactly "mimics" SLD-resolution (with an innermost selection strategy), in the sense that there is a one-to-one correspondence between the set of all the SLD sequences and the set of the narrowing sequences which obey to this refined strategy:

unify2(t1,t2,R) =
current-goal := eq(t1,t2)
occ := O'(eq(t1,t2)) - {<>}
current-subst := empty-subst
1. if occ = ∅ then let eq(t1',t2') = current-goal in
if σ is the mgu of t1' and t2'
then (σ current-subst) is a E-unifier of t1 and t2
else goto 2.
2.**don't-care-nondeterministically-select** from **occ**
an innermost occurrence **u**
(i.e. an occurrence which is not the prefix of any other occurrence in occ)
and **don't-know-nondeterministically-execute** 3 or 4.
3. occ := occ - {**u**}
goto 1.
{corresponding to resolution with X=X}
4. **don't-know-nondeterministically-select l-->r** from R
s.t. **l** and **current-goal/u** syntactically unify;
let σ = mgu (**current-goal/u** , **l**) in
current-goal:= σ(current-goal[**u<--r**])
current-subst:=σ(current-subst)
occ:= (occ-{u}) ∪ {u.v| v is in O'(r)}
goto 1.
{corresponding to resolution with flat(l-->r)}

The algorithm **unify2** achieves exactly the same elimination of redundant computations with respect to unconstrained (basic) narrowing as flat SLD-resolution does, but without requiring the presence of the "compilation" phase with the associated introduction of new variables.

The existence of a one-to-one mapping between innermost-SLD derivations and the derivations obtained with this new algorithm can be easily proved by induction on the length of the sequences.

The algorithm **unify2** is sound because it explores only a subset of the paths followed by **unify1**; so the correctness of flat resolution is confirmed.

Completeness, of course, is direct consequence of completeness of SLD-resolution. An important point to remark is that completeness is only guaranteed if, as in point 3 of the above algorithm, among all the possible narrowing reductions of the subterm selected, also the "null" reduction is taken into account, i.e., also the paths are explored where the subterm selected at each step, instead of being reduced, is excluded from the possible reducible terms for all the subsequent subpaths. That corresponds to resolution against **X=X**, which is necessary in general, although it may be disposed of in particular cases, such as the one of *theories with constructors* : if a distinction is operated between data constructors, which never rewrite, and actual function symbols, and if moreover the actual functions are "everywhere defined", then if the flattening algorithm is modified so as not to apply to data terms, resolution against **X=X**, and therefore "null" narrowing, become useless.

The following is the Prolog program implementing **unify2**, which we are using to carry out comparative experiences:

- **preprocessing on rewrite rules to compute the set of non variable occurrences of rhs:**

```
init :- L-->R, occ(R,OR),assertz(rwr(L,R,OR)),fail.
init.                        ; OR denotes the set O'(R)
occ(T,0)  :- var(T),!.
                             ; 0 indicates that the corresponding term is not to be rewritten
occ(T,[1|Ann]) :- T =.. [F|ARG], occ1(ARG,Ann).
                             ; 1 indicates that the corresponding term is to be rewritten
occ1([],[]).
occ1([TH|TT],[A|Ann]) :-occ(TH,A),occ1(TT,Ann).
```

- **refined narrowing strategy:**

```
unify(T,S):-occ(T,OT),occ(S,OS),!,narrred(T,OT,TR),
                                        narrred(S,OS,SR),TR=SR.
narrred(T,0,T) :- !. ; 0 denotes that this is a term not to be narrowed
narrred(TC,[1|Oarg],TR) :- TC =.. [F|Arg], narrarg(Arg,Oarg,Narg),
                        ; before narrowing a term, its arguments must be narrowed
                                        TC1 =.. [F|Narg],
                        ; now TC1 is an innermost term
                                        narrterm(TC!,TR).
narrterm(T,T).    ; clause corresponding to step 3 of unify2
narrterm(TC,TR) :- rwr(TC,R,OR),narrred(R,OR,TR).
                        ; clause corresponding to step 4 of unify2
```

```
narrarg([],[],[]).
narrarg([A1|Arg],[O1|Oarg],[AR|ArgR]) :- narrred(A1,O1,AR),
                                         narrarg(Arg,Oarg,ArgR).
```

6. Application to Logic/Functional languages

The algorithms presented in the above sections can be most naturally applied to logic programming with equality. Consider a language like the one proposed in [**GM**], for which a program consists of a set of Horn clauses **p:-b1,...,bn**, where the bi's are either predicates or equality, and of an equational theory described by a canonical rewrite system: its execution strategy is the same as the one used for Horn clause programs without equality (Prolog), with syntactic unification replaced by a complete E-unification algorithm. The flattening procedure can be easily extended to deal with this kind of programs (a similar procedure is found in [**TA**]):

flatrule(l-->r) = if r is a variable (also occurring in l)
then l=r
else l=Z :- flatterm(r,Z) (where Z is a new variable)

flatterm(f(t1,...,tn),Z) =
let t_{i1},...t_{iq} be the non-variable arguments
let Zi=ti if ti is a variable
Zi=Xk if ti is t_{ik} in
flatterm(t_{i1},X1),....flatterm(t_{iq},Xq), f(Z1,...,Zn)=Z

flatclause(p(t1,...,pn) :- body) =
let t_{i1},...t_{iq} be the non-variable arguments
let Zi=ti if ti is a variable
Zi=Xk if ti is t_{ik} in
p(Z1,...,Zn) :- flatterm(t_{i1},X1),....flatterm(t_{iq},Xq),flatbody(body)

flatboby(b1,...,bn) = flatgoal(b1),...,flatgoal(bn)

flatgoal(t1=t2) = flat(t1,Z),flat(t2,Z) (where Z is a new variable)

flatgoal(p(t1,...,tn)) =
let t_{i1},...t_{iq} be the non-variable arguments
let Zi=ti if ti is a variable
Zi=Xk if ti is t_{ik} in
flatterm(t_{i1},X1),....flatterm(t_{iq},Xq), p(Z1,...,Zn)

Then, for every goal **G**, a complete set of solutions is found by normal SLD-resolution (provided that the clause **X=X** is added, as usual, to the flattened program).

Alternatively, the selection narrowing algorithm could be used to replace syntactical unification in the resolution procedure running on the original program.

The use of the proposed algorithms reduces the search space both in the unification phase and, by reducing the number of duplicated unifiers, in the overall resolution procedure. Flat SLD-resolution has the advantage of not introducing a different computational mechanism, at the price of a previous compilation stage.

With respect to the amount of computation, flat SLD-resolution and selection narrowing are not equivalent in this context: the first unification algorithm avoids term duplications, and so duplications of narrowing steps introduced by resolution in the second unification algorithm.

This improvement is comparable with the one introduced by basic-chains in the narrowing algorithm.

In spite of this reduction of the search space, completeness is not lost: it is easy, but tedious, to prove that at least all the solutions in normal form (or substitutions more general than them) are computed: starting by a resolution with selection narrowing which computes one of the normalized solutions, it is possible to build a resolution chain where all the occurrences of the same term are narrowed in the same way: this sequence, in turn, is shown to be correspondent to a flat SLD-resolution sequence.

A transformation based on flattening has been used to implement a higher-order functional plus logic programming language [**BG**].

7. Related work

Related work on the subject has been constantly increasing during the last few years. Maybe the closest proposals to the kind of approach here advocated are LEAF [**BB**], already quoted above, and SLOG [**FR2**].

In the LEAF language, based on full Horn-clause logic with equality, the flat-resolution approach is adopted, along with a demand-driven selection strategy which allows to deal with infinite data.

SLOG, on the other hand, adopts the innermost-narrowing approach; as remarked in section 5, since the execution mechanism of SLOG does not admit a step equivalent to "null" narrowing, completeness is only preserved as long as the functions are "everywhere defined"; being the language based on conditional rewrite rules, the interpretation algorithm is also related to the one proposed in [**KA**] (conditional narrowing).

Other similar approaches are those of [**RE**],[**SU**], which use an outermost constructor-driven narrowing strategy: the algorithm in [**SU**] is incomplete, the E-unification algorithm in [**RE**] is based on a notion of equality, called "continous equality", different from the more usual algebraic equality considered in our work. As the pure outermost strategy is incomplete for algebraic equality, an almost-outermost E-unification algorithm was proposed in [**MM**].

The above languages, all based on theories with constructors, do not allow rules whose lhs's contain functional composition (e.g. f(f(X)) --> g(X)), which on the contrary are permitted in the algorithms we have presented. This limitation, which may be undesirable when working with specifications, is sensible if the systems are used as programming languages.

8. Conclusions and future work

As has been remarked in the introduction, the problem - which has a definite importance in connection with attempted extensions of logic programming - of moving from syntactical to so-called "semantical" unification, or E-unification, even though theoretically rather well understood, does not present, in practice, easy solutions. Even if the stepping from a decidable to a semi-decidable procedure is accepted because inherent in the nature of the problem, there still remains a lot of inefficiency researchers who have tried to use narrowing in programming or specification languages [**GA**],[**BE**] including ourselves, feel uncomfortable about.

The algorithms presented in this paper are a step towards the discovery of methods more suitable to practical implementability. Our work also shows how narrowing and resolution, though being quite distinct inference rules, are actually two different versions of a common underlying mechanism, so that refinements found out for resolution can be applied to narrowing as well. The worse behaviour of the usual narrowing-based unification algorithms is therefore merely the result of these straightforward optimizations not being applied to them; when this handicap is eliminated, narrowing becomes as efficient as SLD-resolution.

Nevertheless, what is gained over flat SLD-resolution with this optimized narrowing strategy is a minor advantage, namely the absence of a quite simple compilation phase; that, in our opinion, does not seem to counterbalance the benefit of having just one inference rule, resolution, i.e. one computational model, for which efficient implementations are already available and more efficient ones based on specially-conceived architectures are being developed.

In this paper we have shown how an innermost selection strategy for flat SLD-resolution can easily be compiled; but an innermost selection rule in E-unification has the same drawbacks of innermost strategy in reduction (i.e. call by value): i.e. it performs unnecessary computations. We are therefore trying to define a complete "almost-outermost" strategy for flat SLD-resolutions, where "outermost" literals are selected, so that resolution with clauses different from X=X is only applied on request. This strategy, unlike the innermost case, cannot be implemented by means of a trivial compilation, because the atom selection order is not known statically.

Acknowledgement

This work has been partially sponsored by EEC through ESPRIT Project 415 "Parallel Architectures and Languages for Advanced Information Processing - a VLSI-directed Approach".

9. References

BB **R. Barbuti, M. Bellia, G. Levi** and **M. Martelli**, LEAF: A language which integrates logic, equations and functions. In *Logic Programming: Functions, Relations and Equations* , D. DeGroot and G. Lindstrom, Eds.

(Prentice-Hall, 1985), 201-238.

BE **D. Bert,** personal communication.

BG **P.G. Bosco** and **E. Giovannetti,** IDEAL: an Ideal DEductive Applicative Language. *Proc. 1986 Symp. on Logic Programming* (IEEE Comp. Society Press, 1986), 89-94.

BR **D. Brand**, Proving theorems with the modification method. *SIAM J. Comput.* 4 (1975), 412-430.

CP **P.T. Cox** and **T. Pietrzykowski,** Surface deduction: a uniform mechanism for Logic Programming. *Proc. 1985 Symp. on Logic Programming* (IEEE Comp. Society Press, 1985), 220-227.

FA **M. Fay**, First order unification in an equational theory. *Proc. 4th Workshop on Automated Deduction* (1979), 161-167.

FR1 **L. Fribourg**, A narrowing procedure for theories with constructors. Proc. 7th Int. Conf. on Automated Deduction, *LNCS 170* (Springer Verlag, 1984), 259-301.

FR2 **L. Fribourg**, SLOG: A logic programming language interpreter based on clausal superposition and rewriting. *Proc. 1985 Symp. on Logic Programming* (IEEE Comp. Society Press, 1985), 172-184.

GA **H. Gallaire**, Logic programming: further developments. *Proc. of the 1985 Symp. on Logic Programming* (IEEE Comp. Society Press, 1985), 88-96.

GM **J.A. Goguen** and **J. Meseguer**, Equality, types, modules and (why not?) generics for logic programming. *J. Logic Programming 1* (1984), 179-210.

HU **J.-M. Hullot**, Canonical forms and unification. *Proc. 5th Conf. on Automated Deduction, LNCS 87* (Springer Verlag, 1980), 318-334.

KA **S. Kaplan,** Fair conditional term rewriting systems: Unification, termination and confluence. *Technical Report no. 194* , University ofOrsay (1984).

MM **A. Martelli, C. Moiso** and **G.F. Rossi,** An algorithm for unification in equational theories. *Proc. 1986 Symp. on Logic Programming* (IEEE Comp. Society Press, 1986), 180-186.

RE **U.S. Reddy**, Narrowing as the operational semantics of functional languages. *Proc. 1985 Symp. on Logic Programming* (IEEE Comp. Society Press, 1985), 138-151.

SU **P.A. Subrahmanyam** and **J.-H. You**, FUNLOG = functions + logic: A computational model integrating functional and logic programming. *Proc. 1984 Int. Symp. on Logic Programming* (IEEE Comp. Society Press, 1984), 144-153.

TA **H. Tamaki,** Semantics of a logic programming language with a reducibility predicate. *Proc. of the 1984 Symp. on Logic Programming* (IEEE Comp. Society Press, 1984), 259-264

Extensional Models for Polymorphism

Val Breazu-Tannen
MIT Laboratory for Computer Science
545 Technology Sq., Cambridge, MA 02139, USA

Thierry Coquand
INRIA
Domaine de Voluceau, 78150 Rocquencourt, France

Abstract. We present a general method for constructing extensional models for the polymorphic lambda calculus—the *polymorphic extensional collapse.* The method yields models that satisfy additional, computationally motivated constraints like having only two polymorphic booleans and having only the numerals as polymorphic integers. Moreover the method yields models that prove that the polymorphic lambda calculus can be *conservatively* added to arbitrary algebraic data type specifications, even with complete transfer of the computational power to the added data types.

1 Introduction

The design of functional and object-oriented programming languages has recently witnessed the widespread adoption of polymorphic type systems. A list of examples that is by no means exhaustive includes, in addition to the archetype ML [Gordon *et al.* 1979], such languages as Miranda [Turner 1985], Poly [Matthews 1985], Amber [Cardelli 1985], polymorphic FQL [Nikhil 1984], Ponder [Fairbairn 1982], and Hope [Burstall *et al.* 1980], while an excellent survey of the field is provided by [Cardelli & Wegner 1985].

We adopt the Girard-Reynolds polymorphic lambda calculus (henceforth denoted $\lambda^{\forall}$) as a formal setting for studying properties of such languages. Our concern here will be to construct models for $\lambda^{\forall}$ that satisfy additional constraints computationally motivated. These constraints have to do with the interaction between the type discipline of $\lambda^{\forall}$ and the data types with which we compute, eg. integers, booleans etc. An example follows.

Consider the representation of the integers in $\lambda^{\forall}$ where the numerals are taken to be the closed terms of type

$$\textit{polyint} \stackrel{\text{def}}{=} \forall t.\,(t \to t) \to t \to t\ .$$

The numeral corresponding to the integer n is

$$\tilde{n} \stackrel{\text{def}}{=} \lambda t.\,\lambda f{:}\,t \to t.\,\lambda x{:}\,t.\,f^n x\ .$$

The first author was supported in part by an IBM Graduate Fellowship and in part by NSF Grant DCR–8511190

One can then define

$$Add \stackrel{\text{def}}{=} \lambda u{:}polyint.\ \lambda v{:}polyint.\ \lambda t.\ \lambda f{:}t \to t.\ \lambda x{:}t.\ utf(vtfx) \quad : polyint \to polyint \to polyint$$

and verify that $\lambda^\forall$ proves

(1) $$Add\,\widetilde{m}\,\widetilde{n} = \widetilde{m+n}\ .$$

The arithmetic functions that are numeralwise representable in the same way addition is represented above are exactly the functions which are provably total recursive in second-order Peano arithmetic [Girard 1972], [Statman 1981], [Fortune *et al.* 1983]. To date, no "natural" examples of total recursive functions that are not in this class are known and one can argue that such computational power is adequate for most purposes [Leivant 1983], [Reynolds 1985]. Therefore it appears that $\lambda^\forall$ can be regarded as a programming language already equipped with a type of integers and, as it turns out, also with one of booleans:

$$polybool \stackrel{\text{def}}{=} \forall t.\, t \to t \to t$$

$$True \stackrel{\text{def}}{=} \lambda t.\ \lambda x{:}t.\ \lambda y{:}t.\ x$$

$$False \stackrel{\text{def}}{=} \lambda t.\ \lambda x{:}t.\ \lambda y{:}t.\ y$$

as well as many other familiar data types [Reynolds 1985].

There is a problem, though. While we would like to reason about the terms of type *polyint* as if they actually *are* the integers, the pure $\lambda^\forall$ is *not* sufficient for that. For example, by a simple Church-Rosser argument,

(2) $$Add\,u\,v = Add\,v\,u$$

with arbitrary u, v: *polyint* is *not* provable in $\lambda^\forall$. But if u and v are *numerals* then the equation (2) follows from (1). Hence the question: is it consistent to assume equation (2) as a further axiom of $\lambda^\forall$? This would follow from the existence of a model in which the *only* elements of type *polyint* are the (denotations of the) numerals. [1]

Such a question (actually for *polybool*) was asked in [Meyer 1986]. A positive answer was obtained in two ways using two different model constructions [Moggi 1986a], [Coquand 1986]. Both constructions used partial equivalence relations to interpret types, suggesting that there might be some relationship between them and, indeed, a common generalization was found [Breazu-Tannen 1986].

We are going to present this general construction, which we call *polymorphic extensional collapse*, that has as particular cases both the HEO-like model construction [Mitchell 1986b] [2] (the one used in [Moggi 1986a]) and the closed type/closed term model construction (the one used in [Coquand 1986]).

Another application of our general construction is to show that arbitrary algebras can be fully and faithfully embedded in models of $\lambda^\forall$. Moreover, such embeddings can be achieved in a manner that connects the computational power of $\lambda^\forall$ to the embedded algebras. The *conservative extension* theorems of [Breazu-Tannen & Meyer 1987] then follow as corollaries from our full and faithful embedding results.

The investigation of these conservative extension situations started from the same concern that suggested the question asked in [Meyer 1986], namely, is it possible to have data types with

[1] This account is inspired from [Meyer *et al.* 1987] where another example, involving *polybool*, is presented.

[2] [Mitchell 1986b] also contains a short history of the idea of interpreting types using partial equivalence relations. We want to add one reference to Mitchell's account, namely [Gandy 1956], which introduced the extensional collapse model construction for simple types, later called the "Gandy hull" in [Statman 1980].

"classical" properties live in a computational framework? In [Breazu-Tannen & Meyer 1987] it is remarked that unrestricted recursion is not compatible with "classical" properties. Then, computation done within the framework of the type discipline of $\lambda^\forall$ is offered as an alternative. However, unlike in the above discussion, one does not use the built-in integers, booleans, etc.; instead one *adds* such data types to $\lambda^\forall$ as algebraic data type specifications. The advantage is that we can postulate for these added data types whatever equations we wish, so that problems like the one with equation (2) do not arise.

The conservative extension theorems assure us that we can continue to reason about algebraic data expressions "classically", i.e., using the data type specification, even when these expressions occur in the computational framework provided by $\lambda^\forall$.

It is possible that there are some connections between the model constructions we describe here and the work reported in [Scedrov 1986]. However, [Scedrov 1986] does not give enough details for us to be able to verify this yet.

Finally, we should mention that detailed proofs of most of the new results mentioned here are also included in [Breazu-Tannen].

2 The polymorphic lambda calculus

2.1 Syntax

We assume we have an infinite set of *type variables*. By convention, t will range over type variables while σ, τ will range over *type expressions* which are defined by the grammar:

$$\tau ::= t \mid \sigma \to \tau \mid \forall t.\, \sigma\,.$$

We identify type expressions that differ only in the names of bound variables. The set of free type variables of σ will be denoted $fv(\sigma)$.

We also assume we have a separate infinite set of *variables*. By convention, x will range over variables while M, N will range over *raw terms* which are defined by the grammar:

$$M ::= x \mid MN \mid \lambda x{:}\sigma.\, M \mid M\sigma \mid \lambda t.\, M\,.$$

Again, we identify raw terms that differ only in the names of bound variables. The set of free variables of the term M will be denoted $FV(M)$ while the set of free *type* variables of M will be denoted $fv(M)$.

Type assignments are partial functions that map variables to type expressions and that have *finite* domain. Alternatively, we can regard type assignments as finite sets of pairs $x{:}\sigma$ such that no x occurs twice. We will use Δ to range over type assignments. When we write $\Delta, x{:}\sigma$ we mean a type assignment Δ' that contains $x{:}\sigma$ and such that $\Delta = \Delta' \setminus \{x{:}\sigma\}$.

Typing judgments have the form $\Delta \vdash M : \sigma$. Here are the type-checking rules:

(*variable introduction*) $\qquad x{:}\sigma \vdash x : \sigma$

(*extension*) $\qquad \dfrac{\Delta \vdash M : \sigma}{\Delta, x{:}\tau \vdash M : \sigma} \quad x \notin dom\Delta$

(→ *introduction*)
$$\frac{\Delta, x{:}\sigma \vdash M : \tau}{\Delta \vdash \lambda x{:}\sigma.\, M : \sigma \to \tau}$$

(→ *elimination*)
$$\frac{\Delta \vdash M : \sigma \to \tau \quad \Delta \vdash N : \sigma}{\Delta \vdash MN : \tau}$$

(∀ *introduction*)
$$\frac{\Delta \vdash M : \sigma}{\Delta \vdash \lambda t.\, M : \forall t.\, \sigma} \quad t \notin fv(ran\Delta)$$

(∀ *elimination*)
$$\frac{\Delta \vdash M : \forall t.\, \sigma}{\Delta \vdash M\tau : \sigma[t := \tau]}$$

Equations have the form
$$\Delta \,.\, M = N : \sigma$$
where the role of Δ and σ is to help check that the equational reasoning is type-correct. The *core* proof system for deriving equations, denoted $\lambda^{\forall}$, consists of

(*extension*)
$$\frac{\Delta \,.\, M = N : \sigma}{\Delta, x{:}\tau \vdash M = N : \sigma} \quad x \notin dom\Delta$$

reflexivity, symmetry, transitivity, congruence w.r.t. application,

(ξ)
$$\frac{\Delta, x{:}\sigma \,.\, M = N : \tau}{\Delta \,.\, \lambda x{:}\sigma.\, M = \lambda x{:}\sigma.\, N : \sigma \to \tau}$$

β, η, congruence w.r.t. polymorphic application, *type* ξ,

(*type* β)
$$\Delta \,.\, (\lambda t.\, M)\tau = M[t := \tau] : \sigma[t := \tau]$$
$$\text{where } \Delta \vdash M : \sigma \,,\ t \notin fv(ran\Delta)$$

(*type* η)
$$\Delta \,.\, \lambda t.\, Mt = M : \forall t.\, \sigma$$
$$\text{where } \Delta \vdash M : \forall t.\, \sigma \,,\ t \notin fv(ran\Delta) \,,\ t \notin fv(M)$$

As usual, conversion can be analyzed by a reduction system. We will call "$\beta\eta$-reduction" the notion of reduction consisting of both the "regular" and the "type" β and η. The definition is omitted here.

2.2 Semantics

An *algebra of polymorphic types*, $\mathcal{T}$, consists of the following:

- a non-empty set T of *types*;
- a binary operation $\rightarrow$ on T;
- a non-empty set $[T \Rightarrow T]$ of functions from T to T;
- a map $\forall$ from $[T \Rightarrow T]$ to T;

such that the following inductive definition of an assignment of meanings in T to type expressions in type environments is possible (we define a *type environment* to be a map from type variables to T and we will use η to range over type environments):

1. $[\![t]\!]\eta \;=\; \eta(t)$
2. $[\![\sigma \rightarrow \tau]\!]\eta \;=\; [\![\sigma]\!]\eta \;\rightarrow [\![\tau]\!]\eta$
3. $[\![\forall t.\, \sigma]\!]\eta \;=\; \forall(\lambda a \in T.\, [\![\sigma]\!]\eta\{t{:=}\, a\})$

By "the definition is possible" we understand that each inductive application of step 3 is defined, i.e., $\lambda a \in T.\, [\![\sigma]\!]\eta\{t{:=}\, a\} \;\in\; [T \Rightarrow T]$. Here $\eta\{t{:=}\, a\}$ is the type environment equal to η everywhere except at t where it takes the value a.

A *polymorphic lambda interpretation* (p.l.i.) consists of the following:

- an algebra of polymorphic types, $\mathcal{T}$;
- a set D_a for each type $a \in T$ (the *domain* of a);
- a binary operation $\cdot_{ab} : D_{a\rightarrow b} \times D_a \longrightarrow D_b$ for each pair of types $a, b \in T$ (functional application);
- a binary operation $\cdot_\phi : D_{\forall(\phi)} \times T \longrightarrow \bigcup\{D_a\}$ for each function $\phi \in [T \Rightarrow T]$, such that $p \cdot_\phi a \in D_{\phi(a)}$ (polymorphic application);

Given a type assignment Δ and a type environment η, we define an $\Delta\eta$*-environment* to be a function ρ that maps $dom\Delta$ to $\bigcup\{D_a\}$ such that $\rho(x) \in D_{[\![\Delta(x)]\!]\eta}$ for each variable $x \in dom\Delta$. As with type assignments, we will regard $\Delta\eta$-environments as finite sets of pairs $x{:}\,d$, extending to them the notational convention $\rho, x{:}\,d$. With this, the final component of a polymorphic lambda interpretation is

- a "meaning" map that assigns to every typing judgment $\Delta \vdash M : \sigma$ that is *derivable* and every type environment η a map $[\![\Delta \vdash M : \sigma]\!]\eta$ from $\Delta\eta$-environments to $D_{[\![\sigma]\!]\eta}$ such that

  1. $[\![x{:}\sigma \vdash x : \sigma]\!]\eta\rho \;=\; \rho(x)$
  2. $[\![\Delta, x{:}\tau \vdash M : \sigma]\!]\eta\rho = [\![\Delta \vdash M : \sigma]\!]\eta\rho'$

     where $x \notin dom\Delta$ and $\rho' \stackrel{\text{def}}{=} \rho\,|_{dom\Delta}$

3. $[\![\Delta \vdash MN : \tau]\!]\eta\rho = [\![\Delta \vdash M : \sigma \to \tau]\!]\eta\rho \cdot_{ab} [\![\Delta \vdash N : \sigma]\!]\eta\rho$

   where $a \stackrel{\text{def}}{=} [\![\sigma]\!]\eta$ and $b \stackrel{\text{def}}{=} [\![\tau]\!]\eta$

4. $[\![\Delta \vdash \lambda x{:}\sigma. M : \sigma \to \tau]\!]\eta\rho \cdot_{ab} d = [\![\Delta, x{:}\sigma \vdash M : \tau]\!]\eta\rho'$

   where $a \stackrel{\text{def}}{=} [\![\sigma]\!]\eta$, $b \stackrel{\text{def}}{=} [\![\tau]\!]\eta$, $d \in D_a$ and $\rho' \stackrel{\text{def}}{=} \rho, x{:}d$

5. $[\![\Delta \vdash M\tau : \sigma[t{:=}\tau]]\!]\eta\rho = [\![\Delta \vdash M : \forall t. \sigma]\!]\eta\rho \cdot_\phi [\![\tau]\!]\eta$

   where $\phi \stackrel{\text{def}}{=} \lambda a \in T. [\![\sigma]\!]\eta\{t{:=}a\}$

6. $[\![\Delta \vdash \lambda t. M : \forall t. \sigma]\!]\eta\rho \cdot_\phi a = [\![\Delta \vdash M : \sigma]\!]\eta\{t{:=}a\}\,\rho$

   where $a \in T$ and $\phi \stackrel{\text{def}}{=} \lambda a \in T. [\![\sigma]\!]\eta\{t{:=}a\}$

7. if $\forall t \in fv(ran\Delta) \cup fv(M),\ \eta(t) = \eta'(t)$ then $[\![\Delta \vdash M : \sigma]\!]\eta = [\![\Delta \vdash M : \sigma]\!]\eta'$

An equation $\Delta\,.\,M = N{:}\sigma$ is *valid* in a polymorphic lambda interpretation when $[\![\Delta \vdash M{:}\sigma]\!]\eta = [\![\Delta \vdash N : \sigma]\!]\eta$ for every η.

A p.l.i. is a quite general concept. For example, not even basic axioms like β are necessarily valid in arbitrary p.l.i.'s.

A *model* of the polymorphic lambda calculus is a polymorphic lambda interpretation in which functional and polymorphic applications are *extensional*:

$$(\forall d \in D_a, f \cdot_{ab} d = g \cdot_{ab} d) \Longrightarrow f = g \quad f, g \in D_{a \to b}$$

$$(\forall a \in T, p \cdot_\phi a = q \cdot_\phi a) \Longrightarrow p = q \quad p, q \in D_{\forall(\phi)} \,.$$

This definition is equivalent and, in fact, very close to the one in [Bruce & Meyer 1984].

A model is *trivial* when all its domains have at most one element. It is not hard to check that a model is trivial if and only if it equates *True* and *False* (i.e., $.\ True = False : polybool$ is valid).

It is easy to see that the proof rules of the core system $\lambda^\forall$ are sound for this notion of model. As was recently explained in [Meyer *et al.* 1987], completeness is more complicated. One is, of course, interested in the strong kind of completeness, i.e., completeness of reasoning from additional premises. In [Bruce & Meyer 1984] such a result is stated, but it amounts to completeness of the core proof system extended with the rule:

$$(\textit{discharging}) \qquad \frac{\Delta, x{:}\sigma\,.\,M = N : \tau}{\Delta\,.\,M = N : \tau} \qquad x \notin FV(M) \cup FV(N)$$

for the subclass of models with all types non-empty. (Discharging is *not sound*, in general, in models that can have empty type domains.)

The model definition presented here allows empty types and, in fact, if additional constraints like having only two polymorphic booleans or having only the numerals as polymorphic integers are to hold, then some type domains *must* be empty [Meyer *et al.* 1987].

In [Meyer *et al.* 1987] it is stated that the core proof system $\lambda^\forall$ (no discharging), while sound, is not complete for the class of all models. The paper then gives an extension of the proof system that is sound and complete for all models. This extension involves modifying the syntax of the equations to allow "type emptiness" assertions to be added to the type assignments as well as new axioms and inference rules. Our full and faithful embedding constructions (Subsection 4.3) imply the conservative extension results of [Breazu-Tannen & Meyer 1987] w.r.t. to this new extended proof system.

As far as the *model constructions* described in the present paper, we have noted that it does not matter which of the three proof systems we use to construct our closed term interpretations. Indeed, by Church-Rosser arguments, discharging is a *derived rule* in the pure $\lambda^{\forall}$ theory or in theories axiomatized by additional equations that can be analyzed with *delta reduction* rules, like the ones we use in Subsection 4.3. Thus, the closed type/closed term constructions of Subsections 4.2 and 4.3 are the same as the ones that would be obtained using the extended proof system of [Meyer *et al.* 1987] or the proof system with discharging.

2.3 Logical relations

The concept of second-order logical relation was introduced in [Mitchell & Meyer 1985]. Here we will review only a particular case of this concept, namely, the case that we need for the polymorphic extensional collapse.

Given a polymorphic lambda interpretation, a *logical relation* on it is a family of binary relations $\mathcal{R} = \{R_a | a \in T, R_a \subseteq D_a \times D_a\}$ such that

$$f\ R_{a\to b}\ g \text{ iff } \forall d \forall e\ \ d\ R_a\ e \implies f \cdot_{ab} d\ R_b\ g \cdot_{ab} e$$

and

$$p\ R_{\forall(\phi)}\ q \text{ iff } \forall a\ \ p \cdot_{\phi} a\ \ R_{\phi(a)}\ \ q \cdot_{\phi} a\ .$$

Proposition 2.1 (Fundamental property of logical relations) *Assume we have a logical relation $\mathcal{R}$ on a polymorphic lambda interpretation. For any derivable typing judgment $\Delta \vdash M : \sigma$, any type environment η and any two $\Delta\eta$-environments ρ_1 and ρ_2, if*

$$\forall x \in dom\Delta, \quad \rho_1(x)\ R_{[\![\Delta(x)]\!]\eta}\ \rho_2(x)$$

then

$$[\![\Delta \vdash M : \sigma]\!]\eta\rho_1\ R_{[\![\sigma]\!]\eta}\ [\![\Delta \vdash M : \sigma]\!]\eta\rho_2\ .$$

We will make essential use of this property in the polymorphic extensional collapse and, in fact, the definition of the concept of polymorphic lambda interpretation was engineered to consist of the "minimum necessary" to make the proof of Proposition 2.1 work.

3 Polymorphic extensional collapse

If D is a set, let $per(D)$ denote the set of *partial equivalence* (i.e., symmetric and transitive but not necessarily reflexive) *relations* (p.e.r.'s) on D. Let $R \in per(D)$. We denote by $R[d]$ the p.e.r. class of d w.r.t. R. Note that $R[d] \neq \emptyset$ iff $d\ R\ d$. The *quotient set* D/R is the set of all nonempty p.e.r. classes w.r.t R.

3.1 Factoring by a logical partial equivalence relation

Suppose that we have a polymorphic lambda interpretation $\mathcal{I}$ together with a logical relation $\mathcal{R}$ on it such that each R_a is a p.e.r. We call $\mathcal{R}$ a *logical p.e.r.* Then, we can construct a new polymorphic lambda interpretation, $\mathcal{I}/\mathcal{R}$ (the *quotient* of $\mathcal{I}$ by $\mathcal{R}$), which is actually extensional, *i.e.*, a *model*.

The algebra of types will be the same. As domains we take the quotient sets D_a/R_a. Since $\mathcal{R}$ is logical, it is also a congruence w.r.t. functional and polymorphic application therefore application on the quotient sets is defined straightforwardly.

Claim. Both functional and polymorphic application are extensional.

For polymorphic application this is immediate. For functional application it can be seen that

$$\text{if } f\ R_{a\to b}\ f \text{ and } g\ R_{a\to b}\ g \text{ and } (\forall d\ \ f\cdot_{ab} d\ \ R_b\ \ g\cdot_{ab} d) \text{ then } f\ R_{a\to b}\ g\,.$$

To show how to define the meaning function let us fix a derivable typing statement $\Delta \vdash M : \sigma$ and a type environment η. For any $\mathcal{I}/\mathcal{R}$-$\Delta\eta$-environment $\hat{\rho}$, choose an $\mathcal{I}$-$\Delta\eta$-environment ρ such that

$$\forall x \in dom\Delta,\ \ \hat{\rho}(x) \;=\; R_{[\![\Delta(x)]\!]\eta}[\rho(x)]$$

and then define

$$[\![\Delta \vdash M : \sigma]\!]^{\mathcal{I}/\mathcal{R}}\eta\hat{\rho} \;\stackrel{\text{def}}{=}\; R_{[\![\sigma]\!]\eta}[[\![\Delta \vdash M : \sigma]\!]^{\mathcal{I}}\eta\rho]\,.$$

Indeed, by Proposition 2.1 the definition does not depend on the choice of ρ and also $[\![\Delta \vdash M : \sigma]\!]^{\mathcal{I}}\eta\rho$ is related to itself hence its p.e.r. class is nonempty.

Any equation valid in $\mathcal{I}$ is valid in $\mathcal{I}/\mathcal{R}$. The converse is in general not true since there can be pairs of closed terms whose meanings in $\mathcal{I}$ are distinct but *related* by $\mathcal{R}$ and therefore whose meanings in $\mathcal{I}/\mathcal{R}$ are the same p.e.r. class.

If $\mathcal{I}$ is actually a *model* then the relation consisting of the identity on each of its types is actually logical (because of extensionality) and the model $\mathcal{I}/Id$ is isomorphic to $\mathcal{I}$. Therefore, the class of models obtained as quotients of arbitrary polymorphic lambda interpretations by logical p.e.r.'s is the same as the class of all models.

3.2 Tagging the types with partial equivalence relations

In order to take advantage of the construction in the previous subsection, assuming that one has a p.l.i., how does one construct a logical p.e.r. on it so that one would then obtain a model by taking the quotient?

The idea is the same as the one behind Girard's "candidats de réductibilité": since we don't know in advance which p.e.r.'s we will need, we will put in all of them!

Starting with an arbitrary polymorphic lambda interpretation $\mathcal{I}$ we show how to construct a new one, $\mathcal{I}^{per}$, that has a logical p.e.r. on it and, moreover, the same equations are valid in $\mathcal{I}$ and $\mathcal{I}^{per}$.

First, from the algebra of types $\mathcal{T}$ construct $\mathcal{T}^{per}$ as follows:

- the new types, T^{per}, are pairs $<a, R>$ with $a \in T$ and $R \in per(D_a)$;

- $<a,R> \to <b,S> \stackrel{\text{def}}{=} <a \to b, R \to S>$ where $R \to S$ is defined by

$$f\ R \to S\ g \text{ iff } \forall d \forall e\ d\ R\ e \implies f \cdot_{ab} d\ S\ g \cdot_{ab} e$$

  and is shown to be a p.e.r. also;

- $[T^{per} \Rightarrow T^{per}]$ consists of the functions determined (one-to-one) by pairs $<\phi, H>$ where $\phi \in [T \Rightarrow T]$ and H is a family of maps

$$H_a : per(D_a) \longrightarrow per(D_{\phi(a)})$$

  one for each type $a \in T$;

- $\forall(<\phi, H>) \stackrel{\text{def}}{=} <\forall(\phi), \forall(H)>$ where $\forall(H)$ is defined by

$$p\ \forall(H)\ q \text{ iff } \forall <a,R> \in T^{per}\ \ p \cdot_\phi a\ H_a(R)\ q \cdot_\phi a\ .$$

  and is, of course, also a p.e.r.

To check that this is an algebra of polymorphic types, one further shows that the inductive definition of meaning is possible. Moreover

$$proj_1([\![\sigma]\!]^{T^{per}} \eta) = [\![\sigma]\!]^T (proj_1 \circ \eta)\ .$$

The rest of the definition of the polymorphic lambda interpretation is by "taking the first projection of the types":

- $D_{<a,R>} \stackrel{\text{def}}{=} D_a$;
- $f \cdot_{<a,R><b,S>} d \stackrel{\text{def}}{=} f \cdot_{ab} d$;
- $p \cdot_{<\phi,H>} a \stackrel{\text{def}}{=} p \cdot_\phi a$;
- $[\![\Delta \vdash M : \sigma]\!]^{I^{per}} \eta \stackrel{\text{def}}{=} [\![\Delta \vdash M : \sigma]\!]^I (proj_1 \circ \eta)$.

Clearly, any equation valid in I is valid in I^{per}. The converse is also true since any T-type environment is the first projection of some T^{per}-type environment.

The benefit of all this is that now we have at each type $<a,R>$ a p.e.r., namely R, and, more importantly, this collection of p.e.r.'s, call it $\mathcal{R}^{per}$, is a *logical relation* on I^{per} as one can readily check.

We define the *polymorphic extensional collapse* of I to be the model $I^{per}/\mathcal{R}^{per}$.

The models obtained as polymorphic extensional collapses of arbitrary polymorphic lambda interpretations are not arbitrary at all. For example, it is not hard to see that in all of them the type $\forall t.\, t$ is *empty*. This implies the validity of certain non-trivial equations, for example

$$True\ \forall t.\, t = False\ \forall t.\, t\ .$$

An interesting open question is to obtain a characterization of the set of equations that are valid in all such models.

4 Applications

4.1 HEO-like models

These models are obtained by applying the polymorphic extensional collapse to "erase-types" polymorphic lambda interpretations, i.e., ones in which the terms are interpreted by first erasing the type information and then interpreting the resulting untyped terms in, say, some combinatory algebra (via the usual translation into combinatory terms; see [Barendregt 1984]).

We consider untyped lambda terms built from the same variables used for the polymorphic lambda terms. Again, we identify terms that differ only in the name of the bound variables.

An *untyped lambda interpretation* (called *pseudo-λ-structure* in [Hindley & Longo 1980]) , $\mathcal{U}$, consists of the following:

- a non-empty set D;
- a binary operation $\cdot$ on D (application);
- a "meaning" map that assigns to every untyped lambda term M and every D-environment π an element $[\![M]\!]\pi$ of D (we define a *D-environment* to be a map from variables to D and we will use π to range over D-environments) such that:

  1. $[\![x]\!]\pi = \pi(x)$
  2. $[\![MN]\!]\pi = [\![M]\!]\pi \cdot [\![N]\!]\pi$
  3. $[\![\lambda x.\, M]\!]\pi \cdot d = [\![M]\!]\pi\{x := d\}$ where $d \in D$
  4. if $\forall x \in FV(M),\ \pi_1(x) = \pi_2(x)$ then $[\![M]\!]\pi_1 = [\![M]\!]\pi_2$

If application is also extensional we get the usual concept of *model of the untyped λβη-calculus* [Hindley & Longo 1980], [Meyer 1982], [Barendregt 1984].

Any combinatory algebra yields an untyped lambda interpretation. Namely, the meaning map $[\![M]\!]\pi$ is defined by first translating M into a combinatory term [Barendregt 1984] and then interpreting the result in the algebra.

Now, starting from an arbitrary algebra of polymorphic types $\mathcal{T}$ and an arbitrary untyped lambda interpretation $\mathcal{U}$, we construct the "erase-types" polymorphic lambda interpretation , $\mathcal{I}^{\mathcal{T},\mathcal{U}}$ as follows:

The algebra of types is, of course, $\mathcal{T}$. The domains of all types are equal to D, the domain of $\mathcal{U}$. Functional application is given by the application in $\mathcal{U}$. Polymorphic application simply erases the type:

$$p \cdot_\phi a \stackrel{\text{def}}{=} p\,.$$

Finally, the meaning map is defined by

$$[\![\Delta \vdash M : \sigma]\!]^{\mathcal{I}^{\mathcal{U}}}\eta\rho \stackrel{\text{def}}{=} [\![Erase(M)]\!]^{\mathcal{U}}\pi$$

where π is some D-environment that takes the same values as ρ on $FV(M)$ (by (4) above only these values matter) and $Erase(\lambda x{:}\sigma.\, M) = \lambda x.\, Erase(M)$, $Erase(M\sigma) = Erase(M)$, $Erase(\lambda t.\, M) = Erase(M)$, etc.

We then define the *HEO-like model* with parameters $\mathcal{T}$ and $\mathcal{U}$ to be the polymorphic extensional collapse of $\mathcal{I}^{\mathcal{T},\mathcal{U}}$.

The construction can be further generalized to start from *partial* combinatory algebras, just like the original HEO_2 model [3] [Girard 1972], [Troelstra (ed.) 1973], as was discovered by independently by Gordon Plotkin and Eugenio Moggi.

Moggi's ingenious construction [Moggi 1986a] of a model that has exactly two elements of type *polybool* amounts to—in the terminology of this paper—the HEO-like model whose parameters are the trivial algebra of types (just one type) and the open term model of the untyped lambda calculus.

Such HEO-like models whose second parameters are actually untyped lambda models (untyped application is already extensional) are particularly intriguing. This is because the corresponding "erase-types" polymorphic lambda interpretations are *already* models: functional application is extensional because the untyped application is while polymorphic application is always (trivially) extensional! However, these "erase-types" models are much too coarse: all elements have all types! The point of continuing with a polymorphic extensional collapse—as suggested by Moggi's idea—seems therefore to be the "pruning" of the model, while preserving extensionality.

Another connection is with the *PER models* of [Mitchell 1986b]. PER models are, in general, *not* obtained by (what we defined as) polymorphic extensional collapse (for example, one can construct PER models that have all types non-empty). Nonetheless, we have developed enough terminology to be able to say what they are.

Such models have three parameters: an algebra of polymorphic types $\mathcal{T}$, an untyped lambda interpretation $\mathcal{U}$ [4] and a logical p.e.r. $\mathcal{R}$ on the "erase-types" polymorphic lambda interpretation $\mathcal{I}^{\mathcal{T},\mathcal{U}}$. The model is then defined as the quotient $\mathcal{I}^{\mathcal{T},\mathcal{U}}/\mathcal{R}$.

Any HEO-like model is a PER-model. Indeed, given an HEO-like model with parameters $\mathcal{T}$ and $\mathcal{U}$, we note that $(\mathcal{I}^{\mathcal{T},\mathcal{U}})^{per} \equiv \mathcal{I}^{\mathcal{T}^{per},\mathcal{U}}$. Therefore this model is the same as the PER model with parameters $\mathcal{T}^{per}$, $\mathcal{U}$ and $\mathcal{R}^{per}$.

A characterization of the theories of PER models is given in [Mitchell 1986b]. It essentially says that the only additional equations that hold in PER models—compared to general models— are those obtained by equating terms that look the same when types are erased. It is an open question whether these are also the only additional equations that hold in HEO-like models—compared to general models obtained by polymorphic extensional collapse.

4.2 The closed type/closed term model construction

We start with the observation that the closed type expressions form an algebra of polymorphic types. Indeed, we can take $[T \Rightarrow T]$ to be the set of functions $\omega \longmapsto \sigma[t := \omega]$ determined by the closed polymorphic type expressions $\forall t.\, \sigma$.

Then, for each closed type expression ω we have an equivalence relation on the set of closed terms of type ω:

$$M \cong_{\omega} N \ \ \textit{iff} \ \ \lambda^{\forall} \vdash \ .\, M = N : \omega \ .$$

We take the domain of ω to consist of equivalence classes of closed terms of type ω modulo $\cong_{\omega}$. We can also think of this domain as the set of all closed normal forms of type ω. The definitions of application and the definition of the meaning map by substitution are straightforward. It is

[3] HEO_2 starts from the partial combinatory algebra of integers and "Kleene brackets" application

[4] Actually, Mitchell requires $\mathcal{U}$ to be a lambda model but the construction goes through for interpretations

easy to check that we get a polymorphic lambda interpretation (call it the *closed type/closed term polymorphic lambda interpretation*). Moreover, the elements of type *polyint*, for example, are in one to one correspondence with the numerals. Unfortunately, extensionality fails since, for example, there are no elements of type $\forall t.\, t$ but there are two *distinct* elements of type $(\forall t.t) \to (\forall t.t) \to (\forall t.t)$ namely (the equivalence classes of) $\lambda x{:}\,\forall t.t.\lambda y{:}\,\forall t.t.x$ and $\lambda x{:}\,\forall t.t.\lambda y{:}\,\forall t.t.y$ while by extensionality there should be at most one.

Hence the idea of [Coquand 1986] of combining the closed type/closed term construction with factoring by p.e.r.'s and thus achieving extensionality. This amounts to taking the polymorphic extensional collapse of the closed type/closed term polymorphic lambda interpretation. Let us call the resulting model $\mathcal{C}$. In [Coquand 1986] it is shown that in $\mathcal{C}$ there are exactly two elements of type *polybool* namely (the meanings of) *True* and *False*. In particular, $\mathcal{C}$ is non-trivial. Here we will show that in $\mathcal{C}$ the elements of type *polyint* are exactly the numerals. This will provide a positive answer to the question we asked in the introduction, as well as another proof that $\mathcal{C}$ is non-trivial.

Since the numerals are the only closed normal forms of type *polyint* we need only show that no further identifications between numerals take place.

Suppose that $\vdash \widetilde{m} = \widetilde{n} : polyint$ is valid in $\mathcal{C}$. Then, for any closed type expression ω and for any p.e.r. R on the set of equivalence classes modulo $\cong_\omega$ we must have (recall that $\cong_\omega[M]$ is the equivalence class of M modulo $\cong_\omega$)

$$\cong_{(\omega\to\omega)\to\omega\to\omega}[\widetilde{m}\,\omega]\ \ (R\to R)\to R\to R\ \ \cong_{(\omega\to\omega)\to\omega\to\omega}[\widetilde{n}\,\omega]\ .$$

Define

$$Succ \stackrel{\text{def}}{=} \lambda u{:}\,polyint.\, Add\, u\, \widetilde{1}\ \ : polyint \to polyint\ .$$

Taking $\omega = polyint$ and R to be the identity we have

$$Succ\ R\to R\ Succ \ \text{ and }\ \widetilde{0}\, R\, \widetilde{0}$$

hence

$$\widetilde{m}\ polyint\ Succ\,\widetilde{0} \cong_{polyint} \widetilde{n}\ polyint\ Succ\,\widetilde{0}\ .$$

But

$$\widetilde{m}\ polyint\ Succ\,\widetilde{0} = Succ^m\,\widetilde{0} = \widetilde{m}$$

hence $\widetilde{m} \cong_{polyint} \widetilde{n}$ which implies $m = n$.

Let ω be a closed type. A model is said to be *canonical* at ω if its elements of type ω are in one-to-one correspondence with the closed normal forms of type ω. So far, we have seen that $\mathcal{C}$ is canonical at *polybool* and *polyint*. As it was pointed out to us by Albert Meyer, it follows from a result in [Statman 1983] that this generalizes to all "such" types.

More precisely, let us define an *ML-polymorphic* type to be a closed type of the form $\forall t_1 \ldots \forall t_n.\sigma$ where σ is $\forall$-free [5]. As expected, the "combinatorics" of terms of ML-polymorphic type is essentially that of simply typed terms. The following is a result about simple lambda terms from [Statman 1983], rephrased for ML-polymorphic terms.

Statman's Typical Ambiguity Theorem *Let ω be an ML-polymorphic type and M, N two closed terms of type ω. If M and N are not $\beta\eta$-convertible then there exists a closed term $L : \omega \to polybool$ such that $L\,M = True$ and $L\,N = False$.*

Since $\mathcal{C}$ is non-trivial:

[5] These types correspond to the limited kind of polymorphism allowed in the language ML [Gordon *et al.* 1979]

Corollary 4.1 *The model $\mathcal{C}$ is canonical at all ML-polymorphic types.*

An interesting open problem is to characterize the theory of $\mathcal{C}$. A possibility, suggested by Rick Statman [Moggi 1986b], is that $\mathcal{C}$ is a *minimal* model for $\lambda^{\forall}$, i.e., that any equation that can be consistently added to $\lambda^{\forall}$ is valid in $\mathcal{C}$.

4.3 Full and faithful embeddings of algebras

This subsection is a spin-off from [Breazu-Tannen & Meyer 1987]. The results presented here can be thought of as model-theoretical versions of the conservative extension theorems stated there.

For the conservative extension theorem that corresponds to (and follows from) Theorem 4.2 below, an alternative, purely syntactic, proof is given in [Breazu-Tannen & Meyer 1987]. We know of no such syntactic proof for the conservative extension theorem corresponding to Theorem 4.3. In fact, [Breazu-Tannen & Meyer 1987] refers to Theorem 4.3 in this paper for a model-theoretical proof of the corresponding result.

Let A be an algebra with (say, just for simplicity) just one sort and a binary operation f. Given a model of $\lambda^{\forall}$, we say that (A, f) is *fully and faithfully embedded* in it if there exists a type *alg* and an element $f' \in D_{alg \to alg \to alg}$ such that when regarding f' as a binary operation on D_{alg} the resulting algebra (D_{alg}, f') is isomorphic to (A, f).

Theorem 4.2 *Any many-sorted algebra can be fully and faithfully embedded in a a model of the polymorphic lambda calculus.*

We are going to explain briefly how this is done. Given (again, for simplicity) an algebra (A, f) with one sort and a binary operation f, we construct first an extension of $\lambda^{\forall}$ by adding:

1. a type constant *alg*,
2. for each $a \in A$, a constant q_a and a type-checking axiom $\vdash q_a : alg$,
3. a constant f with $\vdash f : alg \to alg \to alg$,
4. for each $a, b \in A$, an equational axiom $\vdash f\, q_a\, q_b = q_{f(a,b)} : alg$.

Then, we construct the closed type/closed term polymorphic lambda interpretation of this extension. We claim that (A, f) is fully and faithfully embedded here at type *alg*. For this it is sufficient to see that any closed term of type *alg* converts to a term of the form q_a (true because the $\beta\eta$-normal forms of type *alg* are algebraic terms which then convert via the axioms (4) above to terms of the desired form) and that no two distinct terms of the form q_a are convertible to each other (true because the axioms (4) seen as reduction rules from left to right form together with β and η a Church-Rosser system—these are delta rules, see [Klop 1980]).

Next, we can see that the full and faithful embedding "survives" the subsequent polymorphic extensional collapse. This is because in the final model we have the liberty to choose a p.e.r for the interpretation of the type constant *alg* and we choose the *identity* p.e.r. Therefore, we have a full and and faithful embedding of (A, f) at type <*alg*, *identity*>.

In [Mitchell 1986b] it is stated that PER models can be used to obtain faithful but not full embeddings of algebras into models of the polymorphic lambda calculus. Subsequently, John

Mitchell and Eugenio Moggi have discovered how to do faithful *and full* embeddings of algebras into PER models that have empty types (actually HEO-like models) and, if the algebra has all sorts non-empty, even into PER models that have all types nonempty (these *cannot* be HEO-like models)[Mitchell 1986a]. The construction that we have presented here always yields models with empty types and had been obtained by us previously and independently.

While Theorem 4.2 is providing us complete information about the "pure" interaction between the polymorphic type discipline and algebraic data type specifications, its setting is not entirely satisfactory from the computer scientist's point of view. Indeed, the enormous computational power that $\lambda^{\forall}$ has over the numerals is only superficially used over the added data types. However, as shown in [Breazu-Tannen & Meyer 1987], there are *extensions* of $\lambda^{\forall}$ in which a strong connection between the computational power of $\lambda^{\forall}$ and the added data types can be set up and, moreover, the equational theory of the resulting language is still a conservative extension of the data type specifications. Theorem 4.3 below is a model-theoretic version of this result, showing that both full and faithful embedding and (semantic) computational power over the added data types can be simultaneously achieved. The corresponding conservative extension result from [Breazu-Tannen & Meyer 1987] follows as a corollary of the *proof* of Theorem 4.3.

We will assume that the added data type has a set of *observables*—say, character strings or lists or trees—and that we care only about computational behavior on the observables. We will also assume that there is some standard way to enumerate the observables with each observable appearing exactly once in the enumeration. This in turn will yield a one-to-one correspondence between functions on the integers and functions on the observables.

Theorem 4.3 *Let $\mathcal{A}$ be a many-sorted algebra. Let $c_0, c_1, c_2, \ldots$ be a sequence of distinct elements of some sort* obs *of $\mathcal{A}$, called* observables. *Then, there exists a model $\mathcal{E}$ of the polymorphic lambda calculus such that*

(i) $\mathcal{A}$ is fully and faithfully embedded in $\mathcal{E}$, and

(ii) every function on observables which is provably total recursive in second-order Peano arithmetic is in $\mathcal{E}$.

The construction of $\mathcal{E}$ is a refinement of the one we use for Theorem 4.2. Like there, we add a constant type for each sort of $\mathcal{A}$, constants for the elements and operations of $\mathcal{A}$ and axioms corresponding to the "tables" of these operations (items (1)–(4)). Moreover, here we also add the following items:

5. a constant In with $\vdash\ In : obs \rightarrow polyint$,

6. a constant Out with $\vdash\ Out : polyint \rightarrow obs$,

7. for each observable c_n, an axiom $\ .\ In\ q_{c_n} = \tilde{n} : polyint$,

8. for each element a of sort *obs* that is *not* an observable, an axiom $\ .\ In\ q_a = \tilde{0} : polyint$,

9. for each integer n, an axiom $\ .\ Out\ \tilde{n} = q_{c_n} : obs$.

Again, we construct the closed type/closed term polymorphic lambda interpretation of this extension. We claim that $\mathcal{A}$ is fully and faithfully embedded here and moreover the elements of type *polyint* are exactly the numerals.

To see this, note that conversion in the extended calculus can be analyzed with the reduction system consisting of β, η and the delta rules obtained by orienting the axioms, (4), (7), (8) and (9) from left to right. This system is strongly normalizable [Mitchell 1986b] and Church-Rosser [Klop 1980] and, using this, we can argue in the same spirit as in the proof of Theorem 4.2.

Like before, the full and faithful embedding survives the subsequent polymorphic extensional collapse. But, equally important, so do *In* and *Out*. Moreover, no identifications between distinct numerals take place (see the previous subsection). Since the collapse preserves the validity of axioms (7) and (9), we end up in the final model with two maps that establish a bijection between the observables and the numerals. This immediately implies the second part of the theorem.

Acknowledgments

We are grateful to John Mitchell for reading an earlier version and suggesting some corrections and improvements. Any remaining errors are, of course, our responsibility. The first author also benefited from a discussion on full and faithful embeddings with John Mitchell and Eugenio Moggi.

References

[Barendregt 1984] H. P. Barendregt. *The Lambda Calculus: Its Syntax and Semantics.* Volume 103 of *Studies in Logic and the Foundations of Mathematics*, North-Holland, Amsterdam, second edition, 1984.

[Breazu-Tannen] V. Breazu-Tannen. Ph.D. thesis, MIT. Expected Feb.1987.

[Breazu-Tannen & Meyer 1987] V. Breazu-Tannen and A. R. Meyer. Computable values can be classical. In *Proceedings of the 14th Symposium on Principles of Programming Languages*, ACM, 1987. To appear.

[Breazu-Tannen 1986] V. Breazu-Tannen. Communication in the TYPES electronic forum (xx.lcs.mit.edu), July 29th. 1986. Unpublished.

[Bruce & Meyer 1984] K. B. Bruce and A. R. Meyer. The semantics of second order polymorphic lambda calculus. In G. Kahn, D. B. MacQueen, and G. Plotkin, editors, *Semantics of Data Types*, pages 131–144, Springer-Verlag, Berlin, June 1984.

[Burstall *et al.* 1980] R. M. Burstall, D.B. MacQueen, and D.T. Sanella. Hope: an experimental applicative language. In *LISP Conference*, pages 136–143, Stanford University Computer Science Department, 1980.

[Cardelli & Wegner 1985] L. Cardelli and P. Wegner. On understanding types, data abstraction and polymorphism. *Computing Surveys*, 17(4):471–522, 1985.

[Cardelli 1985] L. Cardelli. Amber. In *Combinators and functional programming languages, Proceedings of the 13th Summer School of the LITP*, Le Val D'Ajol, Vosges, France, May 1985.

[Coquand 1986] T. Coquand. Communication in the TYPES electronic forum (xx.lcs.mit.edu), April 14th. 1986. Unpublished.

[Fairbairn 1982] J. Fairbairn. *Ponder and its type system.* Tech. Rep. 31, Computer Laboratory, Univ. of Cambridge, Cambridge, England, November 1982.

[Fortune *et al.* 1983] S. Fortune, D. Leivant, and M. O'Donnell. The expressiveness of simple and second-order type structures. *Journal of the ACM*, 30(1):151–185, January 1983.

[Gandy 1956] R. O. Gandy. On the axiom of extensionality—Part I. *Journal of Symbolic Logic*, 21, 1956.

[Girard 1972] J.-Y. Girard. *Interprétation fonctionelle et élimination des coupures dans l'arithmétique d'ordre supérieure.* Ph.D. thesis, Université Paris VII, 1972.

[Gordon *et al.* 1979] M. J. Gordon, R. Milner, and C. P. Wadsworth. *Edinburgh LCF.* Volume 78 of *Lecture Notes in Computer Science*, Springer-Verlag, Berlin, 1979.

[Hindley & Longo 1980] R. Hindley and G. Longo. Lambda-calculus models and extensionality. *Zeitschrift für Mathematische Logic und Grundlagen der Mathematik*, 26:289–310, 1980.

[Klop 1980] J. W. Klop. *Combinatory reduction systems.* Tract 129, Mathematical Center, Amsterdam, 1980.

[Leivant 1983] D. Leivant. Reasoning about functional programs and complexity classes associated with type disciplines. In *24th Symposium on Foundations of Computer Science*, pages 460–469, IEEE, 1983.

[Matthews 1985] D. C. J. Matthews. *Poly manual.* Tech. Rep. 63, Computer Laboratory, Univ. of Cambridge, Cambridge, England, 1985.

[Meyer *et al.* 1987] A. R. Meyer, J. C. Mitchell, E. Moggi, and R. Statman. Empty types in polymorphic λ-calculus. In *Proceedings of the 14th Symposium on Principles of Programming Languages*, ACM, 1987. To appear.

[Meyer 1982] Albert R. Meyer. What is a model of the lambda calculus? *Information and Control*, 52(1):87–122, January 1982.

[Meyer 1986] A. R. Meyer. Communication in the TYPES electronic forum (xx.lcs.mit.edu), February 7th. 1986. Unpublished.

[Mitchell & Meyer 1985] J. C. Mitchell and A.R. Meyer. Second-order logical relations (extended abstract). In R. Parikh, editor, *Logics of Programs*, pages 225–236, Springer-Verlag, Berlin, June 1985.

[Mitchell 1986a] J. C. Mitchell. Personal communication, August. 1986. Unpublished.

[Mitchell 1986b] J. C. Mitchell. A type-inference approach to reduction properties and semantics of polymorphic expressions. In *LISP Conference*, pages 308–319, ACM, New York, August 1986.

[Moggi 1986a] E. Moggi. Communication in the TYPES electronic forum (xx.lcs.mit.edu), February 10th. 1986. Unpublished.

[Moggi 1986b] E. Moggi. Communication in the TYPES electronic forum (xx.lcs.mit.edu), July 23rd. 1986. Unpublished.

[Nikhil 1984] R. S. Nikhil. *An incremental, strongly typed database query language.* Ph.D. thesis, Univ. of Pennsylvania, Philadelphia, August 1984. Available as tech. rep. MS-CIS-85-02.

[Reynolds 1985] J. C. Reynolds. Three approaches to type structure. In *TAPSOFT advanced seminar on the role of semantics in software development*, Springer-Verlag, Berlin, 1985.

[Scedrov 1986] A. Scedrov. Semantical methods for polymorphism. 1986. Unpublished manuscript, Univ. of Pennsylvania, July 1986.

[Statman 1980] R. Statman. On the existence of closed terms in the typed λ-calculus. In J. P. Seldin and R. Hindley, editors, *To H. B. Curry: Essays in Combinatory Logic, Lambda Calculus, and Formalism*, pages 511–534, Academic Press, New York, 1980.

[Statman 1981] R. Statman. Number theoretic functions computable by polymorphic programs. In *22nd Symposium on Foundations of Computer Science*, pages 279–282, IEEE, 1981.

[Statman 1983] R. Statman. λ-definable functionals and $\beta\eta$ conversion. *Arch. math. Logik*, 23:21–26, 1983.

[Troelstra (ed.) 1973] A. S. Troelstra (ed.). *Metamathematical investigation of intuitionistic arithmetic and analysis.* Volume 344 of *Lecture Notes in Mathematics*, Springer-Verlag, 1973.

[Turner 1985] D. A. Turner. Miranda: a non-strict functional language with polymorphic types. In J.-P. Jouannaud, editor, *Functional programming languages and computer architecture*, pages 1–16, Springer-Verlag, Berlin, September 1985.

A Type Discipline for Program Modules

Robert Harper Robin Milner Mads Tofte
Laboratory for Foundations of Computer Science
University of Edinburgh
Edinburgh EH9 3JZ
UNITED KINGDOM

Abstract

The ML modules system is organized around the notions of *structure*, *signature*, and *functor*. A structure is an encapsulated declaration of data types and values, a signature is a "type" or specification of a structure, and a functor is a function taking structures to structures. We present a static semantics for a fragment of this system in the style of Plotkin's operational semantics. The treatment of structures and signatures has interesting parallels with the type assignment rules for ML given by Damas and Milner. In particular there is a notion of principal typing.

1 Introduction

The ML modules system [Mac86a] is an approach to solving some of the problems that arise in organizing and maintaining large ML programs. The approach taken in ML, as in many other languages, is to define a calculus of environments whereby the programmer may decompose a program into relatively independent components with a well-defined interface. These program units are variously called *modules*, *packages*, and *clusters*; in ML we use the term *structure* to suggest both the idea of an "environment structure" and the mathematical notion of an algebraic structure. It is also standard to ascribe some form of "type" to a module. Such specifications go by names such as *interface* or *package description*; in ML we use the word *signature*, by analogy with the signature of an algebraic structure and with established usage in algebraic data type specifications. Many languages supporting modularization have the ability to define what are often called *parameterized modules*. In ML these appear as functions from structures to structures, called *functors*, a term that suggests their functional character.

The tension between the desire to decompose a program into units that may be understood and maintained in relative isolation from the other components, and the desire to combine these components into a coherent unit is perhaps the fundamental problem in modular program construction. MacQueen's analysis of these problems reveals that, in large measure, they can be expressed as problems of *sharing*. The idea is that two program units may come to depend on one another primarily by sharing a common subunit. For example, the common subunit may allocate, say, a stack, and define a collection of operations on it. Two program units may then cooperate with one another by virtue of the fact that they share a common stack. This is represented in ML by the use of *substructures*, the inclusion of a structure as a component of another. Two structures that include the same substructure are said to share that structure.

This analysis of dependence hinges on an appropriate notion of structure equality. Suppose that the stack structure is implemented by use of a reference to the heap (ML has a primitive similar to the **new** operation in Pascal). Then if two program units are to use a stack cooperatively, it is clear that they must use the *same* stack, so the definition of structure equality must be at least as fine-grained as equality of references. Similar problems of structure equality arise in connection with ML's data types and exceptions, and so the problem is not simply one of references. In order to capture these intuitions the ML convention on structure equality is that two structures are equal if and only if they arise from the same evaluation of the same structure expression.

The problem of sharing is most acute when we consider the dynamics of program construction. As static entities, programs in ML are organized as a hierarchical collection of structures, where the hierarchy is defined in terms of the substructure relationship. As such it would appear unproblematic to ensure that proper sharing is maintained, for all that is necessary is for the programmer to combine the structures together properly, that is, in accordance with the desired sharing between structures. But when we consider the dynamics of program development, it is clear that we must provide some assistance with sharing management. One of the principal reasons for wanting to treat structures independently is so that one structure can be modified in relative isolation from the others. For example, if we correct an error in the stack structure, then we wish to relink (rather than recompile!) the rest of the program with the new stack structure built in. Functors provide the means of performing this relinking: each structure is built as a function of its substructures, and the entire program hierarchy is constructed by applying these structures "bottom up", structures on which a given structure depends being built earlier than that structure.

For example, if structures A and B both employ the stack structure S, then they are built as functions of S by functors F_A and F_B. The structure A is constructed by applying the functor F_A to S, and similarly for B. Notice that functors give us the ability to define several "instances" or "versions" of a structure by applying the appropriate functor more than once. Now if A and B are to be used cooperatively in some structure C, then it is crucial that the functor F_C that is used to build C be applied to compatible instances of A and B, namely those that are built on the *same* stack S. In ML this is expressed by attaching a *sharing specification* to the parameter of F_C that specifies the required sharing between its arguments.

Informal examples of these problem and how they are solved in ML may be found in the papers of MacQueen [Mac86a,Mac86b] and Harper [Har86]. The purpose of this paper is to provide a formal grounding for these ideas. For the sake of perspicuity we limit our attention to a fragment of the full language, called ModL. This fragment consists only of of structures, signatures, and functors, with the entire core language of ML left out. This subset language is sufficiently rich to illustrate the issues that arise in connection with sharing without introducing any of the complexities that are irrelevant for our purposes.

In Section 2 we give some examples of the use of ModL to express modular structure, and make more precise the issues that arise in connection with structure equality and sharing. Then in Section 3 we present a formal static semantics of ModL. By "static" semantics, we mean a collection of inference rules (presented in Plotkin's operational style [Plo81]) that specifies the compile-time correctness conditions on a valid ModL program. In the full language, this encompasses type checking, but here we concentrate on those aspects that involve modules. This semantics bears a close resemblance to the type assignment rules for the core language of ML, as given by Damas and Milner [DM82].

2 Overview of ModL

The syntax of our skeletal language ModL is given in Figure 1. Each syntactic category is defined in terms of its typical elements; the set of phrases in a category is written as a capitalized version of the typical element. For example, *strexp* is a typical element of the set StrExp of structure expressions. The set of identifiers is graded into three sets, StrId for structure identifiers, SigId for signature identifiers, and FunId for functor identifiers. These sets are ranged over by *strid*, *sigid*, and *funid*, respectively. The set Path, of which *path* is a typical member, is the set of finite non-empty sequences of structure identifiers, which we write as a dot-separated list. Paths are sometimes called *qualified names*.

A program is a sequence of declarations, functor bindings, and signature bindings. The basic form of structure expression is an encapsulated declaration, bracketed by `struct` and `end`. Informally, a structure expression denotes an environment assigning meaning to identifiers. In the full language a structure may contain bindings for variables, types, exceptions, and other structures.

dec	::=	**structure** *strid* = *strexp*	structure binding
		$dec_1; \ldots; dec_k$	sequence, $k \geq 0$
strexp	::=	**struct** *dec* **end**	basic
		path	qualified name
		funid(*strexp*)	functor application
spec	::=	**structure** *strid* : *sigexp*	basic
		$spec_1; \ldots; spec_k$	sequence, $k \geq 0$
		spec **sharing** *path*=*path*	equation
sigexp	::=	**sig** *spec* **end**	signature expression
		sigid	signature identifier
prog	::=	*dec*	declaration
		signature *sigid* = *sigexp*	signature binding
		functor *funid*(*strid*: *sigexp*) = *strexp*	functor binding
		prog ; *prog*	sequence

Figure 1: Syntax of ModL

Example 1 (Structure Declaration)

```
structure A =
  struct
    type t = int;
    fun fact(x) = if x=1 then 1 else x*fact(x-1)
  end;

structure B =
  struct
    structure BA = A;
    fun f(x) = BA.fact(x) * BA.fact(x)
  end;

structure C =
  struct
    structure CA = A;
    structure CB = B;
    fun g(x) = CB.f( CA.fact(x) )
  end
```

Structure `A` defines a type `t` and a function `fact`. Structure `B` incorporates `A` as a substructure and in addition defines a function `f` in terms of `fact`. The qualified name `BA.fact` designates the identifier `fact` in structure `BA`. Similarly, `C` incorporates both `A` and `B` as substructures, and defines a function `g` in terms of `CB.f` and `CA.fact`. Note that both `B` and `C` incorporate the same structure `A`.

In our skeletal language ModL we throw away all but substructure declarations within structures. One effect of this is that a structure can be represented as a directed acyclic graph with edges labeled by the substructure identifiers, acyclic because a sturcture cannot be a substructure of itself. Each node of the graph is labeled by the *name* of the structure, which we think of as a kind of absolute designator, or address, for the structure. In the static semantics of ModL, structures are evaluated to just such a DAG, with each structure having its own unique name. For example we might depict structure C (with all but substructures omitted) as in the following example where n is the name of the structure bound to C etc.

Example 2

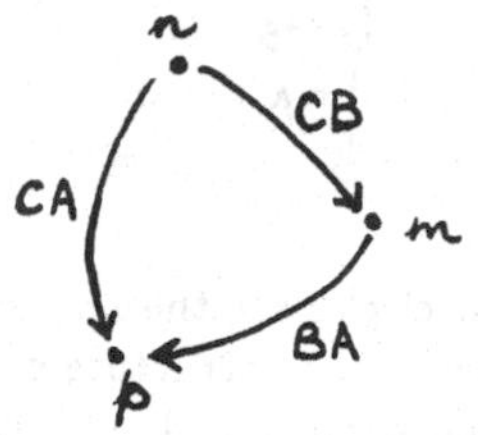

Signatures are specifications of structures. In the full language a specification of a structure describes the types of variables and exceptions, the arities of type constructors, and the signatures of substructures. The basic form of signature expression is an encapsulated *specification*, bracketed by **sig** and **end**. In ModL the only form of specification is the *structure specification*, whereby a signature is attached to a structure identifier.

Example 3 (Signature Declaration)

```
signature SIGA =
  sig
    type t;
    fun fact : int -> int
  end;
signature SIGB =
  sig
    structure BA : SIGA;
    fun f : int -> int
  end;
signature SIGC =
  sig
    structure CA : SIGA;
    structure CB : SIGB
  end
```

The precise definition of what it means for a structure to satisfy, or *match*, a signature is given by the static semantics below. Roughly speaking, the structure must have *at least* the components appearing in the signature, and these components must satisfy the specification of that component. Structure B matches SIGB because the substructure BA matches SIGA, and f is indeed of type int->int. Note that structure C matches SIGC, even though SIGC makes no mention of the component g of C. Since ModL structures contain only structure bindings, signatures specify only structure signatures, and signature matching, at the current level of detail, reduces to recursively matching substructures against their signatures. (This definition makes sense because any structure matches sig end, the empty signature.)

Signatures may also be depicted as DAG's, but there is an important difference as compared with those of structures. Whereas for structures the substructure identifiers designate *fixed* structures, in signatures they are merely formal names that are instantiated during signature matching. The idea is that a structure matches a signature if there is an instantiation of the formal names in the DAG of the signature such that the resulting DAG can be expanded (by adding new edges and nodes) to the DAG of the structure. For example, the following is the DAG representation of signature SIGC.

Example 4

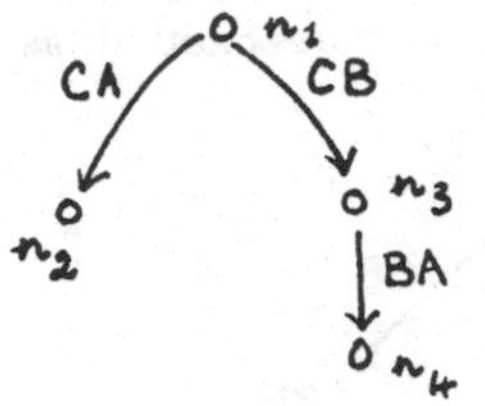

In DAGs representing signatures we draw circles for the nodes with formal names to distinguish them from the nodes with "actual" names used in structure diagrams. In the semantics this will be represented by the fact that the formal names are bound whereas the actual names are free. In fact this is the entire difference between the representations of structures and signatures in the static semantics.

Signatures may contain *sharing specifications* that specify that a certain equation must hold between structures. For example, the following signature is matched by the structure C defined in Example 1.

Example 5 (Signature with Sharing)

```
signature SIGC' =
  sig
    structure CA : SIGA;
    structure CB : SIGB
    sharing CA = CB.BA
  end
```

SIGC' requires that the structures bound to CA and CB.BA be equal. The representation of SIGC' differs from that of SIGC in that it uses the same formal name for CA and CB.BA, as can been seen in the following diagram.

Example 6

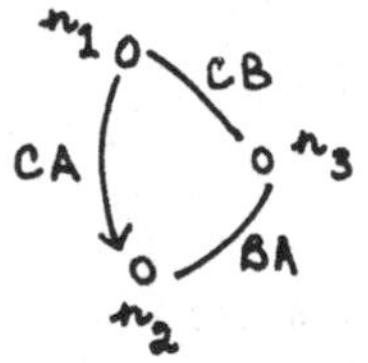

Any instance of this DAG must have the same name for these two components, and thus this convention accurately reflects the intended meaning of the sharing specification.

Sharing specifications may involve non–local structures, thereby limiting the structures tha match that specification to a single, fixed structure.

Example 7 (Non–local Sharing)

```
signature SIG =
  sig
    structure X : SIGA
    sharing X = A
  end
```

This signature can be matched only by structures that have the structure A bound to X. Diagrammatically, this shows up as an uncircled node, since the sharing specification forces the name for to be the name of A.

m, n	$\in$	Names
M, N	$\in$	Fin(Names) i.e., finite subsets of Names
E	$\in$	Env = StrId $\xrightarrow{\text{fin}}$ Str
S *or* (n, E)	$\in$	Str = Names × Env
Σ *or* $(N)S$	$\in$	Sig = Fin(Names) × Str
$[strid, \Sigma, strexp, \mathcal{E}]$	$\in$	Fun = StrId × Sig × StrExp × ProgEnv
F	$\in$	FunEnv = FunId $\xrightarrow{\text{fin}}$ Fun
G	$\in$	SigEnv = SigId $\xrightarrow{\text{fin}}$ Sig
$\mathcal{E}$ *or* (M, F, G, E)	$\in$	ProgEnv = Fin(Names) × FunEnv × SigEnv × Env

Table 1: Semantic Objects

Functors are functions taking structures to structures. In ModL each functor has a single parameter with a specified signature (there is no "signature inference" for functors).

Example 8 (Functor Declaration)

```
functor F( P: SIGC' ) =
  struct
    structure X = P.CA;
    fun f(y) = X.fact(y)+1
  end
```

Each evaluation of a `struct`...`end` expression yields a new structure (*i.e.*, a structure with a new name). For instance each application of `F` yields a new structure.

Example 9 (Functor Application)

```
structure D1 = F( C );
structure D2 = F( C )
```

These two declarations yield two isomorphic but unequal structures.

3 Static Semantics of ModL

In this section we present a formal static semantics for ModL. The semantics will be given in terms of a set of inference rules. Some of the objects occurring in the rules are syntactic and they were defined in the last section. In Section 3.1 we define the remaining objects, called the *semantic objects*. Then we present the rules.

3.1 Semantic Objects

Table 1 contains the recursive definition of the sets of semantic objects together with the variables we shall use to range over them.

In the present section, we shall use the word *structure* to mean a member of the set Str. A structure, S, has the form (n, E), where $n \in$ Names and $E \in$ Env; n is the *name* of the structure, and E is its *environment* binding structures to structure identifiers, one binding for each substructure of S — the set Names of names can be any infinite set. In a richer language, environments would contain other bindings as well (for instance bindings to type and value identifiers).

In terms of the DAG representation introduced in the last section, each node corresponds to a structure, the label of the node is the name of the structure, and the edges emanating from a node are determined by the environment component.

Two structures are equal if and only if their names are equal *and* their environment components are equal as finite functions. This definition reflects the fact that names are used to define a finer–grained equality than that induced by the equality on environments. Notice that the equality is also finer than simply name equality.

A *signature*, Σ, is a pair $(N)S$ consisting of a finite set of names together with a structure. (In the present section, the word *signature* will always have this technical meaning.) The set N binds names within S. Not all names appearing in S need be bound by N; free names in a signature are used to represent non–local sharing. The circled nodes in the diagrammatic representation of a signature are those that are bound by N here.

Functors are represented as *(functor) closures* consisting of the parameter identifier, its signature, the text of the functor body, and the environment in which it was defined. The need for closures is as usual: the body of a functor may contain free identifiers, and so must be packaged with its environment of definition if capture is to be avoided.

A program environment $\mathcal{E}$ is a quadruple (M, F, G, E) consisting of a finite set of names (intuitively, the set of "fixed" names), a functor environment mapping functor identifiers to functor closures, a signature environment mapping signature identifiers to signatures, and an environment. Environments are extended to paths as follows:

$$E(path) = \begin{cases} E(strid) & path = strid \\ E'(path') & path = strid.path',\ E(strid) = (n, E') \end{cases}$$

Structure environments E are extended similarly. We often write $E.path$ for $E(path)$, and $S.path$ for $E.path$, when $S = (n, E)$.

Environments are combined using the "+" operator, defined as follows:

$$(E + E')(i) = \begin{cases} E'(i) & i \in \mathrm{Dom}(E') \\ E(i) & i \notin \mathrm{Dom}(E') \end{cases}$$

Similar definitions apply to signature and functor environments.

Finally, we define "+" on program environments as follows:

$$(M, F, G, E) + (M', F', G', E') = (M \cup M', F + F', G + G', E + E')$$

In cases where some components of an operand are empty, we shall often omit them. For instance, $\mathcal{E} + M'$ means $\mathcal{E} + (M', \emptyset, \emptyset, \emptyset)$.

3.2 Realization Maps and Matching

We shall now define what it is for a structure to match a signature. The relation $\Sigma \geq S$ holds i there is a so–called *realization map* taking $\Sigma = (N)S'$ to S that affects only those substructures o S' whose name appears in N. In this way we obtain an interesting parallel with the polymorphi type discipline of ML [Mil78,DM82] (Table 2). Using the terminology of polymorphism, a struc ture matches a signature precisely if it is a generic instance of that signature, where the generi instantiation relation is defined in terms of realization maps.

Definition 10 (Realization Map) *A* realization map *is a total function* $\phi\colon \mathrm{Str} \to \mathrm{Str}$ *such that for all* $S \in \mathrm{Str}$ *and all* $strid \in \mathrm{StrId}$*, if* $S.strid$ *is defined, then* $\phi(S).strid$ *i defined, and* $\phi(S.strid) = (\phi(S)).strid$*.*

ModL	*Polymorphism*
structure	type
signature	type scheme
realization map	substitution
matching	generic instance

Table 2: ModL *vs.* Polymorphism

There are two important consequences of this definition. Firstly, a realization map may introduce more components (by enlarging the environment contained within a structure), but it may not destroy existing paths: if $S.path$ is defined, then $(\phi(S)).path$ is also defined. Secondly, a realization map may introduce more sharing (by identifying names within a structure), but it must preserve existing sharing: if $S.path = S.path'$, then $(\phi(S)).path = (\phi(S)).path'$, because both of the latter are equal to $\phi(S.path)$.

Example 11 *There is a realization map mapping S_1 to S_2 but none mapping S_2 to S_1, where*

The identity function on Str is a realization map, and if ϕ_1 and ϕ_2 are realization maps, then so is $\phi_2 \circ \phi_1$, where "$\circ$" is ordinary function composition.

The application of a realization map ϕ to an environment E is defined pointwise i.e., $(\phi(E))(strid) = \phi(E(strid))$. Thus the domain of $\phi(E)$ is the same as the domain of E.

We say that ϕ *glides* on a structure $S = (n, E)$ if $\phi(S) = (n, \phi(E))$. Note that this does *not* imply that $\phi(S) = S$, but rather only that ϕ "descends smoothly" into S without changing its name or the domain of its environment. The *support* of a realization map ϕ, written Supp(ϕ), is defined to be the set of structures on which ϕ does not glide.

For every structure, S, we write Names(S) for the set of names occurring in S. Similarly for environments. For every signature, $\Sigma = (N)S$, the *bound names* are the names in N while the *free names*, FN(Σ), are those in Names(S) $\setminus N$. Similarly, a structure S' in S is said to be *bound* in Σ if its name is a member of N, and is said to be free otherwise; BS(Σ) means the set of structures bound in Σ.

Definition 12 (Signature Matching) *A structure S matches a signature $\Sigma = (N)S'$, written $\Sigma \geq S$, if and only if there is a realization map ϕ such that $\phi(S') = S$ and* $\mathrm{Supp}(\phi) \subseteq \mathrm{BS}(\Sigma)$.

In this definition, the restriction of ϕ to S' and its substructures is uniquely determined by S' and S, so S can essentially only match Σ in one way.

Example 13 *The structure S matches the signature Σ, where*

S = 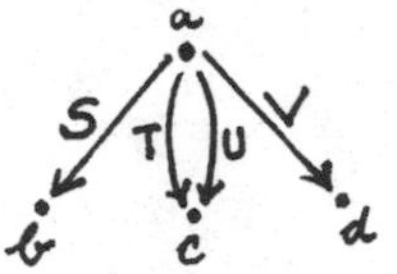

Σ = 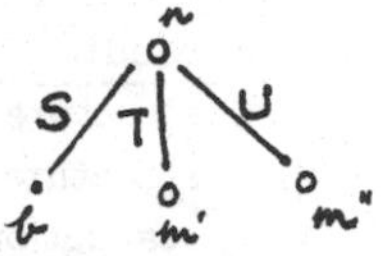

but S does not match either Σ' or Σ'':

Σ' = 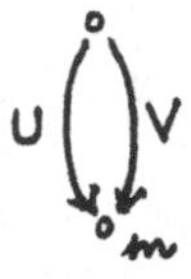

Σ'' = 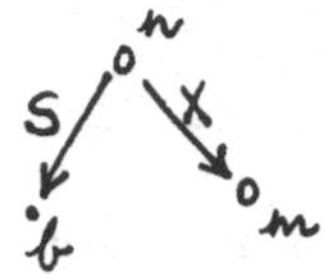

Definition 14 *A signature Σ is said to be* more general than *a signature Σ', written $\Sigma \geq \Sigma'$ if whenever a structure S matches Σ', it also matches Σ. Two signatures are equivalent, $\Sigma \equiv \Sigma'$ if each is more general than the other.*

One can prove that $(N)S \geq (N')S'$ if and only if $(N)S \geq S'$ and no $n' \in N'$ is the name of a free structure in $(N)S$. It can also be shown that two signatures are equivalent if and only if they can be obtained from each other by renaming of bound variables together with the introduction and elimination of spurious bound variables. Note the correspondence with the notion of generic instance defined by Damas and Milner [DM82]. The relation $\geq$ on signatures is a partial ordering on the equivalence classes.

3.3 Inference Rules

We shall now present the inference rules. The rules recursively define relations. For instance $\boxed{\mathcal{E} \vdash dec \Rightarrow E}$ in Figure 2 indicates that we define a ternary relation $(\_ \vdash \_ \Rightarrow \_) \subseteq$ ProgEnv $\times$ Dec $\times$ Env. Let us say that a phrase is *legitimate* in a given program environment if it can be evaluated to a semantic object using the rules.

It is helpful to think of the rules as falling into two categories, "strict" and "liberal". The idea is that the strict rules, given a phrase and a program environment, leave very little choice as to what can follow after the arrow. By contrast, the liberal rules may be used to infer a host of different semantic objects for a given program environment and phrase.

The rules for declarations and structure expressions are strict and appear in Figure 2. Intuitively the first component of a program environment records the names of structures that should be considered "fixed". Hence, in (2) names are accumulated in the program environment. In (3) n is required to be outside M so that it is not the name of a priviously fixed structure, and outside E_1 to avoid circularity in (n, E_1).

Functor applications (5) are evaluated in the usual way, by binding the (value of the) argument S, to the formal parameter identifier, *strid*, and elaborating the body, *strexp*, provided that the argument structure S matches the parameter signature Σ. Notice that M is added to $\mathcal{E}'$ so that we are sure that the names that are chosen during the evaluation of the body are new with respect to the *actual* program environment. This is the all–important reason for having name sets in program environments.

Notice that the only freedom in these rules is the choice of n in Rule 3. By contrast, the rule for specifications and signature expressions are liberal (Figure 3). The key source of freedom is th instantiation rule (12) which says that whenever we can infer a signature for a signature expression then we can also infer any less general signature — as defined in Section 3.2. This is crucial to ge the simple rule for sharing, because the instantiation rule gives us the ability to introduce extr sharing before testing the equality in (7).

$\boxed{\mathcal{E} \vdash dec \Rightarrow E}$

$$\frac{\mathcal{E} \vdash strexp \Rightarrow S}{\mathcal{E} \vdash \texttt{structure}\ strid = strexp \Rightarrow \{\, strid \mapsto S \,\}} \qquad (1)$$

$$\frac{\begin{array}{l}\mathcal{E} \vdash dec_1 \Rightarrow E_1\\ \cdots\\ \mathcal{E} + \mathrm{Names}(E_1) + \cdots + \mathrm{Names}(E_{k-1}) + E_1 + \cdots + E_{k-1} \vdash dec_k \Rightarrow E_k\end{array}}{\mathcal{E} \vdash dec_1\,;\ldots;\,dec_k \Rightarrow E_1 + \cdots + E_k} \qquad (2)$$

$\boxed{\mathcal{E} \vdash strexp \Rightarrow S}$

$$\frac{M, F, G, E \vdash dec \Rightarrow E_1 \qquad n \notin M \cup \mathrm{Names}(E_1)}{M, F, G, E \vdash \texttt{struct}\ dec\ \texttt{end} \Rightarrow (n, E_1)} \qquad (3)$$

$$\frac{E(path) = S}{M, F, G, E \vdash path \Rightarrow S} \qquad (4)$$

$$\frac{\begin{array}{c}F(funid) = [strid, \Sigma, strexp', \mathcal{E}']\\ M, F, G, E \vdash strexp \Rightarrow S \qquad \Sigma \geq S\\ \mathcal{E}' + M + \mathrm{Names}(S) + \{\, strid \mapsto S \,\} \vdash strexp' \Rightarrow S'\end{array}}{M, F, G, E \vdash funid(strexp) \Rightarrow S'} \qquad (5)$$

Figure 2: Rules for declarations and structure expressions

Rule (6) requires that the signature expression determine a signature with no bound names. The reason for this is that the binding of names in signatures is "outermost": no nesting of bound names is allowed within the environment part of a signature.

Rule 9 packages environments into signatures choosing an arbitrary name for it. The generalization rule (11) allows for binding of names in the signature, provided that they are not in M, i.e., not "fixed", and not free in the environment.

Turning to the rules for programs (Figure 3), let us consider functor binding (15). (The notion of principal signature will be explained in Section 4). First, the parameter signature is evaluated to $(N)S$, where N is chosen to be suitably new; this can always be achieved by applications of (12). Then the body of the functor is elaborated in the environment extended with *strid* bound to S, making sure that the names of S are considered fixed. If this succeeds, then we build a closure for the functor and bind it to *funid* in the functor environment. Notice that S' does not occur in the result. In particular, names used during the evaluation of the body may be reused; this is obtained by letting the name set in the result be empty.

4 Principal Signatures

Definition 15 *We say that a signature* Σ *is* principal *for sigexp in* $\mathcal{E}$ *if and only if (a)* $\mathcal{E} \vdash sigexp \Rightarrow \Sigma$, *and (b) whenever* $\mathcal{E} \vdash sigexp \Rightarrow \Sigma'$ *then* $\Sigma \geq \Sigma'$.

Intuitively, a signature for a signature expression is principal if it has the components and the sharing specified by the signature expression, *and no more*.

Returning to (15), let us see why we require the inferred signature to be principal. Suppose a functor declaration has been found legitimate. Then we would expect *any* application of the functor to a structure which matches the formal parameter signature *expression* to be legitimate. However, this requires that the inferred formal parameter signature be principal. So among all the similarities with polymorphic type checking, here is an important difference; in the latter,

$\boxed{\mathcal{E} \vdash spec \Rightarrow E}$

$$\frac{\mathcal{E} \vdash sigexp \Rightarrow (\emptyset)S}{\mathcal{E} \vdash \mathbf{structure}\ strid : sigexp \Rightarrow \{\,strid \mapsto S\,\}} \tag{6}$$

$$\frac{M,F,G,E \vdash spec \Rightarrow E' \qquad (E+E')(path_1) = (E+E')(path_2)}{M,F,G,E \vdash spec\ \mathbf{sharing}\ path_1{=}path_2 \Rightarrow E'} \tag{7}$$

$$\frac{\begin{array}{l}\mathcal{E} \vdash spec_1 \Rightarrow E_1 \\ \cdots \\ \mathcal{E} + E_1 + \cdots + E_{k-1} \vdash spec_k \Rightarrow E_k\end{array}}{\mathcal{E} \vdash spec_1\ ;\ldots;\ spec_k \Rightarrow E_1 + \cdots + E_k} \tag{8}$$

$\boxed{\mathcal{E} \vdash sigexp \Rightarrow \Sigma}$

$$\frac{\mathcal{E} \vdash spec \Rightarrow E_1}{\mathcal{E} \vdash \mathbf{sig}\ spec\ \mathbf{end} \Rightarrow (\emptyset)(n, E_1)} \tag{9}$$

$$\frac{G(sigid) = \Sigma}{M,F,G,E \vdash sigid \Rightarrow \Sigma} \tag{10}$$

$$\frac{M,F,G,E \vdash sigexp \Rightarrow (N)S \qquad n \notin M}{M,F,G,E \vdash sigexp \Rightarrow (N \cup \{\,n\,\})S} \tag{11}$$

$$\frac{\mathcal{E} \vdash sigexp \Rightarrow \Sigma \qquad \Sigma \geq \Sigma'}{\mathcal{E} \vdash sigexp \Rightarrow \Sigma'} \tag{12}$$

$\boxed{\mathcal{E} \vdash prog \Rightarrow \mathcal{E}'}$

$$\frac{\mathcal{E} \vdash dec \Rightarrow E}{\mathcal{E} \vdash dec \Rightarrow (\mathrm{Names}(E), \emptyset, \emptyset, E)} \tag{13}$$

$$\frac{\mathcal{E} \vdash sigexp \Rightarrow \Sigma \qquad \Sigma \text{ principal for } sigexp \text{ in } \mathcal{E}}{\mathcal{E} \vdash \mathbf{signature}\ sigid = sigexp \Rightarrow (\emptyset, \emptyset, \{\,sigid \mapsto \Sigma\,\}, \emptyset)} \tag{14}$$

$$\frac{\begin{array}{c}\mathcal{E} \vdash sigexp \Rightarrow (N)S \qquad \mathcal{E} = (M,F,G,E) \qquad N \cap (M \cup \mathrm{FN}(E)) = \emptyset \\ (N)S \text{ principal for } sigexp \text{ in } \mathcal{E} \\ \mathcal{E} + \mathrm{Names}(S) + \{\,strid \mapsto S\,\} \vdash strexp \Rightarrow S'\end{array}}{\begin{array}{c}\mathcal{E} \vdash \mathbf{functor}\ funid(strid{:}sigexp){=}strexp' \Rightarrow \\ (\emptyset, \{\,funid \mapsto [strid, (N)S, strexp', \mathcal{E}]\,\}, \emptyset, \emptyset)\end{array}} \tag{15}$$

$$\frac{\mathcal{E} \vdash prog_1 \Rightarrow \mathcal{E}_1 \qquad \mathcal{E} + \mathcal{E}_1 \vdash prog_2 \Rightarrow \mathcal{E}_2}{\mathcal{E} \vdash prog_1\ ;\ prog_2 \Rightarrow \mathcal{E}_1 + \mathcal{E}_2} \tag{16}$$

Figure 3: Rules for specifications, signatures, and programs

formal function parameters have types, not type schemes, while in ModL we have signatures as the "types" of formal parameters.

A similar constraint is appropriate on the rule for signature declaration (14). For example it will ensure that in

```
signature SIG =
sig structure A: sig end;
    structure B: sig end;
end;

functor F(S:SIG) = body
```

S.A and S.B will be treated as being different within the functor body.

But *do* signature expressions have principal signatures? The answer is yes, but under certain conditions. We shall not go into details but the most interesting condition is that structure names uniquely determine structures: if $S_1 = (n, E_1)$ and $S_2 = (n, E_2)$ then $E_1 = E_2$. This constraint creates a one–one correspondence between the DAGs and the elements of Str.

The existence of principal signatures is proved constructively by giving an algorithm which either fails or succeeds and succeeds with a principal signature just in case the signature expression is legitimate. The algorithm uses a unification algorithm which generalizes ordinary term unification to structure unification. These algorithms and detailed proofs of their correctness exist and will appear in the last author's forthcoming Ph. D. thesis.

References

[DM82] Luis Damas and Robin Milner. Principal type schemes for functional programs. In *Proceedings of the 9th ACM Symposium on the Principles of Programming Languages*, pages 207–212, 1982.

[Har86] Robert Harper. *Introduction to Standard ML.* Technical Report, University of Edinburgh, September 1986.

[Mac86a] David MacQueen. Modules for Standard ML. In *Standard ML*, by Robert Harper and David MacQueen and Robin Milner, Technical Report ECS–LFCS–86–2, Laboratory for the Foundations of Computer Science, Edinburgh University, March 1986.

[Mac86b] David MacQueen. Using dependent types to express modular structure. In *Proceedings of the 13th ACM Symposium on the Principles of Programming Languages*, 1986.

[Mil78] Robin Milner. A theory of type polymorphism in programming languages. *Journal of Computer and System Sciences*, 17:348–375, 1978.

[Plo81] Gordon Plotkin. *A Structural Approach to Operational Semantics.* Technical Report DAIMI–FN–19, Computer Science Department, Aarhus University, Denmark, 1981.

Theory and practice of canonical term functors in abstract data type specifications

Christoph Beierle
TK LILOG, IBM Deutschland GmbH
Postfach 800880, D-7000 Stuttgart 1
EARN/BITNET: BEIERLE at DSØLILOG

Angelika Voss
GMD, Gruppe Expertensysteme
Postfach 1240, D-5205 St. Augustin 1
USENET: AVOSS%GMDXPS at GMDZI

Abstract: Term algebras have been widely used in the theory of abstract data types. Here, the concept of canonical term algebra is generalized to the notion of canonical term functor, which is useful for various aspects of abstract data type specifications. In particular, we show how canonical term functors provide a constraint mechanism in loose specifications and how they constitute a junction between axiomatic and constructive approaches. These concepts are the semantic base for the specification development language ASPIK which has been implemented as a core component of an integrated software development and verification system.

1. Introduction

During the last decade the field of abstract data type theory has received much attention, yielding numerous papers on various approaches. To mention only a few, there is the initial approach proposed by the ADJ group ([GTW 78], see also [EM 85]) which is based on equational specifications and was later generalized to conditional equations and universal Horn clauses, the terminal approach advocated by e.g. [GGM 76], [Wa 79], [Kam 80], the loose approaches of Clear [BG 80] or CIP-L [CIP 85], the algorithmic approaches of [Cart 80], [KL 84], [Lo 84], etc., for a more complete list of references see e.g. [EM 85].

In many of these approaches term algebras have played an important role, and the concept of canonical term algebra as introduced in [GTW 78] has been used also in e.g. [Pad 79] and [KL 83]. Here we generalize canonical term algebras to the new notion of canonical term functors and show how this notion provides a powerful concept both under theoretical and practical aspects of abstract data types. It eases the stepwise development and verification of specifications, provides a constraint mechanism in loose specifications and can be used as a junction between high level axiomatic and lower level algorithmic or constructive approaches.

The concept of canonical term functor has already been exploited extensively in design and implementation of the specification development language ASPIK which together with its support environment SPESY is a core component of the ISDV system, an integrated software development and verification system [BV 85], [BOV 86].

specifications and fixes our notation. In section 3 we recall the definition of canonical term algebra and show how it can be generalized to canonical term functors. Additionaly, we define strict versions of both concepts, supporting partial operations and a simple error handling mechanism. Composability of canonical term functors and other properties are proved. In section 4 various applications are described, section 5 briefly discusses ASPIK and its support in SPESY, and section 6 contains concluding remarks.

Acknowledgements: This work was performed at the Universität Kaiserslautern and was supported in part by the Bundesministerium für Forschung und Technologie (IT 8302363) and the Deutsche Forschungsgemeinschaft (SFB 314).

2. Preliminaries: Algebraic specifications

A signature $\Sigma = \langle S, Op \rangle$ consists of a set S of sorts or types and an $S^* \times S$ - sorted set Op of typed operation names. For $op \in Op$ the notation $op: s_1...s_n \to s$ means that op has argument sorts $s_1...s_n$ and target sort s.
A Σ-algebra $A = \langle \{A_s \mid s \in S\}, \{op_A: A_{s1} \times ... \times A_{sn} \to A_s \mid op: s_1...s_n \to s \ \in Op\} \rangle$ provides a data set or carrier A_s for each sort s and an operation op_A for each operation symbol op in Op. A Σ-homomorphism $h: A \to A'$ is an S-sorted family of functions $\{h_s: A_s \to A_s' \mid s \in S\}$ such that h commutes with the algebra operations in A and A'. Alg(Σ) denotes the category of all Σ-algebras together with all Σ-homomorphisms.
A specification $SP = \langle \Sigma, E \rangle$ consists of a signature Σ and a set E of sentences over Σ. This defines the class of $\langle \Sigma, E \rangle$-algebras which are all Σ-algebras satisfying the sentences E. According to the ADJ approach the isomorphism class of the initial $\langle \Sigma, E \rangle$-algebra is the abstract data type specified by SP.

The initial approach of the ADJ-group is an example of a so-called fixed approach where a specification has only isomorphic models. Fixed approaches were generalized to so-called loose approaches where a specification $SP = \langle \Sigma, E \rangle$ may also have non-isomorphic models, for example, the class of all Σ-algebras satisfying E is considered, not just the initial ones. Whereas the initial as well as the terminal approach (e.g. [Wa 79], [Kam 80]) have to restrict the types of admissible sentences in order to guarantee the existence of an initial (resp. terminal) model, there is no such need in a loose approach: Equations are considered in [GTW 78], positive conditional equations in [TWW 82], and universal Horn sentences in [EKTWW 80], whereas in the loose approach of [CIP 85] arbitrary first order formulas are allowed. Other loose approaches are e.g. [BG 77, 80, 81], [HKR 80], [SW 82], [ZLT 82] and [EWT 82]. Beside logical formulas, these approaches need so-called constraints as another type of sentences in order to exclude unreachable elements or non-standard interpretations. In sections 4.3 and 4.4 we will show how algorithmic definitions may be used for this purpose.

3. Canonical term functors

We introduce canonical term functors as generialization of canonical term algebras in section 3.1. In section 3.2 we specialize the definition to strict canonical term functors that are better suited as semantics of algebraic definitions. Properties of both types of canonical term functors are given in section 3.3.

3.1 Definition

In the initial approach of the ADJ-group, an abstract data type is defined as the isomorphism class of the initial algebra of an equational specification SP = $\langle \Sigma, E \rangle$. Such an initial algebra can be obtained by taking the free Σ-term algebra T_Σ and imposing the congruence generated by E on the carriers. The resulting quotient algebra $T_{\Sigma/E}$ has equivalence classes as its carrier elements. This definition in terms of equivalence classes is rather abstract. Sometimes, a more concrete definition is preferable, for example in order to compute terms over initial specifications. This role of a concrete initial algebra can be played especially by a canonical term algebra (cta), which exists for every equational specification. Unfortunately, the existence proof is non-constructive [GTW 78], and in general there is no algorithm to generate an initial cta from a specification.

A cta is obtained from the quotient term algebra $T_{\Sigma/E}$ by choosing a representative out of each equivalence class. Two restrictions are imposed on this selection: The first guarantees that the carriers are closed under subterm formation (subterm property), the second guarantees that the carriers are operation-generated. We call this the constructor property since the generating operations are often called constructors.

Definition 3.1 [canonical term algebra, cta]

Let $\Sigma = \langle S, Op \rangle$ be a signature and $A \in Alg(\Sigma)$ an algebra. A is a canonical Σ-term algebra (Σ cta, or just cta) iff

(1) $\forall s \in S .\ A_s \subseteq T_{\Sigma,s}$ (term property)

(2) $\forall op: s_1 \ldots s_n \rightarrow s \in Op$.

$op(t_1, \ldots, t_n) \in A_s$

$\Rightarrow t_1 \in A_{s1}\ \&\ \ldots\ \&\ t_n \in A_{sn}$ (subterm property)

$\&\ op_A(t_1, \ldots, t_n) = op(t_1, \ldots, t_n)$ (constructor property).

The initial approach to ADTs was extended to parameterized ADTs ([TWW 78], [EKTWW 80]). A parameterized specification PSP = $\langle$ FSP, Σ, E $\rangle$ consists of a formal parameter specification FSP = $\langle F\Sigma, FE \rangle$, a signature Σ extending $F\Sigma$ ($F\Sigma \subset \Sigma$) and equations E extending FE ($FE \subseteq E$). The formal parameter specification denotes the class of all FSP-algebras to be parameter algebras. The parameterized specification PSP denotes the free functor $free_{PSP}$: Alg (FSP) $\rightarrow$ Alg ($\langle \Sigma, E \rangle$) that maps every parameter algebra A to its free extension $free_{PSP}(A)$, which can again be defined very abstractly in terms of equivalence classes over the free term algebra $T_\Sigma(A)$ generated from A.

Therefore the same reasons that led to consider a cta instead of a quotient term algebra also apply in the parameterized case: Sometimes it is preferable to have a more concrete definition than just the implicit definition of a free functor by equivalence classes. This role can be played by the so-called canonical term functor (ctf), which we define by a straightforward generalization of the cta definition: Since the parameter algebras must not be affected, a ctf should be strongly persistent, and the term-, subterm-, and constructor properties must now be restricted to the new sorts. In order to ease the precise definition of these ideas we first introduce some auxiliary notions for expressing the cta-requirements relative to a parameter algebra A.

Definition 3.2 [term-, subterm-, constructor property]

Let Σ, Σ' be signatures such that $\Sigma \subseteq \Sigma'$. Let $A \in Alg(\Sigma)$ and $B \in Alg(\Sigma')$.

(1) B has the $(\Sigma' - \Sigma)$-term property w.r.t. A iff

$$\forall s \in \Sigma' - \Sigma.\ B_s \subseteq T_{\Sigma' - \Sigma}(A)_s$$

(2) B has the $(\Sigma' - \Sigma)$-subterm property iff

$$\forall s \in \Sigma' - \Sigma.\ \forall op: s_1 \dots s_n \to s \in \Sigma' - \Sigma.$$
$$op(t_1,\dots,t_n) \in B_s \Rightarrow t_1 \in B_{s1} \ \& \dots \& \ t_n \in B_{sn}$$

(3) A' has the $(\Sigma' - \Sigma)$-constructor property iff

$$\forall s \in \Sigma' - \Sigma.\ \forall op: s_1 \dots s_n \to s \in \Sigma' - \Sigma.$$
$$op(t_1,\dots,t_n) \in B_s \Rightarrow op_B(t_1,\dots,t_n) = op(t_1,\dots,t_n)$$

Definition 3.3 [canonical term functor, ctf]

Let $\iota: \Sigma \to \Sigma'$ be a signature inclusion, and let $C \subseteq Alg(\Sigma)$ and $C' \subseteq Alg(\Sigma')$ be subcategories. A functor $g: C \to C'$ is a canonical (Σ, Σ')-term functor ((Σ, Σ')-ctf, or just ctf iff

(1) g is strongly persistent:

$$Alg(\iota) \cdot g = id_C$$

(2) For every $A \in C$, (2.1) - (2.3) hold:

(2.1) g(A) has the $(\Sigma' - \Sigma)$-term property w.r.t. A

(2.2) g(A) has the $(\Sigma' - \Sigma)$-subterm property

(2.3) g(A) has the $(\Sigma' - \Sigma)$-constructor property

As an example, let ELEM = $\langle\langle \{elem\}, \emptyset \rangle, \emptyset \rangle$ specify all one-sorted algebras as parameters. Let ΣLIST = $\langle$ {elem, list}, {nil, cons, car, cdr} $\rangle$ be the signature of linear lists with elements of sort elem. Define g as a functor g: Alg(ELEM) → Alg(ΣLIST) whose object part extends every parameter algebra $A \in$ Alg(ELEM) by the list carrier {nil, cons(e_1, nil), cons(e_2, cons(e_1, nil)) ... | $e_1, e_2, \dots \in A_{elem}$} and by the usual list operations such that e.g.

$cons_{g(A)}(e_2, cons(e_1, nil)) = cons(e_2, cons(e_1, nil))$

$car_{g(A)}(cons(e_2, cons(e_1, nil))) = e_2$

$cdr_{g(A)}(cons(e_2, cons(e_1, nil))) = cons(e_1, nil)$.

Then g is a ctf for the following reasons:

1. g is strongly persistent since the parameter algebra A is not modified.

2. g(A) has the term property because the list objects are term generated by the new operations nil and cons over the elements of A.
3. g(A) has the subterm property since for every list carrier element $cons(e_i,t)$ t is also in the list carrier.
4. g(A) has the constructor property since for the constructor operations nil and cons we have $nil_{g(A)} = nil$ and $cons_{g(A)}(e_i,t) = cons(e_i,t)$ for every term $cons(e_i,t)$ in the list carrier.

3.2 Strict canonical term functors

So far we have considered all total algebras as models. But there are many reasons to consider also partial algebras, e. g. partially defined operations or non-terminating recursion, c. f. [CIP 85] among others. A particular method to deal with partial algebras is to extend the operation domains by a new element ('undefined'), and to extend the operations such that they are strict w. r. t. the new element. We say that a strict algebra has carriers with a minimal element, called the error element, and strict operations propagating the error elements. Whereas Alg(Σ) denotes the class of all Σ-algebras, we use EAlg(Σ) to denote the class of all strict algebras. To make the error elements addressable in our specifications we introduce error constants error-s for each sort s in a signature Σ yielding the signature Err(Σ). Thus, a strict Σ-algebra in particular is an ordinary Err(Σ)-algebra.

Now we can replace Σ by Err(Σ) and Alg(Σ) by EAlg(Σ) in the definition of cta. Additionally we require that in every carrier the error element is represented by the error constant. The latter requirement is not necessary, but convenient since it allows to define the error constants implicitly.

Definition 3.4 [strict cta]
Let $\Sigma = \langle S,Op \rangle$ be a signature and $A \in EAlg(\Sigma)$ a strict Σ -algebra. A is a strict Σ-cta iff
(1) A is an (ordinary) Err(Σ)-cta
(2) $\forall s \in S$. error-s $\in A_s$.

Just as we obtained the definition of a strict cta from the definition of cta by adding the implicit error constants and the error requirement (2), we define a strict ctf to be a ctf between two categories of strict algebras and add the error requirement w.r.t. the new carriers.

Definition 3.5 [strict ctf]

Let $\iota: \Sigma \to \Sigma'$ be a signature inclusion, and let $C \subseteq EAlg(\Sigma)$ and $C' \subseteq EAlg(\Sigma')$ be subcategories. A functor $g: C \to C'$ is a strict (Σ,Σ')-ctf iff
(1) g is an (Err(Σ), Err(Σ'))-ctf
(2) $\forall s \in \Sigma' - \Sigma$. $\forall A \in C$. error-s $\in g(A)_s$.

As an example consider again the ctf g defining lists over arbitrary elements from section 3.1. Supplementing the missing operation definitions we would have difficulties to define $car_{g(A)}$ (nil) in a total algebra approach. Assuming g as a strict ctf that extends strict ELEM-algebras A, we can define $car_{g(A)}$ (nil) := $error\text{-}elem_A$ to yield the error element of sort elem in algebra A. This corresponds exactly to a partial algebra approach (as in the CIP project [CIP 85]) when we forget the error elements and analogously restrict the algebra operations to partial operations. Thus $car_{g(A)}$(nil) = $error\text{-}elem_A$ means that $car_{g(A)}$(nil) is undefined if g(A) was a partial algebra, and the fact that $cons_{g(A)}(car_{g(A)}(nil), nil)$ would also be undefined in a partial algebra g(A) is reflected in the strictness of the operations in a strict algebra g(A). However, taking the approach of strict algebras we can stay within the simpler framework of total algebras.

3.3 Properties

We motivated the concept of ctfs as concrete counterparts of free functors defined by equivalence classes in the semantics of parameterized specifications, just like ctas are concrete counterparts of initial quotient term algebras in the semantics of non-parameterized specifications. Therefore, we would like to have the following correspondences between ctfs and free functors:

(1) Since a constant free functor defines an initial algebra, a constant ctf should yield a cta.

(2) Since the composition of free functors yields again a free functor, the composition of ctfs should yield again a ctf.

(3) Since the application of a free functor to an initial algebra yields again an initial algebra, the application of a ctf to a cta should yield again a cta.

These properties hold both for ordinary and for strict ctfs due to the following three facts:

Fact 3.6 [constant ctfs are ctas]

Let Σ be a signature, $A \in Alg(\Sigma)$ [resp. $A \in EAlg(\Sigma)$] and

$$1_A: Alg(\langle\emptyset,\emptyset\rangle) \to Alg(\Sigma)$$

$$[\text{resp. } 1_A: EAlg(\langle\emptyset,\emptyset\rangle) \to EAlg(\Sigma)]$$

be the constant functor yielding A. Then we have:

A is a [strict] Σ-cta $\Leftrightarrow$ 1_A is a [strict] $(\langle\emptyset,\emptyset\rangle,\Sigma)$-ctf.

Proof

1_A is strongly persistent since the only object in $Alg(\langle\emptyset,\emptyset\rangle)$ [resp. $EAlg(\langle\emptyset,\emptyset\rangle)$] is the empty algebra with no sorts and no operations, and for $\Sigma - \langle\emptyset,\emptyset\rangle = \Sigma$ [resp. $Err(\Sigma) - Err(\langle\emptyset,\emptyset\rangle) = Err(\Sigma)$], the [strict] Σ-term, [strict] Σ-subterm, and [strict] Σ-constructor properties w. r. t. the empty algebra coincide with the conditions for a [strict] Σ-cta.

The next two facts state that ctfs are closed under composition and that a ctf applied to a cta yields again a cta.

Fact 3.7 [ctfs are closed under composition]

Let $g_1: C_1 \to C_2$ be a [strict] (Σ_1,Σ_2)-ctf and $g_2: C_2 \to C_3$ be a [strict] (Σ_2,Σ_3)-ctf. Then

$$g_2 \cdot g_1: C_1 \to C_3$$

is a [strict] (Σ_1,Σ_3)-ctf.

Proof

$g_2 \cdot g_1$ is strongly persistent since both g_1 and g_2 are strongly persistent. For $A \in C_1$, $g_2(g_1(A))$ has the [strict] $(\Sigma_3-\Sigma_2)$-term property w. r. t. $g_1(A)$ since g_2 is a [strict] (Σ_2,Σ_3)-ctf, and $g_1(A)$ has the [strict] $(\Sigma_2-\Sigma_1)$-term property w. r. t. A since g_1 is a [strict] (Σ_1,Σ_2)-ctf. Thus, $g_2(g_1(A))$ has the [strict] $(\Sigma_3-\Sigma_1)$-term property w. r. t. A since g_2 is strongly persistent. A similar argument shows that $g_2(g_1(A))$ has the [strict] $(\Sigma_3-\Sigma_1)$-subterm and [strict] $(\Sigma_3-\Sigma_1)$-constructor properties.

Fact 3.8 [application of ctfs to ctas]

Let $g: C \to C'$ be a [strict] (Σ,Σ')-ctf, and A a [strict] Σ-cta with $A \in C$. Then $g(A)$ is a [strict] Σ'-cta.

Proof

According to Fact 3.6, A can be identified with the constant functor 1_A, and 1_A can be corestricted to C since $A \in C$. The composition $g \cdot 1_A$ is a [strict] ctf due to Fact 3.7. Since $g \cdot 1_A$ is a constant functor from the category containing just the empty algebra, its value g(a) is a [strict] Σ'-cta according to Fact 3.6.

4. Applications

4.1. Proofs and stepwise verification

The power of the cta concept is demonstrated in [GTW 78] by showing that for every equational specification an initial cta exists. Similarly, we can prove an analogous result for the parameterized case.

Fact 4.1 [existence of a ctf]

Let $PSP = \langle FSP, \Sigma, E \rangle$ be a parameterized equational specification with parameter specification $FSP = \langle F\Sigma, FE \rangle$ such that the induced free functor is persistent. Then there exists a free functor

$$ctf_{PSP}: Alg\,(FSP) \to Alg\,(\Sigma, E)$$

which is a ctf.

As in the non-parameterized cta case the proof of this fact which is given in the appendix is non-constructive, but similarly as for ctas there is often a natural choice for selecting the canonical representatives for a ctf.

Knowing that ctfs exist, we can use them like ctas instead of quotient term algebras with the advantage that one can exploit the term structure in induction proofs (c.f. [GTW 78], [Pad 79], [Kl 83] and - for a variant of ctas - [EM 85]). Moreover, if one has a system of equational parameterized specifications of say sets over lists over some elements and corresponding ctfs one can verify them w.r.t. given properties in a stepwise manner by considering first the set ctf and then the list ctf, or the other way around. This modularization also allows us to do the set verification part only once (e.g. showing that the union operation is commutative) and to use it for other instances like sets over arrays as well. Such a modularization is used extensively in our ISDV system [BV 85, BOV 86].

4.2 Constraints

Whereas in a fixed approach to abstract data type specifications like the initial or terminal one there is no need for a constraint mechanism, such a mechanism is needed in a loose approach where all models of a specification are considered. The reason is that at least for some substructures one wants to allow only a standard interpretation. For example, a specification of the natural numbers should not allow for a model with additional elements like ∞ that cannot be generated by the usual natural numbers operations. The loose approaches of [HKR 80], [BG 80] and [EWT 83] use a constraint mechanism involving a free functor. The hierarchy constraints proposed in [SW 82] are weaker in the sense that - apart from requiring true $\neq$ false - they only exclude unreachable elements ("no-junk" condition) while the other approaches also require that generated elements must be distinct ("no-confusion" condition).

The functor involved in these constraint mechanisms is the free functor defined by equational theories. In [GB 83] the more general case of data constraints in so-called liberal institutions is considered where an institution is liberal if each of its theory morphisms gives rise to a free functor. While the equational institution is liberal, many other institutions like the institution of first order predicate logic are not. Therefore, we propose to allow as definition of the desired functor not only a theory morphism with its induced free functor but any other functors and functor definition methods as well. We illustrate this idea first by introducing a general concept of functor constraints and then by describing a constructive ctf definition method in the next subsection.

Definition 4.2 [functor constraints and their satisfaction]

Let $f: Alg(\Sigma, E) \to Alg(\Sigma \cup \Sigma_{new}, E)$ be a functor, let $\iota: \Sigma \to \Sigma \cup \Sigma_{new}$ be the signature inclusion, and let $\sigma: \Sigma \cup \Sigma_{new} \to \Sigma'$ be a signature morphism. Then the pair (f, σ) constitutes a Σ'-functor constraint.

An arbitrary Σ'-algebra A satisfies (f, σ) exactly if its $(\Sigma \cup \Sigma_{new})$-reduct along σ is generated - up to isomorphisms - from its Σ-reduct by the functor f, i.e.

A satisfies (f, σ)

$$\Leftrightarrow$$

$$Alg(\iota)(Alg(\sigma)(A)) \in Alg(\Sigma, E) \;\&$$
$$Alg(\sigma)(A) \cong f(Alg(\iota)(Alg(\sigma)(A)))$$

where $Alg(\sigma)$ is the forgetful functor corresponding to the signature morphism σ. (For the strict version replace Alg by EAlg.)

As an example, consider the ctf $g: Alg(ELEM) \to Alg(\Sigma LIST)$ from section 3 and an algebra A of lists over the natural numbers. Then A satisfies the functor constraint $(g, id_{\Sigma LIST})$ if the list part of A corresponds exactly to the standard lists over the natural numbers. But an algebra A' obtained from A by adding terms like "default-list" or "cons(overflow, nil)" as new elements of sort list does not satisfy the constraint.

Note that like in the data constraints of [GB 83], the signature component $\sigma: \Sigma \cup \Sigma_{new} \to \Sigma'$ in a functor constraint (f, σ) serves as a means for translating such a Σ' constraint by a signature morphism $\sigma' : \Sigma' \to \Sigma''$ to a Σ''-constraint (g, $\sigma' \bullet \sigma : \Sigma \cup \Sigma_{new} \to \Sigma''$).
This allows us to derive the satisfaction condition for functor constraints; the proof is analogous to the case of data constraint in [GB 83].

Fact 4.3 [satisfaction condition for functor constraints]
Let (g, σ) and σ' be as above, and let $A'' \in Alg(\Sigma'')$ be an algebra. Then $Alg(\sigma')(A'')$ satisfies (g, σ) iff A'' satisfies (g, $\sigma' \bullet \sigma$). (For the strict version replace Alg by EAlg.)

Proof
A'' satisfies (g, $\sigma' \bullet \sigma$) iff $Alg(\iota)(Alg(\sigma' \bullet \sigma))(A'') \in Alg(\Sigma,E)$ and $Alg(\sigma' \bullet \sigma)(A'') \equiv g(Alg(\iota)(Alg(\sigma' \bullet \sigma)(A'')))$ due to Definition 4.2. Since the functor Alg respects composition this is equivalent to $Alg(\sigma \bullet \iota)(Alg(\sigma')(A'')) \in Alg(\Sigma,E)$ and $Alg(\sigma)(Alg(\sigma')(A'')) \equiv g(Alg(\sigma \bullet \iota)(Alg(\sigma')(A'')))$, which in turn is equivalent to $Alg(\sigma')(A'')$ satisfies (g,σ) according to Definition 4.2. (For the strict version replace Alg by EAlg.)

Since the satisfaction condition holds we can extend the types of admissible sentences in a specification (c.f. section 2) by functor constraints and in particular by ctf constraints.

4.3 Parameterized algorithmic definitions

Whereas so far only free functor constraints defined by theory morphisms have been considered in the literature, we now describe a definition method for ctf constraints.

While the implicit definition method for free functors via equational theories or more generally via theory morphisms represents a very high level of abstraction we think that for the more concrete ctfs a more constructive definition method is appropriate. Constructive or algorithmic definition techniques in the framework of abstract data types have been proposed in [Cart 80], [Kl 84], and [Lo 84], but none of them exploits the specific advantages of ctas nor do they support a rigorous parameterized approach. On the other hand, for the definition of ctf domains we would like to allow a broad range of different specification techniques since our ctf concept does not make any specific assumptions about the parameter algebras. Therefore, we distinguish the following two components of our ctf definition method:

(1) definition of the class of parameter algebras
(2) definition of the new carriers and the new operations.

For (1) we can assume an arbitrary loose specification $\langle \Sigma, E \rangle$ denoting the class $Alg(\Sigma, E)$ (resp. $EAlg(\Sigma, E)$ in the strict case) as the domain of the ctf. E may contain just equations or formulas in first order predicate logic, or constraints, etc. For (2) we will describe a definition method for strict ctfs that can be modified to yield a method for the definition of ordinary ctfs.

Since our constructive definition method for strict ctfs has been realized in the specification development language ASPIK [BV 85], we will illustrate it by working through the ASPIK specification LIMITED-STACK as shown in figure 4.4; (this figure was produced by the ASPIK support environment SPESY). The dashed lines in figure 4.4 indicate parts that obey certain syntactic conditions to be discussed in the sequel w.r.t. the individual clauses. These conditions guarantee that every ASPIK specification has a well defined ctf semantics.

1. The use clause contains the two specification names ELEM and LIMIT where ELEM contains just the single sort ELEM and LIMIT extends a specification NAT of the natural numbers by a constant limit of sort nat to be used as the maximal size of the stacks. Semantically, the use clause defines the class of parameter algebras for a ctf which in this case is the class of all one-sorted algebras combined with the natural numbers with an additional natural number constant. As pointed out above, ELEM and LIMIT could have been specified by any suitable specification method.

2. The sorts and ops clauses introduce the names and arities of the new sorts and operations.

3. In the spec-body clause, the new carriers and operations are defined separately

3.1 Definition of new carriers:
The operation symbols empty and push in the constructors clause generate the Herbrand universe of terms over these operation symbols. Prefixing the terms with the symbol `*´, it is the set {*empty, *push(empty, e_1), *push(push(empty, e_1), e_2), ...| $e_i \in A_{elem}$} ∪ {error-stack} of all terms built from empty, push and elem- objects in the parameter algebra A (without error-elem$_A$); the stack error constant is added separately. Thus, the term property is satisfied. Note that the prefix * is used to distinguish data objects from operation applications. Thus, *push(st,e) is an element of the Herbrand universe, while push(st,e) is a term that may evaluate to *push(st,e) or to error-stack depending on the depth of st. The auxiliary function depth is introduced and defined in order to be used in the definition of the characteristic predicate is-stack in the define-carriers clause. This characteristic predicate restricts the term-generated Herbrand universe to stack terms that do not exceed the given limit, yielding the carrier for sort stack. Note that is-stack must respect subterms so that the restricted carrier is still closed under subterms (subterm property). This semantic property is guaranteed by a simple syntactic condition that requires the explicit subterm test in the definition of is-stack, (see figure 4.4).

3.2 Definition of new operations:
In the define-constructor-ops clause the constructors empty and push are defined so as to satisfy the constructor property, which requires empty := *empty and push(st,e) := *push(st, e) for all stack terms st below the limit. To satisfy this requirement the characteristic predicate´s definition can be transformed into definitions of the

```
spec LIMITED-STACK
    /* STANDARD ALGORITHMIC DEFINITION OF A LIMITED-STACK. PUSH ON A FULL  */
    /* STACK, POP OR TOP OF AN EMPTY STACK RESULT IN ERRORS */
  use   ELEM
        LIMIT ;
  sorts STACK;
  ops   EMPTY:   --> STACK
        EMPTY?,FULL?: STACK   --> BOOL
        PUSH: STACK ELEM   --> STACK
        POP: STACK   --> STACK
        TOP: STACK   --> ELEM;
spec-body
   constructors EMPTY
                PUSH;
   auxiliaries DEPTH: STACK   --> NAT;
   define-auxiliaries
       DEPTH(ST) = case ST is
                      * EMPTY : ZERO
                      * PUSH(STO,ELO) : SUC(DEPTH(STO))
                   esac;
   define-carriers
       IS-STACK(ST) = case ST is
                         * PUSH(STO,ELO) : if NOT(IS-STACK(STO))
                                           then FALSE
                                           else (DEPTH(STO) LT LIMIT)
                       otherwise TRUE
                      esac;
   define-constructor-ops
       PUSH(STO,ELO) = if (DEPTH(STO) LT LIMIT)
                       then * PUSH(STO,ELO)
                       else ERROR-STACK
       EMPTY = * EMPTY;
   define-ops
       EMPTY?(ST) = case ST is
                       * EMPTY : TRUE
                       * PUSH(STO,ELO) : FALSE
                    esac
       FULL?(ST) = NOT((DEPTH(ST) LT LIMIT))
       POP(ST) = case ST is
                    * EMPTY : ERROR-STACK
                    * PUSH(STO,ELO) : STO
                 esac
       TOP(ST) = case ST is
                    * EMPTY : ERROR-ELEM
                    * PUSH(STO,ELO) : ELO
                 esac;
endspec
```

Figure 4.4 The ASPIK specification LIMITED-STACK

constructor operations by replacing every true-branch by the *-prefixed constructor term. For every false-branch an arbitrary term may be supplemented. By requiring that it must not contain any *-prefixed constructors it is guaranteed to lie in the restricted carrier. In our example, *push(st, e) is not accepted by is-stack when st is full to the limit. In this case push(st, e) is defined to yield the error element of sort stack. The remaining operations are defined in the define-ops clause using the constructor operations, but again no *-prefixed constructors. As a consequence, these operations are also guaranteed to be closed on the carriers.
Auxiliary operations like depth need not be redefined as new operations, they are closed on the carriers because they, too, must not be defined using the *-prefixed constructors.

All operations may be defined via if-then-else schemes, case-schemes w.r.t. new sorts, and recursion. To explain the semantics of the recursive definitions by a least fixpoint construction we use strict algebras: Their carriers are flat cpos with the error element as bottom. As a consequence the ctfs defined by our language are strict ctfs. Besides, strict algebras provide a simple built-in error handling mechanism that propagates errors via strict operations.

The syntactic clauses discussed above do not contain an explicit definition of the morphism part of a ctf, because it can be derived from the information already given. For example, if $h : A \rightarrow A'$ is a morphism in EAlg(ELEM) the corresponding LIMITED-STACK extension of h maps a stack carrier object $*push(push(empty, a_2), a_1)$ with $a_i \in A_{elem}$ to $*push(push(empty, h(a_2)), h(a_1))$.

In this section we could only indicate the conditions that guarantee that every constructive ctf definition denotes a well defined ctf. [BV 85] contains a denotational semantic definition with a complete set of context sensitive conditions and correctness proofs. The algorithmic approach of [Lo 84] also uses term sets as carriers but in principle there is no syntactic correspondence to the algebra operations like in a cta approach. In [Lo 84] the carriers may be restricted by a characteristic predicate and additionally an algorithmically defined equivalence relation generates congruence classes on the restricted carriers. We think the latter may be better suited for a high level axiomatic approach than for a lower level constructive one.
[Lo 84] does not provide any syntactic conditions for a well-defined semantics: In general, rather complex and difficult proofs may be necessary to ensure that the operations are restrictable to the restricted carriers, that the equivalence operation is reflexive, symmetric, and transitive and that it defines a congruence relation (i.e. it must be compatible with all operations). [Kl 84] allows only primitive recursive definitions which makes a least fixpoint semantics superfluous. If we restrict our ctf definition method to primitive recursive definitions and additionally exclude error elements and constants we obtain a definition method for ordinary ctfs where the same context conditions can be used.

4.4 Integration of axiomatic and constructive techniques

The parameterized constructive ctf definition technique described in the previous subsection can be used as a constraint mechanism according to section 4.2. Since it is independent of the sentences used to specify the parameter class of the ctfs, it can extend many different approaches. In particular, extending axiomatic techniques based on equational logic or first order predicate calculus by ctf constraints, axiomatic and constructive methods presenting different levels of abstraction are integrated in a uniform framework. In such a framework the stepwise development scenario can be realized by moving gradually from high level, purely axiomatic definitions through intermediate forms to completely constructive definitions representing executable prototypes ([BV 85], [BOV 86]).

5. ASPIK and SPESY

ASPIK is a specification development language for the stepwise development of hierarchical, loose specifications, their refinements and implementations. A specification may contain two types of sentences: arbitrary first order formulas and ctf constraints that are defined in the constructive technique described in section 4.3.

The constructive ctf definition technique is highly supported by the ASPIK support environment SPESY:

- Context-sensitive conditions guarantee that every ctf definition has a well defined semantics. SPESY checks these conditions and additionally exploits them to generate parts of a ctf definition automatically. In figure 4.4 these parts are indicated by dashed lines.
- Being constructive, ctf definitions are amenable to interpretation: SPESY provides an interpreter for terms built from constructively defined operations.

Due to the integration of axiomatic and constructive techniques stepwise specification development as sketched in section 4.4 can be carried out within ASPIK. All development steps can be verified formally, e.g. refining an axiomatically specified subpart A by a constructive ctf definition C requires a proof that C satisfies the properties given in A. Such proofs are done stepwise along the hierarchical structure as suggested in section 4.1. The corresponding proof tasks are formulated by SPESY, and passed to one of its associated automatic theorem provers ([Karl 84], [Tho 84]). SPESY processes the results of the provers and a reason maintenance component surveys the validity of proved assertions after any manipulations like editing in the specification hierarchy ([BV 85], [BOV 86]).

6. Conclusions

We introduced the notion of canonical term functor as a generalization of canonical term algebra and defined strict versions for both concepts. After proving some properties of ctfs, we addressed their applications in a constraint mechanism, an integration of axiomatic and constructive techniques, and in the specification development language ASPIK and its support environment SPESY.

Appendix: Proof of Fact 4.1

The free functor $free_{PSP}$: $Alg(FSP) \rightarrow Alg(\Sigma, E)$ can be defined by sending every $A \in Alg(FSP)$ to $T_\Sigma(A)_{/\equiv}$ (c. f. Theorem 7 in [TWW 82]). From $T_\Sigma(A)_{/\equiv}$ we will construct an isomorphic algebra C(A) by selecting a single representative for each equivalence class. Then sending A to C(A) still yields a free functor. By showing that the $F\Sigma$-reduct of C(A) is A and that C(A) has the $(\Sigma - F\Sigma)$-term, -subterm, and -constructor properties w. r. t. A we conclude that this functor is also a ctf.

The rest of this proof generalizes the one for the cta case given in [GTW 78]: We define a family $\langle C_n | n \geq 0 \rangle$ of subsets of $T_\Sigma(A)$ such that $C = \bigcup \{C_n \mid n \geq 0\}$ is the set of representatives. The sets C_n are defined inductively on the depth of terms so that:

(1) $t \in C_n$ implies $depth(t) \leq n$

(2) if $t \in T_\Sigma(A)$ such that the $\equiv$-equivalence class of t has a representative of depth $\leq$ n, then there is a unique representative $t^* \in T_{\Sigma - F\Sigma}(A)$

(3) for any $op: s_1 \dots s_m \to s \in \Sigma$ with $s \in \Sigma - F\Sigma$ $op(t_1, \dots t_m) \in C_n$ implies $\{t_1, \dots, t_m\} \subseteq C_{n-1}$

In the following the elements of $F\Sigma$ are called old, the elements of $\Sigma - F\Sigma$ are called new. For any old sort $s \in F\Sigma$ we observe that $A_s \cong T_\Sigma(A)_{/\equiv,s}$ since the free functor is persistent. Therefore, the elements of A can be taken as unique representatives for all eqivalence classes in $T_\Sigma(A)_{/\equiv,s}$ with $s \in F\Sigma$. For the set $T_0 := \{op: \to s \in \Sigma - F\Sigma \mid s \in \Sigma - F\Sigma\}$ of constants of a new sort s we choose a subset $C'_0 \subseteq T_0$ such that for each $op \in T_0$ there exists a unique $op^* \in C'_0$ with $op \equiv op^*$ (which obviously can be done). Since the elements of A are treated as constants having depth 0 in the definition of $T_\Sigma(A)$, $C_0 := A \cup C'_0$ satisfies conditons (1) - (3).

Now assume that C_n satisfies (1) - (3). Let T_{n+1} be the set of equivalence classes having a representative of depth n + 1, but no representative of depth $\leq$ n. C_{n+1} is given by C_n together with a single representative $op(t_1^*, \dots, t_m^*)$ of depth n +1 for each class in T_{n+1} which can be chosen so that $t_i^* \in C_n$ since C_n contains representatiaves for all terms of depth $\leq$ n. Furthermore, both the target sort s of $op: s_1 \dots s_m \to s$ and op itself must be in $\Sigma - F\Sigma$ since for all old sorts there are representatives of depth 0 due to the peristency of the free functor. Thus, C_{n+1} also satisfies (1) -(3).

C is the carrier of our desired algebra C(A). The operations of C(A) are obtained by restricting the operations in $T_\Sigma(A)_{/\equiv}$ to the representatives, i.e. $op_{C(A)}(t_1^*, \dots, t_m^*) := (op(t_1, \dots, t_m))^*$. The definition of C immediatly guarantees that the $F\Sigma$-reduct of C(A) has the $(\Sigma - F\Sigma)$ - term and subterm properties w.r.t. A. For $s \in \Sigma - F\Sigma$, $op: s_1 \dots s_m \to s \in \Sigma - F\Sigma$, and $op(t_1, \dots, t_m) \in C(A)$ we have $op_{C(A)}(t_1, \dots, t_m) = (op(t_1, \dots, t_m))^* = op(t_1, \dots, t_m)$ since the representatives in C(A) are unique. Thus, C(A) also has the $(\Sigma - F\Sigma)$ - constructor property which completes the proof.

eferences

BG 77] Burstall, R.M., Goguen, J.A.: Putting Theories together to Make Specifications. Proc. 5th IJCAI, 1977, pp. 1045-1058.

BG 80] Burstall, R.M., Goguen, J.A.: The semantics of Clear, a specification language. Proc. of Advanced Course on Abstract Software Specifications, Copenhagen. LNCS Vol.86, pp. 292-332.

BG 81] Burstall, R.M., Goguen, J.A.: An informal introduction to specifications using Clear. in: The Correctness problem in Computer Science (Eds. R.S. Boyer, J.S. Moore). Academic Press 1981.

BOV 86] Beierle, C., Olthoff, W., Voß, A.: Towards a formalization of the software development process. Proc. Software Engineering '86, Southampton, U.K. (Eds. D. Barnes, P. Brown). Peter Peregrinus Ltd., pp. 130-144, 1986.

[BV 85] Beierle, C., Voß, A.: Algebraic Specifications and Implementations in an Integrated Software Development and Verification System. Memo SEKI-85-12, FB Informatik, Univ. Kaiserslautern, (joint SEKI-Memo containing the Ph.D. thesis by Ch. Beierle and the Ph.D. thesis by A. Voß), Dec. 1985.

[Cart 80] Cartwright, R.: A constructive alternative to abstract data type definitions. Proc. 1980 LISP Conf., Stanford University, pp. 46-55, 1980.

[CIP 85] CIP Language Group: The Munich Project CIP, Vol. I: The Wide Spectrum Language CIP-L. LNCS, Vol. 183, 1985.

[EKTWW 80] Ehrig, H., Kreowski, H.-J., Thatcher, J., Wagner, E., Wright, J.: Parameterized data types in algebraic specification languages, Proc. 7th ICALP, LNCS Vol. 85, 1980, pp. 157-168.

[EM 85] Ehrig, H., Mahr, B.: fundamentals of Algebraic Specificiations 1 - Equations and Initial Semantics, Springer Verlag, 1985.

[EWT 82] Ehrig, H., Wagner, E., Thatcher, J.: Algebraic Constraints for specifications and canonical form results. Draft version, TU Berlin, June 1982.

[EWT 83] Ehrig, H., Wagner, E., Thatcher, J.: Algebraic specifications with generating constraints, Proc. ICALP 83, LNCS 154, 1983, pp. 188-202.

[GB 83] Goguen, J.A., Burstall, R.M.: Institutions: Abstract Model Theory for Program Specification. Draft version. SRI International and University of Edinburgh, January 1983, revised 1985.

[GGM 76] Giarratana, V., Gimona, F., Montanari, V.: Observability concepts in abstract data type specifications. 5th MFCS, LNCS 45, 1976, pp. 576-587.

[GTW 78] Goguen, J.A., Thatcher, J.W., Wagner, E.G.: An initial algebra approach to the specification, correctness, and implementation of abstract data types, in: Current Trends in Programming Methodology, Vol.4, Data Structuring (ed. R. Yeh), Prentice-Hall, 1978, pp. 80-144. also: IBM Research Report RC 6487, 1976.

[HKR 80] Hupbach, U.L., Kaphengst, H., Reichel, H.: Initial algebraic specifications of data types, parameterized data types, and algorithms. VEB Robotron, Zentrum für Forschung und Technik, Dresden, 1980.

[Kam 80] Kamin S.: Final data type specifications: a new data type specification method. 7th POPL, Las Vegas, 1979.

[Karl 84] Karl Mark G Raph: The Markgraf Karl Refutation Procedure. SEKI-Projekt, Memo SEKI-MK-34-01, Univ. Kaiserslautern, 1984.

[Kl 83] Klaeren, H.: Algebraische Spezifikation. Springer Verlag, 1983.

[Kl 84] Klaeren, H.: A constructive method for abstract algebraic software specification. TCS, Vol.30, No. 2, pp. 139 - 204, Aug. 1984.

[Lo 84] Loeckx, J.: Algorithmic specifications: A constructive specification method for abstract data types. Bericht A 84/03, Fachrichtung Informatik, Universität des Saarlandes, April 1984. (to appear in TOPLAS)

[Pad 79] Padawitz, P.: Proving the correctness of implementations by exclusive use of term algebras. Bericht Nr. 79-8, TU Berlin, Fachbereich Informatik, 1979.

[Pad 83] Padawitz, P.: Correctness, Completeness, and Consistency of Equational Data Type Specifications. Dissertation, TU Berlin, Fachbereich Informatik, Bericht Nr. 83-15, 1983.

[SW 82] Sannella, D.T., Wirsing, M.: Implementation of parameterized specifications, Proc. 9th ICALP 1982, LNCS Vol. 140, pp 473 - 488.

[Tho 84] Thomas, Ch.: RRLab - Rewrite Rule Labor. Entwurf, Spezifikation und Implementierung eines Software-werkzeuges zur Erzeugung und Vervollständigung von Rewrite-Rule Systemen. SEKI-Projekt, Memo SEKI-84-01, Univ. Kaiserslautern, FB Informatik, 1984.

[TWW 82] Thatcher, J.W., Wagner, E.G., Wright, J.B.: Data Type Specification Parameterization and the Power of Specification Techniques. ACM TOPLAS Vol. 4, No. 4, Oct. 1982, pp. 711-732.

[Wa 79] Wand, M.: Final algebra semantics and data type extensions. J. Comp. Syst. Sci. 19, 1979.

[ZLT 82] Zilles, S.N., Lucas, P., Thatcher, J.W.: A Look at Algebraic Specifications. RJ 3568 (41985), IBM Research Division Yorktown Heights New York, 1982.

AUTHOR INDEX

(I, II indicate the volumes)

Vol. 219: Advances in Cryptology – EUROCRYPT '85. Proceedings, 1985. Edited by F. Pichler. IX, 281 pages. 1986.

Vol. 220: RIMS Symposia on Software Science and Engineering II. Proceedings, 1983 and 1984. Edited by E. Goto, K. Araki and T. Yuasa. XI, 323 pages. 1986.

Vol. 221: Logic Programming '85. Proceedings, 1985. Edited by E. Wada. IX, 311 pages. 1986.

Vol. 222: Advances in Petri Nets 1985. Edited by G. Rozenberg. VI, 498 pages. 1986.

Vol. 223: Structure in Complexity Theory. Proceedings, 1986. Edited by A. L. Selman. VI, 401 pages. 1986.

Vol. 224: Current Trends in Concurrency. Overviews and Tutorials. Edited by J.W. de Bakker, W.-P. de Roever and G. Rozenberg. XII, 716 pages. 1986.

Vol. 225: Third International Conference on Logic Programming. Proceedings, 1986. Edited by E. Shapiro. IX, 720 pages. 1986.

Vol. 226: Automata, Languages and Programming. Proceedings, 1986. Edited by L. Kott. IX, 474 pages. 1986.

Vol. 227: VLSI Algorithms and Architectures – AWOC 86. Proceedings, 1986. Edited by F. Makedon, K. Mehlhorn, T. Papatheodorou and P. Spirakis. VIII, 328 pages. 1986.

Vol. 228: Applied Algebra, Algorithmics and Error-Correcting Codes. AAECC-2. Proceedings, 1984. Edited by A. Poli. VI, 265 pages. 1986.

Vol. 229: Algebraic Algorithms and Error-Correcting Codes. AAECC-3. Proceedings, 1985. Edited by J. Calmet. VII, 416 pages. 1986.

Vol. 230: 8th International Conference on Automated Deduction. Proceedings, 1986. Edited by J.H. Siekmann. X, 708 pages. 1986.

Vol. 231: R. Hausser, NEWCAT: Parsing Natural Language Using Left-Associative Grammar. II, 540 pages. 1986.

Vol. 232: Fundamentals of Artificial Intelligence. Edited by W. Bibel and Ph. Jorrand. VII, 313 pages. 1986.

Vol. 233: Mathematical Foundations of Computer Science 1986. Proceedings, 1986. Edited by J. Gruska, B. Rovan and J. Wiedermann. 650 pages. 1986.

Vol. 234: Concepts in User Interfaces: A Reference Model for Command and Response Languages. By Members of IFIP Working Group 2.7. Edited by D. Beech. X, 116 pages. 1986.

Vol. 235: Accurate Scientific Computations. Proceedings, 1985. Edited by W.L. Miranker and R.A. Toupin. XIII, 205 pages. 1986.

Vol. 236: TEX for Scientific Documentation. Proceedings, 1986. Edited by J. Désarménien. VI, 204 pages. 1986.

Vol. 237: CONPAR 86. Proceedings, 1986. Edited by W. Händler, Haupt, R. Jeltsch, W. Juling and O. Lange. X, 418 pages. 1986.

Vol. 238: L. Naish, Negation and Control in Prolog. IX, 119 pages. 1986.

Vol. 239: Mathematical Foundations of Programming Semantics. Proceedings, 1985. Edited by A. Melton. VI, 395 pages. 1986.

Vol. 240: Category Theory and Computer Programming. Proceedings, 1985. Edited by D. Pitt, S. Abramsky, A. Poigné and D. Rydeheard. VII, pages. 1986.

Vol. 241: Foundations of Software Technology and Theoretical Computer Science. Proceedings, 1986. Edited by K.V. Nori. XII, 519 pages. 1986.

Vol. 242: Combinators and Functional Programming Languages. Proceedings, 1985. Edited by G. Cousineau, P.-L. Curien and Robinet. V, 208 pages. 1986.

Vol. 243: ICDT '86. Proceedings, 1986. Edited by G. Ausiello and Atzeni. VI, 444 pages. 1986.

Vol. 244: Advanced Programming Environments. Proceedings, 1986. Edited by R. Conradi, T.M. Didriksen and D.H. Wanvik. VII, 603 pages. 1986.

Vol. 245: H.F. de Groote, Lectures on the Complexity of Bilinear Problems. V, 135 pages. 1987.

Vol. 247: STACS 87. Proceedings, 1987. Edited by F.J. Brandenburg, G. Vidal-Naquet and M. Wirsing. X, 484 pages. 1987.

Vol. 248: Networking in Open Systems. Proceedings, 1986. Edited by G. Müller and R.P. Blanc. VI, 441 pages. 1987.

Vol. 249: TAPSOFT '87. Volume 1. Proceedings, 1987. Edited by H. Ehrig, R. Kowalski, G. Levi and U. Montanari. XIV, 289 pages. 1987.

Vol. 250: TAPSOFT '87. Volume 2. Proceedings, 1987. Edited by H. Ehrig, R. Kowalski, G. Levi and U. Montanari. XIV, 336 pages. 1987.

Vol. 251: V. Akman, Unobstructed Shortest Paths in Polyhedral Environments. VII, 103 pages. 1987.

Vol. 252: VDM '87. VDM – A Formal Method at Work. Proceedings, 1987. Edited by D. Bjørner, C.B. Jones, M. Mac an Airchinnigh and E. Neuhold. X, 422 pages. 1987.